Professional SAS® Programming Secrets

Updated with New Features of Releases 6.08–6.10

McGraw-Hill

New York San Francisco Washington, D.C. Auckland Bogotá
Caracas Lisbon London Madrid Mexico City Milan
Montreal New Delhi San Juan Singapore
Sydney Tokyo Toronto

McGraw-Hill

A Division of The McGraw-Hill Companies

Paul Nordquist: Editorial consultant

1 2 3 4 5 6 7 8 9 DOC/DOC 9 0 0 9 8 7 6

Library of Congress Cataloging-in-Publication Data

Aster, Rick.
Professional SAS programming secrets / by Rick Aster & Rhena Seidman.
p. cm.
Includes index.
ISBN 0-07-913095-X (pbk.)
1. SAS (Computer file) I. Seidman, Rhena. II. Title.
QA276.4.A84 1996
005.3—dc20 96-17754
CIP

McGraw-Hill books are available at special quantity discounts to use as premiums and sales promotions, or for use in corporate training programs. For more information, please write to the Director of Special Sales, McGraw-Hill, 11 West 19th Street, New York, NY 10011. Or contact your local bookstore.

System options

```
AUTOEXEC= CONFIG= INITSTMT= or IS= SYSIN=
WORKINIT
CAPS CENTER DATE DSNFERR ERRORABEND ERRORS=
FMTERR FORMCHAR= INVALIDDATA= LABEL _LAST_=
LINESIZE= or LS= MISSING= NOTES NUMBER
PAGENO= PAGESIZE= or PS= S= S2= SOURCE
SOURCE2 SYSPARM= VNFERR YEARCUTOFF=
```

```
COMPRESS= FIRSTOBS= OBS= REPLACE REUSE=
```

Dataset options

```
CNTLLEV=MEM or REC COMPRESS=YES FIRSTOBS=n
IN=variable INDEX=(variable or index= variables /UNIQUE
/NOMISS...) KEEP or DROP=variables LABEL= OBS=n
RENAME=(old=new ...) REPLACE=YES REUSE=YES
SORTEDBY=variables TYPE= WHERE=(condition)
```

WHERE operators

```
BETWEEN ... AND
CONTAINS or ?
IS NULL or IS MISSING
LIKE 'pattern'          _=any char    %=any chars
=*   (sounds like)
```

Procs

```
PROC PRINT DATA=SAS dataset UNIFORM SPLIT='\';
BY variables;   ID variables;   VAR variables;
```

```
PROC REPORT DATA=SAS dataset NOWD HEADLINE
HEADSKIP WRAP PANELS=n SPLIT='\';
COLUMN columns;
DEFINE variable or alias / 'header' ... usage
     statistic ORDER= WIDTH= NOPRINT
     FORMAT=format spec  alignment PAGE;
BREAK BEFORE or AFTER variable / break options;
RBREAK BEFORE or AFTER / break options;
COMPUTE variable / LENGTH=n; ... ENDCOMP;
COMPUTE AFTER variable; ...
  LINE @n +n variable format spec 'string' n*'string';
  ENDCOMP;
        Usage: DISPLAY ORDER COMPUTED
               ANALYSIS GROUP ACROSS
        Break options: OL DOL UL DUL
          SKIP PAGE SUMMARIZE SUPPRESS
```

```
PROC SORT DATA=SAS dataset OUT=SAS dataset;
BY variables;
```

```
PROC SUMMARY DATA=SAS dataset NWAY;
CLASS variables;
VAR variables;
OUTPUT OUT=SAS dataset
     statistic=
     statistic(variables)=variables
     ...;
```

```
PROC SUMMARY DATA=SAS dataset NWAY;
CLASS variables;
OUTPUT OUT=SAS dataset;
```

```
PROC CONTENTS DATA=SAS dataset POSITION;
```

```
PROC COPY IN=libref OUT=libref MTYPE=member type;
SELECT members; or EXCLUDE members;
```

```
PROC APPEND DATA=SAS dataset (dataset options)
            OUT=SAS dataset FORCE;
```

```
PROC DATASETS LIBRARY=libref NOLIST KILL;
(delete all members)
```

```
PROC DATASETS LIBRARY=libref MTYPE=member type;
CHANGE member=new name ...;
EXCHANGE member name=member name ...;
AGE members;
DELETE members; or SAVE members;
COPY OUT=libref; SELECT or EXCLUDE members;
APPEND DATA=SAS dataset OUT=SAS dataset FORCE;
CONTENTS DATA=member or _ALL_;
MODIFY member (TYPE=type LABEL='string');
  RENAME vaiable=new name ...;
  LABEL variable='string' ...;
  INFORMAT variables informat specification ...;
  FORMAT variables format specification ...;
  INDEX CREATE variable or index=variables / options;
  INDEX DELETE indexes;
QUIT;
```

```
PROC SQL; SQL expression; ....
```

```
PROC FORMAT LIBRARY=libref;
VALUE format (format options)
    range = value ...;
PICTURE format (format options)
    range = picture (picture option) ...;
INVALUE informat (informat options)
    range = value ...;
             Format options:
       MIN=w MAX=w DEFAULT=w FUZZ=ε
             Informat options:
     MIN=w MAX=w DEFAULT=w UPCASE JUST
             Picture options:
  PREFIX='chars' FILL='char' MULT=x NOEDIT
```

Functions

```
ABS CEIL EXP FLOOR FUZZ INT LOG LOG2 LOG10
SIGN SQRT (x)   DATE DATETIME TIME TODAY ()
DIM HBOUND LBOUND (array, n)    DEQUOTE LEFT
LENGTH LOWCASE RIGHT QUOTE REVERSE SOUNDEX
TRIM TRIMN UPCASE (string)   COMPRESS INDEXC
VERIFY (string, chars) INDEX INDEXW (string, substring)
HOUR MINUTE SECOND (SAS time/datetime)
DAY MONTH QTR WEEKDAY YEAR (SAS date)
DATEPART TIMEPART (SAS datetime)
MOD(x, modulus)  ROUND(x, unit)  TRUNC(x, length)
TRANSLATE(string, to, from)  TRANWRD(string, from, to)
REPEAT(string, n) SCAN(string, n, delimiters) SUBSTR
(string, position, length)   INPUT(string, informat spec)
PUT(value, format spec)    DHMS(d, hr, min, s)
HMS(hr, min, s)   MDY(mon, d, yr)   YYQ(yr, qtr)
```

Statistics

```
CSS CV KURTOSIS MAX MEAN MIN N NMISS RANGE
SKEWNESS STD STDERR SUM USS VAR
```

Informats/Formats

```
$ $ASCII $CHAR $EBCDIC $HEX $QUOTE $UPCASE
COMMA D DOLLAR E HEX IB OCTAL PIB RB
DATE DDMMYY MMDDYY YYMMDD MONYY YYQ TIME
DATETIME lanDFir
```

Informats

```
BZ
```

Formats

```
BEST ROMAN WORDF WORDS Z
WORDDATE WEEKDATE YEAR MONNAME MONTH DAY
YYMON MMYY YYMM QTR QTRR YYQR DOWNAME
WEEKDAY TOD DATETIME TIME HOUR HHMM MMSS
```

Contents

Tables and illustrations

Introduction

So you want secrets? Here's one:

Quite a lot of professional computer programming is done using the SAS programming language. Programmers don't usually like to emphasize that fact, because SAS is usually thought of as a "user's language." SAS programming seems like cheating somehow — a "real" programmer would sweat through the program development process in a "real" language like Cobol, C, or assembly language. Theoretically, these lower-level "programmer's" languages should create more efficient and better suited programs. In practice, the SAS program gets the job done. It also gets written five times as fast, runs faster, and is more likely to work right the first time. It has less than half as many lines of code, yet actually makes sense when you try to read it. But don't try to explain this to a manager who has never written a SAS program — you might have to stop having so much fun and get back to work.

You want more secrets? That's what this book is all about: little-known facts that make SAS programming even more fun; the right and wrong ways to do ordinary things; easy ways to do complicated things; clever techniques that we've developed or discovered in our years as SAS programming consultants; how the SAS System can help you; all the secrets that distinguish the better professional SAS programmers; and all this with the programmer's perspective that you won't find in any other book on the subject.

This book takes a mechanical approach to covering SAS syntax. Th because we've found that — for some reason — SAS programmers to understand SAS syntax in purely symbolic terms never Those who can take the machine point of view, though, are surprise. Besides, programmers ought to be curio computer is really doing, and to the average professio more mechanical explanation will make more sense.

We wrote this book for anyone who works with SAS programs. Because we don't have time to solve all your SAS programming problems personally, this book is the next best thing. It can't actually solve problems for you, but it can probably answer most of your questions.

We had SAS version 6 in mind when we wrote this book — and in particular, SAS releases 6.03 to 6.06. This book will probably work fine with later SAS releases, although one never knows what SAS Institute has up its sleeve. For earlier SAS releases, the general principles are the same, but some details of the syntax are different. For maintenance programmers, we've noted the important differences between version 5 and version 6.

How to read this book

In general, the first half of this book introduces the bits and pieces of SAS programming and the second half puts them together. Each of the four parts assumes familiarity with the topics of the preceding ones, although this is generally not true of the chapters within a part.

You won't find many complete applications programs here. If we had to write a program to illustrate every concept and technique, the book would be twice as heavy, and you would hesitate to carry it around. However, there are enough complete steps and complete programs for you to get the idea.

Complete beginners should stop periodically, especially in the first few chapters, to write and run some SAS programs to try out the new concepts and features. If you like, you can use our programs as starting points — then change them around a dozen different ways to see what you get. With a SAS program, making changes doesn't take long at all to do, and if you do something wrong, the log will tell you.

Beginners should not be concerned that not everything seems to make sense the first time through. The SAS System can be bewildering at first, but you'll be ready to start writing useful SAS programs after reading the first two chapters of this book.

Experienced SAS programmers might prefer to read the book through uninterrupted, skipping through some of the material in the first few chapters. This book can also be used as a reference book, with the index, glossary, and table of contents as starting points.

We focus on the SAS programming language throughout the book. Other aspects of the SAS System are mentioned where they relate to the programming language. Wherever you see the word "SAS" by itself in this book, we mean "the SAS programming language."

Some techniques appear in this book not because we recommend them, but because they are widely used. This is necessary because every professional SAS programmer does some maintenance programming, rewriting and revising existing programs. In some cases we show ways to replace techniques with more efficient ones.

Several typographical conventions are used throughout the book. SAS keywords and names, such as BY and _N_, appear in all capital letters.

```
Programs and code fragments, data files, print files, screen
displays, and any symbols that naturally reside on a computer are
printed in this monospaced typeface.
```

Text in this italic font `represents parts of code fragments for you to fill in. For example:`

```
    IF condition THEN action
```

```
A horizontal line like this one is used to separate a program file
from an input or output file or to mark a page break in print
output.
```

We use icons in the left margin to identify several of this book's recurring themes. Like footnotes (which we *don't* use), the icons can safely be ignored. If you're flipping through the book, though, they can help you find interesting things quickly.

Power.
Especially useful or strongly recommended programming techniques.

Time.
Saving time for programmers (as distinct from saving time for computers). "Power user" techniques.

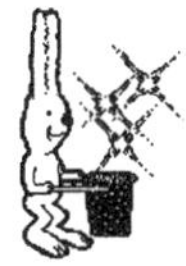

Trick.
Simple, clever techniques and programs. Usually good examples to study. Entertain your friends.

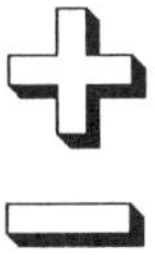

Plus/Minus.
Especially good and bad features of the SAS System — from a programmer's perspective, of course.

Bug.
Surprising behavior of the SAS System that can cause problems for programmers.

Caution.
Common sources of confusion and error. Drive carefully.

Implementation.
Characteristics of a particular SAS release for a particular operating system, or of the operating system itself. Especially for I/O.

Installation.
Characteristics that vary from one computer to another, even within the same implementation. Includes all SAS products other than base SAS, since different installations have different SAS products.

Obsolete.
Important features of the past, especially of SAS version 5.

New.
Recent innovations in the SAS System, especially with SAS release 6.06.

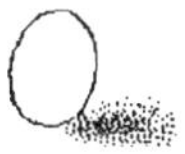

Future.
Speculations on possible future changes in the SAS System.

Incidental note

When we put a topic in a box like this, it means that it's a related topic that isn't really part of the main discussion. You can skip over the boxes without any loss of continuity.

Source code disk

Typing someone else's programs can be an unrewarding task. If you want to run the programs in this book without having to type them, refer to the source code disk packaged with the book. It contains all the programs and many of the code fragments in this book, plus enhanced or alternative versions of some programs.

The source code disk is a floppy disk in MS-DOS format. It contains a series of text files. Use any text editor to copy the program lines you're interested in from the files on the source code disk to your program files.

PART ONE:
For programmers

The large number of user-friendly SAS features presents a challenge to programmers: there is a lot to keep track of.

1 Getting started

We start with an overview of the SAS programming language: its origins and philosophy, the SAS environment, and the building blocks of SAS syntax. This chapter is especially important for programmers who are new to the SAS System.

Origins

The SAS programming language is the visible connecting link between the many diverse capabilities of the sprawling SAS System. However, it still retains much of the character of its simple origins doing statistics on mainframes in the 1970s.

Statistics

"SAS" originally stood for "statistical analysis system," and many of the characteristics of the SAS language can be traced back to its statistical background.

Scientists observe nature and attempt to draw conclusions. One way they do that is by making numerical measurements and looking for patterns in the numbers. The latter part of that process is what we call *statistics*.

In one kind of experiment, the same measuring process is done many different times. For example, the experimenter might count the number of leaves on each plant in a group of plants or have many people complete a questionnaire. Each instance of measuring is called an *observation*, and each different quality that is measured is called a *variable*. That's the source of those two SAS terms and of the form of a SAS dataset.

Ideally, statistical observations are independent — that is, the different observations do not affect or depend upon each other. This simplifies statistical analysis: the data from each observation can be processed separately, without reference to data from the other observations, and the order in which the observations are processed does not affect the conclusions. When the processing is done in a computer program, it makes possible the *observation loop*, a repeated process of reading one observation at a time into memory and extracting the information needed from it. The observation loop became a central part of the design of the SAS System, and it was subsequently found to be useful in all kinds of applications.

Mainframes

When the SAS System first appeared in the 1970s, most statistical analysis was done on IBM mainframes. Only a few programming languages were in common use on mainframes at that time. Fortran and PL/I, the two languages commonly used for scientific programming, had a strong influence on SAS syntax. The use of free-form statements ending in semicolons, comments delimited with `/* */`, the control flow statements, and most of the set of operators can be traced to PL/I. The SAS language also has some similarities to Fortran.

The language also embodies some concepts from the mainframe operating systems of the time, particularly having to do with files. Punch cards, small pieces of stiff paper with holes cut in them to represent data, were in common use in the 1970s. Mainframe files were based on punch card ideas and terminology, and some of these concepts are reflected in the SAS language — the CARDS statement, for example.

There were practical limits on the number of physical files under operating systems like OS, which led to the concept of a library. In a library, a related group of logical files are stored at one physical location. Libraries are still part of the SAS system design, even though they are no longer physical objects under most operating systems.

It was customary on mainframes for output files from programs to be sent directly into the print queue, a special operating system device to support the mainframe's slow, heavily used printers. The SAS System followed this tradition with its standard print file, which is still called file PRINT, and its contents called print output, regardless of whether it ends up on paper.

Modularity

From the start, the SAS system had a modular design. Instead of being one monolithic program, or a small group of related programs that run at different times, it was a large collection of several types of programs that are coordinated by a central program called the *supervisor*. The specifications for each type of program were published, so that it was possible for anyone with the requisite programming skill to expand the system.

Even the SAS System's reading and writing routines were modular, and that made it easy for the system to read data in almost any format in use.

The SAS language's input and output capabilities are still among the most powerful and flexible of any programming language.

Simplicity

The original SAS System did not have most of the features of the SAS System of today. Features like screen support and macrolanguage were added gradually, in patchwork fashion, and the language syntax itself was expanded. Each new addition has gone off in its own direction, but the core of the system still embodies much of the elegance of the original SAS System.

In the 1980s, in the redesign of the SAS System for version 6, many aspects of the system were simplified.

What kind of language is SAS?

Although SAS programs look much like programs written in other programming languages, there are several things that distinguish SAS.

Interpreter

A programming language is usually implemented either as an interpreter or as a compiler. An interpreter runs a program by determining the meaning of each program statement, then carrying it out. A compiler translates an entire program into machine language in a separate file, which can then be executed. Compiled programs run faster, but you have to take the time to compile them. Interpreted programs provide more immediate feedback when an error occurs, but they run more slowly and can only be run when the interpreter is present.

SAS is an interpreted language, but it also has some of the characteristics of a compiler. Some parts of SAS programs are compiled. And most SAS statements, rather than being interpreted and executed one at a time, are grouped into segments called *steps* before being executed.

Step-structured

It is traditional to divide programming languages into structured languages and nonstructured languages. Structured languages allow programmers to compartmentalize sections of a program, keeping the variables and data of that part of the program from affecting any other parts of the program.

In a sense, the SAS language is structured — each step is isolated from every other step in the program — but in another sense, it isn't, because it does not allow traditional techniques of structured programming. Structured programming involves a top-down design in which program units nest inside other program units, but the SAS language only allows steps to run one at a time, one after another. It seems fair to call SAS a step-structured language.

Library

You expect a programming language to come with a library of functions. In addition to a few hundred functions, the SAS System contains *informats* and *formats*, specialized routines that are mainly used for input and output; CALL routines, which do some small useful things; and, of course, procs. *Procs*, known formally as procedures, are the specialized application programs that to most SAS users are the main attraction of the SAS System. Procs do everything from sorting to bar charts.

Shell

Older programming languages were designed with teletype-style terminals in mind. In the highest form of interaction possible with those terminals, the user would type something, and then the computer would type something. Although the SAS System still supports that kind of user interface, it has several special features for more advanced forms of input and output.

It automatically creates two special output files. The log file contains the SAS supervisor's step-by-step account of the execution of the program, including the program statements, notes, warnings, and error messages. The standard print file, sometimes called the *output* file or the *print* file, contains pages of results from programs. Both files are suitable for viewing on screen, printing, or storing.

The SAS System also provides you with temporary storage space for data, primarily in the WORK library, that you can use freely without having to plan it in advance or erase anything afterward.

The SAS System includes a full-screen user interface, the *SAS Display Manager System*, which includes a command line, a text editor, and separate windows for the log, the standard print file, and other information related to the SAS System. The display manager interface is designed primarily for an interactive programming approach, but it can be used in other ways too: for program development, or as an operations center.

Very high-level language

Low-level languages are those in which the components of a program correspond closely to the actual actions taken by the computer. Programs in high-level languages are intended to represent more closely the way the programmer thinks about the program.

For example, high-level languages use data types to represent the different ways memory can be used. The SAS language has two data types, character and numeric, and it will prevent you, for example, from inadvertently assigning a character value to a numeric variable.

SAS has been called a very high-level language because much of its syntax is even more abstract — farther removed from the machine point of view — than most high-level languages. Hopefully, at the same time, its programs represent the ideas of the programmer more clearly and simply.

Storage format

The SAS System has its own storage format, and the SAS language provides high-level access to files in this format, and a similar level of access to many other file formats. Data files that the SAS System accesses this way are called SAS datasets. The simplified access to SAS datasets in SAS syntax eliminates most of the work of programming input and output in SAS programs.

Proprietary

Most programming languages are implemented in several variant forms by several software publishers. The SAS programming language, however, is rooted in the SAS System, which you can only get from SAS Institute, Inc.

Better than BASIC

If you have some experience with the BASIC language, you might find some of the advanced features of the SAS language confusing at first. But there is a way to get the SAS language to act very much like BASIC. You can put BASIC-like statements, translated to SAS syntax, between the statement `DATA _NULL_;` and the statements `STOP; RUN;`. You can use the SUBMIT and RECALL commands in display manager to modify the program and run it again. SAS's advantages over BASIC include more advanced control flow and its large function library.

You can translate most BASIC statements directly to corresponding SAS statements. However, the SAS language has nothing like BASIC's function definitions, and it needs to have arrays declared.

Here is a sample BASIC program and the corresponding literally translated SAS program.

```
100  A = 5
110  B = 10
150  C = 1
200  FOR I = A TO B
210  C = C*(1 + I)
220  NEXT I
230  IF C > 1000 THEN GOTO 600
240  GOTO 700
600  WRITE 'C='; C
610  STOP
700  WRITE 'C < 1000'
710  STOP
```

```
  DATA _NULL_;
    A = 5;
    B = 10;
    C = 1;
    DO I = A TO B;
      C = C*(1 + I);
      END;
    IF C > 1000 THEN GOTO L600;
    GOTO L700;
L600: PUT 'C=' C;
    STOP;
L700: PUT 'C < 1000';
    STOP;
RUN;
```

Up and running

If you've never run a SAS program before, you might be wondering at this point how it's done. An exact answer would describe several ways to do it, each of which would depend on the operating system you're using and some details about the installation. In brief, though, here's what it takes:

1. Get the SAS Display Manager System to appear. We assume you have a computer with the SAS System installed on it. Usually you can get display manager to appear by entering `SAS` at the operating system's command line prompt. You might have to find the right directory first. (Look for one called SAS.)

2. Get the program to appear in the program editor window. It's okay just to type it there. There are several commands you can enter on the command line in the program editor window: INCLUDE to bring in a program from a file, UP and DOWN for scrolling, and HELP if you have questions. The KEYS command also produces interesting results.

3. Enter the SUBMIT command on the command line. The program runs. You might need to put a RUN statement at the end of the program, since the SAS supervisor runs steps only when it's sure it's reached the end of a step. You can use the LOG and OUTPUT commands to go to the log and output windows, or PROGRAM to return to the program editor window.

There is more than this to display manager, and you can find out many interesting things about it by going through the HELP screens, but this ought to be all you need to run a program. Eventually, you'll wonder how to exit display manager; use the ENDSAS or BYE command.

A simple SAS program

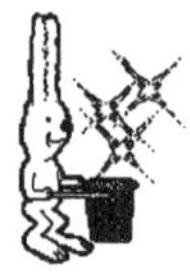

A programmer's traditional first program in a new programming language is the simplest program possible, one that just makes a message such as "Hello, world" appear. There's no reason a SAS program couldn't do this.

```
DATA _NULL_; PUT "Hello, world."; RUN;
```

The typical first SAS program, though, is more like the program that follows. It is a good example of the kinds of things simple SAS programs tend to do.

The program below might have been written by Lisa and Kir, two space aliens trying out several colors for their flying saucer. They made their ship visible in the different colors for varying lengths of time and then monitored people's UFO reports to the local police. They want to know which colors had the greatest tendency to result in UFO reports.

```
* Program to report flying saucer color test statistics;
  DATA UFOS;
    INPUT START TIME8. +3 END TIME8. REPORTS 5. +3 COLOR $CHAR8.;
    IF END >= START THEN LENGTH = END - START;
    ELSE LENGTH = END + 86400 - START;
CARDS;
21:37:01   21:39:33     4     RED
21:59:24   22:00:14     1     YELLOW
22:11:01   22:11:21     0     BLACK
22:18:22   22:19:35     2     GREEN
22:30:00   22:40:00    12     RED
22:52:18   22:52:44     1     CYAN
23:08:15   23:10:15     0     BLACK
23:21:00   23:21:28     1     WHITE
23:41:45   23:42:19     1     CYAN
23:51:05   23:51:49     4     GREEN
23:59:45   00:02:00     1     YELLOW
00:19:02   00:42:52     0     BLACK
;
  PROC SUMMARY DATA=UFOS;
    CLASS COLOR;
    VAR REPORTS LENGTH;
    OUTPUT OUT=UFOSTAT SUM=;
  DATA;
    SET UFOSTAT;
    AVG_RATE = REPORTS/LENGTH;
  PROC PRINT;
RUN;
```

The log

After the program runs, the log is a record of its execution. It is often easier to learn what a SAS program does by reading its log than by reading the program by itself. This makes logs useful as documentation for the program, and thus of any output data it produces. Logs are also the main source of information on syntax errors and other bugs in SAS programs.

This is the log produced by running the UFO program:

```
    1
    2     * Program to report flying saucer color test statistics;
    3       DATA UFOS;
    4         INPUT START TIME8. +3 END TIME8. REPORTS 5. +3 COLOR $8.;
    5         IF END >= START THEN LENGTH = END - START;
    6         ELSE LENGTH = END + 86400 - START;
    7     CARDS;
   20     ;
NOTE: The data set WORK.UFOS has 12 observations and 5 variables.
NOTE: The DATA statement used 8.00 seconds.
   21       PROC SUMMARY DATA=UFOS;
```

```
   22          CLASS COLOR;
   23          VAR REPORTS LENGTH;
   24          OUTPUT OUT=UFOSTAT SUM=;
   25        DATA;
NOTE: The data set WORK.UFOSTAT has 7 observations and 5 variables.
NOTE: The PROCEDURE SUMMARY used 7.00 seconds.
   26          SET UFOSTAT;
   27          AVG_RATE = REPORTS/LENGTH;
   28        PROC PRINT;
NOTE: The data set WORK.DATA1 has 7 observations and 6 variables.
NOTE: The DATA statement used 6.00 seconds.
   29      RUN;
NOTE: The PROCEDURE PRINT used 6.00 seconds.
   30
```

Sequential line numbers appear to the left of the program lines in the log. Messages that the SAS supervisor writes in the log are preceded by the identifiers "NOTE," "WARNING," and "ERROR," reflecting different levels of concern.

Standard print file

The standard print file is the file ordinarily used to hold text output from programs, whether it is sent to a printer, displayed on a screen, or stored for later use. Print files are divided into pages and usually have a title that appears on the first line or first few lines of each page. This program uses the default title, "SAS."

The UFO program produced this standard print file:

```
                                   SAS                                      1

OBS    COLOR     _TYPE_    _FREQ_    REPORTS    LENGTH    AVG_RATE

 1                  0        12         27        2712    0.009956
 2     BLACK        1         3          0        1570    0.000000
 3     CYAN         1         2          2          60    0.033333
 4     GREEN        1         2          6         117    0.051282
 5     RED          1         2         16         752    0.021277
 6     WHITE        1         1          1          28    0.035714
 7     YELLOW       1         2          2         185    0.010811
```

The data step

SAS programs are divided into steps, which are almost like separate programs. There are two kinds of steps: data steps, which begin with the word DATA, and proc steps, which begin with the word PROC.

The UFO program has two data steps. The first one reads input data — in this case, in the data lines following the CARDS statement — and puts it in a SAS dataset so that the proc step that follows can use it. The name of the SAS dataset, UFOS, is given in the DATA statement.

The INPUT statement interprets one input data line, creating values for the variables START, END, REPORTS, and COLOR. Values for START and END are interpreted by the informat `TIME8.` An informat can be thought of as a procedure for interpreting a certain kind of input data. The "8" in the informat is its width; the informat will look for up to 8 characters of input data.

The informat `$8.` is specified for the variable COLOR. This is the informat used for ordinary character variables without leading blanks, with a width of 8. No informat is given for the variable REPORTS, so the default numeric informat is used.

Another variable, LENGTH, gets its value in an assignment statement. The IF . . . THEN . . . ELSE form determines which assignment statement is executed for each observation, depending on whether the time of day of START is earlier than END. If START is later than END, we assume that the test period spanned midnight, and calculate its length accordingly.

The CARDS statement marks the end of the step. At that point, the program writes the values of all the variables named in the step to the output SAS dataset, UFOS, creating an observation. Since there is more than one data line, the data step is executed repeatedly, creating one observation from each input line, until the end of the input lines is reached.

The second data step comes between the two proc steps. Its input data is the SAS dataset UFOSTAT named in the SET statement. It produces an output SAS dataset for which no name is given in the DATA statement, so the SAS supervisor gives it the name DATA1. DATA1 has the same data as UFOSTAT, plus an added variable, AVG_RATE, which is created by the assignment statement.

The proc step

In addition to the two data steps, the program has two proc steps.

The first proc step uses the SUMMARY proc to calculate sums of REPORTS and LENGTH, the two variables listed in the VAR statement. Because COLOR is listed in the CLASS statement, these variables are summed for all observations having the same COLOR value. The output SAS dataset, UFOSTAT, contains one value for each different color, plus an observation representing all colors combined. The output SAS dataset contains all the variables named in the PROC step, plus a few extra identifier variables.

The final step uses the PRINT proc. Because the input SAS dataset is not specified, the most recently created SAS dataset, DATA1, is used. No list of variables is stated, so the procedure uses all of them. The PRINT proc produces a report, in table form, of all the data values in the SAS dataset. This report is the contents of the standard print file that appears above.

SAS datasets

The SAS System provides special support for a particular kind of data file called a *SAS dataset*. SAS datasets are used frequently in SAS programs; there are three SAS datasets, UFO, UFOSTAT, and DATA1, in the program above.

A SAS dataset is like a table. It has a list of variables and can have any number of observations. Each observation consists of values for each of the variables. In addition to the data values, a SAS dataset has a header, which contains identifying information about the SAS dataset and its variables.

SAS datasets are kept in collections called SAS data libraries, which are identified in SAS programs by names called *librefs*. A SAS dataset is identified in a SAS program by a two-level name that identifies the SAS data library and the SAS dataset. For example, the name A.TABLE4 identifies the TABLE4 member of the A library. When a one-level name is used for a SAS dataset, the WORK library is ordinarily assumed. For example, the SAS dataset UFO in the program above is actually WORK.UFO, in the WORK library. That's why messages in the program's log refer to WORK.UFO rather than simply to UFO.

How to read a SAS program

So many things can appear in a SAS program that you need a scorecard to keep track of them all. On the following pages, we describe the main things to look for.

Comments

First, you need to be able to pick out the SAS program among the other things that can be in the program file. The file might also contain data lines, input data that is treated just as if it were in a separate file. The end of a SAS program might be marked in the middle of the program file. And, like just about every programming language, SAS allows comments.

Comments are ignored by the interpreter and are typically used to explain the program or to prevent parts of the program from running. SAS comments come in two forms: a *delimited comment*, between `/*` and `*/`, or a *comment statement*, which starts with a star and ends with a semicolon.

```
/* This is a delimited comment. */
* This is a comment statement;
```

```
*------------------------------------------------------------*
|                                                            |
|  Some programmers like to draw this kind of box around     |
|  large descriptive comments.  It makes the comment much    |
|  easier to see.                                            |
|                                                            |
*------------------------------------------------------------*;
```

Neither kind of comment nests, but you can put one kind of comment inside the other.

```
/* This is a comment with  * Another comment;  inside it. */
  * This is also a /* valid */ comment form;

  /* This /* line */ is an error. */

  * This is also /* an error; because the first semicolon
      marks the end of the comment statement.*/;
```

A comment statement should not begin with the characters */, like this

```
*/ A bad way to start a comment statement /;
```

because the SAS interpreter tends to interpret those characters as the end of a delimited comment, even if there is no delimited comment to end. It then does not recognize the start of the comment statement, and will probably report a syntax error.

Comments are often used to disable parts of a program, especially when a program is being debugged. Statements and parts of statements that are put inside a comment are said to be *commented out*.

```
  * This is one way to comment out a group of statements.
    The stars can form a column because there is only one
    statement on each line. ;
* DATA BETTER;
*   SET RESULTS;
*   FILE PRINT;
*   PUT @5 SECTION $CHAR4. @11 PERCENTL 3.;

    * Only part of the following statement is commented out. ;
    KEEP SECTION PERCENTL /* SCORE1-SCORE17 */ VERSION;

* It is possible to comment out large sections of a program.
  In this example, only US50 gets printed.;

/*PROC PRINT DATA=I44;
    BY STATE;
  PROC PRINT DATA=I55;
    BY STATE;
```

```
  PROC PRINT DATA=I64;
    BY STATE;
  PROC PRINT DATA=I70;
    BY STATE;
*/PROC PRINT DATA=US50;
    BY STATE;
/*PROC PRINT DATA=US67;
    BY STATE;
*/
```

> Under the MVS operating system, /* should not appear at the beginning of an otherwise blank line. There, it might be taken as an end-of-file mark. This is unfortunate, because the beginning of a line would be the most natural place to start a long comment.

Data lines

Lines of data can be included in a program file. Any step can be followed by data lines. The interpreter, though, has to be told where the step ends and the data lines begin. In the data step, the CARDS or CARDS4 statement marks the transition.

The CARDS and CARDS4 statements can also be written as the LINES and LINES4 or DATALINES and DATALINES4 statements.

When the interpreter gets to the CARDS statement, it immediately stops interpreting program statements. Beginning with the following line, and continuing until it comes to a line containing a semicolon, it treats lines in the program file as data lines. Since a semicolon marks the end of every SAS statement, it is a pretty good indication that the statements making up the next step in the program have been reached. But this also means that the data lines cannot contain any semicolons.

To mark data lines that might contain semicolons, you can use the CARDS4 statement. With CARDS4, the signal for the end of the data lines is very specific: a line starting with four semicolons and otherwise blank.

Because the interpreter stops as soon as it gets to the CARDS or CARDS4 statement, that statement has to be the last one in the step. Any statement that follows on the same line will be completely ignored.

```
  DATA WORK.FAVES;
    INFILE CARDS;
    INPUT NAME $ FAVCOL $ FAVPUNC $;
CARDS4;      -- Anything here is ignored by the interpreter! --
KENDRA   YELLOW   !
ALAN     GREEN    $
ANN      BLACK    +
BETH     PINK     =
TOM      BROWN    ;
JASON    RED      /
```

```
SCOTT    PLAID   &
;;;;
```

Data lines can be used in proc steps too, but few procs use them. They work the same way, but the statement at the end of the step and the beginning of the data lines is PARMCARDS or PARMCARDS4.

End of the program

Usually the SAS interpreter keeps interpreting program steps until it gets to the end of the program file, but under certain circumstances it will stop sooner. The end of the program can be marked with the ENDSAS statement:

```
ENDSAS;
```

The ENDSAS statement cannot be combined with any other statement; in particular, you cannot say `IF ... THEN ENDSAS;`.

The ABORT statement, which can be used in a data step, can also cause a program to end early. It is described in chapter 4, "Control flow."

Preprocessing

SAS syntax has a few different types of preprocessor symbols; when they are present, the SAS interpreter uses them to find or generate the statements to be interpreted before it actually interprets each step.

The %INCLUDE or %INC statement identifies one or more external files to be included in the program at that point. This allows you to put your SAS program in more than one file, or to include the same group of statements in several programs.

```
%INCLUDE FROG1;  * FROG1 is a file containing SAS statements. ;
```

There is also a SAS macrolanguage, which is managed by a separate part of the SAS interpreter called the macro processor.

Macrolanguage has two slightly different types of objects that represent SAS code, called macrovariables and macros. It also has an extensive collection of statements, functions, and operators.

The macrovariable is the most common macrolanguage object. A macrovariable reference consists of an ampersand (&) followed by a macrovariable name. (Sometimes more than one ampersand is used.) The macrovariable name might be followed by a period (or several periods, if several ampersands are used) to separate the macrovariable reference from whatever characters follow it. The macrovariable reference is replaced by the string of characters that is the value of the macrovariable.

Macrolanguage statements all begin with a percent sign (%) and a keyword. One common macrolanguage statement is the %LET statement, which assigns a value to a macrovariable.

```
* Assign the value 45A to the macrovariable N;
%LET N = 45A;

  DATA GROUP&N; * Now this statement means DATA GROUP45A;
```

References to macros and macro functions look and act about the same. They consist of a percent sign, then a name, and then possibly a list of parameters or arguments enclosed in parentheses.

```
* Invoke the STORY macro with these 4 parameters;
%STORY(GOLDILOCKS, BEAR, BEAR, BEAR)
```

The main difference is that macros are defined using the %MACRO and %MEND statements, while macro functions are a predefined part of macrolanguage.

Macrolanguage references can come anywhere at all in a program, even in the middle of words. They can even occur within a character constant if it is surrounded by double quotes.

SAS macrolanguage is covered in detail in chapter 7, "Macrolanguage." At this point, the important thing is to be able to identify macrolanguage references when you run across them. Most of the time, ampersands and percent signs indicate the use of macrolanguage.

> The word "macro" comes from the Greek word for "long." Its use goes back to the early days of computer programming, when macro instructions were invented to shorten assembly language programs. A macro instruction represented a long series of instructions used to accomplish a particular task. The term has evolved to include a wide range of situations in software where one thing represents another.

Tokens

The smallest meaningful unit of a program is a token. The SAS language uses three types of tokens — words, symbols, and constants — which are discussed in detail below.

Tokens are grouped into statements. Each SAS statement ends with a semicolon.

SAS is a free-form language, allowing statements to be spread across several lines, and allowing spaces to be added between any two tokens. The use of spaces, blank lines, and indentation can have a considerable effect on the clarity of a program.

Steps

Most of the statements in a SAS program are grouped into steps. There are two kinds of steps: the data step, which includes general programming statements, and the proc step, which runs a proc.

The beginning of a step is marked by a DATA or PROC statement. Sometimes the end of the step is explicitly marked, with the RUN or QUIT statement, or with a CARDS, CARDS4, PARMCARDS, or PARMCARDS4 statement that also signals the beginning of data lines. Otherwise, the step boundary is at the end of the program or the DATA or PROC statement beginning the next step.

The RUN statement is ordinarily the statement that marks the end of a step. However, there are certain interactive *run-group* procs that work differently. Statements in an interactive proc can be executed one at a time or a few at a time, instead of executing all the statements in the step at once, the way most steps work. The RUN statement tells the interactive proc to execute the preceding statements, but does not necessarily mark the end of the step. The QUIT statement can be used to mark the end of the interactive proc step; otherwise, the end of the step is signaled by the next DATA or PROC statement. The DATASETS proc is an example of a run-group proc.

The CANCEL option can appear on the RUN statement to indicate that the preceding step (or run group) is not actually executed:

```
RUN CANCEL;
```

The PGM= option can appear on the RUN, CARDS, or CARDS4 statement at the end of a data step to indicate that the step is being compiled instead of being executed. The use of the PGM= option is described in chapter 2, "The facts."

Statements

SAS statements are named for the words that they start with, except for a few statements that do not begin with keywords.

The different SAS statements are used in different places. Some of them can be used only in data steps, and some can be used only in proc steps. Some of them must appear in a certain position relative to other statements.

Some SAS statements do not really belong to steps. They are called *global* statements because they can be used anywhere in a SAS program. The SAS interpreter executes them immediately when it encounters them, before executing the step they reside in.

Two data step statements do not begin with keywords: the assignment statement and the sum statement. They are both used to change the value of a variable. Both statements start with a reference to a variable: a variable name, array reference, or for the assignment statement, a SUBSTR pseudo-variable. In the assignment statement, the variable reference is followed by an equals sign (=) and an expression that is assigned to the variable. In the sum statement, the variable reference is followed by a plus sign (+) and a value that is added to the variable.

```
DATA _NULL_;
  F = 5;      * Assignment statement -- assigns the value 5
                  to the variable F;
  I + 1;      * Sum statement -- adds 1 to the variable I;
```

There is also a null statement, which is just a semicolon by itself. It can appear anywhere and doesn't do anything (which is not to say that it is meaningless). It is mainly used in certain kinds of control flow programming to specify that no action should take place in a particular case.

The following table categorizes SAS statements according to where they can be used and the kinds of things they do.

Where	Actions	Statements
data and proc steps	set variable attributes	ATTRIB, FORMAT, INFORMAT, LABEL, LENGTH
data and proc steps	input	BY, WHERE
data step	control flow	ABORT, DELETE, DO, END, ELSE, GOTO, IF, LINK, LOSTCARD, OTHERWISE, RETAIN, RETURN, SELECT, STOP, WHEN
data step	input	INFILE, INPUT, MERGE, SET, UPDATE
data step	output	DATA, DROP, ERROR, FILE, KEEP, LIST, PUT, OUTPUT, RENAME
data step	miscellaneous	ARRAY, assignment, CALL, DISPLAY, sum, WINDOW
proc step	run proc	CLASS, FREQ, ID, MODEL, OUTPUT, PROC, VAR, WEIGHT, *other statements, depending on the proc*
anywhere	program parameters	FILENAME, FOOTNOTE, LIBNAME, MISSING, OPTIONS, TITLE
anywhere	immediate actions	DM, SKIP, PAGE, X, *other statements, depending on the implementation*
anywhere	none	null
between steps	mark end of step	CARDS, CARDS4, DATALINES, DATALINES4, LINES, LINES4, PARMCARDS, PARMCARDS4, QUIT, RUN

Statement labels

Most statements in a data step can be preceded by a label, which is followed by a colon (:). Statement labels are used in GOTO statements and other forms of branching in the data step.

```
HERE: A + 1;           * a sum statement with the label HERE;
THERE: ;               * a null statement with the label THERE;
    IF A < 6 THEN GOTO HERE;    * a GOTO statement;
```

Words

Two kinds of words occur in SAS programs. A *keyword* is a word that has a particular meaning in SAS syntax. Keywords occur at the beginnings of statements and at certain specified places within certain statements.

Other words in a SAS program are names. Words that are used as SAS keywords can also be used as names — there might be a variable called DATA, for example — so you have to identify keywords by their location. Most keywords begin statements and are listed in the table of statements above. AND, BETWEEN, CANCEL, CHARACTER, DEFAULT, DESCENDING, EQ, GE, GROUPFORMAT, GT, IN, LE, LIKE, LT, MAX, MIN, NE, NOBS, NOT, NOTIN, NOTSORTED, NUMERIC, OF, OR, OUT, SAME, TO, UNTIL, WHILE, and _PAGE_ are some other common SAS keywords.

Capital letters and lowercase letters are interchangeable in words in SAS programs. For example, `DATA`, `data`, and `DAta` all mean the same thing. By convention, most SAS programmers use capital letters.

Meet PROF and DARA

The SAS interpreter is astute at finding the most likely misspellings of certain of the most popular SAS keywords. DATA, for example, can be misspelled as DAT, DARA, DAATA, DATYA, or with various other simple one-letter errors, without creating a syntax error. CARTS, CARD, and CARDZ will all pass as CARDS, and PROF and PORC are among the recognized misspellings of PROC.

When the interpreter recognizes a misspelling of a SAS keyword, it mentions it in a brief log message, naming the keyword it assumes you mean, and proceeds with interpreting the step.

Names

Names in SAS programs are 1 to 8 characters long. The first character is a letter or underscore. The rest of the characters can be letters, underscores, and digits. Compare the following lists of valid and invalid names:

```
VALID                      NOT VALID
A                          1STNAME
CAT_NAME                   dog-name
X1                         BIORHYTHM
_1                         $C4
homevalu
```

Names of this type are called *SAS names* and are used for variables and arrays, SAS datasets, filerefs, librefs, statements labels, windows, macro-variables, and macros.

Slightly different rules apply for the names for informats and formats. Their names cannot end in a digit, and the names of character informats and character formats begin with a dollar sign ($).

Additional restrictions might apply to the names of librefs and filerefs, because these names have to be valid filenames too under certain operating systems. Filerefs can also use the characters $, #, and @.

The names of functions, procs, and engines might be longer than 8 characters.

Generally, the different classes of objects in SAS programs have different name spaces. That means you can use the same name for different objects, as long as they are not the same kind of object. You could, for example, have a SAS dataset TIME containing a variable TIME. Variables and arrays share a name space, so you cannot use the same name for a variable and an array in the same step. Also, it is a bad idea for an array to have the same name as a SAS function. Only one step runs at a time, so you can use the same name for variables, arrays, and statement labels in different steps.

Special names

Certain names have specific uses in the SAS language. Although it might be possible to use these names for other objects, you should try to avoid doing so. Most of them begin and end with a single underscore (_). The following list is not complete, so to be really safe, you can avoid using any name that begins and ends with a single underscore.

Some names have special meaning as SAS dataset names. In certain contexts, _ALL_ means all the SAS datasets that are available. Using _DATA_ asks the SAS interpreter to make up a new name in the DATA*n* series: DATA1, DATA2, DATA3, etc. _NULL_ means no SAS dataset. _LAST_ means the most recently created SAS dataset.

The SAS interpreter creates automatic variables in the data step and in some proc steps. The most important automatic variables are _N_, which counts the executions of the observation loop, starting at 1, and _ERROR_, which is usually 0, but changes to 1 when some error conditions are encountered. Other examples of automatic variable names SAS sometimes uses are _COL_, _CMD_, _FDBK_, _FREQ_, _I_, _INFILE_, _LABEL_, _MSG_, _NAME_, _RBA_, _ROW_, _TITLES_, _TYPE_, and _WEIGHT_.

A few names are used as abbreviated variable lists, which are discussed below.

There are also many reserved names for macrolanguage objects; unlike other special names, they do not begin and end with an underscore. They are the names of macro functions and automatic macrovariables. The names of automatic macrovariables generally begin with the letters SYS.

Variable lists

Variable lists can occur in many places in SAS programs. You might list variables to be stored in a SAS dataset or to be analyzed by a proc. The keyword OF allows you to use variable lists as arguments to certain functions. Variable lists normally consist of variable names separated by spaces. However, the SAS language also provides several forms of abbreviated variable lists you can use.

The most common form of abbreviated variable list uses a hyphen to indicate variable names with a range of numeric suffixes. For example, `A1-A12` is the same as `A1 A2 A3 A4 A5 A6 A7 A8 A9 A10 A11 A12`. Leading zeroes can be used in the numeric suffixes if they have the same number of digits. `A08-A10` would be `A08 A09 A10`, but `A01-A100` would not be accepted.

In some implementations, a descending numbered range can also be used; `A12-A1` would represent `A12 A11 A10 A9 A8 A7 A6 A5 A4 A3 A2 A1`.

A double hyphen indicates a different kind of range of variables, in the order in which they appear in memory. If a data step has the variables X, Y, Z, and TOTAL defined in that order, then `X--TOTAL` represents the variables `X Y Z TOTAL`. This kind of variable list is called a *named range*.

There are three special variable lists. _ALL_ represents a list of all the variables available, including any automatic variables. Use _NUMERIC_ to get only the numeric variables, or _CHARACTER_ or _CHAR_ to get only character variables.

A named range can be combined with a special variable list by putting the keyword NUMERIC or CHARACTER (or, in some implementations, _NUMERIC_ or _CHARACTER_) between the two hyphens in a named range of variables. For example, `E-NUMERIC-A` includes only the numeric variables located from E to A in memory.

The preceding abbreviated variable lists can be used almost anywhere you use a variable list in a SAS program.

In many procs, a colon can be used to indicate an alphabetic range of variable names. For example, `A:` would be used to identify all variables (or perhaps all numeric variables) whose names begin with the letter A. A group of variables beginning with the letters INC could be identified as `INC:`.

A few procs that operate on SAS datasets or other SAS files use lists of file names that can be abbreviated using forms similar to those of abbreviated variable lists. In particular, the keyword _ALL_ can be used to indicate all the SAS datasets or files available in a particular context.

Arrays

SAS syntax provides a way to refer to a variable list by name in programming statements; a named variable list is called an *array*, and the variables in it are called *elements*. Arrays are defined in the ARRAY statement, which identifies the name of the array, the number of elements, and the names of the elements. This ARRAY statement creates an array SEQUENCE with the 5 elements FIRST, SECOND, THIRD, FOURTH, and FIFTH.

```
ARRAY SEQUENCE{5} FIRST SECOND THIRD FOURTH FIFTH;
```

After the array is defined, its elements can be referred to using the array name and the position of the element in the array, called a *subscript*, which is enclosed in braces. For example, SECOND could be referred to as

```
SEQUENCE{2}
```

The subscript can be any numeric expression; it is often the index variable of a DO loop.

In some implementations, parentheses or brackets can be used instead of braces to enclose array subscripts. However, all implementations allow the use of braces.

There is another kind of array, called an implicitly subscripted array, in which the index value is not actually stated in the array reference itself. It is less commonly used. Arrays are described in chapter 6, "Expressions."

Constants

Constants are values that appear in a program. They're called "constants" to distinguish them from variables — variables also have values, but the value of a variable can change as the program runs. The SAS language has several ways of representing constants for its two data types.

The following are all valid numeric constants in a SAS program:

```
1
-0.0087
.
00750
6.02E23
9.109534E-31
5EX
'4JUL1776'D
'16:30'T
'15AUG1991 09:14.21'DT
```

The following are valid character constants:

```
'Good morning!'
" a"
'534153'X
"'"
```

The meaning of the different forms of constants is described in chapter 6, "Expressions."

Single and double quote marks are used for some forms of constants.

The use of single quotes and double quotes is nearly identical, but they must occur in matched pairs: a closing single quote for every opening single quote, and a closing double quote for every opening double quote. In a constant delimited with single quotes, two consecutive single quotes represent one single quote, while double quotes have no special meaning. Inside double quotes, the reverse is true.

There is an important difference between single quotes and double quotes having to do with SAS macrolanguage. The macro processor attempts to resolve macro references that occur in constants that are enclosed in double quotes. Macro references begin with an ampersand (&) or a percent sign (%). For a character constant to contain an actual ampersand or percent sign, it should be enclosed in single quotes.

```
'AT&T'    /* the right way to write this character constant */
"AT&T"    /* the wrong way, because the macro processor will try
            to substitute the value of the macrovariable T for &T */
```

It's essential to have a closing quote to match every opening quote. Quote marks that don't occur in pairs are called *unbalanced quotes*. A frequent result of unbalanced quotes is that the SAS interpreter thinks the entire rest of the program is a character constant.

The following examples demonstrate the two most common ways of generating unbalanced quotes by accident.

```
    W = 'It's';                       /* odd number of quote marks */

TITLE1 "Topographic Details';         /* mismatched quote marks */
```

Special symbols, including the semicolon and comment delimiters, do not have their usual meaning inside quoted strings. Similarly, quote marks inside comments do not indicate character constants and do not have to be balanced. We discuss some implications of this below.

Symbols

We've already seen several uses for symbols in the SAS language, and there are many more. The following table summarizes the main uses of symbols in SAS programs.

Symbol	Use
	Program Control
/*	the beginning of a comment
*/	the end of a comment
*	the beginning of a comment statement
;	at the end of a statement
;;;;	after data lines
%	part of some keywords, such as %INCLUDE
&	macrovariable reference
% ( )	other macrolanguage references
:	after a statement label
	Statement Syntax
$	declares or identifies character variables
( )	encloses options
=	associates value with option
,	separates expressions in lists
/	separates lists from options
@ @@ & ? ?? / # : +	used in INPUT and PUT statements
, : *	used in ARRAY statement to define subscript range
=	identifies assignment statement
+	identifies sum statement
	Names
- -- :	used to form abbreviated variable lists
.	separates levels in multi-level names
$	begins name of character format or informat
.	follows informat or format name or width specification
	Expressions
+ – * / ** < <= = >= > ^= ¬= ~= : <> >< || & | ^ ¬ ~	operators, used to create expressions
.	missing value; decimal point
–	negative sign in numeric constant
' ' " "	encloses date, time, datetime, and character constants
( )	used for grouping in expressions; encloses SELECT, WHEN, UNTIL, and WHILE expressions; encloses arguments for functions and CALL routines
{ } ( ) [ ]	encloses subscripts in array reference
,	separator
=* ?	additional operators used in WHEN expressions

A few symbols have many different uses. The largest category of symbols is the operators. Operators are used to create expressions and are described in detail in chapter 6, "Expressions."

Start at the beginning

There are several symbols that affect the meaning of parts of the program — particularly the quote marks, the semicolon that marks the end of statements, and the /* and */ or * and ; that mark comments. (There are also some macrolanguage statements and functions that have similar effects.) In addition to controlling the meaning of other symbols, these symbols can affect each other's meaning.

A semicolon inside quotes does not mark the end of a statement, for example. Here, it is the second semicolon that marks the end of the statement:

```
SYMBOL = ';';
```

Double quotes have no special effect inside single quotes, and vice versa. The statement

```
I'd insisted that "it's" wasn't a possessive.
```

could be made a character constant either of these two ways (using two single quotes to represent a single quote in the first constant, and using two double quotes to represent a double quote in the second):

```
ST = 'I''d insisted that "it''s" wasn''t a possessive.';
ST = "I'd insisted that ""it's"" wasn't a possessive.";
```

Quotes have no effect inside comments. That means that this is a valid comment, despite the lone single quote:

```
/* There isn't anything wrong with this comment, */
```

but the statement below is imperfectly commented out, resulting in a troublesome unbalanced quote, because the first semicolon marks the end of the comment statement:

```
* SYMBOL = ';';
```

Comments can't be placed inside character constants. This statement assigns A a 12-character value, not a one-character value:

```
A = '/*CAPITAL*/A';
```

It's possible for some confusion to arise as to which of these symbols are actually in control in a certain section of code. (This especially happens when macrolanguage functions are used.) The way to be sure you know what the program means is to start interpreting it at the beginning of the program, applying the same rules that the SAS interpreter uses.

This code fragment demonstrates the kind of confusion that can arise.

```
  DATA A;                                                    /* line 1 */
TITLE1 'Very Important Report To Underwriters And Lawyers ;
  /* Based on selections from the first two weeks'          ;
     set of case studies                                    ;
  */
    LENGTH A1 A0 $ 3;                                        /* line 6 */
    RETAIN A1 'Yes' A2 'No;'
    SET Q1;
    L = (A =: 'Y');
```

Taken by themselves, lines 3–5 appear to be a descriptive comment. Actually, line 3 is a continuation of the title in line 2, line 4 is a SET statement, and lines 5–6 make up a comment statement. Also notice that the statement on line 7 continues on line 8, even though line 8 looks like a statement in its own right.

Few SAS programs (excluding those that use macrolanguage) are as confusing as this, but it is important to remember that you cannot always determine the meaning of one line in a program without considering the lines that precede it.

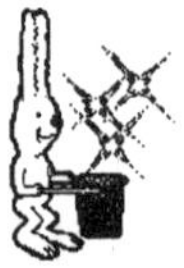

Sometimes the SAS interpreter just doesn't seem to respond to steps that you submit. This is hardly ever due to a SAS bug. The interpreter might be stuck inside an unterminated quoted string, comment, or macro function. In display manager, this condition may be evidenced by an insistent R flag on the bottom line. "R" stands for *running,* and means that the interpreter is between the beginning and the end of a step. In that situation, before you panic, even before you start an investigation, submit this sequence of characters, which almost always returns things to normal:

```
*))%*'"))*/;
```

If that doesn't have any effect, try a line of four semicolons

```
;;;;
```

in case there were data lines following a CARDS4 statement that were never properly terminated, and a `%MEND;` statement in case you are in an unintended macro definition. Then you might want a `RUN CANCEL` statement so that you can start fresh with a new step.

One way to write SAS programs

There are at least as many ways to program as there are programmers. What follows is the general approach we recommend for most SAS programmers most of the time. This approach allows you to break down a programming problem into questions that are small enough to be looked up in books like this one.

Step by step

Before you start programming, be clear about the purpose of the program. A program produces output that has some relation to its input. What output do you intend to get? Consider the data available to be used as input. What parts of it are actually relevant to the output of the program? Is it sufficient data to produce the output data intended?

Determine what processing the data has to go through between the input and the output. Then determine what parts of the process can be done by procs. Write proc steps for the procs to be used, and determine the exact form of the input and output data for the proc steps. Write data steps where needed to bridge the gaps between procs or to handle the input or output data.

You might need data step programming to prepare data for a proc, to modify data produced by a proc, to put input data in a usable form, to put output data in a particular format needed, to combine data from different sources, or to break data into subsets. Several things can be often be done in the same data step; in general, it is better not to have several data steps when one will accomplish the same thing.

Writing a data step

There is little reason to try to write data step statements in the order in which they ultimately appear in the step. You can start with the most obvious part, which is usually the statements controlling either input or output, depending on the position of the step in the program and what steps have been written already.

Output in the data step is controlled by the DATA and OUTPUT statements, for output to SAS datasets, and the FILE and PUT statements for text output. In any case, the first statement in the data step is the DATA statement, which lists the names of SAS datasets that the step creates. For example, a data step creating SAS datasets A and B would start with

```
DATA A B;
```

If the step does not create a SAS dataset, the form of the statement is

```
DATA _NULL_;
```

Input in a data step is controlled by the SET, MERGE, and UPDATE statements, which identify input SAS datasets, or the INFILE and INPUT statements for text input. In simple cases, the input data for the step comes from only one file. If the file is a SAS dataset, it is named in a SET statement.

```
SET C;
```

If the file is a text file, an INFILE statement identifies it and an INPUT statement interprets it.

```
INFILE D;
INPUT E F G H I;
```

After writing the input and output statements, write any statements needed for control flow related to input and output. Then add any other statements needed for processing in the step. You might also need some declaration statements, like an ARRAY statement if you use an array or perhaps a LENGTH statement if you create a character variable.

Writing a proc step

A proc step starts with the PROC statement, which has the word PROC, the name of the proc being used, and usually some options that are appropriate for the particular proc. One common option is the DATA= option, which identifies the input SAS dataset.

Most procs also have additional statements, which might be required or optional. The order of statements after the PROC statement usually does not matter. The BY statement can be used with most analytic procs to cause analysis to be done separately by groups. The syntax of proc steps varies considerably from one proc to another, so you'll need to refer to the individual proc's documentation to know how to program it.

Putting steps together

Output data becomes input data; the output from one step in a SAS program might be input to a later step. A SAS dataset is the usual connection between two steps in a SAS program.

When putting steps together to form a program, you need to make the references to the SAS datasets consistent. Make sure that each SAS dataset has the same name everywhere, that the variable names are the same, and that a variable does not change between the numeric and character data types in any step.

2 The facts

A symbolic understanding of the SAS language might be adequate for writing some SAS programs. However, having a mechanical understanding of some central concepts can make programming easier and more reliable. This chapter concentrates on distinctive characteristics of the SAS programming language and the SAS System.

The parse/execute cycle

A SAS program consists of a number of steps — data steps and proc steps. This division into steps is more than just a rule of syntax; it reflects the way the SAS interpreter goes through a program, alternately parsing and executing steps. First, the interpreter reads lines from the program file, parsing them — dividing them into tokens and statements — until a complete step is formed. Then it executes the step. Then it parses more lines from the program file until it forms another complete step. Then it executes that step. This process continues until the end of the program is reached.

The parse/execute cycle actually consists of a sequence of specific actions. In general, starting at the beginning of the SAS program, the interpreter:

- reads lines from the program to form a statement.
- checks the syntax of the statement. If it is the kind of statement that is executed immediately, it executes it. If there is a syntax error, it generates an error message. Otherwise, it adds the information from the statement to the step being built.
- continues processing statements until it reaches the end of the step.
- executes the step, unless it can't because of syntax errors.

• stops, if the end of the step was the end of the program. Otherwise, it repeats this whole process.

Notice that the SAS interpreter accepts two types of statements, which are processed independently of each other. A step is compiled from the statements that belong to it, while other statements that are interspersed with the step's statements are executed immediately. It can be important to know which statements belong to a step and which do not.

The statements that execute immediately are often called *global* statements or "statements used anywhere." "Anywhere" implies that the statements do not have to be associated with a step. Just about any statement that would make sense to execute immediately belongs to this category, particularly statements that affect the SAS environment, such as the TITLE and OPTIONS statements.

Step boundary

The end of a step can be marked in any of these ways:

• a RUN (or QUIT) statement
• a CARDS, CARDS4, LINES, LINES4, DATALINES, or DATALINES4 statement (in a data step)
• a PARMCARDS or PARMCARDS4 statement (in a proc step)
• the DATA or PROC statement at the beginning of the next step
• the end of the program

The RUN statement is the explicit way to mark the end of a step. This is especially useful when running programs interactively, because you often want to have a step run before you enter the beginning of the next step.

The end of the program can be either the ENDSAS statement or the end of the program file.

Stepping through a program

Let's take this program as an example.

```
  DATA A;
    INFILE A;
    INPUT A B C D;
  PROC FREQ DATA=A;
    TABLES A*B;
TITLE 'Frequency Table';
OPTIONS PAGESIZE=60;
  PROC MEANS;
TITLE 'Descriptive Statistics';
    CLASS B;
```

The SAS interpreter executes this program in this order:

• the data step `DATA A; INFILE A; INPUT A B C D;`

- the TITLE statement `TITLE 'Frequency Table';`
- the OPTIONS statement `OPTIONS PAGESIZE=60;`
- the proc step `PROC FREQ DATA=A; TABLES A*B;`
- the TITLE statement `TITLE 'Descriptive Statistics';`
- the proc step `PROC MEANS; CLASS B;`

The order of execution does not match the order of the statements in the program. The first TITLE statement and OPTIONS statement execute before the FREQ proc step because they are statements that execute immediately, and the interpreter encounters them in the program before it finds the end of the FREQ proc step.

We can rearrange the program many different ways and still have it execute exactly the same way. The TABLES statement, for example, could be put after the OPTIONS statement. Perhaps the most sensible arrangement is to have the statements appear in the order in which they are executed. To do this requires the use of RUN statements to separate each step from the statements that execute between it and the next step.

```
  DATA A;
    INFILE A;
    INPUT A B C D;
RUN;
TITLE 'Frequency Table';
OPTIONS PAGESIZE=60;
  PROC FREQ DATA=A;
    TABLES A*B;
RUN;
TITLE 'Descriptive Statistics';
  PROC MEANS;
    CLASS B;
```

Compare this version of the program with the previous one. It executes the same way. Only its appearance is changed.

Understanding the cycle of parsing and executing becomes particularly important when macrolanguage is used. We discuss this in chapter 7, "Macrolanguage."

Canceling a step

The CANCEL option can be used on a RUN statement to prevent the preceding step from being executed. In an interactive session, it can let you change your mind about a step and start it over. The RUN CANCEL statement cancels the most recent step, but not any global statements that are mixed in with it. For example, when these statements are executed

```
  PROC PRINT;
OPTIONS OBS=40;
RUN CANCEL;
```

the PRINT proc does not run, but the OPTIONS statement, which is not part of the step, does. The OPTIONS statement has already been executed when the interpreter gets to the RUN statement.

Run groups

Interactive procs fall into two categories: the *full-screen* procs, which display data in their own windows, and the *run-group* procs, which, like most procs, display data in the SAS log or standard print file. Full-screen procs are controlled by commands, which are entered in the command lines of the procs' windows. They cannot be used in batch mode.

Run-group procs, like most procs, are controlled by statements in the SAS program file and therefore can be used in either interactive or batch mode. However, the RUN statement can appear between statements in the step, marking off segments called *run groups* that are executed separately, as if they were separate steps. In an interactive session, this allows the user to see the results of the first statements in the proc before deciding what other statements to execute. The QUIT statement is the statement that marks the end of the step. The RUN CANCEL statement can be used to cancel a run group without ending the step.

Some procs, especially run-group procs, execute some of their statements immediately, without waiting for a RUN statement. Thus, some statements in a step or run group might be executed even if there is a syntax error in a later statement or if a RUN CANCEL statement is used. Also, if global statements are used in the step or run group, they would not necessarily be executed before the proc step statements.

Compiling

When a program is compiled, a separate file is created with a machine language or low-level version of the program. Machine language is the code that a computer works with directly, so a machine language file can be run by the computer without having to be interpreted. Running a compiled program is usually faster that interpreting a program.

SAS data steps can be compiled. Compiling a data step creates a SAS file, in a SAS data library, that can be run in a SAS program. The compiled data step is not actually a machine language program, but is parsed code that the SAS System calls "intermediate code."

To compile a data step, use the PGM= option on the RUN statement at the end of the step. The PGM= option specifies a SAS file name where the compiled data step will be stored. When the PGM= option is used, the data step is not executed, but (if there are no syntax errors) is compiled instead.

These statements compile this data step, putting the compiled version in the SAS data library PROJECT, with the member name A:

```
  DATA A;
    INFILE A;
    INPUT A B C D;
RUN PGM=PROJECT.A;
```

A compiled data step can be executed by using the PGM= option on a DATA statement. You can change the names of input SAS datasets (on SET, MERGE, or UPDATE statements) and output SAS datasets (listed on the DATA statement) in the compiled data step by using the REDIRECT INPUT and REDIRECT OUTPUT statements:

```
  DATA PGM=SAS file;
    REDIRECT INPUT  compiled SAS dataset name=actual SAS dataset name ...;
    REDIRECT OUTPUT compiled SAS dataset name=actual SAS dataset name ...;
RUN;
```

> Before SAS release 6.06, the REDIRECT INPUT and REDIRECT OUTPUT statements were simply the INPUT and OUTPUT statements. However, these INPUT and OUTPUT statements were used only when running compiled data steps and had nothing at all to do with the usual INPUT and OUTPUT statements in the data step.

The data step compiled above could be run with these statements:

```
  DATA PGM=PROJECT.A;
RUN;
```

It could also be run this way, in which case the step would create the SAS dataset B instead of the SAS dataset A:

```
  DATA PGM=PROJECT.A;
    REDIRECT OUTPUT A=B;
RUN;
```

It makes sense to use very general descriptive names in compiled data steps that might be used in different situations. For example, if a compiled data step creates only one SAS dataset, you might as well call it OUT, so that the REDIRECT OUTPUT statement can then read

```
    REDIRECT OUTPUT OUT=B;
```

Since the SAS dataset names used in a compiled data step can be changed by the REDIRECT OUTPUT statement, there is no conflict in using the same SAS dataset name (such as OUT) in many different compiled data steps that will be used in the same program.

Similarly, a compiled data step that compared a new SAS dataset against an old SAS dataset might use the names NEW and OLD:

```
  DATA _NULL_;
    FILE PRINT;
    MERGE NEW (IN=NEW) OLD (IN=OLD);
    BY ID;
    ...
RUN PGM=PROJECT.COMPARE;
```

Then, when the compiled data step is run, it is easy to see which input SAS dataset is which.

```
  DATA PGM=PROJECT.COMPARE;
    REDIRECT INPUT NEW=ALABAMA.APR94 OLD=ALABAMA.MAR94;
RUN;
```

A data step's syntax is checked when it is compiled, even though it is not actually run at that point. If the step has input SAS datasets, though, variable and attribute information from those SAS datasets are used in the syntax check; therefore, those SAS datasets must exist before the data step is compiled. The input SAS datasets that are present when the data step is compiled should have the same variables and attributes as the SAS datasets that will be used when the compiled data step is run, but they do not need to have any observations. A separate step could be used to create an empty SAS dataset, using the techniques described in chapter 9, "Operating on SAS datasets."

If a compiled data step will be used with data lines, the PGM= option appears on a CARDS or CARDS4 statement instead of the RUN statement when compiling. However, the RUN statement is still used — instead of a CARDS or CARDS4 statement — when executing the compiled data step. Because the step is not actually run at the time it is compiled, data lines should not be present following the `CARDS PGM=` statement. However, the step will compile successfully even if data lines are present.

There is no compiling feature for proc steps because procs are already compiled programs.

The observation loop

The largest feature inside most SAS steps is the observation loop, which is a special case of a general programming concept, the loop. The purpose of a loop is to execute a specific action or series of actions repeatedly. Usually, the actions of a loop repeat a certain number of times, or until a certain condition is met. In this example, steps 2 and 3 are the loop, and step 3 is the action, which is executed 5 times:

```
Step 1:  a = 0
Step 2:  repeat step 3 until a ≥ 5
       Step 3:  a = a + 1
Step 4:  stop
```

The parse/execute cycle, discussed above, is an example of a loop. The SAS interpreter goes through a series of actions to interpret and execute each program step, stopping after the last step in the program file.

Notice what happens when the algorithm above is changed by adding another action:

```
Step 1:  a = 0
Step 2:  repeat steps 3 through 4 until a ≥ 5
     Step 3:  if a ≥ 1 then stop
     Step 4:  a = a + 1
Step 5:  stop
```

The loop only starts executing twice, and it doesn't finish the second time because step 3 tells it to stop. This illustrates the other way a loop can stop: one of the actions inside the loop can stop it. We could have written the algorithm above this way:

```
Step 1:  a = 0
Step 2:  repeat steps 3 through 4 forever
     Step 3:  if a ≥ 1 then stop
     Step 4:  a = a + 1
Step 5:  stop
```

Steps 2 through 4 now form what is known as an *infinite loop*. The loop itself does not have a stopping mechanism; instead, it depends on one of the actions inside it to stop it — in this case, step 3. Step 3 would not have to say "stop" to stop the loop; it could, instead, say "proceed with step 5" (or some other step outside the loop).

Of course, the use of an infinite loop allows the possibility that the loop (and the program that contains it) could fail to stop — it could continue repeating until something outside the program intervenes (such as turning the computer's power off). Whenever a loop is constructed, some care must be taken to ensure that it will, every time it runs, stop within an appropriate length of time.

> In SAS programs, the DO statement is used to form loops that are directly controlled by the programmer. DO loops are described in chapter 4, "Control flow." An infinite DO loop could most easily be formed with this statement:
>
> ```
> DO WHILE(1);
> ```

The actions in the observation loop read and process a certain amount of input data. There can be other actions in an observation loop, but it is actions related to the input data that are critical. The amount of input data read by one repetition of the observation loop is an *observation*.

(The word *observation* also has a separate, related meaning, referring to a certain amount of stored data.)

The observation loop is an infinite loop of the sort described above; it depends on one of the actions inside it to stop it. Normally, the action that stops the observation loop is the input process, the action that supplies the input observations. When the end of the input data file is reached, the input process stops the step.

Of course, other actions could stop the observation loop. And it's possible to arrange the input processes so that they do not reach the end of the input data file, letting the observation loop repeat forever. (Ways of doing this are described below.)

The observation loop in a proc step is primarily of academic interest to SAS programmers, because with few exceptions, it can't be seen or controlled. However, in the data step, the details of the observation loop are under the control of the programmer. The rest of this section describes the statements and options that affect the observation loop in the data step.

The observation loop in the data step includes all the executable statements in the step. Executable statements are statements that represent specific actions, and include most of the statements that can be used in the data step. The DATA, ARRAY, and CARDS statements are nonexecutable statements; so are statements like RETAIN and KEEP that have the same effect regardless of where they appear in the step.

The observation loop stops normally when a statement reading data from an input file finds the end of the file, or if the STOP statement is executed. It can also end abnormally if certain error conditions occur, or if the ABORT statement is executed.

Vector processor?

Misconceptions abound about the observation loop and the control flow of SAS steps. The most common one is that the SAS System is a *vector processor*, somehow processing all the observations simultaneously instead of one after another.

Actually, that would be impossible. A SAS dataset or a data step can have any number of observations, but the amount of data a computer's central processor can address at one time is very limited.

Nevertheless, a data step variable is sometimes described as having a separate value for each observation. While that is literally true of a SAS dataset, it is only a metaphor in a data step, where a variable can have only one value at a time.

The vector processor concept works as a metaphor in describing INPUT, SET, OUTPUT, and subsetting IF statements. For example, someone might describe a SET statement as "loading a SAS dataset into the data step." However, the metaphor fails when a step has more complicated control flow, and it can create a false picture of the amount of work the computer is doing.

The simple observation loop

The effects of the observation loop depend on the input data — how many files it is in and how much data is read from the file (or files) for each observation. In the simple case, the data is all in one file and the same amount of data is read each time.

If the input data is coming from a text file, you need an INFILE statement to identify the file and an INPUT statement to say how it should be interpreted. Perhaps like this:

```
INFILE FISH;
INPUT @1 AGE 2. @3 SPECIES $11.;
```

Input from a SAS dataset has simpler syntax; you can just name the SAS dataset in a SET statement. The SET statement takes care of getting one observation at a time, finding out the names of the variables, and so on.

```
SET TROPICAL;
```

The INPUT statement or SET statement reads in just one observation. But because the SAS interpreter creates an observation loop for the step, the INPUT statement or SET statement eventually reads every observation in the input file.

In the following example, there is an INPUT statement with several other executable statements. Each statement is executed once for each repetition of the observation loop. In this case, the observation loop repeats once for each input record, a total of seven times. It also starts executing an eighth time, but stops when it gets to the INPUT statement.

```
  DATA _NULL_;
    INFILE CARDS;
    FILE LOG;
    PUT 'Tree: ' @;
    INPUT TREE :$12. CIRC AGE;
    RADIUS = CIRC/(2*3.14159265358979);
    RING = RADIUS/AGE;
    PUT TREE $12. ' Average ring thickness: ' RING 7.3 ' cm';
    CARDS;
OAK      1  1
OAK      9  11
MAPLE     15  7
PINE      16  18
OAK     109  40
FLAGPOLE      16  2
MAPLE     5  3
;
```

Here's how it works: For the first input record, the SAS supervisor executes the INFILE statement, the FILE statement, the PUT statement, the INPUT statement, the two assignment statements, and the second PUT statement. (The DATA and CARDS statements are nonexecutable statements.) Then it goes back to the beginning of the loop for the second input record. It executes the INFILE statement, the FILE statement, the PUT statement, the INPUT statement, the two assignment statements, and the second PUT statement. And so on for the third, fourth, fifth, sixth, and seventh input records.

Finally, the SAS supervisor goes back to the beginning of the loop for an eighth input record. It executes the PUT statement and the INPUT statement. The INPUT statement finds an end of file condition, so it stops the step. The assignment statements and the second PUT statement are not executed an eighth time.

This is the output:

```
Tree: OAK          Average ring thickness:   0.159 cm
Tree: OAK          Average ring thickness:   0.130 cm
Tree: MAPLE        Average ring thickness:   0.341 cm
Tree: PINE         Average ring thickness:   0.141 cm
Tree: OAK          Average ring thickness:   0.434 cm
Tree: FLAGPOLE     Average ring thickness:   1.273 cm
Tree: MAPLE        Average ring thickness:   0.265 cm
Tree:
```

The word "Tree" appears in the output an extra time because the PUT statement appears before the INPUT statement.

We can modify this example to demonstrate in a different way what it means for the observation loop to encompass the entire data step. An added statement makes the step stop after the INPUT statement if we find that someone is trying to slip flagpole data into our tree analysis.

```
  DATA _NULL_;
    INFILE CARDS;
    FILE LOG;
    PUT 'Tree: ' @;
    INPUT TREE :$12. CIRC AGE;
    IF TREE =: 'FLAGPOLE' THEN STOP;
    RADIUS = CIRC/(2*3.14159265358979);
    RING = RADIUS/AGE;
    PUT TREE $12. ' Average ring thickness: ' RING 7.3 ' cm';
    CARDS;
OAK      1  1
OAK      9  11
MAPLE      15  7
PINE      16  18
OAK      109  40
FLAGPOLE      16  2
MAPLE      5  3
;
```

This results in the step stopping between the two PUT statements, on the sixth observation. The step never gets to the seventh input record. so the output looks like this:

```
Tree: OAK          Average ring thickness:   0.159 cm
Tree: OAK          Average ring thickness:   0.130 cm
```

```
Tree: MAPLE        Average ring thickness:   0.341 cm
Tree: PINE         Average ring thickness:   0.141 cm
Tree: OAK          Average ring thickness:   0.434 cm
Tree:
```

The top of the observation loop

Some parts of the observation loop are automatic.

The SAS supervisor sets the values of variables in memory to missing values before each observation. This prevents data from accidentally getting from one observation into the next. The SAS supervisor does this only for certain variables; it does not set the value of a variable to missing if:

- the variable is listed in a RETAIN statement; or
- there is a global RETAIN statement; or
- the variable is used on the left side of a sum statement; or
- the variable comes from a SAS dataset (in a SET, MERGE, or UPDATE statement); or
- the variable is used in an I/O (INFILE, SET, MERGE, UPDATE, or FILE) statement option; or
- the variable is an element of an array, if initial values are given for one or more of the array elements in the ARRAY statement; the array uses temporary variables; a reference to the array is used on the left side of a sum statement; or the array is named in a RETAIN statement.

Most variables start the step with missing values. However, variables used in I/O statement options and variables used on the left side of sum statements are initialized to 0. A few I/O statement options, such as NOBS=, are initialized to data-dependent values. Variables can be given other initial values in a RETAIN or ARRAY statement.

The SAS supervisor also maintains some automatic variables. The observation count, _N_, is set to 1 for the first repetition of the observation loop and increases by 1 on each subsequent repetition. The variable _ERROR_ starts out with a value of 0 at the top of the observation loop (it changes to 1 when certain kinds of error conditions occur). The values of these variables are the same as if they were created by these statements at the beginning of the data step:

```
_N_ + 1;
_ERROR_ = 0;
```

If there is a BY statement, it creates two variables associated with each BY variable, known as FIRST. ("first-dot") and LAST. ("last-dot") variables. The use of these variables is described in chapter 8, "Groups and sorting."

The SAS supervisor resets the current output file (for PUT statements) to LOG and the current input file (for INPUT statements) to CARDS at the top of the loop, just as if these statements appeared:

```
FILE LOG;
INFILE CARDS;
```

The bottom of the observation loop

Something extra happens at the bottom of the observation loop too. After the statements in the data step have executed, there is an implied RETURN statement, which usually directs the step to go on to the top of the observation loop for the next observation. RETURN also has some other specialized uses, to go to a point in the step after the execution of a LINK statement or a HEADER= branch (which is used to put page headings in print files).

If the value of _ERROR_ is 1 at the bottom of the loop, or if a LIST or LOSTCARD statement has been executed, input records read by an INPUT statement (if any) are written in the log. The records are preceded by a ruler to make column locations easier to find.

Output syntax

Output to SAS datasets has a special place in SAS syntax. The DATA statement, the first statement in a data step, lists the SAS datasets being created in the step. If you do not list a name in the DATA statement, the SAS supervisor makes up a name (in the DATA*n* series). You have to specify _NULL_ on the DATA statement (as in the examples above) to avoid creating a SAS dataset in a data step.

The output process is assumed too. The OUTPUT statement is used to write an observation to an output SAS dataset, but if there is no OUTPUT statement, then any RETURN statement (except after a LINK or HEADER= branch) writes an observation to the output SAS datasets — including the implied RETURN statement at the end of the step.

So you can do output to a SAS dataset without having to mention anything about it. This is handy in very informal programming where names don't matter, but it also means that you could be doing extra output that you don't want. To avoid that, when a data step should not create a SAS dataset, use this form of the DATA statement:

```
DATA _NULL_;
```

More than one input file

The observation loop works essentially the same way with more than one input file. However, there are several different ways that multiple input files can be arranged, and it's important to know which one is being used.

If you want every observation to take information from a few input files, you can have a few SET and INPUT statements. We say the different input files are different *input streams* in this case, because they operate completely independently of each other. However, the step stops after only one of the input streams reaches the end of data, which usually means that the data at the end of the other input streams is never reached.

It more often happens that you want the input from different files to be coordinated in some way. There are several ways you can do this. You can *concatenate* them, putting them one after another. In the SET statement, you just list the SAS datasets in the order you want them:

```
SET FIRST SECOND THIRD;
```

Alternatively, if they are in sorted order, you can *interleave* them. Interleaving produces the same set of observations that concatenating does, but keeps them in sorted order. Interleaving is done with the SET statement followed by a BY statement (without the NOTSORTED option) listing the variables that the observations are sorted by.

```
SET ONE TWO;
BY CATEGORY;
```

This input stream would take the observations from SAS dataset ONE with the variable CATEGORY equal to 1 and then observations from TWO with CATEGORY equal to 1 before taking observations from ONE with CATEGORY equal to 2 — and so on.

Alternatively, input observations from two or more SAS datasets could be combined to form each observation. This process is called *merging* and is done with the MERGE statement. Like the SET statement, the MERGE statement can be used with or without the BY statement.

Without the BY statement, the MERGE statement does *one-to-one merging*. The first observation from the first SAS dataset is combined with the first observation from the second SAS dataset, the second observation from the first SAS dataset is combined with the second observation from the second SAS dataset, and so on. When the end of one of the SAS datasets is reached, its variables have missing values for the rest of the observations created by the MERGE statement.

When the MERGE statement is followed by a BY statement, it does *match merging*. Observations from the different SAS datasets with the same BY variable values are combined. If there are several observations with the same BY variable values, they are matched in a manner similar to the one-to-one merging process, except that when one SAS dataset has fewer observations in a BY group than another, the values of its last observation in the BY group are used to form the rest of the observations in the BY group, instead of missing values. But missing values are used when a SAS dataset has no observations in a BY group.

When there is a conflict in the value of a variable (other than a BY variable) between different input SAS data sets in a MERGE statement, the value from the SAS dataset named later in the MERGE statement is used.

The UPDATE loop

The UPDATE statement also provides a way of combining input observations from two SAS datasets, but it generates a specialized form of the observation loop. Because of the nature of the UPDATE loop, the UPDATE statement is useful primarily for the updating process.

Some special terms are used with updating. The first SAS dataset listed in the UPDATE statement is called the *master dataset,* while the second one is the *transaction dataset*. MASTER is the master dataset and TRANS is the transaction dataset in this example:

```
UPDATE MASTER TRANS;
BY ID;
```

For the UPDATE loop to work correctly, there must be a BY statement, the SAS datasets must be sorted by the variable(s) in the BY statement, and there should not be more than one observation in the master dataset with the same value(s) of the BY variable(s).

The UPDATE statement creates observations in almost the same way that MERGE does, except that only nonmissing values from the transaction dataset are used. (Also, the special missing value ._ can be used to update a value to missing.) The UPDATE loop has an implicit OUTPUT at the bottom of the observation loop only for the last observation in the BY group, as if a statement like this one appeared at the end of the step:

```
IF LAST.ID THEN OUTPUT;
```

> The details of the UPDATE loop are undocumented, so it would not be surprising if SAS Institute changed the workings of UPDATE in a future version so that the entire BY group is handled in one execution of the UPDATE statement rather than in repeated executions of the observation loop. That would actually make the UPDATE statement more consistent with the behavior of the SET, MERGE, and INPUT statements. To be safe, you could avoid writing steps that rely on the form of the UPDATE loop.

Input streams

Input files can be coordinated in other ways by using more than one INPUT, SET, or MERGE statement and using programming statements to coordinate the input streams. The END= option on the INFILE, SET, and MERGE statements, which is described in more detail in chapter 5, "I/O," can be used to identify the end of an input stream.

This step does a one-to-one merge of a SAS dataset with an input text file, creating a new SAS dataset:

```
DATA FISSION;
  POTATO = .;
  INFILE FISH END=LAST1;
  IF NOT LAST1 THEN INPUT @1 AGE 2. @3 SPECIES $11.;
  IF NOT LAST2 THEN SET CHIPS (KEEP=POTATO) END=LAST2;
  IF LAST1 AND LAST2 THEN STOP;
```

The conditional INPUT and SET statements read data from the input files but do not attempt to read past the end of either file. Thus, the first observation of the SAS dataset CHIPS is combined with values from the first record of the input file FISH, the second observation is combined with values from the second record, and so on. After the end of either file is reached, its variables have missing values while the remaining data is read from the other file. The conditional STOP statement stops the step only after the end of both files is reached.

Programming statements for combining files in other ways are discussed in chapter 10, "File formats."

Views

SAS data views can represent another way to coordinate data from different files. Views are SAS datasets and can be accessed in SET statements, but they can contain data actually stored in other files, which can be SAS data files or other files.

No observation loop

The SAS interpreter does not create an observation loop for steps that do not have an INPUT, SET, MERGE, UPDATE, or DISPLAY statement. It executes the statements in the data step only once. For example, this data step produces a SAS dataset ONE with one observation and the variables A and B:

```
DATA ONE;
  A = 1;
  B = 1;
```

Even though there is no observation loop, there is still implicit output at the bottom of the step.

Observation loops that never end

In their normal forms, the SET, MERGE, UPDATE, and INPUT statements proceed forward through the input data, and eventually have to reach the end of the input data file and stop the data step. However, with certain terms or options, this might not happen. You should exercise caution when using any of these statements:

- the INPUT statement with the trailing @@
- the direct access SET statement (with the POINT= option)
- the INFILE statement with the EOF= option
- a SET, MERGE, UPDATE, or INPUT statement that executes conditionally
- the INFILE statement with the RECFM=U option

These statements are discussed in detail in chapter 5, "I/O," and chapter 4, "Control flow." Also, a STOP statement is usually essential when a DISPLAY statement is used in a step with no SET, MERGE, or UPDATE statement. The DISPLAY statement is used to display a window and is described in chapter 18, "User interface."

Data in memory

Memory is the internal working space of a computer. It resides on memory chips that retain data for short periods of time. You can think of memory as consisting of a series of locations, each of which contains a certain amount of data. It might help to picture a chalkboard divided into small squares, with a number in each square.

The smallest unit of data is a bit, or a binary digit. A bit has two possible values, either 0 or 1. A combination of eight bits is a byte, which is enough space to represent one character, or a whole number from 0 to 255. Eight bytes, or 64 bits, is the amount of space the SAS System uses for a numeric value.

Larger amounts of memory may be measured in kilobytes, which are 1,000 or 1,024 bytes, and megabytes, which are 1,000 or 1,024 kilobytes. The SAS System might use one megabyte of memory in running a moderate-sized SAS program.

Variables

SAS keeps the values of all variables in a step in a block of memory called the *program data vector* or *PDV*. The size of the PDV is fixed, which limits the number of variables a step can have to a few thousand. Other memory considerations might also limit the number of variables.

In addition to the values of the variables, the SAS supervisor maintains a list of *attributes* for each variable in memory. These variable attributes are described in the next section.

Other uses of memory

The PDV and variable attributes represent a modest part of the SAS System's use of memory. Essentially everything that the SAS System has to keep track of has a place in memory. This can include:

- pointers to all the files being used, including the program file, the log file, the standard print file, and any input files, output files, and libraries being used in the step;
- buffers containing data read from or to be written to each file;
- programs, including the SAS supervisor, the current step, and any proc, functions, CALL routines, informats, and formats being used in the step;
- file names associated with filerefs or librefs in a FILENAME or LIBNAME statement;
- array definitions;
- system options;
- titles;
- macrovariable names and values.

The amount of memory being used should not be a concern until you want to run a step that might need more memory than you have available. When this happens, you could increase the amount of memory you have, or reduce the memory requirements of the program by reducing the use of the objects that take up space in memory.

Variable attributes

Variables in a SAS program have these attributes: name, data type, length, position, informat, format, and label. Attributes can be explicitly or implicitly declared in a SAS program or are set to default values by the SAS interpreter.

SAS variables can appear not only in a SAS program, but also in SAS datasets. SAS datasets are used to store data between SAS steps. They contain a variable's attributes along with its values.

Name

A variable's name usually appears in the SAS step that creates the variable, but even if it doesn't, the variable has a name. When an array is defined without naming the variables in the array, the ARRAY statement creates variable names based on the array name. The rules of SAS names were discussed in chapter 1, "Getting started." The ARRAY statement is described in chapter 6, "Expressions."

Data type

A data type is a way of representing or organizing data in a computer's memory. The SAS programming language has only two data types: numeric and character.

This differs from most high-level languages, which have many different numeric data types. The SAS System's one numeric data type corresponds to the double precision or 8-byte real type of other languages. By using only one data type, the SAS System saves programmers from having to be concerned with the problems of converting between different types. The disadvantage is that SAS programmers cannot get the faster performance that smaller, less precise data types can provide.

The SAS System gets a lot of mileage out of its numeric type. Besides holding numbers, it is used for dates and times and logical (true or false) values.

The SAS language's character data type can be one character or as long as 200 characters. A character variable can hold any type of data.

The SAS interpreter assumes variables created in a data step are numeric variables unless they are declared or first used as the character type. Variables can be identified as character variables in LENGTH, ARRAY, ATTRIB, RETAIN, assignment, INFORMAT, FORMAT, INPUT, and PUT statements.

Length

Every variable has a length. The length of a character variable is the number of bytes, or characters, of memory it uses. All numeric variables use 8 bytes of memory, but their length attribute determines the amount of storage that will be used for the variable if it is stored in a SAS dataset. Lengths shorter than 8 can be used to save storage space and input/output time, but the values stored in the shorter length might not be as precise, because the truncation might result in rounding errors.

The length of a numeric variable is assumed to be 8, but a shorter length can be declared in a LENGTH or ATTRIB statement. The shortest length allowed is 2 or 3, depending on the operating system.

The length of a character variable in a data step can be declared in a LENGTH, ATTRIB, or ARRAY statement. If it is not, its initial value in a RETAIN statement, if any, is used as its length. Otherwise, it takes its length from the length of the first value assigned to it in an assignment, INPUT, SET, MERGE, or UPDATE statement. The minimum length is 1, and the current SAS version does not allow the length to be greater than 200.

Position

The position attribute tells where the value of a variable is kept.

In a SAS program, a variable's position is the index of the location in the program data vector assigned to the variable. The position attribute of a variable stored in a SAS dataset tells where the variable is stored relative to the beginning of each observation.

Usually, a variable's position is of no interest; at any rate, the absolute position cannot be directly controlled. However, the order of variables can be important. It is significant in the `A--B` form of abbreviated variable list, for example, and the APPEND proc can work faster if both SAS datasets have the same variables in the same positions.

The order of variables in the program data vector is determined by the order in which the variables appear in the step. Variables are placed in the PDV in the order in which they appear in statements in the step (other than in dataset options or KEEP, DROP, RENAME, and WHERE statements). This includes variables in SAS datasets in SET, MERGE, and UPDATE statements, in the order in which the SAS datasets are named, using the variables in each SAS dataset in the order in which they occur in the SAS dataset. The automatic variables _ERROR_ and _N_ appear last.

You can control the order in which variables appear by naming them in the intended order at the beginning of the step, in a LENGTH statement, for example.

The order of variables in memory determines the order in which they are used in the special abbreviated variable lists _ALL_, _CHARACTER_ or _CHAR_, and _NUMERIC_, and in named range variable lists formed with the `--` symbol. This statement

```
PUT _ALL_;
```

lists the variables in a data step in order (along with their values).

When a SAS dataset is created, variables are placed in it in the same order in which they appear in the program data vector. The position attribute of variables in a SAS dataset is reported by the CONTENTS proc, along with the other variable attributes.

Informat

The INFORMAT statement is used to associate an informat specification with a variable. The informat specification is then used to read the variable in cases where no informat is specified, as in a list-style INPUT statement or in certain interactive procs.

Format

The FORMAT statement associates a format specification with a variable. The format specification is then used to write the variable in cases where no format is specified, as in a list-style PUT statement or in text output from most procs.

Label

A variable label is a character string that is used in place of the variable name to identify the variable in text output from procs. Labels can be up to 40 characters long, which allows them to be much more descriptive than an 8-character variable name.

Some uses for the label and format attributes are discussed in chapter 11, "Reports."

Declaring attributes in a step

A variable's attributes can be declared in a step in the LENGTH, INFORMAT, FORMAT, and LABEL statements, or in the ATTRIB statement, which combines the effects of the other four statements. These statements work about the same way in data and proc steps.

Variables created in a step also take attributes from variables of the same names in input SAS datasets — in a SET, MERGE, or UPDATE statement in a data step, or in the DATA= option in most proc steps. This is the way variables usually get their attributes in proc steps, and it is common in data steps too.

If a variable's attribute is indicated more than once in a step, either the first or the last appearance of the attribute is used. For the informat, format, and label attributes and the length attribute of a numeric variable, the last appearance of the attribute in the step is what counts. For the other attributes, it is the first appearance that counts. Thus, to override the attributes in an input SAS dataset in a SET statement, a LENGTH statement for character variables would appear before the SET statement, and INFORMAT, FORMAT, and LABEL statements and a LENGTH statement for numeric variables would appear after the SET statement.

There must not be a conflict in the data type of any variable, though, or a syntax error will result.

A variable can be dissociated from an informat or format attribute, returning that attribute to the default value, using an INFORMAT or FORMAT statement in which the variable is named but not associated with a value for that attribute.

Attributes in a SAS dataset

A variable in a SAS dataset inherits the attributes of the step that creates it. You control the attributes of the variables in the SAS dataset by LENGTH, INFORMAT, FORMAT, LABEL, or ATTRIB statements in the step that creates the SAS dataset.

Steps, in turn, get variable attributes when they retrieve a variable from a SAS dataset. As a result, variables and variable attributes can flow through a program in a transparent way. This can save some programming effort, but it can also cause problems if you lose control of the process.

You can change a variable name, informat, format, or label (but not a type or length) in an existing SAS dataset using the DATASETS proc. In a display manager session, attributes can also be changed in the VAR window.

SAS data libraries

The SAS System provides special support for certain kinds of files, which are called *SAS files*. SAS files are organized into collections called *SAS data libraries*. The files in a library are said to be *members* of the library. The two main types of SAS files are *SAS datasets*, which contain data used by SAS steps, and *catalogs*, which contain various data objects used by the SAS System. There are other types of SAS files, including compiled data steps. Most of the stored data created by SAS programs is kept in SAS files.

In a SAS program, a SAS data library is identified by a name called a *libref*. A SAS file is identified by a two-level name, actually two names separated by a period: the libref and the member name.

The different types of SAS files are distinguished by having different *member types*. The member types appear in lists of members of a library, and can be used to restrict processing to specific member types. The common member types are listed in the table below.

Member Type	Description
`DATA`	SAS data file (the common kind of SAS dataset)
`VIEW`	SAS data view (another kind of SAS dataset)
`CATALOG`	SAS catalog
`PROGRAM`	compiled data step
`ACCESS`	access descriptor

Before a SAS data library can be used in a SAS program, it has to be associated with a libref. One way this can be done is with a LIBNAME statement. In its simplest form, the LIBNAME statement states the libref and the name of the storage associated with the SAS data library:

```
LIBNAME libref 'name';
```

The specific details of naming the storage associated with a SAS data library vary by operating system. Under operating systems that implement directories, a SAS data library is usually associated with a directory name. Some operating systems allow or require the use of operating system commands to identify a library.

The reserved librefs WORK, USER, LIBRARY, SASHELP, and SASUSER should not be used except for the specific meanings that they have in the SAS System. The WORK and USER libraries are discussed below.

A libref can be dissociated from a SAS data library by using the CLEAR option on the LIBNAME statement:

```
LIBNAME libref CLEAR;
```

Another form of the LIBNAME statement can be used to list all the librefs currently defined:

```
LIBNAME _ALL_ LIST;
```

In a display manager session, the LIBNAME command can be used to open the LIBNAME window, which contains a similar list.

Access to each SAS data library is managed by a routine called a *library engine*. Each SAS release has a default library engine that is used for most libraries. A *sequential* library engine, called TAPE, is used for libraries on sequential storage devices, such as tape. One or more *transport* library engines (such as XPORT in SAS release 6.06) are used in moving libraries between different SAS environments. There are also *compatibility* library engines, for accessing libraries created by other SAS releases, and *interface* library engines for accessing libraries created by other software systems. Compatibility engines and interface engines have only some of the capabilities of the default library engine. The engine used with a library is identified next to the libref in the list created by the LIBNAME statement or in the LIBNAME window.

The members of a SAS data library can be listed using the DATASETS proc:

```
PROC DATASETS LIBRARY=libref;
```

Statements in the DATASETS proc can be used to copy, delete, modify, and describe the members of the library.

In a display manager session, the DIR command can be used with a libref to list the members of a SAS data library in the DIR window. The DIR window can also be accessed by selecting a SAS data library in the LIBNAME window. Line commands in the DIR window can be used to rename and delete members.

The WORK library

One SAS data library, the WORK library, is created automatically at the beginning of a SAS program or interactive session and automatically deleted at the end of the program or session. It is usually used to store data that is only needed during the program or session.

The WORK libref can be omitted when identifying members of the WORK library — that is, one-level names can be used. For example, the SAS dataset WORK.OUT can be identified as OUT. However, this does not work when there is a USER library, as described next.

The USER library

There is a USER library if a SAS data library has been declared with the USER libref:

```
LIBNAME USER 'name';
```

or if the USER= system option is used to identify another libref to be used as the USER library:

```
OPTIONS USER=libref;
```

After a USER library has been declared, one-level names of SAS files refer to members of the USER library, rather than members of the WORK library. For example, OUT would mean USER.OUT instead of WORK.OUT.

The USER library is often used in debugging, so that the contents of temporary files can be analyzed, and for programs that tend to fail because of system limitations, so that they can be restarted at an intermediate point.

The USER library can be removed from a program or session by using the CLEAR option on the LIBNAME statement:

```
LIBNAME USER CLEAR;
```

or by naming the WORK library in the USER= system option:

```
OPTIONS USER=WORK;
```

SAS datasets

There are basically two kinds of SAS datasets: *SAS data files*, in which the entire SAS dataset is stored in one place, and *views*, in which only part of the SAS dataset is physically present, along with references to other files containing other parts of the data.

A SAS data file can have indexes, which list the file's observations in a different order. The order listed in an index is an increasing order of one or more key variables. Indexes are usually physically separate files but are treated as part of the SAS data file by the library engine.

A SAS data view is treated as a SAS dataset by a SAS program, but depends on the presence of other SAS datasets, text files, database tables, or other files in assembling the data that is presented to the SAS program when the view is accessed. The view is put together by a routine called a *view engine*, sometimes using a SAS file called an *access descriptor*, which describes the format of a data file.

Views that use data in other SAS datasets are created using the SQL proc. Other views are created using SAS/ACCESS®software.

The CONTENTS proc can be used to describe the contents of a SAS dataset.

```
PROC CONTENTS DATA=SAS dataset;
```

In a display manager session, the variables in a SAS dataset can be listed in the VAR window. The VAR window can be reached by using the VAR command with a SAS dataset name, or by selecting a SAS dataset in the DIR window. You can rename variables or change variable attributes in the VAR window.

Catalogs

A SAS catalog can store many kinds of objects used by the SAS System in a single file. Each object in a catalog is called an *entry*. The different kinds of objects are identified by names called *entry types*. Some more commonly used entry types are described in this table:

Entry Type	Description
`TITLE`	title line, footnote line, or note line
`DICTNARY`	spelling dictionary; used by spelling checker
`PMENU`	menu definition
`KEYS`	function keys
`WSAVE`	window definition
`SOURCE`	contents of editor window
`LOG`	contents of LOG window
`OUTPUT`	contents of OUTPUT window
`LIST`	list of values
`FORMAT`	numeric format
`FORMATC`	character format
`INFMT`	numeric informat
`INFMTC`	character informat
`MACRO`	parsed macro
`MSYMTAB`	symbol table (during macro execution)
`GOPTIONS`	SAS/GRAPH® system options
`GRSEG`	output from graphics procedures
`HELP`	definition of help screen
`MENU`	definition of MENU screen (created by BUILD proc)
`PROGRAM`	definition of PROGRAM screen (created by BUILD proc)
`CBT`	definition of a CBT screen (created by BUILD proc)
`SCREEN`	definition of FSEDIT screen
`FORM`	printing instructions
`FONT`	font

Entries are usually identified by four-level names indicating the catalog and entry name and type:

libref.*catalog*.*entry name*.*entry type*

When a catalog has already been identified, an entry can often be identified by a two-level name:

entry name.*entry type*

The entries in a catalog are listed by the CATALOG proc, which is similar to the DATASETS proc. Statements in the CATALOG proc can be used to rename, copy, and delete entries.

In a display manager session, a catalog's entries can be listed in the CATALOG window, which can be reached by using the CATALOG command with the name of a catalog or by selecting a catalog in the DIR window. Commands in the CATALOG window can be used to copy, rename and delete entries.

Missing

In real life, it's possible for a value to be unavailable or unknown. Most computer languages, though, won't let you have a variable without a value. That's because a variable is associated with a certain location in memory, and *something* has to be there.

The SAS programming language provides a way for the value of a numeric variable to be "missing." This is possible because of the details of the double precision format the SAS System uses for all numeric values. The double precision format uses 64 bits, but not just any combination of 64 bits can represents a number; those that do not are sometimes used as nans. A *nan* is a special value related to the use of real numbers; "nan" stands for "not a number." Nans are sometimes used to represent infinity, for example, or as the result of attempting to divide by zero. The designers of the SAS System picked out some nans to use as missing values.

In input text files, a period can be used to represent a missing value:

With most informats, a missing value can also be indicated by leaving an input field completely blank.

A numeric missing value is also represented by a period in a SAS program, in an assignment statement, for example:

```
EDGE = .;
```

SAS programs generate missing values in many different situations:

- When values are missing in input data, the variable is given a missing value.
- When there is an error in interpreting input data, because the input data is not valid for the informat used, or because an INPUT statement ran beyond the end of an input line with the MISSOVER option, the variable is given a missing value.
- Operators produce missing values for certain operands. For example, dividing by 0 produces a missing value. Arithmetic operators produce missing values when they have a missing value as an operand.

• Functions return missing values for certain kinds of arguments. For example, `SQRT(A)` is a missing value if A is a negative number. Many functions return missing values if their arguments are missing.

• At the beginning of a data step, variables are set to missing (except for those initialized to other values in a RETAIN statement).

• At the top of the observation loop in a data step, certain variables are reset to missing.

• In input from more than one SAS dataset in a SET, MERGE, or UPDATE statement, variables that are not available for a particular observation are given missing values.

• Missing values are created as a standard part of output SAS datasets by certain procs, especially when the CLASS statement is used.

Character missing values

The concept of missing values extends to character values. A character missing value is a null string, a string of length 0. Character values are padded with blanks before being assigned to variables, though, so a blank variable value is also considered missing. Character missing values are represented in SAS programs with two quote marks: `''` or `""`.

Character missing values are created by SAS programs in the same situations that result in numeric missing values. Other than that, though, character missing values are treated like ordinary character values.

Special missing values

Numeric values might be missing for different reasons, so the SAS System uses several distinct missing values. In addition to the standard missing value, which is represented by a period in a SAS program, there are 27 special missing values, which are represented by a period followed by a letter or an underscore.

Variables can get special missing values in only two ways. First, they can be assigned or initialized to a special missing value.

```
PRICE = ._;
RETAIN AGE .C;
```

Second, they can be read from an input file, using a letter or underscore to represent the special missing value. Each input character used as a special missing value must first be identified in the MISSING statement. Capital and lowercase letters are listed separately in the MISSING statement. For example, if input data contains both `a` and `A` as special missing values, this statement would be used:

```
MISSING a A;
```

However, `a` and `A` would not be read as distinct values; they both represent the special missing value `.A`.

In the example below, a survey of radio programming, radio listeners recorded the number of minutes of music, news, and commercials in an hour of broadcasting. However, music was timed only on music stations, and commercials only on commercial stations. Special missing values were used to indicate the reasons for not timing a programming component.

```
MISSING C P T N;
  DATA RADIO;
*-----------------------------------------------------------------*
|    Special missing values:                                        |
|        C = college station, noncommercial                         |
|        P = public broadcasting or other noncommercial station     |
|        T = not a music station                                    |
|        N = off the air                                            |
*-----------------------------------------------------------------*;
    INPUT DIAL MUSIC NEWS SPOTS;
    CARDS;
97.3     50.0     2.0      8.9
88.7     58.2     0.0      C
91.1     59.0     0.0      P
100.9     T       7.2     15.3
107.5     0.0     0.0      C
750       T      41.5     18.5
820       N       N        N
1500     26.0     0.0     24.5
;
```

Missing values in comparisons

Missing values can be compared to numbers using the comparison operator or in a sort operation. Missing values always compare less than numbers. The comparison order of numeric values is this:

`._  .  .A  .B  .C  .D  .E  · · ·  .Y  .Z` *negative numbers* 0 *positive numbers*

← *smallest* ——————————————————————— *largest* →

So, for example, the following comparisons are true:

```
._ < .
. < -94573211
0 > .Z
```

The order of character comparisons depends on the collating sequence of the operating system being used. However, missing character values are blanks, which compare less than alphanumeric characters. Still, blanks are not the lowest possible character values; so while missing numeric values compare less than any number, it is not necessarily true that missing character values compare less than any character string.

Options and defaults

An option is a choice. Options are a part of SAS syntax that state choices about the way certain things are done in executing a SAS program.

A default is what results when a choice is not stated. There is a default for almost every option in the SAS language. There are also defaults that apply when certain SAS statements do not appear in a step, or when terms are omitted from certain SAS statements.

An option is specified in one of two ways. For some options, just a keyword is listed; usually there is an opposite keyword to make the opposite choice. For example, the system option NUMBER causes the SAS supervisor to page-number print output, while NONUMBER causes the SAS supervisor not to use page numbers. Other options have a keyword followed by an equals sign that associates it with a value, which could be a constant, a name, a keyword, or a list. The dataset option KEEP is an example of an option associated with a list of names:

```
DATA STATES (KEEP=NAME ABBR AREA POP RANK CAPITAL BIG_CITY);
```

There are three different kinds of options in SAS syntax: system options, statement options, and dataset options. Some system options cannot be used in a SAS program, but only when the SAS System is started; they are called configuration options.

System options

System options control general things about the way the SAS System works. For example, the LINESIZE option determines the width of print output from any step that puts output into a print file.

System options can be changed between steps using the OPTIONS statement. In a display manager session, many system options can also changed in the OPTIONS window. There are also ways of setting system options when starting the SAS System, although the details vary by implementation. Configuration options can only be specified when starting the SAS System.

When a value is given for a system option, it usually stays the same until it is changed later by the program or user, but there are a few system options (such as _LAST_) that are changed by the SAS supervisor.

The general form of the OPTIONS statement is

```
OPTIONS options;
```

(OPTION can also be used as a synonym for OPTIONS.)

For example:

```
OPTIONS LINESIZE=72 PAGESIZE=60 NOCENTER;
```

The following table lists selected system options that can be used in a SAS program. Some of these options are new with SAS release 6.06.

System Option	Negative Form	Description
		The Appearance Of Print Output
CENTER CENTRE	NOCENTER NOCENTRE	center titles and proc tables (horizontally)
PAGENO= PAGNO=		page number for standard print file (use `PAGENO=1` to restart numbering)
NUMBER	NONUMBER	page number on title line
DATE	NODATE	date on title line
LINESIZE= LS=		line width; maximum number of characters in a line
PAGESIZE= PS=		page length; number of lines per page
SOURCE	NOSOURCE	SAS statements from program file in log
SOURCE2 SRC2	NOSOURCE2 NOSRC2	SAS statements from `%INCLUDE` file in log
NOTES LNOTES	NONOTES NOLNOTES	notes in log
ERRORS=		limit on the number of detailed error messages in a step
MISSING=		character to represent standard missing values (default: `MISSING='.'`)
FORMCHAR=		formatting characters used for tables, dividers, boxes
FORMDLIM= FRMDLIM=		a character to be used in place of page breaks; the default, `FORMDLIM=''`, allows actual page breaks
LABEL	NOLABEL	allows procs to use variable labels
OVP	NOOVP	allows lines to be overprinted
STIMER	NOSTIMER	computer performance statistics in log
FULLSTIMER	NOFULLSTIMER	detailed computer performance statistics in log
PROBSIG=0 PROBSIG=1 PROBSIG=2		the precision printed by certain statistical procs
		The Program File
S=		the maximum length of lines in program file
S2=		the maximum length of lines in `%INCLUDE` file (the default, `S2=S`, means that the value of the S= option is used)
CAPS	NOCAPS	translate program file to capital letters
CARDIMAGE	NOCARDIMAGE	treat program lines as 80-character records, allowing tokens to be split between lines (for example, a quoted string in a TITLE statement could continue from one line to the next)
		Routines
SYSPARM=		a character string retrieved by the SYSPARM function
PARM=		parameter string passed to an external program
SORTPGM=		which sort routine to use
FMTERR	NOFMTERR	creates an error condition when a format or informat used as a variable attribute is not found
YEARCUTOFF=		the earliest of 100 years used as 2-digit years by SAS date and SAS datetime informats, formats, and functions
		Processing
ERRORABEND	NOERRORABEND	stops processing after a step containing an error
CLEANUP	NOCLEANUP	automatically frees memory

continues

System Option	Negative Form	Description
		Macrolanguage
SERROR	NOSERROR	creates an error condition when a macrovariable is not found
MERROR	NOMERROR	creates an error condition when a macro is not found
SYMBOLGEN SGEN	NOSYMBOLGEN NOSGEN	prints macrovariable values in log
MPRINT	NOMPRINT	prints statements generated by macros in log
MLOGIC	NOMLOGIC	prints notes on macro control flow in log
IMPLMAC	NOIMPLMAC	allows statement-style macro invocation
MAUTOSOURCE	NOMAUTOSOURCE	allows autocall macro invocation
		Input And Output (especially for SAS datasets)
FIRSTOBS=		the first observation or record to be processed from an input file (default: FIRSTOBS=1)
OBS=		the last observation or record to be processed from an input file (default: OBS=MAX)
REPLACE	NOREPLACE	allows an existing SAS dataset (outside the WORK library) to be replaced by a new SAS dataset with the same name
COMPRESS=YES	COMPRESS=NO	compresses new SAS datasets by default
LAST=		the _LAST_ SAS dataset name (identifies the most recently created SAS dataset)
ENGINE=		the default library engine
REUSE=YES	REUSE=NO	whether free space can be reused in new compressed SAS datasets
USER=		the USER libref; SAS data library assumed for one-level SAS dataset names (default: USER=WORK)
DSNFERR	NODSNFERR	creates an error condition when an input SAS dataset is not found
VNFERR	NOVNFERR	creates an error condition when a variable in an input _NULL_ or dummy SAS dataset is not found
INVALIDDATA=		a character representing the missing value to be assigned for invalid numeric data (default: INVALIDDATA='.')
WORKTERM WRKTERM	NOWORKTERM NOWRKTERM	erases WORK library at end of program or session

The following table lists configuration options:

Configuration Option		Description
CONFIG=		configuration file (containing system options)
AUTOEXEC=		AUTOEXEC file, containing SAS statements to be executed first
ECHOAUTO	NOECHOAUTO	writes AUTOEXEC statements in SAS log
INITSTMT= IS=		a SAS statement or statements to be executed before SYSIN file (but after AUTOEXEC file)
SYSIN=		SAS program file
OPLIST		writes system options set on initialization to log
DMS	NODMS	selects display manager session, instead of interactive line mode
MACRO	NOMACRO	allows use of macro processor and macrovariables
LOG=		file used as SAS log
PRINT=		file used as standard print file
ALTLOG=		file used as copy of SAS log

continues

Configuration Option		Description
`ALTPRINT=`		file used as copy of standard print file
`WORK=`		name of storage used as SAS work library
`WORKINIT` `WRKINIT`	`NOWORKINIT` `NOWRKINIT`	erases WORK library when starting SAS System
`SASAUTOS=`		name(s) of storage used as macro autocall library
`SASUSER=`		the SAS library containing the user profile

The OPTIONS proc produces a list of the current values of system options in the log, along with a brief description of the meaning of each option. The proc requires only one statement:

```
PROC OPTIONS;
```

When you do not specify options, they have default values. The default values of most options are determined by your installation. You can find out the defaults by running the OPTIONS proc immediately after starting the SAS System.

A separate category of system options, called *SAS/GRAPH system options* or *graphics options*, control the form of the graphics output from SAS/GRAPH procs. They are specified in the GOPTIONS statement and can be listed using the GOPTIONS proc.

Statement options

Statement options are part of the syntax of many SAS statements, especially the statements that identify files, the PROC statement, and certain other statements in various procs.

An often used statement option in the data step is the END= option on the INFILE, SET, MERGE, and UPDATE statements. It creates a variable that is initialized to 0 and then set to 1 when the last record or observation from the input data is reached. For example, the option on the INFILE statement below creates the variable NOW, which is set to 1 when the INPUT statement reads the last record in the input file HISTORY. The variable NOW can then be used in an IF . . . THEN statement to execute a block of statements only after the last record is read.

```
INFILE HISTORY END=NOW;
INPUT YEAR MONTH DAY PLACE & $ EVENT & $;
IF NOW THEN DO;
   statements to be executed after last input record
   END;
```

The most common statement option in the proc step is the DATA= option in the PROC statement, which is used to identify the input SAS dataset for most procs. For example, this step prints the SAS dataset INK:

```
PROC PRINT DATA=INK;
```

If the DATA= option is not specified, `DATA=_LAST_` is assumed, and the most recently created SAS dataset is used for input.

Dataset options

Dataset options modify SAS datasets. More precisely, they modify input and output processes related to SAS datasets. On output, they control the data stored in the SAS dataset. On input, they affect the way the SAS dataset appears to the step, but they do not actually change the stored data. Dataset options can be used almost anywhere a SAS dataset name is used in a SAS program; they follow the SAS dataset name, enclosed in parentheses.

Some dataset options are meaningful only when a SAS dataset is being created, and some are only used when a SAS dataset is being used as input.

The following table lists selected dataset options.

Dataset Option	Description
	Variables (input and output SAS datasets)
`KEEP=`*list*	list of variables to be kept
`DROP=`*list*	list of variables not to be kept
`RENAME=` (*old=new ...*)	change variable names
`SORTEDBY=`*list*	declares the sorted order of observations
	Observations (input SAS datasets only)
`FIRSTOBS=`	the first observation to be processed from input file (default: `FIRSTOBS=1`)
`OBS=`	the last observation to be processed from input file
`WHERE=` (*condition*)	a condition for selecting observations from input file. A WHERE expression can include any SAS operator and several other operators; can use any variable from the input SAS dataset; but cannot use any SAS function call. Only observations for which the WHERE expression evaluates as true are used in the step.
`IN=`*variable*	creates a logical variable that tells whether an observation comes from a SAS dataset (used only in data step statements)
`CNTLLEV=MEM` `CNTLLEV=REC`	whether to lock the entire SAS dataset (member) or one observation at a time (record)
	Header Information And Storage (mainly for output SAS datasets)
`COMPRESS=NO` `COMPRESS=YES`	whether the SAS dataset is compressed or not (output only); overrides system option
`REUSE=NO` `REUSE=YES`	in a compressed SAS dataset, whether space can be reused (output only); overrides system option
`TYPE=`	SAS dataset type (used by some procs)
`LABEL=`	creates label for SAS dataset (input or output)
`REPLACE=YES` `REPLACE=NO`	whether to allow an existing SAS dataset (outside the WORK library) to be replaced by a new SAS dataset with the same name (output only); overrides `REPLACE/NOREPLACE` system option
`INDEX=` (*index clause . . .*)	creates indexes (output only)

Dataset Option	Description
	Passwords (for all types of SAS files, except catalogs)
ALTER=*password*	a password for alter-protection or to access an alter-protected SAS file
WRITE=*password*	a password for write-protection or to access a write-protected SAS file
READ=*password*	a password for read-protection or to access a read-protected SAS file
PW=*password*	assigns a password or accesses a protected SAS file

The KEEP= and DROP= options should not be used together on the same SAS dataset. When used with the RENAME= option, the KEEP= or DROP= option applies before the RENAME= option. In the data step, there are KEEP, DROP, and RENAME statements that correspond to the KEEP=, DROP=, and RENAME= options for output SAS datasets. If both the statements and the dataset options are used, the statements are applied before the dataset options.

In any step, the WHERE statement can be used as the equivalent of the WHERE= option for input SAS datasets. In addition to the SAS operators, the following WHERE operators can be used in WHERE expressions:

WHERE Operator	Description
BETWEEN ... AND	tests whether a value falls inside a range
NOT BETWEEN ... AND	tests whether a value falls outside a range
CONTAINS ?	tests whether a character string contains a substring
IS NULL IS MISSING	tests whether a value is missing
IS NOT NULL IS NOT MISSING	tests whether a value is nonmissing
LIKE	tests whether a character string follows a pattern, in which an underscore (_) represents any character and a percent sign (%) represents any character sequence
NOT LIKE	tests whether a character string does not follow a pattern
=*	sounds like; tests whether two character strings sound similar, using the Soundex algorithm

In SAS releases 6.03–6.04, the MIN and MAX operators cannot be used in a WHERE expression, and the CONTAINS, LIKE, and sounds-like operators are not available.

Defaults

A default is a condition that exists automatically, unless you specify otherwise. Most options in the SAS language have defaults. There are also defaults in the operation of the observation loop, which were described above in "The observation loop." There are default informats and formats, which are used for reading and writing variables in data and proc steps when no informat or format has been specified.

Some other defaults occur in proc steps when certain statements are omitted. For example, if there is no VAR statement for an analytic proc, the proc may process all the variables in the input SAS dataset, or perhaps all the numeric variables not listed in a BY or CLASS statement.

The defaults in SAS syntax let you write shorter programs when you want to do the default action. It is important to remember, though, that the default is not the only way to do something. And although the defaults might be the way people most often want a statement or a proc to operate, that doesn't mean that the default will always do what you want.

3 Programs on call

The SAS System is a library of routines containing a central program, called the supervisor, and several specialized types of routines: procs, engines, functions, CALL routines, informats, and formats. Each type of routine is used in SAS programs using its particular SAS syntax rules. For example, to use a proc, you would write a proc step, while a CALL routine would be used in a CALL statement.

The SAS System routines are machine language programs and complex data structures developed mainly using the C programming language. Additional routines could be added simply by coding them correctly and putting them in the right place in the SAS System's libraries, directories, or catalogs. Similarly, routines can be deleted by removing the files associated with them. Thus, different SAS installations might have different sets of routines — and SAS programs might depend on customized routines that are not part of the SAS System itself.

Certain informats and formats can also be created in a SAS program. Some procs and engines are marketed as add-ons for the SAS System. Other added routines are likely to become common after SAS Institute publishes guidelines for creating routines for SAS version 6. When you use any routine other than a base SAS routine in a SAS program, you must make sure that the routine will be available at the installation or installations where the program will be run.

Supervisor

The central program of the SAS System is called the *supervisor*. It interprets and executes SAS programs. It links together the different routines that are used by a SAS program. It includes the macro processor, which implements SAS macrolanguage, and display manager, the SAS System's full-screen interactive user interface. The supervisor also handles interaction between SAS routines and the computer hardware and operating system.

Procs

Procs, or procedures as they are known in formal settings, are specialized applications programs designed to be used in a SAS program.

Most SAS procs use input data from SAS datasets, and many of them produce SAS datasets as output. Many procs produce output in text form, in either the standard print file or, in a few cases, the log. However, there are exceptions; a SAS proc can be almost any kind of program.

Categories of procs

Most procs are analytic; they produce output, either as a SAS dataset or in the standard print file, that represents a summary or description or measurement of the data in an input SAS dataset. A few are reporting procs, which produce visual representations of SAS datasets. There are several interactive procs, which focus on specialized user interfaces for different tasks. There are graphics procs, which create mathematical descriptions of graphic objects, display them on screens, and print them on plotters and graphics printers.

There are several storage procs, which allow you to investigate and manage files and storage. The few other procs are grouped together as *utility* procs. Some of the storage and utility procs put their text output in the log instead of the standard print file.

Proc step syntax

You can use a proc by writing a group of statements called a proc step. A proc step starts with the PROC statement and might contain other statements. The proc being used determines what statements and options are required or allowed. The syntax involved is described in the documentation for the proc.

For procs that take input data from a SAS dataset, you usually identify the input SAS dataset in the DATA= option on the PROC statement. If you omit this option, the SAS dataset most recently created in the program (the _LAST_ SAS dataset) is used.

Proc step syntax is usually kept as simple as possible. For the SORT proc, which sorts SAS datasets, for example, you only need to specify the input SAS dataset, the output SAS dataset, and the sort order intended.

```
PROC SORT DATA=MYKIND OUT=MYSORT;
  BY FRSTNAME LASTNAME;
```

In some cases, the PROC statement options are not needed:

```
PROC SORT;
  BY ZIP_CODE;
```

Most interactive procs have a set of commands you can use with them, which are described in their documentation. They are entered on the proc's command line, which appears after the proc starts executing. However, a few interactive procs are driven by SAS statements in the program file. Even though these procs are called interactive, they can also be used in batch processing.

A proc might need data lines to tell it what to do. These data lines follow a PARMCARDS or PARMCARDS4 statement at the end of the step; the documentation for the proc should specify the contents of the data lines. If the PARMCARDS statement is used, the lines following the line that the PARMCARDS statement is on are data lines, up to the first line containing a semicolon. If the PARMCARDS4 statement is used, the data lines can contain semicolons, but a line starting with four semicolons is needed to mark the end of data lines.

```
  PROC DATALINES;
PARMCARDS;          * or PARMCARDS4;
data lines
;;;;
```

Products from SAS Institute

Procs are licensed by SAS Institute in several packages that they call SAS program products, or just products. The first product, base SAS, is more than just procs; it also includes the SAS supervisor, and all of SAS Institute's functions, CALL routines, informats, and formats. It includes a few dozen procs of the most general interest: storage, reporting, and utility procs, analytic procs having to do with descriptive statistics, and a few others. Most other products consist only of procs.

Every SAS installation has base SAS; the SAS supervisor is required to run any SAS product. The other products are all licensed separately, however, so only some SAS installations have them. You can test whether a product is installed by trying to run one of its procs; the product is not there if a log message says that the proc cannot be found.

SAS/STAT® includes specialized statistical procs, most of them rather technical and requiring statistical training to be used effectively. Other analytic procs are included in SAS/ETS®, which focuses on econometrics and time series; SAS/OR®, which covers operations research, linear programming, and project management; and SAS/QC®, which is intended for industrial-style quality analysis and reporting. SAS/GRAPH® includes most of SAS Institute's graphics procs. SAS/AF® and SAS/FSP® are SAS Institute's general-purpose full-screen interactive procs. There are other, more specialized products. SAS Institute continues to develop new products and expand the capabilities of their existing ones, so SAS users can expect more and better procs in the future.

Even within base SAS, there are more procs than any one programmer can be expected to know well. A better approach is to have a general idea of what procs there are and to become familiar with the ways procs are documented. With that knowledge, you can select and use procs effectively without having to know all about them.

The most commonly used SAS System procs are described below. The few procs that tend to be integrated into the programming process are described at various places throughout this book.

SAS Institute publishes the primary documentation for its procs in manuals called *reference guides* and additional discussions of procs in other manuals. Pithier documentation can also be found in the SAS online help.

SAS/ACCESS® is a SAS product that consists of a system of program screens rather than procs. The screens prompt the user for the information necessary to write SAS steps. Although SAS/ACCESS's windowing approach is a cumbersome way to program in general, it can be a relatively painless way to get started on a new analytic proc — if you're in a display manager session on a computer that has SAS/ACCESS installed.

Reporting procs

The principal purpose of the reporting procs is to produce print files containing representations of data in SAS datasets.

PRINT. The PRINT proc prints the values of a SAS dataset in table form, using observations as rows and variables as columns. If there are too many variables to fit across the page, the page is divided into sections with different variables.

PRINTTO. The PRINTTO proc redirects print output. It affects the standard print output or the log produced by the steps that follow, specifying a target fileref for the output to either file.

FORMS. The FORMS proc prints mailing labels and similar rectangularly tiled forms. Selected variables from one observation are put into each form unit.

CALENDAR. The CALENDAR proc prints month calendars containing schedules, holidays, time series measurements, or other information for each day of the month.

CHART, **PLOT**, and **TIMEPLOT**. The CHART and PLOT procs produce low-resolution graphs formed with characters, suitable for printing on text printers. CHART produces several kinds of graphs, including bar graphs and pie charts. PLOT produces two-dimensional scatter diagrams. The TIMEPLOT proc is similar to PLOT, but specializes in time series and can combine tables with graphs.

REPORT. When the REPORT proc is released, it will provide a more flexible and (optionally) interactive way to produce tables from SAS datasets similar to those produced by the PRINT proc.

Storage procs

Storage procs are used to work with SAS datasets and other files.

DATASETS. The DATASETS proc is used to maintain SAS data libraries. It can rename and delete SAS datasets and other library members, change header information, and create and remove indexes. It includes most of the capabilities of the COPY, APPEND, and CONTENTS procs, using corresponding statements in the DATASETS proc. It can be executed interactively, so that you can generate a list of members to be processed before deciding what processing to do.

CATALOG. A similar proc, the CATALOG proc has capabilities paralleling those of the DATASETS proc, but is used to maintain SAS catalogs rather than SAS data libraries.

CONTENTS. The CONTENTS proc prints information from the header of a SAS dataset. It can produce an output SAS dataset with variable attributes and other information about the SAS dataset

COPY. The COPY proc copies SAS data libraries, and copies SAS files from one library to another. When it copies SAS datasets, it copies the indexes correctly. It cannot change the names of the SAS files it copies.

APPEND. The APPEND proc also copies SAS datasets and can combine the data in two SAS datasets, copying the observations from one onto the end of another.

SORT. The SORT proc sorts the observations of a SAS dataset, using any variable or combination of variables as the sort key. A variable can be used in ascending or descending order. The use of the SORT proc is described in chapter 8, "Groups and sorting."

SQL. The SQL proc was introduced with SAS release 6.06. "SQL" stands for Structured Query Language, a standardized language often used for communicating database inquiries between computers or between programs. The SQL proc implements SQL using SAS datasets as tables. It creates SAS data files, views, and indexes.

TRANSPOSE. The TRANSPOSE proc transposes a SAS dataset, turning observations into variables and variables into observations.

Mainframe storage. Several other storage procs are available on mainframes. CONVERT converts data in several other storage formats to SAS datasets. PDS and PDSCOPY are used with partitioned datasets under the MVS operating system. SOURCE is used to manage and print tape libraries. TAPELABEL prints information from tape volumes with IBM standard labels; TAPECOPY copies tape volumes or tape files. RELEASE releases unused space from a disk dataset under the MVS operating system.

Utility procs

OPTIONS. The OPTIONS proc describes and lists the values of system options.

SPELL. New with SAS release 6.06, the SPELL proc checks spelling in text files and HELP entries, producing a list of possibly misspelled words. It also maintains spelling dictionaries.

FORMAT. The FORMAT proc creates certain types of formats and informats. The use of the FORMAT proc is described at the end of this chapter.

PMENU. The PMENU proc is used in creating user interfaces. It uses source code to define menus and related dialog boxes that can be used in windows defined in the WINDOW statement or elsewhere in SAS programs. It was introduced with SAS release 6.06.

Analytic procs

MEANS, SUMMARY, and **UNIVARIATE.** MEANS and SUMMARY are procs that calculate descriptive statistics, such as mean, standard deviation, minimum, maximum, and sum, for numeric variables in a SAS dataset. The statistics can be printed or stored in an output SAS dataset. The two procs are the same, except for having different defaults.

UNIVARIATE is a similar proc. In addition to most of the statistics that MEANS and SUMMARY calculate, it can determine quantiles. In other respects, it is not as good as MEANS and SUMMARY: its statistics are not as precise, it is slower, and it requires more memory to run efficiently.

TABULATE. The TABULATE proc prints tables of descriptive statistics from the variables of a SAS dataset. It is flexible in the shape and content of the tables it produces.

CORR. The CORR proc computes correlation coefficients between numeric variables in a SAS dataset. It produces print output and an output SAS dataset, which is a TYPE=CORR SAS dataset, containing a correlation matrix and other statistics.

FREQ. The FREQ proc produces frequency tables for variables in a SAS dataset. It prints tables and can produce an output SAS dataset.

STANDARD. The STANDARD proc standardizes the values of numeric variables in a SAS dataset, producing a new SAS dataset as output. When a variable is standardized, a constant is added to it and it is multiplied by a constant to give its distribution a particular mean and variance.

RANK. The RANK proc creates rank variables, which show the comparative magnitude of numeric variables in a SAS dataset. The rank variables are combined with other variables to create an output SAS dataset. Variables are ranked from lowest to highest; the lowest variable value has rank 1, the second lowest has rank 2, and so on. There are several alternative ways of assigning ranks in the case of a tie.

COMPARE. The COMPARE proc compares the values of variables in two SAS datasets, producing a report or an output SAS dataset showing the observations that differ. COMPARE can also compare two variables in the same SAS dataset.

SAS/STAT

Statistics once belonged to base SAS, but with SAS version 6, SAS Institute separated the more technical statistics procedures, of interest mainly to statisticians, into the separate SAS/STAT product.

SAS/STAT has procs to do multivariate analysis, including FACTOR; survival analysis; regression, including NLIN and REG; analysis of variance, including ANOVA and GLM; clustering analysis; and other forms of statistical analysis.

Some statistical procs that use iterative methods allow the use of the programming statements of the data step, which form an iteration loop similar to the observation loop of the data step.

SAS/ETS — Econometrics And Time Series Analysis

SAS/ETS is a collection of procs related to econometrics, time series, and finance.

SAS/OR

The SAS/OR product contains procs that do linear programming, shortest path and maximum flow network analysis, project scheduling, and other operations research.

SAS/QC

SAS/QC is a collection of procs for quality control and quality management. It is mainly designed to be used by quality departments in industrial operations.

Interactive procs

The behavior of the SAS System's interactive procs varies considerably between implementations, reflecting the different personality and display capabilities of each computer model and operating system.

EDITOR and **BROWSE**. A holdover from SAS version 5, in some SAS implementations, EDITOR is a proc that can be used to display and edit a SAS dataset. It works in a line-prompt mode with a set of commands. The BROWSE proc is the same, except that commands to change the SAS dataset have no effect. The EDITOR and BROWSE procs are not documented in SAS version 6, but use the same commands as in version 5.

BUILD. The BUILD proc is the major part of the SAS/AF product. It is used interactively to define full-screen user interfaces for SAS programs. Program parameters that are entered on the screen by the user are put into a program attached to the screen for execution. A separate programming language, called SCL or screen control language, can be used with values entered in or displayed on the screen.

BUILD can also be used to create programmed instruction screens, called *CBT* screens. However, it has little resemblance to the hypermedia programs usually used for this purpose.

The screens created with the BUILD proc are run using the AF display manager command. In SAS version 5, the DISPLAY proc was used for this purpose.

SAS/FSP

SAS/FSP is a collection of interactive procs that all use a full-screen menu interface.

FSEDIT displays a SAS dataset for editing, with each observation on a separate screen. FSBROWSE is the same as FSEDIT except that it cannot change the values in the SAS dataset.

FSPRINT displays a SAS dataset in a window suitable for scrolling. It can be used in edit mode to change values in a SAS dataset. With SAS release 6.06, FSPRINT was replaced by the more powerful FSVIEW proc. The SCL features of SAS/AF can be used with FSEDIT, FSPRINT, and FSVIEW.

FSLIST displays text files. FSLETTER is a word processor, which might be used for form letters using data in SAS datasets.

SAS/IML

The SAS/IML product implements an interactive language for matrix processing.

Graphics procs

The SAS/GRAPH product lets you manipulate graphics objects. It also has some reporting procs that use graphics output.

The GPLOT, GCHART, and GPRINT procs correspond in a general way to the PLOT, CHART, and PRINT procs of base SAS. The GFONT proc allows the definition of fonts to be used in SAS/GRAPH output.

To many people, the most impressive thing about SAS/GRAPH is its ability to draw maps. Maps created with the GMAP proc can present data in many different ways. SAS/GRAPH includes SAS datasets that define map coordinates for most of the world.

Some of the analytic SAS products include procs that create graphics of specialized kinds of graphs.

Engines

The SAS supervisor uses engines to read and write SAS datasets and SAS data libraries. The various engines use data stored in various different formats, but present the data to the SAS supervisor in a standard form.

Engines have varying capabilities. Those that read and write SAS data libraries are called *library* engines. Those that only read (and perhaps modify) SAS data views are called *view* engines.

Certain SAS statements and procs require certain capabilities of an engine. Capabilities that a particular engine might or might not have include:

- creating a SAS dataset
- deleting a SAS dataset
- renaming a SAS dataset
- direct access
- changing data values (in place)
- adding observations (appending)
- changing variable attributes
- SAS dataset labels
- compressed observations
- indexes
- accessing a SAS dataset at the same time as another user

A different set of engines is provided with each SAS implementation. Nevertheless, the engines tend to fall into these general categories:

Engine Type	Used For
default	most SAS libraries
compatibility	older SAS libraries
transport	transporting SAS libraries between computers
compatibility transport	transporting SAS libraries to or from a computer with an earlier SAS release
sequential	sequential storage devices, such as tape
interface	data stored by other software systems
native view	views that refer to data in SAS datasets
interface view	views that refer to data in text files, database files, and other files

Telling the SAS System what engine to use is not usually necessary. However, it can be done on the LIBNAME statement by putting the engine name between the libref and the storage name:

```
LIBNAME libref engine storage name;
```

Functions

A function is a routine that provides a value that can be used in an expression. The value is usually calculated based on a list of values, called *arguments*, provided to the function. A function is said to be *called* when it is used in a program. The resulting value is said to be *returned* by the function.

Most functions take numeric arguments and return numeric values, but there are other types too. There are functions that take character arguments, or a combination of character and numeric arguments, and return either a character value or a number that describes a character string. Some functions accept either type of argument, and return an argument of the same type. A few functions take unusual types of arguments, such as informats, formats, and arrays. Finally, there are functions with no arguments. The SAS interpreter ensures that a function gets the right argument types. Numeric and character arguments can be any valid SAS expression.

Function calls can be used anywhere a SAS expression is allowed. Uses for functions are described in chapter 6, "Expressions." Function calls can even be used as arguments to functions.

Function syntax

A function call is written using the name of the function followed by parentheses. The arguments to the function are listed inside the parentheses. If there is more than one argument, the arguments are separated by commas:

```
FUNCTION(ARGU1, ARGU2, ARGU3)
```

Some functions allow you to use the OF keyword with a variable list as an argument list. Using this convention, the function call above could be rewritten:

```
FUNCTION(OF ARGU1-ARGU3)
```

The most common use of functions is in assignment statements:

```
VARIABLE = FUNCTION(ARG1, ARG2, ARG3)
```

The syntax for a function call is similar to the syntax used for arrays. Because of the similarity, an array should not be given the same name as a function.

Side effects

Functions can be as interesting for the things they do as for the values they return. The actions of a function, other than returning a value, are called *side effects*. Only a few SAS functions have side effects (notably, the LAG functions).

> The term "side effect" used to have a very negative connotation in computer programming, when side effects were usually logical errors resulting from poor coding practices. Most of that connotation is gone now, as side effects are generally accepted as legitimate programming techniques. However, programming purists still discourage the use of functions with side effects.

Functions from SAS Institute

SAS Institute supplies its collection of functions with base SAS software. Many of these functions are described below.

A numeric function written for another purpose can be made into a SAS function without too much difficulty, so you might find functions from various sources being used in SAS programs at some installations.

Mathematical functions

The word *function* comes to computers from mathematics, and most SAS functions are mathematical: the values they return are numbers that are calculated based on the values of one or more numbers used as arguments. A few of these functions have very general uses in programming. The rest have their niches in mathematical and statistical modeling.

All SAS mathematical functions return missing values when missing values are used as arguments. Some have other requirements for arguments and return missing values if the arguments are invalid.

Representational functions

There are close to 2^{64} numbers that can be represented in a SAS program. That's a lot of numbers, but it is a limited subset of the infinitely many real numbers that can exist. Thus, some information about a number might be lost when it is represented as a SAS numeric value.

For example, most SAS implementations do not distinguish between the numbers 713,251,034,119,303.49993 and 713,251,034,119,303.49996, because they are both represented in the double precision format as the number 713,251,034,119,303.5.

The purpose of the SAS representational functions is to create even more limited subsets. They extract a certain kind of information about a number, while disregarding other information. The set of SAS numeric values is mapped into a smaller range of values. The argument itself is returned if it is in the function's range; otherwise, the value returned is a number in the range that represents the argument in some way.

Function	Description	Range
`ABS`	absolute value; negative numbers are multiplied by -1 to make them positive	0 and positive numbers
`CEIL`	ceiling; nonintegers are rounded up	integers
`FLOOR`	floor; nonintegers are rounded down	integers
`FUZZ`	fuzz; numbers very close to (within 10^{-12} of) an integer are rounded to the integer value	integers and numbers not within 10^{-12} of an integer
`INT`	integer truncation; nonintegers are rounded toward 0. For positive values, this is the same as FLOOR. For negative values, it is the same as CEIL.	integers
`MOD`	modulo. The second argument is the modulus. The returned value is the remainder after dividing the number by the modulus. A multiple of the modulus is added to or subtracted from the number to get a result with a magnitude between 0 and the modulus. For positive numbers, the result is between 0 and the absolute value of the modulus. For negative numbers, the result is between 0 and the negative of the absolute value of the modulus.	numbers from 0 to (but not including) `SIGN(`*number*`)*` `ABS(`*modulus*`)`
`ROUND`	rounding. The second argument is the roundoff unit. (It must be positive.) The number is rounded to the nearest multiple of the roundoff unit. If the second argument is omitted, the roundoff unit is 1, and the number is rounded to the nearest integer. The process is equivalent to `CEIL((`*number*/ *roundoff unit*`) - .5)*`*roundoff unit*	multiples of the roundoff unit
`SIGN`	sign; signum; 1 is returned for positive arguments; -1 is returned for negative arguments. For nonmissing arguments, this is equivalent to `(`*number* `> 0) - (`*number* `< 0)`	-1, 0, 1
`TRUNC` 	memory truncation. The second argument is a length in bytes. The number is truncated to that length by erasing the rest of the memory representation of the number. SAS numbers use 8 bytes, so if the length is 3, the 5 least significant bytes are erased. For nonmissing arguments, this has the same rounding effect as storing a number with that length (using the length variable attribute). The function does not accept missing values as arguments.	numbers that can be represented in the number of bytes given

Beginning with SAS release 6.06, the CEIL, FLOOR, and INT functions include an implicit FUZZ function call; that is, the function call `CEIL(X)` actually returns `(CEIL(FUZZ(X))`, `FLOOR(X)` actually returns `(FLOOR(FUZZ(X))`, and `INT(X)` actually returns `(INT(FUZZ(X))`.

Algebraic functions

Algebraic functions are the simpler functions used by mathematicians. They can be represented by a formula constructed using the SAS arithmetic operators `+`, `-`, `*`, `/`, and `**` (with exponents restricted to selected constants). Because these operators are available, there is little need for a library of algebraic functions, but the SAS System does have two: ABS, which is described above, and SQRT, the square root function. `SQRT(X)` is equivalent, in theory at least, to `X**.5`.

Transcendental functions

Mathematicians call functions with more complicated formulas *transcendental functions.*

Function	Description
`EXP`	exponential function; *e* raised to a power; `EXP(X)` is approximately equivalent to `2.718281828459045**X`
`LOG`	natural logarithm; base *e* logarithm
`LOG10`	common logarithm; base 10 logarithm
`LOG2`	base 2 logarithm
`ERF`	error function; `ERF(X)` $= \frac{2}{\sqrt{\pi}} \int_0^X e^{-t^2}\, dt$
`ERFC`	complement of the error function; `1 - ERF`
`GAMMA`	gamma function; $\Gamma(x) = \int_0^\infty t^{x-1} e^{-t}\, dt$
`LGAMMA`	log gamma function; the natural logarithm of the gamma function
`DIGAMMA`	the derivative of the log gamma function
`TRIGAMMA`	the second derivative of the log gamma function

Trigonometric functions

One important category of transcendental functions is the trigonometric functions. Trigonometric functions are used to measure circles and triangles and to describe periodic behavior, among other things.

SAS's trigonometric functions use radian measurements. To use these functions with angles measured in degrees, convert the angle measurements to radians using the formula

$$2\pi \text{ rad} = 360°$$

For example, to get the sine of an angle measured in degrees, use a statement like

```
SIDE = SIN(ANGLE*3.14159265/180);
```

or

```
SIDE = SIN(ANGLE*0.0174532925);
```

The SAS System has an incomplete set of trigonometric functions. The following table shows the SAS trigonometric functions and SAS expressions to calculate other trigonometric functions.

Symbol	Mathematical function name	SAS function or expression
sin	sine	SIN
cos	cosine	COS
tan	tangent	TAN
sec	secant	1/COS(X)
csc	cosecant	1/SIN(X)
cot	cotangent	1/TAN(X)
$\sin^{-1}$	arcsine	ARSIN
$\cos^{-1}$	arccosine	ARCOS
$\tan^{-1}$	arctangent	ATAN
sinh	hyperbolic sine	SINH
cosh	hyperbolic cosine	COSH
tanh	hyperbolic tangent	TANH
sech	hyperbolic secant	1/COSH(X) *or* 2/(EXP(X) + EXP(-X))
csch	hyperbolic cosecant	1/SINH(X) *or* 2/(EXP(X) - EXP(-X))
coth	hyperbolic cotangent	1/TANH(X)

Statistic functions

A *sample* is a group of values, especially ones that result from measurements in an experiment. A *statistic* is a number that is calculated or determined from the values of a sample. The SAS System has several functions that calculate commonly used statistics.

The statistic functions take a list of arguments. The order of arguments does not affect the result. The statistic functions except NMISS ignore missing arguments and require at least one nonmissing argument; some of them need more than one.

This set of functions calculates sample statistics, which means that in calculating the variance and related statistics, a divisor of $n - 1$ instead of n is used. The results correspond to the statistics calculated by the descriptive statistics procs, such as MEANS, with the option `VARDEF=DF` (the default) and with no FREQ or WEIGHT statement.

Function	Description	Minimum number of nonmissing arguments
CSS	corrected sum of squares; sum of squares corrected for the mean	1
CV	percent coefficient of variation (if MEAN ≠ 0)	2
KURTOSIS	kurtosis (if STD ≠ 0)	4
MAX	maximum; highest value	1
MEAN	mean; arithmetic average	1
MIN	minimum; lowest value	1
N	sample size; number of nonmissing values	0
NMISS	number of missing values	0
RANGE	range; difference between highest and lowest value	1
SKEWNESS	skewness (if STD ≠ 0)	3
STD	standard deviation; `SQRT(VAR)`	2
STDERR	standard error of the mean; `SQRT(VAR/N)`	2
SUM	sum; total	1
USS	uncorrected sum of squares	1
VAR	variance	2

Calculating a statistic can be an appropriate time to use the OF keyword and an abbreviated variable list, as shown in this example.

```
DATA _NULL_;
  X1 = 4; X2 = .; X3 = 0; X4 = 5; X5 = 6; X6 = 5;
  CSS = CSS(OF X1-X6);
  CV = CV(OF X1-X6);
  KURTOSIS = KURTOSIS(OF X1-X6);
  MAX = MAX(OF X1-X6);
  MEAN = MEAN(OF X1-X6);
  MIN = MIN(OF X1-X6);
  N = N(OF X1-X6);
  NMISS = NMISS(OF X1-X6);
  RANGE = RANGE(OF X1-X6);
  SKEWNESS = SKEWNESS(OF X1-X6);
  STD = STD(OF X1-X6);
  STDERR = STDERR(OF X1-X6);
  SUM = SUM(OF X1-X6);
  USS = USS(OF X1-X6);
  VAR = VAR(OF X1-X6);
  PUT _ALL_;
  STOP;
```

```
X1=4 X2=. X3=0 X4=5 X5=6 X6=5 CSS=22 CV=58.630196998
KURTOSIS=3.3223140496 MAX=6 MEAN=4 MIN=0 N=5 NMISS=1 RANGE=6
SKEWNESS=-1.744369497 STD=2.3452078799 STDERR=1.0488088482 SUM=20
USS=102 VAR=5.5 _ERROR_=0 _N_=1
```

The ORDINAL function, new in SAS release 6.06, is different from other statistic functions in that the first argument is not considered part of the sample. The function returns one of the remaining arguments, the one with the rank indicated by the first argument.

If the first argument is 1, ORDINAL returns the lowest of the remaining arguments; if the first argument is 2, it returns the second lowest one; and so on. Thus,

```
ORDINAL(5, 1, -1, 2, 4, 6)
```

returns 6, which is the 5th lowest argument, not including the first one.

Also unlike other statistic functions, the ORDINAL function uses missing values as valid arguments.

Probability distributions

Probability distributions represent the behavior of random events. They are used in statistical modeling, probability theory, hypothesis testing, and stochastic simulations.

A probability distribution is associated with several functions. The SAS System includes a distribution function, an inverse distribution function, and a random number function for selected distributions.

Random number functions are unlike other functions in returning a different value each time; the value returned is a random number from a particular probability distribution. The arguments of a random number function are the parameters of the probability distribution and a *seed* argument. The seed controls the way the random number function generates random numbers. A random number function actually generates a long list (or *stream*) of numbers, one at a time; the list repeats itself every few zillion numbers. The seed determines the location in the list where the function starts. A positive seed argument represents an actual seed number, so that a step using a positive seed argument will use the same list of random numbers each time the step is executed. A zero seed argument tells the random number function to start with a different seed each time, taken from the computer's clock. A negative seed argument tells the random number function to take numbers from the computer's clock instead of a random number generator.

The SAS System has random number CALL routines corresponding to the random number functions. Using the CALL routine instead of the function allows the programmer to control seed values directly. This may be important to people who need to be concerned about the quality of their random numbers.

Distribution function calls have the form

```
function(X, parameters)
```

except in a few cases indicated in the table below. Inverse distribution function calls have the form function(P, parameters)

Random number function calls have the form

function(seed, parameters)

Function names and parameters are listed in the following table.

Probability distribution	Distribution function	Inverse distribution function	Random number function	Random number CALL routine	Parameters
beta	PROBBETA	BETAINV			α, β
binomial	PROBBNML (*p*, *n*, *x*)		RANBIN	RANBIN	n, p
Cauchy			RANCAU	RANCAU	α=1, β=1 assumed
chi-squared	PROBCHI	CINV			d.f., noncentrality
exponential			RANEXP	RANEXP	λ=1 assumed
F	PROBF	FINV			numerator d.f, denominator d.f, noncentrality
gamma	PROBGAM	GAMINV	RANGAM	RANGAM	a; b = 1 assumed
hyper-geometric	PROBHYPR (*nn*, *k*, *n*, *x*, *odds ratio*)				
negative binomial	PROBNEGB (*p*, *n*, *x*)				
normal	PROBNORM	PROBIT	RANNOR NORMAL	RANNOR	μ=0, σ=1 assumed
Poisson	POISSON(λ, *x*)		RANPOI	RANPOI	λ
Student's t	PROBT	TINV			d.f., noncentrality
tabled			RANTBL	RANTBL	f(1), f(2), f(3), ...
triangle			RANTRI	RANTRI	hypotenuse (mode); interval [0, 1] assumed
uniform	(*x*)		RANUNI UNIFORM	RANUNI	interval [0, 1] assumed

Time functions

The numeric values used in time functions represent points in time and durations of time. Numeric values represent time in the following ways in SAS routines:

Points in time	SAS date, SAS time, SAS datetime, second, minute, hour, day of week, day of month, month, quarter, year
Durations of time	seconds, minutes, hours, days, weeks, months, quarters, years

Time measurements are discussed in chapter 13, "Numbers."

There are a few functions for returning the current date and time:

Function Call	Value Returned
`DATE()` `TODAY()`	SAS date: today's date
`TIME()`	SAS time: the current time
`DATETIME()`	SAS datetime: the current date and time

Most of the time functions convert between different ways of representing time:

Function Call	Value Returned
`MDY`(month, day, year)	SAS date
`HMS`(hour, minute, second)	SAS time
`DHMS`(SAS date, hour, minute, second)	SAS datetime
`YYQ`(year, quarter)	SAS date: first day of quarter
`DATEPART`(SAS datetime)	SAS date
`TIMEPART`(SAS datetime)	SAS time
`YEAR`(SAS date)	year
`QTR`(SAS date)	quarter
`MONTH`(SAS date)	month
`WEEKDAY`(SAS date)	day of week
`DAY`(SAS date)	day of month
`HOUR`(SAS time *or* SAS datetime)	hour
`MINUTE`(SAS time *or* SAS datetime)	minute
`SECOND`(SAS time *or* SAS datetime)	second

The INTNX and INTCK functions do arithmetic with time units; INTNX does addition, and INTCK does subtraction. The use of these functions is described in chapter 13.

Character functions

The SAS System has several functions that modify character strings. They are described in the table below.

A character value returned by a SAS function, like any SAS character expression, has two different lengths: a *memory length,* which is the amount of memory used for the value, and an *expression length,* which is the actual length of the value. Both of these lengths are distinct from the *visual length* of a character value, which is the index of the last nonblank character in the value, as measured by the LENGTH function.

When an undeclared character variable is given a value in an assignment statement, it is the memory length that is used to set the length of the variable. Most character functions return a value with a memory length of either 200 or the memory length of the string argument — not necessarily the appropriate length for the variable. In general, then, it is advisable to use a LENGTH statement to declare the lengths of character variables that are given values in an assignment statement containing character functions.

<table>
<tr><th>Function Call</th><th>Description</th><th>Expression length returned</th><th>Memory length returned</th></tr>
<tr><td><code>COMPRESS(</code>string<code>)</code></td><td>removes blanks from string</td><td>≤ string length</td><td>memory length of string</td></tr>
<tr><td><code>COMPRESS(</code>string, characters<code>)</code></td><td>removes characters from string</td><td>≤ string length</td><td>memory length of string</td></tr>
<tr><td><code>LEFT(</code>string<code>)</code></td><td>left-aligns string; moves leading blanks to end</td><td>string length</td><td>memory length of string</td></tr>
<tr><td><code>REPEAT(</code>string, n<code>)</code></td><td>repeats string n + 1 times</td><td>string length × (n + 1)</td><td>200</td></tr>
<tr><td><code>REVERSE(</code>string<code>)</code></td><td>reverses order of characters in string (including blanks)</td><td>string length</td><td>memory length of string</td></tr>
<tr><td><code>RIGHT(</code>string<code>)</code></td><td>right-aligns string; moves trailing blanks to beginning</td><td>string length</td><td>memory length of string</td></tr>
<tr><td><code>SCAN(</code>string, n, delimiters<code>)</code></td><td>returns nth token from string.
A token is any sequence of non-delimiter characters. The default delimiters are “ <code>.<(+|&!$*);-/,%>\</code>” plus “^” on ASCII computers and “¬” on EBCDIC computers.
If there are fewer than n tokens, the function returns a blank.</td><td>≤ string length</td><td>200</td></tr>
<tr><td><code>SUBSTR(</code>string, position, length<code>)</code></td><td>substring; returns a part of the string with the specified length beginning at the specified position. (The length must be at least 1.)</td><td>length specified</td><td>memory length of string</td></tr>
<tr><td><code>SUBSTR(</code>string, position<code>)</code></td><td>substring; returns a part of the string beginning at the specified position.</td><td>string length – position + 1</td><td>memory length of string</td></tr>
<tr><td><code>TRANSLATE</code> <code>(</code>string, to, from<code>)</code></td><td>substitutes to characters for from characters in string. The substitution is done character by character.</td><td>string length</td><td>memory length of string</td></tr>
<tr><td><code>TRIM(</code>string<code>)</code></td><td>removes trailing blanks;
shortens expression length to visual length (but not shorter than 1)</td><td>visual length of string
(but at least 1)</td><td>memory length of string</td></tr>
<tr><td><code>UPCASE(</code>string<code>)</code></td><td>capitalizes; changes all lowercase letters to uppercase letters</td><td>string length</td><td>memory length of string</td></tr>
</table>

The following examples demonstrate the use of the character functions.

Function Call	Value Returned
`COMPRESS('  Now is the time  ')`	`'Nowisthetime'`
`COMPRESS('$64,000.00', '$,()')`	`'64000.00'`
`LEFT('    brain    ')`	`'brain         '`
`REPEAT('ho ', 2)`	`'ho ho ho '`
`REPEAT('-', 19)`	`'--------------------'`
`REVERSE('  Now is the time  ')`	`'  emit eht si woN  '`
`RIGHT('  over    ')`	`'      over'`
`SCAN('  Now is the time  ', 1)`	`'Now'`
`SCAN('  Now is the time  ', 2)`	`'is'`
`SCAN('  Now is the time  ', 5)`	`' '`
`SCAN(',,,RELEASE', 1)`	`'RELEASE'`
`SCAN('  PROC PRINT; RUN;', 2, ';')`	`' RUN'`
`TRANSLATE('$64,000.00', '  ', '$¢')`	`' 64,000.00'`
`TRANSLATE('Now is the time','eal','oim')`	`'New as the tale'`
`TRIM('  Now is the time  ')`	`'  Now is the time'`
`UPCASE('  Now is the time  ')`	`'  NOW IS THE TIME  '`

The SUBSTR function has another use, as a pseudo-variable for character substitution, which is described below.

Functions that analyze character strings

The functions in this group return numeric values providing information about character strings.

Function Call	Description
`INDEX(`string, character sequence`)`	the index of the first occurrence of the character sequence in the string. If the character sequence is not found, INDEX returns 0.
`INDEXC(`string, characters`)`	the index of the first occurrence in the string of any of the characters listed. If none of the characters are found in the string, INDEXC returns 0. When searching for one character, INDEX and INDEXC are equivalent.
`LENGTH(`string`)`	the visual length of the string; the index of the last nonblank character. LENGTH always returns at least 1, even for missing values.
`VERIFY(`string, characters`)`	the index of the first character in the string that is not one of the characters listed. If all of the characters in the string are matched, VERIFY returns 0.

The following examples demonstrate the use of these functions.

Function Call	Value Returned
`INDEX('discovery', 'over')`	5
`INDEX('discovery', 're')`	0
`INDEX('discovery', 'i ')`	0
`INDEXC('discovery', 'i ')`	2
`INDEXC('discovery', 'ABCDEFGHIJ')`	0
`LENGTH('discovery')`	9
`LENGTH('discovery      ')`	9
`LENGTH('      discovery')`	15
`LENGTH('')`	1
`VERIFY('A', 'ABCDF')`	0
`VERIFY('A+', 'ABCDF')`	2

Array functions

The array functions are distinctive in two respects: they use an array as an argument, and they are evaluated as a data step is interpreted rather than when it is executed. The purpose of the functions is to determine the size of an array. They are often used as DO loop bounds, so that the size of the array does not have to be explicitly stated in the DO statement.

For one-dimensional arrays, these function calls are used:

Function Call	Function Call (suffix form)	Description
`LBOUND(`array`)` `LBOUND(`array`, 1)`	`LBOUND1(`array`)`	the lower bound of the array index
`HBOUND(`array`)` `HBOUND(`array`, 1)`	`HBOUND1(`array`)`	the upper bound of the array index
`DIM(`array`)` `DIM(`array`, 1)`	`DIM1(`array`)`	the number of elements in the array

For multidimensional arrays, the functions return information about a selected dimension of the array. The dimension can be selected either as a numeric suffix in the function name or as a second argument. The default dimension, if none is stated, is 1.

Function Call	Function Call (suffix form)	Description
LBOUND(array, 1) LBOUND(array, 2) LBOUND(array, 3) ...	LBOUND1(array) LBOUND2(array) LBOUND3(array) ...	the lower bound of the array index for the selected dimension
HBOUND(array, 1) HBOUND(array, 2) HBOUND(array, 3) ...	HBOUND1(array) HBOUND2(array) HBOUND3(array) ...	the upper bound of the array index for the selected dimension
DIM(array, 1) DIM(array, 2) DIM(array, 3) ...	DIM1(array) DIM2(array) DIM3(array) ...	the size of the selected dimension of the array

There is no single function call to return the number of elements in a multidimensional array.

Geographic functions

The geographic functions convert between different codes that might be used to identify a state of the United States. FIPS state codes are used in some U.S. census data. ZIP codes used in these functions are character values with a length of 5, not numeric values. A state's postal code is the two-letter abbreviation commonly used in addresses.

In addition to the 50 states, these functions cover Puerto Rico, District of Columbia, and Guam.

	Convert to (returned value)			
Convert from (argument)	FIPS state code	state name in uppercase	state name in upper and lower case	2-letter postal code
FIPS state code		FIPNAME	FIPNAMEL	FIPSTATE
2-letter postal code	STFIPS	STNAME	STNAMEL	
ZIP code	ZIPFIPS	ZIPNAME	ZIPNAMEL	ZIPSTATE

Financial functions

The SAS financial functions are designed to describe and analyze periodic payments or expenses. They implement classic formulas from financial analysis and accounting.

These functions are expressed in terms of *periods*. In the most familiar uses, the period would be a month, but the functions work exactly the same way if a different period is used. Although it is traditional to express interest rates as annual percentage rates, these functions express rates as periodic fractions. For example, if the payment period is monthly, a 12% annual rate would be expressed as .01.

MORT

The MORT function describes a simple loan, such as a mortgage loan: a certain amount *a* is borrowed, and then paid back in *n* periodic payments, where *p* is the amount of each payment and *r* is the periodic interest rate (compounded periodically). These parameters are related by the formula

$$p = r\,a\,\frac{(1+r)^n}{(1+r)^n - 1}$$

or in SAS syntax,

```
p = r*a*(1 + r)**n/((1 + r)**n - 1);
```

MORT(*a*, *p*, *r*, *n*) calculates any one of these parameters if the other three are given. For example, MORT(., *p*, *r*, *n*) calculates the loan amount, and MORT(*a*, *p*, ., *n*) calculates the periodic interest rate as a fraction.

The MORTGAGE proc does similar loan calculations and produces a detailed report.

SAVING

The SAVING function also describes a sequence of equal, periodic payments. The difference is that these payments are not repaying a loan. You can think of them as being paid into a savings account, with *f* being the value of the account in the future, one period after the last payment is made. The SAVING parameters are related by the formula

$$f = p\,(1+r)\,\frac{(1+r)^n - 1}{r}$$

or in SAS syntax,

```
f = p*(1 + r)*((1 + r)**n - 1)/r;
```

SAVING(*f*, *p*, *r*, *n*) calculates any one of these parameters if the other three are given.

COMPOUND

The COMPOUND function represents savings or a loan with compound interest but without periodic payments. For savings, *a* is the amount deposited, and *f* is the value of the account after *n* periods with a compound interest rate per period of *r*. For a loan, *a* is the amount advanced, and *f* is the amount repaid, including interest. The four parameters are related by the formula

$$f = a\ (1 + r)^n$$

or in SAS syntax,

```
f = a*(1 + r)**n;
```

COMPOUND(*a*, *f*, *r*, *n*) calculates any one of the four parameters if the other three are given.

INTRR and NETPV

Two functions provide ways of analyzing the value of investments and other financial decisions. The investment possibility is represented as a sequence of periodic cash flows (some positive, some negative). Then the INTRR function calculates the *internal rate of return*, essentially an effective interest rate; or the NETPV function calculates the *net present value*, the value at the beginning of the sequence, based on a projected interest rate.

Both functions allow you to use annual interest rates by specifying the number of payment periods per year. The forms of the functions are

```
internal rate of return = INTRR(number of payment periods per year,
     cash flow 1, cash flow 2, cash flow 3, . . .);

net present value = NETPV(interest rate, number of payment periods per year,
     cash flow 1, cash flow 2, cash flow 3, . . .);
```

INTRR and NETPV use interest rates expressed as a fraction. Variations on these functions, IRR and NPV, do the same calculations with interest rates expressed as a percent.

Depreciation functions

A depreciation function approximates the decline in value of an asset for accounting purposes. The SAS System has periodic and accumulated depreciation functions for several different depreciation methods.

The arguments for these functions are

value	the original value of the asset, before depreciation
years	the recovery period; the number of years it takes for the asset to be fully depreciated
period	the year of the recovery period for which depreciation is calculated; 1 for the first year of the recovery period, 2 for the second, etc.
rate	the depreciation rate

The function names and arguments are given in the table below.

Depreciation method	Periodic depreciation function	Accumulated depreciation function	Function arguments
Sum of years digits	DEPSYD	DACCSYD	period, value, years
Straight line	DEPSL	DACCSL	period, value, years
Declining balance	DEPDB	DACCDB	period, value, years, rate
Declining balance switching to straight line	DEPDBSL	DACCDBSL	period, value, years, rate
Table	DEPTAB	DACCTAB	period, value, rate 1, rate 2, rate 3, ...

Miscellaneous functions

These are other SAS functions of interest.

INPUT. The INPUT function applies an informat specification to a character string to create a value. The function takes any of these forms:

```
INPUT(string, informat specification)
INPUT(string, ? informat specification)  /* release 6.06 and later */
INPUT(string, ?? informat specification) /* release 6.06 and later */
```

The informat interprets the characters the same way that it would in reading from a text file in an INPUT statement. If a numeric informat is used, a numeric value is returned. If a character informat is used, INPUT returns a character value with an expression length and memory length determined by the informat. If no informat width is stated, the width used depends on the length of the string argument. Beginning with SAS release 6.06, the ? and ?? format modifiers can be used to suppress invalid data messages, the same as in the INPUT statement.

PUT. The PUT function applies a format specification to a value to create a character string. The function takes either of these forms:

```
PUT(numeric value, numeric format specification)
PUT(character value, character format specification)
```

The format creates the same characters as it would in writing to a text file in a PUT statement. The expression length and memory length of the value returned are the same as the format width.

LAG and DIF functions. Each time a LAG1 function call is executed, it returns the argument passed to it the previous time it was called. The LAG2 function returns the argument passed to it the 2nd previous time. And so on up to LAG100. Each LAG*n* function call returns missing values the first *n* times it is called. The functions can be used with both numeric and character arguments. The LAG1 function can also be called LAG.

Each appearance of a LAG function in a step is independent of each other appearance. Thus, you can use separate LAG function calls for different variables.

```
DATA _NULL_;
  DO I = 1 TO 5;
    A = LAG1(I);
    B = LAG3('B');
    PUT I= A= B=;
    END;
```

```
I=1 A=. B=
I=2 A=1 B=
I=3 A=2 B=
I=4 A=3 B=B
I=5 A=4 B=B
```

The LAG functions should be used with caution. Many programmers believe that the LAG1 function returns the value of a variable in the previous input observation. While it is possible to set up the LAG1 function to do that, that is not really what it does.

The DIF functions work only with numeric arguments and are only slightly different from the LAG functions. Instead of returning the previous argument, the DIF1 function returns the result of subtracting the previous argument from the current argument. The DIF2 function returns the result of subtracting the 2nd previous argument from the current argument, and so on.

SYMGET

The SYMGET function takes a character argument, which is the name of a macrovariable. It returns the value of the macrovariable, or the first 200 characters of it.

> In SAS releases 6.03 and 6.04, the SYMGET function uses memory greedily, grabbing memory hundreds of bytes at a time and not releasing it for the remainder of the SAS session. Although it is usually safe enough to use the function, it is essential not to execute it repeatedly — in an observation loop, for example. Presumably this bug will be fixed for the next release.

The SUBSTR pseudo-variable for character substitution

SUBSTR is the only function that can be used at the beginning of an assignment statement, having a value assigned to it. Used this way, it is a *pseudo-variable*, allowing a part of a character variable to be assigned a value, as if it were an entire variable. The use of SUBSTR as a pseudo-variable follows either of these forms:

SUBSTR(*character variable, position*) = *character expression*;
SUBSTR(*character variable, position, length*) = *character expression*;

This statement replaces characters in the variable beginning at the position indicated with the value on the right side of the equals sign. If a length argument is given, only that many characters are changed; otherwise, characters are changed up to the end of the variable, padding with blanks if needed.

```
DATA _NULL_;
  POINT = 'FINGER';
  SUBSTR(POINT, 4, 1) = 'D';
  PUT POINT=;
```

```
POINT=FINDER
```

The SUBSTR pseudo-variable can be used only on an already existing character variable. If the first appearance of a variable is in a SUBSTR pseudo-array reference, use an earlier LENGTH statement to declare the variable. Unpredictable errors occur when a SUBSTR pseudo-variable is used with an undeclared variable.

CALL routines

CALL routines (sometimes called CALL subroutines) are essentially the same as functions except that they do not return a value. Because they can't be used in an expression, they are used in a separate statement, the CALL statement. Another difference between CALL routines and functions is that CALL routines often change the value of variables used as their arguments.

Like functions, CALL routines are used only in the data step.

Random numbers

CALL routines to generate random numbers have the same arguments as the corresponding random number functions, except that the seed must be a numeric variable, and an additional, final argument, also a numeric variable, contains the random number generated.

For example, this use of the random number function for the binary distribution

```
X = RANBIN(SEED, N, P);
```

is equivalent to this CALL statement:

```
CALL RANBIN(SEED, N, P, X);
```

The names of the random number CALL routines are listed in the probability distributions table in the preceding section.

Other CALL routines

There are a few other CALL routines of interest.

SYMPUT. Probably the most commonly used CALL routine, SYMPUT assigns a value to a macrovariable. The form of the statement is

```
CALL SYMPUT(macrovariable name, string);
```

SYSTEM. The SYSTEM routine executes operating system commands contained in a character string. The argument can be a character variable, constant, or expression. The commands allowed depend on the operating system. The form of the statement is

```
CALL SYSTEM(string);
```

LABEL. LABEL assigns the label attribute of a variable to a character variable. The form of the statement is

```
CALL LABEL(variable, character variable);
```

The arguments must be variables or array elements. The character variable should have a length of at least 40, because that is the length of a variable label.

VNAME. Similarly, VNAME assigns the name of a variable to a character variable. Its form is

```
CALL VNAME(variable, character variable);
```

The arguments must be variables or array elements. The character variable should have a length of 8 or more so that it can hold any variable name.

SOUND. Available in some implementations, the SOUND routine has this form:

```
CALL SOUND(frequency, duration);
```

It creates a beep (or perhaps a nicer tone, depending on the hardware) with the indicated frequency in Hertz and duration in 80ths of a second.

Informats

Reading means determining the meaning of data. When the INPUT statement reads a stream of characters from an input text file, it uses informats to convert them to the numeric values and character values that can be used in a SAS program.

Informats are used wherever the SAS System interprets character data. Besides the INPUT statement, they are used in the INPUT function and in many interactive procs.

An informat that produces a numeric value is called a numeric informat. An informat that produces a character value is called a character informat. Names of character informats begin with a dollar sign ($). Informat names cannot end in a digit.

That's because of the way informat names are used in SAS programs. The informat name is ordinarily followed by a width specification and a period. For example, the $HEX informat with a width of 7 would be written this way:

```
$HEX7.
```

The width tells how many characters the informat should interpret. For some numeric informats, the period can be followed by a decimal specification, indicating the number of implied decimal places in input data that does not contain a decimal point. The width can be omitted, in which case a default width will be used. However, the period must be present to identify the name as an informat name.

Certain limited kinds of informats can be created using the FORMAT proc.

The tables below list selected informats supplied with the SAS System. The characters *w* and *d* indicate width and decimal specifications. Some of these informats were new with SAS release 6.06.

Character informats

Informat	Description
$*w*.	standard character informat; removes leading blanks; treats . as a missing value
$ASCII*w*.	reads ASCII characters; the same as $CHAR on ASCII computers
$BINARY*w*.	character binary; converts each 8 input characters (0s and 1s) to one character
$CHAR*w*.	uninterpreted characters; passes characters through without change
$CHARZB*w*.	changes null characters (zero bytes) to blanks
$EBCDIC*w*.	reads EBCDIC characters; the same as $CHAR on EBCDIC computers
$F*w*.	same as the $ informat (standard character informat)
$HEX*w*.	character hexadecimal; converts each pair of hexadecimal digits to one byte; works the same way as hexadecimal character constants
$OCTAL*w*.	character octal; converts each 3 input characters (digits 0–7) to one character
$VARYING*w*.	varying-length values. This informat is useful only in the INPUT statement. Its use is described in chapter 5, "I/O."

Numeric informats

Informat	Description
w.d	standard numeric informat; reads ordinary numeric data and scientific notation (using E). This is the informat without a name. This informat accepts leading – and + signs, but there cannot be a blank between the sign and the first digit.
BEST*w.d* D*w.d* E*w.d* F*w.d*	same as the standard numeric informat
BINARY*w.d*	binary; reads binary digit characters (0 and 1 characters) as integer values
BITS*w.d*	extracts bits; skips *d* bits, then reads *w* as integer value; used for reading bitfields
BZ*w.d*	same as the standard numeric informat, except that it treats blanks (other than leading blanks) as '0' digits. Blanks between a – or + sign and the first digit are acceptable.
COMMA*w.d* DOLLAR*w.d*	ignores commas, dollar signs, percent signs, blanks, and parentheses; a leading left parenthesis indicates a negative value
COMMAX*w.d* DOLLARX*w.d*	treats commas as decimal points; ignores periods, dollar signs, percent signs, blanks, and parentheses; a leading left parenthesis indicates a negative value
HEX*w.*	hexadecimal integer; nonnegative integers in hexadecimal notation
HEX16.	hexadecimal real number; hexadecimal representation of 8-byte floating-point value
IB*w.d* S370FIB*w.d*	signed integer binary; two's complement notation. IB2. and IB4. correspond to common ways of representing integers in memory in other computer languages. If a decimal specification is used, the number is multiplied by 10 raised to that power. IB corresponds to the computer's memory form for signed integers. S370FIB is similar, but is a portable informat that operates the same way on all computers.
OCTAL*w.d*	octal integer
PD*w.d* S370FPD*w.d*	packed decimal
PERCENT*w.*	percent; same as COMMA, except that if a percent sign (%) follows the numeral, it is divided by 100
PIB*w.d* S370FPIB*w.d*	positive integer binary. PIB is similar to IB, but all values are considered nonnegative. PIB corresponds to the computer's memory form for unsigned integers. S370FPIB is similar, but is a portable informat that operates the same way on all computers.
PK*w.d*	unsigned packed decimal; each half-byte contains one decimal digit
RB*w.d* S370FRB*w.d*	real binary; floating point. RB8. is the way the SAS System ordinarily stores numeric values. RB corresponds to the computer's memory form for double precision floating-point numbers. S370FRB is similar, but is a portable informat that operates the same way on all computers.

Time informats

The informats that produce SAS date values are generally tolerant of extra characters like hyphens, spaces, and slashes in the input data. The values produced when informats read 2-digit years is affected by the YEARCUTOFF= system option.

Informat	Description	Example	Produces
`DATE`*w*`.`	ddMMMyy form of date	`15AUG91`	SAS date
`DDMMYY`*w*`.`	date	`15/08/91`	SAS date
`MMDDYY`*w*`.`	date	`8-15-91`	SAS date
`YYMMDD`*w*`.`	date	`910815`	SAS date
`MONYY`*w*`.`	month and year	`AUG91`	SAS date: first day of month
`YYQ4.` `YYQ6.`	year and quarter: yyQq or yyyyQq	`1991Q3`	SAS date: first day of quarter
`NENGO`*w*`.`	Japanese date: M, T, S, or H, then yymmdd	`H.020101`	SAS date
`TIME`*w*`.`	hh:mm:ss. form of time	`16:57:21.01`	SAS time, or duration in seconds
`DATETIME`*w*`.`	like `DATE.` followed by `TIME.`	`15AUG91 16:57`	SAS datetime

Formats

Writing means preparing data to be read. When the PUT statement writes variable values to an output text file, it uses *formats* to convert the values to a stream of characters that a person or another program will be able to read, a process called *formatting*.

The SAS System uses formats whenever it formats data values. Besides the PUT statement, formats are used in the PUT function and in almost every proc.

In the way they handle data, formats are like the opposite of informats. In other ways, formats are very much like informats. They have the same naming rules, and indeed, some of them have the same names. They have the same width and decimal specifications, but the decimal specifications are more important in formats: they determine where decimal points are placed in numeric formats that have decimal points.

Character formats

Character formats can format only character values. Their names begin with dollar signs ($).

The width of a character format might not match the amount of data to be written. The character format begins writing with the first character, truncating the end of the data or padding with trailing blanks if necessary in order to write the specified width.

These are the most commonly used character formats, including several that were introduced with SAS release 6.06:

Format	Description
$w.	standard character format; removes leading blanks
$ASCIIw.	writes ASCII characters; the same as $CHAR on ASCII computers
$BINARYw.	character binary; converts each character to eight output characters (0s and 1s)
$CHARw.	unformatted characters; passes characters through without change
$EBCDICw.	writes EBCDIC characters; the same as $CHAR on EBCDIC computers
$Fw.	same as the $ format (standard character format)
$HEXw.	character hexadecimal; writes each character as 2 hexadecimal digits
$OCTALw.	character octal; converts each character to 3 output characters (digits 0–7)
$VARYINGw.	varying-length values. This format is useful only in the PUT statement. Its use is described in chapter 5, "I/O."

Numeric formats

Numeric formats can be divided, in a rough way, between those that most people can read — which we could call *display* formats — and those that are intended more for computer programs and computer scientists to read — which we can call *machine* formats.

The formatted numerals produced by a display format do not usually contain the full precision of the floating-point numbers they represent. Display formats round numbers to the nearest value that they can represent. If a number is too large to be written in the space provided using the format specified, most formats switch to the BEST format to try to represent the number. If the number still cannot be represented, the format fills the field with asterisks (***).

Display formats right-align their output, padding with leading blanks to fill the width indicated. You might use the : format modifier in a PUT statement to get left-aligned output.

Format	Description
w.d	standard numeric format
BEST*w*.	formats a number in the way that provides the most precision possible in the width provided. This is the default numeric format.
COMMA*w*.0 COMMA*w*.2	commas separate every three digits
COMMAX*w*.0 COMMAX*w*.2	the same as COMMA, but with periods and commas reversed
DOLLAR*w*.0 DOLLAR*w*.2	leading dollar sign; commas separate every three digits
DOLLARX*w*.0 DOLLARX*w*.2	the same as DOLLAR, but with periods and commas reversed
E*w.d*	scientific notation (using E)
F*w.d*	same as the standard numeric format
FRACT*w*.	fractions in reduced form
HEX*w*.	hexadecimal integer. A negative number is converted to a positive number by adding 16^w. If a number is too large to fit in the width specified, the least significant part (that is, the rightmost digits) of the number is kept.
NEGPAREN*w.d*	negative values in parentheses; commas separate every three digits
PERCENT*w*.	percent; multiplies number by 100, writes percent sign (%) after it, and encloses negative values in parentheses
ROMAN*w*.	Roman numerals, using capital letters (up to 9,999)
SSN11. SSN.	Social Security numbers; hyphens after 3rd and 5th digits, leading zeros
WORDF*w*.	writes number in words; writes hundredths as a fraction; useful for writing checks, perhaps.
WORDS*w*.	writes number in words; writes hundredths in words.
Z*w.d*	zeros; same as the standard numeric format, except with zeros in place of leading blanks.

All the machine formats produce the entire width specified, with no need for leading or trailing blanks.

If a decimal specification is used with a machine format, the value is multiplied by 10 raised to that power before formatting.

The integer binary and hexadecimal formats can write only integers. Noninteger values are truncated to integer values, except that numbers between 0 and –1 are treated as –1. The results of the integer binary formats are not consistent when you try to format a value outside the format's range. The hexadecimal and packed formats simply omit digits on the left (the most significant digits) if there are too many. All these formats format missing values as 0.

Format	Description
`BINARYw.`	formats positive integers as binary numerals (using 0 and 1 characters); truncates nonintegers; writes negative numbers as all 1s.
`HEXw.`	hexadecimal integer. A negative number is converted to a positive number by adding 16^w. If a number is too large to fit in the width specified, the least significant part (that is, the rightmost digits) of the number is kept.
`HEX16.`	hexadecimal real number; hexadecimal representation of 8-byte floating-point value
`IBw.d` `S370FIBw.d`	signed integer binary; two's complement form. IB2. and IB4. correspond to common ways of representing integers in memory in other computer languages. If a number is too large to fit in the width specified, the least significant part (that is, the rightmost digits) of the number is kept. IB corresponds to the computer's memory form for signed integers. S370FIB is similar, but is a portable format that operates the same way on all computers.
`OCTALw.`	octal integer; writes positive integers as octal numerals; truncates nonintegers
`PDw.d` `S370FPDw.d`	packed decimal
`PIBw.d` `S370FPIBw.d`	positive integer binary. PIB is similar to IB, but all values are considered nonnegative. (The way negative values are formatted depends on the computer.) If a number is too large to fit in the width specified, the least significant part (that is, the rightmost digits) of the number is kept. PIB corresponds to the computer's memory form for unsigned integers. S370FPIB is similar, but is a portable format that operates the same way on all computers.
`PKw.d`	unsigned packed decimal; each half-byte contains one decimal digit. For negative arguments, the absolute value is formatted.
`RBw.d` `S370FRBw.d`	real binary; double precision floating point. RB8. is the way the SAS System ordinarily stores numeric values. RB corresponds to the computer's memory form for floating-point numbers. S370FRB is similar, but is a portable format that operates the same way on all computers.

Time formats

Formats for writing time values truncate and punctuate differently depending on the width specifications used. The various possibilities are shown in chapter 13, "Numbers." In any case, they right-align, and those that write whole words use upper- and lowercase letters. The table below lists the formats used with time values. Time of day is always written using a 24-hour clock.

Many of the formats for writing SAS dates are new with SAS release 6.06.

Value	Formats
SAS date (year, month, day)	DATEw., YYMMDDw., MMDDYYw., DDMMYYw., WORDDATEw., WORDDATXw., WEEKDATEw., WEEKDATXw. YEARw., MONNAMEw., MONTHw., DAYw., MONYYw., YYMONw., MMYYw., MMYYCw., MMYYDw., MMYYNw., MMYYPw., MMYYSw., YYMMw., YYMMCw., YYMMDw., YYMMNw., YYMMPw., YYMMSw.
SAS date (quarter)	QTRw., QTRRw., YYQw., YYQCw., YYQDw., YYQNw., YYQPw., YYQSw., YYQRw., YYQRCw., YYQRDw., YYQRNw., YYQRPw., YYQRSw.
SAS date (other)	NENGOw. (Japanese dates), JULDAYw. (day of year), DOWNAMEw. (name of day of week), WEEKDAYw.
SAS datetime	TODw. (time of day), DATETIMEw.d (date and time)
SAS time	TIMEw.d, HOURw.d, HHMMw.
duration of time in seconds	TIMEw.d, HOURw.d, HHMMw.d, MMSSw.d, w.d

Creating formats and informats using the FORMAT proc

The FORMAT proc creates certain kinds of formats and informats. Once they are created, the formats and informats can be used in the program or session in which they are created, or they can be stored for use with later programs.

The LIBRARY= option is used on the PROC statement to store formats and informats for later programs. Details such as the libref and the form of the files created vary by operating system.

One statement defines each format or informat that is created. Any number of formats and informats can be created in a single step.

Ranges

The FORMAT proc works with ranges of values and has syntax rules for specifying ranges. A range can be a constant value or a list of constant values separated by commas, as in these examples:

```
-4.4
1, 2, 5
'a', 'e', 'i', 'o', 'u'
'TEXAS'
```

A range can also include intervals. An interval includes all the values between two named endpoints. The lower endpoint must be listed before the upper endpoint. The symbol between the two endpoints determines whether they are included.

lower-higher	interval including both endpoints

lower<–higher	interval including the higher endpoint
lower–<higher	interval including the lower endpoint
lower<–<higher	interval not including either endpoint

The special values LOW and HIGH can be used as interval endpoints to indicate the lowest and highest possible values. For numeric ranges, LOW does not include missing values.

The range OTHER can be used to encompass all values not included in other ranges.

Value formats

A value format simply associates a range with a character constant, giving the characters to be produced by the format for values in that range. A value format can have up to a few thousand ranges, but runs out of space if you try to use too many.

A value format is created by the VALUE statement, which has this form:

```
VALUE name (format options)
     range = constant
     range = constant
     . . .
     ;
```

The ONEDIGIT format defined in this example attempts to represent numeric values in one character.

```
PROC FORMAT;
  VALUE ONEDIGIT
     0              = '0'
     0    <-<  1    = '/'
     1     -<  1.5  = '1'
     1.5   -<  2.5  = '2'
     2.5   -<  3.5  = '3'
     3.5   -<  4.5  = '4'
     4.5   -<  5.5  = '5'
     5.5   -<  6.5  = '6'
     6.5   -<  7.5  = '7'
     7.5   -<  8.5  = '8'
     8.5   -< 10    = '9'
     10-999999999.5 = '+'
     999999999.5-HIGH = '!'
     LOW   -<  0    = '-'
     ._    -   .Z   = '?'
     ;
```

Normally, ranges should not overlap. In this example, though, the value 999999999.5 appears in two ranges. The FORMAT proc resolves this kind of ambiguity by including the value in the first range in which it appears. So `PUT(999999999.5, ONEDIGIT.)` would be '+' rather than '!'.

The final range, ._–.Z, includes all missing values. It is possible to format different special missing values differently. The next example demonstrates one use of this.

Suppose you are maintaining a weekly "top 100" chart showing records in order of popularity. The chart also shows the previous week's position for each chart entry. Not every chart entry would have been on the previous chart, though; you use the special missing value .N to indicate new records and .R for records re-entering the chart. You could format them using the format LASTWK:

```
PROC FORMAT;
  VALUE LASTWK
      .N = 'NEW ===>'
      .R = 'RE-ENTRY'
      ;
```

When a format's ranges do not include all possible values, values outside the ranges are formatted using the default format. The LASTWK format, then, formats all numbers using the default numeric format (the BEST format), but it provides explanatory labels for the two special missing values .N and .R.

Character value formats can be created the same way. Names of character formats begin with a dollar sign.

```
  VALUE $PF
      'A' -< 'E' = 'PASS'
      'E' -< 'G' = 'FAIL'
      OTHER = ' '
      ;
```

The character strings created by a format cannot be longer than 40 characters. For character formats, the character values that define a range cannot be longer than 16 characters.

Format options

Format options can follow the name of a format created in the FORMAT proc, enclosed in parentheses.

Three options relate to the allowed width of a format or informat. MIN= and MAX= give the range of widths that can be used. DEFAULT= gives the default width, which is the width used if no width is specified when the format is used. The default values for MIN= and DEFAULT= are the length of the longest constant or picture used in the format. You might specify `MIN=1` to allow you to truncate the output of the format. The default value of MAX= is 40, which is the longest value allowed. The DEFAULT= value must be at least as large as the MIN= value but not larger than the MAX= value.

A fourth format option can only be used for numeric value formats. It is the FUZZ= option, which extends each value or interval by the specified *fuzz* amount. In other words, a value being formatted will be treated as matching a listed value if the distance between them is less than or equal to the fuzz amount. The default is `FUZZ=1E-12`.

The following example shows the use of a format with format options.

```
PROC FORMAT;
  VALUE MONL (MIN=1 DEFAULT=3 FUZZ=.5)
         1 = 'January'
         2 = 'February'
         3 = 'March'
         4 = 'April'
         5 = 'May'
         6 = 'June'
         7 = 'July'
         8 = 'August'
         9 = 'September'
        10 = 'October'
        11 = 'November'
        12 = 'December'
     OTHER = ' '
         ;
DATA _NULL_;
  A = 2.7; B = 8; C = 12.2; D = 0;
  PUT 'Using MONL. format:  '
      A= MONL. B= MONL. C= MONL. D= MONL. /
      'Using MONL9. format:  '
      A= MONL9. B= MONL9. C= MONL9. D= MONL9.;
```

```
Using MONL. format:  A=Mar B=Aug C=Dec D=
Using MONL9. format:  A=March B=August C=December D=
```

Picture formats

Picture formats are more complicated than value formats. A picture format can associate a range with a *picture*, rather than simply the characters to be printed. A picture is a character constant, but the digits it contains (called *digit selectors*) represent positions to be used by the *picture processor*, in the process described below.

A picture format is created by the PICTURE statement, which has this form:

```
PICTURE name (format options)
    range = picture  (picture options)
    range = picture  (picture options)
    . . .
    ;
```

Only numeric picture formats can be created.

A picture must begin with a digit. Pictures can be up to 40 characters long; unpredictable errors occur in trying to use a picture format defined with a picture that is longer than 40 characters. A picture can contain no more than 15 digits.

Picture options

Each picture can have *picture options* associated with it. The MULTIPLIER= or MULT= option gives a number that a data value is multiplied by before being put into the picture. If the picture contains a decimal point (a period) and you do not specify a MULT= value, a MULT= value that is the power of 10 needed to shift the integer part of the number to the left of the (first) decimal point is used. (If there is no decimal point, the default is `MULT=1`.)

The PREFIX= option specifies a character constant, one or two characters, to be put before the first digit of the formatted numeral. `PREFIX='$'` is commonly used for money values. `PREFIX='-'` is usually used for negative values, because the picture processor does not produce minus signs by itself.

If there are any leading spaces left, they are filled with the fill character specified in the FILL= option. The default fill character is a blank. `FILL='*'` might be used for writing checks or in other situations where it is important to prevent tampering with a printed number.

The NOEDIT picture option can be used to have the character constant treated as a constant value rather than as a picture. Thus, some ranges in a picture format can be formatted as constant values while others are formatted as pictures.

The picture processor

> The workings of the picture processor are quite complicated and in several respects are counterintuitive. If you need precise results from a picture format, you should walk through the picture processor actions described here using representative values as you design each picture, and then test the completed picture format before relying on it.

The picture processor works only with nonnegative integers. Before formatting numbers, it processes them by multiplying them by the multiplier (from the MULT= picture option), taking the absolute value (to turn negative numbers into positive numbers), and truncating to an integer value (but rounding to the nearest integer if the value is within .00000001 of an integer). In SAS syntax, that would be

```
INTEGER = FLOOR(ABS(NUMBER*MULT) + .00000001);
```

The picture processor converts the integer to a numeral. The numeral has the same number of digits as the picture has, with leading zeros if necessary. If the number is too large to fit in the picture, only the last digits of the numeral are used. To avoid this kind of truncation, include only values that will fit in a picture in the range associated with the picture.

The digits of the numeral are then substituted for the digit selectors in the picture. Zeros at the beginning of the picture (up to the first nonzero digit selector) are not replaced by leading zeros from the numeral, though; instead, they are replaced by fill characters (from the FILL= picture option). If there is a prefix (from the PREFIX= picture option), it is placed in the last one or two fill positions (depending on whether the prefix is one or two characters long).

The prefix and fill characters, then, appear only if there is room for them in the picture. If there is only one fill position for a two-character prefix, the second character of the prefix is used.

Using picture formats

The following picture format formats dollar amounts between –$10 and $100 as a number of cents.

```
PROC FORMAT;
  PICTURE CENT
      0   -< 100 = '0001¢' (MULTIPLIER=100)
      -10 <-<  0 = '0001¢' (PREFIX='-' MULTIPLIER=100)
      LOW -   -10 = '-$$$$' (NOEDIT)
      100 - HIGH = '$$$$$' (NOEDIT)
      ;
```

Using the CENT format, you could print 1.333 as " 133¢", 0 as " 0¢", and 125 as "$$$$$".

If a picture format is used with a width wider than the length of the picture, the picture is right-aligned and one fill character is placed before it. If the width is smaller than the width of the picture, the rightmost part of the picture is used.

If the ranges of a picture format do not include all possible numeric values, other values are printed using the default format (the BEST format). In particular, ordinary missing values are printed as right-aligned periods.

Value informats

Value informats are very much like value formats. They are defined in the INVALUE statement, which is scarcely different from the VALUE statement. The essential difference is that the value informat associates ranges of character strings to be interpreted with constant values — character values or numeric values, depending on whether the informat is a character informat or a numeric informat. Names of value informats cannot be longer than 7 characters.

Informat options can be used on the INVALUE statement. The MIN=, MAX=, and DEFAULT= options are the same as the corresponding format options, but they apply to input values rather than output values. Two new informat options are usually used, beginning with SAS release 6.06: JUST, to ignore leading blanks, and UPCASE, to convert all letters to uppercase letters before applying the informat.

You could use this numeric value informat to interpret small Roman numerals:

```
PROC FORMAT;
  INVALUE ROMAN (MIN=1 MAX=32 UPCASE JUST)
      ' ' = 0 'I' = 1 'II' = 2 'III' =  3 'IV'   = 4  'V'   =  5
      'VI'  =  6 'VII'  =  7 'VIII'  =  8 'IX'   = 9  'X'   = 10
      'XI'  = 11 'XII'  = 12 'XIII'  = 13 'XIV'  = 14 'XV'  = 15
      'XVI' = 16 'XVII' = 17 'XVIII' = 18 'XIX'  = 19 'XX'  = 20
      'XXI' = 21 'XXII' = 22 'XXIII' = 23 'XXIV' = 24 'XXV' = 25
      'XXVI'= 26 'XXVII'= 27 'XXVIII'= 28 'XXIX' = 29 'XXX' = 30
      ;
```

Two special values, _ERROR_ and _SAME_, can be used in place of interpreted values in the definition of a value informat. When the _ERROR_ value is assigned to a range, the informat treats input characters in that range as invalid data.

For a character informat, when the _SAME_ value is used with a range, the input characters are passed through unchanged by the informat. However, the JUST or UPCASE options take effect if they are present. Thus, this informat can be used to capitalize input strings:

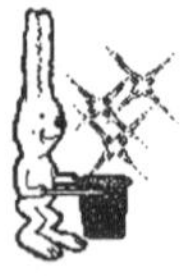

```
PROC FORMAT;
  INVALUE $UPCASE (MIN=1 MAX=40 DEFAULT=1 UPCASE)
      LOW-HIGH = _SAME_;
```

For a numeric value informat, the _SAME_ value results in input characters being interpreted as numbers as well as possible, and treated as invalid data if they cannot be interpreted as numbers.

Storing and editing

Value formats, picture formats, and value informats can be stored in a SAS catalog to be used with later programs. To store informats and formats, use the LIBRARY= option on the PROC FORMAT statement to identify a permanent SAS data library:

```
LIBNAME libref ...;
  PROC FORMAT LIBRARY=libref;
    VALUE ...;
    PICTURE ...;
    INVALUE ...;
```

The syntax is the same whether you are creating a new catalog, adding formats or informats to an existing catalog, or replacing existing formats or informats. The formats and informats are placed in the catalog FORMATS in the library.

The SAS supervisor looks for format and informat entries in the catalog LIBRARY.FORMATS. (It also looks in WORK.FORMATS.) Thus, to use your permanent formats and informats, you need to associate the library with the libref LIBRARY:

```
LIBNAME LIBRARY ...;
```

An informat or format in the catalog can be converted to a SAS dataset for editing, and then converted back into an informat or format, using the CNTLOUT= and CNTLIN= options with the FORMAT proc.

To convert a format or informat entry to a SAS dataset, use the CNTLOUT= option on the PROC FORMAT statement to name the SAS dataset being created, and use a SELECT statement to identify the entry. The entry name of a format is the format name; the entry name of a value informat is an at-sign (@) followed by the informat name.

```
  PROC FORMAT LIBRARY=libref CNTLOUT=SAS dataset;
    SELECT entry;
RUN;
```

The SAS dataset can then be edited, using the FSEDIT proc, perhaps. Each observation in the SAS dataset represents a range. Variables whose values are the same for every observation are FMTNAME, the name of the format or informat; TYPE, which is C for a character value format, N for a numeric value format, P for a picture format, J for a character value informat, or I for a numeric value informat; and DEFAULT, MIN, MAX, and FUZZ, the format or informat option values. The variables START, SEXCL, EEXCL, END, and HLO identify the ranges. SEXCL and EEXCL are N if a range endpoint is included or Y if it is excluded. HLO identifies the special ranges LOW, HIGH, LOW–HIGH, and OTHER using the initials L, H, LH, and O; usually this variable is blank. The variable LABEL is the formatted value of a value format, the picture of a picture format, or the interpreted value of a value informat. Finally, the variables PREFIX, MULT, FILL, and NOEDIT represent picture options.

To convert the edited SAS dataset to a format or informat, use the CNTLIN= option to identify the SAS dataset on the PROC FORMAT statement:

```
  PROC FORMAT LIBRARY=libref CNTLIN=SAS dataset;
RUN;
```

No other statements are needed. The FORMAT proc reads the data in the CNTLIN= SAS dataset to determine the name and type of format or informat to create.

In a CNTLOUT= or CNTLIN= SAS dataset, the UPCASE and JUST options are indicated by the additional codes U and J in the HLO variable. The HLO variable can contain more than one code at a time.

Some other codes that can appear in the HLO variable are N for an informat or format that has no ranges, F for a range that is an informat or format specification to be applied, and I for a range of a numeric informat that is a numeric value.

PART TWO: The rules

SAS is a general programming language. You can get it to do just about anything.

4 Control flow

To a computer, a program is a list of instructions. The instructions could be executed in order, from the beginning of the list to the end, or in any other order. The order of execution of instructions in a program is called *control flow*. The process of determining it is called *program structure, program control*, or just *control*.

Jumping from one spot in a program to another is called *branching*. Looping is a special form of branching, when it causes a section of a program to execute repeatedly.

The SAS programming language has no control flexibility on the largest scale — one step follows another — but within the data step it has an extensive set of control flow statements.

Conditional execution

Let's say you have a statement that you want to execute only some of the time — only when a certain condition is met. You can do this with the IF . . . THEN statement, which has the form

```
IF condition THEN action
```

A condition in a SAS program is expressed as a numeric expression. Any nonzero number is considered to be a true value, while 0 and missing values are considered false.

The action in an IF . . . THEN statement is ordinarily an executable statement. If the condition is true, then the statement is executed.

Consider this example:

```
IF STATE = 'PA' THEN SALESTAX = .01*FLOOR(PURCHASE*6 + .95 -
      (.005 < MOD(PURCHASE, 1) < .105));
```

The condition is the expression `STATE = 'PA'`. When this condition is true, then the assignment statement is executed and the variable SALESTAX is assigned a value.

You can choose between two actions by using the ELSE statement with IF . . . THEN. The ELSE statement appears immediately after the THEN action and provides an action to be taken if the IF condition is false.

You might, for example, want to assign a value to SALESTAX in situations where STATE is something other than 'PA':

```
IF STATE = 'PA' THEN SALESTAX = .01*FLOOR(PURCHASE*6 + .95 -
      (.005 < MOD(PURCHASE, 1) < .105));
ELSE SALESTAX = 0;
```

The statement `SALESTAX = 0;` is executed when the condition `STATE = 'PA'` is false.

It is essential for the ELSE statement to follow immediately after the THEN action. Even a null statement (an extra semicolon) before the ELSE statement is enough to disassociate it from the IF . . . THEN statement, resulting in a syntax error:

```
IF STATE = 'PA' THEN SALESTAX = .01*FLOOR(PURCHASE*6 + .95 -
      (.005 < MOD(PURCHASE, 1) < .105));
;
ELSE SALESTAX = 0;   * syntax error;
```

The IF . . . THEN . . . ELSE construction lets you choose between two actions, but there's no need to stop there. An IF . . . THEN statement can be used as the action in an ELSE statement. With an ELSE IF chain, you can choose among any number of actions.

```
LENGTH SIZE $ 11;
IF WIDTH = 99  AND 191 <= LENGTH <= 193 THEN SIZE = 'Twin';
ELSE IF WIDTH = 137 AND 191 <= LENGTH <= 193 THEN
    SIZE = 'Full';
ELSE IF WIDTH = 152 AND  LENGTH = 203 THEN SIZE = 'Queen';
ELSE IF 193 <= WIDTH <= 198 AND 203 <= LENGTH <= 213 THEN
    SIZE = 'King';
ELSE SIZE = 'Nonstandard';
```

The important thing to remember about IF . . . THEN . . . ELSE is that only one of the statements is executed. In the preceding example, SIZE is assigned only one of the five values, depending on the values of WIDTH and LENGTH.

Executable and nonexecutable

In using control flow statements, keeping track of the difference between executable and nonexecutable statements is essential. Control flow statements cannot be used to control the effects of nonexecutable statements. For example, although the statement

```
IF UNIT = 'NB' THEN TITLE1 'New Brunswick';
```

is syntactically valid, the TITLE1 statement, which is not even really part of the data step, takes effect regardless of the condition `UNIT = 'NB'`.

Executable statements correspond to specific actions that are part of the observation loop in a data step. The order in which executable statements appear is important. I/O and control flow statements and CALL, assignment, and sum statements are executable. INFILE, FILE, LIST, and null statements are considered executable; DATA, BY, and CARDS are not.

Nonexecutable statements take effect regardless of their position in a data step and despite any control flow statements that might be present. Usually, their position in the step does not matter. Statements that declare variable attributes, represent dataset options, or mark places in the step are nonexecutable. The ARRAY and RETAIN statements, and global statements such as TITLE and OPTIONS are nonexecutable.

Blocks

A *block* is a group of statements that is treated as a single statement for control flow purposes. An ordinary block is formed by the DO and END statements, and is often called a *DO block*:

```
DO;
  statements
  END;
```

You can use blocks to extend the use of IF . . . THEN and ELSE statements. Because blocks are treated as statements, you can use a block as a THEN action or an ELSE action:

```
IF condition THEN block
ELSE block
```

This example executes a group of statements when the variable BALANCE is negative, and another statement when BALANCE is 0 or positive:

```
IF BALANCE < 0 THEN DO;
  DEFICIT = -BALANCE;
  BALANCE = 0;
  END;
ELSE DEFICIT = 0;
```

Extending the observation loop

In the simplest case the observation loop executes a group of statements once for each input observation, then stops. The form of the observation loop can be changed, though.

Stopping short

The simplest thing to change in an observation loop is its stopping point.

If you know in advance how much data the step should process, you can cut off the input stream using the OBS= option. To stop after the 250th input observation, you would use the option `OBS=250`. OBS= can be used as a dataset option, an INFILE option, or even a system option. There is a parallel option, FIRSTOBS=, that allows observations or records at the beginning of a file to be skipped. This step reads from an input text file beginning with the 63rd record and going through the 187th record:

```
DATA PLACES;
  INFILE SITES MISSOVER FIRSTOBS=63 OBS=187;
  INPUT @1 ZIP $5. @6 SITE_ID $3. @9 LANDAREA 7. @15 BLDGS 3.
      @18 FLORAREA 10. @28 BLDYR 4.;
```

You don't have to depend on the input stream to stop the observation loop, though. The STOP statement will stop it directly. STOP is usually used conditionally, to stop the observation loop after a certain condition is reached. You could stop after a certain number of observations, for example, by using the automatic variable _N_ that counts input observations:

```
IF _N_ > 250 THEN STOP;
```

Or you could stop after a certain magnitude of data, measured in another way, is reached:

```
DATA PLACES;
  INFILE SITES MISSOVER;
  INPUT @1 ZIP $5. @6 SITE_ID $3. @9 LANDAREA 7. @15 BLDGS 3.
      @18 FLORAREA 10. @28 BLDYR 4.;
  QFLAREA + FLORAREA;
  IF QFLAREA > 50000000 THEN STOP;
```

Or you could stop after a certain data value is reached:

```
IF BLDYR = 1869 THEN STOP;
```

You might want to execute several statements after finding the stopping condition. In that case, STOP would be the last statement in a DO block.

```
IF QFLAREA > 75000 THEN DO;
  FILE LOG;
  PUT 'Area limit exceeded.';
  STOP;
  END;
```

Often, you might want to output the current observation before stopping:

```
OUTPUT;
IF BLDYR <= 1869 THEN STOP;
```

A related statement, ABORT, stops not only the current step but the entire program or session. This is appropriate to do in batch-style processing when you discover that the program's mission has been accomplished, or when an error condition has been found that makes the rest of the program futile.

```
IF TEMP < -273 THEN DO; PUT 'Brrrrr!'; ABORT; END;
```

The observation loop depends on reading input data each and every time the statements in it execute. If for any reason this does not happen, the step stops with an error condition. This is intended to keep steps that have logical errors from looping indefinitely; however, it applies equally where there is no danger of that happening, as in the step below.

The conditional input process in this step makes makes the step fail on the fifth repetition of the observation loop:

```
  DATA _NULL_;
    IF _N_ NE 5 THEN INPUT X @@;
    PUT _ALL_;
CARDS;
1 2 3 4 5 6
;
```

```
X=1 _ERROR_=0 _N_=1
X=2 _ERROR_=0 _N_=2
X=3 _ERROR_=0 _N_=3
X=4 _ERROR_=0 _N_=4
X=. _ERROR_=0 _N_=5
ERROR: DATA STEP stopped due to looping.
```

Before

There are many things you might want to do at the beginning of a data step, before starting to go through the input observations: writing the first few lines of the output file, for example, or calculating an initial value for a variable.

You can just test the value of the automatic counter variable _N_, because it always starts with a value of 1. Statements to be executed before the observation loop can be executed at the beginning of the step on the condition `_N_ = 1`:

```
IF _N_ = 1 THEN initialization action
```

The following code segment reads two variables from the 5-line header of an input text file:

```
DATA ORDER;
  RETAIN R_DATE C_DATE;
  INFILE Q;
  IF _N_ = 1 THEN
      INPUT // @32 R_DATE YYMMDD6. / @17. C_DATE YYMMDD6. /;
  ...
```

After

The end of the observation loop is determined by the input statements, and they can provide a signal that the end is coming. The END= option on the SET, MERGE, UPDATE, or INFILE statement names a logical variable that tells whether the SET, MERGE, or UPDATE statement has read its last observation or whether an INPUT statement has read the last record from a file. This variable can then be used as a condition for statements to be executed at the end of the observation loop.

One thing you might want to do at the end of an observation loop is to finish calculating descriptive statistics and output them.

```
DATA SCORE (KEEP=HTEAM VTEAM WINNER V1 V2 V3 H1 H2 H3 INNINGS);
  SET INNINGS END=OVER;
  V1 + RUNS_V;
  V2 + HITS_V;
  V3 + ERRORS_V;
  H1 + RUNS_H;
  H2 + HITS_H;
  H3 + ERRORS_H;
  IF OVER THEN DO;
    IF H1 > V1 THEN WINNER = 'H';
    ELSE IF V1 > H1 THEN WINNER = 'V';
    ELSE WINNER = ' ';
    IF RUNS_H = . THEN INNINGS = _N_ - .5; ELSE INNINGS = _N_;
    OUTPUT;
    END;
```

In this example, the variable OVER, which has been 0 (false) all along, is given the value 1 (true) at the time when the last observation is read. Then the statements in the DO block are executed. Notice that this step produces only one output observation, when the OUTPUT statement is executed.

With an input text file, the EOF= option can also be used. Instead of using a logical variable, The EOF= option names a statement label that the program jumps to when the INPUT statement attempts to read past the end of a file. EOF= may be preferable to END= when an INPUT statement might read more than one record (as when the FLOWOVER option is being used). The EOF= option prevents the error condition that otherwise occurs when an INPUT statement reaches the end of a file in the middle of the statement. It also prevents the INPUT statement from stopping the observation loop, so you might need a STOP statement.

```
  DATA C;
    INFILE A EOF=THERE;
    INPUT A B / C D;
    RETURN;
THERE: FILE LOG;
    PUT _N_ = A= B=;
    STOP;
```

After an EOF= branch, if no input occurs before a RETURN statement or the bottom of the observation loop, the observation loop stops. This is intended to protect users who might not think to put a STOP statement after the EOF= branch. However, the results can be quite confusing for programmers working with more than one input file in a step. If necessary, use a GOTO statement, with a statement label at the top of the observation loop, instead of a RETURN statement.

Back to the top

The SAS language has four statements for returning to the top of the observation loop, each of them slightly different.

The standard way to return to the top of the observation loop is with the RETURN statement. There is an implicit RETURN statement at the end of every data step. In a data step that has an output SAS dataset, but does not have an OUTPUT statement, there is an implied OUTPUT on each RETURN to the top of the observation loop.

However, RETURN has a different meaning after a LINK statement or a HEADER= branch has been executed. In that case, it returns control to the place in the step where the LINK statement or HEADER= branch was executed. That kind of RETURN does not include an implied OUTPUT. In a step that has a LINK statement or a HEADER= branch, it is important to remember that the meaning of the RETURN statement depends on whether a LINK statement or a HEADER= branch has been executed since the top of the observation loop and since the most recent RETURN statement.

DELETE has no such dual meaning. It simply returns to the top of the observation loop. It does not have an implied OUTPUT; the lack of this feature is what gives the DELETE statement its name. It is commonly used with IF . . . THEN to do a subsetting operation. This statement, for example, would discard any observations with a negative value for NPV, keeping them from further processing or output:

```
IF NPV < 0 THEN DELETE;
```

Besides that use, DELETE is the usual way to return to the top of the observation loop after a LINK statement has been executed. If you want to write the current observation to the output SAS dataset first, you can use the OUTPUT statement — even though OUTPUT and DELETE might not sound like statements that belong together. These statements write the current observation to the output SAS dataset and return to the top of the observation loop when the condition `X >= THRSHLD` is true, regardless of what happens in the rest of the data step:

```
IF X >= THRSHLD THEN DO; OUTPUT; DELETE; END;
```

The subsetting IF statement is like the opposite of the IF . . . THEN DELETE statement. It is an IF statement without the THEN:

```
IF condition;
```

What it means is this:

```
IF NOT condition THEN DELETE;
```

Thus, the following statements are equivalent:

```
IF NPV < 0 THEN DELETE;
IF NOT (NPV < 0);
IF NPV >= 0;
```

Most programmers prefer the subsetting IF statement to the DELETE statement for subsetting, because it is shorter and because it states the subsetting condition in positive terms rather than negative — the condition for acceptance rather than the condition for rejection.

The LOSTCARD statement is somewhat different from the other statements that return to the top of the observation loop. It could have been called the "losecard" statement, because it tells the SAS supervisor to ignore ("lose") one input record ("card") from the most recent INPUT statement. It leaves the file pointer pointing to the second record in the INPUT statement and then returns to the top of the observation loop. Thus, it is primarily useful when more than one record is being read from an input text file in the same statement.

LOSTCARD also puts some things in the log: the message "`NOTE: LOST CARD`" and the same display of input data that the LIST statement produces.

The execution of a LOSTCARD statement does not increment the automatic counter variable _N_.

The LOSTCARD statement is intended to be used when an INPUT statement reads a series of records that are supposed to follow a certain pattern but can't always be relied upon to do so. If something irregular happens in the middle of a file — such as a missing record, or "lost card"

— LOSTCARD will eventually, one record at a time, get the INPUT statement back in sync with the file.

```
  DATA NAMES;
    LENGTH FIRSNAME MIDLNAME LASTNAME $22;
    INFILE CARDS MISSOVER EOF=OOPS;
    INPUT LABEL1 $ FIRSNAME $ / LABEL2 $ MIDLNAME $ /
        LABEL3 $ LASTNAME $ /;
    IF UPCASE(LABEL1) NE: 'FIRST' OR
       UPCASE(LABEL2) NE: 'MIDDLE' OR
       UPCASE(LABEL3) NE: 'LAST' THEN LOSTCARD;
    RETURN;
OOPS: LIST; STOP;
CARDS;

FIRST:  Elisa
MIDdle:  Bazilian
Last:     Banks

FIRST:  Wilna
oops
FIRST: Wilma
middle: Kay
lasT:  Burger

;
```

In this example, the LOSTCARD statement executes three times, for the first, sixth and seventh records. Despite the defects in the file, the step above successfully extracts all the data from it.

The step above also illustrates the use of the EOF= option on the INFILE statement. Control would jump to the LIST statement (with the OOPS label) when the INPUT statement tried to read past the end of the file. This is recommended when an INPUT statement reads more than one record from an undisciplined INPUT file such as this one; it eliminates the possibility of an error occurring if the end of the input file comes at an unexpected place.

Automatic processing

Variables ordinarily have missing values at the beginning of a step, and some of them are reset to missing values at the top of the observation loop. The RETAIN statement can change this, though, giving a variable a different initial value and preventing it from being reset to missing.

RETAIN is a nonexecutable statement, which can appear anywhere in the data step. A step can have any number of RETAIN statements, but usually one is sufficient. Variables listed in the RETAIN statement are not reset to missing at the top of the observation loop. If a constant follows a variable or a list of variables in the RETAIN statement, the variable or variables are given that initial value at the beginning of the step.

When listing character variables in a RETAIN statement, you should generally give them initial values with the appropriate length for the variable, adding trailing blanks if necessary.

The following RETAIN statement gives A and B an initial value of 3, gives C an initial value of 1.25, makes D a character variable of length 4 and gives it an initial value of "STR ", gives E and F an initial value of ., and prevents all these variables from being reset to missing at the top of the observation loop:

```
RETAIN A B 3  C 1.25 D 'STR ' E F;
```

Beginning with SAS release 6.06, an array name can appear in a RETAIN statement, which has the same effect as listing all the elements in the array. However, the ARRAY statement defining the array must appear before the RETAIN statement. To initialize the array elements to different values, you can use an initial value list, a list of constants enclosed in parentheses. Each constant is applied to one variable in the preceding list; if there are fewer constants than variables, the remaining variables are initialized to missing values.

The RETAIN statement below initializes A to 1, B to 2, C to 3, and D and E to missing:

```
ARRAY EARLY{2} B C;
RETAIN A EARLY D (1 2 3) E;
```

Elements of an array can instead be initialized in the ARRAY statement. The use of the ARRAY statement is described in chapter 6, "Expressions."

The abbreviated variable lists _ALL_, _CHARACTER_, and _NUMERIC_ can appear in a RETAIN statement, but they apply only to variables defined in statements that come before the RETAIN statement in the step.

A RETAIN statement with no variables listed is a *global* RETAIN statement, preventing any variable from being reset to missing.

While RETAIN affects an automatic process at the top of the observation loop, LIST creates an automatic process at the bottom of the loop.

> Actually, the top of the observation loop and the bottom of the observation loop are essentially the same place: between observations in the observation loop. The difference is that LIST has to do with the preceding observation, while RETAIN affects the following observation.

In a step with an INPUT statement, LIST causes the input records from the INPUT statement to be written in the log. However, the records are written at the bottom of the observation loop rather than where the LIST statement executes. Thus, executing the LIST statement repeatedly does not cause the same input record to be written more than once. LIST puts a ruler before the first record it writes to help you locate columns in the records.

The group loop

The SAS language doesn't do it for you, but it's possible to have a *group loop*, a loop that executes once for each group of observations, with the observation loop nested inside it. The process is similar to the way you would execute statements before the observation loop using the statement

```
IF _N_ = 1 THEN ...
```

If a data step takes input from a SAS dataset, a BY statement can specify the variable or variables by which the observations are grouped. For example, if observations with the same value of MODEL appear consecutively, the BY statement could read

```
BY MODEL NOTSORTED;
```

The NOTSORTED option is necessary when the observations are not in sorted order.

The BY statement creates FIRST. and LAST. variables for each BY variable. The variable FIRST.MODEL is 1 for the first observation in a group. (That is, it is 1 when the value of MODEL for an observation is different from the value of MODEL in the previous observation.) For other observations, FIRST.MODEL is 0. Similarly, LAST.MODEL is 1 for the last observation in a group and 0 otherwise.

The FIRST. and LAST. variables are used as conditions to implement a group loop:

```
DATA ...;
  RETAIN variables used in group processing;
  SET ...;
  BY GROUP;
  IF FIRST.GROUP THEN DO;
    statements to be executed at beginning of group
    END;
  statements to be executed for each observation
  IF LAST.GROUP THEN DO;
    statements to be executed at end of group
    END;
```

The group loop concept can easily be extended to more than one level by using more than one BY variable.

DO loop

SAS syntax provides for loops inside the observation loop. These loops are created with the DO statement and are called *DO loops.*

A DO loop is a DO block modified in any combination of three ways to make it repeat.

Index

An index variable takes on a different value for each repetition of a DO loop. The values can simply be listed, like this:

```
DO I = 1, 2, 4, 8, 10, 17;
```

The index values do not have to be constants. Any SAS expression is allowed. An index variable can even be a character variable with listed values:

```
DO MON = 'MAR', 'JUN', 'SEP', 'DEC';
```

A range of numeric values can be covered with the TO keyword. In a list of index values, `2 TO 7` is the same as `2, 3, 4, 5, 6, 7` and `2 TO 3.5` is the same as `2, 3`. The default increment is 1, but you can specify a different increment using the BY keyword. This index range:

```
DO I = 2 TO 3.5 BY .4;
```

gives I the values 2, 2.4, 2.8, and 3.2. To count downward from 10 to 1:

```
DO I = 10 TO 1 BY -1;
```

Ranges can be listed along with single values:

```
DO I = 2, 3 TO 7 BY 2, 13, 17, 23;
DO I = 11 TO 14, 21 TO 24, 31 TO 34, 41 TO 44;
```

The DO loop repeats, taking on a different value of the index variable with each repetition. After the end of the index variable list is reached, the loop stops.

Expressions in the index value list are evaluated before the loop begins. This loop repeats 4 times, despite the change in the value of B inside the loop:

```
A = 1;
B = 4;
DO I = A TO B;
  PUT I= B=;
  B = 2;
  END;
```

When a loop is going through a range of values, though, the index variable can be altered to change the number of repetitions of the loop. This loop repeats three times, with the values 1, 3.5, and 4.5:

```
B = 4.5;
DO I = 1 TO B;
  PUT I=;
  IF I = 1 THEN I = 2.5;
  END;
```

When a value is assigned to an index variable in a range, care must be taken to avoid creating an infinite loop. Infinite loops can be created quite easily, as in this example:

```
DO I = 1 TO 10;
  I = 4;                    * infinite loop;
  END;
```

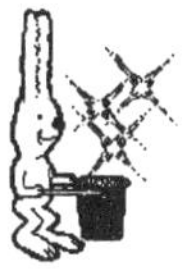

Once or twice

A DO loop that executes 0 or 1 times is effectively a conditional DO block. SAS operators generate the values 0 and 1 for false and true results, making this easy to arrange; the statement `IF` *condition* `THEN DO;` could be replaced with `DO I = 1 TO` *condition*`;`. For a true condition, this would evaluate to `DO I = 1 TO 1;`, and the DO loop would execute once. For a false condition, it would be `DO I = 1 TO 0;`, and the loop would not execute.

A simple extension of this concept lets you execute a loop once or twice, depending on a condition:

```
DO I = 0 TO condition;
```

WHILE condition

A WHILE condition gives a condition for executing a loop. The form is:

```
DO WHILE(condition);
```

The parentheses around the condition are required.

The condition is evaluated at the top of the loop, and the loop executes if the condition is true, but it stops if the condition is false. If the condition is false before the first repetition of the loop, then the loop does not execute at all.

This loop finds the lowest 4-digit number that is a power of 2:

```
DATA _NULL_;
  X = 1;
```

```
DO WHILE(X < 1000);
  X = X + X;
  END;
PUT X=;
```

```
X=1024
```

If you are depending on a WHILE condition to stop a loop, make sure it is a condition that will eventually be false, or the loop could go on forever. The loop above would be an infinite loop, for example, if the value given to X before the loop was not a positive number.

UNTIL condition

An UNTIL condition is the opposite of a WHILE condition in two ways: it gives a condition for loop stopping, and it is evaluated at the bottom of the loop. In other words, an UNTIL condition will let the loop run at least once, and it will let the loop continue if the condition is false, but stop the loop when the condition is true.

Other than that, though, UNTIL conditions act pretty much like WHILE conditions. The example above could be rewritten:

```
DATA _NULL_;
  X = 1;
  DO UNTIL(X >= 1000); X = X + X; END;
  PUT X=;
```

Conditions combined

The index, WHILE condition, and UNTIL condition provide different ways of stopping a loop. Because there is no conflict between them, you can use any combination of them in one loop. The loop repeats until one of the stopping rules stops it.

You might add an index to a loop with a WHILE or UNTIL condition to give it a maximum number of repetitions. This loop, for example, stops after X gets greater than 1000, but if that never happens, it will stop after 10,000 repetitions, rather than repeating forever:

```
DO I = 1 TO 10000 UNTIL(X >= 1000);
  X = X + X;
  END;
```

Using a logical variable for loop stopping

Sometimes the condition for stopping a loop can be too complicated to be put comfortably into a single expression. In that case, the best thing to do is to calculate the stopping condition inside the loop. In other words, use the DO statement

```
DO UNTIL(LOOPSTOP);
```

and then assign a true value to LOOPSTOP when you want the loop to stop (but not before then).

Using loops with arrays

Arrays are often used with loops. Typically, a loop is used to do the same processing for each element of an array. The index variable covers the range of subscript values for an array and is used as the array subscript.

```
ARRAY CHSTATE{4}; ARRAY NSTATE{4};
DO I = 1 TO 4;
  CHSTATE{I} = STNAMEL(NSTATE{I});
  END;
```

A typical use of a loop is to find the total or maximum of the elements of an array:

```
ARRAY A{27} A1-A27;
DO I = 1 TO 27;
  ASUM + A{I};
  IF A{I} > AMAX THEN AMAX = A{I};
  END;
```

— although, in many cases, that might be better done using the SAS System's statistic functions:

```
ASUM = SUM(OF A1-A27);
AMAX = MAX(OF A1-A27);
```

The LBOUND and HBOUND functions can be used to find the range of an array's subscripts. For a one-dimensional array, the LBOUND function returns the lowest subscript of the array, and the HBOUND function returns the highest subscript. This can be useful in assigning index values for a loop that does array processing. For example:

```
DO I = LBOUND(FACTOR) TO HBOUND(FACTOR);
  IF FACTOR{I} < 1 THEN FACTOR{I} = 1;
  IF FACTOR{I} > 2 THEN FACTOR{I} = 2;
  END;
```

For multidimensional arrays, you can get the bounds of each dimension's subscripts using the LBOUND1, LBOUND2 . . . and HBOUND1, HBOUND2, . . . functions, or by using the LBOUND and HBOUND functions with a second argument giving the dimension.

DO OVER

A separate form of the DO loop simplifies processing of implicitly subscripted arrays. The form is

```
DO OVER(array name);
```

The loop uses the index variable of the implicitly subscripted array, giving it all the subscript values the array uses. For example, if the array's index variable is _I_ and its subscripts range from 1 to 7, the DO OVER statement is equivalent to

```
DO _I_ = 1 TO 7;
```

Nested loops

It's possible to put one DO loop inside another. This is called *nesting* loops, and it is what you should do if you want to have more than one index variable. You might do this to process a multidimensional array, for example. It is essential to use different index variables for the different nested loops. If you usually use I as the index variable for every loop, it's time to move on to J for the loop at the second level — and K if you have a third loop inside that.

```
DO I = LBOUND1(MEASURE) TO HBOUND1(MEASURE);
  DO J = LBOUND2(MEASURE) TO HBOUND2(MEASURE);
    AV{I, J} = ROUND((MEASURE{I, J, 1} + MEASURE{I, J, 2})/2);
    END;
  END;
```

Multiple conditional execution with SELECT

A SELECT block selects one statement or block to execute, based on a sequence of conditions.

Conditional SELECT

A conditional SELECT block has the form

```
SELECT;
  WHEN(condition) action;
  WHEN(condition) action;
  WHEN(condition) action;
  . . .
  OTHERWISE action;
  END;
```

SELECT goes through the WHEN conditions in order until it finds one that is true (a nonzero number). It then executes the corresponding WHEN action. SELECT executes only one WHEN action; if more than one WHEN condition is true, SELECT executes only the action for the first one.

Beginning with SAS release 6.06, a WHEN statement can have more than one condition. The conditions are separated by commas; if any one of the conditions is true, that WHEN action is executed. Thus, these two statements

```
WHEN(A > 0) X = 1;
WHEN(B > 0) X = 1;
```

can be combined into this statement:

```
WHEN(A > 0, B > 0) X = 1;
```

If none of the WHEN conditions is true, the OTHERWISE action is executed. If none of the WHEN conditions is true and there is no OTHERWISE statement, the SELECT block generates a runtime error. To avoid runtime errors, there should generally be an OTHERWISE statement.

A WHEN action or OTHERWISE action can be a statement or a block. A null statement (;) can be used to signify no action to be taken. If you just want to ignore cases that don't match any of the WHEN conditions, you can use this statement:

```
OTHERWISE ;
```

Similarly, a null statement could be used as the action for the first WHEN condition to have the SELECT block ignore certain kinds of cases, even though they might have a true value for some of the other WHEN conditions.

If an action needs to encompass more than one statement, you can use a DO block or, if appropriate, a DO loop or SELECT block as the action.

> Be careful not to put any extra statements — not even a null statement — between the SELECT, WHEN, OTHERWISE, and END statements in a SELECT block. Even a comment statement might confuse the SAS supervisor, resulting in a syntax error.

The conditional SELECT block is very much like an ELSE IF chain. The form of the SELECT block presented above is logically equivalent to

```
IF(condition) THEN action;
ELSE IF(condition) THEN action;
ELSE IF(condition) THEN action;
ELSE IF(condition) THEN action;
. . .
ELSE action;
```

The SELECT block is usually preferred over the ELSE IF chain because it executes faster and is often easier to read. However, most programmers use IF . . . THEN . . . ELSE when selecting between only two actions.

Comparison SELECT

The comparison SELECT block is a variation on the SELECT block that simplifies the use of comparisons. It has the form

```
SELECT(expression);
  WHEN(expression) action;
  WHEN(expression) action;
  WHEN(expression) action;
  ...
  OTHERWISE action;
  END;
```

The SELECT expression is compared to the WHEN expressions one at a time, until a match is found, and then the corresponding WHEN action is taken. If no match is found, then the OTHERWISE action is taken, or if there is no OTHERWISE statement, a runtime error results.

As with the conditional SELECT block, a WHEN statement in a comparison SELECT block can have more than one expression, separated by commas, beginning with SAS release 6.06. If any one of the expressions in a WHEN statement is matched, that WHEN action is executed.

The comparison SELECT is logically equivalent to the conditional SELECT, but the conditions are formed by comparing the SELECT expression to the WHEN expression using the equality operator (=). That is, the comparison SELECT block

```
SELECT(S);
  WHEN(A) ...;
  WHEN(B) ...;
  ...
```

is logically equivalent to the conditional SELECT block

```
SELECT;
  WHEN(S = A) ...;
  WHEN(S = B) ...;
  ...
```

The SELECT block is often used to take different actions based on the value of a variable. This block, for example, directs PUT statements to different files depending on the value of the variable SUBGROUP:

```
SELECT(SUBGROUP);
  WHEN('NORTH') FILE N;
  WHEN('WEST') FILE W;
  WHEN('CENTRAL') THEN DO;
    IF STATUS = 'A' THEN FILE CA;
    ELSE FILE CI;
    END;
```

```
WHEN('SOUTH') FILE S;
OTHERWISE FILE LOG;
END;
```

Transferring control

Here we examine the more direct forms of branching. They are not used as often as conditional constructions and loops, but they do have some important uses.

Simple branching

The GOTO statement causes program flow to continue with the statement that has a particular statement label. For example, after the statement

```
GOTO SUMPLACE;
```

is executed, the next statement to execute is the statement with the SUMPLACE statement label, regardless of where in the step it appears. A statement label precedes a statement and is followed by a colon.

```
SUMPLACE:  AVERAGE = SUM_M/SUM_R;
```

Executable statements can have statement labels. Statement labels should not appear on nonexecutable statements, or on the control flow statements that depend on earlier control flow statements — ELSE, END, WHEN, and OTHERWISE. However, it is okay for a statement label to be attached to a null statement.

The use of GOTO should be avoided when other control flow statements such as IF . . . THEN and DO can be used. GOTO is not particularly efficient, and its use tends to obscure the meaning of a program. However, there are situations where only GOTO will do.

A similar kind of branching is done by the EOF= option on the INFILE statement. When an INPUT statement gets to the end of an input file named in an INFILE statement with the EOF= option, control flow jumps to the statement with the statement label named in the EOF= option. This option can be used when you want to do a certain action at the end of the input file, or just to prevent the runtime error that could occur when the end of the file is reached unexpectedly, as in this example:

```
  DATA LETTERS;
    INFILE LETTERS EOF=OVER;
    INPUT A B / C D / E;
GO: more statements
    OUTPUT;
    IF DONE THEN STOP;
```

```
    RETURN;
OVER: DONE = 1;
    IF A NE . THEN GOTO GO; ELSE STOP;
```

Branching out of a loop

In addition to the loop stopping possibilities that the DO statement provides, you can stop a DO loop by branching out of it. Usually, this is done with a conditional GOTO statement:

```
IF condition THEN GOTO label;
```

Alternatively, if the loop is reading from an input text file, an EOF= branch can have the same effect. If the statement you are branching to is before the DO statement or after the END statement, you are branching out of the loop, and the loop is stopped.

The new LEAVE statement, borrowed from another SAS System language, SCL, is designed for branching out of a DO loop. Effectively, it is the same as the GOTO statement described above. It branches to the statement immediately after the end of the DO or SELECT block. If blocks are nested, it exits only the innermost block. The LEAVE statement can be used only inside a block. The statement is simply:

```
LEAVE;
```

Another way to stop a loop is with a RETURN, DELETE, subsetting IF, or LOSTCARD statement. Any of these statements transfer control to the top of the observation loop (or the RETURN statement returns to the place where a LINK statement or a HEADER= transfer was executed). Of course, the STOP and ABORT statements stop a loop, along with the entire data step.

Branching inside a loop

Of course, it is also possible to branch within a loop; doing that does not stop the loop. In some cases it might be convenient to branch to the top of the loop (the first statement following the DO statement) or the bottom of the loop (a null statement before the END statement). Branching to the bottom of the loop has the same effect for a DO loop as the DELETE statement has for the observation loop. For example, if you want to process only nonmissing elements of an array, you could use statements like these:

```
    DO I = LBOUND(AREA) TO HBOUND(AREA);
      IF A{I} <= .Z THEN GOTO NEXT; * Skip missing values;
      ...
NEXT: ;
      END;
```

The CONTINUE statement, also borrowed from SCL, is designed for branching to the bottom of a DO loop. It is equivalent to the `GOTO NEXT` statement in the preceding example. If loops are nested, it stays inside the innermost loop that contains it. The CONTINUE statement cannot be used anywhere except inside a loop. Like the LEAVE statement, it is a one-word statement, simply:

```
CONTINUE;
```

Don't branch into a block

While branching out of a loop might be useful, branching into a loop — or a block of any kind — is not allowed. An ELSE statement also cannot be the target of branching.

Branching and returning

While the GOTO and EOF= forms of branching just go to another place in the step, the LINK statement and HEADER= option go and come back.

The LINK statement is just like the GOTO statement except that, after a LINK statement is executed, a RETURN statement (including the implied RETURN at the end of the step) causes execution to resume at the statement following the LINK statement. BASIC programmers will recognize the LINK statement as the SAS language equivalent of the GOSUB statement in the BASIC language.

This example uses a LINK to calculate a cube root:

```
    X = VOLUME;
    LINK CUBEROOT;
    EDGE = Y;
    . . .
    RETURN;
CUBEROOT: ;       * calculates Y as the cube root of X
                  * using an iterative method;
    HIGH = ABS(X); LOW = -HIGH;
    DO UNTIL(-1E-10 <= E <= 1E-10 OR HIGH - LOW < 1E-10);
      Y = .5*(LOW + HIGH);
      E = Y*Y*Y - X;
      IF E < 0 THEN LOW = Y; ELSE HIGH = Y;
      END;
    RETURN;
```

One time to use LINK is when you need to execute a SET statement at several places in a data step. You can't just use several SET statements, because each SET statement is a different input stream. You can, instead, use a LINK statement to branch to the SET statement.

```
  DATA B;
    LINK SET_A;
```

```
    IF SKIP > 0 THEN DO I = 1 TO SKIP;
      LINK SET_A;
      END;
    IF LEVEL > 4 THEN OUTPUT;
    RETURN;
SET_A: SET A;
    RETURN;
```

HEADER= is an option that can be used in the FILE statement. When a PUT statement writes the end of a page in a print file with the HEADER= option, control flow is transferred to the statement with the statement label names in the HEADER= option. A group of statements there presumably write a header for the new page. Then, when a RETURN statement is executed, control returns to the PUT statement.

5 I/O

I/O is computer jargon for *input and output* — a running program's connections to the outside world. Input refers mainly to the process of transferring data from storage to memory. Output sends data in the opposite direction. To understand input and output, then, it is essential to understand the difference between memory and storage.

The terms *memory* and *storage* have often been used interchangeably, but in careful contemporary usage they mean different things. Memory resides in electronic patterns on silicon chips inside the computer. Data usually stays in memory for, at most, the duration of a running program. (This is true for *RAM*, which stands for *random access memory* and is the type of memory that is available for a program to use. Another type of memory, *ROM*, or *read-only memory*, has its data permanently put into it at the factory.)

Storage, by contrast, is data recorded on a storage medium, usually disk or tape, by a *storage device*, often called a *drive* because of its moving parts. An individual disk or tape is called a *volume*, and is either *fixed*, meaning it is a permanent part of the storage device, or *removable*, so that different volumes can be used on the same device. Storage is especially useful for keeping large amounts of data, for keeping data between programs, and for transporting data from one computer to another.

Speed is the critical difference between memory and storage. It might take a computer 20 milliseconds to access a storage device, compared to perhaps 100 nanoseconds (or .0001 milliseconds) to access a memory chip. Hardware varies and continues to get faster, but storage, with its moving parts, is several orders of magnitude slower than memory.

Because of this enormous speed difference, it makes sense to think of memory being inside the computer and storage being outside, regardless of the form of the physical connection between the storage device and the computer. That's why the terms *input* and *output* make sense.

> Memory and storage are typically used in different characteristic ways, but they don't have to be. Storage used to emulate memory is called *virtual memory*. A block of memory used to emulate a storage device is a *RAM disk*.

Reading and *writing* are terms that are nearly synonymous with *input* and *output*. *Reading* is especially used to describe input when the data is being interpreted in some way. Similarly, *writing* often describes output that involves formatting. *Reading* and *writing* are also the terms used for the physical actions of the storage device in retrieving and storing data.

Storage

Data in storage is organized into logically related sections called *files*. Files are managed by the computer's operating system. The use of files allows a program to use the same routines to access data on different kinds of storage devices in the same way. The operating system makes files on different storage devices look the same to the program.

Files

A *file type* is a standard for organizing data in a file. SAS I/O focuses mainly on two types of files: text files and SAS datasets.

A text file is a sequence of records, with each record consisting of a sequence of characters. A print file is a special type of text file that is designed to be printed by certain types of printers. Program files and the SAS log are text files.

A SAS dataset is a data file organized or recognized by the SAS System as a sequence of observations. The details of SAS datasets are described in the discussion of SAS data libraries in chapter 2, "The facts."

The SAS System can also do input and output on what are called *unorganized* files. These files really do have some kind of structure, but SAS routines do not attempt to understand it; the file is treated simply as a block of data, or a sequence of bytes. I/O for unorganized files essentially involves pretending that they are text files.

Another file type that is important to the SAS System is the executable file, which is a machine language program, ready for the computer to run. The SAS System does not exactly read and write executable files, but it executes them. The uses of executable files in the SAS System are discussed in chapter 3, "Programs on call."

Access methods

Most input and output is done by what is called *sequential access*, meaning that the bytes of data in the file are read or written in their storage order. File access might also be *indexed,* which means that the access appears sequential to the program, even though it might not actually be in storage order.

A different method of access is direct access, in which the data in the file is read or written in an order determined by the program. Direct access is generally slower than sequential access for processing an entire file, but it can be much faster than sequential access if only small parts of the file are of interest.

Sequential storage

Tape was once the dominant computer storage medium, and reels and cartridges of computer tape are still in common use, especially on mainframes and as a backup medium on all computers. Tape users need to be aware of some differences between disk storage and tape storage.

Tape is a linear storage medium; to get from one point on the tape to another, the tape drive has to go through all the points in between. In practical terms, this means that only one place on a tape can be accessed at one time. In a SAS program, only one text file or SAS dataset on a tape volume can be accessed in one step. You cannot, for example, merge two SAS datasets from the same tape. There is also a physical limitation on the number of tape volumes that can be used simultaneously.

There is an important limitation in writing to tape with most computer tape drives: You can write only at the end of the volume! Any file you write to a tape becomes the last file on the volume. If you write a file in the middle of a tape volume, all the files that follow that point on the tape are deleted. If you write to the middle of a file, the end of the file is deleted. Because of this, writing to tape usually means writing the entire volume at one time. Many tape users avoid conflicts by never putting two files on the same tape volume.

Similar restrictions on I/O apply to other linear storage media.

External devices

I/O also includes communication with devices away from the computer, such as a printer, a measuring device, or another computer. The operating system handles these devices so that they appear the same as files to the program.

I/O modes

I/O in SAS programs generally follows a few standard modes, which represent different things that can be done with files.

Input. Input simply involves reading data from a file. Although programmers often talk of "moving" or "bringing in" the data in the file, reading does not actually affect the contents of the file at all.

Because it doesn't change a file, input works exactly the same way on *locked* volumes — volumes that are protected by hardware from being modified. It is the only I/O mode that can be done on read-only or locked volumes.

Output. Output puts data in a new file or changes or replaces the contents of a file. Output is usually sequential. Output to an existing file can either replace the data in the file by writing from the beginning of the file, which is the OLD option in SAS, or by adding data onto the end of the file, which is the MOD option.

Editing. Editing is a process that alternates between input and output on a file, usually to change some of the data while keeping some of it intact. SAS procs like EDITOR and FSEDIT edit SAS datasets. The new SHAREBUFFERS option makes it possible for SAS programs to edit text files.

Copying. Transferring data from one file to another, without any particular concern for the way the data appears in memory, is commonly called *copying*. The source file is unchanged; the target file is created, replaced, or expanded.

SAS datasets can be copied using the COPY proc and several other procs. Operating systems also provide ways to copy files.

Sorting in place. Sorting is usually a variation on copying, with the order of records or observations changed between reading them from the input file and writing them to the output file. However, some sort programs can use the same file as the input and output file; they write the sorted data over the original data, a process called *sorting in place*. It is not without risk; if the sort process fails, the file could be damaged.

Deleting. Removing a file from a storage volume is called *deleting* or *erasing*. SAS datasets can be deleted using the DATASETS proc. Operating systems provide ways of deleting files.

I/O for text files

The SAS language supports sequential input and output for text files. Beginning with SAS release 6.06, the same file can have both input and output in the same step. SAS I/O syntax for text files is more powerful and flexible than that of any of the classic high-level languages.

A text file is a sequence of records, and SAS I/O for text files is record-oriented. Input or output is done for one record or a certain number of records at a time — although it isn't necessary for all the interpreting or formatting for a record to be done in the same statement. Data positions are usually stated in terms of columns, which represent the distance from the beginning of a record.

Other file types can be read and written using the same syntax as text files. Even though they might not literally consist of records, they are treated as records of a certain arbitrary length.

In SAS syntax, a text file is identified by a fileref, which is a SAS name associated with the file. The method of associating filerefs with files varies between implementations; it might be done using the FILENAME statement or using an operating system command. In some implementations, the file name, in quotes, can be used in place of the fileref. Some implementations allow the use of undeclared filerefs.

The simple FILENAME statement just names the fileref and file:

```
FILENAME fileref  file;
```

The file name is normally a character constant, enclosed in quotes. Sometimes options can follow the file name on the FILENAME statement. A device type (such as PRINTER, TERMINAL, TAPE, or DUMMY) can sometimes be given before or in place of the file name; the allowable device types vary by implementation.

The CLEAR option can be used to dissociate a fileref from a file:

```
FILENAME fileref CLEAR;
```

I/O for SAS datasets

The SAS language supports sequential and direct access input from SAS datasets. Sequential input is provided by the SET, MERGE, and UPDATE statements in the data step and the DATA= option and some other options in the proc step. Direct access is done by the SET statement with the POINT= option.

SAS data steps create output SAS data files using the DATA and OUTPUT statements. Some proc steps also create output SAS data files, usually with the OUT= option on the PROC or OUTPUT statement. All output SAS data files are new files, even if a SAS dataset already exists with the same name; in that case, the old SAS dataset is deleted after the successful completion of the step that creates the new one.

A SAS dataset cannot be read in the same step in which it is created. However, a previously existing SAS dataset can be read in the same step in which a new SAS dataset of the same name is created.

SAS data views are created by procs in a completely different process from the creation of SAS data files.

Whether reading or writing, a SAS step first processes the header of a SAS dataset, and then inputs or outputs one observation at a time. Most engines also add more information to the header after writing the last observation.

Some of the details of input or output for a SAS dataset can be controlled using dataset options. Dataset options can be used to rename and exclude variables, to select observations, and to specify physical characteristics of new SAS datasets. Dataset options are described in chapter 2, "The facts."

There are several SAS procs designed for editing SAS datasets, particularly FSEDIT, and the SORT proc for sorting SAS datasets. Unlike most SAS procs, these procs can actually do input and output on the same SAS dataset. However, most view engines cannot be used with these procs. There are also several procs for copying SAS datasets.

Input from text files

The syntax for input from text files involves two statements: INFILE, which provides general identifying information about the input file, and INPUT, which controls the way the input data is interpreted and assigned to variables.

INFILE

The INFILE statement identifies an input text file. Because files are managed by the operating system, and different operating systems have different kinds of files, the options that can be used with the INFILE statement vary considerably between operating systems. The discussion here focuses on the common features of the INFILE statement, which are sufficient for the great majority of files.

The form of the INFILE statement is

```
INFILE fileref options;
```

The fileref identifies the input file. The CARDS fileref refers to data lines in the program file following the CARDS or CARDS4 statement at the end of the data step. LOG and PRINT are special filerefs used for output files; they cannot be used for input.

The INFILE statement is an executable statement; it sets the current input file, which is the file that INPUT statements read. It must be executed before the INPUT statement to which it refers. The current input file is changed to CARDS at the top of the observation loop, so the INFILE statement has to execute in every repetition of the observation loop that executes an INPUT statement.

You can read from more than one input file in a step. To do that, you need separate INFILE statements to identify the different input files.

The INFILE statement can be conditionally executed, to allow you to choose between input files.

```
IF NEXTFILE =: 'A' THEN INFILE A; ELSE INFILE B;
```

INFILE options

Most of the time, you will not need to use any INFILE options. However, there are quite a few of them to handle special situations and detailed input programming. The most generally useful INFILE options are listed in the following table.

INFILE Option	Description
MISSOVER FLOWOVER STOPOVER	determines what the INPUT statement does when it gets to the end of a record before it finds values for all the variables in the record. With MISSOVER, it assigns the remaining variables missing values. With FLOWOVER, it continues reading at column 1 of the next record. With STOPOVER, it creates an error condition, and the step stops running.
RECFM=	record format. Values vary by implementation. F fixed length (given by LRECL= option) V variable length U undefined D data sensitive N no format
LRECL=	logical record length; the number of characters in a record
PAD	pads short input records (shorter than the LRECL= value) with trailing blanks (with RECFM= D or V). Default: NOPAD
LINESIZE= LS=	limits the number of characters in a record available to the INPUT statement. Use this option to prevent the INPUT statement from reading characters past a certain column.
FIRSTOBS=	the number of the first record to be read from the input file. Use this option to skip records at the beginning of the file.
OBS=	the number of the last record to be read from the input file. Use this option to skip records at the end of the file.
N=	the number of lines available to the input pointer. This option might be necessary when an INPUT statement reads a variable number of lines. The default is the largest constant value used with the # line pointer control.
UNBUFFERED UNBUF	tells the SAS supervisor not to look ahead at the next record when reading a record. When this option is used, the END= variable cannot be used to indicate the last line in the input file.
EOF=*label*	The INPUT statement branches to the statement with the statement label indicated if it attempts to read past the end of a file.
END=*variable*	designates a numeric variable that the INPUT statement sets to 1 when it reads the last record in the file. The variable is 0 until then. An END= variable cannot be used for an UNBUFFERED file.
COLUMN=*variable* COL=*variable*	designates a numeric variable that the INPUT statement sets to the column pointer location.
LINE=*variable*	designates a numeric variable that the INPUT statement sets to the line pointer location.
LENGTH=*variable*	designates a numeric variable that contains the length of the input line. The variable can be used with the $VARYING. informat to read entire varying-length records. The value of the variable can be changed between the INPUT statement and a PUT statement to change the length of the _INFILE_ string.
START=*variable*	The numeric variable specified identifies the starting character to be used in the _INFILE_ string. This variable normally has a value of 1. A different value can be assigned before a PUT statement to change the extent of the _INFILE_ string.

continues

INFILE Option	Description
`DELIMITER=` `DLM=`	delimiters used in list input. Default: `DELIMITER=' '`. Either a character constant or a character variable can be specified.
`EXPANDTABS`	converts tab character to blanks, using tab stops every 8 columns. Default: `NOEXPANDTABS`
`FILENAME=` *variable*	The physical name of the input file is assigned to the character variable specified.
`FILEVAR=` *variable*	Changing the value of the character variable specified causes the INFILE statement to close the input file and open the file whose physical name is the value of the variable.
`SHAREBUFFERS` `SHAREBUFS`	Use this option for text files being edited to use the same buffer for input and output.

If there is more than one INFILE statement for the same fileref in a step, an INFILE option needs to be listed on only one of the statements.

INPUT

The INPUT statement consists of a sequence of terms that are executed in the order in which they appear. There are basically two kinds of terms: pointer controls and variable terms. There is also a notational form for grouping terms, using parentheses.

Pointer controls

The INPUT statement uses a *pointer* to keep track of its current position in the input records. The purpose of pointer controls is to set the value of the pointer — in other words, to go to a specific place in the input records.

The at-sign (@) and plus sign (+) are the column pointer controls. The at-sign moves to a specific column in the current record indicated by the value that follows, which can be a numeric constant, a numeric variable, a numeric expression in parentheses, a character constant, a character variable, or a character expression in parentheses. An implicitly subscripted array can be used in place of a variable name, but an explicitly subscripted array reference has to be enclosed in parentheses to be used.

An @ pointer control followed by a numeric value moves the column pointer to the column indicated. Normally, the value is a positive integer. If D is a numeric variable with a value of 20, the following pointer controls all move the pointer to column 20 of the current record:

```
@20
@D
@(4*5)
```

If the value used with the @ pointer control is not positive, the column pointer moves to column 1. If it is not an integer, it is truncated to an integer value.

The @ pointer control followed by a character value locates the sequence of characters in the input file (beginning at the current pointer position) and moves the pointer to the first column after it. You should be quite confident that the specific characters will appear if you use this kind of pointer control. If the character value is not found in the current record, this can move the input pointer to a subsequent record or all the way to the end of the input file — even if the MISSOVER option is in effect.

The + pointer control advances the column pointer a certain number of columns, indicated by the value that follows, which can be a positive numeric constant, a numeric variable, or a numeric expression in parentheses. If the value is not an integer, it is truncated and the integer part is used.

The line pointer controls are the number sign (#) and slash (/). Line pointer controls are necessary when an INPUT statement reads more than one input record. Generally, the two types of line pointer controls should not be used together in the same INPUT statement.

The # pointer control moves the line pointer to the record indicated by the value that follows, which can be a numeric constant, a numeric variable, or a numeric expression enclosed in parentheses. The value should be a positive integer.

The / pointer control moves the line pointer to the next record.

Whenever any line pointer control is used, the column pointer is changed to 1.

The last term in an INPUT statement can be a line hold specifier. Normally, the INPUT statement releases all the input records it uses, but it can hold onto them for the next INPUT statement with a line hold specifier. The line hold specifiers are @ and @@; they are called the *trailing at-sign* and *double trailing at-sign* because they have to appear at the end of the INPUT statement.

If the trailing at-sign is used, the input records are released at the bottom of the observation loop, so that the next observation can use new records. If the double trailing at-sign is used, though, the records are held for the next observation to use. The use of the double trailing at-sign is appropriate when there are several observations on an input record.

> Because of an oversight in the redesign of the SAS System for version 6, the MISSOVER option and the trailing @@ cannot usually be used together. This applies regardless of the number of INPUT statements and / pointer controls that appear in a step. Version 5 programs that use MISSOVER with trailing @@ can be rewritten using a trailing @, replacing the observation loop with a DO loop.

Variable terms

A variable term in an INPUT statement assigns a value to a variable. The first part of the term identifies the variable, using either the variable name or an array reference. The variable can be followed by almost any combination of the following:

=
$
scanning controls
error controls
informat specification or columns

The equals sign indicates named input, which is described below.

The dollar sign identifies a variable as a character variable. It should not be used when an informat is specified. You must use it to identify a character variable if no informat is given and there is nothing in a preceding statement in the step to identify the variable as a character variable.

The scanning controls are & (ampersand) and : (colon). Either one can be used. The effect of the scanning controls is described below under "Scanning and pointer movements."

The error controls are ? (question mark) and ?? (double question mark). They affect the error messages that ordinarily occur when the INPUT statement fails to get a value for a variable because of invalid data in the input record. The ? and ?? error controls prevent the printing of an invalid data message in the log. The ?? error control also prevents the automatic variable _ERROR_ from being set to 1. In any case, the variable that cannot be read is given a missing value.

An informat specification tells the INPUT statement what standards to use in interpreting the input data. It includes an informat name followed by a period. The period might be preceded by a width specification and followed by a decimal specification. If an informat is not named, the informat given in the informat attribute of the variable, usually the standard numeric informat or standard character informat, is used.

Columns can be given for a variable, indicating either a single column or a range of columns containing the value to be read, 4 or 4–6, for example. Columns cannot be used with an informat specification; instead, a pointer control is used if necessary to position the pointer at the correct column. A decimal specification can be given for a numeric variable if columns are given. The decimal specification is a period followed by a number indicating the number of decimal places to be assumed in a numeral that does not contain a decimal point. For example, if an INPUT statement contained the term

```
SIZE 10-12 .2
```

and columns 10-12 contained the characters `556`, the variable SIZE would be given the value 5.56.

Informats

The most common numeric informat is the standard numeric informat, which can read ordinary numeric data and scientific notation. With no name, it is specified simply as *w.* or *w.d*, where *w* is the width of the field to be read, and *d* is an optional decimal specification, telling how many decimal places should be assumed to be present in input data that does not have a decimal point.

The most useful character informats are the standard character informat $*w*., which skips leading blanks and treats a single period as a missing value, and the $CHAR*w*. informat, which passes characters through unchanged. In other words, the $CHAR*w*. informat keeps leading blanks and treats a single period as a single period.

Other common numeric informats are BZ*w.d*, which is like the standard numeric informat but treats blanks as zero digits; COMMA*w.d*, which reads bookkeeping-style numbers; HEX*w*., which reads hexadecimal integers; IB*w.d* and PIB*w.d*, which read signed and unsigned binary integers; and PD*w.d* for reading packed decimal fields. Other character informats of interest are the $HEX*w*. informat, for reading character data expressed in hexadecimal form, and $VARYING*w*., an informat for reading varying-length fields, whose use is described below.

There are many more informats; they are described in chapter 3, "Programs on call."

The $VARYING informat

The $VARYING informat can be used to read character values that may vary in length. The informat specification is followed by the name of a length variable, a numeric variable that indicates the number of characters to be read. The length variable can be read earlier in the INPUT statement, or it can be assigned a value in an assignment statement.

For example, if the record

```
--THREE--------
```

is read with the statements

```
    LENGTH = 5;
    INPUT @3 NUMBER $VARYING80. LENGTH;
```

the variable NUMBER is given the value "THREE".

Scanning and pointer movements

The way the INPUT statement executes a variable term depends on the scanning mode. Normally, scanning is off. However, if there is no informat specification or columns, or if either of the scanning controls : and & are used, scanning is on. When scanning is on, : scanning is done unless the & scanning control is present.

Reading starts with the present pointer location, unless columns are given for the variable. The pointer location at the beginning of an INPUT statement is line 1, column 1, unless records were held from an earlier INPUT statement with a trailing @.

With scanning off, the INPUT statement reads the indicated number of characters using the indicated informat. If no informat is indicated, the informat from the informat attribute for the variable is used. The default informats are the standard numeric informat for numeric variables and the standard character informat for character variables. The column pointer is left at the column after the last column read.

With scanning on, the INPUT statement looks for values separated by blanks. It looks for a nonblank character beginning at the current pointer location. It then applies the informat to the characters from that point up to the first blank character, or in the case of & scanning, two consecutive blank characters. It leaves the column pointer at the character after the blank character (or, for & scanning, after the second blank character). The final pointer position does not depend on the informat width used.

If the column pointer is moved past the end of a record by a pointer control, or if an attempt is made to read a value beyond the end of the record, the action taken depends on the INFILE options used. If the FLOWOVER option is used, the pointer is moved to the first column of the next record. If the MISSOVER option is used, the pointer is invalidated, and any variables to be read from that location are given missing values. If the STOPOVER option is used, an error condition is created and the step stops running.

Grouping with parentheses

SAS syntax allows variables and informats to be listed separately using a Fortran-like notation. A group of variables can be listed in parentheses, followed by a list of informats, pointer controls, and similar information in parentheses. The first list is called a *variable list*; the second list is an *informat list*. For example, this statement reads FIRST using the term `:$16.`, INITIAL with the term `:$1.`, and LAST with the term `&$27.`:

```
INPUT (FIRST INITIAL LAST) (:$16. :$1. &$27.);
```

Commas can be used, if necessary, to separate terms in the informat list.

If the number of informats is fewer than the number of variables, the informat list is repeated as needed. You could, for example, specify one informat for a list of variables. This example uses an abbreviated variable list:

```
INPUT (SCORE1-SCORE20) (3. +1);
```

After all the variables in the variable list are read, the rest of the informat list is ignored. For example, this statement

```
INPUT (A B C D) (5. +1 4. +7);
```

is equivalent to

```
INPUT A 5. +1 B 4. +7 C 5. +1 D 4.;
```

rather than

```
INPUT A 5. +1 B 4. +7 C 5. +1 D 4. +7;
```

If the informat list does not include informat specifications for every variable, you might have to use commas to separate information that applies to different variables. For example, the comma in

```
INPUT (A B) ($, 4.);
```

is necessary to distinguish it from

```
INPUT (A B) ($4.);
```

You can use an informat or other item several times by preceding it with a number and an asterisk. For example, `3*$5.` indicates that the `$5.` informat is used 3 times. The statement

```
INPUT (A B1-B4) ($4. 5.2 3*3.);
```

is equivalent to

```
INPUT A $4. B1 5.2 B2 3. B3 3. B4 3.;
```

Arrays

The elements of an explicitly subscripted array can be used in an INPUT statement by using the special subscript `*`. The ARRAY statement must appear before the INPUT statement.

```
ARRAY B{4} B1-B4;
INPUT (A B{*}) ($4. 5.2 3*3.);
```

The variables can be associated with formats in a format list, as in the examples above, or read using list input, which is described next. Arrays with temporary variables cannot be read this way.

List input

Input with no pointer controls, columns, or informat specifications is called *list input*. List input is appropriate for reading records in which values do not contain blanks and are separated by blanks. With the & scanning control, list input can also read a value containing single blanks, as long as the value is followed by two consecutive blanks. List input normally uses the standard numeric and standard character informats, so it is most useful for ordinary numbers and character data. (If a different informat has been associated with a variable in an INFORMAT or ATTRIB statement, that informat is used.)

Suppose, for example, each record in a file contains a name, phone number, and vocal range in this format:

```
KEN LORIN  606/555-8309 TENOR
GEORGIA MARAUDER  609/555-1411 SOPRANO
JEFF MASON  212/555-8119 BARITONE
```

You could read the file using these statements:

```
    LENGTH NAME $ 45 PHONE $ 12 RANGE $ 10;
    INPUT NAME $ & PHONE $ RANGE $;
```

It is usually necessary to declare the lengths of character variables read using list input before the INPUT statement, as is done in this example in the LENGTH statement. Otherwise, in most cases, a default length of 8 will be used.

If characters other than blanks separate values, the INFILE option DELIMITER= can be used to specify other characters to be used as delimiters for list input.

```
  DATA _NULL_;
    INFILE CARDS DELIMITER=',:;';
    INPUT A B C;
    PUT _ALL_;
CARDS;
1: 2: 3
,6,,,50,,,,81,,,,
;
```

```
A=1 B=2 C=3 _ERROR_=0 _N_=1
A=6 B=50 C=81 _ERROR_=0 _N_=2
```

Several consecutive delimiter characters count the same as a single delimiter, which is not what is usually meant by comma-delimited lists. If you need to read delimited fields that might be empty, see chapter 10, "File formats."

If the values of variables might extend beyond one record, they can still be read with list input if the FLOWOVER option is used on the INFILE statement.

Named input

The named input mode is indicated by an equals sign (=) following a variable. It is similar to list input, but the variable name and an equals sign must precede the value in the input record. Because variable names are present in the input data, the variables do not have to appear in any particular order. Named input data cannot be followed by any other data on the same input record.

Any variable that was previously declared in the data step can appear in the input record and will be given a value if it appears, even if is not named in the INPUT statement. If a variable name in the input record has not been declared or listed in the INPUT statement, or if data other than named input data appears, it is treated as invalid data. Values containing blanks can be read if two blanks come between the equals sign and the value and two blanks follow the value.

If a slash (/) appears at the end of the named input record, the INPUT statement continues reading named input data on the next record.

Reading fixed-field records

It is very common for records in data files to have data fields in fixed column positions. Such records are called *fixed-field* records. The location of fields in the record is defined by a document called a *record layout*. All the records in a file might have the same record layout, or several record layouts might be grouped together in a fixed sequence.

There is no standard form for a record layout, but it should contain enough information to let you determine for each field

- the starting and ending column;
- what data the field contains;
- what format the data is in.

You should be able to translate that information directly into an INPUT statement of the form

```
INPUT
    @column   variable   informat specification
    @column   variable   informat specification
    . . .
    ;
```

If an observation takes up more than one record, you can use the same form but add the line pointer controls #1, #2, ...

The INPUT statement without terms

You can have an INPUT statement without any terms; that is,

```
INPUT;
```

This statement does not assign values to variables, but it does have an effect. If it is used after an INPUT statement with a trailing @, it releases the input record or records. Otherwise, it puts a record from the input file into the _INFILE_ buffer and releases the record, and if there are COLUMN=, LINE=, LENGTH=, or END= variables (defined by INFILE options), it gives them new values.

Special missing values

You can read special missing values in an INPUT statement using any numeric informat, but the special missing values you use must first be identified in a MISSING statement. The missing values can then be indicated in input fields by the appropriate letters or underscores.

To read the missing value .G, for example, you would name G or g in a MISSING statement, and then use that character in the input data. In this step, the variable X has the value .G in the third and fifth observations:

```
MISSING g;
  DATA;
    INPUT X;
CARDS;
11
24
g
16
g
1
```

The MISSING statement stays in effect for all steps until a new MISSING statement appears. Thus, if you want to read several special missing values in the same step, you need to name them all in the same MISSING statement:

```
MISSING A B D E;
```

Input from SAS datasets

Sequential input from SAS datasets uses the SET, MERGE, and UPDATE statements. The SET statement can also do direct access input.

SET

Input from a SAS dataset is considerably simpler than input from a text file. You can just name the SAS dataset in a SET statement, which has the form

```
SET SAS dataset   options;
```

The options that can be used on the SET statement are NOBS=, POINT=, and END=. The NOBS= option creates a numeric variable that is initialized to the number of observations in the SAS dataset. The NOBS= option cannot be used on SAS datasets whose format does not include the number of observations in the header (such as TAPE format SAS datasets). The POINT= option is used for direct access input, which is described below. The END= option creates a logical variable that the SET statement sets to 1 when it reads its last observation. The use of the END= option was described in chapter 4, "Control flow."

A SET statement can name more than one SAS dataset. The SAS datasets are concatenated — that is, the SET statement reads all the observations from the first SAS dataset, then all the observations from the second SAS dataset, and so on. The END= variable is set to 1 when the last observation is read from the last SAS dataset.

If a BY statement, without the NOTSORTED option, follows a SET statement, and the SAS datasets are in sorted order, the SET statement interleaves them, so that the sorted order is maintained.

The behavior of the SET statement used with a BY statement with the NOTSORTED option is inconsistent. In releases 6.03 and 6.04, it does a normal concatenation, making it possible to concatenate SAS datasets while using FIRST. and LAST. variables. However, in release 6.06, at least as initially released, it attempts to interleave the SAS datasets. There is no way to concatenate SAS datasets in release 6.06 while using FIRST. and LAST. variables (unless the SAS datasets do not have BY variable values in common).

MERGE

The MERGE statement is used for combining observations from two or more SAS datasets. Typically, different variables come from the different SAS datasets. The form of the MERGE statement is

```
MERGE SAS dataset   SAS dataset   ...   option;
```

The END= option can be used with the MERGE statement. It has the same effect as the END= option on the SET statement.

The action of the MERGE statement depends on whether a BY statement is present. Without a BY statement, MERGE does a *one-to-one merge;* with a BY statement, it does a *match merge.*

A one-to-one merge of two SAS datasets combines the first observation from the first SAS dataset with the first observation from the second SAS dataset, then the second observation from the first SAS dataset with the first observation from the second SAS dataset, then the third observations, and so on. After one of the SAS datasets runs out of observations, its variables have missing values. After the last SAS dataset runs out of observations, the merging process stops.

A match merge combines the observations of SAS datasets sorted by the same variables, which are listed in the BY statement. The sort order is maintained, and only observations with the same BY values are combined. If one of the SAS datasets does not have any observations for a particular BY group, its variables have missing values for that BY group. If the SAS datasets have unequal numbers of observations in a BY group, all the observations are used, and the values from the last observation in the BY group of a SAS dataset with a lesser number of observations are retained through the end of the BY group. Thus, you could, for example, merge a SAS dataset with only one observation per BY group with a SAS dataset that has many observations in each BY group.

The NOTSORTED option can be used on the BY statement in match merging to get a match merging process that does not use a sort order. BY groups are formed in the same way as with a sorted match merge. However, after a BY group is completed, the next BY group is determined by the value of the BY variables in the first SAS dataset named in the MERGE statement. This contrasts with a sorted match merge, in which each SAS dataset is checked to find the next BY value. If the first SAS dataset in the MERGE statement contains at least one observation in each BY group, and the BY groups are in the same order in each SAS dataset, a NOTSORTED match merge can form the same observations that a sorted match merge would.

UPDATE

The UPDATE statement combines BY groups in two SAS datasets, which are called the *master dataset* and the *transaction dataset.* The form of the UPDATE statement is

```
UPDATE master dataset   transaction dataset   option;
```

Like the SET and MERGE statements, the UPDATE statement can use the END= option.

For the UPDATE process to work correctly, both SAS datasets must be sorted; there must be a BY statement showing the sorted order; and the master dataset should have no more than one observation per BY group.

For variables that are in both SAS datasets, nonmissing values in the transaction dataset take precedence over values in the master dataset. In addition, variables with a value of ._ or '_' in the transaction dataset are given standard missing values. Otherwise, the values from the master dataset are used. If the master dataset does not have any values for a particular BY group, then the values from the transaction dataset are used for that BY group. Only one output observation is created for each BY group.

More than one SET, MERGE, or UPDATE statement

Each SET, MERGE, and UPDATE statement is a separate input stream. This allows you to access the same SAS dataset more than once in a step, but it also means that all references to the same input stream must use the same SET, MERGE, or UPDATE statement.

The step

```
DATA C;
  SET B;
  SET B;
```

is not the same as

```
DATA C;
  DO I = 1 TO 2;
    SET B;
    END;
```

The two SET statements in the first step are simply redundant; they each read the first observation of B in the first repetition of the observation loop, the second observation of B in the second repetition of the observation loop, and so on. The SAS dataset C is simply a copy of B. The second step achieves the effect of producing a SAS dataset C containing the even-numbered observations of B.

DATA=

In a proc step, the input SAS dataset is usually named in the DATA= option on the PROC statement. If no SAS dataset is named, `DATA=_LAST_` — the most recently created SAS dataset — is the default. Procs that might have input from more than one SAS dataset have different input syntax.

Subsetting

You can select observations from input SAS datasets using the FIRSTOBS=, OBS=, and WHERE= dataset options. The dataset options follow the SAS dataset name and are enclosed in parentheses.

The FIRSTOBS= option identifies the first observation of the SAS dataset to be read; the OBS= option identifies the last observation to be read. The option `OBS=0` is sometimes used in testing the syntax of a step, without having it process any data. This step reads (and prints) only the second and third observations from the SAS dataset SIGNS:

```
PROC PRINT DATA=SIGNS (FIRSTOBS=2 OBS=3);
```

The WHERE= dataset option allows a program to test the values of variables in an observation before deciding whether to use it. This step prints only those observations from SIGNS where the value of YEAR is at least 1990:

```
PROC PRINT DATA=SIGNS (WHERE=(YEAR >= 1990));
```

A WHERE expression can use most of the features that are allowed in a SAS expression. A WHERE expression can have:

- variables in the SAS dataset
- constants
- SAS operators
- the operator `IS MISSING` or `IS NULL` as a synonym for `<= .Z` (for a numeric value) or `= ' '` (for a character value)
- the operator `BETWEEN` *value* `AND` *value* to test whether a value falls in a range
- the operator `CONTAINS` or `?` to test whether a string contains a substring
- the operator `LIKE` to test whether a character value fits a pattern specified as a character string in which _ represents a position that can be occupied by any character, % represents a position that can be occupied by any number of characters, and other characters have to match exactly
- the operator `=*` to test whether two character values sound similar.

However, a WHERE expression cannot use a SAS function.

In SAS releases before release 6.06, a WHERE expression cannot use the SAS operators MIN, MAX, or || or the WHERE operators CONTAINS, LIKE, or =*.

The WHERE statement can be used in either a data or proc step as the equivalent of the WHERE dataset option. The step above, for example, could be rewritten:

```
PROC PRINT DATA=SIGNS;
  WHERE YEAR > 1990;
```

If the WHERE= option is used together with the KEEP= or DROP= option on the same SAS dataset, variables that are dropped by the KEEP= or DROP= option cannot be used in the WHERE= option.

Direct access

Direct access input from a SAS dataset is done using the SET statement with the POINT= option. Usually, only one SAS dataset is used, but you can use more than one, in which case they are treated as if they had been concatenated.

The POINT= option names a numeric variable that tells which observation to read. For example, these statements read the 7th observation from the SAS dataset ELEMENTS:

```
AT = 7;
SET ELEMENTS POINT=AT;
```

The SET statement with the POINT= option does not reach the end of input data in the same sense that a sequential SET statement does. Thus, it cannot be expected to stop the observation loop or set an END= variable to 1. In a step in which a direct access SET statement is the only input stream, you will need a STOP statement to stop the observation loop.

The NOBS= option might be helpful. NOBS= creates a numeric variable that tells the number of observations in the SAS dataset.

Direct access input is done with ordinary SAS data files. It cannot work with

- SAS data views
- compressed SAS data files
- transport or sequential engines
- the index of a SAS dataset
- a BY statement
- a WHERE= dataset option or WHERE statement

> The direct access SET statement is much slower than the sequential SET statement, so you should usually use the direct access SET statement only when you need to read the observations of a SAS dataset out of sequence. Use the FIRSTOBS= and OBS= dataset options if you want to read a few observations in the middle of the SAS dataset. Use a subsetting IF statement or WHERE= dataset option or put the SET statement in a DO loop with an UNTIL condition if you want to skip observations at various places in the SAS dataset.

Variables and attributes

You can determine which variables are read from an input SAS dataset by using the KEEP= or DROP= dataset option. If the KEEP= option is used, only the variables listed are read. This statement reads only two variables, CYCLE and LATEST, from the file SYSTEM.PARM:

```
SET SYSTEM.PARM (KEEP=CYCLE LATEST);
```

The DROP= option can be used instead to specify variables not to be read. The KEEP= and DROP= options should not be used together. If neither option is present, all the variables in the input SAS dataset are read.

The dataset option IN=, which can only be used for SAS datasets in SET, MERGE, and UPDATE statements, creates a variable that tells whether the SAS dataset contributed values to the current observation. These statements use the IN= variables to create the variable MONTH, whose value reflects the SAS dataset an observation came from.

```
SET JUN (IN=IN6) JUL (IN=IN7) AUG (IN=IN8);
IF IN6 THEN MONTH = 6;
ELSE IF IN7 THEN MONTH = 7;
ELSE IF IN8 THEN MONTH = 8;
```

When a variable in a step comes from a SAS dataset, its attributes (name, type, length, label, informat, and format) come too. If you want variables to have different length, label, informat, or format attributes in the step than they have in the SAS dataset, you can declare the attributes you want in the step.

For example, in this step, the variables A and B have a length of 8 regardless of their length in the SAS dataset AB:

```
DATA C;
  SET AB (KEEP=A B);
  LENGTH A B 8;
```

You can use a different name for the variable by using the RENAME= dataset option. If, for example, the SAS dataset BEST contains the variables ALPHA, BETA, and DELTA, but you want the variables to be called A, B, and D in the step, you can use a statement like this:

```
SET BEST (RENAME=(ALPHA=A BETA=B DELTA=D));
```

If the KEEP= and RENAME= options are used together, the old names are used in the KEEP= option:

```
SET BEST (KEEP=ALPHA BETA DELTA
          RENAME=(ALPHA=A BETA=B DELTA=D));
```

If, in a match merging, interleaving, or updating process, a BY variable has different names in the different input SAS datasets, it can be renamed using the RENAME= dataset option so that the names match in the step. If the key variable in the SAS dataset IN is called PRIO, while in the SAS dataset OUTSIDE it is called PRIORITY, and both SAS datasets are properly sorted, they can be match merged using these statements:

```
MERGE IN (RENAME=(PRIO=PRIORITY)) OUTSIDE;
BY PRIORITY;
```

When more than one input SAS dataset contains a variable, the different SAS datasets could have different attributes for the variable. SAS syntax rules determine which attributes are used in that situation. Each attribute is determined separately, so that a variable could, for example, get a length attribute from one SAS dataset and a label attribute from another.

Explicitly specified attributes are used in preference to default attributes. In confiicts between explicit attributes, the later ones are usually used. If several input SAS datasets appear in the same statement, the SAS datasets mentioned later in a statement override SAS datasets mentioned earlier in the statement. Statements that appear later in the data step override earlier statements. Thus, INFORMAT, FORMAT, and LABEL statements should appear after SET, MERGE, or UPDATE statements to override variable attributes that might appear in input SAS datasets. The same is true for a LENGTH statement for numeric variables.

However, the length of a character variable is determined by its first appearance in a step, rather than its last appearance. The first place a character variable appears in the step (other than the DATA statement or a KEEP, DROP, or WHERE statement) determines its length.

The data type of a variable cannot be changed. If there is any conflict about the data type of a variable, a syntax error results. If two input SAS datasets in the same step contain variables of the same name but with different data types, one of the variables must be dropped or renamed in a dataset option.

Changing the type of a variable

You can't directly change the type of a variable from an input SAS dataset. You can do it indirectly, though. First, use the RENAME= dataset option to rename the original variable so that the variable name will be available for use without conflicting. Then create a new variable with that name, based on the value of the original (now renamed) variable. Finally, drop the old variable (with its new name) from any output SAS dataset.

```
DATA B (DROP=CODECHAR);              * Drop old, renamed variable;
  SET A (RENAME=(CODE=CODECHAR));    * Rename old variable;
  CODE = INPUT(CODECHAR, 12.);       * Create new variable;
```

You will also need to do this when you need to use the value of a variable that has different types in different input SAS datasets in a step. Apply the process above to the SAS dataset in which the variable has the wrong type.

This process will not resolve a conflict in the type of a BY variable between two SAS datasets. A separate step is needed to change the type of a BY variable — and the SAS dataset might then have to be sorted again to put the observations in the right order.

Output to text files

Output to text files mainly uses the FILE and PUT statements, which are strongly analogous to the INFILE and INPUT statements.

FILE

The FILE statement, which identifies an output text file, has the form

```
FILE fileref options;
```

The fileref identifies the output file. The LOG fileref refers to the SAS log. The PRINT fileref refers to the SAS standard print file. CARDS is a special fileref used for an input file; it cannot be used for output.

The FILE statement, like the INFILE statement, is an executable statement. It sets the current output file, which is the file that PUT statements refer to. The FILE statement must be executed before a PUT statement in order to direct the PUT statement to a particular output file. The current output file is changed to LOG at the top of the observation loop, so the FILE statement has to execute in every repetition of the observation loop that executes a PUT statement.

You can write to more than one output file in a step. To do that, you need separate FILE statements to identify the different output files. The FILE statements can be conditionally executed, to allow you to choose between files.

FILE options

Many of the FILE options are the same as or similar to the corresponding INFILE options. There are also several other FILE options that are mainly used for print files. The most generally useful FILE options are listed in the following table.

FILE Option	Description
PRINT NOPRINT	tells whether a file is a print file or a non-print file
RECFM=	record format. Values vary by implementation. F fixed length V variable length U undefined D data sensitive N no format
LRECL=	logical record length; the number of characters in a record
PAD NOPAD	determines whether short output records (shorter than the LRECL= value) are padded with trailing blanks. Default: PAD for fixed-length records; NOPAD for variable-length records.
LINESIZE= LS=	limits the number of characters that can be written to a record by the PUT statement.

continues

FILE Option	Description
`OLD` `MOD`	tells where in the output file to put output records. If the OLD option is used, the step writes output records at the beginning of the file, replacing the previous contents of the file (if any). If the MOD option is used, the step begins writing output records at the end of the file, adding records to the previous contents of the file.
`NOTITLES` `NOTITLE`	tells the SAS supervisor not to put the current titles (defined in TITLE statements) at the top of each page of a print file.

`N=`
`N=PAGESIZE`
`N=PS`
	the number of lines available to the output pointer. This option might be necessary when a PUT statement writes a variable number of lines. Using N=PAGESIZE or N=PS makes the number of lines available to the pointer the same as the number of lines on the page. Use N=PS when you want to control the page format in one PUT statement or a group of related PUT statements.

`PAGESIZE=` `PS=`	the number of lines per page. The default is the value given in the system option of the same name.
`HEADER=` *statement label*	When the PUT statement writes the end of a page, it branches to the HEADER= statement label to execute a group of statements there until a RETURN statement is reached. These statements are usually used to write a page header.
`COLUMN=`*variable*	designates a numeric variable that the PUT statement sets to the column pointer location.
`LINE=`*variable*	designates a numeric variable that the PUT statement sets to the line pointer location.
`LINESLEFT=` *variable* `LL=`*variable*	designates a numeric variable that tells the number of lines remaining on the current page (including the current line pointer position)
`FILENAME=` *variable* 	The physical name of the output file is assigned to the character variable specified.
`FILEVAR=` *variable* 	Changing the value of the character variable specified causes the FILE statement to close the input file and open the file whose physical name is the value of the variable.

If there is more than one FILE statement for the same fileref in a step, the FILE options need to be listed on only one of the statements. If a FILE statement refers to the same fileref as an INFILE statement in the same step, the options that the INFILE and FILE statements have in common can only be specified on the INFILE statement.

PUT

The PUT statement consists of a sequence of terms, which are executed in the order in which they appear. There are basically four kinds of terms: pointer controls, character constants, variable terms, and keywords. There is also a notational form for grouping terms, using parentheses.

Pointer controls

The PUT statement uses a pointer similar to the INPUT statement's pointer, and it has a similar set of pointer controls.

The at-sign (@) and plus sign (+) are the column pointer controls. They both move the column pointer according to the value that follows, which can be a numeric constant, a numeric variable, or a numeric expression in parentheses.

An @ pointer control moves the column pointer to the column indicated. The value should be a positive integer.

The + pointer control advances the column pointer a certain number of columns. The value should be an integer; if it is a negative number, it must be enclosed in parentheses.

The line pointer controls are the number sign (#) and slash (/) and the keyword OVERPRINT. Line pointer controls are necessary when a PUT statement writes more than one input record. The # pointer control is not usually used together with the other line pointer controls.

The # pointer control moves the line pointer to the record indicated by the value that follows, which can be a numeric constant, a numeric variable, or a numeric expression enclosed in parentheses. The value should be a positive integer.

The / pointer control moves the line pointer to the next record.

The OVERPRINT pointer control can only be used for print files with the FILE option N=1. It releases the current record, and then moves the line pointer to a new record that overprints it. This feature is most often used for underlining.

```
FILE OVER PRINT N=1;
PUT @11 'Extra Texture' OVERPRINT @11 '_____ ________';
```

```
          Extra Texture
```

Not all printers support overprinting.

Whenever a line pointer control is used, the column pointer is changed to 1.

The last term in a PUT statement can be the line hold specifier @. Normally, the PUT statement releases all the output records it uses, but it can hold onto them for the next PUT statement with a line hold specifier. The line hold specifier is @, the same trailing at-sign that is used in the INPUT statement. The double trailing at-sign does not need to be used in the PUT statement, but if it is used, it has the same effect as the trailing at-sign.

Character constants

Character constants can be used as terms in the PUT statement. The character values are simply put in the output lines beginning at the current pointer location. For example, this statement

```
PUT @11 'A' 'B' +1 'C ' 'D' @21 'eeee eeee';
```

produces this output line:

```
          AB C D    eeee eeee
```

A character constant can be printed more than once by preceding it with a number and an asterisk (*). For example, the statement

```
PUT 9*'la ';
```

produces the output line

```
la la la la la la la la la
```

In addition to character literals, character hexadecimal constants can appear in PUT statements. They might be useful in sending escape sequences or control strings to a printer.

Variable terms

A variable term in a PUT statement writes the value of a variable to the output file. The first part of the term identifies the variable, using either the variable name or an array reference. The variable can be followed by almost any combination of the following:

=
$
:
format specification or columns
alignment specification (in SAS release 6.06 or later)

The equals sign (=) indicates that the variable's name and an equals sign precede the value. This form is called *named output* and is described below.

The dollar sign ($) identifies a variable as a character variable. It is only necessary when a character variable has not been identified as a character variable in any previous statement in the data step and no format is specified for it — a very unusual occurrence.

The colon (:) modifies the output from the format used, by removing leading and trailing blanks and then adding one trailing blank — the same process that is done in list output.

A format specification tells the PUT statement how to format the variable. It includes a format name followed by a period. The period might be preceded by a width specification and followed by a decimal specification. If a format is not named, the BEST. format or standard character format is used. If an alignment specification is present, it overrides the format's default alignment. Valid alignment specifications are `-L` to left-align, `-R` to right-align, or `-C` to center the formatted characters within the specified format width.

Columns can be given for a variable, indicating either a single column or a range of columns to containing the formatted value. Columns cannot be used with a format specification; instead, a pointer control is used if necessary. A decimal specification can be given for a numeric variable if columns are given. The decimal specification is a period followed by a number indicating how many decimal places to be used in writing the value. If a decimal specification is present, the standard numeric format is used to format the variable.

Formats

The most commonly used numeric formats are the standard numeric format, *w.d*, which writes numeric values with a fixed number of decimal places, and the BEST*w*. format, which writes as much information about the number as possible in the width available.

The most useful character formats are the $CHAR*w*. format, which passes characters through unchanged, and the standard character format $*w*., which skips leading blanks.

Other common numeric formats are Z*w.d*, which writes leading zeros instead of blanks; COMMA*w.d*, which writes numbers with commas between every three digits; DOLLAR*w.d*, which is like COMMA but precedes the number with a dollar sign; E*w*., which writes scientific notation using E and a signed exponent; HEX*w*., which writes hexadecimal integers; IB*w.d* and PIB*w.d*, which write signed and unsigned binary integers; and PD*w.d* for writing packed decimal fields. Other character formats of interest are the $HEX*w*. format, for writing characters as hexadecimal digits, and $VARYING*w*., a format for writing varying-length fields, whose use is described below.

There are many more formats; they are described in chapter 3, "Programs on call."

The $VARYING format

The $VARYING format is similar to the $VARYING informat. It is used to write character values that may vary in length. The format specification is followed by the name of a length variable, a numeric variable that indicates the number of characters to be written. The length variable is usually assigned a value in an assignment statement.

For example, the statements

```
ALPHABET = 'ABCDEFGHIJKLMNOPQRSTUVWXYZ';
LENGTH = 9;
PUT '-----' ALPHABET $VARYING26. LENGTH '-----';
```

produce the output record

```
-----ABCDEFGHI-----
```

Note that if you simply want to trim leading and trailing blanks from a value, that can be done by using the : format modifier with the $ format.

Formatting and pointer movements

Normally, a column specification or format width specification indicates the number of characters to be written for a variable. If a format is specified without a width, the format's default width is used. For character formats, this is usually the width of the variable. Writing begins at the current pointer location unless columns are specified. After the variable is written, the pointer is left at the column after the last character written.

However, if no format or columns are specified, or if the : format modifier is used, writing begins with the current pointer location, leading and trailing blanks are omitted, one blank is put after the value, and the pointer is left at the column after the blank.

Named output works the same way, except that before the value is written, the variable name and an equals sign are written.

A character constant is written beginning at the current column position. The pointer is left at the column after the last character written.

If the column pointer is moved past the end of a record by a pointer control, the pointer is moved to the first column of the next record. If an attempt is made to write a value that will not completely fit on the current record, the value is written at the beginning of the next record.

Grouping with parentheses

The PUT statement uses the same grouping notation as the INPUT statement. A variable list, enclosed in parentheses, is followed by a *format list*, which is made up of format specifications, pointer controls, character constants, and similar information in parentheses.

If the number of formats is fewer than the number of variables, the format list is repeated as needed. After all the variables in the variable list are written, the rest of the format list is ignored. If the format list does not include format specifications for every variable, you might have to use commas to separate information that applies to different variables.

An abbreviated variable list can be used as part of a variable list — for example, `(LEVEL1-LEVEL3)` to stand for `(LEVEL1 LEVEL2 LEVEL3)`. The elements of an explicitly subscripted array can be used by using the special array subscript `*`. For example, `(FAR{*})` would be a variable list of all the elements of the array FAR. Arrays with temporary variables cannot be used this way.

You can use a format, character constant, or other item several times by preceding it with a number and an asterisk. For example, `5*$CHAR6.` indicates that the `$CHAR6.` format is used 5 times.

The following example demonstrates the kind of flexibility a format list that includes pointer controls can have.

```
  DATA _NULL_;
    INFILE CARDS MISSOVER;
    INPUT (P1-P40) ($CHAR1.) ;
    PUT (P1-P40)
        (+4 $CHAR1. +(-3) $CHAR1. +2 $CHAR1. +(-3) $CHAR1.);
CARDS;---1----+----2----+----3----+----4
This step scrambles the output lines by
changing the character order within each
block of four characters. . .
;
```

```
hsTise t cpsabrme lsh teupottlu nsieb  y
hncaiggnte hca hatrcroe drrewt ii hnahec
lcbo fkofu o hrcrcaaestr..   .
```

Keywords

The keywords _PAGE_ and _INFILE_ can appear as terms in the PUT statement. In print files, _PAGE_ releases the current output lines and starts a new page. Using _PAGE_ has no effect in non-print files.

The _INFILE_ term writes the _INFILE_ string, which is normally the last record read from the current input file, but can be truncated by assigning values to variables named in the INFILE options LENGTH= and START=. It has the same pointer effects as a character constant term: it begins writing at the current pointer position and leaves the pointer at the column after the last character written.

> _INFILE_ is not a SAS character variable. Its length is determined by the length of the input record or by the LENGTH= and START= variables and might be longer than 200 characters. It cannot be used in an expression.

Abbreviated variable lists can also be used as terms in the PUT statement. The most commonly used abbreviated variable list is _ALL_, which represents all the variables defined in the step. When _ALL_ is used as a separate term, all the variables in the step are written using named output. In other words, these two statements are equivalent:

```
PUT _ALL_;
PUT (_ALL_) (=);
```

The `PUT _ALL_;` statement produces output like this:

```
NAME=Sonja Mantle ID=00-4434 A1= A2=X A3= A4= A5= A6= A7= A8=X A9=
A10= A11= A12=X A13=B A14=E A15=A A17=A A18=E A19=C A20=E _ERROR_=0
_N_=540
```

The special variable lists _CHARACTER_, _CHAR_, and _NUMERIC_ can be used only if they appear in parentheses, as part of a variable list:

```
(_CHARACTER_)
(_NUMERIC_)
```

List output

Output with no pointer controls, columns, or format specifications is called *list output*. List output is the most compact way of writing ordinary data, because it removes leading and trailing blanks. A file written with list output can be read with list input, as long as the values do not contain leading or embedded blanks.

By default, list output uses the BEST and $ formats, so it is most useful for ordinary numbers and character data where leading and trailing blanks are not significant. If another format has been associated with a variable using the FORMAT or ATTRIB statement, that format is used; however, using the $CHAR format produces results identical to the $ format, because leading and trailing blanks are removed by the list output process.

One blank character is put after each value. If the values do not all fit on one output line, additional lines are used.

```
A = '    a   '; B = 'BBB'; C = 34.55; D = 171E44;
PUT A B C D;
```

```
a BBB 34.55 1.71E46
```

To do list output for an explicitly subscripted array, specify the array name followed by `{*}`.

Named output

Variable terms with the = symbol are written using named output. Named output works the same way as list output, except that a variable name and = are written before the formatted value.

```
A = '    a   '; B = 'BBB'; C = 34.55; D = 171E44;
PUT (A B C D) (=);
```

```
A=a B=BBB C=34.55 D=1.71E46
```

When named output is used with a column specification, the columns should be wide enough to hold the variable name and an equals sign in addition to the variable value.

Writing fixed-field records

Fixed-field records can usually be written using the same statement terms used for reading fixed-field records, as described above under "Reading fixed-field records." Just change the keyword INPUT to PUT, and make sure the format specifications are valid and appropriate. Occasionally you will need to use informats and formats with different names for a particular record layout. If a numeric field is supposed to have leading zeros, for example, you might read it with the statement

```
INPUT   @47 AMOUNT 11.;
```

but write it with

```
PUT     @47 AMOUNT Z11.;
```

Overwriting

It is possible for a term in a PUT statement to write to a position that was already written by a previous PUT statement or by a previous term in the same PUT statement. The earlier characters are erased by the new ones, a process called *overwriting*.

Overwriting can be considered the opposite of overprinting, because while overprinting allows more than one character to appear in the same position, overwriting does not.

Suppose you want to write positive numbers with blanks, instead of commas, between every three digits. You could write the numeral with the COMMA format, and then overwrite the commas with blanks:

```
PUT @11 HEIGHT COMMA9. @12 ' ' @16 ' ';
```

To overwrite in a successive PUT statement, you can use the trailing @ to hold onto the current output line. Suppose you want to write numbers with blanks between every three digits, but some of the numbers might be negative. You then have to take precautions not to overwrite the negative sign.

```
PUT @11 ALTITUDE COMMA9. @;
IF ABS(ALTITUDE) > 999999.5 THEN PUT @12 ' ' @;
IF ABS(ALTITUDE) >    999.5 THEN PUT @16 ' ';
```

The trailing @ holds an output line even between observations. That feature is used in the program below, which copies records from one text file to another. If there are several records with the same value of ID, though, only the last one appears in the output file, overwriting the previous ones.

```
DATA _NULL_;
  INFILE FROM;
```

```
FILE TO;
INPUT @5 ID $CHAR4.;
IF ID NE LAST_ID THEN PUT;
LAST_ID = ID;
PUT _INFILE_ @;
```

It is possible to change selected parts of a file being copied by overwriting parts of the _INFILE_ string. Some examples of this are found below, under "Copying text files."

The PUT statement without terms

You can have a PUT statement without any terms; that is,

```
PUT;
```

Usually, this statement puts a blank record into the current output file. If it is used after a PUT statement with a trailing @, it releases the output record or records. If the file has the N=PAGESIZE option, it simply moves the pointer to the beginning of the next record.

ERROR

The ERROR statement is designed to report errors that a program detects. It writes to the log file only, using all the same terms as the PUT statement. (However, the # line pointer control should generally not be used in writing to the log.) In addition to its output, the ERROR statement sets the value of the automatic variable _ERROR_ to 1.

Numeric missing values

Standard missing values are usually printed as a period. The character used to format standard missing values is controlled by the MISSING= system option. The default is `MISSING='.'`, but any one character can be used instead. A special missing value is printed using the capital letter or underscore associated with it.

```
OPTIONS MISSING='?';
  DATA _NULL_;
    A = .;
    B = .M;
    PUT _ALL_;
```

```
A=? B=M _ERROR_=0 _N_=1
```

If you need to print numeric missing values using more than one character, you could use a value format to format them.

Output to SAS datasets

SAS data files are created in a data step with the DATA and OUTPUT statements, and sometimes the RETURN statement. In proc steps, output SAS datasets are usually identified by the OUT= option. SAS data views are created only by specialized procs and cannot be created in a data step.

DATA

The first statement in a data step is the DATA statement, which lists the output SAS datasets for the step. For example,

```
DATA A B;
```

The special SAS dataset names _DATA_, _NULL_, and _LAST_ can also be used. The statement

```
DATA _DATA_;
```

or just

```
DATA;
```

tells the SAS interpreter to make up a SAS dataset name in the DATA*n* series: DATA1, DATA2, DATA3, ... The statement

```
DATA _NULL_;
```

is used for data steps that do not create any SAS datasets. It is also possible, though unusual, to specify _LAST_ in the DATA statement, indicating that the name of the most recently created SAS dataset should be used — thus replacing that SAS dataset.

Dataset options can be used for the SAS datasets named in the DATA statement.

OUTPUT

In its simple form,

```
OUTPUT;
```

the OUTPUT statement writes an observation to each SAS dataset named in the DATA statement. Output can also be selective, naming one or more of the SAS datasets in order to have output to one or some of the SAS datasets but not all of them.

```
OUTPUT A B;
```

For example, if you want to write observations to different SAS datasets depending on the value of a variable or other condition, you could use a step like this one:

```
DATA D E F;
  SET C;
  SELECT(TYPE);
    WHEN(1) OUTPUT D;
    WHEN(2) OUTPUT E;
    OTHERWISE OUTPUT F;
    END;
```

This step splits the observations in SAS dataset C into three groups. Observations with a TYPE value of 1 are put into SAS dataset D; those with a value of 2 are put into SAS dataset E; and others are put into SAS dataset F.

Dataset options cannot appear in the OUTPUT statement.

RETURN

In steps with no OUTPUT statement, a RETURN statement that returns to the top of the observation loop puts an observation in each output SAS dataset, an action called *implicit output*. There is an implied RETURN statement as the last executable statement of each data step, so in simple data steps, output can occur even though no OUTPUT or RETURN statement appears in the step.

After a LINK statement or HEADER= branch is executed, the RETURN statement has a different meaning and does not do implicit output.

The RETURN statement also does not write output observations in a step that has an OUTPUT statement anywhere in it.

> Some programmers have found that implicit output sometimes happens on RETURN statements even though they have an OUTPUT statement, if the OUTPUT statement is deeply nested in blocks and conditionals. To work around this, if it happens to you: use a DELETE statement at the end of the step or in place of RETURN statements.

OUT=

Output SAS datasets of a proc step are usually identified in the OUT= option on the PROC statement, or sometimes on the OUTPUT statement or another statement in the step. The specific syntax varies from one proc to another.

Variables

Normally, all the variables in a data step appear in the output SAS datasets, except for:

- the automatic variables _N_ and _ERROR_
- FIRST. and LAST. variables
- POINT= and NOBS= variables in a SET statement
- IN= and END= variables in a SET, MERGE, or UPDATE statement
- variables named in INFILE options or FILE options
- _I_, the automatic index variable of implicitly subscripted arrays

These variables are not included in output SAS datasets, no matter what you do, regardless of where the variables came from or what else they were used for. If you need the value of one of these variables in the output data, you can assign it to a variable with a different name.

Each proc determines what variables appear in the output SAS datasets it creates.

The KEEP= or DROP= dataset option can be used to control the variables that appear in the output SAS datasets. In a data step, dataset options for output SAS datasets can appear only in the DATA statement. Dataset options appear, in parentheses, immediately after the SAS dataset name. The KEEP= dataset option lists variables to be stored in the output SAS dataset. Alternatively, the DROP= dataset option lists variables not to be stored. It is important that neither a KEEP= or DROP= list include any variables of the types listed above; they are not included in output SAS datasets no matter what you do, and listing them in a dataset option could confuse the SAS interpreter.

The RENAME= dataset option allows you to store variables with a different name from the name used in the data step. If the KEEP= option and RENAME= option are used together, the old names are used in the KEEP= option.

```
DATA A (KEEP=S RENAME=(S=A));
  INFILE A;
  INPUT S;
```

There are nonexecutable data step statements, the KEEP, DROP, and RENAME statements, that have the same effect as the dataset options on the DATA statement. These statements can be more concise in a step that creates several SAS datasets all having the same variables. For example,

```
DATA A (KEEP=YELLOW MAGENTA CYAN BLACK)
     B (KEEP=YELLOW MAGENTA CYAN BLACK)
     C (KEEP=YELLOW MAGENTA CYAN BLACK);
```

could be written

```
DATA A B C;
  KEEP YELLOW MAGENTA CYAN BLACK;
```

If a KEEP, DROP, or RENAME statement is used in the same step as dataset options on an output SAS dataset, the statement is applied before the dataset options.

Attributes

The attributes of variables in SAS datasets come from the attributes of the variables in the step that created the SAS dataset. The length attribute directly affects the way a variable is stored, but the informat, format, and label attributes are generally only significant after the variables have been read into a SAS step. It is important to store a variable with informat, format, and label attributes that will be sensible for the variable to have in another step, particularly a proc step.

Creating SAS data views

A SAS data view is a SAS dataset that is not self-contained. Typically, it contains header information, but gets data values from other files. Creating a view essentially involves describing what files to use and how the data is formed into a SAS dataset. Views that use data values from other SAS datasets are created using the SQL proc. SAS/ACCESS software is used to create views that use data values from files other than SAS datasets.

Views are mainly used in database applications. The uses of the SQL proc are described in chapter 9, "Operating on SAS datasets."

Editing text files

With SAS release 6.06 and later releases, it is possible to use the same text file for input and output in the same data step. This makes it possible for a SAS program to edit a text file.

The same fileref is used in both the INFILE and FILE statements. Any options that could ordinarily be specified on either the INFILE or FILE statement must be stated on the INFILE statement; they are ignored if they appear on the FILE statement.

The step should ordinarily use one INPUT statement followed by programming statements and one PUT statement. The input and output pointers are independent, even though they point to the same file, so the INPUT and PUT statements should process the same amount of data and execute the same number of times in order to keep them in sync.

```
* The general form of a step to edit a text file;
  DATA _NULL_;
    INFILE TEXT;
    FILE TEXT;
    INPUT variables;
    . . .
    PUT variables;
```

The SHAREBUFFERS option can be used on the INPUT statement to make the file use the same buffer for both input and output. This means that any positions skipped over by the PUT statement will stay the way they were before. Normally, positions in an output record that the PUT statement does not write to are filled with blanks. Thus, the SHAREBUFFERS option makes it possible to change some fields in a file without processing other fields.

This step uses the SHAREBUFFERS option to capitalize the address field in a mailing list file:

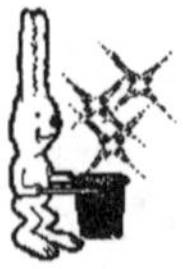

```
DATA _NULL_;
  INFILE FRIENDS SHAREBUFFERS;
  FILE FRIENDS;
  INPUT @36 ADDRESS $CHAR41.;
  ADDRESS = UPCASE(ADDRESS);
  PUT   @36 ADDRESS $CHAR41.;
```

Copying text files

Operating systems provide ways for copying text files, but if you want to do it in a data step, it is easy. The _INFILE_ keyword in the PUT statement simplifies the process and also provides flexibility. To copy an entire text file, you can use this step.

```
DATA _NULL_;
  INFILE FROM;
  INPUT;
  FILE TO;
  PUT _INFILE_;
```

Because the _INFILE_ string contains the entire input record, this step can copy variable-length records correctly, without truncating or blank padding. The _INFILE_ string refers to the last record read from the current input file, the file named in the last INFILE statement executed before the PUT statement.

There are also INFILE options that can affect the extent of the _INFILE_ string: LENGTH= and START=. The LENGTH= option names a variable that contains the length of the current record. The length of the _INFILE_ string can be changed by assigning a different value to the LENGTH= variable. Similarly, the START= variable can be assigned a value to determine the first column to be used in the _INFILE_ string.

This example demonstrates the meaning of _INFILE_ in different situations:

```
DATA _NULL_;
  INFILE A LENGTH=L_A;
  INPUT;
  L_A = 31;
  INFILE CARDS;
  INPUT #2;
  INFILE A;
  PUT 'A record from the current input file, A:'
      / _INFILE_ /;
  INFILE CARDS;
```

```
    PUT 'A record from the current input file, CARDS:'
        / _INFILE_ /;
    INPUT /;
    PUT 'A record from the current input file, CARDS:'
        / _INFILE_ /;
    STOP;
CARDS;
AH 9C 9D 10H QD
2C JC 2H 4S 8S
10S KS JS 3S 7S
9S 4D 4H 4S KC
;
```

```
A record from the current input file, A:
1234567890123456789012345678901

A record from the current input file, CARDS:
2C JC 2H 4S 8S

A record from the current input file, CARDS:
9S 4D 4H 4S KC
```

The first _INFILE_ refers to the current record from file A because A is the current input file, even though records have more recently been read from the CARDS file. The LENGTH= variable has been used to truncate the _INFILE_ string to 31 characters. The second _INFILE_ is the second record from CARDS, because two lines were read from CARDS. Similarly, the third _INFILE_ is the fourth record from CARDS.

An advantage of copying a text file in a data step is the flexibility you can have. If you want to copy the input file to the end of an existing output file, use the MOD option on the FILE statement:

```
FILE TO MOD;
```

You can select records from the beginning, middle, or end of the input file by using the OBS= and FIRSTOBS= options in the INFILE statement. For example, to copy the second thousand records:

```
INFILE FROM FIRSTOBS=1001 OBS=2000;
```

Of course, you can also do programming to select records. For example, this step copies only records which have a blank in column 1 and the letter B in column 5:

```
DATA _NULL_;
  INFILE FROM MISSOVER;
  INPUT @1 BLANK $CHAR1.  @5 B_CODE $CHAR1.;
  IF BLANK = ' ' AND B_CODE = 'B';
  FILE TO;
  PUT _INFILE_;
```

Making several copies

To make more than one copy of a text file, you just need to have more than one FILE and PUT statement:

```
DATA _NULL_;
  INFILE FROM;
  INPUT;
  FILE TO1;
  PUT _INFILE_;
  FILE TO2;
  PUT _INFILE_;
```

Line numbers

Line numbers, also called *sequence numbers,* were essential for keeping punch cards in the right order, and are part of older operating systems designed for use with punch cards. They typically appear at the beginning or end of a record.

Under the MVS operating system, variable-length text files may have line numbers in the first 8 columns. This program copies such a file, removing the line numbers.

```
DATA _NULL_;
  INFILE FROM START=S;
  INPUT;
  S = 9;
  FILE TO;
  PUT _INFILE_;   * Use  PUT @9 _INFILE_  if you don't want the
                    data shifted to the left.   ;
```

Fixed-length text files might have line numbers in the last 8 columns. This program copies a file with a record length of 80, using a LENGTH= variable to remove the line numbers from columns 73–80.

```
DATA _NULL_;
  INFILE FROM LENGTH=L;
  INPUT;
  L = 72;
  FILE TO;
  PUT _INFILE_;
```

This program generates new line numbers incremented by 100.

```
DATA _NULL_;
  INFILE FROM;
  INPUT;
  FILE TO;
  LINE_NO + 100;
  PUT _INFILE_ @73 LINE_NO Z8.;
      * Alternatively, you could use @73 _N_ Z6. '00';
```

Print files

The output of computer programs often ends up on paper; paper is the standard form of business communications, and it provides a higher-resolution image than a video screen. Machines that transfer computer data to paper are called *printers*.

A printer could simply put the characters of a text file on paper. However, files sent to a printer can also contain *print control characters*, which tell the printer where to put the characters on the printed page.

Output text files that contain print control characters are called *print files*, while those that do not are called *non-print files*. The log and standard print files (filerefs LOG and PRINT) are print files, as is the text output from procs. Data steps can produce both print and non-print files, depending on the PRINT or NOPRINT option on the FILE statement, or on the characteristics of the files.

Print control characters

Print control characters are different in different operating systems, and can even differ somewhat between different printer models. The SAS System only really needs two print control characters: the new page character, and the overprint character.

The new page character marks the beginning of a printed page.

The overprint character causes a record to be printed on the same line as the previous record, so that more than one character can be put in the same position on the page. Not all printers can do overprinting, and might ignore a record with the overprint character or print it on a separate line.

There are other print control characters the SAS supervisor sometimes uses: to skip a line on the output page, for example, or to skip two lines or three lines.

Redirecting print files

The standard print file is ordinarily the same file for an entire SAS program. However, you might want to have print output from different steps stored in different files. The PRINTTO proc lets you do this, even with proc steps. The statement that redirects standard print output is

```
PROC PRINTTO PRINT=fileref;
```

The standard print output of subsequent proc steps, and output directed to file PRINT in data steps, is sent to the fileref indicated. The NEW option can be used on the `PROC PRINTTO` statement to start writing at the beginning of the file, rather than at the end, which is the default. In other words, the NEW option erases the current contents of the file before writing to it.

To maintain compatibility with the syntax of the PRINTTO proc in SAS version 5, the UNIT= option can be used in place of the PRINT= option. A two-digit numeral is specified in the UNIT= option, which forms a fileref of the form `FTnnF001`. For example, `PROC PRINTTO UNIT=16;` is equivalent to `PROC PRINTTO PRINT=FT16F001`.

The SAS log can also be redirected using the LOG= option on the `PROC PRINTTO` statement.

Later, to return standard print output or the log to its usual file, use the step `PROC PRINTTO PRINT=PRINT;` or `PROC PRINTTO LOG=LOG;`. To return both output streams to their default files, you can use the step

```
PROC PRINTTO;
```

which is equivalent to `PROC PRINTTO PRINT=PRINT LOG=LOG;`.

Overprinting

Overprinting is used for underlining errors in the SAS log, and at other places in print files produced by SAS programs. However, it is only done if the system option OVP is in effect. If NOOVP is in effect, the SAS supervisor does its underlines with hyphens on a separate line.

If OVP is in effect, overprinting can be done in a PUT statement writing to a print file that has the FILE option N=1 using the OVERPRINT pointer control.

Pages

A page, traditionally, is one side of a sheet of paper. In a print file, though, a page is all the characters between two new page characters. Usually there should be a one-to-one correspondence between the pages in a print file and the pages produced by the printer. To make this happen, you can define the characteristics of the print file in the SAS program.

The essential characteristic of a page, as far as the SAS supervisor is concerned, is its size: *line size*, the number of characters that can appear on a line, and *page size*, the number of lines that can fit on a page. These characteristics can be controlled by the system options LINESIZE= (or LS=) and PAGESIZE= (or PS=).

Usually, all print files produced by a program (or by a step, at least) are printed by the same printer on the same kind of page, so the system options are sufficient. Sometimes, though, one file needs to have a different page definition. A print file produced by a data step can have its line size and page size defined by FILE options, which override the system options.

The simple thing to do is to match the declared size of a page to the size used by the printer. You might make the line size slightly smaller to have a larger right margin, or make the page size slightly smaller for a larger bottom margin.

Various kinds of trouble can arise if the line size is too large. Some printers will just ignore the extra characters; some impact printers will print them on the platen; and some will put them on a new line.

If there are more lines in a print page than the printer can put on a page, it will put the extra lines on an additional page. This can result in lots of wasted paper in a report if you have slightly overestimated the printer page height, for example, by setting `PAGESIZE=66` when the printer only uses 54 or 60 lines on each page.

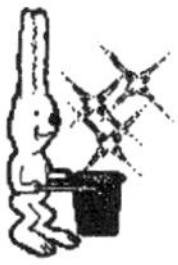

It also has its uses. In this example, the value of PAGESIZE is twice the size of the printer page, to prevent headings from being repeated on subsequent pages in a table.

```
TITLE 'Two Page Table With Headings Only On The First Page';
OPTIONS PAGESIZE=108 LINESIZE=63 NODATE NONUMBER;
  PROC PRINT DATA=CARPET SPLIT='>';
    BY BUILDING; PAGEBY BUILDING;
    VAR COLOR STYLE AREA LENGTH WIDTH LOCATION;
    LABEL COLOR='>Color' STYLE='>Style' AREA='Size>(sq.m.)'
      LENGTH='Length>(m)' WIDTH='Width>(m)' LOCATION='Room>Number';
```

Two Page Table With Headings Only On The First Page 1

---------------------BUILDING=ANNEX C---------------------

OBS	Color	Style	Size (sq.m.)	Length (m)	Width (m)	Room Number
1	GRAY	FLAT	40	40	1	90
2	RED	PLUSH	25	5	5	112
3	RED	PLUSH	25	5	5	113
4	RED	PLUSH	25	5	5	114
5	RED	PLUSH	25	5	5	115
6	WHITE	MARBLE	3200	80	40	100
7	RED	PLUSH	25	5	5	118
8	RED	PLUSH	20	4	5	119
9	RED	PLUSH	25	5	5	122
10	GRAY	FLAT	40	40	1	190
11	RED	PLUSH	25	5	5	121
12	RED	PLUSH	25	5	5	120
13	BROWN	TEXTURED	19	6	3	144
14	BROWN	TEXTURED	20	7	3	148
15	RED	PLUSH	20	5	4	130
16	GRAY	FLAT	40	40	1	191
17	GREEN	TURF	36	12	3	132
18	RED	FLAT	4	2	2	142
19	YELLOW	MATTE	14	7	2	139
20	RED	PLUSH	25	5	5	149
21	RED	PLUSH	25	5	5	141
22	GRAY	FLAT	40	40	1	192
23	RED	PLUSH	25	5	5	211
24	RED	PLUSH	25	5	5	212
25	RED	PLUSH	25	5	5	213
26	RED	PLUSH	45	9	5	215
27	RED	PLUSH	25	5	5	216
28	TAN	MATTE	2	2	1	217
29	GRAY	FLAT	40	40	1	290
30	RED	FLAT	70	10	7	222
31	RED	FLAT	48	8	6	223
32	RED	FLAT	49	7	7	224
33	WHITE	PLUSH	28	7	4	234
34	RED	PLUSH	25	5	5	225
35	RED	PLUSH	25	5	5	226
36	RED	PLUSH	25	5	5	227
37	RED	PLUSH	25	5	5	228
38	RED	PLUSH	25	5	5	229
39	RED	PLUSH	30	6	5	230
40	BROWN	MATTE	72	9	8	234

41	TAN	FLAT	12	4	3	237
42	GRAY	FLAT	40	40	1	291
43	RED	FLAT	12	4	3	242
44	RED	FLAT	12	4	3	243
45	RED	FLAT	12	4	3	244
46	RED	FLAT	12	4	3	245
47	GRAY	FLAT	40	40	1	292
48	GREEN	TURF	9	3	3	240
49	WHITE	MARBLE	21	7	3	300
50	RED	FLAT	6	3	2	311
51	RED	FLAT	9	3	3	312
52	TAN	FLAT	10	5	2	316
53	BROWN	FLAT	21	7	3	317
54	GRAY	FLAT	40	40	1	391
55	WHITE	TEXTURED	16	4	4	313
56	WHITE	TEXTURED	16	4	4	314
57	WHITE	TEXTURED	16	4	4	315
58	WHITE	TEXTURED	16	4	4	319
59	WHITE	TEXTURED	16	4	4	310
60	GRAY	FLAT	40	40	1	390
61	GRAY	FLAT	40	40	1	392
62	BROWN	TEXTURED	19	6	3	325
63	BROWN	TEXTURED	19	6	3	327
64	RED	PLUSH	25	5	5	321
65	BROWN	TEXTURED	19	6	3	320
66	RED	PLUSH	45	9	5	331
67	RED	PLUSH	25	5	5	332
68	RED	PLUSH	25	5	5	337
69	RED	PLUSH	25	5	5	333
70	RED	PLUSH	30	6	5	335
71	GRAY	FLAT	40	40	1	390
72	RED	FLAT	40	40	1	460
73	WHITE	FLAT	320	20	8	440
74	GRAY	PLUSH	140	20	7	401
75	WHITE	FLAT	400	40	10	408
76	WHITE	FLAT	375	25	15	402
77	GRAY	FLAT	40	40	1	490
78	PURPLE	FLAT	555	37	15	400
79	BLACK	PLUSH	416	26	16	404

Larger declared page sizes might also be used for tiling, which is described below.

In the PUT statement, a new page is started the first time a step writes to a file, when the _PAGE_ keyword appears, or when the pointer moves past the end of the last line on the page.

You should think of _PAGE_ as marking the beginning of a page, rather than the end. If you use _PAGE_ at the end of every page, the report will end with a blank page (blank, that is, except for any title lines or HEADER= lines).

If _PAGE_ is the first thing you write to a file in a step, it does not create a blank page at the beginning of the report.

The pointer can move past the end of the last line on the page if you use a column pointer control that is larger than the line size, or if you try to put too many variables on the line using list output, as in this example:

```
FILE A PRINT NOTITLES PS=60 N=PS;
PUT #60 X1-X45 @;
```

Perhaps X1–X15 will appear on line 60, and X16–X45 will appear on the first few lines of the next page, depending on how the width of the values compares to the line size.

There are several FILE options that can help you control the placement of things on the page.

The LINESLEFT= (or LL=) option names a numeric variable whose value is the number of lines left on the current page. The variable can then be used in deciding where to put a page break, or to put notes at the right place at the bottom of the page.

The count includes the line that contains the current line pointer. Thus, the value of the LINESLEFT= variable ranges from 1 to the number of lines available on the page — except at the beginning of the step, before the first FILE statement for the step is executed, when the value of the LINESLEFT= variable is 0.

In the example below, an observation takes up either one or two lines, depending on the data values. The variable NN is assigned the number of lines needed, and then the condition `NN >= LL` is used to determine whether enough lines remain on the current page to write the observation. This prevents an observation from being split between two pages. The additional condition `FIRST.GROUP` is used to start a new page at the beginning of each BY group.

```
FILE REPORT PRINT N=PS LL=LL;
SET THINGS;
BY GROUP;
IF LENGTH(NAME) > 49 THEN NN = 2; ELSE NN = 1;
IF NN >= LL OR FIRST.GROUP THEN PUT _PAGE_ @;
PUT NAME +3 @;
IF NN = 2 THEN PUT;
PUT CAT +2 SERIAL +2 YEAR= +2 COPY=;
```

The COLUMN= option identifies a variable that tells the current column pointer location. It can be used in deciding where to put line breaks in reports with variable formatting.

Using the option N=PS makes all the lines on a page available for access using the line pointer controls. You then do not have to write the lines in the order in which they appear on the page. When N=PS is used, the LINE= option identifies a variable whose value is the current line pointer location.

Values can be assigned to the LINE=, COLUMN=, and LINESLEFT= variables, just like any variable, but doing so does not move the output pointer, and changes the value of the variable only until the next PUT statement is executed.

The N=PS option does not make the number of lines available to the output pointer equal the page size unless the NOTITLES option is used. If title or footnote lines appear on the print page, the number of lines available to the PUT statement is reduced by the number of title and footnote lines.

In most procs that produce print output, if a BY statement is used, output for different BY groups appears on separate pages. In the PRINT proc, the PAGEBY statement is used with the BY statement to identify the variables that trigger page breaks.

Parts of a page

A page in a print file has several parts, which are identified in this diagram.

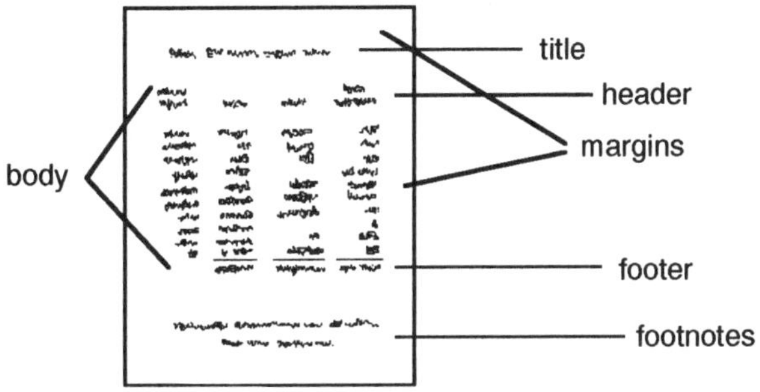

Titles

At the top of the page, there can be up to ten title lines. At the right side of the first title line, if there is one, the date and a page number can appear. At the bottom of the page, there can be up to ten footnote lines.

Titles are defined in the TITLE statements, TITLE1 through TITLE10. TITLE1 can also be written as TITLE. A TITLE statement has a title expressed as a character constant, for example:

```
TITLE1 'This Is The Title';
```

A title defined in a title statement remains in effect until a later title statement changes or removes it. A title statement removes all previous higher numbered titles. For example, a new TITLE5 statement removes any previously defined TITLE6, TITLE7, TITLE8, TITLE9, or TITLE10 title lines.

To remove titles without adding new titles, you can use a TITLE statement without a title. The statement

```
TITLE1;
```

removes all titles.

If no first title line is in effect, the default title "SAS" is used. To prevent this title from appearing you can use the statement

```
TITLE1 ' ';
```

The title line will still appear, but with a blank title. In print files produced by data steps, you can prevent title lines from appearing by using the NOTITLES option on the FILE statement.

The number of title lines is determined by the highest-numbered title currently in effect. For example, after the statements

```
TITLE1 'First Title Line';
TITLE2 'Second Title Line';
TITLE7 'Seventh Title Line';
```

there are seven title lines, with the third, fourth, fifth and sixth title lines blank.

In a display manager session, title lines can also be added and removed in the TITLES window.

System options or FILE options control whether the date and page number appear on the first title line. If the NODATE option is in effect, the date does not appear; if the NONUMBER option is in effect, the page number does not appear. FILE options take precedence over system options. Because the NOTITLES option prevents the title line from appearing, it also prevents the date and page numbers from appearing.

The page number of the standard print file can be set by using the PAGENO= system option. To start numbering pages at 1, use the statement

```
OPTIONS PAGENO=1;
```

When a title is longer than the line size of a file, it is shortened to fit on one line by omitting characters at the end. If DATE and NUMBER options are in effect, and the first title line is too long to fit on the same line with the date and time and the page number, the date and time and page number are moved to the first title line where they fit — or onto their own line, if necessary.

Character hexadecimal constants do not seem to work in TITLE and FOOTNOTE statements.

Footnotes

Footnotes are like titles, but appear at the bottom of the page. There can be up to ten footnote lines, which are defined by the FOOTNOTE statements, FOOTNOTE1 through FOOTNOTE10. As with titles, the number of footnote lines is determined by the highest numbered footnote in effect; a FOOTNOTE statement removes all higher numbered footnote lines;

and the lower numbered footnotes appear above the higher numbered footnotes.

The display manager FOOTNOTES window also contains footnote lines.

In some implementations, footnote lines appear only on pages produced by those procs that know to look for them.

Footnotes do not appear in files that have the NOTITLES option.

Margins

Printers often do not print right up to the edge of the paper. Some space at the edge of the paper is left as margins. If the printer margins are not large enough, you can get larger margins by not using the areas around the edge of the page.

Using a smaller page size value will increase the bottom margin. You can increase the top margin by defining blank title lines. Similarly, you could define blank footnote lines to increase the bottom margin. These statements define five blank title lines and five blank footnote lines:

```
OPTIONS NODATE NONUMBER;
TITLE1 ' ';
TITLE5 ' ';
FOOTNOTE1;
FOOTNOTE5 ' ';
```

Body

The lines on the page between the titles and the footnotes are the body lines, available for the PUT statement or the proc to use. If there are 4 title lines and no footnote lines on a page with 60 lines, for example, there are 56 body lines.

Even though they are lines 5–60 on the page, they are identified as lines #1 through #56 using the # line pointer control in the PUT statement for a file with the N=PS option.

If a page has no title or footnote lines (because of the NOTITLES option), then all the lines on the page are body lines.

Headers and footers

Headers and footers are conceptual objects, rather than being part of SAS syntax. A header is identifying material that appears at the top of the page, such as headings for columns in a table; a footer is identifying material or notes appearing at the bottom of the page. Headers and footers are part of the body of the page, though, which means they appear below any title lines and above any footnote lines that are present.

The HEADER= option on the FILE statement is sometimes useful in writing headers, and it can also be used for footers and for any other text that appears at a fixed place on the page. The statement label named in the HEADER= option identifies a statement or group of statements that are executed when a PUT statement starts a new page. The statement is usually a single PUT statement, although it could be any sequence of executable statements. The PUT statement writes lines on the new page.

The HEADER= option is most useful for writing a header when each observation or each execution of the PUT statement writes one line to the print file, and there is no footer and no direct control over page breaks. In most other cases, there is no advantage in using the HEADER= option.

> Variables can be used in the HEADER= statements, but in the ordinary case, the values will be those of the last observation on the previous page, which is not usually what you want. There are ways around this, by ending PUT statements with a trailing @, for example, but usually the simple solution is not to use the HEADER= option for writing the header.

Headers and footers are typically the first or last thing to be written on a page. Usually, it is simplest to write the header right after the page break. If the FILE option N=PS is used, you can write a footer, and any other text that appears at a fixed place on the page, in the same statement as the header.

This step uses the LL= variable to decide where to put a page break. Then it writes the header and footer for the page, leaving the line pointer at the beginning of line 7 (`#7 @;`) for the first observation to be written on the page. Note that the footer is written on the last line of the page, which is #55 because the page size is 56 and there is 1 title line.

```
TITLE1 'Writing Header And Footer In The Same Statement';
  DATA _NULL_;
    INFILE A;
    INPUT A $CHAR80. / B $CHAR80. / C $CHAR80. / D $CHAR80.;
    FILE B PRINT PS=56 N=PS LL=LL;
    IF LL < 9 OR _N_ = 1 THEN PUT _PAGE_
        #2 @11 'Line A'              /* header */
        #3 @11 'Line B'
        #4 @11 'Line C'
        #5 @11 'Line D'
        #55 @11 '*a footnote'       /* footer */
            +8 '**another footnote'
        #7 @;
    PUT @11 A $CHAR80. /
        @11 B $CHAR80. /
        @11 C $CHAR80. /
        @11 D $CHAR80. /;
```

Centering

The CENTER system option controls the centering of titles, footnotes, and most tables produced by procs. If the CENTER system option is in effect, each title and footnote line is centered on the line, and tables are centered horizontally. If the NOCENTER system option is in effect, titles, footnotes, and tables are aligned with the left side of the page.

Generally speaking, the CENTER option is appropriate when the center of a page is the easiest part to read, while NOCENTER is appropriate when the left side of the page is easier to read than the right side. Using the NOCENTER option also generally runs slightly faster, makes a smaller print file, and prints faster on some printers.

When the CENTER option is used, it is especially important to have the appropriate value for the LINESIZE= option.

Boxes

The FORMCHAR= system option identifies formatting characters used in print output from several procs for boxes and table outlines. The FORMCHAR characters can also be used by procs for other purposes. The default characters used are

```
OPTIONS FORMCHAR='|----|+|---+=|-/\<>*';
```

The first 11 characters are the ones used in boxes and table outlines. The next 9 characters are used primarily by the CALENDAR proc. The following table shows the uses of the individual FORMCHAR characters.

Character	Default	Use
1	|	vertical bar
2	-	horizontal bar
3	-	upper left corner
4	-	upper middle corner
5	-	upper right corner
6	-	middle left corner
7	-	middle middle corner
8	-	middle right corner
9	-	lower left corner
10	-	lower middle corner
11	-	lower right corner
12	+	start or end of event line
13	=	special event
14	|	
15	-	
16	/	separator in event line
17	\	
18	<	left arrow
19	>	right arrow
20	*	highlighting

You can alter the appearance of boxes and table outlines produced by procs by changing the FORMCHAR characters. To get tables with no outlines, you can specify blanks:

```
FORMCHAR='  '
```

To get horizontal rules but no vertical rules, you could use a blank vertical bar and a hyphen for all the corner characters:

```
FORMCHAR=' ----------+=|-/\<>*'
```

The MS-DOS operating system's standard character set contains characters intended to be used in boxes and table outlines. You can use those characters with single, double, or no horizontal bars and single, double, or no vertical bars, using these values:

Horizontal Bars	Vertical Bars	FORMCHAR=
None	None	'2020202020202020202020202B3D7C2D2F5C3C3E2A'X
	Single	'B320B3B3B3B3B3B3B3B3B32B3D7C2D2F5C3C3E2A'X
	Double	'BA20BABABABABABABABABA2B3D7C2D2F5C3C3E2A'X
Single	None	'20C4C4C4C4C4C4C4C4C4C42B3D7C2D2F5C3C3E2A'X
	Single	'B3C4DAC2BFC3C5B4C0C1D92B3D7C2D2F5C3C3E2A'X
	Double	'BAC4D6D2B7C7D7B6D3D0BD2B3D7C2D2F5C3C3E2A'X
Double	None	'20CDCDCDCDCDCDCDCDCDCD2B3D7C2D2F5C3C3E2A'X
	Single	'B3CDD5D1B8C6D8B5D4CFBE2B3D7C2D2F5C3C3E2A'X
	Double	'BACDC9CBBBCCCEB9C8CABC2B3D7C2D2F5C3C3E2A'X

In the FREQ, CALENDAR, and TABULATE procs, the FORMCHAR= option can be used on the PROC statement to change the FORMCHAR string or individual FORMCHAR characters for that step only.

Tiling

If a printer cannot produce a page as large as you want, you can print several pages and tape or glue them together, a process called *tiling*. The arrangement of printer pages into a single page is sometimes called a *mosaic*. To produce a page taller than the printer can produce, set the page size to the number of lines you want the page to have. The printer will then produce several sheets of paper for each print page, which you can combine to form a single large page.

To produce a page wider than the printer can produce, you can write to two different print files in a data step, being sure to write the same number of lines to each file.

This method will not work well for most procs. What you can do, though, is to set the line size to the width you want to use, then read through the print file that is produced, copying the beginning of each line to one file and the rest of the line to a second file, but putting the same print control characters in both files.

Because print control characters vary between operating systems, the program used for splitting a print file will vary somewhat. On mainframes and some minicomputers, print control characters occupy the first column of a record in a print file, so the process of splitting a print file works like this:

```
  PROC PRINTTO UNIT=40;
OPTIONS LINESIZE=160;
TITLE 'A Wide Report';
  PROC PRINT;
RUN;
OPTIONS LINESIZE=80;
  DATA _NULL_;
    INFILE FT40F001;
    INPUT CONTROL $CHAR1. LEFT $CHAR80. RIGHT $CHAR80.;
    FILE LEFT NOPRINT;
    PUT CONTROL $CHAR1. LEFT $CHAR80.;
    FILE RIGHT NOPRINT;
    PUT CONTROL $CHAR1. RIGHT $CHAR80.;
```

6 Expressions

An expression is a group of symbols that resolve to a single value when the statement containing them is executed. SAS expressions can include constants, variables, array references, function calls, and operators.

There are two types of expressions, corresponding to the SAS language's two data types. Character expressions resolve to character values; numeric expressions resolve to numeric values. The values of a character expression can be from 0 to 200 characters in length. SAS numeric values in expressions are represented as 8-byte floating-point numbers.

Expressions belong in specific places in SAS syntax. An expression can be used in an assignment or sum statement, as an operand, as an argument to a function or CALL routine, as an index value for a DO loop, as a condition in a control flow statement or a value to be matched in a comparison SELECT block, as an array subscript, or as a pointer control value in an INPUT or PUT statement.

Constants

Constants are data values that are part of a program. They're called "constants" because, although they are used by the program, the program cannot change them. There are several ways of representing constants for the two SAS data types.

The different forms of constants correspond to different informats. The SAS interpreter actually uses the SAS informats in interpreting constant values in a SAS program. The different forms of constants and their corresponding informats are shown in the following table. Informats are described in more detail in chapter 3, "Programs on call."

Constant Form / Example	Informat / Example
Decimal `663`	standard numeric `INPUT('663', 3.)`
Missing `.`	(Any numeric informat can read missing values, including special missing values named in the MISSING statement) `INPUT('.', 1.)`
Scientific Notation `14E-4`	standard numeric `INPUT('14E-4', 5.)`
Hexadecimal `0F6X`	`HEX.` `INPUT('0F6', HEX3.)`
SAS Date `'7JAN98'D`	`DATE.` `INPUT(' 7JAN98', DATE7.)`
SAS Time `'12:10'T`	`TIME.` `INPUT('12:10', TIME5.)`
SAS Datetime `'04MAY1814 02:24'DT`	`DATETIME.` `INPUT('04MAY1814 02:24', DATETIME15.)`
Character Literal `'Word'`	none (or `$CHAR.`) `'Word'`
Character Hexadecimal `'534153'X`	`$HEX.` (with an even width) `INPUT('534153', $HEX6.)`

Constants can appear anywhere an expression is allowed and at many other places in SAS programs. Character constants can appear in TITLE and FOOTNOTE statements and in PUT statements, for example. They are used in specifying labels, commands, and file names that appear in SAS statements. Constants can be used as pointer controls in the INPUT and PUT statements, and they appear in many SAS options. Numeric constants are used to indicate the number of elements an array has or the range of subscripts in an ARRAY statement, and to indicate width and decimal places in informat and format specifications.

The following statements include several examples of uses of constants other than as expressions.

```
OPTIONS FORMCHAR=' ----------' ERRORS=6;
TITLE1 'This Is A Character Constant';
  ARRAY OFFICE{7};
  SET WORK.GOVT (FIRSTOBS=1040 OBS=2125);
  FILE SA LINESIZE=68 PAGESIZE=56 N=1;
  PUT @1 'Division' +1 DIVISION $CHAR7. @22 AVG DOLLAR9.2 @;
```

Decimal constants

The decimal constant is the ordinary, familiar way of writing numbers on computers. It uses base 10 numerals that can have a decimal point or leading minus sign but cannot have commas.

```
0
-3.7
64000.00
0440
```

Missing values

Missing values represent, in effect, the lack of a value for a variable or expression. A missing value can be represented as a single period (.).

There are 27 special missing values, which are represented by a period followed by a letter or underscore.

```
.
.T
._
```

Scientific notation

Scientific notation, also called E-notation, is a variation on the decimal constant.

The number to the left of the E is multiplied by the power of 10 indicated by the number to the right of the E. Thus, the first numeric constant below represents the number 299,790,000.

```
2.9979E8              /* 2.9979*(10**8) */
9.109534E-31          /* 9.109534*(10**-31) */
```

Hexadecimal constants

The SAS language also uses hexadecimal (base 16) notation, using the digits 0–9 and A–F or a–f. Hexadecimal constants are identified by the letter X or x that appears immediately after the last digit.

A hexadecimal constant cannot begin with an alphabetic character, because that would make it look like a name. Use a leading 0 if necessary.

```
0FFFFFFFFX
0C1X
5EX
```

Hexadecimal? What's that?

Hexadecimal notation uses 16 digits to represent numbers: the familiar digits 0–9, and the letters A–E to represent the numbers 10–15. Sixteen is written as hexadecimal 10, seventeen as hexadecimal 11, and so on.

In general, a hexadecimal number can be interpreted as the rightmost digit, plus the second rightmost digit times 16^1, plus the third rightmost digit times 16^2, and so on. For example,

```
1DEA5X
```

is $5 + 10 \times 16^1 + 14 \times 16^2 + 13 \times 16^3 + 1 \times 16^4$, or 122,533.

Time constants

Constant SAS dates, SAS times, and SAS datetimes can appear in SAS programs, using the forms that the DATE, TIME, and DATETIME informats read. The value is enclosed in quotes and followed immediately by the letters D, T, or DT.

```
'12JAN89'D
'7MAY1990'D
'9:00'T
'17:15'T
'00:05:11.04'T
'12JAN1989 12:00'DT
```

Character literals

An ordinary character constant in a SAS program is called a *literal* because the characters don't just represent the value of the constant — they *are* the value.

The characters in a character literal are enclosed in quotes. For more on quoting, see "Quoting," below.

The following are all valid SAS character constants:

```
'Good morning!'
'"It''s" is a contraction.'
"'"
'10538'
" a"
```

A missing character value is a string of length 0. Because a character variable cannot have a length of 0, and character strings are padded with blanks before being assigned to variables, blank variable values are also considered missing values. A missing character value is represented by two quote marks: `''` or `""`. Trailing blanks are irrelevant for most purposes in SAS programs, so missing character values are often written as a blank enclosed in quotes: `' '` or `" "`.

Character hexadecimal constants

A character hexadecimal constant has an even number of hexadecimal digits enclosed in quotes, followed by an X. Each two hexadecimal digits represent one byte, or character, of the character value.

```
'534153'X
```

Character hexadecimal constants can be used for codes and might be a convenient way to represent characters that do not appear on your keyboard.

> Character hexadecimal constants should not be used in TITLE and FOOTNOTE statements.

Quoting

Quotes, or quotation marks, are used to enclose symbols that represent the value of a constant. There are two kinds of quotes, which are roughly equivalent:

single quote	'
double quote	"

Quotes have to be used in matched pairs. Either two single quotes or two double quotes can be used to enclose a constant. The characters enclosed by the quotes are called a *quoted string*.

Inside single quotes, two single quotes represent a single quote. Inside double quotes, two double quotes represent a double quote. The extra quote characters are a notational convention and are not actually part of the quoted string.

> Characters in quoted strings represent data rather than being part of the syntax of the statement they occur in. Inside quotes, characters such as ; and /* do not have any particular meaning. Inside single quotes, the double quote character does not have any particular meaning. Inside double quotes, the single quote character does not have any particular meaning.

A quoted string can extend from one program line to the next. It does not include any carriage return or line feed characters that might occur between program lines.

The maximum length of a quoted string is 200 characters. If a quoted string is too long, the SAS interpreter issues an error message.

That effectively limits the length of a character value represented by a character hexadecimal constant to 100 characters.

The macro processor resolves macrolanguage references that appear inside double quotes. Strings that contain ampersands and percent signs that are not macrolanguage references should be enclosed in single quotes to avoid confusion. In fact, it's a good idea to use single quotes most of the time, to keep the SAS interpreter from having to look for macrolanguage references in quoted strings.

Every character constant has to have both an opening quote and a matching closing quote. Unbalanced quotes — those that do not occur in matched pairs — may lead the SAS interpreter to treat the remainder of the program as a character constant. The problems of unbalanced quotes are described in chapter 1, "Getting started."

Variables

A variable is a data object whose value can be changed by a program. The term "variable" is used to distinguish them from constants, which do not change.

Variables can be referred to by name or, sometimes, by an array reference. Variables can appear in expressions. They also have other uses, separate from expressions. Certain arguments to functions and CALL routines must be variables — for example, the first argument of SUBSTR when it is used as a pseudo-variable for character substitution. Variables appear in ARRAY, RETAIN, INPUT, PUT, and BY statements, in the statements that declare variable attributes, in dataset options, in I/O statement options, and in various statements in proc steps.

Automatic variables

Two variables, _N_ and _ERROR_, automatically appear in every data step.

The automatic variable _N_ counts the number of times the observation loop has begun executing in a step. It is as if the statement

```
_N_ + 1;
```

appeared as the first executable statement in each data step.

_N_ always has the value 1 at the beginning of a data step, and its value increases by 1 whenever a RETURN statement is executed, including the implicit RETURN statement at the end of the data step, except when returning after a LINK statement or HEADER= transfer is executed. The value of _N_ also increases by 1 when a DELETE statement is executed or when a subsetting IF is executed with a false condition. However, the value of _N_ is not incremented by the LOSTCARD statement.

The automatic variable _ERROR_ starts each execution of the observation loop with a value of 0. Its value is changed to 1 when certain events occur, including these:

- an ERROR or LOSTCARD statement is executed
- an informat finds invalid data
- sometimes when a function or CALL routine has invalid arguments
- division by 0
- a direct access SET statement with a value for the POINT= variable that is not an observation number in the input SAS dataset

The value of _ERROR_ can also be changed by an assignment statement. You could set _ERROR_ to 0, for example, if a condition occurs that you do not want treated as an error. At the bottom of the data step, if _ERROR_ is nonzero, the values of the variables in the step are printed in the log.

Arrays

A SAS array is a variable list with a name.

In practically every other programming language, arrays actually contain data. Ordinary SAS arrays are different. In the SAS language, an array is usually an indexed list of variable names. Using an array reference is equivalent to using the name of the variable.

An array is defined in an ARRAY statement in a data step. The ARRAY statement should appear before any reference to the array in the step. (To use the same array definition in more than one step, repeat the ARRAY statement in each step.)

The ARRAY statement specifies the array name, the range of subscripts allowed, and the variable list. The variables must all be the same data type. If they are character variables, there should be a dollar sign ($) before the variable list in the ARRAY statement. You can also specify a length for variables in the list that have not previously been assigned a length.

The simplest kind of array is a one-dimensional array, with subscripts beginning at 1:

```
ARRAY S{5} FIRST SECOND THIRD FOURTH FIFTH;
```

This statement defines the array S with one subscript, which can have the values 1 through 5. In the step containing this statement, referring to `S{2}` is the same as referring directly to the variable SECOND.

```
DATA _NULL_;
  ARRAY S{5} FIRST SECOND THIRD FOURTH FIFTH;
  S{2} = 2.22;
  I = 3;
  S{3} = 33333;
  FIRST = 1; S{4} = FIRST; S{5.9} = S{1};
  PUT _ALL_;
```

```
FIRST=1 SECOND=2.22 THIRD=33333 FOURTH=1 FIFTH=1 _N_=1 ERROR=0
```

Any numeric expression can be used as an array subscript. The subscript is truncated if it is not an integer. If the subscript is not in the range of subscripts defined for the array, an error results.

Braces are usually used to enclose array subscripts, but in some SAS implementations, parentheses or brackets can be used instead of braces. This is done to accommodate terminals and printers (mostly older ones) that do not support the brace characters. You avoid ambiguity by using braces, because the brace symbols are not used for anything else in SAS syntax.

You can specify `{*}` for the subscript range in an array definition, and the SAS interpreter will assign the subscripts 1, 2, 3, . . . to the variables in the list. Alternatively, you can omit variable names. The SAS interpreter then makes up variable names by appending the numerals 1, 2, 3, . . . to the array name. Thus, the following array definitions are equivalent:

```
ARRAY A{33} $;
ARRAY A{33} $ A1-A33;
ARRAY A{*} $ A1-A33;
```

The same variable can appear more than once in an array. In this example, SCHEDULE{1} and SCHEDULE{7} both refer to the variable WEEKEND:

```
ARRAY SCHEDULE{7} WEEKEND WEEKDAY WEEKDAY WEEKDAY
                  WEEKDAY WEEKDAY WEEKEND;
```

A variable can also appear in different arrays in the same step.

Initial values for array elements can be specified in the ARRAY statement, in a list in parentheses at the end of the statement. For example, this statement gives the variable A1 the initial value 3 and the variable A2 the initial value 0

```
ARRAY A{2} (3 0);
```

just as if these statements had been used:

```
RETAIN A1 3 A2 0;
ARRAY A{2};
```

If there are fewer initial values than array elements, the remaining array elements are initialized with missing values. Specifying initial values for array elements in an ARRAY statement prevents the array elements from being reset to missing at the top of the observation loop, the same as if the variables were listed in a RETAIN statement. This applies to all the elements in the array, even if initial values are given for only some of the elements.

Besides appearing in ARRAY statements and array references, array names can appear in the RETAIN statement, to initialize the array elements and keep them from being reset to missing; as arguments to the LBOUND, HBOUND, and DIM functions; and with the special subscript {*} in the INPUT and PUT statements to read or write all the elements of an array.

Data arrays

In order to create an array that actually does contain data, instead of being an indirect way to access variables, use the keyword _TEMPORARY_ in place of variable names in the array definition. The array elements are then what are called *temporary variables*, which are not really SAS variables. They do not have names or other variable attributes (except for type and, for character arrays, length), they cannot be stored in a SAS dataset, and they can be referenced only through the array reference. Temporary variables are not kept in the program data vector and are not included in any abbreviated variable list, such as _ALL_. Other than these differences, though, they can be used just the same way as any other array element.

Using a data array instead of a variable list array is more efficient when there is no need to store the array elements in a SAS dataset.

Array variations

Array subscripts do not need to begin at 1. You can specify both the lower and upper bounds of the range of a subscript, separating the numbers with a colon. This is useful, for example, when the array subscript represents a year. The following array definition associates GNP{1969} with the variable GNP1, GNP{1970} with GNP2, and so on.

```
ARRAY GNP{1969:1994};
```

You can define multidimensional arrays, arrays that have more than one subscript. The subscripts are separated by commas. In this example, M{1, 13} is M1, M{1, 14} is M2, M{2, 13} is M3, M{2, 14} is M4, and so on.

```
ARRAY M{4, 13:14} $ 3 M1-M8;
M{2, 14} = 'Did';
```

> One-dimensional arrays with subscripts beginning at 0 execute the fastest.

Simulating a multidimensional array in one dimension

Occasionally it may be useful to declare an array with one dimension even though it logically represents two or more dimensions. This was necessary in SAS version 5 for mainframes, for example, because that implementation did not support multidimensional arrays. You might use this approach so that you can treat an array as having different dimensions at different times.

It's just a matter of doing the subscript arithmetic yourself. Let's say you want to have a two-dimensional array with dimensions *m* by *n*. That's a total of $m \times n$ elements, so declare the array as

```
ARRAY A{m × n};
```

Then, instead of using the subscripts `{I, J}`, use the expression `{J + (I - 1)*N}` as the one subscript.

For example, a 4 by 5 array called GRID would be declared as

```
ARRAY GRID{20};
```

and the 3, X element of the array would be

```
GRID{X + (3 - 1)*5}
```

This process can be extended to arrays with three or more dimensions.

Another way to simulate multidimensional arrays is with implicitly subscripted arrays, which are described next.

Implicitly subscripted arrays

There is a second kind of array in the SAS language called the *implicitly subscripted* array. Instead of having a subscript enclosed in braces, its subscript is the value of a specified variable, which is called the *index variable* of the array. The ARRAY statement defining an implicitly subscripted array might look like

```
ARRAY NAME (INDEX) ELEMENT1 ELEMENT2 ELEMENT3;
```

or

```
ARRAY NAME ELEMENT1 ELEMENT2 ELEMENT3;
```

where NAME is the name of the array, INDEX is the index variable, and the rest of the names are the elements of the array. If the index variable is not named, the variable _I_ is used.

To use an implicitly subscripted array, you assign a subscript value to the index variable, and then use the array name in the same manner as an a variable name. These statements, for example, give the variable E the value 20 and give the variable M the value 40:

```
RETAIN TEN 10 TWENTY 20 THIRTY 30 FORTY 40;
ARRAY TENS (_I_) TEN TWENTY THIRTY FORTY;
_I_ = 2;
E = TENS;
_I_ = 4;
M = TENS;
```

If two implicitly subscripted arrays are used in the same statement, they must have different index variables, unless they should always have the same subscript value.

Implicitly subscripted arrays can themselves be array elements. This feature has sometimes been exploited in using implicitly subscripted arrays to simulate a multidimensional array. To create the effect of a two-dimensional array, one array is declared with the first index variable, and several arrays, which are elements of the first array, are declared with the second index variable. Using this approach, you could generate an array that isn't exactly a standard rectangular array.

This example sets up a 4 by 4 array.

```
ARRAY FROM1 (TO) FROM1TO1-FROM1TO4;
ARRAY FROM2 (TO) FROM2TO1-FROM2TO4;
ARRAY FROM3 (TO) FROM3TO1-FROM3TO4;
ARRAY FROM4 (TO) FROM4TO1-FROM4TO4;
ARRAY TRANSNET (FROM) FROM1-FROM4;
```

To use the array, you would assign values to both index variables FROM and TO, and then use the name TRANSNET.

```
FROM = 3;
TO = 4;
DISTANCE = TRANSNET;
```

Array subscripts

Any SAS expression can be used as an array subscript. Even an array reference or a function call can appear in a subscript expression.

The expression should resolve to a value within the range of subscripts defined for the array. If the value of the expression is a noninteger, it is truncated to an integer value as if the INT function were present. If an array subscript is outside the range defined for the array, it is called *out of bounds*, and the SAS interpreter will issue an error message and stop processing the step.

If necessary, you can check whether a variable is a valid subscript value before using it as a subscript.

```
ARRAY D{4:7}
IF 4 <= X <= 7 THEN A = D{X}; ELSE A = .;
```

Alternatively, you might use the MIN and MAX operators to restrict the value of a subscript to valid values.

```
ARRAY D{4:7}
A = D{4 MAX X MIN 7};
```

Arrays in DO loops

The LBOUND and HBOUND functions and the DIM function can be useful in processing the elements of an explicitly subscripted array using a DO loop. A special form of the DO loop, DO OVER, processes all the elements of an implicitly subscripted array. The use of DO loops with arrays is described in chapter 4, "Control flow."

Assignment statement

The assignment statement changes the value of a variable. Its usual form is

```
variable = expression;
```

The expression on the right side of the equals sign is evaluated, and the resulting value is assigned to the variable on the left side of the equals sign. For example, the statement

```
SIZE = 2;
```

gives the variable SIZE the value 2, while

```
NEXT = THIS + 1;
```

gives the variable NEXT a value that is 1 more than the value of THIS.

Instead of a variable name, the left side of an assignment statement can be an array reference. The value on the right side of the statement is assigned to the variable referred to by the array reference. For example, these statements give the variable A a value of `'7'`:

```
ARRAY EASY{3} $ A B C;
I = 1;
EASY{I} = '7';
```

The SUBSTR function can be used as a pseudo-variable on the left side of an assignment statement to change some of the characters of a character variable. The form of the assignment statement with the SUBSTR pseudo-variable is

```
SUBSTR(character variable, index of first character to be replaced,
        number of characters to be replaced) = character expression;
```

These statements give the variable EVENT the value `'Deadline'`:

```
EVENT = 'Headline';
SUBSTR(EVENT, 1, 1) = 'D';
```

Trailing blanks are added if the value of the expression is shorter than the number of characters to be replaced. These statements give GO the value `'RIGHT OVER'`:

```
GO = 'REDISCOVER';
SUBSTR(GO, 2, 5) = 'IGHT';
```

If the third argument of SUBSTR is omitted, characters are replaced up to the end of the variable. For example, these statements give MOVE the value `'PROPER    '`:

```
MOVE = 'PROPELLER';
SUBSTR(MOVE, 6) = 'R';
```

Sum statement

Like the assignment statement, the sum statement changes the value of a variable. It changes the value of a numeric variable by a certain amount. The form of the statement is

```
numeric variable + numeric expression;
```

The value of the expression is added to the variable. For example, the statements

```
X = 3000;
X + 4000;
```

give X a value of 7000.

The sum statement is essentially equivalent to an assignment statement with the SUM function. For example, the statement

```
COUNT + -1;
```

has the same effect as

```
COUNT = SUM(COUNT, -1);
```

A numeric array reference can be used in place of a variable name for the left side of a sum statement.

Variables used on the left side of a sum statement are handled slightly differently by the automatic processing of the observation loop. They are given initial values of 0 and are not reset to missing for each observation, just as if they were named in a RETAIN statement with an initial value of 0:

```
RETAIN COUNT 0;
```

Operators

An *operator* is a symbol or keyword that does something with expressions to create new expressions. The expressions that an operator operates on are called *operands*. An operator is either *unary*, with one operand on its right, or *binary*, with two operands, one on the left and one on the right. Many binary operators are *commutative*, meaning that you can swap the positions of the operands without changing the result.

An operator can be a *character operator*, taking character operands and producing character values, or a *numeric operator*, taking numeric operands and producing numeric values, or both. There is also a class of *comparison operators*, which take either character or numeric values, but produce a logical true or false value, which they represent as the numeric values 1 (true) and 0 (false).

Character operators

Only a few SAS operators produce a character value. The concatenation operator (||) is the only one that works exclusively with character values. As the name suggests, it combines two character strings.

Trailing blanks from both character strings appear in the resulting character string.

<table>
<tr><th>Expression</th><th>Evaluates To</th></tr>
<tr><td><code>'Break' || 'fast '</code></td><td><code>'Breakfast '</code></td></tr>
<tr><td><code>'BROKE   ' || 'N'</code></td><td><code>'BROKE   N'</code></td></tr>
</table>

The TRIM function can be used to remove trailing blanks from a string before concatenating:

<table>
<tr><th>Expression</th><th>Evaluates To</th></tr>
<tr><td><code>TRIM('BROKE   ') || 'N'</code></td><td><code>'BROKEN'</code></td></tr>
</table>

The length of the expression resulting from concatenation is the sum of the lengths of the operands.

The MAX and MIN operators, which are described below, also work on character operands to produce a character value.

Numeric operators

The SAS operators that work exclusively with numeric values make up two categories: arithmetic operators and logical operators.

The SAS language has the usual collection of arithmetic operators: + (plus) for addition, – (minus) for subtraction, * (times) for multiplication, / (divided by) for division, and ** (raised to the power) for exponentiation.

There are two unary arithmetic operators. Placed before a quantity, – means negation, and + doesn't change the number it's applied to, but it's included for the sake of completeness.

Expression	Evaluates To
`4 + 3`	`7`
`4*13`	`52`
`2**-3`	`.125`
`-(8)`	`-8`
`+8`	`8`
`10.1 - .2`	`9.9`
`9/4`	`2.25`
`4736261*63881`	`302557088941`

When missing values are used with any arithmetic operator, the result is a standard missing value. In addition, SAS writes a warning message on the log, saying that "missing values were generated as a result of operations on missing values." However, the unary + operator does not change the operand it is applied to and does not create a warning message.

Expression	Evaluates To
`9 + .`	`.`
`-.`	`.`
`+.H`	`.H`

True and false values are represented by numbers in the SAS language, so the logical operators are numeric operators. There are three logical operators:

AND &
OR |
NOT ^ ¬ ~

These operators have their usual logical meaning. If both of the operands of AND are true, the expression is true; otherwise, it is false. If either of the operands of OR is true, the expression is true; otherwise, it is false. If the value that NOT precedes is true, the expression is false; otherwise, it is true.

Any numeric expression can be used with the logical operators. Missing values and zero are considered false; positive and negative numbers are considered true. The results of the logical operators are 1 for true and 0 for false.

Expression	Evaluates To
NOT 34	0
NOT .	1
NOT 0	1
NOT NOT -7.2	1
-5 OR 0	1
2 OR 3	1
1 AND -1	1
0 AND 1	0

Comparison operators

The classic group of comparison operators appear in the SAS language. These operators check for a certain condition about two values, resulting in a true (1) or false (0) value. Some of these operators can be written in many different forms, but the symbols on the left in the table below are the ones most widely accepted and are used exclusively in this book.

<	is less than	also: LT, ^>=, ~>=, ¬>=, NOT>=, NOT GE, ^GE, ~GE, ¬GE
<=	is less than or equal to	also: LE, =<, ^>, ~>, ¬>, NOT>, NOT GT, ^GT, ~GT, ¬GT
=	equals	also: EQ
>=	is greater than or equal to	also: GE, =>, ^<, ~<, ¬>, NOT>, NOT LT, ^LT, ~LT, ¬LT
>	is greater than	also: GT, ^<=, ~<=, ¬<=, NOT<=, NOT LE, ^LE, ~LE, ¬LE
NE	is not equal to	also: ^=, ¬=, ~=, NOT=, NOT EQ

A distinctive feature of the SAS comparison operators is the way you can string them together. In most languages, an expression like `0 < X < 5` would be meaningless, but the SAS interpreter evaluates it as if an AND were present between the two comparisons, as `0 < X AND X < 5`. This matches the meaning of the expression in mathematical notation.

Numeric comparisons work just the way you'd expect for numbers. Comparisons can be used with missing values too. Missing values compare less than any number. Different missing values are not equal; their order, from lowest to highest, is ._, ., .A, ..., .Z.

Expression	Evaluates To
4 = 3	0
2 >= 3	0
. < -99999999	1
0 NE 0	0
-10 < 0 < 10	1
1 < 4 NE 5	1
._ = .	0

Rounding errors can lead to results you don't expect when comparing approximately equal numbers. See chapter 13, "Numbers," for more on rounding.

The meaning of character comparisons might be less obvious, but technically, it is a simple process. Each character is represented in memory by an integer between 0 and 255. In comparing two characters, the one with the lower number is less than the one with the higher number.

In comparing two character strings, SAS compares the first characters first, then the second ones, and so on, until it finds an inequality. If one character string is shorter than the other, SAS extends it by adding blanks to the end for the purposes of the comparison.

The order in which characters compare is known as the collating sequence, which is a property of the operating system of the computer. Most computers use a variation of the ASCII collating sequence, which (from smallest to largest) is:

```
blank !"#%&'()*+,-./0123456789:;<=>?@
ABCDEFGHIJKLMNOPQRSTUVWXYZ[\]^_`
abcdefghijklmnopqrstuvwxyz{|}~
```

The one big exception is IBM mainframes, which traditionally have used the EBCDIC collating sequence, based on punch-card codes:

```
blank ¢.<(+|&!$*);¬-/¦,%_>?`:#@'="
abcdefghijklmnopqr~stuvwxyz
{ABCDEFGHI}JKLMNOPQR\STUVWXYZ
0123456789
```

Alphabetization by word works for capital letters, because the blank character is lower than other characters in the collating sequence, and the capital letters are in the right order. Alphabetic comparisons also work for lowercase letters, but they don't necessarily work when capital and lowercase letters are mixed.

Digits are in the expected order too, so you can get a mathematically correct result comparing digit strings that have the same length (ZIP codes, for example).

Expression	Evaluates To
`'A' = 'A     '`	1
`'the' >= ' the'`	0
`'g' = 'G'`	0
`'' < 'T'`	1
`'0' NE '0'`	0
`'B' <= 'B' <= 'C'`	1
`'a' < 'an' < 'ant' < 'antler'`	1
`'10025' <= '44074'`	1

Normally, when comparing strings of different lengths, the comparison operators extend the shorter string with trailing blanks for the comparison. However, the : modifier can be used with a comparison operator to have it truncate the longer string for the comparison, resulting in these operators:

`<:`	also: `LT:`, `^>=:`, `~>=:`, `¬>=:`, `NOT>=:`, `NOT GE:`, `^GE:`, `~GE:`, `¬GE:`
`<=:`	also: `LE:`, `=<:`, `^>:`, `~>:`, `¬>:`, `NOT>:`, `NOT GT:`, `^GT:`, `~GT:`, `¬GT:`
`=:`	also: `EQ:`
`>=:`	also: `GE:`, `=>:`, `^<:`, `~<:`, `¬>:`, `NOT>:`, `NOT LT:`, `^LT:`, `~LT:`, `¬LT:`
`>:`	also: `GT:`, `^<=:`, `~<=:`, `¬<=:`, `NOT<=:`, `NOT LE:`, `^LE:`, `~LE:`, `¬LE:`
`NE:`	also: `^=:`, `¬=:`, `~=:`, `NOT=:`, `NOT EQ:`

When comparing two variables, the characters in the shorter variable are compared to an equal number of characters in the longer variable. For example, in this comparison of the variables A and B,

```
LENGTH A $ 3 B $ 5;
A = 'A';
B = 'ABCDE';
Z = (A >: B);
```

only the first three characters of A and B are compared, because 3 is the length of the shorter variable, A. The value 0 is assigned to Z.

In general, when expressions are being compared with truncation, the expression length of the shorter expression is used. The expression length is the number of characters in the value, including any trailing blanks.

Expression	Evaluates To
`'J' =: 'JAY'`	1
`'BEE' >: 'B'`	0
`'ME' <=: 'M  '`	0
`'ME' <=: TRIM('M  ')`	1
`'9' >=: '7.283' >=: '7'`	1
`'>' =: '>='`	1

> The equality operator looks just like the assignment symbol in the assignment statement, so be careful not to get them confused. An equals sign that follows a variable name, array reference, or SUBSTR function call at the beginning of a statement is an assignment symbol; an equals sign in an expression is the equality comparison operator.
>
> In the statement below, the first equals sign is an assignment symbol, and the second one is a comparison operator. The statement assigns the variable A the result of the comparison `B = C`:
>
> ```
> A = B = C;
> ```
>
> Similarly, this sum statement adds the result of the comparison `B = C` to the variable A:
>
> ```
> A + B = C;
> ```

Two additional operators, IN and NOTIN, allow comparisons to be made against lists of constants. IN extends the use of the = comparison. The left operand of the IN operator can be any expression, but the right operand has to be a list of constant values in parentheses:

```
expression IN (constant, constant, ...)
```

If the left operand is equal to any one of the constants in the list on the right, the result of the IN comparison is true (1). If the left operand does not match any of the constants, the result of the IN comparison is false (0).

Expression	Evaluates To
'J' IN ('WHY', 'JAY', 'KAY')	0
4 IN (1, 2, 3, 4, 5)	1
1E3 IN (1000)	1
2.5 IN (2, 3)	0

The opposite operator, NOTIN, extends the use of the NE operator in the same way. NOTIN can also be written NOT IN, ^IN, ~IN, or ¬IN.

Expression	Evaluates To
'J' NOTIN ('A', 'B', 'C')	1
2.5 NOTIN (1, 2, 3, 4, 5)	1
1000 NOTIN (10, 100, 1000)	0

The : modifier for comparison operators described above also works with the IN and NOTIN operators. The IN: and NOTIN: operations do the same comparisons as the =: and NE: operators, respectively.

Expression	Evaluates To
'J' IN: ('WHY', 'JAY', 'KAY')	1
'ME' IN: ('M', 'NA', 'NBA')	1
'be' NOTIN: ('a', 'e')	1

The "stringing" feature of the comparison operators does not apply to the IN and NOTIN operators. See the discussion below, under "Order of evaluation."

Bit testing

Bit testing is a special use of the equality comparison operator that can be used for testing bits in a value in memory. In bit testing, the binary form of a value is compared against a bit mask. A bit mask consists of 0s and 1s corresponding to the values of bits to be tested, and periods in the places of bits that are not tested. (Blanks can be included in the bit mask for the sake of clarity.) The bit mask is enclosed in quotes and is followed by a B. The bit testing process work differently for character and numeric values.

In bit testing of character values, the SAS supervisor compares the digits of the bit mask against the corresponding bits in the character value. The comparison works from left to right, comparing the first character of the bit mask against the first bit of the value, then comparing the second character of the bit mask against the second bit of the value, and so on. It produces a true result if all the digits match, and a false result if any digits do not match. This expression tests a one-byte character variable (or the first byte of a character variable) to see whether the 8th bit is 1:

```
C = '.......1'B
```

The SAS supervisor converts numeric values to 32-bit signed integers before bit testing, perhaps by using the `S370FIB4.` format. It compares the digits of the bit mask against the corresponding bits in the signed integer. (Thus, the bit mask could meaningfully be up to 32 bits long.) The comparison works from right to left, comparing the last character of the bit mask against the least significant bit of the integer, then comparing the second last character of the bit mask against the second least significant bit of the value, and so on.

Expression	Evaluates To
`'14'X = '00010100'B`	1
`'14'X = '00.1'B`	1
`3 = '0'B`	0
`11 = '0000 1.11'B`	1
`'61'X = '0.......'B`	1
`'61'X = '0000....'B`	0

Bit testing can be used to check for multiples of powers of 2. For example, the bit mask `'0'B` tests for even numbers, `'1'B` tests for odd numbers, `'00'B` tests for multiples of 4, and `'0000'B` tests for multiples of 16.

To test whether a small integer is negative, you can just check the sign bit, which is the first bit of the 32-bit signed integer form. If the first bit is 1, the number is negative; if it is 0, the number is 0 or positive.

```
IF NUMBER = '1....... ........ ........ ........'B THEN
    PUT 'The number is negative.';
```

Bit masks are used only in bit testing. They cannot be used in expressions or assigned to variables.

Operators for both numeric and character values

The MAX and MIN operators work the same way with either numeric or character operands. The MIN operator, also written as ><, compares the expressions on both sides of it, selecting the lesser one. The MAX or <> operator does just the opposite. The comparison is done the same way as the comparison operators do it, which means that you can use MIN and MAX with missing values.

Expression	Evaluates To
`'A' MAX 'B'`	`'B'`
`' t' MIN '11'`	`' t'`
`34 MIN .`	`.`
`0 MAX 5 MAX -11`	`5`
`. MAX .X`	`.X`
`0 MAX 60 MIN 100`	`60`

For nonmissing numeric values, the MIN and MAX operators have the same results as the MIN and MAX functions.

Order of evaluation

In expressions with more than one operator, parentheses can be used to control the order in which operators are evaluated. Expressions enclosed in parentheses are evaluated first.

<table>
<tr><th>Expression</th><th>Evaluates To</th></tr>
<tr><td><code>0 MIN (10 MAX 100)</code></td><td><code>0</code></td></tr>
<tr><td><code>(0 MIN 10) MAX 100</code></td><td><code>100</code></td></tr>
<tr><td><code>(1 < 2) + ('1' < '2')</code></td><td><code>2</code></td></tr>
<tr><td><code>('X' MIN 'XX') || '*'</code></td><td><code>'X*'</code></td></tr>
</table>

In the absence of parentheses, other priority rules are followed. These rules are intended to result in the evaluation that people are most likely to expect. For example, people would generally expect `4*1 < 3*4` to mean `(4*1) < (3*4)`, or 1 (true), rather than `4*(1 < 3)*4`, or 16, so multiplication is done before comparisons.

<table>
<tr><th>Priority</th><th>Operations</th><th>Order of evaluation</th></tr>
<tr><td>0 (first)</td><td>expressions in parentheses</td><td></td></tr>
<tr><td>1</td><td>unary operators (NOT, –, +), MIN, MAX, **</td><td>←</td></tr>
<tr><td>2</td><td>multiplication (*) and division (/)</td><td>→</td></tr>
<tr><td>3</td><td>addition (+) and subtraction (–)</td><td>→</td></tr>
<tr><td>4</td><td>concatenation (||)</td><td>→</td></tr>
<tr><td>5</td><td>comparison (<, <=, =, >=, >, NE, IN, NOTIN)</td><td>→</td></tr>
<tr><td>6</td><td>AND</td><td>→</td></tr>
<tr><td>7 (last)</td><td>OR</td><td>→</td></tr>
</table>

Most operators evaluate from left to right. For example, `A - B - C` is evaluated as `(A - B) - C`. The priority 1 operators are the exception, evaluating in the opposite direction. For example, `A**B**C` is evaluated as `A**(B**C)`.

Expression	Evaluates To
`2**3**2`	`512`
`NOT 11 MIN 0`	`1`
`4 + 2*5`	`14`
`4 + 1 NE 3 + 4`	`1`
`'t' MAX 'd' || 'read'`	`'tread'`
`60/6/2`	`5`

The IN and NOTIN operators belong in the same level of priority as the other comparison operators, but they do not associate with them. An expression such as

```
A < B IN (0, 1)
```

simply confuses the SAS interpreter. That expression should be written out:

```
A < B AND B IN (0, 1)
```

Functions

A function is a routine that returns a value. A function is used in an expression by a function call, which consists of the function name followed by the list of arguments in parentheses. Each function has its own rules about the number and types of arguments that can be used with it. The argument types are usually character or numeric, but there are exceptions.

The type of a function is the type of the value it returns. Functions are either the character or numeric type, except for the INPUT function, which might return either type, and the SUBSTR function when used as a pseudo-variable for character substitution.

SAS functions are described in detail in chapter 3, "Programs on call." Some uses of functions are shown in the rest of this chapter and in chapters 13 and 14. This list shows some of the most commonly used character and numeric functions.

Character Functions
COLLATE
COMPRESS
LEFT
PUT
REPEAT
REVERSE
RIGHT
SUBSTR
TRANSLATE
UPCASE

Numeric Functions	
ABS	LOG10
CEIL	MAX
EXP	MEAN
FLOOR	MIN
FUZZ	MOD
INDEX	N
INDEXC	ROUND
INT	SIGN
LENGTH	SQRT
LOG	SUM
LOG2	

Type conversions

The SAS interpreter automatically converts character values to numeric values and numeric values to character values when necessary. You can also use the INPUT and PUT functions to convert between types.

The SAS interpreter converts character values to numeric values when:

- a character value is assigned to a numeric variable
- a character value is used with a numeric format in the PUT function
- a character expression is an operand of an arithmetic or logical operator
- the operands of a comparison operator or the MAX or MIN operator are a character expression and a numeric expression
- a character expression is used as an array subscript
- a character expression is used as an index value in a DO statement with a numeric index variable
- a character expression is used as a numeric argument to a function or CALL routine
- a character expression is used as a condition in an IF, DO, or WHEN statement
- a character expression is used as a SELECT or WHEN expression in a comparison SELECT block that contains at least one numeric SELECT or WHEN expression

The standard numeric informat is used in automatic conversions from character to numeric.

The SAS interpreter converts numeric values to character values when:

- a numeric expression is assigned to a character variable
- a numeric expression is used with a character format in the PUT function
- a numeric expression is used as an argument of the INPUT function
- a numeric expression is an operand of the || operator
- a numeric expression is used as a character argument of a function or CALL routine
- a numeric expression is used as an index value in a DO statement with a character index variable

The SAS interpreter uses the `BEST12.` format in most situations in which it automatically converts a numeric value to a character value. However, when a numeric expression is assigned to a character variable, it uses the BEST format with a width equal to the length of the character variable.

Expression	Equivalent Expression	Evaluates To
`-"42"`	`-INPUT("42", 2.)`	`-42`
`+"1"`	`+INPUT("1", 1.)`	`1`
`'1' OR 0`	`INPUT('1', 1.) OR 0`	`1`
`NOT '0'`	`NOT INPUT('0', 1.)`	`1`
`'TAKE' || 1`	`'TAKE' || PUT(1, BEST12.)`	`'TAKE           1'`
`-2 || 3`	`PUT(-2, BEST12.) || PUT(3, BEST12.)`	`'          -2           3'`
`'10025' >= 19053`	`INPUT('10025', 5.) >= 19053`	`0`
`36 = '36.0'`	`36 = INPUT('36.0', 4.)`	`1`
`21 MAX "17"`	`21 MAX INPUT("17", 2.)`	`21`
`LEFT(4.8)`	`LEFT(PUT(4.8, BEST12.))`	`'4.8`
`4**'.50'`	`4**INPUT('.50', 3.)`	`2`

Whenever the SAS interpreter does an automatic type conversion, it writes a message on the log, telling the locations in the program where type conversions took place.

It is a good practice to program type conversions explicitly using the INPUT and PUT functions. An automatic type conversion might be thought to be a programming error; a type conversion programmed with the INPUT or PUT function clearly shows the programmer's intention.

Converting a character value to a numeric value is done with the INPUT function and a numeric informat. Converting a numeric value to a character value is done with the PUT function and a numeric format. The table above shows how automatic type conversions can be programmed explicitly using the default formats. Other informats and formats can be used for different types of conversions; for example, if a character value is a numeral containing commas, you could convert to a numeric value using the COMMA informat:

```
POP = INPUT('5,410,000,000', COMMA13.);
```

Whether the conversion of a character value to a numeric value is explicit or implicit, it uses a numeric informat, and an error can result if the informat cannot interpret the character value — that is, if the character value is something other than a numeral. When this happens, a missing value is used, and a warning message is written on the log, and the automatic variable _ERROR_ is set to 1.

Informats do not have any trouble with a blank character value, however. Most numeric informats interpret a blank value as a missing value, although the BZ informat, for example, interprets a blank value as 0.

7 Macrolanguage

SAS macrolanguage is a language in its own right. It appears in SAS program files, but it is not part of the SAS language proper. Instead, it acts on the SAS language. It allows the use of symbols to stand for the characters that make up a program, instead of having the characters themselves appear.

Using macrolanguage adds a level of complexity to SAS programming. It makes debugging SAS statements more difficult, because a statement might not appear literally in the program file. It also introduces the possibility of macrolanguage bugs, which tend to be much more troublesome than SAS language bugs.

Yet macrolanguage has its uses. It makes it possible to write a whole category of similar programs, in effect, at the same time. It allows programs to be adjusted in various ways to run in different situations. Sometimes macros can be more self-documenting than the SAS code they represent. Macrolanguage can also be used to implement a simple user or operator interface.

In addition, it is possible to do certain kinds of programming that involve macro objects. You can write a program that modifies itself, or you can use macrolanguage objects as data objects in a SAS program.

Macrolanguage objects

The simplest macrolanguage object is the macrovariable. It is simply characters that are identified by name. Macroexpressions are roughly similar to SAS character expressions; they can include macrovariables, constant text, macro functions, and macro operators. There are macro statements, which act on macrolanguage objects in various ways. Finally, the macro is a stored macrolanguage object that can be very simple or very complex.

Macrovariables

A macrovariable is a little like a SAS character variable. It is a string of characters associated with a name. Unlike a SAS character variable, though, macrovariables can change in length and are not limited to a maximum length of 200.

The %LET statement is the standard way to assign a value to a macrovariable. The form of the statement is

```
%LET macrovariable = macroexpression;
```

In simple cases, the macroexpression is constant text, that is, simply characters. For example, this statement assigns the macrovariable IS the value `IIIII`:

```
%LET IS = IIIII ;
```

The characters assigned to a macrovariable in a %LET statement ordinarily cannot include a semicolon, because the semicolon marks the end of the macro statement.

After a macrovariable is defined, it can be used by putting an ampersand (&) followed by the macrovariable name in the SAS program. The macrovariable name can optionally be followed by a period to separate it from any following characters. So, for example, the statement

```
PROC SORT DATA=&IS;
```

or

```
PROC SORT DATA=&IS.;
```

is equivalent to having

```
PROC SORT DATA=IIIII;
```

The use of a period after a macrovariable name is necessary when the name might be followed by a letter, digit, or underscore. Otherwise, those characters would be considered part of the macrovariable name. For example, `&IS.3` would be

```
IIIII3
```

but `&IS3` would be the value of the macrovariable IS3, whatever that might be.

Several automatic macrovariables are created by the macro processor. Their names tend to begin with the letters SYS. Some of the more useful ones are listed in this table:

Macrovariable Reference	Description
`&SYSVER`	SAS release number
`&SYSSCP`	Operating system
`&SYSENV`	FORE if display manager is active; BACK otherwise

`&SYSDATE`
`&SYSDAY`
`&SYSTIME`
	Date, day of week, and time
	when the program or session started running

`&SYSPARM`	The string specified in the SYSPARM= system option; same as the SYSPARM function
`&SYSMSG`	Message to be displayed in window; the same as _MSG_ in data step
`&SYSCMD`	Unrecognized command line from window; the same as _CMD_ in data step
`&SYSLAST`	2-level name of the _LAST_ SAS dataset
`%SUBSTR(&SYSDSN, 1, 8)`	Libref of the _LAST_ SAS dataset
`%SUBSTR(&SYSDSN, 9, 8)`	Member name of the _LAST_ SAS dataset

Macroexpressions

The simplest kind of macroexpression is constant text. In any macro object or in a SAS program, any characters that are not macro keywords, macro operators, or names of macro objects are constant text. Any consecutive string of constant text characters (which might extend over several lines) is a single constant text object.

Macrolanguage objects are designed to be concatenated. Concatenating macrovariables with constant text, as shown above, is the most familiar example of this, but other macrolanguage objects concatenate in the same way.

Macro functions act on macroexpressions in various ways. A macro function call has the form

`%`*function* (*arguments*)

The %UPCASE, %SUBSTR, %SCAN, %LEFT, %INDEX, %TRIM, and %VERIFY functions have the same effects as the corresponding SAS functions. The %LENGTH function returns the length of its argument.

The %EVAL function evaluates expressions involving macro operators. It is needed when using macro operators outside of macro statements, or in the places in macro statements where a macroexpression is not expected.

There are many macro quoting functions, each differing only slightly from the others. Each macro quoting function disables the effects of certain special characters in certain situations. The commonly used macro quoting function is %STR, which can be used in the %LET statement to assign values to macrovariables that contain semicolons or other special characters. For example, this statement assigns the characters PROC PRINT; to the macrovariable PROCESS:

```
%LET PROCESS = PROC PRINT%STR(;);
```

The statement could also be written this way:

```
%LET PROCESS = %STR(PROC PRINT;);
```

In arguments to the %STR function, an unmatched parenthesis or quote mark must be preceded by a percent sign (%). A percent sign that precedes a parenthesis or quote mark must be written as two percent signs (%%).

Another quoting function, %NRSTR, is almost the same as %STR, but also removes the special meaning from the % and & characters. Any macro function with a Q in its name is also a quoting function. The macro quoting functions are all very specialized and differ from each other only slightly, which accounts for the large number of them. The distinctions between them can be critical in complicated macro definitions, though. There is also an %UNQUOTE function that undoes the effect of macro quoting.

All of the SAS arithmetic, comparison, and logical operators can be used as macro operators. In the macrolanguage context, however, the arithmetic operators do only integer arithmetic. The comparison operators can be used with integer operands, resulting in a numeric comparison, but if either operand is not an integer, the expressions are compared as character strings. The %EVAL function is needed to evaluate expressions using the macro operators when they do not appear in macro statements.

Routines used with macrolanguage objects

Two routines can be used in the data step to process macrovariables.

SYMPUT is a CALL routine that assigns a value to a macrovariable. Its first argument is the name of the macrovariable. The second argument is the value to be assigned to the macrovariable. For example, this step

```
DATA _NULL_;
  CALL SYMPUT('WHERE', 'HERE');
```

assigns the value HERE to the macrovariable WHERE, much the same as

```
%LET WHERE = HERE;
```

Any character expression can be used for either argument. The LEFT and TRIM functions are often useful with expressions or variables used as the second argument of SYMPUT to remove leading and trailing blanks. In this example, the TRIM and LEFT functions result in A being given a two-character value, rather than seven characters, including five leading blanks:

```
A = 11;
CALL SYMPUT('SIDE', TRIM(LEFT(PUT(A, 7.))));
```

The SYMGET function does the opposite, returning the value of a macrovariable. For example, this statement assigns the value of the macrovariable SIDE to the character variable S:

```
S = SYMGET('SIDE');
```

If the length of a macrovariable is more than 200, the SYMGET function returns only the first 200 characters.

Macro statements

Macro statements are used mainly in macro definitions. However, there are a few macro statements that can appear outside macros. Every macro statement begins with a percent sign and a keyword and ends in a semicolon.

The %LET statement, described above, assigns a value to a macrovariable. The %PUT statement writes a one-line macroexpression to the log. For example:

```
%LET B = BETA;
%PUT THE VALUE OF B IS &B..;
```

```
THE VALUE OF B IS BETA.
```

The %SYSEXEC statement executes an operating system command, much the same as the X statement or SYSTEM CALL routine.

Macros

A macro is a stored macrolanguage object that is referred to by name. It is defined by the %MACRO and %MEND statements, using the form

```
%MACRO name;
macroexpression
%MEND;
```

For example, these lines define the macro PRINTL, which consists only of constant text:

```
%MACRO PRINTL;
OPTIONS NOCENTER;
  PROC PRINT DATA=_LAST_;
RUN;
%MEND;
```

After a macro is defined, it is invoked by its name after a percent sign:

```
%PRINTL
```

This is similar to the form that is used for macro functions and macro keywords, so a name chosen for a macro should not be the same as the name of a macro function or macro keyword.

The use of a macro containing constant text is essentially equivalent to the use of a macrovariable. We could just as well have defined a macrovariable

```
%LET PRINT_L = %STR(
OPTIONS NOCENTER;
  PROC PRINT DATA=_LAST_;
RUN;                    );
```

and used it instead:

```
&PRINT_L
```

The difference is that a macrovariable is kept in the macro processor's table of macrovariables in memory, while a macro is stored in a file.

Macros can have parameters, which appear in parentheses after the macro name. The form of the %MACRO statement then changes to

```
%MACRO name(parameter list);
```

and the macro invocation changes to

```
%name(parameter list);
```

The parameters are simply values for macrovariables that are used inside the macro.

There are two kinds of macro parameters: positional parameters and keyword parameters. Positional parameters appear in a fixed position in the parameter list. Keyword parameters follow the last positional parameter. A keyword parameter is written as the macrovariable name followed by an equals sign and a value.

In the %MACRO statement, the names of the parameters are given, and default values for keyword parameters can be given. In the macro invocation, values for the parameters are given. The value for a keyword parameter is preceded by the parameter name and an equals sign. Parameters do not have to appear in a macro invocation; ones omitted are given default values. The default value of a positional parameter is a *null value,* a constant text value of length 0.

This is an example of a macro with parameters:

```
%MACRO DOPROC(PROC, DATA=_DATA_, OUT=, OPTIONS=, BY=, CLASS=,
              VAR=, STMTS=, TIMES=1, TITLE1="", TITLE2=);
TITLE1 &TITLE1;
TITLE2 &TITLE2;
%DO I = 1 %TO &TIMES;
  PROC &PROC DATA=&DATA
      %IF &OUT NE  %THEN %DO; OUT=&OUT %END;
      &OPTIONS;
    %IF &BY NE  %THEN BY &BY;;
    %IF &CLASS NE  %THEN %STR(CLASS &CLASS;);
    %IF &VAR NE  %THEN VAR &VAR;
    &STMTS;
%END;
RUN;
%MEND;
```

The macro DOPROC has one positional parameter, PROC. It is a positional parameter because it appears at the beginning of the parameter list and is not followed by an equals sign. The rest of the parameters are keyword parameters. Three of the keyword parameters are assigned default values: DATA, TIMES, and TITLE1.

If the macro were invoked this way

```
%DOPROC(SORT, DATA=PRIOR, OUT=PRIOR, BY=DESCENDING INTEREST)
```

then the parameter PROC would have the value SORT, the parameters DATA and OUT would have the value PRIOR, the parameter BY would have the value DESCENDING INTEREST, the parameters DATA, TIMES, and TITLE1 would have their default values, and the rest of the parameters would have null values. This invocation

```
%DOPROC(PRINT, OPTIONS=UNIFORM)
```

would give PROC the value PRINT and OPTIONS the value UNIFORM. The rest of the parameters would have default or null values.

The DOPROC macro also demonstrates the use of some of the macro statements that are used inside macros. There are control flow statements %DO, %END, %IF . . . %THEN, %ELSE, and %GOTO that correspond to the SAS control flow statements DO, END, IF . . . THEN, ELSE, and GOTO. There is also a macro comment statement %* that corresponds to the SAS comment statement.

Autocall macros

An *autocall* macro is one that is defined separately from the program that invokes it. The MAUTOSOURCE system option is required to use the autocall feature. The SASAUTOS= system option identifies the autocall libraries that are used in a particular program or session. Several autocall macros are supplied with the SAS System.

The macro processor

A macro object can appear anywhere in a SAS program, even in the middle of a token. When the SAS interpreter encounters something that looks like a macro object — specifically, a word preceded by a percent sign or an ampersand — it calls the macro processor to handle the object.

> It is possible to define a macro so that it can have a statement-style invocation. This is set in the %MACRO statement by the STMT option. The IMPLMAC system option must be in effect for statement-style macro invocations to be used. The macro invocation can then look like a SAS statement, with the macro name (no %) followed by the parameter list, separated by blanks instead of commas, and ending in a semicolon. For example:
>
> ```
> DOPROC PRINT OPTIONS=UNIFORM;
> ```
>
> With the IMPLMAC system option in effect, the SAS interpreter has to call the macro processor to check every SAS statement. This can slow down the SAS interpreter noticeably.

Scanning

The actions of the macro processor depend on the type of object. If the object is a macrovariable, a macro function, or a macro, it *scans* the object, substituting the constant text resulting from the object for the object in the program. Then it *rescans* the resulting constant text, in case it contains any macrolanguage objects. Rescanning repeats until no macrolanguage objects remain.

If the object is a macro statement, it executes the statement. If the object is a %MACRO statement, it begins to compile the macro: it translates the constant text, macrovariables, and macro statements into a token stream, which it stores in a file. Macro compilation stops when the %MEND statement is reached.

> A macro is not compiled in the sense that programmers mean when they talk about compiling a computer program. It is *not* turned into a machine language file. It's actually *parsed* — broken up into its meaningful components. If SAS statements are produced by the macro when it is executed, those statements are interpreted in the normal way by the SAS interpreter.

The macro processor scans macrolanguage objects in quoted strings if they are enclosed in double quotes, but not if they are enclosed in single quotes.

Scanning results in warning or error messages when the macro processor cannot identify a macro object. Error conditions also commonly result from unbalanced quotes, unbalanced parentheses in macro functions, and the use of the ampersand (&) as the AND operator. Subtle errors can result if macro objects have unintended leading or trailing blanks; it is often necessary to use the LEFT and TRIM functions on a SYMPUT argument.

Rescanning for macrovariable subscripts

If the macro processor encounters two consecutive ampersands (&&), it changes them to a single ampersand (&). This can be used to create an effect similar to subscripts in macrovariables.

For example, after the macrovariables I and FILE5 are given these values

```
%LET I = 5;
%LET FILE5 = LPT1;
```

this macrovariable reference

```
&&FILE&I
```

is interpreted as `LPT1`. On the first scan, the `&&` is changed to `&`, and `5`, the value of I, is substituted for `&I.`, resulting in

```
&FILE5
```

The value of FILE5 is then substituted to get `LPT1`.

Macro execution

When a macro is invoked, the process of turning it into constant text is called *macro execution*. First, values are assigned to the macro's parameters based on the values in the parameter list in the macro invocation. Then the macro is scanned and rescanned to interpret the macrolanguage objects in it.

The macro control flow statements, such as %DO and %GOTO, affect the flow of scanning. They can keep some parts of a macro from being scanned at all, cause other parts to be scanned several times, and change the order of scanning. They can also cause macro execution to fail completely if they are used incorrectly.

This invocation of the DOPROC macro defined above

```
%DOPROC(SORT, DATA=PRIOR, OUT=PRIOR, BY=DESCENDING INTEREST)
```

would resolve all the macrolanguage objects in the first scan, resulting in these SAS statements:

```
TITLE1 "";
TITLE2 ;
PROC SORT DATA=PRIOR OUT=PRIOR ;
BY DESCENDING INTEREST;
;
;
RUN;
```

System options used with macrolanguage

Several system options affect the use of macrolanguage. The MACRO configuration option makes the macro processor available. The MPRINT, SYMBOLGEN, and MLOGIC options affect the notes written in the log about macrolanguage objects. The MERROR and SERROR options determine how unrecognized macro objects are treated. System options are described in chapter 2, "The facts."

Step boundaries and the macro processor

The SAS supervisor alternately interprets and executes steps in a SAS program. If a step changes the value of macrolanguage objects that are part of the code of the step that follows, it might be necessary to put a RUN statement between the steps so that the macro processor does not attempt to resolve the macrolanguage objects before they are given the correct values. Because a step is interpreted before it executes, a step cannot change any macrolanguage object values that are part of its own code.

The log and debugging

An important feature of the SAS log is its ability to point to syntax errors in SAS programs. However, this feature has serious limitations when macrolanguage is used. The log can report that an error occurred inside a particular macrolanguage object, but cannot point to the place in the program that actually caused the error.

The log can, at least, report the tokens that are produced by macrolanguage objects, if the system options MPRINT and SYMBOLGEN are used. Those tokens, though, are not as readable as a program written by a SAS programmer. Tokens produced by macrovariables are reported separately, on a separate line. Macros are even worse: the reconstituted program statements of a macro look little like the source code that defined the macro.

To the extent possible, it is best to do debugging before putting in macrolanguage features. In some cases, you can simply comment out macro statements to run a program without macros:

```
*%MACRO PROGRAM;
   program lines
*%MEND;
*%PROGRAM;
```

Macrolanguage can be a shortcut in the sense that it can reduce the number of keystrokes involved in typing a program. This is a good feature for programs being written and run in an improvisational style, or perhaps when programs are dictated over the telephone. It is not much help in serious programming, though, because typing source code is usually a very small part of the process.

The use of macrolanguage tends to slow down the debugging process. This is especially true when macros call macros or when macro control flow statements are used. In general, the use of macrolanguage can save programming time only when a program is initially coded with no errors at all.

Macrolanguage also tends to interfere with the clarity of a program — a problem that is addressed below.

Uses for macrolanguage

Macrolanguage can be used to implement program parameters and flexcode, as described in chapter 12, or a user interface, as described in chapter 18. It can also be used for macro control flow or for compression and encryption.

Macro control flow

The use of macros allows the use of macro control flow statements, which might add to the brevity and clarity of the program or might provide some needed flexibility.

As an example, suppose you want to merge several SAS datasets, but the number of SAS datasets to merge might vary. Inside a macro, you could use a macro %DO loop like this one

```
MERGE %DO I = 1 %TO &NDAYS;
    DAY&I (KEEP=DEPT NPAGE RENAME=(NPAGE=NPAGE&I)) %END;;
```

to generate a statement like this:

```
MERGE
    DAY1 (KEEP=DEPT NPAGE RENAME=(NPAGE=NPAGE1))
    DAY2 (KEEP=DEPT NPAGE RENAME=(NPAGE=NPAGE2))
    DAY3 (KEEP=DEPT NPAGE RENAME=(NPAGE=NPAGE3))
    DAY4 (KEEP=DEPT NPAGE RENAME=(NPAGE=NPAGE4))
    ...;
```

Compression and encryption

A macro is stored in a compact form compared to the SAS statements it generates. This can sometimes result in faster execution times, particularly when the NOMPRINT, NOMLOGIC, and NOSYMBOLGEN system options are in effect. The increase in speed is usually inconsequential, but might be significant for long programs that process small numbers of observations or for programs that are run many times. Of course, the speed of a SAS program depends mainly on the amount of data being processed and the way SAS statements are used, and not on the use of macros or other preprocessing issues.

The fact that macros are more difficult to read can be an advantage if you are distributing a program that you don't want the user to read. Although you can't currently prevent an experienced SAS programmer from finding out the contents of a macro, you could at least make it difficult for the average SAS user.

Quasi-structured programming

The use of macros in a quasi-structured programming approach is one of the most loved and hated aspects of SAS programming. On the one hand, quasi-structured programming with macros allows programmers to define and name "building blocks" that they can use to assemble a SAS program. On the other hand, having to debug another programmer's quasi-structured macro programming — or even one's own underdocumented macros from a few weeks ago — is a SAS programmer's worst nightmare. In evaluating the usefulness of quasi-structured macro programming, it is important to understand the similarities and differences between it and real structured programming.

In structured programming, a program is divided into logically separate program units usually called *routines*. Each routine, ideally, has a clearly defined and described purpose and operation. Routines can call other routines. Each routine can have its own variables that are protected from being accidentally altered by any other routine. This protection of variables makes programs more reliable. The logical separateness of routines makes it possible to test and debug each routine separately.

A SAS program cannot be structured, but macrolanguage has some of the characteristics of structured programming. Macros can call each other, and each macro can have its own macrovariables, although these macrovariables are not actually protected from being altered by other macros.

There is a fundamental difference between macros in a SAS program and routines in a structured program, though: a routine can do any of the things that a computer program might do, while a macro just generates characters and tokens to be used in a SAS program. Macros are not logical

SAS program units — steps are. Because a macro might contain only part of a step or parts of two steps, it might not be possible to execute the statements produced by a macro by themselves the way a routine can be executed. If macros create whole steps, they are more similar to routines.

As a brief example of quasi-structured programming, consider these macros:

```
* SORTCOPY macro:  make a sorted copy of a SAS dataset;
%MACRO SORTCOPY(BY, DATA=, OUT=_DATA_);
  PROC SORT DATA=&DATA OUT=&OUT;
    BY &BY;
RUN;
%MEND;

*PRINTOUT macro:  print a SAS dataset;
%MACRO PRINTOUT(DATA=_LAST_, BY=, PAGEBY=, FILEREF=);
%IF &FILEREF NE  %THEN %DO; PROC PRINTTO PRINT=&FILEREF; %END;
  PROC PRINT DATA=&DATA;
    %IF &BY =  %THEN %DO; BY &BY; %END;
    %IF &PAGEBY =  %THEN %DO; PAGEBY &PAGEBY; %END;
RUN;
%MEND;
```

The %SORTCOPY macro creates a SORT proc step. The %PRINTOUT macro creates a PRINT proc step. They are combined in the following %SORTPRN macro, which is used to print a sorted copy of a SAS dataset:

```
%MACRO SORTPRN(DATA=, BY=);
%SORTCOPY(DATA=&DATA, BY=&BY)
%PRINTOUT(BY=&BY)
%MEND;
```

The person using the %SORTPRN macro does not need to know the syntax of the SORT and PRINT proc steps, just that of the %SORTPRN macro. This macro call

```
%SORTPRN(DATA=RULES, BY=DATE)
```

can be used in place of these four SAS statements:

```
  PROC SORT DATA=RULES OUT=_DATA_;
    BY DATE;
  PROC PRINT;
    BY DATE;
```

The macro call is more compact than the statements it replaces. More importantly, the person using the macro does not have to know the syntax of the two procs being used — a significant advantage to a nonprogrammer. SAS macros, in fact, were invented to make the SAS System more accessible to "power SAS software users," who are not necessarily familiar with SAS syntax.

On the other hand, the SORT and PRINT procs have numerous options that the %SORTPRN macro does not access, and the procs are thoroughly documented, while the macro is not. The macro is less readable — a SAS programmer would have to study the program to determine the meaning of the macro call, while the four statements it replaces would be clear instantly.

Readability is a paramount concern in more serious programming projects, which might seem to preclude most uses of macros. However, quasi-structured programming can be used to implement a sort of source code control system, an advantage that outweighs the readability problems for some projects.

Also, there are situations in which the use of macros can actually improve the readability of a program. Probably the best example of this is in creating ANNOTATE= datasets, which are used with SAS/GRAPH software. Each observation in an ANNOTATE= dataset represents an action to be taken in creating graphics. The actions are controlled by the values of variables such as X, Y, FUNCTION, TEXT, and COLOR. An ANNOTATE= dataset can be creating using assignment statements and output statements:

```
DATA TRIANGLE; LENGTH FUNCTION COLOR $ 8;
  X = 4; Y = 7; FUNCTION = 'MOVE'; OUTPUT;
  X = 3; Y = 7; FUNCTION = 'DRAW'; COLOR = 'RED'; OUTPUT;
  X = 3; Y = 8; FUNCTION = 'DRAW'; COLOR = 'RED'; OUTPUT;
  X = 4; Y = 7; FUNCTION = 'DRAW'; COLOR = 'RED'; OUTPUT;
```

The use of macros allows a more compact notation that gives more emphasis to the drawing process:

```
DATA TRIANGLE; LENGTH FUNCTION COLOR $ 8;
  %MOVE(4, 7)
  %DRAW(3, 7, RED)
  %DRAW(3, 8, RED)
  %DRAW(4, 7, RED)
```

In general, it makes sense to use macros when they actually simplify (and do not merely shorten) a program. Conversely, do not use them when they distract you from the underlying SAS statements that make up the program.

Demacroizing

If you have to debug or modify another programmer's weird-looking quasi-structured macro programming — or even your own — you will probably find taking the macros out to be a good way to get started. It might seem like a lot of work, but it usually isn't nearly as bad as it looks — and it will probably turn out to be more expeditious than struggling with a mysterious set of macros. (Of course, you might consider the possibility of starting fresh and writing a completely new program — sometimes that's faster.)

There can be other reasons for removing macrolanguage constructions, such as efficiency. For example, a macro %DO loop or a series of macro calls might be used to accomplish similar processing of related groups of data. However, the same effect can usually be accomplished much more efficiently and easily using BY group processing.

To take out macros, start at the beginning of the program and interpret each macrolanguage object the same way the macro processor would. You'll have to keep notes on the values of the macrolanguage objects defined by the program. The program's log, created with the MLOGIC, MPRINT, and SYMBOLGEN options in effect, can be helpful as a guide.

You can often replace macro control flow with SAS control flow statements. Macro %DO loops involving whole steps can almost always be turned into BY groups. If you end up needing a macro for macro control flow purposes, you can make it smaller; it's okay for a macro to consist of nothing more than a macro %DO loop, for example.

After you're done, compare the demacroized program against the original program to make sure they do the same things. Then you can work directly with the SAS statements and steps that make up the program.

8 Groups and sorting

Ordinarily, the order of observations in a SAS dataset does not matter, because each observation gets the same treatment in the observation loop. However, there are certain kinds of processing that depend on the order of observations.

Observations can form groups, identified by distinct values of one or more variables, called *key variables*, or collectively, the *key*. To process the groups, it helps to have all the observations in each group together.

In other cases, it is important to have the key variables in a defined order so that if there is an observation with a particular key value, it can be found easily. This is important, for example, in match merging.

Sorting

In everyday life, *sorting* usually means classifying or putting into categories. After sorting beans, for example, you might end up with a pile of red beans, a pile of white beans, and a pile of gravel and dirt.

Sorting has a different meaning in data processing. It means putting a set of objects, such as records or observations, in a particular order. There are many different sort algorithms, but they all do basically the same thing: rearrange objects until the objects are in the right order.

The sort order is determined by a rule that tells which of two objects should come first. Often only a part of the object is identified as the key for sorting: one or more key fields in a record or key variables in an observation. Most of the time, people want to sort in ascending order, that is, putting lower key values toward the beginning and higher key values toward the end. That's how the familiar process of alphabetization works, for example.

The meanings of lower and higher are the *comparison order*. Theoretically, any set of rules can be used as the comparison order, as long as they produce consistent and transitive results. In a SAS program, the comparison order in sorting is the same as for the less than comparison operator (<), which is described in chapter 6, "Expressions."

The SORT proc

SAS is distinctive among programming languages in providing a routine for sorting data files within a program. The SORT proc sorts SAS datasets using one or more variables as the sort key. The form of the SORT proc is:

```
PROC SORT DATA=SAS dataset OUT=SAS dataset   options;
  BY key variables;
```

The DATA= option names the input SAS dataset. If it is omitted, DATA=_LAST_, the most recently created SAS dataset, is used. The OUT= option names the output SAS dataset. If it is omitted, the output data from the proc replaces the input SAS dataset.

The NODUPKEY option can be used to eliminate observations with duplicate key values. If more than one observation has the same values of all the BY variables, this option discards all but one of them.

Other options are not available in all current SAS implementations.

The NODUPLICATES or NODUPS option is not the same as the NODUPKEY option. The NODUPLICATES option eliminates duplicate observations only if the values of all the variables are the same.

The EQUALS or NOEQUALS option controls the order of observations with identical key values. EQUALS keeps the order of two observations with the same key values the same as in the input SAS dataset. NOEQUALS does not necessarily maintain the order of such observations.

The FORCE option is required when the OUT= option is not used and a WHERE expression is used or the input SAS dataset is indexed. FORCE tells the SORT proc that you really intend to delete observations or indexes from the SAS dataset. If FORCE is required and is not present, the proc issues an error message and does not replace the SAS dataset.

The BY statement lists the key variables, in order of priority. Each variable is sorted in ascending order unless the variable name is preceded by the DESCENDING option in the BY statement.

The SORT proc first puts variables in order according to the first key variable. Then, any group of observations with the same value for the first key variable are put in order according to the values of the second key variable. This process continues until all the key variables are considered.

BY statement

In any step other than a SORT step, the BY statement is used to announce the already sorted order of an input SAS dataset. If the observations are not sorted in that order, SAS creates a runtime error. Thus, the BY statement can be used to verify the sort order of a SAS dataset.

The BY statement is also used to process observations in groups. That use of the BY statement is discussed below.

Other procs with sorted output

For certain kinds of analysis, sorted data can be produced without using the SORT proc. The SUMMARY proc creates descriptive statistics (such as sum, minimum, maximum, and mean) for groups of observations with the same key values without requiring the observations to be grouped by those key values. The key values are named in the CLASS statement, and SUMMARY produces an output SAS dataset with an observation for each key value found in the input data. Other procs use the CLASS statement to achieve the same effect for different kinds of analysis.

The order of the output observations produced by a proc with the CLASS statement is, by default, in increasing order of key values. Thus, it produces sorted output regardless of whether the input data is sorted.

Sorting large files is one of the most intensive tasks computers do. If you can avoid sorting, by using the SUMMARY proc, for example, you can make a program run much faster.

Sort priority code

If the order of observations you intend is something other than simple ascending or descending order of existing variables, you can create a separate variable that specifies the priority of an observation in sorting. That variable can then be used as the sort key. The sort priority code variable can be either a numeric or character variable.

In letter-by-letter alphabetization, for example, blanks and punctuation marks are ignored, and lowercase characters are considered to be equivalent to uppercase letters. A sort priority code variable can be created by extracting and capitalizing the letters from the character variable to be alphabetized.

```
DATA PHRASES;
  INFILE TEXT;
  INPUT PHRASE $CHAR80.;
  PRIORITY = UPCASE(COMPRESS(PHRASE,
                   ' ,.:;''"/?-!()[]{}$¢@#%^&*_0123456789'));
PROC SORT DATA=PHRASES;
  BY PRIORITY;
```

Sometimes items are, as a matter of habit or convention, put in a particular order that does not happen to be alphabetic or numeric. Instead of listing the provinces of Canada in alphabetical order, for example, they are often listed from west to east: British Columbia, Alberta, Saskatchewan, Manitoba, Ontario, Quebec, New Brunswick, Nova Scotia, Prince Edward Island, Newfoundland. As another example, the instruments in a drum set might be listed in a particular order, such as this one: bass drum, snare drum, high tom, mid tom, low tom, floor tom, hi-hat, ride cymbal, crash cymbal. In a case like this, it can be convenient to store these values using a code that embodies the intended sort order, such as

1 = bass drum
2 = snare drum
3 = high tom
4 = mid tom
5 = low tom
6 = floor tom
7 = hi-hat
8 = ride cymbal
9 = crash cymbal

A value format can be associated with the code variable for displaying and printing the code numbers as names. The value format for the drum set could be created with this step:

```
PROC FORMAT;
  VALUE DRUMSET (MIN=5)
      1 = 'bass drum'
      2 = 'snare drum'
      3 = 'high tom'
      4 = 'mid tom'
      5 = 'low tom'
      6 = 'floor tom'
      7 = 'hi-hat'
      8 = 'ride cymbal'
      9 = 'crash cymbal'
      ;
```

A SAS dataset DRUMS with a variable INSTR having the values 1–9, which represent instruments using this code, can be sorted by INSTR, and then printed using these steps:

```
PROC SORT DATA=DRUMS;
  BY INSTR;
PROC PRINT DATA=DRUMS;
  FORMAT INSTR DRUMSET12.;
```

Shuffling a SAS dataset

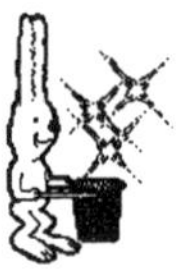

You might be able to re-sort an already sorted SAS dataset by interleaving the first half of the SAS dataset with the second half, a process we call *shuffling* because it resembles the process by which a deck of cards is reordered.

For example, if a SAS dataset HALVES is sorted by HALF and WHO, with the first 1,477 observations having one value for HALF and the rest having another value for HALF, you can make a copy of it sorted by WHO and HALF using this step:

```
DATA TOGETHER;
 SET HALVES (FIRSTOBS=1 OBS=1477)
```

```
    HALVES (FIRSTOBS=1478);
BY WHO HALF;
```

You can use the WHERE= dataset option instead (although if you know the observation numbers, the FIRSTOBS= and OBS= options are more efficient).

```
SET HALVES (WHERE=(HALF = 1))
    HALVES (WHERE=(HALF = 2));
BY WHO HALF;
```

When this shuffling technique works, it is much faster than sorting again using the SORT proc. The same process can be done for a SAS dataset with more than two groups, as long as there aren't too many (20 or 30 ought to work okay).

It's possible to use this technique even if you can't know in advance how many groups there will be or how many observations are in each group. See chapter 12, "Flexcode," for the details.

Reversing

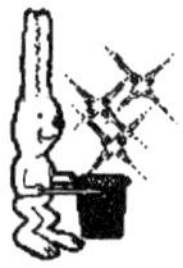

A data step can be used to reverse the order of observations in a SAS dataset. This step creates the SAS dataset CBA, which has observation in the reverse order of SAS dataset ABC:

```
DATA CBA;
  DO POINT = NOBS TO 1 BY -1;
    SET ABC POINT=POINT NOBS=NOBS;
    OUTPUT;
    END;
  STOP;
```

Tag sort

The *tag sort* is a different way to sort a file. In a tag sort, a separate file containing the key variables and indexes of the original observations is sorted, and the sorted file is then constructed using the sorted index values. If a file is too large to fit in memory all at once, and less than half of the length of the observation consists of key variables, tag sorting is usually much more efficient. It uses less memory, uses less temporary storage space, and runs much faster.

In some SAS implementations, tag sorting can be done by specifying the TAGSORT option with the SORT proc.

```
PROC SORT DATA=SAS dataset OUT=SAS dataset  TAGSORT  options;
  BY key variables;
```

Essentially the same process can be done in three SAS steps, and even if you just use the SORT proc with the TAGSORT option, studying the logic involved in the program below can help you understand the tag sorting process. The first step creates a SAS dataset that contains the sort variables from the input SAS dataset, BIG. It also has an index variable, a variable containing the observation number in BIG. The index SAS dataset, SMALL, is then sorted, and the index variable is used as the POINT= variable in a direct access SET statement to retrieve the observations of the large SAS dataset in sorted order.

```
DATA SMALL;
  SET BIG (KEEP=SORT);
  OBS = _N_;
PROC SORT DATA=SMALL;
  BY SORT;
DATA BIGSORT;
  SET SMALL (KEEP=OBS);
  SET BIG POINT=OBS;
```

Sort programs

There are many programs designed for sorting text files. Sometimes a sort program is provided as part of a computer's operating system. It is often easier to sort a text file using one of these sort programs before reading it in a SAS program, rather than transferring the data into a SAS dataset and sorting the SAS dataset using the SORT proc.

Sorting arrays

Occasionally, you might need to sort the variables in an array. For example, in a gaming simulation, you might simulate a roll of several dice and then need to know what the largest dice are. The principle in sorting an array is the same as in sorting a SAS dataset: exchange objects until they are in the right order.

Perhaps the simplest general sort algorithm is the *bubble sort*. It compares each element in the array to the next element and exchanges them if they are in the wrong order, repeating the process enough times to ensure that the elements are sorted.

In this example, the elements of the array A are sorted.

```
ARRAY A{7} A1-A7;
SIZE = DIM(A);

DO R = 1 TO SIZE - 1;
  DO I = 2 TO SIZE;
    IF A(I - 1) > A(I) THEN DO;
      SWAP = A(I - 1);
      A(I - 1) = A(I);
      A(I) = SWAP;
      END;
    END;
  END;
```

The outer loop causes the program to pass over the array 6 times — one fewer than the number of elements in the array. This is the theoretical maximum number of passes needed to put the elements in order. The inner loop examines each consecutive pair of elements in the array, exchanging them where indicated.

A similar process can be used to sort the characters in a character variable, using the SUBSTR function and the REVERSE function to swap characters.

```
SIZE = LENGTH(RIGHT(A));

DO R = 1 TO SIZE - 1;
  DO I = 1 TO SIZE - 1;
    IF SUBSTR(A, I, 1) > SUBSTR(A, I + 1, 1) THEN
        SUBSTR(A, I, 2) = REVERSE(SUBSTR(A, I, 2));
    END;
  END;
```

The bubble sort is simple, and it is efficient enough for small arrays. There are many different sort algorithms that are appropriate for different sorting situations; you can find them in books on sorting or algorithms. If you are sorting an array of several hundred elements, you might want to use an algorithm that is more efficient than the bubble sort, such as the Shell sort or quicksort.

Groups

When consecutive observations are related in some way, they can be processed as a group. The BY statement is used in SAS steps to divide a SAS dataset into groups; consecutive observations with the same values for the BY variables are in the same group. For example, the statements

```
SET PEOPLE;
BY GROUP NOTSORTED;
```

divides the observations in the SAS dataset PEOPLE into groups according to the values of the variable GROUP.

The BY statement results in an independent analysis of each group in most analytic procs. Essentially, the results are the same as if the observations in each group had been in separate SAS datasets analyzed in different steps.

The NOTSORTED option is needed at the end of the BY statement if the observations are not in sorted order by the BY variables. If it is not present, and the observations are not in sorted order, the SAS supervisor creates a runtime error.

The BY statement is used only for input from SAS datasets. It must immediately follow a SET, MERGE, or UPDATE statement and applies only to that statement. Thus, you can, for example, have a MERGE statement with a BY statement, and in the same step, have a SET statement without the BY statement.

```
DATA RNSPO;
  MERGE HALL OATES;
  BY QUARTER;
  SET SMITH;
```

In this example, the SAS dataset SMITH in the SET statement does not have to contain the variable QUARTER, even though QUARTER is a BY variable for a match merge in the same step.

The length of a character BY variable is significant. The variable's length in the data step is the length considered for matching, even if the variable has a longer length in the SAS dataset. You can use a LENGTH statement before the MERGE statement to match on the initial characters, or this can happen by accident if the the variable is longer in the second SAS dataset than in the first SAS dataset.

Formatted grouping

Certain procs optionally group observations using the formatted values of the key variables rather than the actual values. This is especially relevant when a format attribute has been associated with a numeric key variable. If the format specification `3.` is used, for example, the values 3.7 and 4.1 are both written as `4`. Thus, they would belong to the same group if observations are grouped using formatted values, even though they would normally belong to separate groups. An option on the PROC statement is usually used to specify that formatted groups are used.

With SAS release 6.06 and later releases, the same kind of grouping can be done in a data step by using the GROUPFORMAT option before the variable name in the BY statement. The GROUPFORMAT option cannot be used in a proc step.

Any sort of grouping of the values of a variable can be created by using an appropriate value format.

FIRST. and LAST. variables

The BY statement in the data step creates FIRST. and LAST. variables for each BY variable. For example, the statement

```
BY COLOR;
```

creates the variables FIRST.COLOR and LAST.COLOR.

The FIRST. variable is 1 for the first observation in the group, and 0 for all other observations. The LAST. variable is 1 for the last observation in the group, and 0 otherwise. If there are several BY variables, groups form hierarchically. When a FIRST. variable is 1, then all the later FIRST. variables are 1. For example, with the BY statement

```
BY A B;
```

when the value of A changes, both FIRST.A and FIRST.B are 1. FIRST.B is also 1 when the value of B changes.

A SAS dataset with these values

COLOR	SHAPE	SIZE
ORANGE	CIRCLE	5
ORANGE	CIRCLE	6
ORANGE	LINE	6
RED	LINE	6
RED	SQUARE	1
RED	SQUARE	5
RED	SQUARE	5
RED	SQUARE	5
YELLOW	CIRCLE	1

used with the BY statement `BY COLOR SHAPE SIZE;` would create these FIRST. and LAST. variable values:

COLOR	FIRST. COLOR	LAST. COLOR	SHAPE	FIRST. SHAPE	LAST. SHAPE	SIZE	FIRST. SIZE	LAST. SIZE
ORANGE	1	0	CIRCLE	1	0	5	1	1
ORANGE	0	0	CIRCLE	0	1	6	1	1
ORANGE	0	1	LINE	1	1	6	1	1
RED	1	0	LINE	1	1	6	1	1
RED	0	0	SQUARE	1	0	1	1	1
RED	0	0	SQUARE	0	0	5	1	0
RED	0	0	SQUARE	0	0	5	0	0
RED	0	1	SQUARE	0	1	5	0	1
YELLOW	1	1	CIRCLE	1	1	1	1	1

FIRST. and LAST. variables can be used as conditions for actions that should be done only once for each group. For example, a quantity that is calculated based on a BY variable only needs to be calculated when the BY variable changes.

In the step below the variable AREA is calculated at the beginning of each BY group — on the condition FIRST.SIZE. The RETAIN statement is needed to make the value available to subsequent observations in the BY group.

```
DATA AREAMAX;
  RETAIN AREA;
  SET MAX;
  BY COLOR SHAPE SIZE;
  IF FIRST.SIZE THEN SELECT(SHAPE);
    WHEN('SQUARE') AREA = SIZE*SIZE;
    WHEN('CIRCLE') AREA = SIZE*SIZE*3.14159265*.25;
    WHEN('LINE')   AREA = SIZE*.125;
    WHEN('OVAL')   AREA = SIZE*SIZE*(1 + 3.14159265*.25);
    OTHERWISE      AREA = 0;
    END;
```

Selecting one per group

Sometimes the objective of group processing is to select one observation from each group. You might want to list the different values of the BY variable, for example. Or you might have a rule for selecting an observation to represent the group.

Returning to the previous example, you could create a SAS dataset containing all the values of the variable COLOR using this step:

```
DATA PALETTE (KEEP=COLOR);
  SET MAX;
  BY COLOR;
  IF FIRST.COLOR;
```

To find the youngest person in each group, you could sort by GROUP and AGE, and then take the first observation in each group:

```
BY GROUP AGE;
IF FIRST.GROUP;
```

Alternatively, if you sorted by GROUP and BIRTHDAT, you would want the last observation in each group:

```
BY GROUP BIRTHDAT;
IF LAST.GROUP;
```

Descriptive statistics

You might want to calculate descriptive statistics for groups. There are several descriptive statistics procs that can do this, or you can program it in any data step that does grouped processing.

The sum statement is useful for this. You set counter and accumulator variables to 0 at the beginning of the group, add in the appropriate amounts for each observation, and then do something with the results at the end of the group.

To count the number of observations in a group, use these statements:

```
IF FIRST.GROUP THEN COUNT = 0;
COUNT + 1;
```

If you want to count observations that have a certain characteristic, you can add a Boolean expression in the sum statement:

```
IF FIRST.GROUP THEN NEGS = 0;
NEGS + NET < 0;
```

These statements count the number of observations in each group that have a value of NET that is negative or missing.

To calculate totals for certain variables in each group, add those variables to an accumulator variable in a sum statement.

```
IF FIRST.GROUP THEN GPOINTS = 0;
GPOINTS + POINTS;
```

To count the number of groups, use a sum statement with a FIRST. variable:

```
GROUPS + FIRST.GROUP;   /* or IF FIRST.GROUP THEN GROUPS + 1; */
```

At the end of the group, you could put the group totals in a report or an output SAS dataset. The example below calculates all the statistics mentioned above, writes them in the log, and puts them in a SAS dataset. It also computes mean values.

```
DATA GROUPS (KEEP=GROUP GPOINTS GSIZE GAV NEGS RFREQ);
  SET EVERYONE END=LAST NOBS=NOBS;
  BY GROUP NOTSORTED;
  IF FIRST.GROUP THEN DO;
    GROUPS + 1;
    GPOINTS = 0;
    GSIZE = 0;
    NEGS = 0;
    END;
  GPOINTS + POINTS;
  GSIZE + 1;
  NEGS + NET < 0;
  IF LAST.GROUP THEN DO;
    RFREQ = GSIZE/NOBS;
    GAV = GPOINTS/GSIZE;
    PERCENT = NEGS/GSIZE*100;
    OUTPUT GROUPS;
    FILE LOG;
    PUT 'Group #' GROUPS 3. +2 GROUP '  SIZE=' GSIZE +3 RFREQ 4.3
        / 'Points=' GPOINTS '  Average Points=' GAV
        / 'Number With Negative Net=' NEGS +2 PERCENT 5.1 '%' /;
    IF LAST THEN DO;
      PUT 'Total Number Of Groups=' GROUPS;
      END;
    END;
```

Reshaping

Reshaping means changing the shape of a SAS dataset without changing the data. There are two ways this can happen: by reducing the number of observations and increasing the number of variables, thus changing a group to an observation; or the reverse, increasing the number of observations and decreasing the number of variables, changing an observation to a group.

In changing an observation to a group, several variables in the observation become one variable in the group. You might also want a variable to identify which variable a value belonged to originally. Several

OUTPUT statements are needed to create several output observations for each input observation.

```
DATA TALL (KEEP=NAME AGE MONTH);
  SET WIDE (KEEP=NAME AGE1 AGE2 AGE3 AGE4 AGE5 AGE6
               AGE7 AGE8 AGE9 AGE10 AGE11 AGE12);
  MONTH = 1;  AGE = AGE1;  OUTPUT;
  MONTH = 2;  AGE = AGE2;  OUTPUT;
  MONTH = 3;  AGE = AGE3;  OUTPUT;
  MONTH = 4;  AGE = AGE4;  OUTPUT;
  MONTH = 5;  AGE = AGE5;  OUTPUT;
  MONTH = 6;  AGE = AGE6;  OUTPUT;
  MONTH = 7;  AGE = AGE7;  OUTPUT;
  MONTH = 8;  AGE = AGE8;  OUTPUT;
  MONTH = 9;  AGE = AGE9;  OUTPUT;
  MONTH = 10; AGE = AGE10; OUTPUT;
  MONTH = 11; AGE = AGE11; OUTPUT;
  MONTH = 12; AGE = AGE12; OUTPUT;
```

The process can be simplified by the use of an array and a loop:

```
DATA TALL (KEEP=NAME AGE MONTH);
  ARRAY AGEX{12} AGE1-AGE12;
  SET WIDE (KEEP=NAME AGE1 AGE2 AGE3 AGE4 AGE5 AGE6
               AGE7 AGE8 AGE9 AGE10 AGE11 AGE12);
  DO MONTH = 1 TO 12;
    AGE = AGEX{MONTH};
    OUTPUT;
    END;
```

Changing a group to an observation is the reverse process. An OUTPUT statement should be executed only at the end of the group in order to create one output observation for each input group.

```
DATA WIDE (KEEP=NAME AGE1 AGE2 AGE3 AGE4 AGE5 AGE6
             AGE7 AGE8 AGE9 AGE10 AGE11 AGE12);
  ARRAY AGEX{12} AGE1-AGE12;
  RETAIN AGE1-AGE12;
  SET TALL (KEEP=NAME AGE MONTH);
  BY NAME NOTSORTED;
  IF 1 <= MONTH <= 12 THEN AGEX{MONTH} = AGE;
  IF LAST.NAME THEN OUTPUT;
```

The TRANSPOSE proc can also be used to do this kind of reshaping.

Identification codes

When each group should have only one observation, then the value of the group variable can be called an identification code.

One reason to be concerned with identification codes is to ensure that there is, in fact, only one observation for each identification code. If the identification code variable is ID, the uniqueness of an observation is given by the expression

```
FIRST.ID AND LAST.ID
```

To be the only observation in a group, an observation must be the first and last observation in the group.

If you want to eliminate duplicate observations, without concern for which observation in each group you keep, you can use a subsetting IF statement with a FIRST. or LAST. variable:

```
IF FIRST.ID;
```

or

```
IF LAST.ID;
```

If you simply want to note or investigate the presence of the duplicate observations, you could put the values in the log.

```
IF NOT (FIRST.ID AND LAST.ID) THEN PUT _ALL_;
```

You might have a criterion for selecting an observation from among duplicates. For example, you might want the observation with the most recent (highest) ADD_DATE value in each group. In this case, you would sort the observations by the ID variable and the ADD_DATE variable, and then subset:

```
PROC SORT DATA=DUPS;
  BY ID ADD_DATE;

DATA NODUPS;
  SET DUPS;
  BY ID ADD_DATE;
  IF LAST.ID;
```

In some cases, you might want to keep track of the number of duplicate records you're discarding. You can count the number of observations in each group, and then output the last observation in the group:

```
DATA CLEAN;
  SET EXTRA;
  BY NAME;
  IF FIRST.NAME THEN TIMES = 0;
  TIMES + 1;
  IF LAST.NAME THEN OUTPUT;
```

Duplicate records

You can't have a BY statement with an INPUT statement, so you can't use FIRST. and LAST. variables to check for duplicate records in a sorted or grouped input text file. Instead, you can maintain a variable containing the most recent value of the group variable.

These statements select observations in which either of the variables ID and MONTH has a different value from the previous observation:

```
LENGTH LASTID $ 11 LASTMON $ 1;
RETAIN LASTID LASTMON;
INPUT @1 ID $CHAR11. @12 MONTH $HEX2. @14 HOURS 4.;
IF NOT (ID = LASTID AND MONTH = LASTMON);
LASTID = ID;
LASTMON = MONTH;
```

You could test whether an entire record is the same as the preceding record by assigning the entire record to a variable, and comparing it to the value of the preceding record:

```
LENGTH LASTREC $ 40;
RETAIN LASTREC;
INPUT @1 RECORD $CHAR40. @;
IF RECORD NE LASTREC;
LASTREC = RECORD;
INPUT (read variables from input record);
```

To count the longest string of duplicate records in an input text file, and the longest consecutive run of different records, you could use statements like these:

```
DATA _NULL_;
  LENGTH LASTREC $ 40 MAXREP NOREPMAX;
  RETAIN LASTREC MAXREP NOREPMAX;
  INFILE SOMEREPS END=LAST;
  INPUT RECORD $CHAR40.;
  IF RECORD = LASTREC THEN DO;
    REP + 1;
    MAXREP = REP MAX MAXREP;
    NOREP = 0;
    END;
  ELSE DO;
    NOREP + 1;
    NOREPMAX = NOREP MAX NOREPMAX;
    NREPS = 0;
    LASTREC = RECORD;
    END;
 IF LAST THEN PUT
    'MOST DUPLICATES OF A RECORD IS: ' MAXREP /
    'MOST CONSECUTIVE RECORDS WITHOUT A DUPLICATE IS: ' NOREPMAX;
```

If you simply want to copy a text file, removing (consecutive) duplicate records, you can use the overwriting capabilities of the PUT statement, using statements like these:

```
LENGTH LASTKEY $ 16; RETAIN LASTKEY;
INPUT KEY $CHAR16.;
IF _N_ > 1 AND LASTKEY NE KEY THEN PUT;
PUT @1 _INFILE_ @;
LASTKEY = KEY;
```

Related variables

Another way an identification code can appear is as a variable related to a key variable. Even though the identification variable is not itself a key variable, it has only one value in each group. This is the kind of variable that is ordinarily listed in the ID statement in some procs.

In a situation where an ID variable is missing or incorrect in some observations in a group, you can give the variable correct values in a two-step process. In the first step, determine the correct ID value for each group. In the second step, change all the ID values to the correct value for each group.

Suppose, for example, that observations in the SAS dataset BLDG are grouped by CAMPUS, and each value of CAMPUS should be associated with a value for ZIP. The first nonblank ZIP value for each group could be found in this step:

```
DATA BZIP (KEEP=CAMPUS BZIP);
  RETAIN BZIP '     ';
  SET BLDG (KEEP=CAMPUS ZIP);
  BY CAMPUS NOTSORTED;
  IF FIRST.CAMPUS THEN BZIP = '';
  IF BZIP = '' AND ZIP NE '' THEN BZIP = ZIP;
  IF LAST.CAMPUS THEN OUTPUT;
```

and then applied to all the observations in the group in this step:

```
DATA BLDG;
  MERGE BLDG (DROP=ZIP) BZIP (RENAME=(BZIP=ZIP));
  BY CAMPUS NOTSORTED;
```

Matching

When two SAS datasets have identification variables, then a matching process is possible, in which an observation is found in the second SAS dataset with the same identification code value as the observation in the first SAS dataset.

Matching occurs most often in match merging. It also happens in table lookup. Matching is particularly important in database applications.

Match merging

Match merging is done with the MERGE statement and the BY statement. The MERGE statement names two or more SAS datasets to be merged. The BY statement names the variables that identify the observations — the variables to be matched. The SAS datasets have to be sorted by the BY variables. Match merging is described in chapter 5, "I/O."

Eliminating duplicate observations in the match merging process is as easy as it is with a single SAS dataset, if you just want to take the first observation in each group:

```
MERGE A B;
BY ID;
IF FIRST.ID;
```

It is often a good idea to keep track of the number of duplicates and nonmatches in the match merging process. That can be done using statements like these:

```
MERGE A (IN=INA) B (IN=INB) END=END;
BY ID;
IF FIRST.ID THEN OUTPUT;

NA + INA;
NB + INB;
IF FIRST.ID THEN DO;
  MISSA + NOT INA;
  MISSB + NOT INB;
  MATCH + INA AND INB;
  END;
ELSE DO;
  DUPA + INA;
  DUPB + INB;
  END;
FILE LOG;
IF END THEN PUT //
    NA 'observations in SAS dataset A'
    / NB 'observations in SAS dataset B'
    / MATCH 'observations matched in A and B'
    / MISSA 'observations in B not matched against A'
    / MISSB 'observations in A not matched against B'
    / DUPA 'extra observations in A'
    / DUPB 'extra observations in B'
    ;
```

Table lookup

Table lookup, sometimes known simply as lookup, involves finding the value of a lookup variable in the row or observation in which a key variable has a certain value. Match merging is the most widely known way to do table lookup in a SAS program, but there are other ways. Table lookup techniques are covered in chapter 15.

Folding a SAS dataset

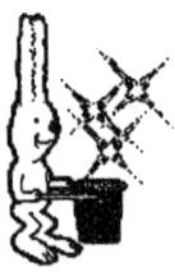

It is sometimes possible to match merge the first half of a SAS dataset with the second half, a process called *folding*. It is similar to the shuffling technique described earlier in this chapter. Because the first half and second half of a SAS dataset have the same variables, folding would mainly be done as a form of reshaping, to increase the number of variables while reducing the number of observations.

The RENAME= dataset option is used to change the variable names so that the variables from the first half of the SAS dataset do not conflict with the variables from the second half.

In this example, the SAS dataset SPEED contains "before and after" test results for several people. The variable TIME contains the value `'B'` for "before" tests, and `'A'` for "after" tests. The SAS dataset is sorted by TIME and ID, using the DESCENDING option with TIME, so that the first 2,405 observations are the results of "before" tests and the remaining observations are the results of "after" tests.

This step folds the SAS dataset so that there is one observation for each person, showing both "before" and "after" values in different variables in the same observation.

```
DATA;
  MERGE SPEED (FIRSTOBS=1 OBS=2405
         KEEP=NAME ID       DATE AGE NEWS TECH FICT COMP
         RENAME=(DATE=B_DATE AGE=B_AGE NEWS=B_NEWS
                 TECH=B_TECH FICT=B_FICT COMP=B_COMP))
      SPEED (FIRSTOBS=2406
         KEEP=NAME ID PHONE DATE AGE NEWS TECH FICT COMP
         RENAME=(DATE=A_DATE AGE=A_AGE NEWS=A_NEWS
                 TECH=A_TECH FICT=A_FICT COMP=A_COMP));
  BY ID;
```

As with shuffling, folding can also be done with a SAS dataset that has more than two major groups, and the WHERE= dataset option can be used instead of the FIRSTOBS= and OBS= dataset options.

Crossing

What do you get when you cross a SAS dataset with another SAS dataset? The process is similar to merging, in that each resulting observation combines an observation from each of the two input SAS datasets. However, in crossing, each observation from one SAS dataset is combined with each observation from the other SAS dataset, resulting in a number of output observations equal to the *product* of the numbers of observations in the two input SAS datasets. In merging, by comparison, the number of output observations is less than or equal to the *sum* of observations in the input SAS datasets.

The uses for crossing are not as prevalent as those for merging. You can imagine it being done in a dating service, where the profile of every woman in the club is put together with the profile of every man in order to find the combinations with the highest predicted compatibility.

The program below crosses the SAS dataset MEN with the SAS dataset WOMEN, calculates a "compatibility score" for each combination, and creates an output SAS dataset with the compatibility scores. The compatibility formula used in the program is unrealistically simple: it just subtracts points for each measured difference in interest, attitude, etc.

In crossing, sequential access is used for one of the input SAS datasets, in this case WOMEN, and direct access is used for the other one, in this case MEN. Which SAS dataset is accessed which way usually does not matter, but it does determine the order of the output observations.

```
DATA PAIRS (KEEP=F_NAME M_NAME CO);
  SET WOMEN (RENAME=(NAME=F_NAME AGE=F_AGE HEIGHT=F_HEIGHT
       WEIGHT=F_WEIGHT ZIP=F_ZIP WORK=F_WORK MGCT=F_MGCT
       ATD1=F_ATD1 ATD2=F_ATD2 ATD3=F_ATD3
       ATD4=F_ATD4 ATD5=F_ATD5 ATD6=F_ATD6
       INT1=F_INT1 INT2=F_INT2 INT3=F_INT3 INT4=F_INT4
       INT5=F_INT5 INT6=F_INT6 INT7=F_INT7 INT8=F_INT8));
  DO POINT = 1 TO NOBS;
    SET MEN (RENAME=(NAME=M_NAME AGE=M_AGE HEIGHT=M_HEIGHT
         WEIGHT=M_WEIGHT ZIP=M_ZIP WORK=M_WORK MGCT=M_MGCT
         ATD1=M_ATD1 ATD2=M_ATD2 ATD3=M_ATD3
         ATD4=M_ATD4 ATD5=M_ATD5 ATD6=M_ATD6
         INT1=M_INT1 INT2=M_INT2 INT3=M_INT3 INT4=M_INT4
         INT5=M_INT5 INT6=M_INT6 INT7=M_INT7 INT8=M_INT8))
        POINT=POINT NOBS=NOBS;
    CO = 100 - ABS(F_AGE - M_AGE) - ABS(F_HEIGHT - M_HEIGHT)
        - ABS(F_WEIGHT - M_WEIGHT) - ABS(F_MGCT - M_MGCT)
        - (F_ZIP NE M_ZIP)
        - (F_WORK > 0 AND M_WORK > 0 AND F_WORK NE M_WORK)
        - ABS(F_ATD1 - M_ATD1) - ABS(F_ATD2 - M_ATD2)
        - ABS(F_ATD3 - M_ATD3) - ABS(F_ATD4 - M_ATD4)
        - ABS(F_ATD5 - M_ATD5) - ABS(F_ATD6 - M_ATD6)
        - (F_INT1 NE M_INT1) - (F_INT2 NE M_INT2)
        - (F_INT3 NE M_INT3) - (F_INT4 NE M_INT4)
        - (F_INT5 NE M_INT5) - (F_INT6 NE M_INT6)
        - (F_INT7 NE M_INT7) - (F_INT8 NE M_INT8);
    OUTPUT;
    END;
```

An OUTPUT statement must be used whenever a cross produces an output SAS dataset.

Match crossing

Crossing entire SAS datasets is not done often. A more common process is match crossing, in which corresponding groups in two SAS datasets are crossed. Match crossing is the same as match merging if every BY group contains one observation in one SAS dataset and at least one in the other SAS dataset. However, when both SAS datasets contain two or more observations in a group, each observation in the group in the first SAS dataset is combined with each observation in the group in the second SAS dataset. Also, in match crossing, a group that is present in one SAS dataset but not in the other produces no observations.

Match crossing is done, for example, in accounting systems when expenses for a project are allocated to the departments that "own" the project. One SAS dataset would contain expense data for various projects, while another would list the departments' shares in each project. Match crossing would allow expense figures to be associated with departments. Expense totals by department could then be calculated.

Like match merging, match crossing requires that the input SAS datasets be sorted by the BY variables. Match crossing requires two steps. In the first step, an index dataset is created that uses one observation to represent each group in one of the input SAS datasets. The index dataset is then match merged with the other input SAS dataset, and direct access is used to read the actual observations in the indexed SAS dataset.

```
DATA INDEX (KEEP=GROUP FIRST LAST);
  RETAIN FIRST;
  SET B;
  BY GROUP;
  IF FIRST.GROUP THEN FIRST = _N_;
  IF LAST.GROUP THEN DO; LAST = _N_; OUTPUT; END;

DATA CROSSED;
  MERGE A (IN=IN1) INDEX (IN=IN2);
  BY GROUP;
  IF IN1 AND IN2;
  DO POINT = FIRST TO LAST;
    SET B POINT=POINT;
    OUTPUT;
    END;
```

It is possible to extend the crossing and match crossing processes to combine more than two SAS datasets, but it is more difficult and not often done. In crossing several SAS datasets, one of them is read sequentially, and all the rest use direct access SET statements. In match crossing, a separate index dataset would have to be created for each of the SAS datasets to be read using direct access.

Match crossing can also be done by the CREATE TABLE AS statement in the SQL proc.

Sequence numbers

Sorting and matching depend on the presence of one or more key variables with values in a certain order. Grouped processing with the BY statement also depends on the presence of a key variable whose value is different for different groups. If there is no variable or group of variables that can be used as a key, then you can create a key variable.

Suppose observations appear in the right order, even though there is no key variable. You could create a variable containing sequence numbers:

```
SEQUENCE = _N_;
```

Then when you have to change the order of observations for some reason, such as match merging, you can use the sequence numbers as the sort variable to put the observations back in their original order:

```
PROC SORT;
  BY SEQUENCE;
```

In a similar way, you can create serial numbers for groups:

```
BY GROUP NOTSORTED;
GSERIAL + FIRST.GROUP;   * or IF FIRST.GROUP THEN GSERIAL + 1;
```

Creating group numbers is especially important when there is no variable identifying which group an observation belongs to. Perhaps, instead, the first observation of each group is marked in some way. For example, there could be a variable NEWGROUP that has the value x for the first observation in each group. Then you could create group serial numbers with this statement:

```
GSERIAL + (NEWGROUP = 'X');
```

Alternatively, there might be sequence numbers within each group, starting at 1 for the first observation for the group. The statement to create group serial numbers would then look like this:

```
GSERIAL + (SEQUENCE = 1);
```

SAS dataset indexes

An index of a SAS dataset is an related file that, among other things, allows the observations in the SAS dataset to be read in sorted order even though they are not stored in sorted order. The sorted order maintained by a SAS dataset index is the increasing order of one or more variables. Indexes are a new feature of SAS release 6.06, and currently can only be applied to ordinary SAS data files.

An index can be created by either the DATASETS or SQL procs. After an index is created, most procs that change the values in the SAS dataset maintain the index by changing it to reflect the changes in key variables. However, sorting the SAS dataset or copying it using the APPEND proc or a data step removes the indexes.

An index on one variable is called a *simple index* and has the same name as the key variable. A step using the DATASETS proc to create a simple index has this form:

```
  PROC DATASETS LIBRARY=libref;
    MODIFY SAS dataset;
      INDEX CREATE variable;
QUIT;
```

A step using the SQL proc to create a simple index has this form:

```
PROC SQL;
  CREATE INDEX variable ON libref.SAS dataset (variable);
```

A *unique* index is one that allows only one observation per key value. It is appropriate, in general, when the key variable is an identification code. If you attempt to create a unique index and duplicate key values exist, an error condition results. After a unique index is created, SAS procs will not add observations to the SAS dataset that duplicate previous key values.

Create a simple unique index using this step

```
  PROC DATASETS LIBRARY=libref;
    MODIFY member;
      INDEX CREATE variable / UNIQUE;
QUIT;
```

or this one

```
  PROC SQL;
    CREATE UNIQUE INDEX variable ON SAS dataset (variable);
```

A *composite* index, one that uses two or more variables, has to be given a name that is *not* the name of a variable in the SAS dataset. The index name might be used later in describing or deleting the index.

Creating a composite index is similar to creating a simple index. If the DATASETS proc is used, the step has this form:

```
  PROC DATASETS LIBRARY=libref;
    MODIFY member;
      INDEX CREATE index=(variable variable ...);
QUIT;
```

Or using the SQL proc:

```
  PROC SQL;
    CREATE INDEX index ON SAS dataset (variable, variable, ...);
```

The UNIQUE option can be used in the same way in creating a composite index.

To use an index with a SAS dataset, use a BY statement (with no options) listing the variables (or the first variable or variables) in the index. The SAS dataset will be read in sorted order according to the index, even though the observations are not actually stored in sorted order. Reading a SAS dataset in this manner is not as fast as actually reading sequentially, but it is often faster than sorting the SAS dataset to read it, especially if the key variables of the index make up less than half the length of the observation in the SAS dataset.

Indexes are also occasionally used in reading a SAS dataset when a WHERE expression is used. Indexes can make WHERE processing much faster when a single value or a small range of values of a key variable is used. However, the rules the SAS supervisor uses in deciding when to use an index for WHERE processing are very complicated, so that it might not be possible to predict whether an index will be used in a particular step.

To remove an index, you can use the DATASETS proc:

```
  PROC DATASETS LIBRARY=libref;
    MODIFY member;
      INDEX DELETE index;
QUIT;
```

or the SQL proc:

```
  PROC SQL;
    DROP INDEX index FROM SAS dataset;
```

If a SAS dataset is deleted or is sorted in place, all its indexes are automatically deleted.

In a typical use for indexing, it can be used instead of sorting before a match merging step:

```
  PROC SQL;
    CREATE INDEX AB ON FIRST (A B);
    CREATE INDEX AB ON SECOND (A B);
  DATA _NULL_;
    MERGE FIRST SECOND;
    BY A B;
    ...
```

9 Operating on SAS datasets

SAS datasets are mainly used in the sorts of input and output processes described in chapter 5, "I/O," in which observations are used one at a time. However, there are other operations that can be done to SAS datasets and other SAS files as a whole, such as renaming and deleting. There are also operations that do not involve individual observations, such as changing variable attributes.

> The SQL proc used throughout this chapter is new with SAS release 6.06. Among other things, the SQL proc creates views and indexes, which are also new with SAS release 6.06.

Creating

SAS datasets are usually created by data steps, or as output from a proc step that either follows a standard form or is based on the form of an input SAS dataset. However, it is possible to use certain procs to define the variables in a new, empty SAS dataset.

When the SAS dataset specified for editing in the FSEDIT proc does not exist, the proc prompts the user to name and define the variables to be used in the SAS dataset.

In the SQL proc, the CREATE TABLE statement can be used to define a new table. The form of the step is:

```
PROC SQL;
  CREATE TABLE SAS dataset
      ( variable definition,
       variable definition,
       . . . ) ;
```

The variable definition for a character variable is

```
variable CHARACTER (length) INFORMAT=informat specification
    FORMAT=format specification LABEL='label'
```

The variable definition for a numeric variable is

```
variable NUMERIC INFORMAT=informat specification
    FORMAT=format specification LABEL='label'
```

The length, informat, format, and label attributes can be omitted.

A data step can be used in a similar way to create an empty SAS dataset. The data step can consist merely of a DATA statement, naming the SAS dataset, and a LENGTH statement, naming the variables and identifying them as character or numeric.

```
DATA SAS dataset;
  LENGTH list of numeric variables 8
        character variable $ length
        ...;
RUN;
```

Different lengths can be specified for variables if appropriate. INFORMAT, FORMAT, LABEL, or ATTRIB statements can be used to specify other variable attributes. The step runs and creates the SAS dataset even though there are no executable statements.

You can also create an empty SAS dataset with the same variables and variable attributes as an existing SAS dataset. This process is described below, under "Copying a header only."

Copying

Oddly, there is no single good way to copy a SAS dataset. The COPY proc is the most efficient and makes the best copies, but it cannot copy SAS datasets within the same library or change the name of a SAS dataset as it is copied. No other copying method maintains the indexes of an indexed SAS dataset.

COPY

The COPY proc can copy SAS datasets from one library to another without changing their names. The form is

```
PROC COPY IN=libref OUT=libref MTYPE=(DATA VIEW);
  SELECT SAS dataset names;
```

The `MTYPE=(DATA VIEW)` option specifies that the step copies SAS datasets, and not any of the other types of files that can be in a SAS data library. Any number of SAS datasets can be copied from the IN= SAS data library to the OUT= SAS data library. If the SELECT statement is omitted, all the SAS datasets in the IN= library are copied.

Other member types can be used with the MTYPE= option. The member type DATA identifies SAS data files; VIEW members are views; CATALOG members are catalogs; and PROGRAM members are compiled data steps. The default is `MTYPE=ALL`.

The system options OBS= and FIRSTOBS= affect the COPY proc. To copy all the observations in a SAS dataset, you should have the default values `FIRSTOBS=1` and `OBS=MAX`.

This step makes a copy of the SAS dataset WORK.COVERS called EARLY.COVERS:

```
PROC COPY IN=WORK OUT=EARLY MTYPE=DATA;
  SELECT COVERS;
```

The same process can be done, using almost the same syntax, in the DATASETS proc. The syntax is then

```
PROC DATASETS LIBRARY=WORK MTYPE=DATA;
  COPY OUT=EARLY;
    SELECT COVERS;
```

When indexed SAS datasets are copied using the COPY proc or COPY statement, the indexes are also copied. This is currently the only way to copy a SAS dataset with its indexes.

SQL

The CREATE TABLE statement in the SQL proc can be used to copy a SAS dataset. The step has this form:

```
PROC SQL;
  CREATE TABLE new SAS dataset AS SELECT * FROM original SAS dataset;
```

The new SAS dataset is a SAS data file, even if a view is being copied.

APPEND

The APPEND proc copies observations from one SAS dataset to another. If the output SAS dataset exists, APPEND copies the observations after any existing observations. If the output SAS dataset does not exist, APPEND creates a new SAS data file.

The form of the APPEND proc is

```
PROC APPEND DATA=FROM OUT=TO;
```

The DATA= option can also be specified as NEW=. The OUT= option can also be specified as BASE=.

The same process can be done using the APPEND statement in the DATASETS proc:

```
PROC DATASETS;
  APPEND DATA=FROM OUT=TO;
```

If you want to replace an existing SAS dataset, you can delete it using the DATASETS proc and then copy to it using the APPEND proc:

```
PROC DATASETS NOWARN;
  DELETE TO (MTYPE=DATA);
PROC APPEND DATA=FROM OUT=TO;
```

If you are using the APPEND proc to combine observations from two SAS datasets, the SAS datasets have to be reasonably similar. Ideally, they have all the same variables in the same order with the same types and lengths. When that is the case, APPEND works much faster. At the very least, the input SAS dataset must have at least one variable that is in the output SAS dataset, and there must not be any type conflicts. The observations from the input SAS dataset are added to the end of the output SAS dataset.

If a variable is shorter in the input SAS dataset than in the output SAS dataset, it is extended to fill the space. If a variable in the output SAS dataset is not in the input SAS dataset, that variable is given missing values in the added observations.

If a variable is longer in the input SAS dataset than in the output SAS dataset, or if any variable in the input SAS dataset is not in the output SAS dataset, the option FORCE must be used on the PROC statement to prevent a syntax error. Variables are dropped and truncated as needed.

The SORT proc

In a case where you want a copy of a SAS dataset to be sorted differently from the original, the SORT proc is the appropriate choice. The form of the SORT proc is

```
PROC SORT DATA=SAS dataset  OUT=SAS dataset ;
  BY key variables;
```

The BY statement lists the variables by which the observations are sorted. Sorting is discussed in chapter 8, "Groups And Sorting."

Copying in the data step

Using a data step to copy a SAS dataset is usually not as efficient as using a proc step, but the syntax is simple enough:

```
DATA TO;
  SET FROM;
```

A data step is more efficient than a proc step for copying if, for some reason, you need to make several copies of a SAS dataset:

```
DATA TO1 TO2 TO3 TO4;
  SET FROM;
```

Copying in the data step is also more efficient if you need to read the input SAS dataset in the step for any other reason. And it is an appropriate way to make a SAS data file out of a SAS data view, or an unindexed SAS dataset out of an indexed SAS dataset.

The main advantage of copying in the data step is its greater flexibility. You can use programming statements to select observations, recode variables, and calculate new variables. You can declare different variable attributes. You can also use dataset options to rename or select variables or to select observations.

Copying a header only

Copying the header of a SAS dataset results in a new SAS dataset with the same variables and variable attributes, but no observations. You can do it with this data step:

```
DATA TO;
  SET FROM;
  STOP;
```

The STOP statement stops the step before the first observation is written, but not before the header is created for the new SAS dataset. The new SAS dataset has all the same variables and variable attributes as the old SAS dataset.

You can make the new SAS dataset different by dropping and renaming variables (with dataset options on either the input or the output SAS dataset), adding variables, or changing variable attributes (using a LENGTH statement for character variables before the SET statement, and FORMAT, INFORMAT, and LABEL statements and a LENGTH statement for numeric variables after the SET statement).

In the SQL proc, a LIKE clause can be used to copy the header of a SAS dataset:

```
PROC SQL;
  CREATE TABLE new SAS dataset LIKE existing SAS dataset;
```

The dataset option DROP= or KEEP= can be used to create a new SAS dataset with some of the variables of an existing SAS dataset.

Operating system commands and file utilities

SAS datasets are files, and as such, they can be copied by operating system commands, such as the COPY command in several operating systems. However, doing so would invalidate any physical addressing information in the SAS dataset's header or indexes, possibly causing problems when you try to access the data.

This is a problem only for SAS dataset formats that have addressing information in the header — usually those whose engines support direct access reading. Views and compressed, transport, and sequential format SAS data files should not have a problem in being copied or moved. However, views might no longer be valid if copied to a different SAS data library.

Some file utility programs, such as disk optimizers, also move files around, which can cause the same problems if any of the files being moved are SAS data files or indexes. If you plan to use a disk optimizing program on a disk that contains SAS datasets, you should tell the program not to move the SAS datasets, store the SAS datasets in moveable formats such as compressed or transport format, or move the SAS datasets to another disk using the COPY proc before doing the disk optimizing, and then move them back using the COPY proc afterward.

Deleting

SAS datasets can be deleted using the DATASETS proc. To empty out a SAS data library, deleting all the SAS datasets and any other members, use the step

```
PROC DATASETS LIBRARY=libref  NOLIST KILL;
```

If LIBRARY= is not specified, LIBRARY=WORK is used.

To delete specific SAS datasets, use this step:

```
PROC DATASETS LIBRARY=libref  MTYPE=DATA NOWARN;
  DELETE SAS dataset names;
```

The MTYPE=DATA option limits processing to SAS data files. Other member types could be used to delete other SAS files. You might use the NOWARN option, which tells the proc not to issue a warning message if a SAS dataset to be deleted does not exist.

For example, to delete the SAS dataset WORK.OBSOLETE:

```
PROC DATASETS MTYPE=DATA NOWARN;
  DELETE OBSOLETE;
```

The SAVE statement can be used to delete all members except for those listed. If the MTYPE= option appears in the PROC DATASETS statement, only members of the listed member types are deleted by the SAVE statement. This step deletes all files from the work library except for a format catalog:

```
PROC DATASETS LIBRARY=WORK NOWARN;
  SAVE FORMATS / MTYPE=CATALOG;
```

The AGE statement in the DATASETS proc, which is described below, also deletes SAS files.

The DROP TABLE and DROP VIEW statements in the SQL proc delete one or several SAS datasets. The DROP TABLE statement deletes SAS data files; the DROP VIEW statement deletes SQL views.

```
PROC SQL;
  DROP TABLE SAS data file;
  DROP TABLE SAS data file, SAS data file, ...;
  DROP VIEW SQL view;
  DROP VIEW SQL view, SQL view, ...;
```

Most engines store SAS datasets as separate physical files, which can be deleted using operating system commands. However, you should avoid doing this during the execution of a SAS program that uses that SAS data library. Also, if indexed SAS datasets are deleted, the files containing the indexes should also be deleted.

Deleting SAS datasets, however it is done, can invalidate any SAS data views that refer to the deleted SAS datasets.

> Exercise caution when you delete files. Be certain that you are not deleting the wrong files or deleting files at the wrong time. Deleted files cannot normally be recovered.

Renaming

SAS datasets and other SAS files can be renamed in the DATASETS proc, using the CHANGE, EXCHANGE, and AGE statements.

The CHANGE statement does for SAS files what the RENAME statement does for variables: an old name is associated with a new name. This step renames the SAS dataset WORK.PLACE as WORK.SPACE:

```
  PROC DATASETS LIBRARY=WORK MTYPE=(DATA VIEW);
    CHANGE PLACE=SPACE;
QUIT;
```

The option `MTYPE=(DATA VIEW)` restricts processing to SAS datasets.

The EXCHANGE statement exchanges the names of two SAS files. This step renames the SAS data file WORK.PLACE as WORK.SPACE while also renaming WORK.SPACE as WORK.PLACE:

```
  PROC DATASETS LIBRARY=WORK;
    EXCHANGE PLACE=SPACE / MTYPE=DATA;
QUIT;
```

The AGE statement renames a list of files and deletes the last one in the list. Each file in the list is given the name of the next file in the list. For example, in this step

```
  PROC DATASETS LIBRARY=WORK;
    AGE NEXTYEAR THISYEAR LASTYEAR YEARB4 / MTYPE=DATA;
QUIT;
```

the SAS dataset NEXTYEAR is renamed THISYEAR, while THISYEAR is renamed LASTYEAR and LASTYEAR is renamed YEARB4. YEARB4, if it exists, is deleted.

Describing

The CONTENTS proc describes the contents of SAS datasets. The usual form of the step is

```
  PROC CONTENTS DATA=SAS dataset;
```

The CONTENTS statement in the DATASETS proc is equivalent to the `PROC CONTENTS` statement.

The CONTENTS proc produces print output showing the essential information from the header of the SAS dataset; the exact information varies by implementation. It includes a table showing the variables in the SAS dataset and all their attributes. The variables are usually shown in order by name, but the POSITION option can be used to print them in position order. The SHORT option can be used to print only the variable names and no other attributes.

The OUT= option can be used to create a SAS dataset containing most of the same information that the CONTENTS proc prints. The output SAS dataset contains one observation for each variable in the input SAS dataset.

For a SAS file other than a SAS dataset, the CONTENTS proc identifies the member type of the file.

In a display manager session, the variables and variable attributes of a SAS dataset can be browsed in the VAR window.

A SAS dataset can have a dataset label or dataset type. The dataset label, like a variable label, is a descriptive character string up to 40 characters long. The dataset type is a SAS name that certain procs check to determine whether a SAS dataset has a particular meaning — for example, `TYPE=CORR` identifies a SAS dataset as a certain kind of correlation matrix. Usually, only certain procs create SAS datasets with dataset types. The dataset label and dataset type can be specified using dataset options when a

SAS dataset is created or read. For an existing SAS dataset, the dataset label or dataset type can be changed in the MODIFY statement, with this form:

```
PROC DATASETS LIBRARY=libref;
  MODIFY SAS dataset (TYPE=type LABEL='label');
```

Variables

The names and other attributes of variables in a SAS dataset can be changed in the DATASETS proc. The step has this form:

```
PROC DATASETS LIBRARY=libref;
  MODIFY SAS dataset;
    INFORMAT variable ... informat specification ...;
    FORMAT variable ... format specification ...;
    LABEL variable='label' ...;
    RENAME old name=new name ...;
```

The INFORMAT, FORMAT, LABEL, and RENAME statements have essentially the same syntax as in the data step.

In a display manager session, variable attributes can be changed using the R (rename) line command in the VAR window.

SQL table operations

So far, the SQL proc has been used to do things like creating and deleting SAS datasets. These are just incidental abilities of the proc, though. The SQL proc implements an entire programming language — SQL, or Structured Query Language — that treats SAS datasets in a very different way from data steps and most procs. A complete discussion of SQL would be a book of its own; however, we present the essential features here.

In SQL, a SAS dataset is a table, a variable is a column, and an observation is a row. A table is mainly treated as being made up of columns. This is reversed from the usual view of a SAS dataset, which is treated by data steps and procs as being made up mainly of observations, with the variables being part of each observation.

The SQL language is designed to create, modify, combine, summarize, and retrieve data from tables, using the relational database model. It can do essentially the same things as the PRINT, SUMMARY, and SORT procs, and processing like match merging, subsetting, and calculated variables, but the SQL statements look very different from the corresponding SAS statements. For one thing, every SQL statement stands alone, creating output of one form or another without reference to other statements. In that sense, an SQL statement is the equivalent of a SAS step.

Consider this SQL statement, which prints the two variables DATE and ACT from the SAS dataset CONCERTS:

```
PROC SQL;
  SELECT DATE FORMAT=DATE9., ACT FROM CONCERTS
      ORDER BY DATE;
```

The ORDER BY clause specifies the sorted order of the printed output — equivalent to having a SORT proc step before a PRINT proc step.

Instead of being printed out, the resulting table could be defined as a SAS data view:

```
CREATE VIEW SLATE AS
    SELECT DATE FORMAT=DATE9., ACT FROM CONCERTS
    ORDER BY DATE;
```

Once it is defined, the view could be printed using a SELECT statement

```
SELECT * FROM SLATE;
```

or, just as easily, using the PRINT proc:

```
PROC PRINT DATA=SLATE NOOBS;
```

The view can also be used in a SET statement or in most places where a SAS dataset can be used.

The view SLATE uses the data in the SAS dataset CONCERTS. If CONCERTS is changed, the changes show up in SLATE. On the other hand, if CONCERTS is deleted, the SLATE view can no longer be used.

The SQL proc can also create SAS data files; however, there is no provision for sorting SAS data files themselves.

The SQL proc can combine SAS datasets, although in different ways from the ways SAS datasets are combined in data step programming. It can create indexes for SAS datasets, a process described in chapter 8, "Groups And Sorting." It can also modify a SAS dataset, adding or deleting observations or variables, and changing the values of variables.

SQL statements are executed in the order in which they appear. The SQL proc is an exception to the rules of the order of execution of SAS statements. After the `PROC SQL` statement, statements are executed one at a time, until the next DATA or PROC statement.

SQL statements and SAS global statements can both appear and are executed one at a time, in order. Global statements are not executed before the proc starts running, as they are in most steps.

RUN statements are not needed in the SQL proc and are ignored if they appear. There is no way to mark the end of an SQL step, except by a DATA or PROC statement beginning a new step.

PART THREE: Techniques

To avoid programming, find an existing program and copy it.

10 File formats

The SAS programming language is known for its versatile I/O features; it can read almost any data file format. I/O syntax was covered in chapter 5. This chapter covers data formats that require specific programming techniques.

Delimited fields

A common form for exchanging tables between database management systems, spreadsheet programs, and similar kinds of software represents each row as one record, and separates the columns, or fields, within each record using a delimiter, which could be any character or sequence of characters that does not appear in the data. Often the tab character (ASCII character `'09'x`) or the comma is used.

An advantage of delimited-field files is that they can be more compact than fixed-field files, because they take advantage of variations in the lengths of values.

The examples in this section use the backslash character (\) as the delimiter. You'll have to adjust the programs to reflect the delimiter you'll actually use. This is an example of part of a delimited-field file with the backslash as the delimiter:

```
1\Meister\Ferd\N.\\609\555-3729\23 Flight St.\\W. Brunswick\NJ\0801
2\Cutter\Deanne\\\609\555-1071\20713 Cove Rd.\#411\Pennsauken\NJ\08
3\Friendly\I.\B.\Jr.\609\555-0011\6 Harold Circle\\Cherry Hill\NJ\0
```

In the first record, the first field is `1`, the second field is `Meister`, the third field is `Ferd`, the fourth field is `N.`, the fifth field is empty, the sixth field is `609`, and so on.

There are several ways of handling different kinds of delimited field I/O; the SCAN function and || operator might be used, for example. The advantage of the methods presented here is their general applicability. Other approaches might not work for records longer than 200 characters, or if fields are empty, for example.

If the delimiter is the blank character, and there are no empty fields, then list input and list output can be used to read and write delimited fields. List input can also be used with any single-character delimiter. List input and output are described in chapter 5, "I/O."

Input

The input process for delimited fields is simpler when an array of character variables is used to hold the character values of the fields. Each field is read into a buffer variable, here called VALUE, and then the part of the buffer that represents the field is copied into the character array. After all the fields in the record have been read, the values in the character array are assigned to variables, using the INPUT function to convert the character values to numeric values.

The approach presented here pads the values with trailing blanks. Where trailing blanks are significant, this approach has to be modified.

This example reads data in the form presented above.

```
DATA FOLKS (KEEP=SEQUENCE NAME_L NAME_F NAME_M NAME_E
        AREACODE PHONE ADDRESS1 ADDRESS2 LOCALITY STATE ZIP);
  ARRAY TOKEN{12} $ 40;
  INFILE FOLKS MISSOVER;
  COLUMN = 1;
  DO I = 1 TO 12;
    INPUT @COLUMN VALUE $CHAR200. @;
    FIELDMK = INDEX(VALUE, '\');
    TOKEN{I} = SUBSTR(VALUE, 1, (FIELDMK - 1) MAX 0);
    COLUMN + FIELDMK;
    END;

  * Additional statements to assign fields to variables;
  LENGTH NAME_L $ 24 NAME_F $ 19 NAME_M $ 14 NAME_E $ 8
         AREACODE $ 3 PHONE $ 13 ADDRESS1 $ 40 ADDRESS2 $ 40
         LOCALITY $ 28 STATE $ 2 ZIP $ 3;
  SEQUENCE = INPUT(TOKEN1, 10.);
  NAME_L = TOKEN2;
  NAME_F = TOKEN3;
  NAME_M = TOKEN4;
  NAME_E = TOKEN5;
  AREACODE = LEFT(TOKEN6);
  PHONE = LEFT(TOKEN7);
  ADDRESS1 = TOKEN8;
  ADDRESS2 = TOKEN9;
  LOCALITY = LEFT(TOKEN10);
  STATE = LEFT(TOKEN11);
  ZIP = INPUT(TOKEN12, $HEX5.);
```

The length of the variables in the TOKEN array is 40 here, but it might have to be longer if longer values are being read. This code assumes that the length of a field plus the length of the delimiter is no more than 200 characters; the program could be modified to handle longer fields, but in any case, no more than 200 characters could be assigned to a variable.

The LENGTH statement and KEEP= option are necessary to store the right variables in the SAS dataset, with the right lengths for character variables (instead of, in this case, 40).

Output

If leading and trailing blanks in the output fields are acceptable, then output of delimited-field files is simple, using ordinary formatted output:

```
PUT SEQUENCE 10. '\' NAME_L $CHAR24. '\' NAME_F $CHAR19. '\'
    NAME_M   $CHAR14. '\' NAME_E $CHAR8. '\'
    AREACODE $CHAR3.  '\' PHONE $CHAR13. '\'
    ADDRESS1 $CHAR40. '\' ADDRESS2 $CHAR40. '\'
    LOCALITY $CHAR28. '\' STATE $CHAR2. '\' ZIP $HEX5. '\';
```

To remove all leading and trailing blanks, you can use list output, or use the : format modifier, with the `+(-1)` pointer control to remove the one blank that the PUT statement leaves after a value:

```
PUT SEQUENCE +(-1) '\' NAME_L +(-1) '\' NAME_F +(-1) '\'
    NAME_M   +(-1) '\' NAME_E +(-1) '\'
    AREACODE +(-1) '\' PHONE  +(-1) '\'
    ADDRESS1 +(-1) '\' ADDRESS2 +(-1) '\'
    LOCALITY +(-1) '\' STATE +(-1) '\' ZIP :$HEX5. +(-1) '\';
```

If leading blanks are significant, you can remove trailing blanks while keeping leading blanks by using the $VARYING format. This approach is also useful if you want to write actually empty fields, rather than writing a single blank in an empty field.

```
LENGTH VALUE FIELD1 FIELD12 $ 40;

* Convert variables to character form and put in array;
ARRAY FIELD{12} $ FIELD1 NAME_L NAME_F NAME_M NAME_E
    AREACODE PHONE ADDRESS1 ADDRESS2 LOCALITY STATE FIELD12;
FIELD1 = LEFT(PUT(SEQUENCE, 10.));
FIELD12 = PUT(ZIP, $HEX5.);

DO I = 1 TO 12;
  LEN = LENGTH(FIELD{I}) - (FIELD{I} = ' ');
  IF LEN THEN PUT FIELD{I} $VARYING200. LEN '\' @;
  ELSE PUT '\' @;
  END;
PUT;
```

Hierarchical files

A hierarchical file is a kind of sequential text file that has different record types that are at different levels. Different kinds of data values are stored in each different record type. Each record is associated with the most recent record of the next higher level.

A SAS observation corresponds to a record at the lowest level in the hierarchical file, and combines values from records at all levels.

Typically, the first character in a record identifies the record type.

Input

To form a SAS dataset from a hierarchical file, you need to retain the values from the higher-level records, and output an observation only after reading a lowest-level record.

This example reads a hierarchical file with four levels. When a higher-level record is read, all the values from the lower levels are set to missing.

```
DATA MUSIC;
  INFILE CARDS;
  RETAIN;
  INPUT @1 TYPE $CHAR1. @;
  SELECT(TYPE);
    WHEN('1') DO;
      INPUT @2 LABEL $CHAR24. @26 DIST $CHAR24.;
      ARTIST = ''; ALIAS = '';
      CAT = ''; TITLE = '';
      SONG = ''; RIGHTS = ''; LENGTH = .;
      DELETE;
      END;
    WHEN('2') DO;
      INPUT @2 ARTIST $CHAR28. @30 ALIAS $CHAR28.;
      CAT = ''; TITLE = '';
      SONG = ''; RIGHTS = ''; LENGTH = .;
      DELETE;
      END;
    WHEN('3') DO;
      INPUT @2 CAT $CHAR10. @12 TITLE $CHAR44.;
      SONG = ''; RIGHTS = ''; LENGTH = .;
      DELETE;
      END;
    WHEN('4') INPUT @2 SONG $CHAR44. @50 RIGHTS $CHAR12.
          @62 LENGTH MMSS5.;
    OTHERWISE DELETE;
    END;
  * Additional processing statements could be put here;
```

```
CARDS;---1----+----2----+----3----+----4----+----5----+----6----+--
1TAXMAN                  A&B
2REMINISCENT
31099-G    CAREER CAREEN
4CAREER CAREEN                                   BMI          4:06
4FLOWERS(TAKING OVER THE GARDEN)                 BMI         11:38
4WARNER DAYS                                     BMI          3:18
4TYRANNOSAUR                                     BMI          4:05
4HACKSAW                                         BMI          5:19
4RUNNING OUT OF BURBANK                          BMI          3:10
31099-X    LIME-LIGHT
4RIGHT                                           BMI          6:00
4EASTERN BLVD.                                   BMI          4:38
4RICHER THAN RICHARD                             BMI          5:43
4THE MOTELS                                      BMI          4:12
4GLASS HOUSES                                    BMI          4:01
4WATER BLVD.                                     BMI          3:30
4TRAIN TO ANTARCTICA                             BMI          9:22
2REZ
3W-4-8891  ANONYMOUS
4FREE RADIOS & TVS                               BMI          3:47
4HIGHWAY 42 S                                    BMI          3:14
4(DON'T TRY TO PARK AT) SHADY GROVE              BMI          2:57
```
and so on

Output

For a SAS dataset to be written as a hierarchical file, it should be sorted or at least grouped by the identifying variables in each level of the output hierarchy. Write the higher-level records at the beginning of the appropriate BY groups, and write a lowest-level record for each observation.

This example writes lines in the same format that is read by the previous example.

```
DATA _NULL_;
  SET MUSIC;
  BY LABEL ARTIST CAT NOTSORTED;
  FILE HIER;
  IF FIRST.LABEL THEN
      PUT '1' @2 LABEL $CHAR24. @26 DIST $CHAR24.;
  IF FIRST.ARTIST THEN
      PUT '2' @2 ARTIST $CHAR28. @30 ALIAS $CHAR28.;
  IF FIRST.CAT THEN PUT '3' @2 CAT $CHAR10. @12 TITLE $CHAR44.;
  PUT '4' @2 SONG $CHAR44. @50 RIGHTS $CHAR12. @62 LENGTH MMSS5.;
```

Binary files

There are three commonly used approaches for reading or writing a binary file: sequentially, one byte at a time; sequentially, several bytes at a time; or by using byte addresses for direct access.

To read through a file sequentially, one byte at a time, use the INFILE options `RECFM=F` (fixed length records) and `LRECL=1` (records 1 byte long). Then read the byte using the `$CHAR1.` or `PIB1.` informat or any appropriate informat with width 1.

```
INFILE BINARY RECFM=F LRECL=1 EOF=EOF;
INPUT BYTE $CHAR1.;
```

To read the file in pieces that vary in size, use the INFILE option `RECFM=U` (unorganized). This disables all line pointer movements, and has the effect of having a trailing @@ at the end of each INPUT statement. You can then read the entire file sequentially using formats of any width. You can also use the + pointer control to move forward or backward a certain number of bytes in the file.

This code fragment reads a binary file that consists of a sequence of Pascal strings (which are described later in this chapter).

```
    INFILE BINARY RECFM=U EOF=EOF;
    DO WHILE(1);
      INPUT LENGTH PIB1.;
      IF LENGTH <= 200 THEN INPUT STRING $VARYING200. LENGTH;
      ELSE INPUT STRING $CHAR200. +(LENGTH - 200);
      OUTPUT;
      END;
EOF: STOP;
```

Some binary files have particular items at specified locations. Those files can be treated as one large fixed-field record, using the INFILE option `RECFM=U` and the @ column pointer control. If the 2,033rd and 2,034th bytes in a file contain a two-character code, for example, you can read it using these statements:

```
INFILE BINARY RECFM=U EOF=EOF;
INPUT @2033 CODE $CHAR2.;
```

The output syntax for binary files perfectly mirrors the input syntax. The RECFM= and LRECL= options can be use in the same way on the FILE statement, and the pointer controls then work the same way in the PUT statement. In addition, with the FILE option `RECFM=U`, character constants can be written to the binary file. This step creates a 7-byte file that just contains the character constant indicated:

```
DATA _NULL_;
  FILE BINARY RECFM=U;
```

```
PUT 'Binary?';
STOP;
```

Binary formats, such as PIB, IB, and RB, are often found in binary files. These formats and the corresponding informats are described in chapter 3, "Programs on call."

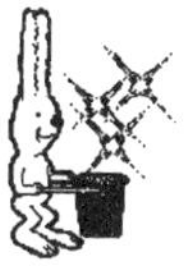

Sending control sequences to printers is an application of binary output. Under the MS-DOS operating system, the printer can usually be addressed as file PRN. If ASCII escape-E is the sequence that tells the printer to use bold characters, and escape-F tells the printer to use roman characters again, you could switch to bold print by running this program

```
* BOLD.SAS    Sends escape-E sequence to printer.;
  DATA _NULL_; FILE 'PRN' RECFM=U; PUT '1A'X 'E';
```

and back to roman print by running this program

```
* ROMAN.SAS    Sends escape-F sequence to printer.;
  DATA _NULL_; FILE 'PRN' RECFM=U; PUT '1A'X 'F';
```

Text files

The SET and MERGE statements provide ways of concatenating, interleaving, and match merging SAS datasets. Here we present ways of doing the same thing with text files.

Concatenating

Concatenating text files is just a matter of keeping track of what file you're reading from, and moving to the next file when you get to the end of a file. This example creates both a SAS dataset and an output text file from the concatenated files FROM1, FROM2, and FROM3:

```
  DATA CONCATN8;
    RETAIN FILE 1;
TOP:SELECT(FILE);
      WHEN(1) INFILE FROM1 EOF=NEXT;
      WHEN(2) INFILE FROM2 EOF=NEXT;
      WHEN(3) INFILE FROM3 EOF=NEXT;
      OTHERWISE STOP;
      END;

    INPUT variables;
    FILE TO;
    PUT _INFILE_;
    RETURN;

NEXT: FILE + 1; GOTO TOP;
```

This program, like the ones that follow, uses the EOF= option instead of the END= option so that it will still work if one of the files is empty.

The FILEVAR= INFILE option can also be used to switch between input text files for concatenating, beginning with SAS release 6.06.

Most operating systems also provide ways to concatenate text files.

Interleaving

Interleaving is the process by which all the observations (or records) in several files are copied to a single file, in sorted order; in the example here, we use ascending order with three files. Interleaving two files can be done simply by eliminating all references to the third file from the step below. Interleaving four or more files can be done by extending the pattern.

This step obtains the key field from the current record in each file, and then reads the rest of the record from the file with the lowest key field. It also keeps track of which files it has reached the end of, so that it does not attempt to read past the end of a file.

```
  DATA INTERLV (DROP=KEY1 KEY2 KEY3 END1 END2 END3);
    LENGTH KEY1-KEY3 $ 5;
    FILE TO;
    INFILE FROM1 MISSOVER EOF=EOF1; LINK I1;
    INFILE FROM2 MISSOVER EOF=EOF2; LINK I2;
    INFILE FROM3 MISSOVER EOF=EOF3; LINK I3;

    DO WHILE(1);
      * Set variables to missing;
      OTHER = '         ';

      * Find lowest key value in open file;
      SELECT;
        WHEN(END1 AND END2 AND END3) STOP;
        WHEN(END1 AND END2) KEY = KEY3;
        WHEN(END1 AND END3) KEY = KEY2;
        WHEN(END2 AND END3) KEY = KEY1;
        WHEN(END1) KEY = KEY2 MIN KEY3;
        WHEN(END2) KEY = KEY1 MIN KEY3;
        WHEN(END3) KEY = KEY1 MIN KEY2;
        OTHERWISE KEY = KEY1 MIN KEY2 MIN KEY3;
        END;

      * Find all observations with key value;
      DO WHILE(KEY = KEY1 AND NOT END1); LINK IO1; END;
      DO WHILE(KEY = KEY2 AND NOT END2); LINK IO2; END;
      DO WHILE(KEY = KEY3 AND NOT END3); LINK IO3; END;
      END;

IO1:
    INFILE FROM1;
    INPUT @6 OTHER $CHAR9.;
    OUTPUT;
I1: INPUT @1 KEY1 $CHAR5. @@;
    RETURN;
```

```
IO2:
    INFILE FROM2;
    INPUT @6 OTHER $CHAR9.;
    OUTPUT;
I2: INPUT @1 KEY2 $CHAR5. @@;
    RETURN;

IO3:
    INFILE FROM3;
    INPUT @6 OTHER $CHAR9.;
    OUTPUT;
I3: INPUT @1 KEY3 $CHAR5. @@;
    RETURN;

EOF1: END1 = 1; RETURN;
EOF2: END2 = 1; RETURN;
EOF3: END3 = 1; RETURN;
```

Match merging

Match merging is similar to interleaving, in that it combines data from different files in sorted order. In match merging, however, records in the different files with the same key value are combined to form a single output observation.

This step match merges the input files FROM1, FROM2, and FROM3, each of which has a KEY field and one other field.

```
  DATA MERJ (DROP=KEY1 KEY2 KEY3 END1 END2 END3);
    LENGTH KEY1-KEY3 $ 5;
    FILE TO;
    INFILE FROM1 MISSOVER EOF=EOF1; LINK I1;
    INFILE FROM2 MISSOVER EOF=EOF2; LINK I2;
    INFILE FROM3 MISSOVER EOF=EOF3; LINK I3;

    DO WHILE(1);
      * Set variables to missing;
      A = .; B = .; C = .;

      * Find lowest key value in open file;
      SELECT;
        WHEN(END1 AND END2 AND END3) STOP;
        WHEN(END1 AND END2) KEY = KEY3;
        WHEN(END1 AND END3) KEY = KEY2;
        WHEN(END2 AND END3) KEY = KEY1;
        WHEN(END1) KEY = KEY2 MIN KEY3;
        WHEN(END2) KEY = KEY1 MIN KEY3;
        WHEN(END3) KEY = KEY1 MIN KEY2;
        OTHERWISE KEY = KEY1 MIN KEY2 MIN KEY3;
        END;

      * Find all observations with key value;
      DO WHILE((KEY = KEY1 AND NOT END1)
            OR (KEY = KEY2 AND NOT END2)
            OR (KEY = KEY3 AND NOT END3));
        IF KEY = KEY1 AND NOT END1 THEN LINK R1;
        IF KEY = KEY2 AND NOT END2 THEN LINK R2;
```

```
          IF KEY = KEY3 AND NOT END3 THEN LINK R3;
          OUTPUT;
          END;
        END;

R1: INFILE FROM1;
    INPUT @6 A 3.;
I1: INPUT @1 KEY1 $CHAR5. @@;
    RETURN;

R2: INFILE FROM2;
    INPUT @6 B 4.;
I2: INPUT @1 KEY2 $CHAR5. @@;
    RETURN;

R3: INFILE FROM3;
    INPUT @6 C 3.;
I3: INPUT @1 KEY3 $CHAR5. @@;
    RETURN;

EOF1: END1 = 1; RETURN;
EOF2: END2 = 1; RETURN;
EOF3: END3 = 1; RETURN;
```

A similar approach can be used with SAS datasets when a BY statement cannot be used, as when the defined order of the group variable is something other than simple ascending or descending.

Data formats

Many data formats in files can be handled directly by SAS informats and formats, but there are also some common data formats that require special attention.

Signed numerals

The standard numeric informat has no trouble reading the most common kinds of numeric fields. However, some effort might be necessary to read numerals with + or – signs.

The standard numeric informat can handle signs only if they appear right before the digits, with no blanks in between, for example:

```
    INPUT A 6.;
CARDS;
   +80
   -64
  -5.0
```

Some programs write numeric fields with the sign in the first position of the field, followed by blanks and then digits. Provided these numerals are right aligned (that is, with no trailing blanks), they can be read by the BZ informat, which treats leading blanks as zeros:

```
    INPUT A BZ6.;
CARDS;
+   80
-   64
-  5.0
```

If the numerals are not right aligned, you can read them using a character informat, right align them using the RIGHT function, and then interpret them using the BZ informat:

```
    LENGTH C $ 8;
    INPUT C $CHAR8.;
    C = RIGHT(C);
    A = INPUT(C, BZ8.);
CARDS;
+   80
-   64
-    5.0
```

Old-fashioned adding machines used to write negative numbers with a trailing minus sign, such as `12-` for –12, and some programs (especially ones written in Cobol) still represent numbers this way. There are two slightly different forms: using a separate field for the sign, + or –; and a minus sign as the last character in a numeric field.

You can read these numbers by reading the field as a character string, determining whether there is a minus sign, and negating the number if there is.

```
  DATA ADDING;
    INPUT NUMBER 10. SIGN $CHAR1.;
    IF SIGN = '-' THEN NUMBER = 0 - NUMBER;
CARDS;
      3092+
      4384-
         0+
     23974-
;

  DATA MINUS;
    INPUT FIELD $CHAR10.;
    IF SUBSTR(FIELD, 10) = '-' THEN NUMBER = -INPUT(FIELD, 9.);
    ELSE NUMBER = INPUT(FIELD, 10.);
CARDS;
      3092
     4384-
        0
    23974-
;
```

If you have to write a numeric field with a specific nonstandard form, often the easiest way to do it is to create a character variable containing the field, using character functions and operators, and then write the variable using the $CHAR format. For example, to write an 8-character numeric field with the value of the variable A, with the minus sign appearing in the first character of the field, you could code it this way:

```
C = PUT(ABS(A), 8.);   * Unsigned numeral;
IF .Z < A < 0 THEN SUBSTR(C, 1, 1) = '-'; * Sign, if negative;
```

Scientific notation

There are several forms of scientific notation. The E format writes one form, and the standard numeric and E informats read scientific notation that follows certain rules. Here we consider the problem of reading and writing other forms of scientific notation.

Languages like Fortran write floating point numbers in various ways. They might use a D instead of an E, or just have a + or – sign between the mantissa and the exponent. The mantissa might have 1 or 0 digits before the decimal point. Or you might be using engineering notation, which uses exponents that are multiples of 3 and mantissas between 1 and 1000.

In reading and writing these other scientific notation formats, you will be handling the mantissa and the exponent separately. In reading, you can just combine the mantissa and the exponent to get the value; in writing, you'll need to calculate the exponent and use it to calculate the mantissa.

The following steps show the input process.

```
  DATA DOUBLE (KEEP=VALUE);
    INPUT MANTISSA 10. +1 EXPONENT 3.;
    VALUE = MANTISSA*10**EXPONENT;
CARDS;
1.54372823D-43
5.29376630D019
;
  DATA SIGN (KEEP=VALUE);
    INPUT MANTISSA 7. EXPONENT 3.;
    VALUE = MANTISSA*10**EXPONENT;
CARDS;
.928374-43
64.2343+06
;
```

This step writes various different forms for two numeric values.

```
  DATA _NULL_;
    INPUT A 19.;

    IF A = 0 THEN EXPONENT = 0;
    ELSE EXPONENT = FLOOR(LOG10(ABS(A)));
    MANTISSA = A/10**EXPONENT;

    PUT MANTISSA Z7.5 'D' EXPONENT Z3.;
    ABSEXP = ABS(EXP);
    IF EXP >= 0 THEN EXPSIGN = '+'; ELSE EXPSIGN = '-';
    PUT MANTISSA Z7.5 'D' EXPSIGN ABSEXP Z3.;
    PUT MANTISSA Z7.5 EXPSIGN ABSEXP Z3.;
```

```
    PUT 'Fractional mantissa:    ' @;
    IF A = 0 THEN EXPONENT = 0;
    ELSE EXPONENT = FLOOR(LOG10(ABS(A))) + 1;
    MANTISSA = A/10**EXPONENT;
    ABSEXP = ABS(EXP);
    IF EXP >= 0 THEN EXPSIGN = '+'; ELSE EXPSIGN = '-';
    PUT MANTISSA Z8.7 EXPSIGN ABSEXP Z3.;

    PUT 'Engineering notation:    ' @;
    IF A = 0 THEN EXPONENT = 0;
    ELSE EXPONENT = 3*FLOOR(LOG10(ABS(A))/3);
    MANTISSA = A/10**EXPONENT;
    ABSEXP = ABS(EXP);
    IF EXP >= 0 THEN EXPSIGN = '+'; ELSE EXPSIGN = '-';
    PUT MANTISSA 10.6 EXPSIGN ABSEXP Z3.;
CARDS;
84030572387841267
.000000002346782346
;
```

```
8.40305D016
8.40305D+016
8.40305+016
Fractional mantissa:    .8403057+017
Engineering notation:    84.030572+015

2.34678D-09
2.34678D-009
2.34678-009
Fractional mantissa:    .2346782-008
Engineering notation:     2.346782-009
```

Implied decimal points

Sometimes numbers are written in data files with implied decimal points — meaning that there are decimal places in the number, but the decimal point does not actually appear in the file. This especially happens with money values; $8.98 might appear in a file as

```
898
```

A SAS program can read this kind of field using the standard numeric informat. For example, this statement

```
INPUT PRICE 5.2;
```

reading the data line above would give PRICE the value 8.98.

To write a field with an implied decimal point, you could multiply the number by the appropriate power of 10, and then write the result using the standard numeric format:

```
PRICE100 = PRICE*100;
PUT PRICE100 5.;
```

It is also possible to create a picture format that writes a field with a certain number of implied decimal places. The MULT= picture option is used to multiply the number by a factor before formatting it. For example, this step

```
PROC FORMAT;
  PICTURE MONEY (MIN=1)
     0-HIGH = '000000000000001' (MULT=100);
```

creates a format that could be used to write numeric fields with two implied decimal places (at least for positive values that fit in the field). The field above could then be written by these statements:

```
PRICE = 8.98;
PUT PRICE MONEY5.;
```

Fields with implied decimal places are often written with leading zeros instead of leading blanks. To do that, use the Z format instead of the standard numeric format, or use 1s instead of 0s in the picture of a picture format — that is:

```
PROC FORMAT;
  PICTURE MONEY (MIN=1)
     0-HIGH = '111111111111111' (MULT=100);
```

Picture formats are discussed in more detail under "Creating formats and informats using the FORMAT proc" in chapter 3, "Programs on call."

Pascal strings

In Pascal, the first byte of a character string is a number telling the length of the string, from 0 to 255. To read Pascal strings in a SAS program, you can read the length byte using the PIB1. informat, then read the characters using the $VARYING informat. The input pointer will then be positioned to read the next field in the input record, if any, provided that the length of the Pascal string is 1 to 200 characters.

```
INPUT LEN PIB1. STRING $VARYING200. LEN;
```

To write Pascal strings, first write the length byte using the PIB1. format, then write the character value using the $VARYING format. In this example, the length value is calculated to omit trailing blanks from the field.

```
LEN = LENGTH(STRING) - (STRING = '');
PUT LEN PIB1. STRING $VARYING200. LEN;
```

Variable number of fields

Some records are defined to have fields of a fixed length that vary in number. Usually a preceding field tells the number of fields that are present in each group of fields. The @ column pointer is not much use in reading these records, because fields may not appear at fixed positions.

Consider a record defined this way, for example:

Width	Format	Description
2	integer	number of packages
11	character	package ID (× number of packages)
4	integer	weight of shipment
14	character	invoice number

There is a variable number of package ID fields — conceivably, any number from 0 to 99. In the example below, the package IDs are assigned to variables in an array. It is expected that there will not be more than 12 package IDs; if there are more, the extra IDs are discarded, but the + pointer control is used to put the pointer in the correct position to read the next field.

The trailing @ is needed to allow the input record to be read using several INPUT statements. Normally, the INFILE option MISSOVER is used when reading a defined record such as this one.

```
ARRAY PACKAGE{12} P_1-P_12;
INPUT PACKAGES 2. @;
DO I = 1 TO PACKAGES;
  IF I <= 12 THEN INPUT PACKAGE{I} $CHAR11. @;
  ELSE INPUT +11 @;
  END;
INPUT WEIGHT 4. INVOICE $CHAR14.;
```

11 Reports

A report is output produced by a computer, usually on paper, for a person to read. Most SAS programs create reports, and in many cases, that is the main purpose of the program.

Design

In designing a report, a programmer determines the form in which the data will be presented. The design of a report has to balance various requirements such as clarity, brevity, and completeness. Often, related reports should be given the same or similar designs. This is easier to program and makes the reports easier to read and compare.

Decisions about the content of a report and the design of a report are closely related. Generally, the information that is presented on a report represents a compromise between the most important data and the data that is easiest to present. The form of a report can usually be the simplest and most obvious way to present the data. If possible, it should emphasize the most important information on the report.

There are two main forms that reports tend to follow: tables, which have rows and columns, and the prose or narrative form, which reads left to right, top to bottom, and sometimes forms sentences. Essentially, tables are two-dimensional, while prose is one-dimensional, or linear. Tables and prose might be mixed in a report or on a page.

Most reports also have a title or other identifying material at the top or bottom of every page.

In designing a report, it can be helpful to start by sketching a page design on paper.

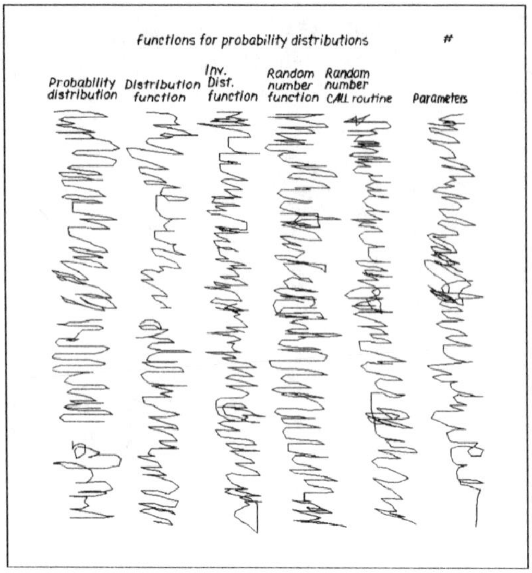

For more exacting report designs, you might use graph paper, with each square representing one character. You could also use a text editor to create a mock-up of a report.

Print files and non-print files

Reports are usually written in print files, which are text files with print control characters. Print files are described at the end of chapter 5, "I/O."

Reports can also be written in non-print files, with the N= option on the FILE statement set to the number of lines per page used by the printer. For example, if the printer puts 60 lines on a page, the FILE statement would have the N=60 option. You would use the # pointer control to move from one line to another. Each PUT statement would end with a trailing @ to stay on the same page, or the pointer control `#60` to move to the end of the page.

```
FILE REPORT NOPRINT N=60;
PUT #1 ... @;
more PUT statements and other statements
PUT #60; * the end of the page;
```

Other software

If a report seems difficult to get exactly right in a SAS program, consider other software you can use with the SAS program. You can have the SAS program produce a roughly formatted report, and then do the final formatting using a text editor, word processor, or page layout program.

This approach is faster in some cases, especially if you're doing the report only a few times, and it can give you more control over the form of the report — perhaps you might like to use bold type in the report or put the report in the middle of a memo or other document.

Tables

A table is a two-dimensional array of text, with rows and columns. The intersection of a row with a column is called a *cell*. Usually there are column headings at the top of each column, and there is often a column of labels at the left side of the rows.

Most of the time, when a SAS dataset is put into a table, each observation in the SAS dataset corresponds to one row in the table, and the columns represent variables. There are other possibilities, though: an observation might take up several rows of a table, even an entire page; or there might be several observations in a row; or columns might represent observations, with rows representing variables.

> **Columns, columns, columns**
>
> The word *column* is pretty generic, referring to just about any vertical arrangement of things. In the INPUT and PUT statement and in data files, column 1 is made up of the character in each line or record, and might simply refer to the first character of a record. In a table, column 1 consists of the first cell in each row. We use the term *column* with both of those meanings in this book; it's not likely to be confusing as long as you remember that there are different kinds of columns.
>
> Another kind of column, used in newspapers and magazines, is formed by dividing the width of the page into a few parts. That meaning is not used much in this book. Where it is, we call that kind of column a *stripe* to avoid confusion with a table column.

Building tables

In a simple case, you might receive the data in the same shape that you intend the report to have. In other cases, you might have to assemble it, organize it, or modify it in some way to build the table you want to print.

If the data is in two or more SAS datasets, you will have to combine them to print them in the same table. If the report is printed in a data step, you can usually combine the SAS datasets in the same step, just by listing them in the same SET or MERGE statement. If the report is printed by a proc, though, you'll have to combine the SAS datasets in a separate step.

SAS datasets are combined in various ways: concatenating, interleaving, and merging, which are described in chapter 5, "I/O"; and crossing, which is described in chapter 8, "Groups and sorting."

A single SAS dataset might be sorted, to put its observations in a particular order; or reshaped, changing the amount of data that makes up an observation. Sorting and reshaping are described in chapter 8. The contents of a SAS dataset might be changed by subsetting, to select observations; or by recoding, to change the appearance of data.

You might calculate descriptive statistics, or summary statistics, either using an analytic proc or using the techniques described in chapter 17, "Applications." Analytic procs generally produce print output, but many of them, including the SUMMARY and FREQ procs, can produce output SAS datasets. This lets you print a report with the summary data that differs in design from the report produced by the proc.

Recoding

Recoding involves substituting one code, or way of presenting information, for another. It is usually a simple process of lookup, as described in chapter 15.

If the only purpose of recoding is to print a variable with different values, that can be accomplished with a value format. For example, if a variable has the values "1" and "0", which you want to print as "yes" and "no", you can define the format $YESNO.

```
PROC FORMAT;
  VALUE $YESNO (MIN=1)
      '1' = 'yes'
      '0' = 'no';
```

and then associate that format with the variable in the step that produces the report, either in a FORMAT statement

```
FORMAT ANSWER $YESNO3.;
```

or in a PUT statement.

```
PUT ANSWER $YESNO3.;
```

Subsetting

Selecting observations to be processed, stored, or printed is called *subsetting*. Almost any subsetting can be done with the FIRSTOBS=, OBS=, and WHERE= dataset options, which can be used in both data and proc steps. This use of dataset options is described in chapter 5, "I/O."

Transposing

Transposing a SAS dataset means turning observations into variables and variables into observations. The TRANSPOSE proc can transpose an entire SAS dataset or each BY group within a SAS dataset.

The form of the TRANSPOSE proc step is

```
PROC TRANSPOSE DATA=input SAS dataset OUT=output SAS dataset
                PREFIX=characters NAME=name LABEL=name LET;
  VAR variables;
  ID variable;
```

If a BY statement is present, each BY group is transposed; otherwise, the entire SAS dataset is transposed.

Variables are turned into observations. The VAR statement lists the variables to be turned into observations. If there is no VAR statement, all numeric variables are used. The name of each input variable is assigned to an output character variable (with length 8), which is called _NAME_ unless another name is given for it in the NAME= option in the PROC statement. The label of each input variable is assigned to an output character variable (with length 40), which is called _LABEL_ unless another name is given for it in the LABEL= option in the PROC statement. The label variable is not created if none of the input variables have a label.

Observations are turned into variables. Either the ID statement or the PREFIX= option on the PROC statement can be used to provide variable names for the output variables. The ID statement identifies a variable whose value is used as the name of an output variable. (The formatted value of the variable is used, with invalid characters converted to valid characters or omitted. If the first character of the formatted value is a digit, the variable name begins with an underscore, as in the example below.) If the PREFIX= option is used instead, the SAS interpreter makes up names by appending the numerals 1, 2, 3, ... to the characters given in the PREFIX option, similar to the way it generates names for array elements. For example, with `PREFIX=A`, the output variables are called A1, A2, A3, ... If the ID statement is used, there can also be an IDLABEL statement to name an input variable whose values are used as the labels of the output variables. The IDLABEL variable can be the same as the ID variable. If the LET option is not present on the PROC statement, the proc stops with an error condition if duplicate values of the ID variable occur.

In the example below, the SAS dataset PROD is transposed to produce the SAS dataset TRANPROD, which is then printed using the PRINT proc.

```
  DATA PROD;
    INPUT YEAR CORN TOMATOES WHEAT SOYBEANS;
CARDS;
          1985  107     38.1     90   35
          1986   99     37.0     98   34
          1987  108     37.8     97   46
          1988  109     40.6     97   46
          1989   85     42.0     98   50
          1990  102     45.5    106   51
;
  PROC TRANSPOSE DATA=PROD OUT=TRANPROD NAME=CROP;
    VAR CORN TOMATOES WHEAT SOYBEANS;
    ID YEAR;
    IDLABEL YEAR;
RUN;
%PUT After transposing:;
  DATA _NULL_;
    SET TRANPROD;
    PUT _ALL_;
  PROC PRINT DATA=TRANPROD SPLIT='\';
```

```
    ID CROP; LABEL CROP='Crop';
    VAR _1985 _1986 _1987 _1988 _1989 _1990;
RUN;
```

```
After transposing:
CROP=CORN _1985=107 _1986=99 _1987=108 _1988=109 _1989=85 _1990=102
_ERROR_=0 _N_=1
CROP=TOMATOES _1985=38.1 _1986=37 _1987=37.8 _1988=40.6 _1989=42
_1990=45.5 _ERROR_=0 _N_=2
CROP=WHEAT _1985=90 _1986=98 _1987=97 _1988=97 _1989=98 _1990=106
_ERROR_=0 _N_=3
CROP=SOYBEANS _1985=35 _1986=34 _1987=46 _1988=46 _1989=50 _1990=51
_ERROR_=0 _N_=4
```

Crop	1985	1986	1987	1988	1989	1990
CORN	107.0	99	108.0	109.0	85	102.0
TOMATOES	38.1	37	37.8	40.6	42	45.5
WHEAT	90.0	98	97.0	97.0	98	106.0
SOYBEANS	35.0	34	46.0	46.0	50	51.0

Before transposing, the SAS dataset has 6 observations and 5 variables. After transposing, it has 4 observations (because the variable YEAR was used to create the variable names instead of becoming an observation) and 7 variables (with an extra variable, CROP, being created from the former variable names).

The output SAS dataset is printed in a data step before the PRINT proc step so that you can see that the variable names begin with underscores. Underscores were added by the TRANSPOSE proc because a variable name cannot begin with a 1. The underscores do not appear in the PRINT proc output because the variable labels are used, and underscores were not added to the labels.

Procs with table output

If you need a table to look orderly, but don't need precise control over its appearance, you can probably produce it with a proc step. PRINT, TABULATE, FORMS, SUMMARY, FREQ, and most procs produce output in table form, and they usually allow some control over the column headings, formats, etc., used in the report.

Reports from procs go to the standard print file. They contain the current titles and footnotes on each page, and they can have page numbers and the current date and time on the first title line. To avoid getting titles, footnotes, date, time, and page numbers on a report from a proc, use these statements before the proc step:

```
TITLE1 ' ';
FOOTNOTE1;
OPTIONS NODATE NONUMBER;
```

Usually, a proc will, by default, present all the variables in a SAS dataset (or all the numeric variables). However, the variables that are processed, and the order in which they appear, can usually be controlled with the VAR statement. The KEEP= or DROP= dataset option could also be used to affect the variables used by the proc.

The format a proc uses to write a variable can be controlled using the FORMAT statement. For example, this step prints the variable R with the format `7.2` and the variable X with the format `6.2`:

```
  PROC PRINT DATA=BUD;
    VAR R X;
    FORMAT R 7.2 X 6.2;
RUN;
```

Similarly, for procs that print values of variables, the text used to label the variables can sometimes be controlled using the LABEL statement. Often a PROC statement option has to appear to indicate that labels will be used. This step is the same as the preceding step, except for the use of variable labels:

```
  PROC PRINT DATA=BUD LABEL;
    VAR R X;
    FORMAT R 7.2 X 6.2;
    LABEL R='Revenue' X='Expenses';
RUN;
```

If the LABEL statement cannot be used with a particular proc, you can use the RENAME= dataset option to change variable names to names more suitable for printing. If the KEEP= dataset option is used with the RENAME= option to list the variables to be used with a proc, the old variable names, before renaming, are listed.

```
  PROC PRINT DATA=BUD (KEEP=R X RENAME=(R=REVENUE X=EXPENSES));
```

The PRINT proc

The PRINT proc is the most popular and simplest proc for printing SAS datasets. It prints tables with observations as rows and selected variables as columns.

The BY, VAR, and ID statements identify the variables that appear in the PRINT proc's output, and also the order in which the variables appear. If there is a BY statement, the BY variables appear in a horizontal line above the table. The variables in the VAR statement appear in the order in which they are listed. If there is an ID statement, the ID variables appear to the left of the VAR variables.

The leftmost column contains observation numbers unless there is an ID statement or the NOOBS option appears on the PROC statement.

If there is no VAR statement, all the variables in the SAS dataset are used.

Variable names are normally used as headings of the columns produced by the PRINT proc. However, if the LABEL or SPLIT= option appears in the PROC statement, variable labels can be used as headings. Labels can be given in the LABEL statement.

The SPLIT= option identifies a character that separates lines in labels. With the SPLIT= option, labels can have up to 3 lines.

These fundamental characteristics of the PRINT proc are demonstrated in this example:

```
TITLE 'Variables in PRINT Proc';
OPTIONS NOCENTER NODATE NONUMBER;
  PROC PRINT DATA=ALPHA SPLIT='\';
    BY GROUP NOTSORTED;
    ID NAME;
    VAR DIAMETER MASS ALBEDO;
    LABEL GROUP='\Object\Category' NAME='\Object\Name'
      DIAMETER='Diameter' ALBEDO='Albedo\\(%)';
```

```
Variables in PRINT Proc

------------------ \Object\Category=PLANETS ------------------

                                                    Albedo
  Object
   Name         Diameter          MASS               (%)

A.C.-1            2520          8737188             24
A.C.-2            7400        201743637             28
A.C.-3B          11022       1837827219             44
...
```

Notice the effects of the split character, \. The variable name MASS, in capital letters, is used as a column heading because no label is given for that variable. The variable DIAMETER is assigned a label so that the column heading can appear in upper- and lowercase. That label does not contain a split character, so the column heading appears on one line.

Each variable's format attribute is used as the format for printing the variable. If no format is associated with a variable, default formats are used: `BEST12.` for numeric variables, and `$.` for character variables. A FORMAT statement can be used to specify different formats for variables. Formats can be used to control the widths of columns, especially with numeric variables.

Normally, every observation from the input SAS dataset appears in the report, but you can use dataset options to select observations. The FIRSTOBS=, OBS=, and WHERE= dataset options are the most commonly used. This step prints only 51 selected observations from the SAS dataset TREEFARM:

```
PROC PRINT DATA=TREEFARM (FIRSTOBS=50 OBS=100);
```

> When the FIRSTOBS= or WHERE= dataset option is used with the PRINT proc, the OBS numbers printed represent the actual locations of the observations in the SAS dataset, rather than being 1, 2, 3, ... So, in the previous example, the numbers in the OBS column would go from 50 to 100, rather than going from 1 to 51.

The PRINT proc tries to conserve space by making columns narrower when possible. You can use the UNIFORM option on the PROC statement to prevent it from doing this. The UNIFORM option usually makes the PRINT proc run faster, and it guarantees that variables will be in the same place on each page.

The PRINT proc also "rotates" variable names in column headings, printing them vertically, when doing so appears to save space. Sometimes this is appropriate — especially when the SAS dataset contains twenty or thirty short character variables with long names — but just as often, it is a nuisance. To prevent variable names from rotating, use the SPLIT= option on the PROC statement and provide a label for at least one variable.

The system option CENTER or NOCENTER determines whether the PRINT proc spreads columns across the page or puts them close together at the left side of the page. With the NOCENTER option, the proc runs faster, but the tables produced with the CENTER option can be aesthetically better.

If the total width of columns is wider than the page, the PRINT proc produces several tables for each group of observations. The ID variables or OBS numbers appear in each table. With an ordinary page size, the PRINT proc puts two tables on each page.

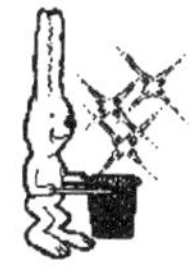

> To have more control over the placement of variables when the total width of variables is greater than the page width, you could print the SAS dataset using several PRINT proc steps. Use VAR statements to select the variables to appear in each step.

Several additional features of the PRINT proc let you control details of the output. The N option on the PROC statement produces an extra line at the end of the report (or at the end of each BY group, if there is a BY statement) showing the number of observations:

```
N=42
```

The SUM statement produces sum lines, which show the totals of values of selected numeric variables. If there is a BY statement, you can use the PAGEBY statement to force page breaks when the value of a certain BY variable changes, and the SUMBY statement to identify which levels of BY groups get sum lines.

Analytic procs

Most analytic procs produce reports, usually showing the results of some specialized kind of analysis. Of the analytic procs, the SUMMARY (or MEANS), FREQ, and TABULATE procs produce the most generally useful reports. This section provides a very brief description of the use of these procs. Detailed information can be found in the documentation of each proc.

The SUMMARY proc calculates descriptive statistics on the values of variables. The most popular statistic is the SUM statistic, which adds together the different values of a variable. Other generally useful statistics are MEAN, MAX, and MIN.

The SUMMARY proc produces printed output if the PRINT option is used on the PROC statement. The statistics to be calculated are listed as options on the PROC statement. Each statistic is calculated for each numeric variable listed in the VAR statement.

The BY statement and CLASS statement can be used to generate statistics for subsets of the SAS dataset defined by the combinations of values of the BY and CLASS variables. In general, a variable is used as a BY variable if the SAS dataset is grouped by that variable, or as a CLASS variable otherwise. The proc uses less memory with BY variables than with CLASS variables, but the SAS dataset must be sorted or grouped by the BY variables.

The TABULATE proc has a similar syntax and calculates the same numbers, but presents them in a different kind of table, which is defined by the TABLE statement. The TABULATE proc can produce multilevel tables with up to three dimensions, and the TABLE statement can be correspondingly complex. A simple TABLE statement names one or two CLASS variables, an analysis variable, and a descriptive statistic. In this example, R and C are CLASS variables, AMOUNT is an analysis variable, and SUM is the descriptive statistic used.

```
PROC TABULATE;
  CLASS R C;
  VAR AMOUNT;
  TABLE R,
      C*AMOUNT*SUM;
```

Output from TABULATE proc

	C			
	1	2	3	4
	AMOUNT	AMOUNT	AMOUNT	AMOUNT
	SUM	SUM	SUM	SUM
R				
1	7.00	8.00	9.00	10.00
2	8.00	9.00	10.00	11.00
3	9.00	10.00	11.00	12.00
4	10.00	11.00	12.00	13.00
5	11.00	12.00	13.00	14.00
6	12.00	13.00	14.00	15.00
7	13.00	14.00	15.00	16.00
8	14.00	15.00	16.00	17.00
9	15.00	16.00	17.00	18.00
10	16.00	17.00	18.00	19.00

(CONTINUED)

The specifications for each dimension are separated by commas. An asterisk separates different levels in each dimension. The TABLE statement above puts different values of R in different rows and different values of C in different columns. Each cell then contains the sum of values for the AMOUNT variable for the observations having that combination of R and C values.

The FREQ proc is specialized for reporting relative and absolute frequencies. It can produce tables showing the frequencies of the different values of one variable or of combinations of the values of two or more variables. The FREQ proc has a TABLES statement, which is similar to the TABLE statement of the TABULATE proc, but produces only two-dimensional tables with one variable on each axis. If there are more than two variables, the FREQ proc prints a separate table for each combination of values of the other variables.

The simplest form of the TABLES statement names one variable for a one-way frequency table, or two or more variables separated by asterisks for a table with variables crosstabulated:

```
PROC FREQ DATA=ACIDRAIN;
  TABLES STATE;
```

```
Output from FREQ proc

                                      Cumulative  Cumulative
STATE   Frequency   Percent    Frequency     Percent
-----------------------------------------------------------
    1           5      62.5            5        62.5
   22           3      37.5            8       100.0
```

```
PROC FREQ DATA=ACIDRAIN;
  TABLES STATE*MONTH;
```

```
Output from FREQ proc

TABLE OF STATE BY MONTH

STATE      MONTH

Frequency|
Percent  |
Row Pct  |
Col Pct  |       1|       2|       3|  Total
---------+--------+--------+--------+
       1 |      2 |      2 |      1 |      5
         |  25.00 |  25.00 |  12.50 |  62.50
         |  40.00 |  40.00 |  20.00 |
         |  66.67 |  66.67 |  50.00 |
---------+--------+--------+--------+
      22 |      1 |      1 |      1 |      3
         |  12.50 |  12.50 |  12.50 |  37.50
         |  33.33 |  33.33 |  33.33 |
         |  33.33 |  33.33 |  50.00 |
---------+--------+--------+--------+
Total           3        3        2        8
            37.50    37.50    25.00   100.00
```

The FREQ proc can also calculate certain kinds of multivariate statistics.

Both the TABULATE and FREQ procs normally print one table on a page. If a table is too large to fit on a page, the procs use tiling techniques to print pages that can be pasted up to form a single printed table.

The FORMS proc

The FORMS proc is designed for printing mailing labels and similar rectangular blocks of data. It takes its name from computer center jargon, where the term "forms" refers to any special kind of paper used in a computer printer. The FORMS proc is not really related to the better-known "forms" software that uses a computer printer to fill in the blanks of preprinted pages such as invoices, checks, and tax forms.

SQL

The SELECT statement of the SQL proc generates tables similar to those of the PRINT proc. In the simplest case, it prints an entire SAS dataset:

```
  PROC SQL;
SELECT * FROM FITNESS;
```

You can select a list of variables, separated by commas. You can also use WHERE and ORDER BY clauses to select and sort observations:

```
SELECT LASTNAME, FIRSNAME, SITUPS FROM FITNESS
    WHERE SITUPS < 40   ORDER BY SITUPS;
```

The PRINTTO proc

Normally, print output from procs and the output directed to the PRINT file in data steps goes to the standard print file. The PRINTTO proc redirects the output, so that subsequent steps are sent to a different file. This is especially useful in batch jobs, to send the output from a program's different proc steps to different print files. The use of the PRINTTO proc is described in chapter 5, "I/O."

Programming table output

The advantage of programming reports is flexibility. You can put any character in any position on the page. The # and @ pointer controls allow you to think of locations on the page in terms of coordinates. For example, a PUT statement would use the terms `#5 @17` to move to line 5, column 17.

Because the @ pointer control can be used with variables, we recommend defining variables to identify the columns in a table. You can have columns A, B, C, etc., spreadsheet-style, if those variable names are available. You can define the column locations in a RETAIN statement

```
RETAIN  A 1  B 12  C 23  D 34  E 45  F 56  G 67;
```

and then use the terms `@A`, `@B`, etc., to move to the different columns.

There are many advantages in using this approach. All items in PUT statements that appear in the same column can easily be identified, because they all have the same column letter preceding them. It is easier to change the position of columns, add space between columns, add new columns, remove columns, and make similar changes, because only one line needs to be changed. Last but not least, you can code the PUT statements without having to determine spacing first, because it is easy to adjust the spacing later.

The specific techniques used to create tables depend on the shape of the group of cells produced by each observation — something that we call a *form* in the discussion that follows.

Line forms

Usually an observation is printed on one line. In that case, the step just has to create the line for each observation and, usually, column headers at the top of each page. The HEADER= option can be used to create the column headers.

```
TITLE1 'Physical Fitness';
TITLE2 'June 7, 1990';
TITLE3 '----------------------';
  DATA _NULL_;
    RETAIN  A 1  B 20  C 28  D 38  E 48;
    SET FITNESS;
    FILE PRINT HEADER=HEADER N=1;
    PUT @A LASTNAME +(-1) ', ' FIRSNAME
        @B +2 SITUPS 3. @C +3 PUSHUPS 3.
        @D +2 MILETIME MMSS5. @E CLIMBHT 6.;
    RETURN;
HEADER: PUT / @D 'Mile Run' @E 'Rope Climb' /
      @B 'Situps' @C 'Pushups' @D '(min:s)' @E +3 '(m)' /;
```

```
                      Physical Fitness
                        June 7, 1990
                  ----------------------

                                   Mile Run  Rope Climb
                  Situps  Pushups  (min:s)      (m)

BRAVELY, JANE       30        3      7:20        12
COOPER, ALLEY       29        8      6:49        12
EHMAN, SID          80       10      7:11        12
FASTER, RICK        48       12      5:36        12
GETTY, LEE          52       17      5:29        12
HATTER, HEATHER     40       12      5:05        12
MASTERS, KRIS       28        9      6:06        12
NICELY, MARTY       41        9      6:59        12
```

Observations

You might want to include only selected observations in a report. You can give the condition for using an observation in a subsetting IF statement, a WHEN option, or an IF . . . THEN statement controlling the PUT statement for each observation:

```
    IF SITUPS > 40 THEN PUT @A LASTNAME +(-1) ', ' FIRSNAME
        @B +2 SITUPS 3. @C +3 PUSHUPS 3.
        @D +2 MILETIME MMSS5. @E CLIMBHT 6.;
```

```
EHMAN, SID          80       10      7:11        12
FASTER, RICK        48       12      5:36        12
GETTY, LEE          52       17      5:29        12
NICELY, MARTY       41        9      6:59        12
```

Alternatively, you might want to include identifying information (in this example, the name) for the omitted observations.

```
PUT @A LASTNAME +(-1) ', ' FIRSNAME @;
IF SITUPS > 40 THEN PUT @B +2 SITUPS 3. @C +3 PUSHUPS 3.
    @D +2 MILETIME MMSS5. @E CLIMBHT 6.;
```

```
BRAVELY, JANE
COOPER, ALLEY
EHMAN, SID              80        10        7:11        12
FASTER, RICK            48        12        5:36        12
GETTY, LEE              52        17        5:29        12
HATTER, HEATHER
MASTERS, KRIS
NICELY, MARTY           41         9        6:59        12
```

Or you could leave a blank line for each omitted observation:

```
IF SITUPS > 40 THEN PUT @A LASTNAME +(-1) ', ' FIRSNAME
    @B +2 SITUPS 3. @C +3 PUSHUPS 3.
    @D +2 MILETIME MMSS5. @E CLIMBHT 6.;
ELSE PUT;
```

```


EHMAN, SID              80        10        7:11        12
FASTER, RICK            48        12        5:36        12
GETTY, LEE              52        17        5:29        12


NICELY, MARTY           41         9        6:59        12
```

Including a blank line between every five rows of data sometimes makes a table more readable, especially for wide tables of numbers. A statement like

```
IF NOT MOD(_N_, 5) THEN PUT;
```

at the appropriate place in the step can accomplish this.

```
  DATA _NULL_;
    RETAIN  A 1  B 20  C 28  D 38  E 48;
    SET FITNESS;
    FILE PRINT HEADER=HEADER N=1;
    PUT @A LASTNAME +(-1) ', ' FIRSNAME
        @B +2 SITUPS 3. @C +3 PUSHUPS 3.
        @D +2 MILETIME MMSS5. @E CLIMBHT 6.;
    IF NOT MOD(_N_, 5) THEN PUT;
    RETURN;
HEADER: PUT / @D 'Mile Run' @E 'Rope Climb' /
      @B 'Situps' @C 'Pushups' @D '(min:s)' @E +3 '(m)' /;
```

```
                                      Mile Run  Rope Climb
                    Situps  Pushups   (min:s)      (m)

BRAVELY, JANE         30        3       7:20        12
COOPER, ALLEY         29        8       6:49        12
EHMAN, SID            80       10       7:11        12
FASTER, RICK          48       12       5:36        12
GETTY, LEE            52       17       5:29        12

HATTER, HEATHER       40       12       5:05        12
MASTERS, KRIS         28        9       6:06        12
NICELY, MARTY         41        9       6:59        12
```

Groups

When a report is produced with grouped observations, you can put a blank line between groups to separate them visually.

```
DATA _NULL_;
  RETAIN  A 1  B 9  C 15  D 22  E 28;
  PILE PRINT N=PS LL=LL;
  SET FX;
  BY GROUP;
  IF _N_ = 1 OR LL < 5 THEN PUT _PAGE_ @A 'Effect'
      @B 'Test' @C 'Rating' @D 'Price' @E +1 'S/N' @F +1 'THD' /;
  IF FIRST.GROUP THEN PUT;
  PUT @A GROUP @B +1 TEST
      @C RATED 4. @D PRICE 5. @E SN 4. @F THD 4.;
```

```
Effect  Test  Rating Price  S/N            THD

Comp/L   A       8     395   76            -28
Comp/L   B       7     495   81            -33

ParaEQ   A      10    1199   84            -36
ParaEQ   B      10     895   82            -37
```

Or you might put the groups on separate pages:

```
DATA _NULL_;
  RETAIN  A 1  B 9  C 15  D 22  E 28;
  PILE PRINT N=PS LL=LL;
  SET FX;
  BY GROUP;
  IF FIRST.GROUP OR LL < 5 THEN PUT _PAGE_ @A 'Effect'
      @B 'Test' @C 'Rating' @D 'Price' @E +1 'S/N' @F +1 'THD' /;
  PUT @A GROUP @B +1 TEST
      @C RATED 4. @D PRICE 5. @E SN 4. @F THD 4.;
```

```
Effect  Test  Rating Price  S/N  THD

Comp/L   A       8     395   76  -28
Comp/L   B       7     495   81  -33
```

```
Effect   Test  Rating Price  S/N   THD

ParaEQ   A       10    1199   84   -36
ParaEQ   B       10     895   82   -37
```

You might be interested in printing a line of totals for each group at the end of the group. This involves calculating the totals.

```
DATA _NULL_;
  RETAIN  A 1  B 9  C 15  D 22  E 28  QR QP QS QT;
  PILE PRINT N=PS LL=LL;
  SET FX;
  BY GROUP;
  IF _N_ = 1 OR LL < 5 THEN PUT _PAGE_ @A 'Effect'
      @B 'Test' @C 'Rating' @D 'Price' @E +1 'S/N' @F +1 'THD' /;
  PUT @A GROUP @B +1 TEST
      @C RATED 4. @D PRICE 5. @E SN 4. @F THD 4.;

  IF FIRST.GROUP THEN DO; QR = 0; QP = 0; QS = 0; QT = 0; END;
  QR + RATED; QP + PRICE; QS + SN; QT + THD;
  IF LAST.GROUP THEN PUT /
      @C  ' ----' @D '-----' @E '----' @F '----' /
      @B 'Total' @C QR 4. @D QP 5. @E QS 4. @F QT 4. /;
```

```
Effect   Test  Rating Price  S/N   THD

Comp/L   A        8     395   76   -28
Comp/L   B        7     495   81   -33
               ----  ----- ----  ----
         Total   15     890  157   -61

ParaEQ   A       10    1199   84   -36
ParaEQ   B       10     895   82   -37
               ----  ----- ----  ----
         Total   20    2094  166   -73
```

Instead of totals, you could report averages.

```
DATA _NULL_;
  RETAIN  A 1  B 9  C 15  D 22  E 28  QR QP QS QT N;

  PILE PRINT N=PS LL=LL;
  SET FX;
  BY GROUP;
  IF _N_ = 1 OR LL <= 5 THEN PUT _PAGE_ @A 'Effect'
      @B 'Test' @C 'Rating' @D 'Price' @E +1 'S/N' @F +1 'THD' /;
  PUT @A GROUP @B +1 TEST
      @C RATED 4. @D PRICE 5. @E SN 4. @F THD 4.;

  IF FIRST.GROUP THEN DO;
    QR = 0; QP = 0; QS = 0; QT = 0; N = 0; END;
  QR + RATED; QP + PRICE; QS + SN; QT + THD; N + 1;
  IF LAST.GROUP THEN DO;
    AR = QR/N; AP = QP/N; AS = QS/N; AT = QT/N;
```

```
PUT /
  @C   ' ----' @D '-----' @E '----' @F '----' /
  @B 'Av.' @C AR 4. @D AP 5. @E AS 4. @F AT 4. /;
END;
```

```
Effect  Test  Rating Price  S/N   THD

Comp/L   A       8    395   76    -28
Comp/L   B       7    495   81    -33
               ---- ----- ----   ----
        Av.      8    445   79    -30

ParaEQ   A      10   1199   84    -36
ParaEQ   B      10    895   82    -37
               ---- ----- ----   ----
        Av.     10   1047   83    -36
```

Page breaks

The LL= (or LINESLEFT=) variable and LINE= variable created by the FILE statement can be useful in determining where to put a page break in a report. The LL= variable tells how many lines are left on the page, including the current line; the LINE= variable tells which line of the page the line pointer is on if the N=PS option is used.

Page breaks should be put in the right place to create the intended bottom margin, or just to keep the report from flowing over the end of the page onto the next page. The headers, if the report has any, can be written in the same statement as the page break. In that case, the condition `_N_ = 1` or a similar condition should be part of the condition for this statement so that the header can appear on the first page. This was done in the examples above:

```
IF _N_ = 1 OR LL <= 5 THEN PUT _PAGE_ header;
```

It's possible to write a header that tells the range of observations printed on the page. The header is written on the first observation on the page, except for the part identifying the last observation on the page. That kind of header appears in this alphabetical telephone listing:

```
DATA _NULL_;
  RETAIN  A 1  B 23;
  LENGTH LASTNAME $ 6;
  FILE PHONLIST PRINT N=PS LL=LL LINE=LINE;
  SET PHONE END=LAST;

  IF _N_ = 1 OR LINE = 1 THEN DO;
    LASTNAME = SCAN(NAME, 1, ',');
    PUT _PAGE_ @A 'SharkCorp USA'
        #2 @A 'Telephone Listing 05/91'
        #1 @(B - 7) LASTNAME $CHAR6. '-'
        #4 @;
    END;
```

```
PHONE1 = SUBSTR(PHONE, 3, 1);
PHONE2 = SUBSTR(PHONE, 4);
PUT / @A NAME $CHAR22.
      @B PHONE1 $CHAR1. '-' PHONE2 $CHAR4. @;
IF LL = 1 OR LAST THEN DO;
  LASTNAME = SCAN(NAME, 1, ',');
  PUT #1 @B LASTNAME $CHAR6. @;
  END;
```

```
SharkCorp USA  Sawyer-Shark
Telephone Listing 05/91

Sawyer, Bea             4-0115
Sears, Greta            7-9237
Sellers, Tim            4-2382
Sellers, Patricia       4-2387
Sexton, Apollo          5-4322
Shark, Abby             5-2483
Shark, Andrew J.        4-2379
Shark, Andrew W.        4-0047
Shark, Andrew W.        4-0048
Shark, Charles          7-3428
Shark, Emma S.          7-1154
Shark, Fitzgerald       5-3234
Shark, Kevin            4-2343
Shark, Mack             4-9905
Shark, Noah             4-0156
```

For some reports with grouped data, it is appropriate to keep a page break from appearing in the middle of a group. This assumes that no group has too many observations to fit on a single page. To put as many groups as possible on a page without breaking up a group, the report step needs to know how many observations are in each group, something that can be counted in a previous step.

```
* Count observations in each group;
DATA COUNT;
  SET PERSONEL;
  BY GROUP;
  IF FIRST.GROUP THEN COUNT = 1;
  ELSE COUNT + 1;
  IF LAST.GROUP THEN OUTPUT;

DATA _NULL_;
  FILE PRINT NOTITLE LL=LL PS=20;
  MERGE PERSONEL COUNT;
  BY GROUP;
  IF FIRST.GROUP THEN DO;
    * Compare number of lines needed for group to lines on page;
    IF COUNT + 2 > LL THEN PUT _PAGE_ @;
    ELSE PUT;
    PUT 'LEVEL:  ' GROUP;
    END;
  PUT PARTIC @5 NAME;
```

```
LEVEL:  Chief Executive Officer
*    Jeremy O'Clock

LEVEL:  Entry Level Prof/Tech
     Marcus Downe
     Helena Handbasket
     Loudon Obnoxious
     Barnaby Wilde

LEVEL:  Executive Vice President
*    John Lum
```

```
LEVEL:  Manager
*    Gerry Bacon
*    Max Burns
     Guy Charles
*    Canilla Ford
     Cosmic Jones
     Hiroshi Ko
     Bryan Lennain
*    Judith Mister
     Alan Ozone
     Zoey Pack
     Warren Peace
     Keith Riot
     Mona Sparks
     Fred Young
```

Multiple-line forms

It is possible to print more than one line from each observation. The only complications are making sure that column headers are meaningful and that page breaks come at appropriate places. It might be appropriate to put a blank line before or after each observation.

The step below uses the condition `LL < 4` to check whether it is getting near the bottom of the print page. The LL= option on the FILE statement defines LL as a variable that tells the number of lines left on the page.

```
TITLE1 'Total Physical Fitness Guaranteed Program';
TITLE2 'Total Fitness Test Results';
TITLE3 ' ';
  DATA _NULL_;
    RETAIN  A 1  B 16  C 20  D 29  E 38;
    FILE PRINT LS=64 LL=LL N=PS;
    SET _LAST_ (KEEP=LASTNAME AGE SITUPS1 SITUPS2 SITUPS3
                PUSHUPS1 PUSHUPS2 PUSHUPS3 DATE1 DATE2 DATE3);
    IF LL < 5 OR _N_ = 1 THEN PUT _PAGE_
        #2 @A 'Name' @B 'Age' @C 'Date' @D 'Pushups' @E 'Situps'
        #3 @A '-------------' @B '---' @C '--------' @D '-------'
        @E '------' #2 @;
    PUT // @A LASTNAME @B AGE 3.
        @C DATE1 MMDDYY8. @D PUSHUPS1 7. @E SITUPS1 6. /
        @C DATE2 MMDDYY8. @D PUSHUPS2 7. @E SITUPS2 6. /
        @C DATE3 MMDDYY8. @D PUSHUPS3 7. @E SITUPS3 6. @;
```

```
          Total Physical Fitness Guaranteed Program
                  Total Fitness Test Results


Name           Age Date     Pushups  Situps
-------------  --- -------- -------  ------
Olive           23 09/09/90       2      11
                   10/10/90       4      15
                   11/11/90       7      40

Oliver          31 09/09/90       6      17
                   10/10/90       8      15
                   11/11/90      17      20

Poppy           22 09/09/90      32      71
                   10/10/90      34     100
                   11/11/90      27     100
```

Page forms

Sometimes each observation has enough data to take up a whole page by itself. This is especially appropriate with a two-dimensional array.

Usually you can use a single PUT statement to write the entire page:

```
DATA _NULL_;
  RETAIN  A 1  B 8  C 18  D 28  E 38  F 48;
  FILE PRINT;
  MERGE SKED  (KEEP=STUDENT A1-A5 B1-B5 C1-C5 D1-D5 E1-E5 F1-F5
          G1-G5 H1-H5 I1-I5 J1-J5 K1-K5 L1-L5 M1-M5 O1-O5 P1-P5)
        CLASS (KEEP=STUDENT NAME CLASS);
  BY STUDENT;
  PUT _PAGE_ / @B NAME $CHAR44. /
      @B STUDENT $HEX10. @E 'CLASS:   ' CLASS $CHAR9. //
      @A 'Time' @B 'Monday' @C 'Tuesday' @D 'Wednesday'
      @E 'Thursday' @F 'Friday' //
      @A ' 8:00' @B (A1-A5) ($CHAR10.) /
      @A ' 8:30' @B (A1-A5) ($CHAR10.) /
      @A ' 9:00' @B (B1-B5) ($CHAR10.) /
      @A ' 9:30' @B (C1-C5) ($CHAR10.) /
      @A '10:00' @B (D1-D5) ($CHAR10.) /
      @A '10:30' @B (E1-E5) ($CHAR10.) /
      @A '11:00' @B (F1-F5) ($CHAR10.) /
      @A '11:30' @B (G1-G5) ($CHAR10.) /
      @A '12:00'                       /
      @A '12:30'                       /
      @A ' 1:00' @B (H1-H5) ($CHAR10.) /
      @A ' 1:30' @B (I1-I5) ($CHAR10.) /
      @A ' 2:00' @B (J1-J5) ($CHAR10.) /
      @A ' 2:30' @B (K1-K5) ($CHAR10.) /
      @A ' 3:00' @B (L1-L5) ($CHAR10.) /
      @A ' 3:30' @B (M1-M5) ($CHAR10.) /
      @A ' 4:00' @B (N1-N5) ($CHAR10.) /
      @A ' 4:30' @B (O1-O5) ($CHAR10.) /
      @A ' 5:00' @B (P1-P5) ($CHAR10.) / ;
```

```
        PIERRE ALMAN
        0375489A01                    CLASS:  SENIOR

Time    Monday     Tuesday    Wednesday Thursday   Friday

 8:00   Mu 160     Ma 190     Mu 160               Mu 160
 8:30   Mu 160     Ma 190     Mu 160               Mu 160
 9:00
 9:30              EE 311               EE 311
10:00              EE 311               EE 311
10:30              EE 311               EE 311
11:00   EE 417                EE 417               EE 417
11:30   EE 417                EE 417               EE 417
12:00
12:30
 1:00
 1:30
 2:00              Ch 105
 2:30              Ch 105
 3:00   Ma 250     Ch 105     Ma 250               Ma 250
 3:30   Ma 250     Ch 105     Ma 250               Ma 250
 4:00              Ch 105
 4:30              Ch 105
 5:00
```

Column forms

Writing an observation as a column is often preferable to writing it as a row. It is especially convenient when the total width of variables is greater than the line size and the number of variables is less than the number of lines on the page.

For example, some SAS datasets contain a certain measurement for each of the 50 U.S. states, Puerto Rico, and the District of Columbia. Those 52 variables could not fit in a row, but can be printed in a column.

You have to write the row labels on each new page and keep track of the number of observations appearing on each page. The page break, heading, and row labels are written after the specified number of observations have been put on a page.

In this example, values for 12 months appear in each observation and are written as a column. Up to 6 observations are printed on each page.

```
DATA _NULL_;
  RETAIN  A 1  B 11  C 19  D 27  E 35  F 43  G 51  COLUMN 8;
  ARRAY CIRC{12};
  ARRAY COL{7} A B C D E F G;
  FILE PRINT N=PS;

  SET BOOKMON (KEEP=BRANCH CAT CIRC1-CIRC12);
  IF COLUMN > 7 THEN DO;
    PUT _PAGE_ #2 @A 'Branch' #3 @A 'Category'
        #5  @A 'January   ' #6  @A 'February ' #7  @A 'March    '
        #8  @A 'April     ' #9  @A 'May      ' #10 @A 'June     '
        #11 @A 'July      ' #12 @A 'August   ' #13 @A 'September'
        #14 @A 'October   ' #15 @A 'November ' #16 @A 'December '
```

```
        #18 @A 'Total' @;
     COLUMN = 2;
     END;
   TOTAL = SUM(OF CIRC1-CIRC12);
   PUT #2  @(COL{COLUMN}) BRANCH $CHAR7.
       #3  @(COL{COLUMN}) CAT $CHAR7.
       #4  @(COL{COLUMN}) '-------'
       #5  @(COL{COLUMN}) CIRC1  COMMA7.
       #6  @(COL{COLUMN}) CIRC2  COMMA7.
       #7  @(COL{COLUMN}) CIRC3  COMMA7.
       #8  @(COL{COLUMN}) CIRC4  COMMA7.
       #9  @(COL{COLUMN}) CIRC5  COMMA7.
       #10 @(COL{COLUMN}) CIRC6  COMMA7.
       #11 @(COL{COLUMN}) CIRC7  COMMA7.
       #12 @(COL{COLUMN}) CIRC8  COMMA7.
       #13 @(COL{COLUMN}) CIRC9  COMMA7.
       #14 @(COL{COLUMN}) CIRC10 COMMA7.
       #15 @(COL{COLUMN}) CIRC11 COMMA7.
       #16 @(COL{COLUMN}) CIRC12 COMMA7.
       #17 @(COL{COLUMN}) '-------'
       #18 @(COL{COLUMN}) TOTAL  COMMA7. @;
   COLUMN + 1;
```

Branch Category	Mudd LC	Mudd Dewey	Mudd Fiction	Con LC	Con Scores	Math LC
	-------	-------	-------	-------	-------	-------
January	16,012	875	2,496	1,472	4,263	148
February	28,637	1,426	2,034	1,574	3,104	116
March	25,788	1,734	2,633	1,494	3,344	88
April	29,047	1,333	2,757	1,001	2,952	105
May	17,435	1,058	260	962	3,045	90
June	2,155	298	164	106	267	6
July	1,729	158	363	103	227	7
August	5,820	554	1,706	664	1,065	11
September	28,543	1,643	1,853	1,554	3,405	121
October	26,722	1,075	2,264	1,576	3,054	89
November	25,338	1,655	2,340	1,616	3,724	89
December	25,509	1,354	624	1,244	3,387	51
	-------	-------	-------	-------	-------	-------
Total	232,735	13,163	19,494	13,366	31,837	921

Cell forms

Sometimes several observations must be be combined to form one row of a table. If each observation produces one cell, then the observation must usually contain additional information that indicates in which column the cell should be printed. There must also be a variable indicating how the cells are grouped into rows. The row variable should be a BY variable and can be printed at the beginning of the row.

In the example below, the row variable is CORP, and the WEEKDAY function is used with the variable DATE to determine what column to print an observation in.

```
TITLE1 'Closing Stock Prices';
```

```
TITLE2 'Week Of 7/2/90-7/6/90';
  DATA _NULL_;
    RETAIN  A 1  B 19  C 27  D 35  E 43  F 51;
    ARRAY COLUMN{2:6} B C D E F;
    SET STOCK (KEEP=CORP DATE CLOSE);
    BY CORP;
    FILE PRINT HEADER=HEADER LS=64;

    IF FIRST.CORP THEN PUT / @1 CORP @;
    PUT @(COLUMN{WEEKDAY(DATE)}) CLOSE BEST7. @;
    RETURN;
HEADER: PUT / @B +3 'MON' @C +3 'TUE' @D +3 'WED'
              @E +3 'THU' @F +3 'FRI' /
         @B +2 '-----' @C +2 '-----' @D +2 '-----' @E +2 '-----'
         @F +2 '-----';
```

```
                    Closing Stock Prices
                    Week Of 7/2/90-7/8/90

                     MON     TUE      WED      THU     FRI
                    -----   -----    -----    -----   -----

AAAAce                 5    5.125       5        5     4.75
ABC                   44   45.125   45.25     48.5       51
AcmeEx                30       30      30   30.375     30.5
```

The next example demonstrates a situation in which more than one observation may be associated with a combination of row and column labels. The program has to keep track of the maximum number of lines printed in a cell in the current row in order to know where to start the next row.

```
DATA _NULL_;
  RETAIN A 1  B 15  C 30  D 45  BASELINE 5;
  FILE PRINT N=PS LINE=LINE LL=LL;
  SET _LAST_ (KEEP=NAME COMMITEE EXPDATE);
  BY EXPDATE COMMITEE;
  IF FIRST.COMMITEE THEN DO;
    IF FIRST.EXPDATE THEN DO;
      IF _N_ = 1 OR LL < 7 THEN PUT _PAGE_
         #1 @C +3 'Committee'
         #2 @B '-----------------'
            @C '-----------------'
            @D '--------------'
         #3 @A 'Term Expires'
            @B 'Finance' @C 'Planning' @D 'Rules'
         #4 @A '-------------'
            @B '--------------'
            @C '--------------'
            @D '--------------'
         #3 @;
      PUT // @A EXPDATE 4. @;
      BASELINE = LINE - 1;
      LINEMAX  = LINE;
      END;
    PUT #BASELINE @;
```

```
    END;
  SELECT(SUBSTR(COMMITEE, 1, 1));
    WHEN('F') PUT / @B NAME $CHAR14. @;
    WHEN('P') PUT / @C NAME $CHAR14. @;
    WHEN('R') PUT / @D NAME $CHAR14. @;
    OTHERWISE;
    END;
  LINEMAX = LINE MAX LINEMAX;
  IF LAST.EXPDATE THEN PUT #LINEMAX @;
RUN;
```

```
                                  Committee
              -------------------------------------------
Term Expires  Finance         Planning        Rules
------------  --------------  --------------  --------------
1992          R. Bacon        L. Cupertino
                              D. Yttri
                              H. Franklin

1993          A. Hamilton     F. Houser       G. Kennedy
                                              D. Kay

1994          J. Lumski       J. Tee          C. Angel
                                              C. Waters
```

Block forms

Finally, we consider observations that take up a rectangular area that is more than a single cell, but neither the whole width nor the whole height of the page.

A familiar example of this is mailing labels, 30 or 33 of which are often printed in 3 columns on a standard-size printed page. From a programming standpoint, mailing labels can most easily be produced in a non-print file, with each row of labels taking up 6 lines. However, this might require more work in operating the printer, because the margins must be set to create a page size that is a multiple of 6 and the first line of each label falling slightly below the top of the label. Therefore, we demonstrate here how to create mailing labels in a print file.

The step below prints names and addresses from the SAS dataset PEOPLE, with the variables NAME, ADDRESS1, ADDRESS2, ADDRESS3, CITY, ST, and ZIP. ADDRESS2 and ADDRESS3 are printed only if they are not blank. Printing for each label begins with NAME on the second line of the 6-line block associated with the label. Eleven rows of labels, with three labels in each row, are printed.

```
DATA _NULL_;
  RETAIN  A 1  B 23  C 46  ROW 0 COLUMN 3;
  ARRAY COL{3} A B C;
  FILE MAILING PRINT NOTITLE N=PS PS=66;

  SET PEOPLE (KEEP=NAME ADDRESS1 ADDRESS2 ADDRESS3 CITY ST ZIP);
```

```
COLUMN + 1;
IF COLUMN > 3 THEN DO; ROW + 1; COLUMN = 1; END;
IF ROW > 11 THEN DO; PUT _PAGE_ @; ROW = 1; END;
BASELINE = ROW*6 - 4;

PUT #BASELINE @(COL{COLUMN}) NAME /
    @(COL{COLUMN}) ADDRESS1 @;
IF ADDRESS2 NE ' ' THEN PUT / @(COL{COLUMN}) ADDRESS2 @;
IF ADDRESS3 NE ' ' THEN PUT / @(COL{COLUMN}) ADDRESS3 @;
PUT / @(COL{COLUMN}) CITY +(-1) ST ZIP @;
```

To print 10 rows of labels, with 3 lines skipped at the top of the page, use the appropriate number of blank TITLE lines and the PRINT option but not the NOTITLES option on the FILE statement:

```
TITLE1 '';
TITLE2 '';
TITLE3 '';
  ...
    FILE MAILING PRINT N=PS PS=66;
    ...
```

Another way to divide a page is represented by newspaper columns, sometimes called "snaking" columns, because of the way the end of one column connects to the beginning of the next column. We call these newspaper-style columns "stripes" to avoid confusion between them and the columns of a table or of a print file. Stripes are used in printing tables when the width of the table is a fraction of the width of the page; several table segments can be placed, side by side, on each page.

A revision of the earlier telephone listing example demonstrates how this can be done. When you near the bottom of the page, instead of automatically starting a new page, you move to the next stripe, which can either be on the same page or on the next page.

The example uses the implicitly subscripted arrays A and B for the two table columns. The table columns are associated with different column pointer locations depending on which stripe is being printed.

```
DATA _NULL_;
  RETAIN  A1 1  B1 23  A2 31  B2 53  STRIPE 2;
  ARRAY A (STRIPE) A1-A2;
  ARRAY B (STRIPE) B1-B2;
  LENGTH LASTNAME $ 6;
  FILE PHONLIST PRINT N=PS LL=LL LINE=LINE;
  SET PHONE (KEEP=NAME PHONE) END=LAST;

  IF _N_ = 1 OR LINE = 1 THEN DO; * Begin new page;
    LASTNAME = SCAN(NAME, 1, ',');
    PUT _PAGE_ @A1 'SharkCorp USA'
        +4 'Telephone Listing 05/91'
        #1 @(B2 - 7) LASTNAME $CHAR6. '-'
        #3 @;
    STRIPE = 1;
    END;
  PHONE1 = SUBSTR(PHONE, 3, 1);
```

```
PHONE2 = SUBSTR(PHONE, 4);
PUT / @A NAME $CHAR22. @B PHONE1 $CHAR1. '-' PHONE2 $CHAR4. @;

IF LINE >= 12 AND STRIPE < 2 THEN DO; * End of stripe;
  STRIPE + 1;
  PUT #2 @;
  END;
ELSE IF LINE >= 12 OR LAST THEN DO; * End of page;
  LASTNAME = SCAN(NAME, 1, ',');
  PUT #1 @B2 LASTNAME $CHAR6. @;
  END;
```

```
SharkCorp USA    Telephone Listing 05/91     Sawyer-Shark

Sawyer, Bea            4-0115  Shark, Emma S.         7-1154
Sears, Greta           7-9237  Shark, Fitzgerald      5-3234
Sellers, Tim           4-2382  Shark, Kevin           4-2343
Sellers, Patricia      4-2387  Shark, Mack            4-9905
Sexton, Apollo         5-3222  Shark, Noah            4-0156
Shark, Abby            5-3283  Shark, Pamela          4-7711
Shark, Andrew J.       4-2379  Shark, Patrick         7-0050
Shark, Andrew W.       4-0047  Shark, Rhonda          4-2472
Shark, Andrew W.       4-0048  Shark, Theodore E.     5-3285
Shark, Charles         7-3428  Shark, Wendy           5-3201
```

Rules

Rules can be created between rows and columns, and boxes can be printed around objects, using characters such as +, -, and |. Usually the rules can be printed as an extension of the header. The telephone listing program above is revised here to have rules on each page.

```
DATA _NULL_;
  RETAIN  A1 3  B1 25  A2 34  B2 56  STRIPE 2;
  ARRAY A (STRIPE) A1-A2;
  ARRAY B (STRIPE) B1-B2;
  LENGTH LASTNAME $ 6;
  FILE PHONLIST PRINT N=PS LL=LL LINE=LINE;
  SET PHONE (KEEP=NAME PHONE) END=LAST;

  IF _N_ = 1 OR LINE = 1 THEN DO; * Begin new page;
    LASTNAME = SCAN(NAME, 1, ',');
    PUT _PAGE_ @A1 'SharkCorp USA'
        +4 'Telephone Listing 05/91'
        #1 @(B2 - 7) LASTNAME $CHAR6. '-'
        #2  '+------------------------------'     /* horizontal */
            '+------------------------------+'    /* rules      */
        #13 '+------------------------------'
            '+------------------------------+'
        #3 @;
  DO L = 3 TO 12;        /* vertical rules */
    PUT '|' @;
    DO OVER B; PUT @B +7 '|' @; END;
    PUT;
    END;
```

```
PUT #2 @;
STRIPE = 1;
END;
PHONE1 = SUBSTR(PHONE, 3, 1);
PHONE2 = SUBSTR(PHONE, 4);
PUT / @A NAME $CHAR22. @B PHONE1 $CHAR1. '-' PHONE2 $CHAR4. @;

IF LINE >= 12 AND STRIPE < 2 THEN DO; * End of stripe;
  STRIPE + 1;
  PUT #2 @;
  END;
ELSE IF LINE >= 12 OR LAST THEN DO;  * End of page;
  LASTNAME = SCAN(NAME, 1, ',');
  PUT #1 @B2 LASTNAME $CHAR6. @;
  END;
```

```
  SharkCorp USA    Telephone Listing 05/91      Sawyer-Shark
+------------------------------+------------------------------+
| Sawyer, Bea            4-0115 | Shark, Emma S.        7-1154 |
| Sears, Greta           7-9237 | Shark, Fitzgerald     5-3234 |
| Sellers, Tim           4-2382 | Shark, Kevin          4-2343 |
| Sellers, Patricia      4-2387 | Shark, Mack           4-9905 |
| Sexton, Apollo         5-3222 | Shark, Noah           4-0156 |
| Shark, Abby            5-3283 | Shark, Pamela         4-7711 |
| Shark, Andrew J.       4-2379 | Shark, Patrick        7-0050 |
| Shark, Andrew W.       4-0047 | Shark, Rhonda         4-2472 |
| Shark, Andrew W.       4-0048 | Shark, Theodore E.    5-3285 |
| Shark, Charles         7-3428 | Shark, Wendy          5-3201 |
+------------------------------+------------------------------+
```

Formatting

There are basically two ways variable values can be converted to characters in a print file: by using a format, or by associating character constants with specific variable values in a SELECT block or in IF . . . THEN . . . ELSE statements. There is also a hybrid approach, combining these two approaches.

Most of the time, a format is all that is needed to format a variable. A variable term containing the format appears in a PUT statement:

```
PUT QUANTITY 7.;
```

In addition to the formats included in the SAS System, two kinds of formats can be created by the FORMAT proc. Formats are described in chapter 3, "Programs on call."

Instead of having a variable term in the PUT statement, you could use a constant term, with the variable value appearing in a SELECT, WHEN, or IF condition. These statements, for example, print either "Yes" or "No" depending on the value of the variable ANSWER:

```
SELECT(ANSWER);
  WHEN(0) PUT 'No';
```

```
OTHERWISE PUT 'Yes';
END;
```

A variable could appear both as a condition and in a PUT statement, to format different values using different format specifications, or to print some values as a constant and others using a format:

```
IF QUANTITY > 0 THEN PUT QUANTITY 7.; ELSE PUT '   None';
```

Omitting zero quantities improves the appearance of some tables. To print only nonzero quantities, determine whether a variable is nonzero before printing it:

```
IF QUANTITY THEN PUT @C QUANTITY 7. @;
```

Standard missing values are ordinarily printed as a single period, but the character used can be changed with the MISSING= system option. Specifying

```
OPTIONS MISSING=' ';
```

would print standard missing values as a blank, while

```
OPTIONS MISSING='*';
```

might be used to call attention to missing values.

Numeric formats print special missing values as the corresponding capital letter or underscore; for example, .A is printed as A. If you do not want to distinguish between different special missing values, you can print them using a character constant:

```
IF AMOUNT <= .Z THEN PUT '      .';
ELSE PUT AMOUNT 7. @;
```

A similar effect can be achieved using a picture format:

```
PROC FORMAT;
  PICTURE MISSDOT (MIN=1)
      ._-.Z  = '.' (NOEDIT)
      LOW-<0 = '000000000001' (PREFIX='-')
      OTHER  = '000000000001';
RUN;
...
    PUT AMOUNT MISSDOT7.;
```

The way a variable is formatted can depend on the value of another variable. A variable might, in some cases, be printed only if another variable has a certain value. For example, a variable representing an excess amount might be printed only when another variable indicates that an excess exists:

```
PUT LEVEL $ @;
IF LEVEL = 'EXCESS' THEN PUT +2 XSAMT :8. @;
```

```
    PUT;
```

```
BASIC
BASIC
EXCESS    10000
EXCESS    25000
EXCESS    1000000
```

Footnotes

If the same footnotes appear on every page, they can be written in the same statement that writes the header.

```
  DATA _NULL_;
    SET INDATE;
    FILE PRINT N=PS LL=LL PS=55;
    IF LL < 7 OR _N_ = 1 THEN PUT _PAGE_
        'This header appears on every page.'
        #50 'This footer appears on every page.' #8 @;
    ...
```

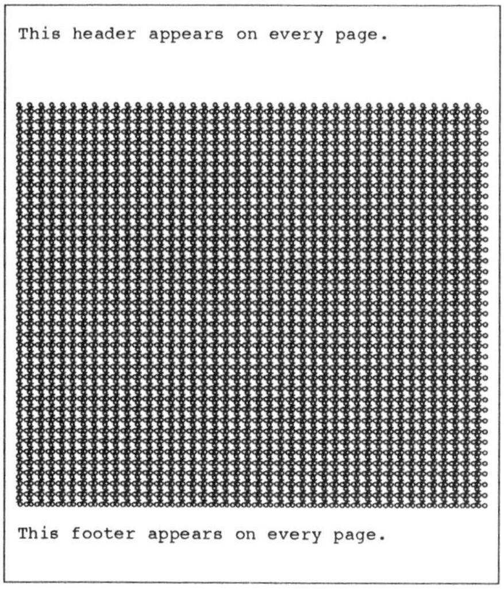
This header appears on every page.
This footer appears on every page.

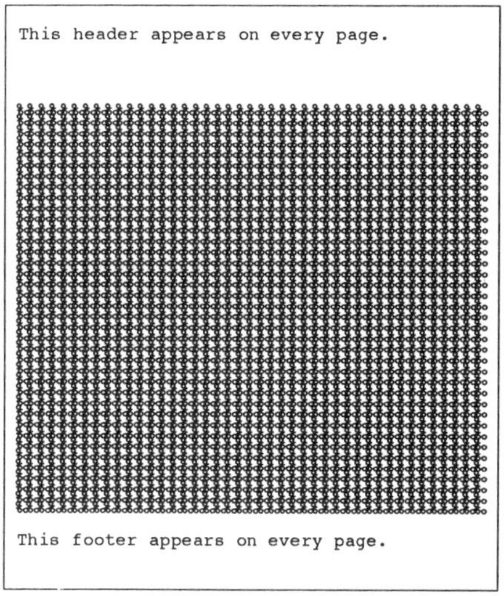
This header appears on every page.
This footer appears on every page.

If the footnotes depend on the data on the page, they can be printed after the last observation on the page. You should keep track of the number of footnotes being used on each page to make sure that there are enough lines left on the page to write them.

If there are 8 possible footnotes, you can use the variables DONOTE1–DONOTE8 to keep track of which notes appear on a page. The footnote variables are set to 0 at the beginning of each page, and are set to 1 in the course of the page when the need for a footnote is ascertained from the values of a variable.

```
  DATA _NULL_;
    RETAIN DONOTE1-DONOTE8 0  A 11  B 21  C 31  D 41  E 51;
```

```
FILE PRINT LS=64 PS=60 N=PS NOTITLE LL=LL;

SET STOCKS END=LAST;
IF _N_ = 1 OR LL <= 3 THEN PUT _PAGE_ @;
PUT / @A YEAR 4.  @B LEVEL1 COMMA9. @;
IF NOTE1 NE ' ' THEN PUT @C '(' NOTE1 $CHAR1. ')' @;
PUT @D LEVEL2 COMMA9. @;
IF NOTE2 NE ' ' THEN PUT @E '(' NOTE2 $CHAR1. ')' @;
IF NOTE1 = 'a' OR NOTE2 = 'a' THEN DONOTE1 = 1;
IF NOTE1 = 'b' OR NOTE2 = 'b' THEN DONOTE2 = 1;
IF NOTE1 = 'c' OR NOTE2 = 'c' THEN DONOTE3 = 1;
IF NOTE1 = 'd' OR NOTE2 = 'd' THEN DONOTE4 = 1;
IF NOTE1 = 'e' OR NOTE2 = 'e' THEN DONOTE5 = 1;
IF NOTE1 = 'f' OR NOTE2 = 'f' THEN DONOTE6 = 1;
IF NOTE1 = 'g' OR NOTE2 = 'g' THEN DONOTE7 = 1;
IF NOTE1 = 'h' OR NOTE2 = 'h' THEN DONOTE8 = 1;

IF LL < (3 + SUM(OF DONOTE1-DONOTE8)) MAX 5 OR LAST THEN DO;
  PUT;
  IF DONOTE1 THEN PUT / '(a) projected  ' @;
  IF DONOTE2 THEN PUT / '(b) budgeted   ' @;
  IF DONOTE3 THEN PUT / '(c) predicted  ' @;
  IF DONOTE4 THEN PUT / '(d) anticipated' @;
  IF DONOTE5 THEN PUT / '(e) expected   ' @;
  IF DONOTE6 THEN PUT / '(f) forecast   ' @;
  IF DONOTE7 THEN PUT / '(g) mandated   ' @;
  IF DONOTE8 THEN PUT / '(h) reported   ' @;
  DONOTE1 = 0; DONOTE2 = 0; DONOTE3 = 0; DONOTE4 = 0;
  DONOTE5 = 0; DONOTE6 = 0; DONOTE7 = 0; DONOTE8 = 0;
  END;
```

```
        1987      101,933              441,234
        1988       70,858              591,432
        1989      282,640              962,724
        1990      879,011              467,722
        1991       23,000 (e)           12,560
        1992       23,000 (b)          119,000 (f)
        1993      955,000 (a)          701,000 (a)

(a) projected
(b) budgeted
(e) expected
(f) forecast
```

With a narrow table, notes of this sort could be written at the right side of the page.

```
DATA _NULL_;
  RETAIN DONOTE1-DONOTE8 0  A 1  B 8  C 18  D 25  E 35  F 42;
  FILE PRINT LS=64 PS=60 N=PS NOTITLE LL=LL;

  SET STOCKS END=LAST;
  IF _N_ = 1 OR LL <= 3 THEN PUT _PAGE_ @;
  PUT / @A YEAR 4.  @B LEVEL1 COMMA9. @;
  IF NOTE1 NE ' ' THEN PUT @C '(' NOTE1 $CHAR1. ')' @;
  PUT @D LEVEL2 COMMA9. @;
  IF NOTE2 NE ' ' THEN PUT @E '(' NOTE2 $CHAR1. ')' @;
```

```
IF NOTE1 = 'a' OR NOTE2 = 'a' THEN DONOTE1 = 1;
IF NOTE1 = 'b' OR NOTE2 = 'b' THEN DONOTE2 = 1;
IF NOTE1 = 'c' OR NOTE2 = 'c' THEN DONOTE3 = 1;
IF NOTE1 = 'd' OR NOTE2 = 'd' THEN DONOTE4 = 1;
IF NOTE1 = 'e' OR NOTE2 = 'e' THEN DONOTE5 = 1;
IF NOTE1 = 'f' OR NOTE2 = 'f' THEN DONOTE6 = 1;
IF NOTE1 = 'g' OR NOTE2 = 'g' THEN DONOTE7 = 1;
IF NOTE1 = 'h' OR NOTE2 = 'h' THEN DONOTE8 = 1;

IF LL < 2 OR LAST THEN DO;
  PUT #6 @;
  IF DONOTE1 THEN PUT @F '(a) projected  ';
  IF DONOTE2 THEN PUT @F '(b) budgeted   ';
  IF DONOTE3 THEN PUT @F '(c) predicted  ';
  IF DONOTE4 THEN PUT @F '(d) anticipated';
  IF DONOTE5 THEN PUT @F '(e) expected   ';
  IF DONOTE6 THEN PUT @F '(f) forecast   ';
  IF DONOTE7 THEN PUT @F '(g) mandated   ';
  IF DONOTE8 THEN PUT @F '(h) reported   ';
  DONOTE1 = 0; DONOTE2 = 0; DONOTE3 = 0; DONOTE4 = 0;
  DONOTE5 = 0; DONOTE6 = 0; DONOTE7 = 0; DONOTE8 = 0;
  END;
```

```
1987     101,933            441,234
1988      70,858            591,432
1989     282,640            962,724
1990     879,011            467,722
1991      23,000 (e)         12,560        (a) projected
1992      23,000 (b)        119,000 (f)    (b) budgeted
1993     955,000 (a)        701,000 (a)    (e) expected
                                           (f) forecast
```

Hierarchical table

A hierarchical table design can be used for appropriate kinds of data. It is similar to the hierarchical file described in the previous chapter, but with these differences:

- Data is formatted to be read easily.
- Different record types are usually identified by indentation.
- There are header lines on each page.
- A group line is repeated, with the word "continued," at the top of a new page if a page break occurs in the middle of the group.

Hierarchical tables with two levels are the kind most commonly seen. (They are similar to the tables produced by the PRINT proc with a BY statement). This program prints a hierarchical table with three levels.

```
TITLE1 'Phonylog';
TITLE2 'Jan. 5, 1990';
  DATA _NULL_;
    SET ALBUMS;
    BY ARTIST TITLE NOTSORTED;
```

```
FILE PRINT LS=64 PS=28 N=PS LL=LL;
IF LL < FIRST.TITLE + FIRST.ARTIST + 1 OR _N_ = 1 THEN DO;
  PUT _PAGE_ #2 'Artist' #3'-------------------------------'
      #4 @4 'Title   Label   Catalog Number'
      #5 @4 '------------------------------------------'
      #6 @8 'Song' @54 'Time  PPR'
      #7 @8
      '---------------------------------------------------'
      @53 '-----' @59 '-----'
      #8 @;
  IF NOT FIRST.ARTIST THEN PUT / ARTIST +2 'continued' @;
  IF NOT FIRST.TITLE THEN PUT / @4 TITLE +2 'continued' @;
  END;
IF FIRST.ARTIST THEN PUT / ARTIST @;
IF FIRST.TITLE THEN PUT / @4 TITLE +2 LABEL +1 CAT @;
PUT / @8 SONG $CHAR44. @53 TIME MMSS5. @ 59 PPR $CHAR5. @;
```

```
                        Phonylog
                      Jan. 5, 1990
ARTIST
-------------------------------
   Title   Label   Catalog Number
   ------------------------------------------
       Song                                         Time  PPR
       --------------------------------------------- ----- -----
RED ZEPPELIN
   VI   Swanson  5-01311
       Shaken All Over                               7:06 BMI
       In Through The Up Escalator                   5:01 BMI
       Green Dog                                     4:30 BMI
       Going To Colorado                             7:03 BMI
       Airline To Heaven                            12:44 BMI
   The Same Old Song   Swanson  5-01770
       Airline To Heaven                            32:01 BMI
       When The Story Breaks                         7:22 BMI
       Hamburger                                     3:21 BMI
NO
   The No Album   Pacific  9 00010-3
       Galactic Highway Patrol                      14:02 BMI
       Over The Edge                                20:21 BMI
```

```
                        Phonylog
                      Jan. 5, 1990
ARTIST
-------------------------------
   Title   Label   Catalog Number
   ------------------------------------------
       Song                                         Time  PPR
       --------------------------------------------- ----- -----
NO   continued
   The No Album   continued
       The Frog                                      3:12 BMI
       This Side Of The Sky                          7:45 BMI
   Nostrums   Pacific 9 00045-0
       The Redeeming Silence Of Gold                20:41 BMI
       The Renumbering                              21:05 BMI
```

```
The Enchanting                                      20:31 BMI
Rock 'N Roll                                        19:27 BMI
```

Word wrap

Word wrap, also known as text wrap, is the process of printing or displaying a character value on several lines because it is too long to fit on one line. It is usually associated with word processing programs and rarely attempted by SAS programmers, but is actually not too difficult. You just need to identify the range of characters in the character string to be printed on each line, and then extract those characters using the SUBSTR function.

```
DATA _NULL_;
  LENGTH TEXT $ 100;
  RETAIN CS 26; * Column width for word wrap;
  IF _N_ = 1 THEN PUT
      'Tent/number of people/seasons/description' /;
  SET TENTS;
  PUT @1 ITEM  @15 OCC 3. SEAS 3. @;
  C = 1;
  LENGTH = LENGTH(TEXT);
  DO UNTIL(C > LENGTH OR SUBSTR(TEXT, C MIN 100) = ' ');
    C + VERIFY(SUBSTR(TEXT, C), ' ') - 1;  * Skip blanks;
    IF C + CS > LENGTH THEN L = LENGTH + 1 - C; * Last line;
    ELSE DO;
      L = CS;
      BREAK = 0;
      DO I = (C + CS - 1) TO C - 1 BY -1 UNTIL(BREAK);
        IF      SUBSTR(TEXT, I + 1, 1) = ' '
            OR SUBSTR(TEXT, I + 1, 2) = '--'
            OR (SUBSTR(TEXT, I, 1) = '-'
                AND SUBSTR(TEXT, I + 1, 1) NE '-')
            THEN DO; BREAK = 1; L = I + 1 - C; END;
        END;
      END;
    LINE = SUBSTR(TEXT, C, L);
    PUT @24 LINE;
    C + L;
    END;
```

```
Tent/number of people/seasons/description

Mt. St. Helens  2  3   Its competitive price and
                       light weight (2 kg) make
                       it ideal for summer
                       backpacking.
Adventure Pup   2  4   This traditional design is
                       sturdy and durable, to
                       withstand stormy weather
                       reliably.
```

Formatted cell datasets

With very complicated table designs, it can be easier to do the formatting for a table in an separate step from the step that prints the table. The formatted data can be stored in a SAS dataset that contains the page, row, and column position of each cell to be printed and the characters to be printed in the cell. Each observation represents one formatted cell, so we call the SAS dataset a *formatted cell dataset.*

For example, this formatted cell dataset

PAGE	ROW	COLUMN	CELL
1	1	2	TOP
1	17	2	MIDDLE
1	33	2	BOTTOM
1	11	1	1
1	11	2	2
1	11	3	3
1	1	3	PAGE 1
2	1	3	PAGE 2
2	10	1	4
2	33	3	etc.

might be printed as these pages

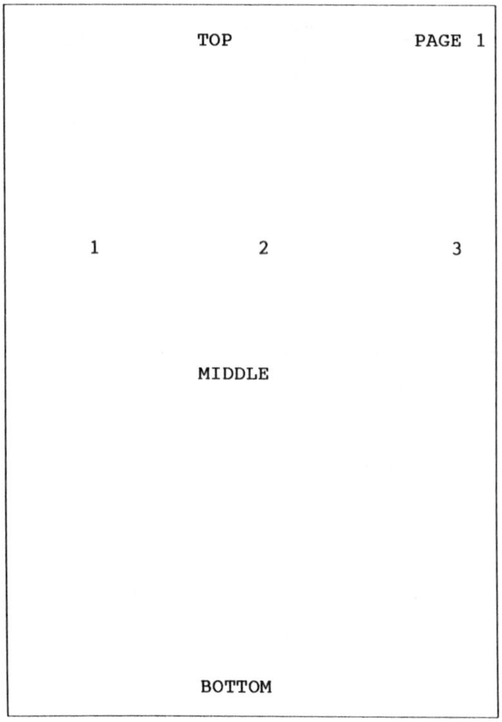

It's important to stay within the concept of a formatted cell dataset: only assign each cell once, and only use rows and columns that will actually appear on the page.

The COLUMN variable could represent either table columns or column pointer locations. Using table columns allows the same formatted cell dataset to be printed with different column spacing by making minor changes in the step that prints the formatted cell dataset.

A formatted cell dataset must, at the very least, be grouped by page to be printed. Sorting by page, row, and column produces the most consistent results.

The following steps print the formatted cell dataset shown above (assuming it has the name FCELLS). The column values 1, 2, and 3 are mapped to the column pointer locations 1, 16, and 31. The expression `LBOUND(COL) <= COLUMN <= HBOUND(COL)` is used to test whether COLUMN is one of the columns defined in the step; if not, the cell is not printed.

```
PROC SORT DATA=FCELLS;
  BY PAGE ROW COLUMN;
DATA _NULL_;
  RETAIN  A 1  B 16  C 31  R_MARGIN 132;
  ARRAY COL{*} A B C;
  FILE PRINT NOTITLES PAGESIZE=40 N=PS;
  SET FCELLS;
  BY PAGE ROW;
  IF FIRST.PAGE THEN PUT _PAGE_ @;   * Put header (if any) here;
  IF FIRST.ROW THEN PUT #ROW @;
  IF LBOUND(COL) <= COLUMN <= HBOUND(COL) THEN DO;
    LENGTH = LENGTH(CELL) MIN (R_MARGIN - COL{COLUMN});
    PUT @(COL{COLUMN}) CELL $VARYING. LENGTH @;
    END;
```

The $VARYING format is used for each cell, because the width of cells can vary. The length variable, LENGTH, is assigned the visible length of the cell in the example above; however, if a cell is so long that it would run off the right edge of the page, only the length that fits on the page is printed. Doing this is essential; otherwise the PUT statement might move cells to different lines. The variable R_MARGIN contains the column pointer position of the right side of the page, and should not be greater than the value of the LS= option.

Titles can appear in a printed formatted cell dataset either by having TITLE statements (and not having the NOTITLES option in the FILE statement) or by including a header in the step, right after the page break. If necessary, the formatted cells could be moved down the page by a few lines, by using the line pointer control `#(ROW + 2)` instead of `#ROW`, for example.

```
IF FIRST.PAGE THEN DO;
  PAGE_NO + 1;
  PUT _PAGE_ @12 'Formatted Cells' @C +7 PAGE_NO 5.;
  END;
IF FIRST.ROW THEN PUT #(ROW + 2) @;
```

Overflow

Consider the problem of programming a series of tables, each of which has an arbitrary number of rows and columns. Only the data will tell whether a table will fit on one page; it might flow over the right side of the page (too many columns) or the bottom of the page (too many rows) or both. Because data has to be in sorted order by page before it can be printed in a data step, the data first has to be assigned to pages. The use of a formatted cell dataset then becomes the most practical approach to take.

In the example that follows, the data represents bird counts taken at various times and locations. A separate table is printed for each location, with a separate column for each different visit and a separate row for each different variety of bird. Up to 40 rows (varieties) and 4 columns (visits) can fit on a page. Thus, a location with 30 varieties and 10 visits would take 3 pages, while one with 50 varieties and 10 visits would take 6 pages — 2 "down" and 3 "across."

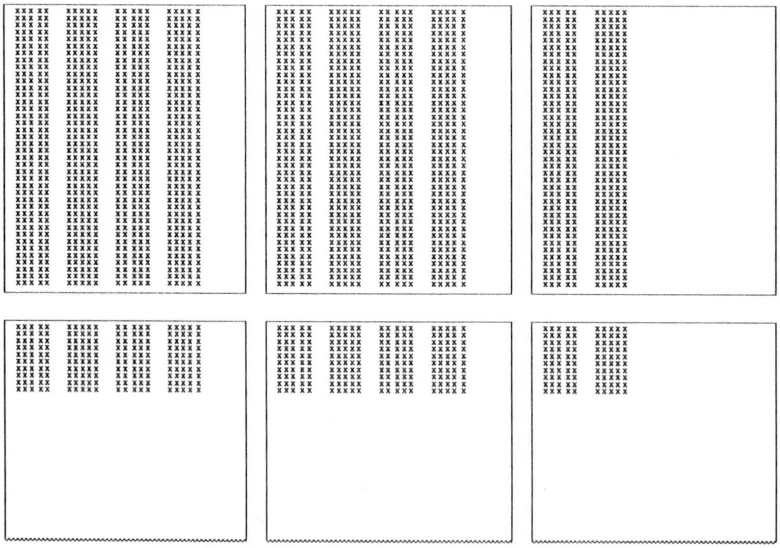

The input data for the example has these variables:

LOCATION	DATE	TIME	SPECIES	COUNT
London	04/07/90	PM	Robin	7
London	04/07/90	PM	Pigeon	522
London	04/07/90	PM	Falcon	1
Asherwood	01/01/90	AM	Blue Jay	7
Asherwood	01/01/90	AM	Crow	4

This example actually uses two formatted cell datasets, which are interleaved in the print step.

```
PROC SORT DATA=BIRDSITE;
  BY LOCATION DATE TIME;

* Count columns (visits) at each location;
PROC SORT DATA=BIRDSITE (KEEP=LOCATION DATE TIME)
          OUT=C1 NODUPKEY;
  BY LOCATION DATE TIME;
PROC FREQ DATA=C1;
  TABLES LOCATION / MISSING NOPRINT OUT=C2 (KEEP=LOCATION COUNT);
* Assign chronological index numbers to visits;
DATA C3 (KEEP=LOCATION DATE TIME VISIT);
  SET C1;
  BY LOCATION;
  IF FIRST.LOCATION THEN VISIT = 0;
  VISIT + 1;

* Count rows (varieties) at each location;
PROC SORT DATA=BIRDSITE (KEEP=LOCATION SPECIES) OUT=R1 NODUPKEY;
  BY LOCATION SPECIES;
PROC FREQ DATA=R1;
  TABLES LOCATION / MISSING NOPRINT OUT=R2 (KEEP=LOCATION COUNT);

* Determine number of pages for each table;
DATA CR (KEEP=LOCATION DATE TIME VISIT P_ACROSS P_DOWN);
  MERGE C2 (RENAME=(COUNT=C)) R2 (RENAME=(COUNT=R)) C3;
  BY LOCATION;
  P_ACROSS = CEIL(C/4);  * Number of pages across;
  P_DOWN = CEIL(R/40);   * Number of pages down;

* Place columns on pages;
DATA B1 (KEEP=LOCATION DATE TIME VISIT SPECIES COUNT
              P_ACROSS P_DOWN)
     COLL (KEEP=PAGE ROW COLUMN CELL);
  LENGTH CELL $ 40;
  RETAIN PREPAGE LASTPAGE 0;

  MERGE BIRDSITE CR;
  BY LOCATION DATE TIME;
  OUTPUT B1;

  * Create cells containing column labels;
  IF FIRST.LOCATION THEN DO;
    PREPAGE = LASTPAGE;
    LASTPAGE + P_ACROSS*P_DOWN;
    COLUMN = 1;
    DO PAGE = PREPAGE + 1 TO LASTPAGE;
      ROW = 4; CELL = '  Variety  '; OUTPUT COLL;
      ROW = 5; CELL = '-----------'; OUTPUT COLL;
      END;
    END;
  IF FIRST.TIME THEN
  DO PAGE = PREPAGE + CEIL(VISIT/4) TO LASTPAGE BY P_ACROSS;
    COLUMN = MOD(VISIT, 4) + 2;
    ROW = 3;
    CELL = 'Visit ' || LEFT(PUT(VISIT, 12.)); OUTPUT COLL;
    ROW = 4; CELL = PUT(DATE, MMDDYY8.) || TIME; OUTPUT COLL;
    END;
```

```
* Sort by row;
  PROC SORT DATA=B1 OUT=B2;
    BY LOCATION SPECIES;

* Assign rows to pages.  Create the rest of the cells;
  DATA CELLS (KEEP=PAGE ROW COLUMN CELL);
    LENGTH CELL $ 40;
    RETAIN PREPAGE LASTPAGE PAGE ROW COLUMN 0;

    SET B2;
    BY LOCATION SPECIES;

    IF FIRST.LOCATION THEN DO;
      PREPAGE = LASTPAGE;
      LASTPAGE + P_ACROSS*P_DOWN;
      * Create cells containing page header for each page in table;
      DO PAGE = PREPAGE + 1 TO LASTPAGE;
        ROW = 1;
        COLUMN = 1; CELL = 'LOCATION:  '||Location; OUTPUT;
        COLUMN = 5; CELL = '   Page ' || LEFT(PUT(PAGE, 12.));
        OUTPUT;
        END;
      LSPECIES = 0;
      END;

    IF FIRST.SPECIES THEN DO; * Create cells containing row labels;
      LSPECIES + 1;
      ROW = MOD(LSPECIES - 1, 40) + 6;
      COLUMN = 1; CELL = SPECIES;
      DO PAGE = PREPAGE + (CEIL(LSPECIES/40) - 1)*P_ACROSS + 1 TO
                PREPAGE + CEIL(LSPECIES/40)*P_ACROSS BY P_ACROSS;
        OUTPUT;
        END;
      END;

      * Create ordinary data cells;
      PAGE = PREPAGE + CEIL(VISIT/4)
                     + (CEIL(LSPECIES/40) - 1)*P_ACROSS;
      COLUMN = MOD(VISIT, 4) + 1;
      CELL = PUT(COUNT, COMMA10.); OUTPUT;

* Print cells;
  PROC SORT DATA=CELLS;    * Contains most cells;
    BY PAGE ROW COLUMN;
  PROC SORT DATA=COLL;     * Contains column label cells;
    BY PAGE ROW COLUMN;
  DATA _NULL_;
    RETAIN  A 1  B 18  C 31  D 44  E 57  R_MARGIN 68;
    ARRAY COL{5} A B C D E;
    FILE PRINT NOTITLES N=PS;

    SET COLL CELLS;
    BY PAGE ROW COLUMN;
    IF FIRST.PAGE THEN PUT _PAGE_ @;
    IF FIRST.ROW THEN PUT #ROW @;
    IF LBOUND(COL) <= COLUMN <= HBOUND(COL);
    LENGTH = LENGTH(CELL) MIN (R_MARGIN - COL{COLUMN});
    PUT @(COL{COLUMN}) CELL $VARYING. LENGTH @;
```

```
LOCATION:  Asherwood                                                    Page 1

                 Visit 1       Visit 2       Visit 3       Visit 4
  Variety        01/01/90AM    01/04/90AM    01/06/90AM    01/06/90PM
-----------
Blue Jay                                8             2
Crow                                                  4             2
Falcon                                  1
Robin                   10              9            12             4
Swan                                    1             2             4
```

```
LOCATION:  Asherwood                                                    Page 2

                 Visit 5
  Variety        01/11/90PM
-----------
Blue Jay
Crow                     4
Falcon
Robin
Swan                     4
```

Prose

Prose reports tend to be short, usually less than a page in length. They can be organized into sentences, or they can be designed as fields in fixed positions. Observations are not usually a relevant part of the data in a prose report; if the data comes from a SAS dataset, either only one observation is used or there is a separate page for each observation.

Sentences

List output can help you maintain normal spacing when you write sentences that include variable values used as words. List output trims leading and trailing blanks and adds one blank after the value. The same thing is done by the : format modifier. You'll need to provide the blank before the word.

```
PUT 'We discovered ' NFISHS :COMMA11. 'new species of fish.';
```

```
We discovered 42 new species of fish.
```

You'll need to write over the blank that follows a value if you want to have a punctuation mark there. The term `+(-1)` can be used for "backspacing" in a PUT statement.

```
PUT 'The number of new species of fish we discovered was '
    NFISHS :COMMA11. +(-1) '.';
```

```
The number of new species of fish we discovered was 42.
```

Fixed fields

It can be simpler, and sometimes easier to read, to dispense with the sentence form, and instead put a value at a fixed position with a label — producing a more traditional "computerish" report.

```
PUT @5 'New species of fish:' @32 NFISHS COMMA11. /;
```

```
    New species of fish:                42
```

Word wrap

The word wrap techniques described earlier in the chapter for table reports can be used in the same way for prose reports.

```
TITLE1 'Expo Committees';
TITLE2 '---------------';
  DATA _NULL_;
    RETAIN INDENT;
    SET COMMTS;
    BY COMMITEE;
    FILE PRINT COL=COL LS=64 LL=LL;
    IF FIRST.COMMITEE AND LL < 7 OR _N_ = 1 THEN PUT _PAGE_;
    IF FIRST.COMMITEE THEN DO;
      PUT // @1 COMMITEE 'Committee:  ' @;
      INDENT = COL;
      END;
    IF COL > 56 THEN PUT / @INDENT  @;
    PUT MEMBER +2 @;
```

```
                          Expo Committees
                          ---------------


Finance Committee:  R. Bacon   A. Hamilton   S. Coverly
                    J. Tee

Publicity Committee:  F. Houser   G. Kennedy   C. Ruler
                      M. Newton   Y. Pack   L. Marion
```

Control report

A control report summarizes the activities of a program. It might contain information such as the number of records in an input file, the number of observations in a SAS dataset, totals, and averages. Typically, the data comes from SAS datasets produced in various places throughout the program. They can be combined using a one-to-one merge, so a control report can generally be written with these six statements:

```
TITLE1 'Control Report';
  DATA _NULL_;
    MERGE SAS datasets;
    FILE PRINT;
    PUT report;
    STOP;
```

One of the common values to appear in a control report is the number of observations in a SAS dataset. The CONTENTS proc can be used to find this number, using a step like this:

```
  PROC CONTENTS DATA=FOLKS NOPRINT
    OUT=NFOLKS (KEEP=NOBS RENAME=(NOBS=NFOLKS));
```

This step counts the number of observations in the SAS dataset FOLKS, putting the result in the variable NFOLKS in the SAS dataset NFOLKS.

12 Flexcode

Flexcode refers to any program that modifies itself while running. SAS programs can do this in two ways: using macrovariables, which are given values by the SYMPUT routine; and writing program lines using the PUT statement and then including them in the program using the %INCLUDE statement. Each method is better for some things than for others.

An important limitation of each method limits its use. The longest value that a data step can assign to a macrovariable is 200 characters. The parts of a program in an %INCLUDE file have to be complete statements.

Program parameters

Program parameters are values that can be changed to affect the way a program operates. They are values that are constant while a program is running, but that might change eventually or might be different each time the program is run. For example, the name of an input SAS dataset could be a program parameter if the same SAS dataset is not used for input every time the program is run. Program parameters are usually implemented as macrovariables.

The easiest way to assign values to the macrovariables is using %LET statements at the beginning of the program file.

```
%LET DEADLINE = 'MONDAY';
%LET NAMELEN = 49;
```

The length of a variable is part of a program, for example, but you could allow for the length to change. For example, instead of coding

```
    LENGTH ACCOUNT $ 8;
```

in several places in a program, you might code

```
LENGTH ACCOUNT $ &ID_LEN;
```

and at the beginning of the program, set the value of the macrovariable:

```
%LET ID_LEN = 8; * Number of digits in account ID numbers;
```

Then if the length of the variable is changed later, you'll only have to change the %LET statement. For example, to change the length to 12, you would change the %LET statement to

```
%LET ID_LEN = 12;
```

and that would change the LENGTH statements in the program.

Parameter file

There are some advantages in creating a file of program parameters and reading them into the program in a data step. You can then keep a copy or printout of the file as a record of the program parameters. Also, you might be able to automate the process of creating the parameter file.

The easiest way to set up a parameter file is with the name and value for one macrovariable on each record. The first word on a record would be a macrovariable name, and the rest of the line would be the value to be assigned to it. The step below reads a parameter file, with the fileref PARM, and assigns the values to macrovariables.

```
DATA _NULL_;
  INFILE PARM MISSOVER;
  LENGTH VARIABLE $ 8;
  INPUT VARIABLE $ VALUE $78.;
  CALL SYMPUT(VARIABLE, TRIM(VALUE));
RUN;
```

For example, if the PARM file contained these lines,

```
          A_LIB       D9804
TEST (G >= 5 AND NOT ID = '15507*')
WEEKDAY      MONDAY
```

the step would create the macrovariables A_LIB, TEST, and WEEKDAY, and assign the value `D9804` to the macrovariable A_LIB, the value `(G >= 5 AND NOT ID = '15507*')` to the macrovariable TEST, and the value `MONDAY` to the macrovariable WEEKDAY.

You can give default values to parameters by assigning values to the macrovariables before the parameter file step. Those values will be replaced by values from the parameter file if they are present. The presence of a default value that represents the most common situation allows you to put that parameter in the parameter file only for exceptional cases.

Similarly, you can create macrovariables that depend on values in the parameter file — for example, creating a macrovariable WEEKEND when certain values appear in the parameter file for the parameter WEEKDAY.

The steps below create default values for the macrovariables DATE and PERIOD, and then assign a value for WEEKDAY to match the value of DATE.

```
%LET PERIOD = 1;
  DATA _NULL_;
    CALL SYMPUT('DATE', PUT(TODAY(), DATE9.));
RUN;
  DATA _NULL_;
    INFILE PARM MISSOVER;
    LENGTH VARIABLE $ 8;
    INPUT VARIABLE $ VALUE $78.;
    CALL SYMPUT(VARIABLE, TRIM(VALUE));
RUN;
  DATA _NULL_;
    CALL SYMPUT('WEEKDAY',
                SCAN(PUT(WEEKDAY("&DATE"D), WEEKDATE9.), 1));
RUN;
```

Data in SAS statements

Expressions cannot be used in many SAS statements, such as SET and TITLE. However, expressions can be used in constructing such statements.

Creating a title

For example, you might want to put a calculated value in a title. You could calculate the value, write the TITLE statement, and include it in the program with statements like these:

```
  PROC SUMMARY DATA=PERFECT;
    VAR T;
    OUTPUT OUT=RANGE MIN(T)=MIN MAX(T)=MAX;
  DATA _NULL_;
    SET RANGE;
    FILE PINC;
    PUT "TITLE2 'FROM " MIN "TO " MAX "';";
    STOP;
RUN;
TITLE1 'PERFECT SUMMARY';
%INCLUDE PINC;
```

```
TITLE2 'FROM .505 TO 33.7 ';
```

Essentially the same thing could be done using macrovariables and the SYMPUT routine:

```
  PROC SUMMARY DATA=PERFECT;
    VAR T;
    OUTPUT OUT=RANGE MIN(T)=MIN MAX(T)=MAX;
  DATA _NULL_;
    SET RANGE;
    CALL SYMPUT('TITLE2', 'FROM '||TRIM(LEFT(PUT(MIN, BEST12.)))||
                          ' TO '||TRIM(LEFT(PUT(MAX, BEST12.))));
    STOP;
RUN;
TITLE1 'PERFECT SUMMARY';
TITLE2 "&TITLE2";
```

In both cases, the RUN statement ensures that the TITLE statements are interpreted after, and not before, the step that creates the value for TITLE2.

Selecting variables for a proc

The same approach can be used to determine the variables that appear in the VAR statement for a proc. For example, suppose you want the PRINT proc to print only variables that have positive values in at least one observation in a SAS dataset. You could accomplish that with these steps:

```
  DATA _NULL_;
    RETAIN;
    SET DUBIOUS END=LAST;
    IF A > 0 THEN PA = 1;
    IF B > 0 THEN PB = 1;
    IF C > 0 THEN PC = 1;
    IF D > 0 THEN PD = 1;
    IF E > 0 THEN PE = 1;
    IF F > 0 THEN PF = 1;
    IF LAST THEN DO;
      FILE PINC;
      PUT '    VAR' @;
      IF PA THEN PUT ' A' @;
      IF PB THEN PUT ' B' @;
      IF PC THEN PUT ' C' @;
      IF PD THEN PUT ' D' @;
      IF PE THEN PUT ' E' @;
      IF PF THEN PUT ' F' @;
      PUT ';'
RUN;
  PROC PRINT;
%INCLUDE PINC;
RUN;
```

```
    VAR A C E F;
```

This could be done in much the same way by concatenating the variable names to create the variable list and using the SYMPUT routine to create a macrovariable.

Reversing the order of variables in a SAS dataset

Ordinarily, the order of variables in a SAS dataset does not matter. However, if it is necessary to change the order of variables in a SAS dataset, it can be done by using flexcode for a LENGTH or similar statement. This step creates the SAS dataset REORDER, which contains the variable of the SAS dataset ORDER, but in the reverse order:

```
  PROC CONTENTS DATA=ORDER NOPRINT
      OUT=POS (KEEP=NAME NPOS TYPE LENGTH);
  PROC SORT DATA=POS OUT=REPOS;
    BY DESCENDING NPOS;
  DATA _NULL_;
    SET REPOS END=LAST;
    FILE PINC;
    IF _N_ = 1 THEN PUT @5 'LENGTH';
    PUT @9 NAME $CHAR8. @;
    IF TYPE =: 'C' THEN PUT +1 '$' @;
    PUT +1 LENGTH;
    IF LAST THEN PUT @9 ';';
RUN;
  DATA REORDER;
%INCLUDE PINC;  * LENGTH statement;
    SET ORDER;
RUN;
```

Meta-control flow

Flexcode can allow more complicated control flow than can be done using SAS syntax alone. Simple meta-control flow can be done using the techniques shown above.

Conditional ENDSAS

The ABORT statement can be used to stop a SAS program in the middle of a data step. However, there are situations in which the use of an ABORT statement is not appropriate. Sometimes the program should be stopped after the completion of the step, rather than interrupting it. Also, under some operating systems, the ABORT statement causes the SAS supervisor to report an error condition to the operating system — a circumstance programmers usually like to avoid. In these cases, the best thing would be to have an ENDSAS statement that would only execute sometimes. An `IF ... THEN ENDSAS` statement is not allowed, but something a bit more indirect can be done.

Suppose, for example, the later steps of a program should execute only if the program is run after a certain date. This step checks the current date using the DATE function, and stops the program if doing so is indicated.

```
%LET ACTION = ;

  DATA _NULL_;
    IF DATE() < '01JAN2000' THEN CALL SYMPUT('ACTION', 'ENDSAS');
RUN;

&ACTION;
```

The line `&ACTION;` resolves either to a null statement or an ENDSAS statement. Again, the RUN statement is needed to separate the data step from the macrovariable reference.

Conditional %INCLUDE

The same approach could conditionally use an %INCLUDE file. Suppose certain steps should only be executed on Monday. The program file containing those steps could be associated with the fileref MONDAY, and then would be executed or not using these statements:

```
%LET ACTION = ;

  DATA _NULL_;
    IF WEEKDAY(DATE()) = 2 /* If today is Monday */
        THEN CALL SYMPUT('ACTION', '%INCLUDE MONDAY;');
RUN;

&ACTION;
```

The same kind of logic could be used to decide among several %INCLUDE files to be used in different situations.

Options that can appear on the %INCLUDE statement might be useful. %INCLUDE statement options appear at the end of the statement, preceded by a slash (/). The SOURCE2, NOSOURCE2, and S2= options have the same meanings as the corresponding system options, but apply only to that %INCLUDE statement. Other options are available in different implementations.

Control flow driven by data

More complicated meta-control flow, in which input data values determine the shape of the program, can be done by using ordinary SAS control flow to control PUT statements writing an %INCLUDE file, or by having macrovariables control macro control flow statements. The former approach is more flexible and easier to learn, and is similar to techniques that can be used with SCL, so we'll demonstrate it.

Consider the situation of a person keeping track of the spot prices of different models of used computers in different cities. Such a person might use the program below to plot recent price trends of selected models.

The first two steps create a SAS dataset grouped by computer model. The third step adds the new data to a separate archival file for each model and creates a separate TITLE statement and PLOT proc step for each model that has a large range in recent prices.

```
DATA SPOT;
  INFILE SPOT;
  INPUT @1 DATE YYMMDD6. @7 CITY $CHAR22.
      @29 MODEL $CHAR8. @37 PRICE 8.;
PROC SORT; BY MODEL PRICE;
DATA _NULL_;
  RETAIN LOWPRICE;
  FILE PINC;
  SET SPOT; BY MODEL;
  IF FIRST.MODEL THEN DO;
    LOWPRICE = PRICE;
    PUT '  PROC APPEND BASE=PRICES.' MODEL /
        '        DATA=SPOT (FIRSTOBS=' _N_ @;
  IF LAST.MODEL THEN DO;
    PUT 'OBS=' _N_ ');'
    IF LOWPRICE/PRICE < .65 THEN PUT
        '  DATA;' /
        '    SET PRICES.' MODEL $8. ';' /
        '    IF DATE >= TODAY() - 28;' //
        'TITLE ''Spot Prices for' @23 MODEL $8.''';'
        '  PROC PLOT;'/
        '    PLOT PRICE*DATE;'/
        '    FORMAT DATE MMDDYY5.;';
    END;
RUN;
%INCLUDE PINC;
RUN;
```

Shuffling a SAS dataset

Shuffling a SAS dataset is a way of changing the sort order to switch the priority of the sort variables. For example, if a SAS dataset is sorted by COLOR and FLAVOR, it could be shuffled to make it sorted by FLAVOR and COLOR. The concept was introduced in chapter 8, "Groups and sorting."

The number of values of the first sort variable before shuffling must not be more than about 30 for this technique to work well. In simple cases, though, it can be much faster than the SORT proc.

The use of flexcode can make shuffling work without having to know in advance the number of values of the first sort variable and the observations belonging to each one. A preliminary step scans the SAS dataset to determine this information and write the SET statement for the shuffling step.

These steps, for example, result in the SAS dataset CARMFR, which has all the observations of CARS, but is sorted by MFR and BODYTYPE instead of BODYTYPE and MFR:

```
PROC SORT DATA=CARS;
  BY BODYTYPE MFR;
```

```
  DATA _NULL_;
    SET CARS (KEEP=BODYTYPE);
    BY BODYTYPE;
    FILE PINC (END=LAST);
    IF _N_ = 1 THEN PUT '    SET';
    IF FIRST.BODYTYPE THEN PUT '        CARS (FIRSTOBS=' _N_ @;
    IF LAST.BODYTYPE THEN PUT 'OBS=' _N_ +(-1) ')';
    IF LAST THEN PUT '        ;';
RUN;
  DATA CARMFR;
%INCLUDE PINC; * SET ...;
    BY MFR BODYTYPE;
```

```
    SET
        CARS (FIRSTOBS=1 OBS=818)
        CARS (FIRSTOBS=819 OBS=1106)
        CARS (FIRSTOBS=1107 OBS=1488)
        CARS (FIRSTOBS=1489 OBS=1950)
        CARS (FIRSTOBS=1951 OBS=2544)
        ;
```

> The FIRSTOBS= dataset option runs much faster with uncompressed SAS datasets using the default engine or other engines that support direct access.

Writing other languages

There is no reason why the PUT statement can't create programs in languages other than SAS. Any time you need a program to contain values from a SAS program or to run with a SAS user interface, this is a useful technique.

You can even use this technique to access operating system commands with more detail and flexibility than the X statement allows.

Write and submit a JCL deck

You can have a SAS program write and submit a background job. Under the MVS operating system, this involves writing a JCL deck in a file and then submitting the file as a background job using the TSO SUBMIT command.

This program, for example, submits a JCL deck to run a SAS program that includes a date as part of the name of a file:

```
TSO 'ALLOC DATASET(DECK.CNTL) FILE(DECK) OLD';

  DATA _NULL_;
    FILE DECK;
    TODAY = TODAY();
```

```
     PUT '//DAY JOB (,,)' /
         '// EXEC SAS' /
         '//OUT DD DSN=PR' TODAY YYMMDD6. '.LIST,UNIT=SYSDA,' /
         '//     DISP=(NEW,CATLG,DELETE),SPACE=(CYL,1,1)' /
         '//ACT DD DSN=ACTIVITY.SDS,DISP=SHR' /
         '//SYSIN DD *' /
         '  PROC PRINT DATA=ACT.PR' TODAY YYMMDD4. ';' /
         'RUN;';
RUN;
TSO 'SUBMIT DECK.CNTL';
```

```
//DAY JOB (,,)
// EXEC SAS
//OUT DD DSN=PR900508.LIST,UNIT=SYSDA,
//     DISP=(NEW,CATLG,DELETE),SPACE=(CYL,1,1)
//ACT DD DSN=ACTIVITY.SDS,DISP=SHR
//SYSIN DD *
  PROC PRINT DATA=ACT.PR9005;
RUN;
```

Writing a batch file under MS-DOS

Under the MS-DOS operating system, a batch file is a series of MS-DOS commands that are executed when the batch file is executed. Batch files generally have the extension .BAT.

This program writes and executes a batch file to copy a certain file from drive `C:` to drive `A:`:

```
  DATA _NULL_;
    TODAY = TODAY();
    FILE '\TEMP.BAT';
    PUT 'ECHO INSERT DISK IN DRIVE A:' /
        'PAUSE' /
        'COPY C:\ACT\PR' TODAY YYMMDD6. '.PRN A:' /
        'ERASE \TEMP.BAT';
RUN;
X '\TEMP';
```

```
ECHO INSERT DISK IN DRIVE A:
PAUSE
COPY C:\ACT\PR900508.PRN A:
ERASE \TEMP.BAT
```

13 Numbers

Computers are named for their ability to work with numbers, so you wouldn't expect numbers to present a problem in programming. Most computation can be accomplished directly using the arithmetic, comparison, and logical operators and numeric functions. This chapter covers some of the issues that can arise in programming with numbers.

Rounding

When working with precise values, you need to be aware of the computer's tendency to round numbers. Because the SAS System can represent integers exactly up to about 10^{16}, rounding is mainly a problem with noninteger values.

The SAS System uses 64 bits to represent numbers, which means that it can only represent about 2^{64} or 10^{19} different numbers — the set of double precision numbers. When it encounters a number that it can't represent exactly, it rounds it to the nearest double precision number. The difference between the double-precision number and the number it tries to represent is called the *rounding error*. When operations are done on numbers that are already rounded, the rounding error can become even larger.

Rounding errors can lead to results you don't expect. For example, two numbers might both print out as .44444444444 and theoretically be equal to 4/9, yet might be slightly different because of the way they were calculated. To avoid this problem, you can check the difference between two numbers that might have rounding errors rather than comparing them directly. Instead of `X = Y`, your condition might be

```
-1E-12 < X - Y < 1E-12
```

The FUZZ function can be useful for comparing integers that might have rounding errors. For values that are within 10^{-12} of an integer, it returns the integer. For example, `FUZZ(11.00000000000091)` is 11.

Larger rounding errors can be produced by storing a number in a SAS dataset in a variable with a length shorter than the default length of 8. The TRUNC function can be used to simulate the effect of storing a number with a particular length. For example, `TRUNC(.3, 4)` would be the same value as would be produced by storing a variable with the value .3 in 4 bytes. The TRUNC function does not work for special missing values, however.

Rounding is also something you might want to do deliberately, to reflect the natural resolution of a quantity. Many quantities are only meaningful in integer amounts, such as a variable that represents a number of people. Money amounts in many countries are represented in hundredths. The SAS rounding functions INT, FLOOR, CEIL, and ROUND apply different rounding rules.

Rounding can be used to counteract the effects of rounding errors. If two numbers are both approximately –6, but not equal because of rounding errors, then rounding can be used to make them equal.

Expressions for doing different kinds of rounding are shown below. Most often, you would round a quantity before assigning it to a variable. For example, if you want to assign the expression

```
RANUNI(99)*1024
```

to the variable T, except that you want T to have an integer value, you might use the statement

```
T = ROUND(RANUNI(99)*1024);
```

Another time to use rounding is when you want to compare the rounded values of variables. To select observations in which the value of the variable X is closer to 14 than to 13 or 15, you could use the subsetting IF statement

```
IF ROUND(X) = 14;
```

The following expressions are stated in terms of the variable X, but any expression could be used.

To round a number to the nearest integer:

```
ROUND(X)
```

To round a number to the next lower integer:

```
FLOOR(X)
```

To round a number to the next higher integer:

```
CEIL(X)
```

To truncate a number to three decimal places:

```
(INT(X*1000)*.001)
```

Integer truncation:

```
INT(X)
```

To round a number to the nearest hundredth (or cent):

```
ROUND(X, .01)
```

To round a number to the next higher hundredth:

```
   (CEIL(X*100)*.01)
or ROUND(X + .005, .01)
```

To round a number to the next lower hundredth:

```
   (FLOOR(X*100)*.01)
or ROUND(X - .005, .01)
```

To round to the nearest million:

```
ROUND(X, 1000000)
```

To round a number to the nearest multiple of N:

```
ROUND(X, N)
```

To round a number to the next higher multiple of N:

```
   CEIL(X/N)*N
or ROUND(X + N*.5, N)
```

To round a number to the next lower multiple of N:

```
   FLOOR(X/N)*N
or ROUND(X - N*.5, N)
```

Testing numbers

A test of the value of a number is the most common kind of condition used in IF, DO, and WHEN statements. Several expressions for testing numbers are shown below. Of course, these expressions can also be assigned to variables or used anywhere else an expression is allowed.

Parentheses are shown surrounding expressions that use operators, because they are sometimes needed when an expression is with operators to create another expression. The = symbol that appears in most of these expressions is the equality comparison operator (also known as EQ), not the assignment symbol.

A typical use of one of these expressions is as the condition in an IF . . . THEN statement. To do a certain action only when the value of the observation number _N_ is even, for example, you could use the statement

```
IF MOD(_N_, 2) = 0 THEN action;
```

To test an integer for evenness:

```
      (MOD(X, 2) = 0)
or    (X = ROUND(X, 2))
or    (X/2 = FLOOR(X/2))
or    (X/2 = CEIL(X/2))
or    (X/2 = INT(X/2))
```

To test an integer for oddness:

```
      (MOD(X, 2) = 1)
or    (X NE ROUND(X, 2))
or    (X/2 NE FLOOR(X/2))
or    (X/2 NE CEIL(X/2))
or    (X/2 NE INT(X/2))
```

To test whether a number is an integer:

```
      (X = FLOOR(X))
or    (X = CEIL(X))
or    (X = INT(X))
or    (X = ROUND(X))
or    (MOD(X, 1) = 0)
```

To test whether a number is a multiple of N:

```
      (MOD(X, N) = 0)
or    (X = ROUND(X, N))
or    (X/N = FLOOR(X/N))
or    (X/N = CEIL(X/N))
or    (X/N = INT(X/N))
```

To test for a negative value:

```
(.Z < X < 0)
```

To test for a positive value:

```
(X > 0)
```

To test for a missing value:

```
(._ <= X <= .Z)
```

To test for a standard missing value:

```
(X = .)
```

To test for a special missing value:

```
(X NE --X)
```

To test whether two numbers are approximately equal (within .005):

```
(ABS(X - Y) < .005)
```

Numeric effects

These expressions produce a number that depends in some way on the value of another number — which could be any numeric expression, but is represented here by the variable X.

To limit a value to a maximum of 100 ("cap" at 100):

```
(X MIN 100)
```

To limit a value to a minimum of 0 (also converts missing values to 0):

```
(0 MAX X)
```

To limit a value to the range from 0 to 100:

```
(0 MAX X MIN 100)
```

To limit a value to the range from A to B (with A ≤ B):

```
(A MAX X MIN B)
```

To double a number:

```
    (2*X)
or  (X + X)          /* slightly faster  */
```

To square a number:

```
    (X**2)
or  (X*X)             /* faster and more precise */
```

To cube a number:

```
    (X**3)
or  (X*X*X)           /* faster and more precise */
```

The square root of a number:

```
SQRT(X)
```

The cube root of a number:

```
    (X**(1/3))
or  (SIGN(X)*EXP(LOG(ABS(X))/3))    /* if X is not 0 */
or  (EXP(LOG(X)/3))                 /* if X is positive */
```

A random number (uniformly distributed) in the range from A to B:

```
((B - A)*RANUNI(99) + A)
```

A random roll of a die:

```
CEIL(6*RANUNI(99))
```

A random integer (uniformly distributed) in the range from A to B:

```
(CEIL((B - A + 1)*RANUNI(99) + A - 1))
```

Missing values in numeric expressions

The effect of using a missing value in a numeric expression depends on how the missing value is used.

When a missing value is used with an arithmetic operator, the result is a missing value. This phenomenon is called *propagation of missing values.* The SAS supervisor prints a warning message telling where and how many times this happens.

Comparison operators and logical operators produce only 1 and 0 values, even if missing values are used as operands. With comparison operators, a missing value is considered to be less than any number. With logical operators, missing operands are considered false values, the same as 0.

Most numeric functions do not accept missing values as arguments, even those that meaningfully could. If any argument is missing, they return a missing value, with the same warning message that arithmetic operators generate.

The statistic functions, such as SUM, MAX, and MEAN, are an exception. They take any number of arguments, but they only use the nonmissing arguments, ignoring arguments that have missing values. Each statistic function requires a minimum number of nonmissing arguments, however, and returns a missing value if not enough nonmissing arguments are present. The exception is NMISS, which ignores its nonmissing arguments and never returns a missing value.

Some of the financial functions are intended to be called with one missing argument, and the rest nonmissing. They return missing values if they are called with the wrong number of missing arguments.

Functions can also return missing values when arguments have values that are not meaningful for the function. The LOG function, for example, only works for positive arguments; `LOG(0)` returns a missing value. ARCOS requires arguments between –1 and 1.

The INPUT function can return a missing value if it is unable to apply the informat argument to the string argument. It generates a warning message. This statement, for example, gives YEAR a missing value:

```
YEAR = INPUT('MMVI', 4.);
```

The same thing can happen in an implicit type conversion:

```
LENGTH YEAR 8;
YEAR = 'MMVI';
```

Type conversions are discussed in chapter 6, "Expressions."

The SUM function and + operator both do addition, but they handle missing values differently. The + operator results in a missing value if one operand is missing, while the SUM function returns a missing value only if all its arguments are missing.

The sum statement works the same way as the SUM function.

```
DATA _NULL_
  A = 3 + .;
  B = SUM(3, .);
  C = .;
  C + 3;
  D = 3;
  D + .;
  PUT _ALL_;
```

```
A=. B=3 C=3 D=3 _ERROR_=0 _N_=1
```

Similarly, the MAX and MIN operators are equivalent to the MAX and MIN functions for numbers, but do not necessarily produce the same results for missing values. The MAX and MIN functions, being statistic functions, ignore missing values, while the MAX and MIN operators do not.

The MAX operator and the MAX function produce the same results except for special missing values. The MAX function returns a standard missing value if all its arguments are missing, while the MAX operator actually compares different missing values to find the larger one.

The MIN operator and MIN function produce different values when comparing missing values with nonmissing values. The MIN function returns the lowest nonmissing value. The MIN operator returns the missing value when its operands are one missing value and one nonmissing value. The MIN operator can be used to compare two different missing values.

```
DATA _NULL_
  A = . MIN 1;
  B = MIN(., 1);
  C = .C MIN .E;
  D = MIN(.C, .E);
  W = 64 MAX .;
  X = MAX(64, .);
  Y = .E MAX .Y;
  Z = MAX(.E, .Y);
  PUT _ALL_;
```

```
A=. B=1 C=C D=. W=64 X=64 Y=Y Z=. _ERROR_=0 _N_=1
```

Input data might contain other codes for missing values, such as the number –9. You can convert those values to missing values after an INPUT statement with a statement like

```
IF X = -9 THEN X = .;
```

You can use the SUM function to convert missing values to zero without changing nonmissing values:

```
X = SUM(X, 0);
```

Any arithmetic operator other than the unary + will convert special missing values to standard missing values. These expressions do so without affecting other values:

```
   X = --X;
or X = X + 0;
```

Logic

The subject of logic mainly comes up in connection with conditional execution, which was discussed in chapter 4, "Control flow." Conditions appear in several SAS control flow statements: UNTIL and WHILE conditions in the DO statement, IF conditions in the IF . . . THEN and subsetting IF statements, and WHEN conditions in the conditional SELECT block.

A logical expression in the SAS language is any numeric expression considered to represent a true or false value. Positive and negative numbers represent true, and 0 and missing values represent false. Logical expressions are the conditions in SAS control flow statements and the operands for the logical operators AND, OR, and NOT.

Boolean algebra

The logical operators are numeric operators, allowing logic problems to be represented mathematically. This use of mathematical operations to do logical analysis is the basis of Boolean algebra, the branch of mathematics that deals with logic, so logical operators are sometimes called *Boolean operators.*

The use of 1 and 0 to represent true and false is also a convention of Boolean algebra. A 1 or 0 used as a logical true or false value is called a *Boolean value.* The SAS logical and comparison operators produce Boolean values. A logical expression consisting of an operator with Boolean operands is a *Boolean expression.*

The NOT operator can be used twice to conform a logical expression to a Boolean value: –7, 1, and 8000 all represent true, so `NOT NOT -7`, `NOT NOT 1`, and `NOT NOT 8000` all resolve to the value 1. Similarly, `NOT NOT .` and `NOT NOT 0` both resolve to 0.

The comparison operators also have a particular meaning with Boolean operands. The = operator can be used, in particular, to compare two Boolean values that should be the same, either both true or both false. The MAX operator is equivalent to OR, and MIN is equivalent to AND, when they have Boolean operands.

Any logical expression can be written several ways; it is generally better to use the simpler or more intuitive form. These two expressions are equivalent, for example, and in different situations one or the other of them might appear more meaningful:

```
NOT A AND NOT B
NOT (A OR B)
```

Truth tables

Truth tables show how the values of Boolean expressions depend on the values of operands. They can be useful in determining equivalent forms of Boolean expressions. They can also be used to define the results of Boolean operators.

The truth tables below are presented in graphical table form, with shaded cells representing true values for the expression and unshaded cells representing false values. The upper left cell, for example, would be shaded if the expression being represented is true when both A and B are false.

The first two tables show the effects of the AND and OR operators:

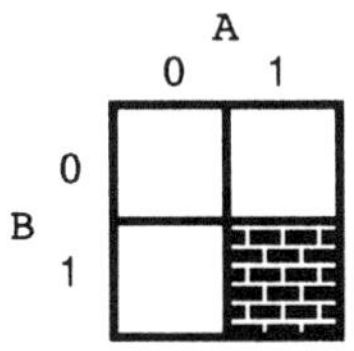

A AND B
A MIN B

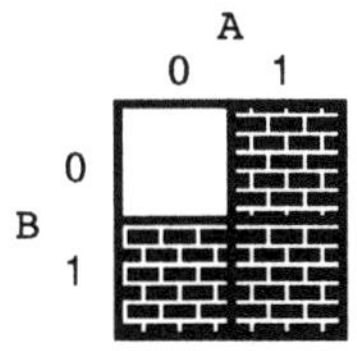

A OR B
A MAX B

These tables can also be inverted (using the NOT operator) to produce these two truth tables:

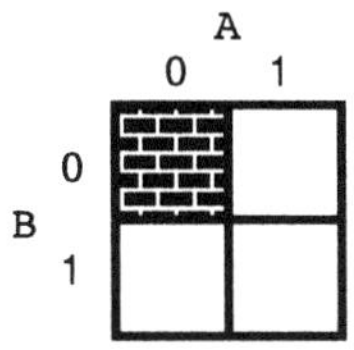

NOT A AND NOT B
NOT (A OR B)

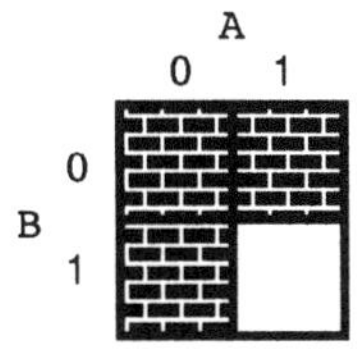

NOT A OR NOT B
NOT (A AND B)

The = and NE operators have effects corresponding to the statement "A is true if and only if B is true" and the inverse of that:

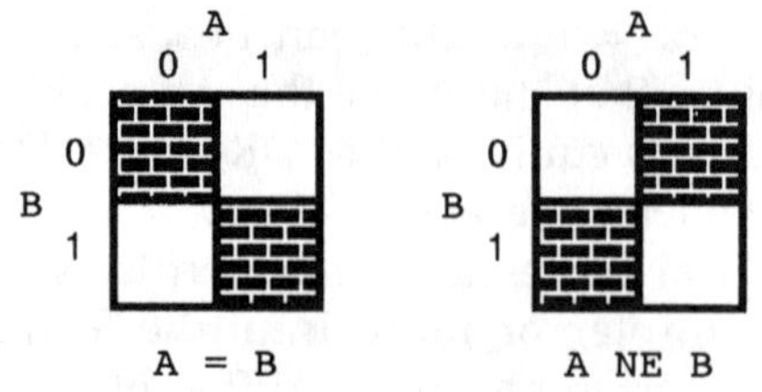

Comparison operators produce these logical results consistently only when they are used with 1 and 0 operands. The other four comparison operators form patterns that can be stated almost as easily using logical operators:

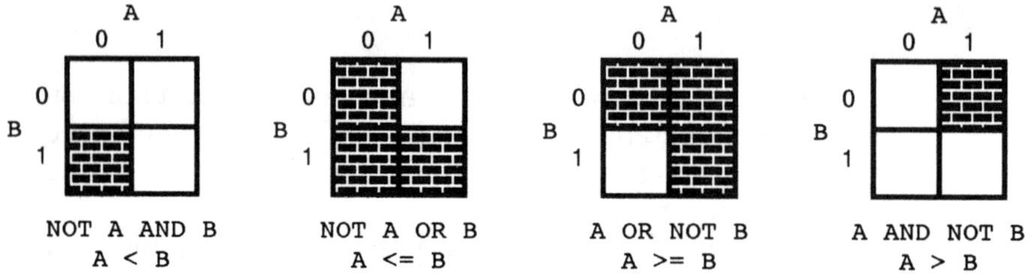

With four cells, each of which can have either of two values, there must be 2^4 or 16 possible truth tables. The remaining six are the simpler ones and are included for the sake of completeness:

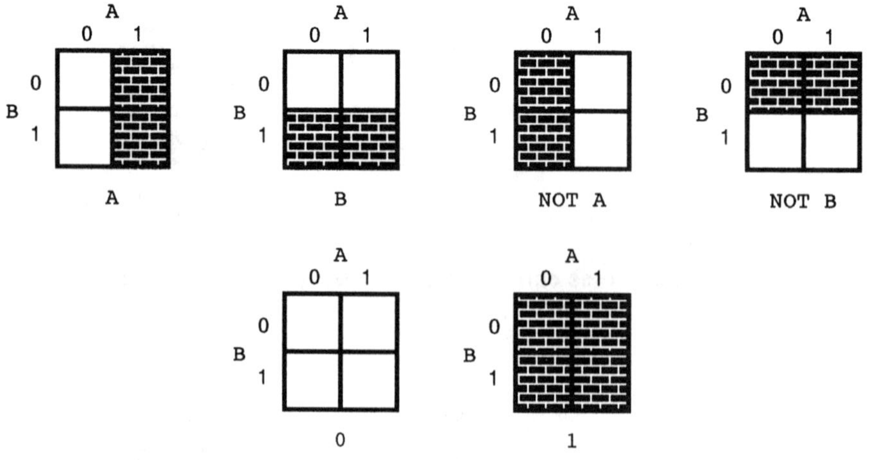

Logical expressions

Logical expressions are usually created as comparisons, using the comparison operators, but in some cases, it is easier to construct logical expressions in other ways.

There is rarely a need to use the NE operator with a 0 operand. Instead of

```
IF X NE 0;
```

you can usually just say

```
IF X;
```

The only time this won't work is when you really need to distinguish missing values from 0 values. Similarly, the expression

```
IF X = 0;
```

can often be simplified to

```
IF NOT X;
```

An important use of testing for zeros is when dividing, to avoid dividing by 0. Instead of coding

```
RATIO = N/D;
```

which can result in warning messages and missing values if D is 0, you might code

```
IF D THEN RATIO = N/D; ELSE RATIO = 0;
```

The ELSE action assigns a result in cases where you can't divide. You'll have to consider what value is appropriate. A zero value or missing value or 1 is appropriate in some situations. The ELSE action is not always necessary, particularly when the quotient variable has been initialized to missing by the observation loop since the last time it was assigned a value:

```
DATA;
  INPUT N D;
  IF D THEN RATIO = N/D;
```

Several SAS functions return values that can be used as logical values, even though they aren't just 0 and 1 values. Several examples of these functions can be found earlier in this chapter under "Testing numbers" and in the next chapter under "Testing strings."

Testing groups of variables

The longest expressions commonly found in SAS programs are logical expressions involving several variables. For example, to find out if any of the variables PRIOR1–PRIOR20 have the value 1, you would use the expression

```
(  PRIOR1  = 1 OR PRIOR2  = 1 OR PRIOR3  = 1 OR PRIOR4  = 1
OR PRIOR5  = 1 OR PRIOR6  = 1 OR PRIOR7  = 1 OR PRIOR8  = 1
```

```
OR PRIOR9  = 1 OR PRIOR10 = 1 OR PRIOR11 = 1 OR PRIOR12 = 1
OR PRIOR13 = 1 OR PRIOR14 = 1 OR PRIOR15 = 1 OR PRIOR16 = 1
OR PRIOR17 = 1 OR PRIOR18 = 1 OR PRIOR19 = 1 OR PRIOR20 = 1)
```

(Instead of this expression, you could code a DO loop with an array, as four out of five programming students would do, but there is no advantage in coding it that way.)

There are some cases where this kind of expression can be simplified using SAS statistic functions. First, if you want to test whether any one of a group of variables is positive, instead of testing each one individually

```
(A1 > 0 OR A2 > 0 OR A3 > 0 OR A4 > 0 OR ... )
```

you could just check the maximum value among them, using the MAX function:

```
(MAX(OF A1-A20) > 0)
```

The same form can be used to test whether any of the variables are above any particular value.

Similarly, if you want to test whether any of a group of variables is negative, you could use the MIN function to find the lowest value, and see if it is negative:

```
(.Z < MIN(OF A1-A20) < 0)
```

(Remember that the MIN function ignores missing values.)

The previous two expressions could be combined to test whether any of a group of variables is nonzero and nonmissing. If both the maximum and minimum value (ignoring missing values) in the group is zero, then every variable in the group must be 0 or missing. Otherwise, the following expression will be true:

```
(MAX(OF A1-A20) OR MIN(OF A1-A20))
```

That expression might win the prize for brevity, but this longer form is clearer and faster:

```
(A1 OR A2 OR A3 OR A4 OR A5 OR A6 OR A7 OR A8 OR A9 OR A10
OR A11 OR A12 OR A13 OR A14 OR A15 OR A16 OR A17 OR A18 OR
A19 OR A20)
```

Arithmetic with Boolean values

Boolean values can be used in arithmetic. The most common use of them is in counting. For example, you could count the number of nonblank variables among a group of variables using this expression:

```
((A1 NE ' ') + (A2 NE ' ') + (A3 NE ' ') + (A4 NE ' '))
```

A Boolean value can be used with a counter variable in a sum statement to count the number of observations with a certain characteristic. For example, the variable COUNT_A in this step counts observations that have positive values for the variable A:

```
DATA B;
  SET A (KEEP=A);
  COUNT_A + A > 0;
```

Boolean values can also be used in more complicated arithmetic. This expression, for example, tells the number of days in a month of a non-leap year:

```
(31 - (MONTH IN (4, 6, 9, 11)) - 3*(MONTH = 2))
```

When a Boolean value is multiplied by a value in an expression, it has the effect of making that term conditional. For example,

```
D = 7*(A <= 8) + (M + 14)*(A > 8);
```

has the same effect as

```
IF A <= 8 THEN D = 7;
IF A > 8 THEN D = M + 14;
```

Logical variables

When the same condition is used in several places, it may be appropriate to evaluate the condition and assign the result to a numeric variable, which is then a *logical variable.* (If the variable can only have the values 1 and 0, it can be called a *Boolean variable.*) For example, in the following step, the rather lengthy condition `HOUR < 8 OR HOUR >= 18 OR WDAY = 'SATURDAY' OR (WDAY = 'SUNDAY' AND HOUR < 12)` appears several times:

```
DATA CHARGE;
  SET SERVICE;
  C_USAGE = USAGE*1.99;
  IF HOUR < 8 OR HOUR >= 18 OR WDAY = 'SATURDAY'
    OR (WDAY = 'SUNDAY' AND HOUR < 12) THEN
    C_USAGE = C_USAGE*.75;
  IF LEVEL < 50 AND 0.00 < C_USAGE < 5.00 THEN C_USAGE = 5.00;
  IF NOT (HOUR < 8 OR HOUR >= 18 OR WDAY = 'SATURDAY'
    OR (WDAY = 'SUNDAY' AND HOUR < 12)) THEN
    C_ACCESS = 5.00;
  ELSE C_ACCESS = 0.00;
  IF (HOUR < 8 OR HOUR >= 18 OR WDAY = 'SATURDAY'
    OR (WDAY = 'SUNDAY' AND HOUR < 12)) AND C_USAGE > 5.00 THEN
    Q_DISC + 1;
```

The step can be shortened and simplified by assigning the condition to a variable:

```
DATA CHARGE;
  SET SERVICE;
  OFF_PEAK = HOUR < 8 OR HOUR >= 18 OR WDAY = 'SATURDAY'
    OR (WDAY = 'SUNDAY' AND HOUR < 12);
  C_USAGE = USAGE*1.99;
  IF LEVEL < 50 AND 0.00 < C_USAGE < 5.00 THEN C_USAGE = 5.00;
  IF OFF_PEAK THEN C_USAGE = C_USAGE*.75;
  IF OFF_PEAK THEN C_ACCESS = 0.00; ELSE C_ACCESS = 5.00;
  Q_DISC + OFF_PEAK AND C_USAGE > 5.00;
```

Logical variables can also be useful in testing combinations of conditions. In this example, a different action is taken for each different combination of two conditions.

```
N_ZONE = 204 < THETA < 207.1 AND .61 < R < .64 AND Z < .5;
CLASS_M = ATMOS = 'N O' AND .8 < GRAVITY < 1.4;
SELECT;
  WHEN(N_ZONE AND CLASS_M) SHIP = 'ENTERPRISE';
  WHEN(N_ZONE) SHIP = 'VALIANT';
  WHEN(CLASS_M) SHIP = 'ORION';
  OTHERWISE SHIP = 'STARFLEET';
  END;
```

When a condition acts as a parameter that affects an entire step, it might be assigned to a logical variable. For example, if a step needs to do various things only when the day it is run on is a Monday, you could create the logical variable MONDAY

```
RETAIN MONDAY;
IF _N_ = 1 THEN MONDAY = (WEEKDAY(TODAY()) = 2);
```

and then use that variable as the condition:

```
IF MONDAY THEN Monday actions;
```

Boolean variables are necessary when a logical value is needed in output data. Boolean values might also appear in input data, as answers to yes/no questions in a questionnaire, for example.

The SAS supervisor creates several Boolean variables on its own. The automatic variable _ERROR_, present in every data step, reflects the presence or absence of certain types of input errors. When a data step has a BY statement, there are FIRST. and LAST. variables for each BY variable, with Boolean values that tell whether an input observation is the first or last in a BY group. The IN=, END=, and other options in the INFILE, SET, MERGE, and UPDATE statements create Boolean variables that reflect certain conditions of the input files. There are also SAS procs that create Boolean variables.

The MIN, MAX, and SUM functions can be used to shorten expressions involving groups of Boolean variables. For Boolean values, MAX has the same effect as OR. For example, if CR1–CR6 are Boolean variables,

```
(CR1 OR CR2 OR CR3 OR CR5 OR CR6)
```

is equivalent to

```
MAX(OF CR1-CR6)
```

In a similar way, the MIN function is equivalent to the AND operator.

The SUM function can be for counting. With Boolean values, the result of the SUM function is the number of true arguments.

You could use the SUM function with IN= variables when doing a merge to determine how many input SAS datasets an observation came from. This example uses a subsetting IF statement to select observations that came from at least three of the input SAS datasets.

```
DATA SEL_COLL;
  MERGE LOCATION (IN=IN1) DEPTS (IN=IN2) PRESTIGE (IN=IN3)
        SPORTS (IN=IN4) EQUIP (IN=IN5) AC_LEVEL (IN=IN6);
  BY COLLEGE;
  IF SUM(OF IN1-IN6) >= 3;
```

Time

There are two different kinds of time data: points in time and durations of time. They are mainly represented by numbers, but can also be represented in character forms. The SAS System uses several numeric standards for representing points in time, and there are many other ways of representing time values.

You can do arithmetic with time values, compare them, and convert between different time forms. There are functions, informats, and formats that are designed to be used with time values.

Points in time

Points in time are the times represented on a clock or a calendar. Two points in time can be compared to determine which is earlier and which is later.

Time intervals, such as a day or a month, are treated as points in time. An interval is represented in SAS data by its beginning point. For example, the SAS date value for 1991 is the same as the SAS date value for January 1, 1991.

SAS date

A SAS date is the number of days since the beginning of 1960. The SAS date value for January 1, 1960 is 0. You can also have negative SAS dates, counting backward from 1960 as far back as Friday, October 15, 1582, when Pope Gregory XIII adopted the current Gregorian calendar. (SAS routines accept SAS dates as far back as January 1, 1582.)

This table shows SAS date values corresponding to a few selected dates:

Date	SAS Date Value
October 15, 1582	-137774
July 4, 1776	-67019
October 15,1951	-3000
January 1, 1960	0
May 19, 1987	10000
December 31, 1999	14609
April 7, 6565	1682038

SAS date constants can be used as a more readable form of SAS date value. A SAS date constant has the day of the month, the three-letter month abbreviation, and the year, in quotes, followed by the letter D. So, for example, SAS date constants to represent the dates in the table above would be `'15OCT1582'D`, `'4JUL1776'D`, `'15OCT1951'D` (or `'15OCT51'D`), `'1JAN1960'D`, `'19MAY1987'D`, `'31DEC1999'D`, and `'7APR6565'D`.

The DATE or TODAY function checks the computer's clock to determine the current date as a SAS date.

> SAS date values are numbers, and therefore are naturally associated with the numeric data type. This is also true of SAS time values and SAS datetime values.
>
> Some other languages, and especially database management systems, have a separate data type for dates, but the SAS System does not. SAS date formats, such as DATE. and MMDDYY., are numeric formats, which format numeric variables. SAS date informats are numeric informats. There are several SAS functions that use SAS date arguments. The SAS interpreter checks only that the argument of the WEEKDAY function (for example) is a numeric expression. It is up to the programmer to make sure that it is a valid SAS date value. On the other hand, using SAS date values with the numeric data type makes time arithmetic easy.

Date

Dates are represented in many different character forms. There are SAS informats and formats that convert between some of these forms and SAS date values.

In the tables of informats and formats below, the letters used in the forms have these meanings:

MM	month number	05
DD	2-digit day of month	09
MMM	three-letter month abbreviation	APR
YY	2-digit year	96
YYYY	4-digit year	1996
Q	quarter number	2
QQQ	quarter as roman numeral	II

This table shows the informats and formats used to convert between SAS date values and some character forms used to represent dates. When more than one format or no informat is shown, you have to convert the parts of the date separately.

Example	Form	Informat	Format
10	MM		MMDDYY2.
1026	MMDD		MMDDYY4.
10/26	MM/DD		MMDDYY5.
102696	MMDDYY	MMDDYY6.	MMDDYY6.
10/26/96	MM/DD/YY	MMDDYY8.	MMDDYY8.
10/26/1996	MM/DD/YYYY		MMDDYY5. '/' Z4.
26	DD		DDMMYY2.
2610	DDMM		DDMMYY4.
26/10	DD/MM		DDMMYY5.
261096	DDMMYY	DDMMYY6.	DDMMYY6.
26/10/96	DD/MM/YY	DDMMYY8.	DDMMYY8.
26/10/1996	DD/MM/YYYY		DDMMYY5. '/' Z4.
19961026	YYYYMMDD		Z4. MMDDYY4.
96	YY		YYMMDD2.
961026	YYMMDD	YYMMDD6.	YYMMDD6.
9610	YYMM		YYMMDD4.
1996/10/26	YYYY/MM/DD		Z4. '/' MMDDYY5.
96/10/26	YY/MM/DD	YYMMDD8.	YYMMDD8.
96/10	YY/MM		YYMMDD5.
26OCT1996	DDMMMYYYY	DATE9.	DATE9.
26OCT96	DDMMMYY	DATE7.	DATE7.
26OCT	DDMMM		DATE5.
OCT96	MMMYY	MONYY5. *(first day of month)*	MONYY5.
OCT1996	MMMYYYY	MONYY7. *(first day of month)*	MONYY7.
96Q4	YYQQ	YYQ4. *(first day of quarter)*	YYQ4.
1996Q4	YYYYQQ	YYQ6. *(first day of quarter)*	YYQ6.

The informats that produce SAS date values are generally tolerant of extra characters like hyphens, spaces, and slashes in the input data. Just how tolerant are they? Consider these examples:

```
  DATA _NULL_;
    INPUT DATE MMDDYY32.;
    PUT DATE DATE9. +1 @;
CARDZ;
Saturday 12, 1, 90, more or less
$10.10x2500
6.02E23
MONTH=5 DAY=11 YEAR=1995
5.5.5.5.5
7=9=11!!!!
;
```

```
01DEC1990 10OCT2500 02JUN1923 11MAY1995 05MAY1905 09JUL1911
```

The formats that print SAS date values truncate and punctuate differently depending on the width specification used. They usually right-align, printing leading blanks, if the number of characters they produce is less than the width specification used. However, if the output they produce is a single word, they left-align, padding with trailing blanks.

Many formats for writing SAS date values as years, months, and quarters were introduced with SAS release 6.06. Their use is shown here:

Example	Form	Format	Example	Form	Format
10/96	MM/YY	MMYYS5.	96Q3	YYQQ	YYQ4.
10-96	MM-YY	MMYYD5.	96:3	YY:Q	YYQC4.
10.96	MM.YY	MMYYP5.	96/3	YY/Q	YYQS4.
1096	MMYY	MMYYN4.	96-3	YY-Q	YYQD4.
10:96	MM:YY	MMYYC5.	96.3	YY.Q	YYQP4.
10M96	MMMYY	MMYY5.	963	YYQ	YYQN3.
10/1996	MM/YYYY	MMYYS7.	1996Q3	YYYYQQ	YYQ6.
10-1996	MM-YYYY	MMYYD7.	1996:3	YYYY:Q	YYQC6.
10.1996	MM.YYYY	MMYYP7.	1996/3	YYYY/Q	YYQS6.
101996	MMYYYY	MMYYN6.	1996-3	YYYY-Q	YYQD6.
10:1996	MM:YYYY	MMYYC7.	1996.3	YYYY.Q	YYQP6.
10M1996	MMMYYYY	MMYY7.	19963	YYYYQ	YYQN5.
96/10	YY/MM	YYMMS5.	96III	YYQQQ	YYQRN5.
96-10	YY-MM	YYMMD5.	96QIII	YYQQQQ	YYQR6.
96.10	YY.MM	YYMMP5.	96:III	YY:QQQ	YYQRC6.
9610	YYMM	YYMMN4.	96/III	YY/QQQ	YYQRS6.
96:10	YY:MM	YYMMC5.	96-III	YY-QQQ	YYQRD6.
96M10	YYMMM	YYMM5.	96.III	YY.QQQ	YYQRP6.
1996/10	YYYY/MM	YYMMS7.	1996III	YYYYQQQ	YYQRN7.
1996-10	YYYY-MM	YYMMD7.	1996QIII	YYYYQQQQ	YYQR8.
1996.10	YYYY.MM	YYMMP7.	1996:III	YYYY:QQQ	YYQRC8.
199610	YYYYMM	YYMMN6.	1996/III	YYYY/QQQ	YYQRS8.
1996:10	YYYY:MM	YYMMC7.	1996-III	YYYY-QQQ	YYQRD8.
1996M10	YYYYMMM	YYMM7.	1996.III	YYYY.QQQ	YYQRP8.
96OCT	YYMMM	YYMON5.	3	Q	QTR1.
1996OCT	YYYYMMM	YYMON7.	III	QQQ	QTRR3.

Another four formats write SAS dates using names. The WORDDATE and WORDDATX formats write the month name, day, and year. The value formatted in the examples below is 11549.

Format Specification	Example
WORDDATE3.	Aug
WORDDATE9.	August
WORDDATE12.	Aug 15, 1991
WORDDATE18.	August 15, 1991
WORDDATX3.	Aug
WORDDATX9.	August
WORDDATX12.	15 Aug 1991
WORDDATX18.	15 August 1991

The WEEKDATE and WEEKDATX formats also write the weekday:

Format Specification	Example
`WEEKDATE3.`	`Thu`
`WEEKDATE9.`	`Thursday`
`WEEKDATE15.`	`Thu, Aug 15, 91`
`WEEKDATE17.`	`Thu, Aug 15, 1991`
`WEEKDATE23.`	`Thursday, Aug 15, 1991`
`WEEKDATE29.`	`Thursday, August 15, 1991`
`WEEKDATX3.`	`Thu`
`WEEKDATX9.`	`Thursday`
`WEEKDATX15.`	`Thu,  15 Aug 91`
`WEEKDATX17.`	`Thu,  15 Aug 1991`
`WEEKDATX23.`	`Thursday,  15 Aug 1991`
`WEEKDATX29.`	`Thursday,  15 August 1991`

SAS time

A SAS time value represents the time of day as the number of seconds since midnight. This table shows SAS time values representing some times of day:

Time	SAS Time Value
midnight	`0`
8:00 a.m.	`28800`
noon	`43200`
4:30 p.m.	`59400`
11:59:59.9 p.m.	`86399.9`

SAS time constants, similar to SAS date constants, can appear in SAS programs to represent SAS times. They consist of an hour number, and optionally minute and second, separated by colons, in quotes, followed by a T. The times of day in the table above correspond to the SAS time constants `'0:00'T`, `'8:00'T`, `'12:00'T`, `'16:30'T`, and `'23:59:59.9'T`.

Time of day

Time of day can be represented in character form in many different forms. This table shows the informats and formats used to convert between SAS time values and some character forms used to represent time of day.

Example	Form	Informat	Format
`11`	`HH`		`HHMM2.` or `TIME2.`
`1130`	`HHMM`		`HHMM4.`
`11:30`	`HH:MM`	`TIME5.`	`HHMM5.` or `TIME5.`
`11:30:00`	`HH:MM:SS`	`TIME8.`	`TIME8.`
`11:30:00.00`	`HH:MM:SS.SS`	`TIME11.`	`TIME11.2`

The SAS System's routines ordinarily represent time of day using the 24-hour clock, with hours from 00 to 23. It's also possible to use time of day values in a 12-hour clock format, with hours 12, 1, 2, ...,11.

Interpreting 12-hour clock hours involves converting the 12s to 0s, and adding 12 hours to p.m. values.

```
CLOCKT = ' 9:11 PM';
TIME = MOD(INPUT(CLOCKT, TIME5.), 43200);
IF UPCASE(SUBSTR(CLOCKT, 7, 1)) = 'P' THEN TIME + 43200;
```

The MOD function is needed to read the hour 12 correctly. The third statement adjusts for p.m. times; there are 43,200 seconds in a half day. The statements above interpret 12:00 a.m. as midnight and 12:00 p.m. as noon.

These statements reverse the process, producing a string containing a 12-hour clock time from a SAS time value:

```
TIME = '21:11'T;
LENGTH CLOCKT $ 8;
PM = TIME >= 43200;
TIME12 = MOD(TIME, 43200);
IF TIME12 < 3600 THEN TIME12 + 43200;
IF PM THEN CLOCKT = PUT(TIME12, TIME5.) || ' PM';
ELSE       CLOCKT = PUT(TIME12, TIME5.) || ' AM';
PUT CLOCKT=;
```

```
CLOCKT=9:11 PM
```

SAS datetime

A SAS datetime is the number of seconds since the beginning of 1960. SAS datetime values are valid over the same range of time as SAS date values, and have millisecond precision over the range of values that people tend to think about.

A SAS datetime constant, which combines the form of the SAS date constant and SAS time constant, can be used to represent a SAS datetime in a program. For example, the statement

```
WHEN = '10OCT1960 12:00'DT;
```

could be used to assign to the variable WHEN a SAS datetime value representing noon on October 10, 1960.

The DATETIME informat and DATETIME format can be used to read and write SAS datetimes that follow the same form as a SAS datetime constant. The DATETIME format can be used with a small width to write only the date part of the SAS datetime. The TOD format writes the time of day of a SAS datetime value.

Year

Year numbers are normally the years of the Gregorian calendar. This calendar has been adopted by one country after another over the last four centuries, but is far from universal. The SAS System has the NENGO informat and format for reading and writing Japanese years.

In some contexts, a year value might represent a fiscal year, which is a period of a year ending on a certain date used by an organization for accounting purposes. Usually the number of the fiscal year is the year number of its last day. For example, a fiscal year ending September 30, 1992, would be called fiscal 1992.

The YEAR function extracts the year of a SAS date. Thus, the current year would be returned by the function call

```
YEAR(TODAY())
```

In SAS release 6.06, there is a YEAR format that writes the year of a SAS date. The `YEAR2.` format specification writes the last two digits of the year.

The meaning of a two-digit year (that is, a year value from 0 to 99) in a SAS informat or function is determined (beginning with SAS release 6.06) by the YEARCUTOFF= system option, which specifies the first year of a hundred-year period for which two-digit years can be represented. The option also affects the meaning of SAS date and SAS datetime constants. The default is (currently) `YEARCUTOFF=1900`. Thus, two-digit years are considered to be between 1900 and 1999. If the system option were changed to

```
OPTIONS YEARCUTOFF=1921
```

a two-digit year would be a year between 1921 and 2020, and the SAS date constant `'15AUG11'D` would represent August 15, 2011.

Still, people and SAS formats will write the years of any century shortened to two digits. Even with the YEARCUTOFF= option, this kind of abbreviation should only be used for values that fall within a span of under 100 years. You might want to avoid using two-digit years for birthdates or the dates of real estate transactions, for example.

End of the century

It is also prudent to avoid doing a simple comparison of two-digit year values to determine which event came first, or using a two-digit year value as a sort key to put a SAS dataset in chronological order.

Despite the obvious shortcomings of two-digit years, surprisingly many programs rely on them and assume that years belong to the 1900s. Even some serious, expensive, professional programs that corporations rely on to operate their computer and accounting systems will come to a crashing halt when the January 2000 data starts coming in. Perhaps the writers of this "twentieth century software" just aren't looking ahead as far as the new millennium.

Quarter

A SAS quarter is three months rather than being precisely a fourth of a year. SAS routines use the codes

1 for January, February, and March,
2 for April, May, and June,
3 for July, August, and September,
4 for October, November, and December.

Organizations with fiscal years are likely to use fiscal quarters. Some organizations assign fiscal quarters with a set number of days rather than by month.

Month

SAS System routines use the month codes 1 for January, 2 for February, 3 for March, etc. Organizations with fiscal years usually use fiscal months.

The SAS function MONTH and, beginning with SAS release 6.06, the MONTH format extract the month number from a SAS date.

As character values, months may be represented by their names or by abbreviations. In English, the longest month name, "September," is 9 characters. Three-letter abbreviations, consisting of the first three letters of the month, are often used. The initials of month names are sometimes used in output, mostly in time-series charts and graphs, even though the initials A, J, and M appear more than once:

```
J F M A M J J A S O N D
```

To convert a month name or three-character abbreviation to a month number, you can use this value informat:

```
PROC FORMAT;
  INVALUE MON (MIN=3 MAX=3 UPCASE)
      'JAN' = 1
      'FEB' = 2
      'MAR' = 3
      'APR' = 4
      'MAY' = 5
      'JUN' = 6
      'JUL' = 7
      'AUG' = 8
      'SEP' = 9
      'OCT' = 10
      'NOV' = 11
      'DEC' = 12
      OTHER = .
      ;
```

After the MON informat is defined, you can use it to convert a month name or abbreviation to a month number using a statement like

```
NUMBER = INPUT(NAME, MON3.);
```

You can also use the informat in INPUT statements for reading data from files.

To convert a month number to a month name, abbreviation, or initial, you can convert the month number to a SAS date value and use the WORDDATE format. Because the WORDDATE format right-aligns, you might want to use the LEFT function to left-align the resulting month name. Because the minimum width of the WORDDATE format is 3, you have to use the SUBSTR function to extract the first letter (although this is unnecessary if you are assigning the result to a variable of length 1).

```
LENGTH NAME $ 9 ABBR $ 3 INITIAL $ 1;
NAME = LEFT(PUT(MDY(MONTH, 1, 1999), WORDDATE9.));
ABBR = PUT(MDY(MONTH, 1, 1999), WORDDATE3.);
INITIAL = SUBSTR(PUT(MDY(MONTH, 1, 1999), WORDDATE3.), 1, 1);
PUT NAME= ABBR= INITIAL=;
```

```
NAME=January ABBR=Jan INITIAL=J
NAME=February ABBR=Feb INITIAL=F
```

Beginning with SAS release 6.06, you can use the simpler MONNAME format instead. It has a minimum width of 1, allowing you to write month initials directly:

```
INITIAL = PUT(MDY(MONTH, 1, 1999), MONNAME1.);
```

You can use the UPCASE function if you need to convert the formatted values to uppercase letters.

Day

Days can be numbered sequentially within any time interval: weeks, months, years, fiscal years, hostage crises, and so on.

The functions DAY and WEEKDAY return the day of month and day of week numbers from a SAS date value.

Beginning with SAS release 6.06, there are the corresponding formats DAY and WEEKDAY and two related formats: DOWNAME, to write the name of the day of the week, and the quaintly named JULDAY to write the day of year.

When using day of year values, remember that the values for February 29 through December 31 are different in non-leap years and leap years. Many large corporations use the year and day of year as their standard way of identifying dates in files.

SAS weekdays represent the days of the week using the codes

1 = Sunday
2 = Monday
3 = Tuesday
4 = Wednesday
5 = Thursday
6 = Friday
7 = Saturday.

Some people use different codes. It is common in business and in many countries to consider Monday the first day of the week, so you might find the codes 1 = Monday, ..., 5 = Friday, ... The simplest way to convert these codes to SAS weekdays is using a conditional formula:

```
IF WORKDAY < 7 THEN WEEKDAY = WORKDAY + 1;
ELSE WEEKDAY = WORKDAY - 6;
```

It is also possible to do the conversion as a single expression:

```
WEEKDAY = MOD(WORKDAY + 0, 7) + 1;
```

(Add a value other than 0 to WORKDAY to convert to a different scheme for numbering weekdays.)

As character values, the days of the week may be represented by their names or by abbreviations. In English, the longest name of a day of the week is 9 characters: "Wednesday." Two-letter and three-letter abbreviations, consisting of the first letters of the weekday name, are often used. The initials of weekdays are sometimes used in output, mostly in calendars and time-series charts, although the initials S and T are each used twice:

```
S M T W T F S
```

To convert a weekday name or abbreviation to a SAS weekday number, you can use the value informat below. This value informat also includes 1-letter abbreviations that are sometimes used for some of the days of the week.

```
PROC FORMAT;
  INVALUE WEEKDAY (MIN=2 MAX=2 UPCASE JUST)
      'SU', 'S' = 1
      'MO', 'M' = 2
      'TU', 'T' = 3
      'WE', 'W' = 4
      'TH', 'R' = 5
      'FR', 'F' = 6
      'SA',     = 7
      OTHER     = .
      ;
```

After the WEEKDAY informat is defined, you can use it to convert a month name or abbreviation to a month number using a statement like

```
NUMBER = INPUT(NAME, WEEKDAY2.);
```

You can also use the informat in INPUT statements for reading data from files.

To convert a SAS weekday to a weekday name or abbreviation, you can convert the weekday number to a SAS date value in order to use the WEEKDATE format. It happens that adding 1 accomplishes this. Because the WEEKDATE format right-aligns, you might want to use the LEFT function to left-align the resulting weekday name. Because the minimum width of the WEEKDATE format is 3, you will need the SUBSTR function to extract the first letter or first two letters (although this is not really necessary if you are assigning the result to a variable of the appropriate length).

```
LENGTH NAME $ 9 ABBR3 $ 3 ABBR2 $ 2 INITIAL $ 1;
NAME = LEFT(PUT(WEEKDAY + 1, WEEKDATE9.));
ABBR3 = PUT(WEEKDAY + 1, WEEKDATE3.);
ABBR2 = UPCASE(SUBSTR(PUT(WEEKDAY + 1, WEEKDATE3.), 1, 2));
INITIAL = SUBSTR(PUT(WEEKDAY + 1, WEEKDATE3.), 1, 1);
PUT WEEKDAY= NAME= ABBR3= ABBR2= INITIAL=;
```

```
WEEKDAY=2 NAME=Monday ABBR3=Mon ABBR2=MO INITIAL=M
```

Beginning with SAS release 6.06, you can use the DOWNAME format, which has a minimum width of 1:

```
NAME = LEFT(PUT(WEEKDAY + 1, DOWNAME.));
ABBR3 = PUT(WEEKDAY + 1, DOWNAME3.);
ABBR2 = UPCASE(PUT(WEEKDAY + 1, DOWNAME2.));
INITIAL = PUT(WEEKDAY + 1, DOWNAME.);
```

Hour, minute, second

SAS hour values go from 0 to 23. The hour from 4:00 p.m. to 5:00 p.m. is hour 16, for example. SAS hour values occasionally contain fractional parts of hours, in which case they can range from 0 up to (but not including) 24.

The conventional way to represent hours on a clock is much more complicated: it begins at 12, then covers 1 through 12, then 1 through 11, with an indicator "a.m." or "p.m." indicating whether the hour is in the first half or second half of the day. There is no agreement as to whether noon should be included in a.m. or p.m., and there is the same problem with midnight. Strictly speaking, noon should be represented as "noon" and midnight as "midnight," which are often abbreviated as "n." and "m." To further complicate matters, "m." is occasionally used as an abbreviation for noon! (Those who know the Latin roots of "a.m." and "p.m." will understand why "m." seems to belong between them.) To avoid confusion, some people (like the bus lines) avoid scheduling anything at exactly noon or midnight.

Minute values representing a fraction of an hour and second values representing a fraction of a minute range from 0 to (but not including) 60. It is common for second values to include fractional parts of seconds.

Converting between points in time

The following tables show expressions for converting between different numbers that may represent a point in time.

convert to ⇒ ⇓convert from	SAS date	day of month	day of year	month	quarter
SAS date		`DAY(DATE)`	`DATE + 1 - MDY(1, 1, YEAR)`	`MONTH(DATE)` *for month name:* `PUT(DATE, MONNAME.)`	`QTR(DATE)`
day of month	`MDY(MONTH, DAY, YEAR)`		`MDY(MONTH, DAY, YEAR) - MDY(1, 1, YEAR)`		
day of year (nonleap year)	`MDY(1, 1, YEAR) + YEARDAY - 1`	`DAY (YEARDAY - 365)`		`MONTH (YEARDAY - 365)`	`QTR (YEARDAY - 365)`
day of year (leap year)		`DAY (YEARDAY)`		`MONTH (YEARDAY)`	`QTR (YEARDAY)`
month	`MDY(MONTH, DAY, YEAR)`			*for name:* `PUT( MDY(MONTH, 1, 0), MONNAME.)`	`CEIL (MONTH/3)`
quarter	`YYQ(YEAR, QUARTER)`			`QUARTER*3 - 2`	

convert to ⇒ ⇓convert from	SAS datetime	SAS date	day of week	quarter	year
SAS datetime		`DATEPART (DATE)`	`WEEKDAY (DATEPART (DATE))`	`QTR (DATEPART (DATE))`	`YEAR (DATEPART (DATE))`
SAS date	`DATE*86400`		`WEEKDAY(DATE)` *for name of day of week:* `PUT(DATE, DOWNAME.)`	`QTR(DATE)`	`YEAR(DATE)`
day of week		`MDY(8, WEEKDAY, 1999)`	*for name:* `PUT(WEEKDAY + 1, DOWNAME.)`		
quarter	`YYQ(YEAR, QUARTER) *86400`	`YYQ(YEAR, QUARTER)`			
year	`MDY(MONTH, DAY, YEAR) *86400`	`MDY(MONTH, DAY, YEAR)`			

convert to ⇒ ⇓convert from	second	minute	hour	p.m.?	SAS time	SAS datetime
hour, minute, second				`HOUR >= 12`	`HMS(HOUR, MINUTE, SECOND)`	`DHMS(DAY, HOUR, MINUTE, SECOND)`
SAS time	`SECOND (TIME)`	`MINUTE (TIME)`	`HOUR (TIME)`	`TIME >= 43200`		`DATE*86400 + TIME`
SAS datetime	`SECOND (DATETIME)`	`MINUTE (DATETIME)`	`HOUR (DATETIME)`		`TIMEPART (DATETIME)`	

Time issues

When doing precise work with points in time you might have to adjust for time zones and daylight savings time.

The usual adjustment for daylight savings time is to subtract one hour (3600 seconds) to convert a daylight time to a non-daylight time. In addition to affecting the time of day of an event, this might affect the date. If DLTIME is a SAS time value in daylight savings time, then this statement converts it to non-daylight time TIME:

```
TIME = MOD(DLTIME - 3600, 86400);
```

If the SAS time value for an event in daylight savings time is less than 3600, converting it to non-daylight time will move the event to the previous day.

If DT is a SAS datetime value in daylight savings time, this statement converts it to non-daylight time:

```
DT + -3600;
```

When working with time values from several time zones, the easiest approach is usually to convert them all to the same time zone. If no time zone is the obvious reference point, Greenwich time is a commonly used standard.

> Time zones are used so that time values around Earth can correspond roughly to local sun time, measured by the position of the sun in the sky. Greenwich time, the local time in the British Isles, Iceland, Portugal, and much of West Africa, is often used in international treaties, astronomical observations, and other situations where local time is not important or appropriate. Greenwich time is named for Greenwich, England, whose astronomers invented standard time and longitude.

The SAS System has a group of functions that can be used to obtain the current time. TIME returns the current time of day as a SAS time. DATETIME returns the current date and time of day as a SAS datetime. DATE returns the current date as a SAS date. TODAY is another name for the DATE function. None of these functions have arguments.

These functions get their values by referring to the computer's clock. The returned values will only be correct if the clock has been set correctly. Single-user computers with dead batteries and some older personal computer models that do not use batteries will have the correct time only if the date and time of day are set after the computer is turned on. On most multiuser systems, the clock can be relied upon to be within a few minutes of the correct time (except, perhaps, right after a daylight savings time change).

Comparing points in time

There are three possibilities when comparing two points in time:

`A < B`	A is earlier than B
`A = B`	A is at the same time as B
`A > B`	A is later than B

To compare two points in time using SAS comparison operators, they must be in the same form. That is, you would compare SAS date values to SAS date values, SAS datetime values to SAS datetime values, SAS time values to SAS time values, hour values to hour values, etc. The form must be appropriate to the comparison intended; for example, to test whether two values are in the same calendar year, you should convert them to the year form before comparing. To test whether the SAS dates BUYDATE and SELLDATE were in the same year, you would use the expression:

```
YEAR(BUYDATE) = YEAR(SELLDATE)
```

To test whether one event happens at a later time of day than another (regardless of the specific days the events occur on), you would convert both values to SAS time values before comparing.

All numeric point in time forms can be compared using the comparison operators, and some character forms can too. In particular, the YYMMDD form can be compared if the dates are in the same century.

Durations of time

The SAS System's routines use durations of time measured in seconds, minutes, hours, days, weeks, months, quarters, and years. Primarily, though, durations of time are counted in seconds.

A duration of time in seconds is very much like a SAS time. SAS time values represent time of day, but you can think of them as representing a duration of time: the duration of time in seconds since midnight.

Hours, minutes, and seconds are often represented in character form in the same form used for a time of day. For example, 3:59 might represent 3 minutes and 59 seconds or 3 hours and 59 minutes, or it might represent a time of day, 1 minute before 4 a.m. For very long races and other long-running events, elapsed time is sometimes measured in days, hours, minutes, and seconds, with the different numbers separated by colons.

The TIME informat can also be used to read durations of time written in hours and minutes or hours, minutes, and seconds. SAS time constants can be used the same way. The values produced are durations of time in seconds.

The SAS System includes several formats that can be used with durations of time measured in seconds, to write them in all the usual forms. These are the same formats that are used with SAS time values, because a

SAS time is, in essence, a duration of time in seconds. A few of these formats can also be used for durations of time in minutes.

to format . . .	**as . . .**	**use . . .**
minutes	hours	`MMSS2.` format (really!)
minutes	hours and minutes	`MMSS5.` format (or wider)
seconds	hours	`HHMM2.` format
seconds	hours and minutes	`TIME5.` format
seconds	hours, minutes, and seconds	`TIME8.` format (or wider)
seconds	minutes and seconds	`MMSS5.` format (or wider)
seconds	seconds	standard numeric format

To format a duration in seconds as days, hours, minutes, and seconds requires formatting the days separately from the hours, minutes and seconds. Suppose the variable CLOCK is a duration of time in seconds that should be formatted as days, hours, minutes, and seconds. You can determine the number of whole days in CLOCK by using the DATEPART function (even though this is not quite what that function was designed to do):

```
DAYS = DATEPART(CLOCK);
```

Similarly, you can extract the fractional part of a day using the TIMEPART function. Then you can format the two values separately, putting a colon between them:

```
PARTDAY = TIMEPART(CLOCK);
PUT DAYS 3. ':' PARTDAY TIME8.;
```

In a similar manner, you could format the value as days, hours and minutes:

```
DAYS = DATEPART(CLOCK);
PARTDAY = TIMEPART(CLOCK);
PUT DAYS 3. ':' PARTDAY HHMM5.;
```

You can read in a duration of time in hours and minutes or hours, minutes, and seconds using the TIME informat. To read in a duration of time in any other form requires reading each part of the value separately.

This step shows the process of reading a value in minutes and seconds and a value in days, hours, minutes, and seconds:

```
  DATA TIMES;
    INFILE CARDS;
    INPUT MINUTES 2. +1 SECONDS 2. @;
    SHORT = 60*MINUTES + SECONDS;

    INPUT +4 DAYS 2. +1 PARTDAY TIME8.;
    LONG = DAYS*86400 + PARTDAY;
CARDS;
 7:06     3:07:21:01
;
```

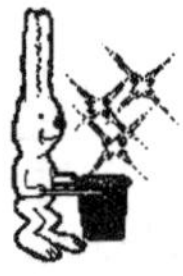

Longitude and latitude

Angles are most often measured in degrees, with 360 degrees in a complete circle. A degree can be divided into smaller units called minutes, which are 1/60 of a degree, and seconds, which are 1/60 of a minute.

If a variable holds an angle measure in degrees, you can write it in degrees and minutes or degrees, minutes, and seconds by multiplying it by the right factor and using the MMSS or TIME format, and then overwriting the symbols °, ', and " for degrees, minutes, and seconds.

To write a degree value as degrees and minutes:

```
MINUTES = DEGREES*60;
PUT MINUTES MMSS7. +(-3) '°' +2 "'";
```

```
-137°02'
```

To write a degree value in degrees, minutes and seconds:

```
SECONDS = DEGREES*3600;
PUT SECONDS TIME10. +(-6) '°' +2 "'" +2 '"';
```

```
-137°01'32"
```

Converting between time units

You can convert between time units just by multiplying by the right factor. The lengths of months, quarters, and years vary, so the numbers for converting them are averages:

from \ to	seconds	minutes	hours	days	weeks	months	quarters	years
seconds	1	.01666667	2.7778E-4	1.1574E -5	1.64366E-6	3.80265E-7	1.26755E-7	3.16887E-8
minutes	60	1	.01666667	6.94444E-4	9.92063E-5	2.28159E-5	7.6053E-6	1.90132E-6
hours	3600	60	1	.041666667	.00595238	.001369	4.56318E-4	1.1408E-4
days	86400	1440	24	1	.14285714	.032854884	.010951628	.002737907
weeks	604800	10080	168	7	1	.229984128	.0766614	.01916535
months	2629746	43829.1	730.485	30.436875	4.348125	1	.333333333	.083333333
quarters	7889238	131487.3	2191.455	91.310625	13.044375	3	1	.25
years	31556952	525949.2	8765.82	365.2425	52.1775	12	4	1

You can use expressions to determine the exact number of days in a month, quarter, or year. First of all, a year is defined as a leap year if the day after February 28 is in February:

```
(MONTH(MDY(2, 28, YEAR) + 1) = 2)
```

Thus, the number of days in a year is

```
(365 + (MONTH(MDY(2, 28, YEAR) + 1) = 2))
```

The number of days in a month in a non-leap year is

```
(31 - (MONTH IN (4, 6, 9, 11)) - 3*(MONTH = 2))
```

The number of days in a month in a leap year is

```
(31 - (MONTH IN (4, 6, 9, 11)) - 2*(MONTH = 2))
```

The number of days in a month is

```
(31 - (MONTH IN (4, 6, 9, 11))
    - (3 - (MONTH(MDY(2, 28, YEAR) + 1) = 2))*(MONTH = 2))
```

The number of days in a quarter is

```
(91 + (QUARTER >= 3)
    - (QUARTER = 1 AND NOT MONTH(MDY(2, 28, YEAR) + 1) = 2))
```

You can also use the INTNX function to find the number of days in a time period, as described below.

Comparing durations of time

Comparison operators can be used to compare durations of time, provided that the two values use the same time units. If two time values have different units, you can convert one of them to the units used by the other before comparing. For example, if DAYS is a number of days, and HOURS is a number of hours, you can compare them with the expression

```
(DAYS*24 >= HOURS)
```

Time arithmetic

You can do certain kinds of arithmetic with time values. You can take the difference between two points in time, which results in a duration of time. You can do the reverse, changing a point in time by a duration of time to get another point in time. You can add and subtract duration values.

That's about all the time arithmetic you'll find. It wouldn't be meaningful to add together two points in time, or to multiply two time values.

In doing time arithmetic, you need to match time units. The duration between two year values, for example, is a number of years. SAS date values use days as their time unit. The time unit of SAS time values and SAS datetime values is seconds.

For example, if A and B are SAS datetime values with A > B, then `A - B` is the length of time in seconds between A and B.

As another example, to find out what day is 7 days in the future, you could get today's date as a SAS date value, using the DATE function, and then add 7 days:

```
NEXTWEEK = TODAY() + 7;
PUT 'A week from today will be ' NEXTWEEK WORDDATE29.;
```

The INTCK and INTNX functions do time arithmetic for time values representing whole periods of time, ignoring fractional parts of time periods and fractional numbers of time periods. Both functions have as their first argument a code telling both the time unit used to measure the time interval and the type of value representing the points in time. They handle the conversion of time units for SAS dates, SAS times, and SAS datetimes.

INTCK does subtraction, determining the length of time between two SAS dates, two SAS times, or two SAS datetimes. It truncates the points in time to the beginnings of fixed calendar intervals before subtracting, so that the number it returns is always a whole number. It then subtracts the second argument from the third argument. For example, the value returned by `INTCK('MONTH', '26FEB1992'D, '1MAR1992'D)` is 1, because the second date is 1 calendar month later than the first date. The interval beginning for a week is considered to be Sunday. The arguments and types used for the INTCK function are shown in this table.

Function Call	Value Returned
`INTCK('YEAR',` SAS date, SAS date`)`	years
`INTCK('QTR',` SAS date, SAS date`)`	quarters
`INTCK('MONTH',` SAS date, SAS date`)`	months
`INTCK('WEEK',` SAS date, SAS date`)`	weeks
`INTCK('DAY',` SAS date, SAS date`)`	days
`INTCK('HOUR',` SAS time, SAS time`)`	hours
`INTCK('MINUTE',` SAS time, SAS time`)`	minutes
`INTCK('SECOND',` SAS time, SAS time`)`	seconds
`INTCK('DTYEAR',` SAS datetime, SAS datetime`)`	years
`INTCK('DTQTR',` SAS datetime, SAS datetime`)`	quarters
`INTCK('DTMONTH',` SAS datetime, SAS datetime`)`	months
`INTCK('DTWEEK',` SAS datetime, SAS datetime`)`	weeks
`INTCK('DTDAY',` SAS datetime, SAS datetime`)`	days
`INTCK('HOUR',` SAS datetime, SAS datetime`)`	hours
`INTCK('MINUTE',` SAS datetime, SAS datetime`)`	minutes
`INTCK('SECOND',` SAS datetime, SAS datetime`)`	seconds

You can use the INTCK function to test whether a date is at the beginning or end of a time interval. If DATE is the first day of a month, then

```
INTCK('MONTH', DATE - 1, DATE)
```

is 1; most of the time, though, it is 0. Similarly, if DATE is the last day of the month, this expression is 1:

```
INTCK('MONTH', DATE, DATE + 1)
```

The INTNX function does addition. Like the INTCK function, it truncates points in time to the beginnings of fixed calendar intervals, and it also ignores fractional parts of time duration arguments. So, for example, `INTNX('YEAR', '15AUG1990'D, 2)` is `'1JAN1992'D`, because 1992 is 2 years after 1990. The combinations of arguments allowed for the INTNX function is shown in this table.

Function Call	Value Returned
`INTNX('YEAR'`, SAS date, years`)`	SAS date
`INTNX('QTR'`, SAS date, quarters`)`	SAS date
`INTNX('MONTH'`, SAS date, months`)`	SAS date
`INTNX('WEEK'`, SAS date, weeks`)`	SAS date
`INTNX('DAY'`, SAS date, days`)`	SAS date
`INTNX('HOUR'`, SAS time, hours`)`	SAS time
`INTNX('MINUTE'`, SAS time, minutes`)`	SAS time
`INTNX('SECOND'`, SAS time, seconds`)`	SAS time
`INTNX('DTYEAR'`, SAS datetime, years`)`	SAS datetime
`INTNX('DTQTR'`, SAS datetime, quarters`)`	SAS datetime
`INTNX('DTMONTH'`, SAS datetime, months`)`	SAS datetime
`INTNX('DTWEEK'`, SAS datetime, weeks`)`	SAS datetime
`INTNX('DTDAY'`, SAS datetime, days`)`	SAS datetime
`INTNX('HOUR'`, SAS datetime, hours`)`	SAS datetime
`INTNX('MINUTE'`, SAS datetime, minutes`)`	SAS datetime
`INTNX('SECOND'`, SAS datetime, seconds`)`	SAS datetime

The INTNX function always returns the beginning of a time period. So with 0 as the third argument, INTNX can be used to find the beginning of the time period containing a particular point in time. For example, the first day of a month containing the day DATE is

```
INTNX('MONTH', DATE, 0)
```

The last day of a month is the day before the first day of the next month:

```
(INTNX('MONTH', DATE, 1) - 1)
```

You can use also the INTNX function to find the length of a time period. If a month contains the day DATE, then the length of the month is the number of days from the beginning of the month to the beginning of the following month:

```
(INTNX('MONTH', DATE, 1) - INTNX('MONTH', DATE, 0))
```

Similarly, you could calculate the length of a year:

```
(INTNX('YEAR', MDY(YEAR, 1, 1), 1) - MDY(YEAR, 1, 1))
```

Of course, if you are calculating the number of days in a week

```
(INTNX('WEEK', DATE, 1) - INTNX('WEEK', DATE, 0))
```

you should always get 7 as a result!

14 Data types

The SAS programming language has fewer data types than most languages, but the two it has are versatile. All kinds of numbers are represented in its one numeric type, along with logical values. Character data is potentially even more diverse; any type of data can be represented in the character data type.

Working with character strings

Character values are most often used as character strings, consisting of printable characters and blanks. There are three general categories of expressions involving character strings: those that test strings, producing a true or false value, those that measure strings, producing a number, and those that change strings, producing new strings.

Testing strings

The expressions we present here represent common questions about strings. These expressions are stated in terms of the variable STRING, but any expression could be used. Expressions using operators are shown enclosed in parentheses; the parentheses might be needed if the expression is used with another operator to form another expression.

To test whether a string is blank (also known as missing):

```
(STRING = '')
```

To test whether a string is nonblank:

```
(STRING NE '')
```

To test whether a string contains a blank:

```
INDEXC(STRING, ' ')
```

To test whether a string contains a blank, other than trailing blanks:

```
INDEXC(TRIM(STRING), ' ')
```

To test whether a string contains the character 'H':

```
INDEXC(STRING, 'H')
```

To test whether a string contains a capital letter:

```
INDEXC(STRING, 'ABCDEFGHIJKLMNOPQRSTUVWXYZ')
```

To test whether a string contains two consecutive blanks:

```
INDEX(STRING, '  ')
```

To test whether a string contains the word 'TRIBBLE':

```
INDEX(STRING, 'TRIBBLE')
```

To test whether a nonblank string is left-aligned:

```
   (STRING NE: ' ')
or (STRING = LEFT(STRING))
```

To test whether a string begins with the character 'C':

```
(STRING =: 'C')
```

To test whether a string begins with the characters '$(':

```
(STRING =: '$(')
```

To test whether a string falls in the alphabetic range L–Mo:

```
('L' <=: UPCASE(STRING) <=: 'MO')
```

To test whether a string is a valid SAS name:

```
(NOT VERIFY(UPCASE(SUBSTR(STRING, 1, 1)),
      'ABCDEFGHIJKLMNOPQRSTUVWXYZ_')
 AND NOT VERIFY(UPCASE(TRIM(STRING)),
      'ABCDEFGHIJKLMNOPQRSTUVWXYZ_0123456789')
 AND LENGTH(STRING) <= 8
 )
```

To test whether a string contains a lowercase letter:

```
(STRING NE UPCASE(STRING))
```

To test whether a string is a valid 2-letter state postal code:

```
STFIPS(STRING)
```

To test whether a character is a letter (or whether all characters in a string are letters):

```
(NOT VERIFY(STRING,
   'ABCDEFGHIJKLMNOPQRSTUVWXYZabcdefghijklmnopqrstuvwxyz'))
```

To test whether a character is a digit (or whether all characters in a string are digits):

```
(NOT VERIFY(STRING, '0123456789'))
```

Measuring strings

There are several things you can count in a string, and the expressions that follow can be used to measure some of the more interesting characteristics of a string. All these expressions end up being expressed in terms of the length of something.

The visible length of a string:

```
(LENGTH(STRING) - (STRING = ' '))
```

The expression length of a nonblank string:

```
LENGTH(RIGHT(STRING))
```

The number of nonblank characters in a string:

```
(LENGTH(COMPRESS(STRING)) - (STRING = ' '))
```

The number of times the character `'*'` appears in a string:

```
(LENGTH(LEFT(STRING)) - LENGTH(COMPRESS(LEFT(STRING), '*'))
 + (LEFT(STRING) = '*'))
```

The number of leading blanks in a string:

```
(LENGTH(STRING) - LENGTH(LEFT(STRING)))
```

The number of trailing blanks in a string:

```
(LENGTH(RIGHT(STRING)) - LENGTH(STRING))
```

The number of embedded blanks in a string:

```
(LENGTH(LEFT(STRING)) - LENGTH(COMPRESS(STRING)))
```

String effects

Each of the following expressions transforms a string in some way.

A string with letters converted to uppercase:

```
UPCASE(STRING)
```

A string with letters converted to lowercase:

```
TRANSLATE(STRING, 'abcdefghijklmnopqrstuvwxyz',
                  'ABCDEFGHIJKLMNOPQRSTUVWXYZ')
```

A string with letters converted to lowercase with an initial uppercase letter:

```
UPCASE(SUBSTR(STRING, 1, 1)) ||
TRANSLATE(SUBSTR(STRING, 2), 'abcdefghijklmnopqrstuvwxyz',
                             'ABCDEFGHIJKLMNOPQRSTUVWXYZ')
```

A string with leading blanks removed:

```
REVERSE(TRIM(REVERSE(STRING)))
```

A string with trailing blanks removed:

```
TRIM(STRING)
```

A string with leading and trailing blanks removed:

```
TRIM(LEFT(STRING))
```

A string with all blanks removed:

```
COMPRESS(STRING)
```

A left-aligned string:

```
LEFT(STRING)
```

A right-aligned string:

```
RIGHT(STRING)
```

A centered string:

```
SUBSTR(RIGHT(STRING), CEIL(.5*(LENGTH(RIGHT(STRING))
                        - LENGTH(LEFT(STRING)))) + 1)
```

A digit string right-aligned with leading blanks converted to zeros:

```
(REPEAT('0', LENGTH(RIGHT(STRING))
           - LENGTH(LEFT(STRING)) - 1)
 || LEFT(STRING))
```

A string shifted to the right one character:

```
(' ' || STRING)
```

A string shifted to the right N characters:

```
(REPEAT(' ', N - 1) || STRING)
```

A string shifted to the left N characters:

```
SUBSTR(STRING, N + 1)
```

The first character of a string:

```
SUBSTR(STRING, 1, 1)
```

The last character of a string:

```
SUBSTR(REVERSE(STRING), 1, 1)
```

The first nonblank character of a string:

```
    SUBSTR(LEFT(STRING), 1, 1)
or  INPUT(STRING, $1.)
```

The last nonblank character of a string:

```
    SUBSTR(LEFT(REVERSE(STRING)), 1, 1)
or  SUBSTR(REVERSE(RIGHT(STRING)), 1, 1)
```

The digits of a phone number (with the characters "/-() " removed):

```
COMPRESS(STRING, '/-() ')
```

A phone number with a leading 1 removed:

```
    TRIM(TRANSLATE(SUBSTR(LEFT(STRING), 1, 1), ' ', '1'))
    || SUBSTR(LEFT(STRING), 2)

or  TRIM(LEFT(TRANSLATE(SUBSTR(LEFT(STRING), 1, 1), ' ', '1')
        || SUBSTR(LEFT(STRING), 2)))
```

A phone number with letters converted to digits:

```
TRANSLATE(STRING, '22233344455566677778889990',
                  'ABCDEFGHIJKLMNOPQRSTUVWXYZ')
```

The digits of a phone number with a leading 1, blanks, and special characters removed and letters converted to digits (combining the previous three effects):

```
TRANSLATE(
  COMPRESS(
    TRANSLATE(SUBSTR(LEFT(STRING), 1, 1), ' ', '1')
    || SUBSTR(LEFT(STRING), 2),
  '/-() '),
'22233344455566677778889990',
'ABCDEFGHIJKLMNOPQRSTUVWXYZ')
```

Encryption

Encryption is the process of coding data to make it difficult to read. The usual reason is for security — to make it more difficult for unauthorized people to get certain information.

There is security and then there is security. An encryption process that is written down in a SAS program can be no more secure than the program itself, but it might protect data from casual observers and confused spies.

We present here two of the easiest ways to encrypt the value of a SAS variable: character substitution and transposition.

In character substitution, each character in a set of characters replaces one other character in the set. For example, the letter E might replace M, while M replaces F, F replaces H, and so on. In this example, we use only capital letters, but you could apply the same process with a more inclusive set of characters.

```
RETAIN ALPHABET 'ABCDEFGHIJKLMNOPQRSTUVWXYZ'
       ENCODING 'IORBPMAFNLDCEUZHKYTGSWXQJV';
CRYPT = TRANSLATE(STRING, ENCODING, ALPHABET);
```

The letters in ALPHABET also appear in ENCODING, but in scrambled order. The code characters are substituted for the characters in STRING to produce CRYPT. For example, if STRING is

```
PRIORITY A-3
```

then CRYPT is

```
HYNZYNGJ I-3
```

Decrypting is just the opposite process:

```
RETAIN ALPHABET 'ABCDEFGHIJKLMNOPQRSTUVWXYZ'
       ENCODING 'IORBPMAFNLDCEUZHKYTGSWXQJV';
DECRYPT = TRANSLATE(CRYPT, ALPHABET, ENCODING);
```

To make the process slightly more secure, you could avoid keeping the ENCODING string in a program file. You could, for example, make it a compiled macro, which would make it a bit more difficult to find. Trying to memorize the ENCODING string is probably a bad idea.

Transposition just changes the order of the characters in a value. It is especially appropriate for values that have a fixed length. If the value is a 10-digit phone number, for example, you might decide to put the characters in the order 3 6 10 4 2 7 5 9 1 8.

```
CRPYT = SUBSTR(PHONE, 3, 1) ||
        SUBSTR(PHONE, 6, 1) ||
        SUBSTR(PHONE, 10, 1) ||
        SUBSTR(PHONE, 4, 1) ||
        SUBSTR(PHONE, 2, 1) ||
```

```
          SUBSTR(PHONE, 7, 1) ||
          SUBSTR(PHONE, 5, 1) ||
          SUBSTR(PHONE, 9, 1) ||
          SUBSTR(PHONE, 1, 1) ||
          SUBSTR(PHONE, 8, 1);
```

or

```
LENGTH CRYPT $ 10;
SUBSTR(CRYPT, 1, 1) = SUBSTR(PHONE, 3, 1);
SUBSTR(CRYPT, 2, 1) = SUBSTR(PHONE, 6, 1);
SUBSTR(CRYPT, 3, 1) = SUBSTR(PHONE, 10, 1);
SUBSTR(CRYPT, 4, 1) = SUBSTR(PHONE, 4, 1);
SUBSTR(CRYPT, 5, 1) = SUBSTR(PHONE, 2, 1);
SUBSTR(CRYPT, 6, 1) = SUBSTR(PHONE, 7, 1);
SUBSTR(CRYPT, 7, 1) = SUBSTR(PHONE, 5, 1);
SUBSTR(CRYPT, 8, 1) = SUBSTR(PHONE, 9, 1);
SUBSTR(CRYPT, 9, 1) = SUBSTR(PHONE, 1, 1);
SUBSTR(CRYPT, 10, 1)= SUBSTR(PHONE, 8, 1);
```

If PHONE is

```
5095551437
```

then CRYPT is

```
9575015354
```

Note that a character variable cannot be created using the SUBSTR pseudo-variable. If that is its first reference in a step, its length should be declared first using a LENGTH statement.

Decrypting the coded phone number involves reversing the transposition process:

```
LENGTH DECRYPT $ 10;
SUBSTR(DECRYPT, 3, 1) = SUBSTR(CRYPT, 1, 1);
SUBSTR(DECRYPT, 6, 1) = SUBSTR(CRYPT, 2, 1);
SUBSTR(DECRYPT, 10, 1)= SUBSTR(CRYPT, 3, 1);
SUBSTR(DECRYPT, 4, 1) = SUBSTR(CRYPT, 4, 1);
SUBSTR(DECRYPT, 2, 1) = SUBSTR(CRYPT, 5, 1);
SUBSTR(DECRYPT, 7, 1) = SUBSTR(CRYPT, 6, 1);
SUBSTR(DECRYPT, 5, 1) = SUBSTR(CRYPT, 7, 1);
SUBSTR(DECRYPT, 9, 1) = SUBSTR(CRYPT, 8, 1);
SUBSTR(DECRYPT, 1, 1) = SUBSTR(CRYPT, 9, 1);
SUBSTR(DECRYPT, 8, 1) = SUBSTR(CRYPT, 10, 1);
```

In practice, you would probably make an array out of the transposition sequence and do the encryption and decryption in a DO loop. The encryption process is then:

```
LENGTH PHONE CRYPT $ 10;
ARRAY SEQUENCE{10} _TEMPORARY_ (3 6 10 4 2 7 5 9 1 8);
DO I = 1 TO 10;
  SUBSTR(CRYPT, I, 1) = SUBSTR(PHONE, SEQUENCE{I}, 1);
  END;
```

and decryption is

```
    LENGTH CRYPT DECRYPT $ 10;
    ARRAY SEQUENCE{10} _TEMPORARY_ (3 6 10 4 2 7 5 9 1 8);
    DO I = 1 TO 10;
      SUBSTR(DECRYPT, SEQUENCE{I}, 1) = SUBSTR(CRYPT, I, 1);
      END;
```

This approach allows you to change the transposition sequence just by typing in a new list of numbers. (You could even hide away the ARRAY statement somewhere, perhaps in an %INCLUDE file or compiled macro.)

Character substitution and transposition are considered elementary encryption methods that cannot be expected to keep secrets from a serious cryptographer. That does not mean they are not useful, though. Either one is usually more than enough to keep ordinary business data, or data in an experiment, from being found by accident. For more sensitive data, there are more serious encryption methods you can use.

Length of character expressions

The length of a SAS character value is not a simple matter. There are actually three different ways to measure the length of a character value, and understanding the difference between them is essential for avoiding programming errors when working with character expressions.

If you did not consider the effects of the lengths of character values, you might expect the following step to give the variable B a nonblank value.

```
  DATA A;
    INPUT C $;
    IF C =: 'X' THEN A = REPEAT('*', 10);
    ELSE A = C;
    IF A =: '*' THEN B = C;
    ELSE B = UPCASE(REVERSE(A));
    PUT _ALL_;
CARDS;
sub
radar
trop
liar
;
```

```
C=sub A=sub B= _ERROR_=0 _N_=1
C=radar A=radar B= _ERROR_=0 _N_=2
C=trop A=trop B= _ERROR_=0 _N_=3
C=liar A=liar B= _ERROR_=0 _N_=4
```

Declaring the lengths of the variables solves this particular case of the missing B. The reasons this is important are described below.

```
  DATA A8;
    LENGTH A B C $ 8;
    INPUT C $;
    IF C =: 'X' THEN A = REPEAT('*', 10);
    ELSE A = C;
```

```
    IF A =: '*' THEN B = C;
    ELSE B = UPCASE(REVERSE(A));
    PUT _ALL_;
CARDS;
sub
radar
trop
liar
;
```

```
A=sub B=BUS C=sub _ERROR_=0 _N_=1
A=radar B=RADAR C=radar _ERROR_=0 _N_=2
A=trop B=PORT C=trop _ERROR_=0 _N_=3
A=liar B=RAIL C=liar _ERROR_=0 _N_=4
```

The visual length of a character value is how long it looks — the length of the value not counting trailing blanks. The expression length is the actual number of characters in the value, including blanks. The memory length is the number of bytes of memory that the SAS supervisor uses for the characters in the value. These three lengths are related by the inequality

$$\text{visual length} \leq \text{expression length} \leq \text{memory length} \leq 200$$

The memory length is determined in the compilation phase of a data step, before the step starts running. It is the same for an expression in a step every time that expression executes. The expression length and visual length can vary, depending on the data.

A related concept is the length of a character variable. Length is an attribute of a character variable, which can be declared in a LENGTH statement or can be determined by the first appearance of the variable in the data step. The length of a variable is determined by the SAS interpreter before the step starts running. A character variable's length determines both its memory length and its expression length.

When a character array reference is used in an expression, its memory length is the length of the longest variable in the array, but the expression length is the variable length of the actual variable being used.

The expression length and memory length of a character constant are the same, equal to the number of characters in the quoted string of a character literal or half the number of hexadecimal digits in a character hexadecimal constant.

Different character functions return different lengths, and usually the expression length and memory length are different. Lengths returned by functions are shown in the table of character functions in chapter 3, "Programs on call." The memory length returned by most character functions is the length of the string argument; other functions return a memory length of 200. The expression length usually varies depending on the values of the function's arguments, but some functions, such as LEFT and UPCASE, always return an expression length the same as the expression length of their arguments.

The operators that produce character values produce the lengths you would expect. The concatenation operator, ||, produces a memory length that is the sum of the memory lengths of its two operands and an expression length that is the sum of the expression lengths of its two operands (but not greater than 200). The MAX and MIN operators each produce a memory length that is the greater of the memory lengths of the two operands and an expression length that is the expression length of the appropriate operand.

A character value produced by an informat, whether in an INPUT statement or an INPUT function call, has an expression length and memory length determined by the informat specification. The length is the width of the informat, except for informats like the $HEX informat, which turn two or more input characters into one character. These statements give both A and B a length of 4, because of the informat widths used:

```
DATA _NULL_;
  INPUT A $HEX8. B $4.;
```

Character variables read using list input, and other character variables whose lengths are not indicated in any way where they are initialized, are given a default length of 8.

In the rare cases when a variable is introduced in a PUT statement, its length is determined in a similar way by the format specification.

The expression length and memory length of a character value produced by a format in a PUT function call is the width of the format. This also applies to an automatic type conversion from numeric to character; the default format specification, `BEST12.`, creates a character value of length 12. The length produced by a format does not, in any case, depend on the specific data being formatted.

The PUT function can be used with the $CHAR format to create a character expression of a specific length. For example, the expression

```
PUT(A, $CHAR40.)
```

has a memory length and expression length of 40, regardless of the length or value of the variable A.

When an expression is assigned to a variable, its length is changed to match the length of the variable. If the expression length is shorter than the variable length, blanks are added to the end, a process called *blank padding.* If the expression length is longer than the variable length, the value is *truncated,* omitting characters at the end.

For example, these statements

```
LENGTH NAME $ 8;
NAME = 'Ali';
```

give the variable NAME the value `'Ali     '`. These statements

```
LENGTH NAME $ 8;
NAME = 'Desdemona';
```

give NAME the value `'Desdemon'`.

If a character variable is created in an assignment statement, the memory length of the expression — not the expression length — is used as the length of the variable. For example, in this step,

```
DATA _NULL_;
  A = '1234';
```

the variable A has a length of 4, because the expression length of the value assigned to it is 4.

Returning to the example that started this section, the variable C is given a length of 8 by the list input process. The variable B first appears with the variable C being assigned to it, giving it the same length. The variable A first appears in an assignment statement, with the value returned by the REPEAT function. It gets a length of 200. When the value of C is assigned to A, 192 blanks are appended to fill in the length of A. The expression `UPCASE(REVERSE(A))` creates an expression length of 200, but it is truncated; only the first 8 characters are assigned to B.

Note that the output lines produced by the PUT statement are not an indicator of the length of a variable. In named output and list output, leading and trailing blanks are omitted; the number of characters printed might be fewer than the length produced by the format.

The lengths of variables in a SAS dataset are the same as the lengths those variables had in the step that created them. The CONTENTS proc can be used to determine the lengths of variables in a SAS dataset, and thus the lengths of variables in a data step.

```
PROC CONTENTS DATA=A;
```

```
Data Set Name:  WORK.A                          Type:
Observations:   4                               Record Len: 220
Variables:      3
Label:

          -----Alphabetic List of Variables and Attributes-----

#  Variable  Type  Len  Pos  Label
2  A         Char  200   12
3  B         Char    8  212
1  C         Char    8    4
```

Codes

A code is a symbol or group of symbols that represents something. Codes are often called numbers: Social Security number, payroll number, serial number, license plate number, account number, phone number. But codes are different from what we usually think of as numbers. They are not used in arithmetic, and they often contain letters or other symbols in addition to digits.

Codes have become part of everyday life in the computer age, largely because of system designers' need to identify data with unique values of a fixed length. In SAS programs, all variables have a fixed length, and unique values are necessary for operations like match merging.

Data types for codes

Codes can be either numeric or character values. Most codes should be character values; however, in deciding whether to use character or numeric variables for a particular code, consider the following:

- Character codes can be any length from 1 to 200 characters.
- Numeric codes can be up to 8 bytes, or about 16 digits.
- Numeric codes can only have digits (or perhaps – or .).
- Character codes can contain any character.
- Many people think of codes as being numbers.
- Digit strings take less space and use less run time as hexadecimal character values.

Processes with codes

Programs typically do only three processes with codes: input, output, and comparison. The comparison operators most commonly used with codes are = and NE. They might be used with the : modifier (=: and NE:) to test only the first few characters of a code. The other comparison operators might be used when ranges of codes are meaningful.

Character codes

Codes that might contain any letter or digit are character codes. Character codes do not have to be interpreted or formatted, so the $CHAR informat and format should be used with them. A constant value for a character constant would be represented as a character literal.

Columbia Records, for example, uses a system of catalog numbers that consist of two to four letters, followed by a blank, followed by five digits. This step reads in these catalog numbers and selects those that are part of the JC 30000 series:

```
DATA JC_30000;
  INFILE RECORDS;
  INPUT CAT_NO $CHAR10.;
  IF 'JC 30000' <= CAT_NO <= 'JC 39999';
```

Digit strings

Codes consisting entirely of digits are *digit strings*. The most efficient way to handle a digit string is in *packed hexadecimal* form, which is read and written with the $HEX informat and format. A character variable half the length of the digit string can then be used. For example, a code 8 digits long would fit in a character variable of length 4. A constant code value would be represented as a character hexadecimal constant.

This step prints addresses, including a ZIP code, except for those with ZIP codes less than 00600. Note that the constant 00600 is represented as `'006000'x`, with an extra 0 at the end to produce an even number of digits. The length of the ZIP variable in this step is 3.

```
DATA _NULL_;
  LENGTH ZIP $ 3;
  SET MAILLIST;
  FILE PRINT;
  IF ZIP < '006000'X /* 00600 */ THEN RETURN;
  PUT / NAME / ADDRESS1;
  IF ADDRESS2 NE ' ' THEN PUT ADDRESS2;
  IF ADDRESS3 NE ' ' THEN PUT ADDRESS3;
  PUT CITY +(-1) ', ' ST ZIP $HEX5.;
```

Character hexadecimal constants have to be an even number of digits, so you have to append a 0 to the code value if the code value has an odd number of digits. If an extra 0 is too confusing, you can use the INPUT function instead:

```
  IF ZIP < INPUT('00600', $HEX5.) THEN RETURN;
```

The $HEX informat and format work with odd lengths, but they can't be relied on to create variables of the right length. For some reason, the SAS interpreter rounds down after dividing by two to determine the length of a variable created with the $HEX informat. For example, in this step

```
DATA PLACES;                        /* wrong */
  INPUT ZIP $HEX5.;
```

the variable ZIP is given the length 2, only enough space to hold 4 hexadecimal digits. So you'll need to declare the length of a variable created with the $HEX informat with an odd width, to keep the last digit from being truncated:

```
DATA PLACES;
  LENGTH ZIP 3;
  INPUT ZIP $HEX5.;
```

Hexadecimal values can also contain the letters A–F, so those letters can also appear in this kind of code. This might be useful in ranking systems that use the ranks A1, A2, B1, etc.

Serial numbers

Serial means "sequential," and literally serial numbers are generated by adding 1 to the number previously assigned in the series. This can be done easily enough even if the serial number is a character code. There are just three steps: convert the last serial number to a number, add 1, and convert the result to the code format as the new serial number.

The PK informat and PK format can be used to convert between packed digit string formats and numbers. So if NEWEST is a packed 8-digit (4-byte) serial number, the next serial number can be assigned to the variable NEXT using this statement:

```
NEXT = PUT(INPUT(NEWEST, PK4.) + 1, PK4.);
NEWEST = NEXT;
```

If NEWEST was 00001001, NEXT is 00001002. The PK4. format also nicely implements a wrap-around feature for these serial numbers. If the last serial number to be assigned was the highest possible one, then the next one that is assigned is 0. In this example, if NEWEST is 99999999, then NEXT is 00000000.

Custom data types

The fact that a character value can hold any kind of data means that you can, in effect, create your own data types. You just have to figure out a way to get the data into and out of the form you devise.

This can be done with formats and informats. You use a format to put the data into a custom data type, and an informat to retrieve it.

> That means you'll be using a format when you give a variable a value, after you read the value from a file, for example, and an informat when you use the variable's value, in writing a report, for example. If that seems backward, look at it this way: a format turns a value into characters, which could either be the characters in a text file or the characters of a character variable. An informat does the reverse, interpreting characters to produce a value.

In this rest of the chapter, we present several custom data types and uses for them.

Byte variables

A character is a byte, or 8 bits, so it can have a total of 2^8 or 256 different values. If you think of the values as integers, you can represent the integers 0 to 255, as an unsigned byte, or the integers -128 to 127, as a signed byte.

An unsigned byte variable is declared as a character variable of length 1 and given its value using the `PIB1.` format. For example, the variable BYTE is given a value of 95 with this statement:

```
BYTE = PUT(95, PIB1.);
```

The value can then be retrieved using the `PIB1.` informat. For example, to write the value, you would use the statements:

```
NUMBER = INPUT(BYTE, PIB1.);
PUT NUMBER=
```

```
NUMBER=95
```

Similarly, a signed byte variable is assigned a value using the `IB1.` format, and the value is retrieved using the `IB1.` informat.

To do arithmetic with byte variables, you have to convert them to numeric form, do the arithmetic, and convert the result to byte variable form — a rather messy process:

```
BYTESUM =
    PUT(INPUT(BYTE1, PIB1.) + INPUT(BYTE2, PIB1.), PIB1.);
```

However, unsigned byte variables can be compared and sorted just as easily as numeric variables — faster, in fact, because an unsigned byte variable is only an eighth the size of a SAS numeric variable. You can compare unsigned byte values to each other or to hexadecimal numbers written as character hexadecimal constants.

You could use an unsigned byte variable for age, for example, and then select observations with an age value greater than 5:

```
INPUT NUMBER;
AGE = PUT(NUMBER, PIB1.);
IF AGE > '05'X;
```

The main reason to use byte variables is to reduce the size of a SAS dataset with many observations, thus saving storage space and I/O time. An integer value between 0 and 255 can be stored as an unsigned byte variable, in a third the space it would take as a numeric variable of length 3.

Integers

Integer variables don't have to be just one byte long. Using the PIB and IB formats and informats, unsigned and signed integer variables of any length from 1 to 8 bytes can be used. Despite the fact that they represent numbers, integer variables belong to the character data type.

In concert data, for example, you might use a 3-byte unsigned integer variable to hold attendance figures.

```
ATTEND = PUT(NUMBER, PIB3.);
```

The table below shows the range of values that integer variables of various lengths can hold. The largest integer value is nowhere near the largest possible double precision numeric value; still, Earth's population fits comfortably in an 5-byte integer value.

Length	Range of unsigned values	Range of signed values
1	0 to 255	–128 to 127
2	0 to 65,535	–32,768 to 32,767
3	0 to 16,777,215	–8,388,608 to 8,388,607
4	0 to 4,294,967,295	–2,147,483,648 to 2,147,483,647
5	0 to 10^{12}	-5.4×10^{11} to 5.4×10^{11}
6	0 to 2.8×10^{14}	-1.4×10^{14} to 1.4×10^{14}
7	0 to 7.2×10^{16}	-3.6×10^{16} to 3.6×10^{16}
8	0 to 1.8×10^{19}	-9.2×10^{18} to 9.2×10^{18}

Forward and backward

While there is a standard for the bits that represent integers in binary form on a computer, and the order of bits in a byte, there is no standard for the order of the bytes. Some computers put the bytes forward while others have them reversed!

"Forward" and "reversed" are determined by comparison to character values, which form our visual frame of reference. The hexadecimal numeral `0100X` represents the number 256, but when a computer reads the character value `'0100'X` using the `PIB2.` informat, does it read 256? If it does, then it represents numbers with the bytes in forward order. Or does it read the bytes in the other order, 00 and then 01, and get the value 1?

This step applies that test to determine whether a computer represents numbers in forward or reversed order.

```
DATA _NULL_;
  NUMBER = INPUT('0100'X, PIB2.);
  IF NUMBER = 0100X THEN
```

```
      PUT 'Numbers on this computer have bytes in forward order.';
    IF NUMBER = 0001X THEN
      PUT 'Numbers on this computer have bytes in reversed order.';
RUN;
```

Computers based on Intel 8086-series microprocessors, such as MS-DOS computers, have numbers in reversed order. VAX computers also have numbers reversed. Most other computers have them in forward order.

It shouldn't matter how a computer organizes its memory, as long as it works. However, there are advantages in the having unsigned integer values in forward order. You can then:

- get mathematically correct results with the <, <=, >=, and > comparison operators
- use an unsigned integer variable as a sort key
- use character hexadecimal constants as integer constants (it helps if you can read hexadecimal numerals)
- print unsigned integer variables as hexadecimal numerals using the $HEX format

You might also need to be concerned with orders of bytes in numbers when moving data from one kind of computer to another. This is a general problem, which is not specific to the SAS System.

Because of any of these reasons, you might want to use a forward integer variable on a computer that naturally represents numbers with bytes reversed. To do that, you can use the S370FPIB or S370FIB format and informat instead of the PIB or IB format and informat. The S370F series of informats and formats put numbers in forward order regardless of what the computer running the SAS System does more naturally. All the S370F informats and formats operate the same way on all computers, so you can use them for data that will be moved between computers.

Of course, you can also use the REVERSE function to reverse the order of bytes in an integer value.

Integer variables

Integer variables are the most compact way to store an integer, which can be a significant advantage in storing a large SAS dataset. On the other hand, they are harder to work with in the data step, and useless in most procs.

Integer variables are especially appropriate for variables that have to be stored but are used infrequently. The use of integer values can also be appropriate in structures and pseudo-arrays, which are described next, because the disadvantages of integer values are similar to those of structures.

Structures

Structures make it possible to have more than one value in a variable. You simply divide the bytes of the variable into elements, each of which has a different value. The SUBSTR function is used to access the different values separately.

For example, a structure of length 2 could have a character in byte 1 and an integer in byte 2. This might be a useful way to store grades that are given in both letter and number form. To assign the letter grade, you could use a statement like

```
SUBSTR(GRADE, 1, 1) = 'A';
```

To assign the number grade, you would use a statement like this one:

```
SUBSTR(GRADE, 2, 1) = PUT(SCORE, PIB1.);
```

To print out both parts of the GRADE structure, you would use statements like these:

```
NUMBER = INPUT(SUBSTR(GRADE, 2, 1), PIB1.);
PUT NAME= +2
    GRADE= $CHAR1. /* letter grade */
    +1 NUMBER 3.   /* number grade */;
```

The use of structures can simplify programming when several values are used together and are assigned or compared together. Structures can also be used as SELECT expressions, DO index values, or anywhere else a single value is required and you need to use two values together.

Consider, for example, the codes used for adult shoe sizes in the United States: a number for length, followed by a letter or multiple letter for width. Combining the length and width into a single variable makes it easier to use in a SELECT block:

```
SELECT(SHOESIZE);
  WHEN(' 9B') ...;
  WHEN(' 9C') ...;
  WHEN('10B') ...;
  WHEN('10D') ...;
  WHEN('10EE') ...;
  ...
```

Array of structures

The use of an array of structures can simplify programming in cases where there is a group of related arrays.

For example, consider a questionnaire in which people are asked about several broad subject areas, such as business and investment, sports, outdoor activities, cars, computers, and so on. They are asked the same twelve questions about each subject: their level of interest in it, the percent of their disposable income they spend on it, the numbers of hours per week they spend on it, the number of magazines on the subject that they read regularly, and so on.

This data could be organized as twelve arrays, one for each question:

```
ARRAY INT{17} $ 1;
ARRAY IPCT{17};
ARRAY WKHR{17};
ARRAY MAG{17};
. . .
```

but it might be easier to manage if organized as a single array of structures. Each structure would correspond to a subject area and would contain twelve elements, representing the answers to the twelve questions.

```
ARRAY ACT{17} $ 25;
```

Types

The type of a structure is defined by the location, form, and meaning of its elements, which you might keep track of with a table like this:

Bytes	Form	Description
1		level of interest 0=none, 1=low, 2, 3, 4, 5=high
2	PIB1.	percent of disposable income spent
3	PIB1.	number of hours per week spent
4	PIB1.	number of magazines read regularly
5		belong to organization (Y, N)
	. . .	

Any kind of data can be part of a structure. Even a structure can be a structure element. Some more custom data types that could be used are described at the end of this chapter.

> The organization of a structure is very much like a record layout for a file. In fact, in some programming languages, Pascal for one, structures are called records.

The main limitation on the form of a structure is that the entire structure cannot be longer than 200 bytes, the limit on the length of a SAS character value.

If two structure variables are the same type, you can use an assignment statement to assign the entire value of one structure to the other:

```
B_ACT = A_ACT;
```

Pseudo-arrays

A pseudo-array is a structure in which all the elements have the same form. In a pseudo-array, elements can be retrieved using an index, in a manner similar to the use of an array.

This familiar example consists of 26 1-byte character elements — that is, each character is a different element.

```
RETAIN ALPHABET 'ABCDEFGHIJKLMNOPQRSTUVWXYZ';
```

To retrieve the 3rd element of the pseudo-array, you would use the SUBSTR function:

```
LETTER = SUBSTR(ALPHABET, 3, 1);
PUT LETTER=;
```

```
LETTER=C
```

You could retrieve the elements of the pseudo-array one at a time using a loop, just as you might do with an array:

```
DO I = 1 to 26;
  LETTER = SUBSTR(ALPHABET, I, 1);
  PUT I LETTER;
  END;
```

```
 1 A
 2 B
 3 C
 4 D
 5 E
 6 F
 7 G
 8 H
 9 I
10 J
11 K
12 L
13 M
14 N
15 O
16 P
17 Q
18 R
19 S
20 T
21 U
22 V
23 W
24 X
25 Y
26 Z
```

You probably would not want to change an element of ALPHABET, but you could do it using the SUBSTR pseudo-variable:

```
SUBSTR(ALPHABET, 9, 1) = 'i';
```

Notice that, as with an array, the same tokens are used both for retrieving and assigning values for an element in a pseudo-array. This is possible because of the dual nature of the SUBSTR function.

Pseudo-arrays can have elements that are not treated as characters. This example demonstrates the use of a pseudo-array of one-byte unsigned integers:

```
RETAIN AB 'A1BB050709A1B01F'X;
FACTOR = INPUT(SUBSTR(AB, CODE, 1), PIB1.)*.01;
```

Length of elements

When the length of elements in a pseudo-array is greater than 1, the arguments for the SUBSTR function have to be calculated. If the length of array elements is LENGTH, the variable name of the pseudo-array is VAR, and the index of the element to be accessed is INDEX, you can access an element of a pseudo-array using the expression

```
SUBSTR(VAR, (INDEX - 1)*LENGTH + 1, LENGTH)
```

So if the length of elements is 10, the 7th element is

```
SUBSTR(VAR, (7 - 1)*10 + 1, 10)
```

or

```
SUBSTR(VAR, 61, 10)
```

You might find pseudo-array references easier to use if implemented as a macro:

```
%MACRO SOY(VAR, INDEX, LENGTH);
SUBSTR(VAR, (&INDEX - 1)*&LENGTH + 1, &LENGTH)
%MEND;
```

You could then use a macro call to access an element of a pseudo-array. To assign a value to the fifth element in a pseudo-array POST, which has elements of length 4:

```
%SOY(POST, 5, 4) = 'STR ';
```

Remember that the size of the entire pseudo-array cannot be over 200 bytes. That means you can have a maximum of 200 elements if the elements are 1 byte long, but no more than a mere 11 if the length is 18.

Other data types

Character strings, codes, digit strings, and packed hexadecimal values, which were discussed earlier in this chapter, can be used in structures. These are some other data types that you can use in structures or as separate variables.

Floating point

Floating point form is the form of the SAS numeric data type. To use it in a structure, you would use the RB (real binary) format and informat. The length of a floating point number can be 3 to 8 bytes (or 2 bytes, on some computers).

To put the full precision of a SAS numeric variable in a structure, you would use the `RB8.` format in a statement like

```
SUBSTR(STRUCT, 17, 8) = PUT(NUMBER, RB8.);
```

A statement like this would retrieve the value:

```
NUMBER = INPUT(SUBSTR(STRUCT, 17, 8), RB8.);
PUT NUMBER= BEST8.;
```

The S370FRB format and informat are portable routines that can be used instead of RB for data that might be moved between computers.

SAS date integer

An integer variable is usually the most compact way to store a date. A SAS date value is the number of days since January 1, 1960; if that value is stored as a 2-byte integer, it can cover a period of 65,536 days, or almost 180 years. A 2-byte signed integer can hold dates from 1871 through 2048. A 2-byte unsigned integer can hold dates from 1960 through 2138. If that doesn't go far enough into the past or the future for you, you could use a 3-byte integer, which covers a period of over 45,000 years.

To read a date from input data and store it as a SAS date integer, you would use the appropriate date informat to read the date into a SAS date value, and then the `PIB2.` or `IB2.` format to put the value in integer form. The process would be reversed for output.

```
  DATA DAYS (KEEP=DATE_INT);
    LENGTH DATE_INT $ 2;
    INPUT N_DATE DATE9.;
    DATE_INT = PUT(NDATE, PIB2.);
CARDS;
01MAR1984
23DEC2045
;
  DATA _NULL_;
    SET DAYS;
```

```
N_DATE = INPUT(DATE_INT, PIB2.);
PUT N_DATE= 'which represents ' N_DATE :WORDDATE18.;
```

```
N_DATE=8826 which represents March 1, 1984
N_DATE=31403 which represents December 23, 2045
```

Time of day

A 3-byte integer can represent time of day as the number of hundredths of a second since midnight. This .01-second precision is better than a standard SAS time value provides — it takes 4 bytes to store a SAS time value that is accurate to the nearest second.

You would use the `PIB3.2` format to translate a SAS time value into a 3-byte unsigned integer representing the number of hundredths of a second since midnight, and the `PIB3.2` informat to do the reverse.

Union

Union is a term borrowed from the C programming language to describe an instance of putting two different types of values in the same space. Of course, you can only have one of them there at a time, and you have to keep track of which one is there. Nevertheless, this can be a way to save storage space, when space or I/O time is critical.

Unions are often used when a SAS dataset contains two slightly different kinds of observations. For example, in a sales system, the same variable that contains the purchase order number for mail order sales might contain the salesperson's initials for showroom sales.

Boolean character

A Boolean variable can be stored in one byte. You could use a one-byte integer variable, with the values 1 and 0, but it is even easier to use the characters '1' and '0', and you can then read and print the variable. To create a Boolean character variable, use the PUT function with the `1.` format:

```
ONTIME = PUT(DATE <= DEADLINE, 1.);
```

You don't need to use an informat to use the Boolean character variable in an expression. You can just use a comparison operator:

```
IF ONTIME = '1' THEN
    PUT 'Thank you for getting this done on time.';
```

You could use any pair of characters to represent a logical value in one byte: T and F, perhaps, or Y and N.

Bitfield

It might occur to you that there ought to be room for eight Boolean values in a character, because a character is a byte, which is 8 bits. In fact, there is, and it can be worth doing if saving storage space in a file is a top priority. A byte treated this way is called a *bitfield* and is essentially like an 8-element array in one character.

If you think of a byte as a binary number, each digit represents (when 1) a different amount of magnitude — specifically, a different power of 2. The last digit represents 1, or 2^0; the second last, 2, or 2^1; the third last, 4, or 2^2; and so on up to 128. If all the digits are 1, they add up to 255, which is the largest value a byte can have.

We'll use this concept in putting eight Boolean values into a byte. Let's say the Boolean variables are called A1–A8 and each have a value of 1 or 0. Then we can determine an integer from 0 to 255 to represent all the possible combinations using this formula

```
128*A1 + 64*A2 + 32*A3 + 16*A4 + 8*A5 + 4*A6 + 2*A7 + A8
```

If you experiment with this formula, you'll find that each combination of values for the eight variables results in a different number, between 0 and 255. We can put that number in a byte variable, then, using this statement:

```
BITFIELD = PUT(
    128*A1 + 64*A2 + 32*A3 + 16*A4 + 8*A5 + 4*A6 + 2*A7 + A8,
    S370FPIB1.);
```

This process can be implemented in a DO loop using this approach:

```
ARRAY A{8} A1-A8;
BINARY = 0;
DO I = 1 TO 8;
  IF A{I} THEN BINARY + 2**(8 - I);
  END;
BITFIELD = PUT(BINARY, S370FPIB1.);
```

Retrieving the values from the bitfield, although not too difficult, can hardly be described as the reverse of the above process.

Use the MOD function to remove higher powers of 2 (earlier digits) in order to determine whether each power of 2 is present in the byte variable.

```
BINARY = INPUT(BITFIELD, S370FPIB1.);
A1 = BINARY >= 128;
A2 = MOD(BINARY, 128) >= 64;
A3 = MOD(BINARY, 64) >= 32;
A4 = MOD(BINARY, 32) >= 16;
A5 = MOD(BINARY, 16) >= 8;
A6 = MOD(BINARY, 8) >= 4;
A7 = MOD(BINARY, 4) >= 2;
A8 = MOD(BINARY, 2) >= 1;
```

This process can be implemented in a DO loop this way:

```
ARRAY A{8};
BINARY = INPUT(BITFIELD, S370FPIB1.);
DO I = 1 TO 8;
  A{I} = MOD(BINARY, 2**I) >= 2**(I - 1);
  END;
```

A bitfield does not have to be exactly 8 bits. It can be any number from 1 to 64 (which are the limits of the S370FPIB format). You can use the DO loops above, changing the 8s to the size you want. You'll need to declare the bitfield variable as an appropriate length, 1 character for each 8 bits, and use the appropriate width for the S370FPIB format and informat.

The PIB informat and format can be used in place of S370FPIB, especially for 1-byte bitfields.

The $BINARY informat and $BINARY format of SAS release 6.06 simplify the use of bitfields by making it easy to convert between a bitfield and a string of 1s and 0s. For example, if the string `'11010111'` represents 8 Boolean values, it can be converted to a bitfield and stored in just one byte:

```
LENGTH STRING $ 8 BITFIELD $ 1;
STRING = '11010111';
BITFIELD = INPUT(STRING, $BINARY8.);
```

A loop can be used with the SUBSTR pseudo-variable to put an array of Boolean values in to the string. The string is then converted to a bitfield:

```
ARRAY A{8} A1-A8;
STRING = '00000000';
DO I = 1 TO 8;
  IF A{I} THEN SUBSTR(STRING, I, 1) = '1';
  END;
BITFIELD = INPUT(STRING, $BINARY8.);
```

To retrieve a single value, use a formula like this one:

```
A{I} = INPUT(SUBSTR(PUT(BITFIELD, $BINARY8.), I, 1), 1.);
```

The retrieved value can even be used directly as a condition, without having to be assigned to a variable, as in this example:

```
DO I = 1 TO 8;
  IF INPUT(SUBSTR(PUT(BITFIELD, $BINARY8.), I, 1), 1.) THEN
      PUT 'Bit #' I 'set';
  END;
```

```
Bit #1 set
Bit #2 set
Bit #4 set
Bit #6 set
Bit #7 set
```

```
Bit #8 set
```

If you want to print a bitfield compactly, you can print it as a string using the $BINARY format in a PUT statement:

```
PUT '12345678' / BITFIELD $BINARY8.;
```

```
12345678
11010111
```

With the $BINARY informat and format, bitfields can be any length up to 25 bytes or 200 bits, using informat and format widths in multiples of 8 up to the maximum of 200.

Pascal string

SAS character variables are fixed in length, which can make it difficult to use character data that must vary in length. You can keep a separate variable telling the number of characters that are significant in a character variable, but that means you need two variables.

Following the practice of the Pascal programming language, you can implement a variable-length string as a structure, with the first byte containing the length of the string, and the rest of the structure containing the characters — up to 199 of them, using a SAS variable.

Bytes	Form	Description
1	PIB1.	length of string
2–200	char	characters of string

A constant Pascal string can be written as two concatenated constants: a 2-digit character hexadecimal constant, showing the length as a hexadecimal numeral, and the character string.

```
'27'X || 'The length of this Pascal string is 39.'
```

To assign a value to a Pascal string requires two expressions, one for each element of the structure. If they are the variables LEN and CHARS, and the Pascal string variable is PASCAL, the variable declaration and assignment statement would be

```
LENGTH PASCAL $ 200;
PASCAL = PUT(LEN, PIB1.) || CHARS;
```

To use the Pascal string, then, you would use the expression

```
SUBSTR(PASCAL, 2, INPUT(PASCAL, PIB1.))
```

For example, you could concatenate two Pascal strings, PASCAL1 and PASCAL2, assigning the result to PASCAL3. The length of PASCAL3 would be the sum of the lengths of the PASCAL1 and PASCAL2, but no more than 199:

```
LENGTH PASCAL1-PASCAL3 $ 200;
PASCAL1 = '04'X || 'BOX ';
PASCAL2 = '03'X || '256';
PASCAL3 = PUT((INPUT(PASCAL1, PIB1.) + INPUT(PASCAL2, PIB1.))
              MIN 199, PIB1.)
          || SUBSTR(PASCAL1, 2, INPUT(PASCAL1, PIB1.))
          || SUBSTR(PASCAL2, 2, INPUT(PASCAL2, PIB1.));
```

To print the value of a Pascal string, you need to assign the two fields to different variables so that they can be used by the PUT statement:

```
CHAR = SUBSTR(PASCAL3, 2);
LEN = INPUT(PASCAL3, PIB1.);
PUT '****' CHAR $VARYING. LEN '****';
```

```
****BOX 256****
```

You can compare two Pascal strings:

```
IF SUBSTR(PASCAL1, 2, INPUT(PASCAL1, PIB1.))
   >= SUBSTR(PASCAL2, 2, INPUT(PASCAL2, PIB1.));
```

You can assign the value of one Pascal string to another using a simple assignment statement:

```
PASCAL2 = PASCAL1;
```

You can change the length of an existing Pascal string variable using the SUBSTR pseudo-variable:

```
SUBSTR(PASCAL1, 1, 1) = PUT(3, PIB1.);
```

You can change the characters of the Pascal string variable without changing the length in a similar manner.

A Pascal string variable can be declared with a length shorter than 200, which is a good idea if it will only be used with short string lengths.

C string

In the C programming language, instead of having a length byte, variable-length character strings are null-terminated: a null character (`'00'x`) follows the last significant character in the string. This string type is closer in form to a normal SAS character string. In fact, because nulls print as blanks (or not at all) on most printers, C strings can be printed using ordinary SAS character formats. C strings can also be compared just like SAS strings, and can be used as sort keys.

To convert a SAS character string variable to a C string just requires putting in the null terminator. It's usually also a good idea to change all the characters following the null terminator to blanks. This can be done with the SUBSTR pseudo-variable. If the length is the variable LEN, this statement would make STRING a C string:

```
SUBSTR(STRING, LEN + 1) = '00'X;
```

An existing C string can be shortened in the same way. (A purist would pad with nulls instead of blanks, but that's more difficult.)

A character string expression can be assigned to a C string variable just by appending a null character. Constant C string values are represented this way:

```
LENGTH STRING $ 200;
STRING = 'The length of this C string is 36.   ' || '00'X;
```

Determining the length of a C string is just a matter of searching for the null terminator:

```
INDEXC(STRING, '00'X) - 1
```

To use a C string in an expression, you would extract the significant characters using the SCAN function:

```
SCAN(STRING, 1, '00'X)
```

(The expression `SUBSTR(STRING, 1, INDEXC(STRING, '00'X) - 1)` would also work, but isn't as concise.)

Concatenating C strings is easier than concatenating Pascal strings — in fact, it is less troublesome than concatenating SAS strings. These statements concatenate the C string variables STRING1 and STRING2, assigning the result to STRING3:

```
LENGTH STRING1-STRING3 $ 200;
STRING1 = 'BOX ' || '00'X;
STRING2 = '256' || '00'X;
STRING3 = SCAN(STRING1, 1, '00'X) || STRING2;
PUT STRING3=;
```

```
STRING3=BOX 256
```

The null terminator from STRING2 is used for STRING3.

It's just as easy (and more efficient) to append a C string to an existing C string variable, using the SUBSTR pseudo-variable:

```
LENGTH STRING1 STRING2 $ 200;
STRING1 = 'BOX ' || '00'X;
STRING2 = '256' || '00'X;
SUBSTR(STRING1, INDEXC(STRING1, '00'X)) = STRING2;
PUT STRING1=;
```

```
STRING1=BOX 256
```

As with Pascal strings, C string variables can be declared with lengths less than 200. With either a C string variable or a Pascal string variable, the variable length has to be at least 1 character greater than the maximum string length that could be used.

Converting between C and Pascal string types is easy enough. To convert a Pascal string to a C string:

```
C_STRING = SUBSTR(PASCAL, 2, INPUT(PASCAL, PIB1.)) || '00'X;
```

To convert a C string to a Pascal string:

```
PASCAL = PUT(INDEXC(C_STRING, '00'X) - 1, PIB1.)
         || SCAN(STRING, 1, '00'X);
```

15 Table lookup

Table lookup is a way to add a variable to a data step. The variable added is called a *lookup variable,* and its value depends on the value of another variable, called a *key variable.* The connection between key values and the value of the lookup variable is listed in a table, which is sometimes called a *relation* or *dictionary.* Mathematically speaking, the connection is that of a *function* or *mapping.*

Table lookup encompasses these processes, which are fundamentally very similar to each other:

Categorizing or **classifying**, determining what category or class something belongs to. For example, if you know a ZIP code, you can look up what state it is in.

Recoding, substituting one code or form of information for another. For example, given the name of a chemical element, you can look up its atomic number.

Stratifying, dividing values into layers based on magnitude. For example, you could assign ages 0–12 to age group 1, 13–19 to group 2, 20–35 to group 3, and so on. Or you could describe frequencies between 3 and 30 megahertz as HF, those between 30 and 300 as VHF, and those between 300 and 3000 as UHF.

Grading, when a measurement is used to put something into one of several consecutive categories, which usually have names. For example, ranges of test scores could be assigned grades A, B, etc.

Related information. For example, given a catalog number, you can look up the product name, price, description, shipping weight, and so on.

Validating, determining that a code actually belongs to a certain specified set of codes. For example, you might look up a credit card number to see if a credit card is legitimate.

Spell checking, looking up words to see whether they appear on a list of words, with the hope of catching misspelled words.

Graphically, table lookup can be represented this way:

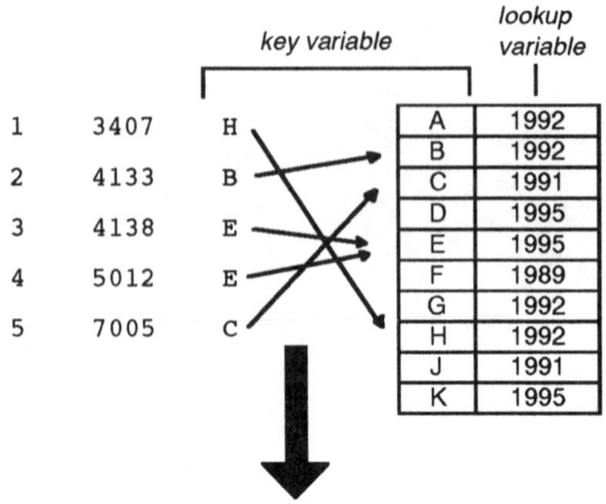

1	3407	H	1992
2	4133	B	1992
3	4138	E	1995
4	5012	E	1995
5	7005	C	1991

There is no single good way to do table lookup in a SAS program. Instead, there are several methods, making use of different syntax features, which are appropriate in different situations.

SELECT

The comparison SELECT block is conceptually the simplest form of table lookup and is therefore the standard to which all the other forms are compared. It is not particularly efficient, but its simplicity makes it the method of choice for small tables used in only one step.

Table lookup using the SELECT block follows the form

```
SELECT(key variable);
  WHEN(value) lookup variable = value;
  WHEN(value) lookup variable = value;
  WHEN(value) lookup variable = value;
  . . .
  OTHERWISE;
  END;
```

For example, if the key variable is KEY and the lookup variable is LOOKUP, the table lookup statements might look like this:

```
SELECT(KEY);
  WHEN(1) LOOKUP = 'ONE';
  WHEN(2) LOOKUP = 'TWO';
```

```
  WHEN(3) LOOKUP = 'THREE';
  OTHERWISE LOOKUP = 'LOTS';
  END;
```

Looking up prices for products is a familiar table lookup application:

```
SELECT(CATALOG);
  WHEN('102') PRICE = 46.00;
  WHEN('201') PRICE = 24.00;
  WHEN('202') PRICE = 18.00;
  WHEN('204') PRICE = 22.00;
  WHEN('301') PRICE = 40.00;
  WHEN('302') PRICE = 24.00;
  WHEN('304') PRICE = 12.00;
  WHEN('306') PRICE = 18.00;
  WHEN('307') PRICE = 32.00;
  WHEN('401') PRICE = 18.00;
  WHEN('402') PRICE = 34.00;
  WHEN('404') PRICE = 32.00;
  WHEN('415') PRICE = 24.00;
  WHEN('505') PRICE = 34.00;
  WHEN('506') PRICE = 34.00;
  WHEN('511') PRICE = 36.00;
  WHEN('512') PRICE = 34.00;
  WHEN('513') PRICE = 36.00;
  WHEN('514') PRICE = 34.00;
  WHEN('515') PRICE = 36.00;
  WHEN('516') PRICE = 34.00;
  OTHERWISE;
  END;
```

When there are fewer lookup values than key values, lists of values can be used in the WHEN expression (in SAS release 6.06 and later) to shorten the SELECT block:

```
SELECT(CATALOG);
  WHEN('304') PRICE = 12.00;
  WHEN('202', '306', '401') PRICE = 18.00;
  WHEN('204') PRICE = 22.00;
  WHEN('201', '302', '415') PRICE = 24.00;
  WHEN('307', '404') PRICE = 32.00;
  WHEN('402', '505', '506', '512', '514', '516') PRICE = 34.00;
  WHEN('511', '513', '515') PRICE = 36.00;
  WHEN('301') PRICE = 40.00;
  WHEN('102') PRICE = 46.00;
  OTHERWISE;
  END;
```

(In releases 6.03–6.04, the IN operator can be used to achieve this effect.)

The conditional SELECT block can also be used for table lookup, making it possible to use ranges of key values. This conditional SELECT block duplicates the results of the SIGN function:

```
SELECT;
  WHEN(KEY <= .Z) LOOKUP = .;
  WHEN(KEY <  0 ) LOOKUP = -1;
```

```
WHEN(KEY <= 0 ) LOOKUP = 0;
OTHERWISE       LOOKUP = 1;
END;
```

This example illustrates an important feature of the SELECT block: only one WHEN action is executed. If more than one of the WHEN conditions is true, the action associated with the first WHEN condition that is true is executed. In table lookup, this means that if ranges overlap, the first range that contains the key value is the one that counts.

Boolean

Boolean lookup means checking whether something is on a predefined list. The lookup variable could be 1 (true) for key values found on the list, and 0 (false) otherwise — or it could be the reverse. In addition to all the other lookup techniques, the IN or NOTIN operator can be used for Boolean lookup. The expression in this statement determines whether an element is a metal, based on its atomic number:

```
METALLIC = NUMBER NOTIN (1, 2, 5, 6, 7, 8, 9, 10,
     14, 15, 16, 17, 18, 33, 34, 35, 36, 52, 53, 54, 85, 86);
```

Array

Table lookup using arrays is simplest and fastest when the values of the key variable are more or less a sequence of counting numbers. The key variable (or some number derived from it) can then be used as the array subscript.

Atomic numbers, for example, are the integers from 1 to about 107, so you could look up the symbols for elements, given their atomic number, using statements like this:

```
RETAIN E1 'H' E2 'He'  E3  'Li'  E4  'Be'  E5  'B'   E6  'C'
   E7  'N'   E8  'O'   E9  'F'   E10 'Ne'  E11 'Na'  E12 'Mg'
   E13 'Al'  E14 'Si'  E15 'P'   E16 'S'   E17 'Cl'  E18 'Ar'
   E19 'K'   E20 'Ca'  E21 'Sc'  E22 'Ti'  E23 'V'   E24 'Cr'
   E25 'Mn'  E26 'Fe'  E27 'Co'  E28 'Ni'  E29 'Cu'  E30 'Zn'
   E31 'Ga'  E32 'Ge'  E33 'As'  E34 'Se'  E35 'Br'  E36 'Kr'
   E37 'Rb'  E38 'Sr'  E39 'Y'   E40 'Zr'  E41 'Nb'  E42 'Mo'
   E43 'Tc'  E44 'Ru'  E45 'Rh'  E46 'Pd'  E47 'Ag'  E48 'Cd'
   E49 'In'  E50 'Sn'  E51 'Sb'  E52 'Te'  E53 'I'   E54 'Xe'
   E55 'Cs'  E56 'Ba'  E57 'La'  E58 'Ce'  E59 'Pr'  E60 'Nd'
   E61 'Pm'  E62 'Sm'  E63 'Eu'  E64 'Gd'  E65 'Tb'  E66 'Dy'
   E67 'Ho'  E68 'Er'  E69 'Tm'  E70 'Yb'  E71 'Lu'  E72 'Hf'
   E73 'Ta'  E74 'W'   E75 'Re'  E76 'Os'  E77 'Ir'  E78 'Pt'
   E79 'Au'  E80 'Hg'  E81 'Tl'  E82 'Pb'  E83 'Bi'  E84 'Po'
   E85 'At'  E86 'Rn'  E87 'Fr'  E88 'Ra'  E89 'Ac'  E90 'Th'
   E91 'Pa'  E92 'U'   E93 'Np'  E94 'Pu'  E95 'Am'  E96 'Cm'
   E97 'Bk'  E98 'Cf'  E99 'Es' E100 'Fm' E101 'Md' E102 'No'
   E103 'Lr' E104 'Unq'  E105 'Unp'  E106 'Unh'  E107 'Uns' ;
```

```
ARRAY ELEMENTS{107} E1-E107;

SYMBOL = ELEMENTS{NUMBER};
```

One use for table lookup is to hold calculated values that are used frequently. Suppose, for example, that the mass of a sphere depends on its radius, and that the spheres come in only four sizes. That means that the mass of a sphere is one of four numbers, and you could calculate those four numbers in advance rather than having to do a separate calculation for each observation.

```
DATA BALL2 (DROP=R RADIUS);
  ARRAY SPH_MASS{9} _TEMPORARY_;
  IF _N_ = 1 THEN DO R = 4, 7, 8, 9;
    SPH_MASS{R} = 4/3*3.14159265358979*R*R*R*4.151*.001;
    END;

  SET BALL1;
  MASS = SPH_MASS{RADIUS};
```

If the values of the key variable are not counting numbers, but the values of the lookup variable are distinct counting numbers, the lookup process is almost as simple. You can use the lookup variable as the array index.

The example below is essentially the reverse of the earlier elements example. It uses the symbol of an element to find the atomic number.

```
ARRAY ELEMENTS{107} $ 3 _TEMPORARY_ (
    'H',  'He', 'Li', 'Be', 'B',  'C',  'N',  'O',  'F',  'Ne',
    'Na', 'Mg', 'Al', 'Si', 'P',  'S',  'Cl', 'Ar', 'K',  'Ca',
    'Sc', 'Ti', 'V',  'Cr', 'Mn', 'Fe', 'Co', 'Ni', 'Cu', 'Zn',
    'Ga', 'Ge', 'As', 'Se', 'Br', 'Kr', 'Rb', 'Sr', 'Y',  'Zr',
    'Nb', 'Mo', 'Tc', 'Ru', 'Rh', 'Pd', 'Ag', 'Cd', 'In', 'Sn',
    'Sb', 'Te', 'I',  'Xe', 'Cs', 'Ba', 'La', 'Ce', 'Pr', 'Nd',
    'Pm', 'Sm', 'Eu', 'Gd', 'Tb', 'Dy', 'Ho', 'Er', 'Tm', 'Yb',
    'Lu', 'Hf', 'Ta', 'W',  'Re', 'Os', 'Ir', 'Pt', 'Au', 'Hg',
    'Tl', 'Pb', 'Bi', 'Po', 'At', 'Rn', 'Fr', 'Ra', 'Ac', 'Th',
    'Pa', 'U',  'Np', 'Pu', 'Am', 'Cm', 'Bk', 'Cf', 'Es', 'Fm',
    'Md', 'No', 'Lr', 'Unq', 'Unp', 'Unh', 'Uns');

NUMBER = .;
DO I = 1 TO 107 UNTIL(NUMBER);
  IF SYMBOL = ELEMENTS(I) THEN NUMBER = I;
  END;
```

When neither the key variable nor the lookup variable can be used as an array subscript, you need two arrays: one containing the key variable values, and the other with the corresponding lookup variable values. This example looks up the name of an element, given the symbol:

```
ARRAY ELEMENTS{107} $ 3 _TEMPORARY_ (
    'H',  'He', 'Li', 'Be', 'B',  'C',  'N',  'O',  'F',  'Ne',
    ...
    'Md', 'No', 'Lr', 'Unq', 'Unp', 'Unh', 'Uns');
```

```
ARRAY ELEMENTN {107} $ 16 _TEMPORARY_ (
    'Hydrogen', 'Helium', 'Lithium', 'Beryllium', 'Boron',
    ...
    'Unnilhexium', 'Unnilseptium');

NAME = '';
DO I = 1 TO 107 UNTIL(NAME NE '');
  IF SYMBOL = ELEMENTS(I) THEN NAME = ELEMENTN(I);
  END;
```

When a SAS dataset is created in a step with array table lookup, it should have a KEEP or DROP list so the extra variables used in the lookup process are not stored in the output observations. The statements above, for example, use the index variable I, which should not be included in the output data, so you could use the dataset option `DROP=I`. The lookup table itself is usually made up of temporary variables, which are automatically excluded from the output data.

Search methods

The two preceding code fragments are examples of a *linear search*: The key values are examined, one by one, until one is found that matches.

The linear search is just one search method. It is efficient when the key value being sought is early in the table, but less so if the value is late in the table or not there at all. Nevertheless, the linear search performs acceptably for most applications involving arrays in memory.

Efficiency is more critical when the lookup table is in storage, so search methods are discussed later, under "Table in storage." The search methods described there can be applied in the same way to arrays.

Loading table from SAS dataset

If a table is in the form of a SAS dataset, you can still use the array method. You can load the table into the array at the beginning of the data step. There is a limit on the total size of variables in a data step, depending on how much memory you have, but two arrays of 1000 temporary variables each should always fit. Much larger arrays might be possible, depending on the operating system used, how much memory is available, and other uses of memory.

In the code fragment below, AKEY1–AKEY1000 are the key values and AL1–AL1000 are the corresponding lookup values. The variable AMAX keeps track of the size of the lookup table. If the lookup SAS dataset has more than 1000 observations, the extra observations are simply ignored.

```
RETAIN AMAX 0;
ARRAY AKEY{1000} _TEMPORARY_;
ARRAY AL{1000} _TEMPORARY_;

* Read table into memory at beginning of step;
IF _N_ = 1 THEN DO I = 1 TO 1000 UNTIL(END);
  SET TABLE (KEEP=KEY LOOKUP RENAME=(KEY=LKEY LOOKUP=LLOOKUP))
```

```
        END=END;
    AKEY{I} = LKEY;
    AL{I} = LLOOKUP;
    AMAX = I;
    END;

  * Table lookup;
  DO I = 1 TO AMAX UNTIL(LOOKUP NE .);
             * Use (LOOKUP NE '') for character lookup variable;
    IF KEY = AKEY{I} THEN LOOKUP = AL{I};
    END;
```

Pseudo-array

Table lookup using a pseudo-array is essentially the same as with an array. It is simplest when the elements of the pseudo-array are one character in length and the key variable is used as the index value.

The example below uses counting number codes for states, in the variable STATE. The NF pseudo-array contains the value E for each state that has an "effective" no-fault automobile insurance law. This step subsets the SAS dataset DRIVER, which has observations representing drivers. It produces a subset NFDRIVER that contains only drivers in states with an "effective" no-fault law.

```
DATA NFDRIVER;
  RETAIN NF '   N EENNEEE    EE  NEEE     NE E E  NN NN NE N    ';
  SET DRIVER;
  IF SUBSTR(NF, STATE, 1) = 'E';
```

The next example converts numeric grades to letter grades. Because the numbers 0–4 correspond to the letter grades, 1 is added to the number grade to produce the index value.

```
LENGTH L_GRADE $ 1;
RETAIN GRADES 'FDCBA';
L_GRADE = SUBSTR(GRADES, N_GRADE + 1, 1);
```

The INDEX and INDEXC functions can be used for the reverse form of table lookup, when the lookup variable has counting number values. This example reverses the previous example, converting letter grades to numbers.

```
RETAIN GRADES 'FDCBA';
N_GRADE = INDEXC(GRADES, L_GRADE) - 1;
```

The next example converts compass angle directions to the eight compass points: N, NW, W, SW, and so on. Notice how the 360° range of lookup values is mapped into ranges using the ROUND function. Also notice that N is both the first and last element in the lookup table, so that it captures both 1° and 359°.

```
RETAIN COMPASS 'N NWW SWS SEE NEN ';
POINT = SUBSTR(COMPASS, ROUND(ANGLE/45)*2 + 1, 2);
```

This process can also be reversed. It is prudent to allow blanks between the elements of a pseudo-array when using the INDEX function for lookup. The MOD function can also be used to make sure the index returned by the INDEX function is actually the beginning of an element:

```
RETAIN COMPASS 'N  NW W  SW S  SE E  NE N  ';
IF MOD(INDEX(COMPASS, POINT), 3) = 1 THEN
    ANGLE = (INDEX(COMPASS, POINT) - 1)*15;
ELSE ANGLE = .;
```

Macroarray

Lookup ability is built into the macro processor. It maintains a table of the currently defined macrovariables, and looks up their values whenever it resolves a macrovariable reference. It is sometimes possible to use this feature for table lookup in the data step, using the SYMGET function.

The key variable values are made part of the macrovariable name. In the example below, the macrovariables used for table lookup begin with the T_ prefix, followed by the key values. *Macroarray* is a rather imprecise term for a group of macrovariables associated in this way.

(In principle, this kind of lookup could be done without a prefix, just using the key values as macrovariable names, but that would tend to conflict with any other use of macrovariables. The prefix is also necessary if the key values are numerals.)

To set up this kind of table lookup, you first need to create the appropriate macrovariables. This could be done using %LET statements. This example involves symbols and names for elements, as in some earlier examples.

```
%LET T_H = Hydrogen;
%LET T_He = Helium;
%LET T_Li = Lithium;
...
```

(Uppercase and lowercase letters are interchangeable in macrovariable names. Normally, we use uppercase letters. Here, we are using uppercase and lowercase letters for clarity.)

Rather than write over one hundred %LET statements, you could create the macrovariables in a data step:

```
DATA _NULL_;
  LENGTH SYMBOL $ 3 NAME $ 16;
  INPUT NUMBER SYMBOL $ NAME $ @@;
  CALL SYMPUT('T_' || TRIM(SYMBOL), TRIM(NAME));
CARDS;
```

```
1 H Hydrogen 2 He Helium 3 Li Lithium 4 Be Beryllium 5 B Boron
6 C Carbon 7 N Nitrogen 8 O Oxygen 9 F Fluorine 10 Ne Neon
11 Na Sodium 12 Mg Magnesium 13 Al Aluminum 14 Si Silicon
15 P Phosphorus 16 S Sulfur 17 Cl Chlorine 18 Ar Argon
19 K Potassium 20 Ca Calcium 21 Sc Scandium 22 Ti Titanium
23 V Vanadium 24 Cr Chromium 25 Mn Manganese 26 Fe Iron
27 Co Cobalt 28 Ni Nickel 29 Cu Copper 30 Zn Zinc 31 Ga Gallium
32 Ge Germanium 33 As Arsenic 34 Se Selenium 35 Br Bromine
36 Kr Krypton 37 Rb Rubidium 38 Sr Strontium 39 Y Yttrium
40 Zr Zirconium 41 Nb Niobium 42 Mo Molybdenum 43 Tc Technetium
44 Ru Ruthenium 45 Rh Rhodium 46 Pd Palladium 47 Ag Silver
48 Cd Cadmium 49 In Indium 50 Sn Tim 51 Sb Antimony 52 Te Tellurium
53 I Iodine 54 Xe Xenon 55 Cs Cesium 56 Ba Barium 57 La Lanthanum
58 Ce Cerium 59 Pr Praseodymium 60 Nd Neodymium 61 Pm Promethium
62 Sm Samarium 63 Eu Europium 64 Gd Gadolinium 65 Tb Terbium
66 Dy Dysprosium 67 Ho Holmium 68 Er Erbium 69 Tm Thulium
70 Yb Ytterbium 71 Lu Lutetium 72 Hf Hafnium 73 Ta Tantalum
74 W Tungsten 75 Re Rhenium 76 Os Osmium 77 Ir Iridium
78 Pt Platinum 79 Au Gold 80 Hg Mercury 81 Tl Thallium 82 Pb Lead
83 Bi Bismuth 84 Po Polonium 85 At Astatine 86 Rn Radon
87 Fr Francium 88 Ra Radium 89 Ac Actinium 90 Th Thorium
91 Pa Protactinium 92 U Uranium 93 Np Neptunium 94 Pu Plutonium
95 Am Americium 96 Cm Curium 97 Bk Berkelium 98 Cf Californium
99 Es Einsteinium 100 Fm Fermium 101 Md Mendelevium 102 No Nobelium
103 Lr Lawrencium 104 Unq Unnilquadium 105 Unp Unnilpentium
106 Unh Unnilhexium 107 Uns Unnilseptium
;
```

After the macrovariables are created, the table lookup can be done with the SYMGET function. The concatenate operator (||) is used to create the argument for the function.

```
NAME = SYMGET('T_' || TRIM(LEFT(SYMBOL)));
```

Table lookup via the macro processor is the most trouble-prone of the methods described in this chapter, but it is sometimes the fastest.

Function

Ideally, table lookup would be handled by a function, which would take the key variable as an argument and return the lookup variable:

lookup variable = *function*(*key variable*) ;

Using a function has the advantage of removing the mechanics of the table lookup process from the data step and the program data vector.

The SAS System does include some functions that do table lookup. The geographic functions, FIPNAME, FIPNAMEL, FIPSTATE, STFIPS, STNAME, STNAMEL, ZIPFIPS, ZIPNAME, ZIPNAMEL, and ZIPSTATE, convert between different ways of representing geographic locations, particularly states. But because the SAS System doesn't create functions, that's all the table lookup you can do with functions using the SAS language by itself.

SAS functions are written in other languages — particularly C, Fortran, and assembly language. Programming SAS functions is described in chapter 21, "Languages." If you did write a function to do table lookup, you would use the array technique described above or a variation of it using one of the search methods described below under "Table in storage."

Value format

If the SAS programming language does not create functions, it does create value formats, which are almost as good as functions for table lookup purposes. Value formats are created by the VALUE statement in the FORMAT proc and are used in the PUT function.

Value formats are appropriate for most table lookup in SAS programs.

In the example below, a value format is used to look up symbols for elements, based on atomic numbers. First, the format is defined in a proc step:

```
  PROC FORMAT;
    VALUE ELEMENTS (MIN=2)
  1 = 'H'     2 = 'He'    3 = 'Li'    4 = 'Be'    5 = 'B'     6 = 'C'
  7 = 'N'     8 = 'O'     9 = 'F'    10 = 'Ne'   11 = 'Na'   12 = 'Mg'
 13 = 'Al'   14 = 'Si'   15 = 'P'    16 = 'S'    17 = 'Cl'   18 = 'Ar'
 19 = 'K'    20 = 'Ca'   21 = 'Sc'   22 = 'Ti'   23 = 'V'    24 = 'Cr'
 25 = 'Mn'   26 = 'Fe'   27 = 'Co'   28 = 'Ni'   29 = 'Cu'   30 = 'Zn'
 31 = 'Ga'   32 = 'Ge'   33 = 'As'   34 = 'Se'   35 = 'Br'   36 = 'Kr'
 37 = 'Rb'   38 = 'Sr'   39 = 'Y'    40 = 'Zr'   41 = 'Nb'   42 = 'Mo'
 43 = 'Tc'   44 = 'Ru'   45 = 'Rh'   46 = 'Pd'   47 = 'Ag'   48 = 'Cd'
 49 = 'In'   50 = 'Sn'   51 = 'Sb'   52 = 'Te'   53 = 'I'    54 = 'Xe'
 55 = 'Cs'   56 = 'Ba'   57 = 'La'   58 = 'Ce'   59 = 'Pr'   60 = 'Nd'
 61 = 'Pm'   62 = 'Sm'   63 = 'Eu'   64 = 'Gd'   65 = 'Tb'   66 = 'Dy'
 67 = 'Ho'   68 = 'Er'   69 = 'Tm'   70 = 'Yb'   71 = 'Lu'   72 = 'Hf'
 73 = 'Ta'   74 = 'W'    75 = 'Re'   76 = 'Os'   77 = 'Ir'   78 = 'Pt'
 79 = 'Au'   80 = 'Hg'   81 = 'Tl'   82 = 'Pb'   83 = 'Bi'   84 = 'Po'
 85 = 'At'   86 = 'Rn'   87 = 'Fr'   88 = 'Ra'   89 = 'Ac'   90 = 'Th'
 91 = 'Pa'   92 = 'U'    93 = 'Np'   94 = 'Pu'   95 = 'Am'   96 = 'Cm'
 97 = 'Bk'   98 = 'Cf'   99 = 'Es'  100 = 'Fm'  101 = 'Md'  102 = 'No'
 103 = 'Lr'  104 = 'Unq'   105 = 'Unp'   106 = 'Unh'   107 = 'Uns' ;
 RUN;
```

Then the format can be used in a data step for table lookup:

```
    SYMBOL = PUT(NUMBER, ELEMENTS3.);
```

The use of ranges in a value format is convenient when several consecutive key values have the same lookup value.

A format always creates a character value. However, the use of a value format for table lookup is also appropriate when both the key variable and the lookup variable are numeric. The character value resulting from the value format can be converted to a numeric value using the INPUT function.

If the lookup variable is numeric and the key variable is character, you should use a value informat instead of a value format.

Value informat

Value informats can be used for table lookup in essentially the same way as value formats. With value informats, the lookup variable can be numeric. Value informats are defined by the INVALUE statement in the FORMAT proc and are used in the INPUT function.

Using a value informat is appropriate for Boolean table lookup. In this example, table lookup is used to separate categories of fibers:

```
PROC FORMAT;
  INVALUE NFIBER
      'COTTON', 'LINEN', 'RAMIE', 'RAYON', 'SILK', 'WOOL' = 1
      OTHER = 0;

DATA NFIBERS SFIBERS;
  SET FIBERS;
  IF INPUT(FIBER, NFIBER.) THEN OUTPUT NFIBERS;
  ELSE OUTPUT SFIBERS;
```

Limitations

There is a certain maximum size that a value format or value informat can have. If the INVALUE or VALUE statement contains more than a few thousand values, the informat or format will not be created, and there will be a cryptic error message. You will need to determine by experimentation what the practical limit for the number of values is in your applications.

When using a value format for table lookup, the maximum length of a character key value is 16 characters. The maximum length of a lookup value is 40 characters.

Flexcode

The trouble with using value formats for table lookup is writing the VALUE statement for each lookup table. Using a flexcode approach, though, you can have the program write the VALUE statement. You just need to have the table values in a readable form in a text file or SAS dataset.

Suppose, for example, you have data on elements in a text file in this form:

```
1 H   Hydrogen          1.008 G    .09
2 He  Helium            4.003 G    .18
3 Li  Lithium           6.940 S    .53
4 Be  Beryllium         9.012 S   9.01
5 B   Boron            10.810 S  10.81
6 C   Carbon           12.011 S   2.30
7 N   Nitrogen         14.007 G   1.25
8 O   Oxygen           15.999 G   1.43
9 F   Fluorine         18.998 G   1.70
```

```
 10 Ne  Neon              20.180 G    .90
                           ...
```

This step writes a proc step to create the ELEMENTS format.

```
  DATA _NULL_;
    INFILE ELEMENT;
    INPUT NUMBER 3. +1 SYMBOL $3. END=LAST;
    FILE PINC;
    IF _N_ = 1 THEN PUT @3 'PROC FORMAT;' /
        @5 'VALUE ELEMENTS (MIN=3)';
    PUT @9 NUMBER 3. " = '" SYMBOL $CHAR3. "'";
    IF LAST THEN PUT @9 ';';
RUN;
%INCLUDE PINC;
```

```
  PROC FORMAT;
    VALUE ELEMENTS (MIN=3)
          1 = 'H  '
          2 = 'He '
          3 = 'Li '
          4 = 'Be '
          5 = 'B  '
          6 = 'C  '
          7 = 'N  '
          8 = 'O  '
          9 = 'F  '
         10 = 'Ne '
           ...
        ;
```

The process of defining a value format from data in a SAS dataset or for defining a value informat works almost exactly the same way.

It's also possible to define a value format or value format by creating a control dataset, a SAS dataset with a particular set of variables that can be used with the CNTLIN= option on the `PROC FORMAT` statement. This is a more efficient approach if your lookup table is a SAS dataset and you can create a view based on it that can be used as the control dataset. Once you create the view, you can run the same proc step to update the value format or value informat each time any changes are made in the lookup table.

Control datasets are described at the end of chapter 3, "Programs on call." Only the FMTNAME, START, and LABEL variables are required; they can all be character variables. The FMTNAME variable contains the name of the value format or the character @ followed by the name of the value informat. START is the key variable; LABEL is the lookup variable.

Table in storage

The preceding methods all dealt with ways of having a table in memory. Tables can also be kept in storage, which is much slower than memory but can handle larger tables.

A SAS dataset is the usual form of a table in storage. Other types of direct access files might be used in SAS implementations that support them, but there would be no advantage in doing that except when the data is already in such a file.

The SAS dataset used as a lookup table is accessed with a direct access SET statement, using the POINT= option.

Observation number as key variable

Table lookup in storage is simplest and fastest, though still slower than table lookup in memory, if the key variable is the observation number of the SAS dataset containing the table. Then you just need to assign the correct observation number to the POINT= variable and execute the direct access SET statement.

The element symbol lookup that was done earlier using an array could also be done with a SAS dataset. You would need to create a SAS dataset with the symbol for element 1 in observation 1, the symbol for element 2 in observation 2, and so on. With that SAS dataset called CHEMICAL.ELEMENT containing a variable SYMBOL with the element's symbol, and with the atomic number a variable called NUMBER, the table lookup would look like this:

```
POINT = NUMBER;
SET CHEMICAL.ELEMENT (KEEP=SYMBOL) POINT=POINT;
```

The NUMBER variable could, in theory, be used as the POINT variable (that is, `SET CHEMICAL.ELEMENT (KEEP=SYMBOL) POINT=NUMBER;`), but that would prevent the NUMBER variable from being kept in any output SAS dataset. POINT= variables are not kept, even if they appear in a KEEP= list for a SAS dataset.

The KEEP= option in the example above selects the variable to be read from the lookup SAS dataset. Without the KEEP= option, all the variables in the SAS dataset would be read. Selecting one variable makes the statement run faster and prevents unwanted variables from creeping into the step. The KEEP= option also makes it easy for someone reading the program to see the source of the variable SYMBOL.

Search methods

Usually, the observation number of the lookup observation is not known, and you'll need to try several before arriving at the one you want. There are several ways of deciding what observation to try next, called *search methods*. A search method should minimize the number of observations that are examined without being unduly complex. Some suggested search methods are described next.

In considering search methods, it might help to think of an old-fashioned kind of database: a card catalog in a library. A card catalog is a sequence of cards, filed in alphabetical order in many small drawers, which describe the books in a library. Think of the entire card catalog as the lookup table and each individual card (including any continuation cards) as one observation.

The importance of having the cards in sorted order is immediately evident. That provides a way to find a card other than by checking cards one by one. If there are only a few cards, having the cards organized is less important. If only a few of the cards are used often, it might be convenient to take them out of the larger catalog and put them in a separate place.

In the same spirit, a SAS dataset used as a lookup table should usually be sorted by the key variable and should not include many extra observations.

Linear search

A linear search is slow and simple: you examine the observations one by one, in order, until you come to the one you want or determine that it is not present. This is accomplished with a DO loop and a direct access SET statement.

```
LOOKUP = .;
DO POINT = 1 TO NOBS UNTIL(LOOKUP NE .);
  SET TABLE (KEEP=KEY LOOKUP RENAME=(KEY=LKEY LOOKUP=LLOOKUP))
      POINT=POINT NOBS=NOBS;
  IF KEY = LKEY THEN LOOKUP = LLOOKUP;
  END;
```

It's important to keep the variables straight here. KEY is the key variable and LOOKUP is the lookup variable in the data step. KEY and LOOKUP are also the names of the corresponding variables in the lookup SAS dataset. Because we can't have two variables with the same name, the variables read from the SAS dataset are renamed as LKEY and LLOOKUP using the RENAME= dataset option in the SET statement. LKEY is the variable we are checking to see if it matches the key value; if it does, then the value of LLOOKUP is the lookup value we want to assign to the "real" lookup variable, LOOKUP.

If the lookup SAS dataset is in sorted order, you can shorten the time spent looking for key values that are not present by stopping when the values of the key variable in the lookup SAS dataset becomes greater than the value being looked for.

```
LOOKUP = .;
DO POINT = 1 TO NOBS UNTIL(LKEY >= KEY);
  SET TABLE (KEEP=KEY LOOKUP RENAME=(KEY=LKEY LOOKUP=LLOOKUP))
      POINT=POINT NOBS=NOBS;
  IF KEY = LKEY THEN LOOKUP = LLOOKUP;
  END;
```

The step below shows how a linear search might be used. This step starts with a list of people in the SAS dataset DRUMMERS, and it prints a report listing their phone numbers, which it looks up in the SAS dataset ADDRESS.

```
DATA _NULL_;
  SET DRUMMERS;
  DO POINT = 1 TO NOBS UNTIL(LNAME >= NAME);
    SET ADDRESS
        (KEEP=NAME PHONE RENAME=(NAME=LNAME PHONE=LPHONE))
        POINT=POINT NOBS=NOBS;
    IF NAME = LNAME THEN PHONE = LPHONE;
    END;
  PUT NAME +2 PHONE;
```

The linear search tends to check a lot of observations before finding the right one. In any particular lookup it checks any number from one to all of them. On average, if all the observations are equally likely to be looked up, and all the key values being looked up are present, it checks half of them. This is too slow if there are more than about 100 observations.

Binary search

For large tables, a more directed approach is needed for deciding which observations to check. The binary search is perhaps the most obvious organized method, and at the same time the most powerful. For the binary search to be used, the lookup table has to be sorted by the key variable.

The binary search starts by determining whether the observation is in the first half or second half of the table. If it is in the first half, it then determines whether it is in the first quarter or second quarter. If it is in the second quarter, it then determines whether it is in the third eighth or the fourth eighth. The search process continues this way until the observation is found.

```
LO = 1;
HI = NOBS;
DO UNTIL(LO > HI);
  POINT = FLOOR((LO + HI)*.5); * Midway between LO and HI;
  SET TABLE (KEEP=KEY LOOKUP RENAME=(KEY=LKEY LOOKUP=LLOOKUP))
      POINT=POINT NOBS=NOBS;
  SELECT;
    WHEN(KEY > LKEY) LO = POINT + 1;
    WHEN(KEY < LKEY) HI = POINT - 1;
    WHEN(KEY = LKEY) DO;
      LO = POINT + 1;
      HI = POINT - 1;
      LOOKUP = LLOOKUP;
      END;
    END;
  END;
```

The phone number example above is modified here to use a binary search method. It is also modified to add the phone numbers to the DRUMMERS SAS dataset rather than writing a report.

```
DATA DRUMMERS (KEEP=NAME PHONE);
  SET DRUMMERS;
  LO = 1;
  HI = NOBS;
  DO UNTIL(LO > HI);
    POINT = FLOOR((LO + HI)*.5);
      SET ADDRESS
          (KEEP=NAME PHONE RENAME=(NAME=LNAME PHONE=LPHONE))
          POINT=POINT NOBS=NOBS;
    SELECT;
      WHEN(NAME > LNAME) LO = POINT + 1;
      WHEN(NAME < LNAME) HI = POINT - 1;
      WHEN(NAME = LNAME) DO;
        LO = POINT + 1;
        HI = POINT - 1;
        PHONE = LPHONE;
        END;
      END;
    END;
```

With as few as 10 observations in the lookup table, the binary search is faster than the linear search, and for large lookup tables, it is much faster. The average number of observations the binary search reads is approximately the base 2 logarithm of the number of observations in the table. With 5,000,000,000 observations in the lookup SAS dataset, the binary search would check on average about 32 before finding the right one — faster than a linear search on a mere 100 observations!

The cost of the binary search method in comparison to the linear search is just six or so extra lines of code and the extra LO and HI variables.

Stratified search

You might notice, in the binary search method, that the middle observation in the table is read every time. Further, the observation one fourth of the way through the table and the observation three fourths of the way through the table are each read half the time, and other observations at regular intervals in the table are also read frequently.

It would make the search more efficient if these observations were read into memory. The search could then be narrowed to a range between two of the key values in memory before starting to read observations from the table in storage.

This kind of search is a *stratified* search. In the card catalog analogy, it corresponds to the labels on the front of the drawers. You find the drawer that a card is in before starting to look at the cards themselves.

Generally speaking, the more layers, the better. This code fragment uses 1001 of them, which is about as many as you can be sure of fitting in a typical SAS data step. Of course, if the lookup table is small enough to fit in memory, you would do better to put the entire table in arrays, using the array technique described earlier.

```
ARRAY AN{1000} _TEMPORARY_; ARRAY AKEY{1000} _TEMPORARY_;
IF _N_ = 1 THEN DO I = 1 TO 1000;           * Establish layers;
  POINT = I*(1 MAX FLOOR(NOBS/1000)) MIN NOBS;
  SET TABLE (KEEP=KEY RENAME=(KEY=LKEY)) POINT=POINT NOBS=NOBS;
  AN{I} = POINT;
  AKEY{I} = LKEY;
  END;

LO = 1;
HI = NOBS;
DO I = 1 TO 1000 UNTIL(HI < NOBS);                * Find layer;
  IF KEY <= AKEY{I} THEN HI = AN{I};
  IF KEY >= AKEY{I} THEN LO = AN{I};
  END;

DO UNTIL(LO > HI);                     * Ordinary binary search;
  POINT = FLOOR((LO + HI)*.5);
  SET TABLE (KEEP=KEY LOOKUP RENAME=(KEY=LKEY LOOKUP=LLOOKUP))
      POINT=POINT;
  SELECT;
    WHEN(KEY > LKEY) THEN LO = POINT + 1;
    WHEN(KEY < LKEY) THEN HI = POINT - 1;
    WHEN(KEY = LKEY) THEN DO;
      LO = POINT + 1;
      HI = POINT - 1;
      LOOKUP = LLOOKUP;
      END;
    END;
  END;
```

You might notice that this example uses a linear search method to find the key values in memory closest to the key value being looked up (which are assigned to the variables LO and HI). A binary search would be faster, but not enough to justify the added programming complexity.

A stratified search takes more memory (mainly for the arrays) and a dozen more program statements than an ordinary binary search, but it can be considerably faster. With 1000 key values in memory, the number of observations to be read in an average lookup is reduced by 10. Even if the lookup table has 80,000 observations, this speeds up the lookup process by more than 60%.

Match merge

Match merging is not really the same thing as table lookup. Match merging is a way of combining the data from two or more SAS datasets. It is done using the MERGE statement, which lists the SAS datasets to be combined, with the BY statement listing the variable or variables to be matched. The SAS datasets have to be sorted by the BY variables before the match merge is done.

Table lookup, by contrast, does not necessarily involve variables in a SAS dataset. All the table lookup methods discussed so far can be used in any data step. The key variable and lookup variable do not even have to be actual variables — they can just be expressions.

However, a match merging process can be used to do table lookup. It has advantages: it's familiar, it's simple, it's recommended by SAS Institute. But it's usually less efficient, taking several steps, instead of fitting into an existing step. It requires that you create a SAS dataset (we'll call it the main SAS dataset) to be combined with the lookup table, which is not necessary with other table lookup techniques. Both the main SAS dataset and the lookup SAS dataset have to be sorted, a potentially time-consuming process.

You sort the two SAS datasets and merge them with the key variable as the BY variable, keeping only observations that appear in the main SAS dataset. Afterward, you can sort the master SAS dataset to restore its original order, if necessary. The process is coded like this:

```
PROC SORT DATA=TABLE;
  BY KEY;
PROC SORT DATA=A;
  BY KEY;
DATA A;
  MERGE A (IN=IN) TABLE (KEEP=KEY LOOKUP);
  BY KEY;
  IF IN;
PROC SORT DATA=A;
  BY GROUP;
```

Suppose you have a SAS dataset SALES containing one observation for each customer purchase, and you would like to calculate a total bill for each customer. The prices are stored in another SAS dataset, called PRICES.

```
* Sort main SAS dataset;
PROC SORT DATA=SALES (KEEP=CUSTOMER ITEM_ID QUANTITY);
  BY ITEM_ID;

* Sort lookup table;
PROC SORT DATA=PRICES (KEEP=ITEM_ID PRICE);
  BY ITEM_ID;

* Match merge;
DATA SALES;
  MERGE SALES (IN=SALES) PRICES;
  BY ITEM_ID;
  IF SALES;

* Restore order of main SAS dataset;
PROC SORT DATA=SALES;
  BY CUSTOMER;

* Calculate bills for customers;
DATA _NULL_;
  SET SALES;
  BY CUSTOMER;
  CUSTBILL + PRICE*QUANTITY;
  IF LAST.CUSTOMER THEN DO;
    FILE BILLS;
    PUT 'Customer #' CUSTOMER 'owes '
        CUSTBILL :DOLLAR12.2 +(-1) '.';
```

```
    CUSTBILL = 0;
    END;
```

Compare the above program, though, to the program below, which uses the value informat technique to do the table lookup in just one step. The program below is simpler and more efficient. (In this case, the customer sales SAS dataset was sorted by customer.)

```
DATA _NULL_;
  SET SALES;
  BY CUSTOMER;
  CUSTBILL + INPUT(ITEM_ID, PRICE.)*QUANTITY;
  IF LAST.CUSTOMER THEN DO;
    FILE BILLS;
    PUT 'Customer #' CUSTOMER 'owes '
        CUSTBILL :DOLLAR12.2 +(-1) '.';
    CUSTBILL = 0;
    END;
```

Beginning with SAS release 6.06, indexing can be done instead of sorting before match merging. Indexes are more efficient than sorting if the SAS dataset has several variables; less efficient if it has only two.

```
PROC SQL;
  CREATE INDEX KEY ON TABLE (KEY);
  CREATE INDEX KEY ON A (KEY);
DATA A;
  MERGE A (IN=IN) TABLE (KEEP=KEY LOOKUP);
  BY KEY;
  IF IN;
PROC SORT DATA=A;
  BY GROUP;
```

If the main SAS dataset is or needs to be sorted by the key variable anyway, then the match merge process is much simpler. In this example, in calculating the sales volume per item, you can add up the quantities of the items using the SUMMARY proc, which produces a sorted output SAS dataset.

```
PROC SUMMARY DATA=SALES NWAY;
  CLASS ITEM_ID;
  VAR QUANTITY;
  OUTPUT OUT=ITEMS SUM=;
DATA _NULL_;
  MERGE ITEMS (IN=IN) PRICES;
  BY ITEM_ID;
  IF IN;
  ITEMVOL = PRICE*QUANTITY;
  FILE VOLUME;
  PUT 'Item #' ITEM_ID 'volume is ' ITEMVOL;
```

Indirect match merge

If the main SAS dataset is large and has several variables, it can take a long time to sort twice. That can be avoided, though, by creating a smaller SAS dataset for sorting, containing only the key variable and the observation numbers from the large SAS dataset, but the same number of observations. The small SAS dataset can then be match merged with the lookup table and recombined with the main SAS dataset.

The program below adds the variable LOOKUP to the SAS dataset BIG to create the SAS dataset BIGGER. The smaller SAS dataset KEY has the same number of observations as BIG. The match merge creates the SAS dataset LOOKUP. LOOKUP is then sorted by the variable N, which corresponds to the observation number in BIG, to put its observations in the same order as BIG. Then it can be merged with BIG to create BIGGER. Note that the final merge has to be a one-to-one merge, because LOOKUP and BIG do not have any variables in common that could be used as BY variables.

```
DATA KEY;
  SET BIG (KEEP=KEY);
  N = _N_;
PROC SORT DATA=KEY;
  BY KEY;
DATA LOOKUP (KEEP=N LOOKUP);
  MERGE KEY (IN=IN) TABLE (KEEP=KEY LOOKUP);
  IF IN;
PROC SORT DATA=LOOKUP;
  BY N;
DATA BIGGER;
  MERGE BIG LOOKUP (KEEP=LOOKUP);    * One-to-one merge;
```

Selecting a lookup method

With all these table lookup techniques, how do you decide which one to use? You need to balance the importance of coding simplicity and run speed while taking into account the specific characteristics of the lookup table. Occasionally, other factors, such as memory limitations, might be important.

For most purposes, you won't go wrong using a value format or value informat. Of course, you should use a function if there is one. For a very small table that's used only once that you don't mind "hard coding," a SELECT block might be best. For a table with counting number lookup values, the array technique might be slightly faster than a value format.

If the lookup value is longer than 40 characters or the key variable is longer than 16 characters, you won't be able to use a value format. If the table is small enough, you can use an array. Otherwise, you have to use a table in storage.

The storage approach is also the only way to do a very large table, because only a few thousand observations can fit in a value format or an array. The stratified binary search technique is usually the most efficient. The binary search technique is slightly simpler and slower. The match merge technique is often used, but is an efficient approach only if the lookup variable is being added to a SAS dataset that is already sorted (or nearly so) by the key variable.

The following table summarizes the features of the different table lookup techniques.

Technique	Table Location	Requires Sorting?	Speed	Major Features
Function	memory	no	fast	only a few of them exist
Value format	memory	no	fast	requires FORMAT proc step to create value format; use especially with character key variable; there is a maximum number of key values; key value can be up to 16 characters; lookup value can be up to 40 characters
Value informat	memory	no	fast	use especially with numeric key variable; otherwise the same as value format
SELECT block	memory	no	fast	hard coded
IN operator	memory	no	fast	hard coded Boolean
array	memory	no	fast	maximum table size depends on memory available; table can be hard-coded or in file; if table is too large, use stratified binary search on SAS dataset instead
linear search on SAS dataset	storage	no	too slow	
binary search on SAS dataset	storage	sorted table	slow	
stratified binary search on SAS dataset	storage	sorted table	depends on table size	use array technique instead if table will fit in memory
match merging	storage	2 SAS datasets	slowest of all	requires several steps; simple; use when both SAS datasets exist and are already sorted

16 Efficiency

A SAS program's use of computer resources can sometimes be an issue. How fast a program runs is important if you are sitting there waiting for it or if it runs on a multiuser computer with other jobs waiting. Its use of storage is important because storage costs money, might be in short supply, and contributes to the time it takes the program to run. Memory becomes an issue when a program threatens to use more memory than is available.

A program is described as efficient if it is conservative in its use of storage, memory, run time, and perhaps other resources; however, the relative importance of the different resources depends on the circumstances in which the program is used and cannot be objectively established. Often there is a tradeoff between the use of one resource and another; a faster program, for example, often requires more memory.

Saving steps

The single most important issue in the efficiency of SAS programs, more important than all others combined, is the use of extra steps, with temporary SAS datasets passing data from one step to another. This practice can slow down a program by a factor of 2, 5, 10, or more — the sky's the limit. Because nearly all SAS programmers write programs with many more steps and more temporary SAS datasets than are needed, most SAS programs can be made to run at least three times as fast just by combining steps. At the same time, the amount of temporary storage used by the program can be reduced considerably.

A typical SAS step reads a SAS dataset from disk storage, processes it, and writes a SAS dataset to disk.

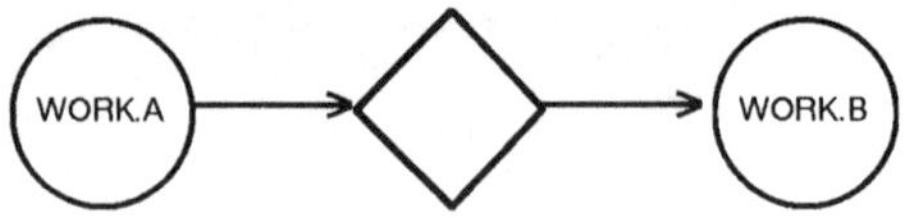

There might be several such steps in a row.

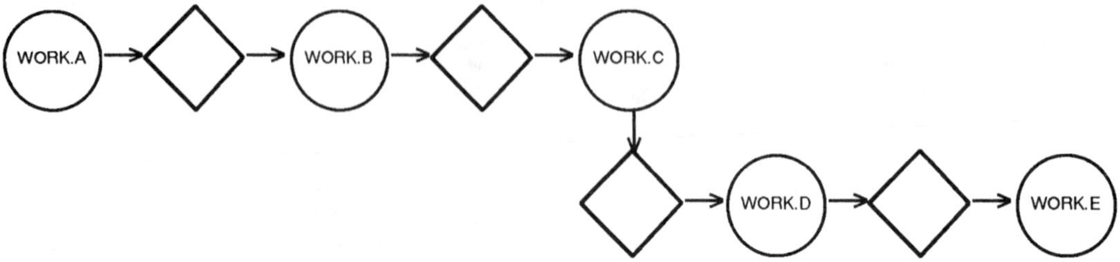

Because disk I/O is a slow process, compared to the other things computers do, it usually takes up most of the time spent in processing a step. (Floppy disk and tape I/O are even slower.) In the diagram above, there are disk accesses at 8 places — 2 for each step. The program could be sped up by about a factor of four by combining the four steps into one step, with only 2 disk accesses:

In addition to the data I/O, there is a certain amount of overhead involved in each step. The SAS supervisor goes through a specific sequence of processes for each step, and that processing increases with each additional step.

Stream-of-consciousness programming

Choppy programming, with many short steps, often reflects a kind of "stream of consciousness" programming technique, in which each step in the program embodies one complete thought (documented, perhaps, by a one-sentence comment).

For example, suppose a stream-of-consciousness SAS programmer wants to read in data from a text file, select certain observations, sort the data by a certain variable, and recode two variables. The program might go something like this:

```
*** Stream-of-consciousness style -- not recommended! ***;

* Read in data from file;
  DATA A;
    INFILE TEXT;
    INPUT CITY $CHAR16. CONTN $CHAR16. LONG LAT POP;
```

```
* Select observations with north latitude;
  DATA B;
    SET A;
    IF LAT > 0;

* Sort by continent;
  PROC SORT DATA=B;
    BY CONTN;

* Express population in thousands;
  DATA C;
    SET B;
    POP = ROUND(POP/1000);
    IF POP < 1 THEN POP = 1;

* Abbreviate continent name;
  DATA D (DROP=CONTNAME);
    SET C (RENAME=(CONTN=CONTNAME));
    SELECT(CONTNAME);
      WHEN('Africa       ') CONTN = 'Af';
      WHEN('Antarctica   ') CONTN = 'An';
      WHEN('Asia         ') CONTN = 'As';
      WHEN('Australia    ') CONTN = 'Au';
      WHEN('Europe       ') CONTN = 'Eu';
      WHEN('North America') CONTN = 'NA';
      WHEN('South America') CONTN = 'SA';
      OTHERWISE;
      END;
```

The fact that the programmer is unable to think of descriptive names for the SAS datasets A, B, C, and D should be a hint that they contain roughly the same data, and therefore, quite possibly not all of them are needed. Actually, the program above can be done in only two steps:

```
*** Streamlined ***;

  DATA D;
    LENGTH CONTN $ 2;  * Abbreviate continent name;
    * Read in data from file;
    INFILE TEXT;
    INPUT CITY $CHAR16. CONTN $CHAR16. LONG LAT POP;
    * Select observations with north latitude;
    IF LAT > 0;
    SELECT(CONTN);
      WHEN('No') CONTN = 'NA';
      WHEN('So') CONTN = 'SA';
      OTHERWISE;
      END;
    POP = ROUND(POP/1000) MAX 1; * Express population in thousands;

* Sort by continent;
  PROC SORT DATA=D;
    BY CONTN;
```

These two steps cannot be combined, because sorting has to be done by the SORT proc, and every proc requires a separate step.

Air travel

Lack of confidence may make a SAS programmer want to code short steps.

Air travel is an apt analogy for this. A new pilot might, understandably, want to fly only a short distance. But an experienced pilot (or air traveller) will prefer to fly all the way to the destination whenever possible, because taking off and landing are the most troublesome parts of flying an airplane.

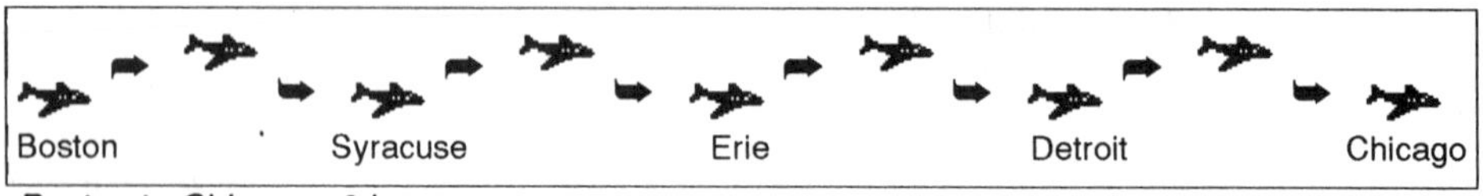

Boston to Chicago: 8 hours

Similarly, disk I/O is ordinarily the most time-consuming part of a SAS program. Thus, the program should "fly" as far as it can in a step, rather than stopping for disk storage at several intermediate points.

Boston to Chicago: 3 hours

Looking for extra steps

So where are these extra steps? How can you identify two steps in a program that can be combined? To be considered for combining, two steps should have some I/O in common: the same (or overlapping) input data; output from the first step that is input data for the second step; or output from two steps that is merely combined in a later step. When those situations occur, you can examine the steps to see if the control flow involved in combining the steps would be practical. This section lists and demonstrates some common patterns of steps that could be combined.

The log tells how much time each step takes. By comparing logs of a program run before and after revisions (using the same input data, to make the times comparable), you can see how much run time the revisions save.

> If you'd rather have an epigram, so you can skip the rest of this section, here it is: Consider every SET statement with suspicion.

Merge. You can merge several SAS datasets in one step. This is easiest when the SAS datasets are all match merged by the same variables.

Extra Steps

```
DATA AB;
  MERGE A B;
  BY X;
DATA A B C;
  MERGE AB C;
  BY X;
DATA DE;
  MERGE D E;
  BY X;
DATA ABCDE;
  MERGE DE ABC;
  BY X;
```

Better

```
DATA ABCDE;
  MERGE D E A B C;
  BY X;
```

or if you need all those SAS datasets . . .

```
DATA ABCDE AB (KEEP=...)
     ABC (KEEP=...)
     DE (KEEP=...);
  MERGE A (IN=A) B (IN=B)
     C (IN=C) D (IN=D)
     E (IN=E);
  BY X;
  IF A OR B THEN OUTPUT AB;
  IF D OR E THEN OUTPUT DE;
  ELSE OUTPUT ABC;
  OUTPUT ABCDE;
```

Dataset options. To extract a part of a SAS dataset doesn't usually require a step. You can "remove" variables from a SAS dataset with the KEEP= and DROP= options.

Extra Step

```
DATA SMALL (KEEP = X XX XXX);
  SET BIG;
PROC SORT DATA=SMALL;
  BY X;
```

Better

```
PROC SORT
     DATA=BIG (KEEP=X XX XXX)
     OUT=SMALL;
  BY X;
```

The OBS=, FIRSTOBS=, and WHERE= options can be used to extract a subset of the observations in a SAS dataset.

Related files. Related SAS datasets and text files can often be created in one step. The SAS datasets created in a step do not have to have the same variables or the same observations.

Extra Steps

```
DATA MAIN (KEEP=X A B C);
  additional statements
DATA PART1 (KEEP=X A);
  SET MAIN;
  IF A > 0;
DATA PART2 (KEEP=X B);
  SET MAIN;
  IF B > 0;
```

Better

```
DATA MAIN (KEEP=X A B C)
     PART1 (KEEP=X A)
     PART2 (KEEP=X B);
  additional statements
  OUTPUT MAIN;
  IF A > 0 THEN OUTPUT PART1;
  IF B > 0 THEN OUTPUT PART2;
```

Extra Step

```
DATA PRODUCE;
  INFILE PRODUCE;
  INPUT YEAR $CHAR4.
      COUNTRY $CHAR12.
      LETTUCE 8.
      ORANGES 7.
      CARROTS 7.
      APPLES 8.
      NUTS 8.;
DATA BRZ_ORNJ
     (KEEP=YEAR ORANGES);
  SET PRODUCE;
  IF COUNTRY = 'Brazil';
```

Better

```
DATA PRODUCE BRZ_ORNJ (KEEP=
              YEAR ORANGES);
  INFILE PRODUCE;
  INPUT YEAR $CHAR4.
      COUNTRY $CHAR12.
      LETTUCE 8.
      ORANGES 7.
      CARROTS 7.
      APPLES 8.
      NUTS 8.;
  OUTPUT PRODUCE;
  IF COUNTRY = 'Brazil' THEN
      OUTPUT BRZ_ORNJ;
```

Input text file. You don't need to have a separate step just to read a text file. Often you can create all the SAS datasets and reports you need from the data in the file in just one step. Both programs below produce the SAS datasets MAZETIME and HUMOR, but the one on the right is simpler and more than twice as fast.

Extra Steps

```
DATA EXPMT;
  INFILE EXPMT;
  INPUT AGE PAY TIME HUMORQ;
DATA MAZETIME;
  SET EXPMT (KEEP=AGE TIME);
  IF TIME > 0;
DATA HUMOR;
  SET EXPMT (KEEP=AGE HUMORQ);
  IF HUMORQ > .;
PROC SUMMARY DATA=EXPMT;
  VAR PAY;
  OUTPUT OUT=TOTAL
    SUM=SUM N=N;
DATA _NULL_;
  SET TOTAL;
  FILE PRINT;
  PUT 'Maze Performance and '
      'Humor Experiments' //
      'Number of subjects:  '
      N / 'Total amount paid '
      'to subjects:  $' SUM;
```

Better

```
DATA EXPMT
     MAZETIME (KEEP=AGE TIME)
     HUMOR (KEEP=AGE HUMORQ);
  INFILE EXPMT END=LAST;
  INPUT AGE PAY TIME HUMORQ;
  IF TIME > 0 THEN
      OUTPUT MAZETIME;
  IF HUMORQ > . THEN
      OUTPUT HUMOR;
  SUM + PAY;
  FILE PRINT;
  IF LAST THEN PUT
      'Maze Performance and '
      'Humor Experiments' //
      'Number of subjects:  '
      _N_ /
      'Total amount paid '
      'to subjects:  $' SUM;
```

Report. Many programmers habitually start a step that produces a report with these statements:

```
DATA _NULL_;
  SET ...
```

but steps with different structures can be used. A report can be produced by a step with a MERGE statement, and SAS datasets can be created in the same step as a report.

Extra Step

```
DATA M;
  MERGE A B;
DATA _NULL_;
  SET M;
  PUT _ALL_;
```

Better

```
DATA _NULL_;
  MERGE A B;
  PUT _ALL_;
```

Duplicate observations. If you want to sort a SAS dataset and then eliminate duplicate observations or observations with duplicate key values, that can be done in one step.

Extra Step

```
PROC SORT DATA=DUP;
  BY ID;
DATA SORTED;
  SET DUP;
  BY ID;
  IF FIRST.ID;
```

Better

```
PROC SORT DATA=DUP OUT=SORTED
          NODUPKEY;
  BY ID;
```

Replacing procs. Sometimes the effects of a proc can be programmed in the same step that produces the input data, especially when the proc is just calculating descriptive statistics.

Extra Steps

```
DATA SCORES;
  INFILE SCORES;
  INPUT SCORE;
PROC MEANS;
```

Faster (but not as concise)

```
DATA _NULL_;
  INFILE SCORES EOF=EOF;
  INPUT SCORE;
  N + 1;
  SCORETOT + SCORE;
  RETURN;
  EOF:
  SCORETOT = SCORETOT/N;
  PUT
     'SCORE MEAN: ' SCORETOT /
     'NUMBER OF SUBJECTS: ' N;
```

Copies. It's possible to make several copies of a SAS dataset in one data step. The copies can be subsets or modifications of the input SAS dataset.

Fresh data. When the input data in a data step comes from only one SAS dataset, created earlier in the same program, the two data steps can usually be combined. The later step becomes a block in the earlier step. This might not work, though, if the SAS dataset has been sorted in the interim or if the later step depends on FIRST. and LAST. variables.

Extra Steps

```
DATA LARGER;
  INFILE INFO;
  INPUT ANIMAL $ MINERAL $
      VEG $;
  IF ANIMAL NE 'DOG' THEN
      OUTPUT;
  ELSE PUT _ALL_;
DATA SMALLER;
  SET LARGER;
  L = LENGTH(MINERAL);
  additional statements
```

Better

```
DATA LARGER SMALLER;
  INFILE INFO;
  INPUT ANIMAL $ MINERAL $
      VEG $;
  IF ANIMAL NE 'DOG' THEN DO;
    OUTPUT LARGER;
    L = LENGTH(MINERAL);
    additional statements
    END;
  ELSE PUT _ALL_;
```

Count steps, not statements

Notice that the "better" versions of the programs above do not look very different from the versions with extra steps. In some cases the better versions actually have more statements — yet they run 2 to 5 times as fast. The number of steps is a more reliable indicator of the run time of a program than the number of statements.

Simplifying

For every simple way of expressing something, there are infinitely many complicated ways. The simpler approaches are usually preferred in SAS programming, because they usually execute faster and use less memory.

The goal in simplifying expressions is, roughly, to minimize the number of operations involved. This is especially something to look for in logical expressions, so that, for example,

```
IF X < 0 AND X NE 5;
```

becomes

```
IF X < 0;
```

The same goal applies to algebra that spreads over several statements. Reducing the process to a single statement, if possible, is usually preferable, so that

```
ARRAY PAY{4}; ARRAY OWE{4};
CREDIT = 0;
DO I = 1 TO 4;
  IF PAY{I} = OWE{I} THEN CREDIT + 1;
  END;
```

or

```
CREDIT = 0;
IF PAY1 = OWE1 THEN CREDIT + 1;
IF PAY2 = OWE2 THEN CREDIT + 1;
IF PAY3 = OWE3 THEN CREDIT + 1;
IF PAY4 = OWE4 THEN CREDIT + 1;
```

becomes

```
CREDIT = (PAY1 = OWE1) + (PAY2 = OWE2) + (PAY3 = OWE3)
        + (PAY4 = OWE4);
```

In Boolean algebra, truth tables like those shown in chapter 13, "Numbers," can be helpful in finding the simplest way to express something.

In simplifying control flow, the main goal is to minimize the amount of branching that is done. Instead of checking the same condition several times

```
IF X > 12 THEN action 1;
IF X > 12 THEN action 2;
IF X > 12 THEN action 3;
```

it is better to check the condition once and form a DO block:

```
IF X > 12 THEN DO;
  action 1;
  action 2;
  action 3;
  END;
```

Also, if one condition depends on another condition, the first condition might be put inside the DO block formed by the second condition. For example, in a step with a BY statement, the expression `_N_ = 1` can be true only if all the FIRST. variables are 1; so

```
IF _N_ = 1 THEN ...;
IF FIRST.GROUP THEN DO;
  ...;
  END;
```

can be rewritten

```
IF FIRST.GROUP THEN DO;
  IF _N_ = 1 THEN ...;
  ...;
  END;
```

In multiple choice situations, SELECT blocks are an improvement over IF . . . THEN and ELSE statements.

Compressing

Smaller data takes less space in a file and less time to read and write, and might take less space in memory.

Variable lengths

Numeric variables naturally have a length of 8 bytes, but they can be stored with a shorter length if a length is declared in a LENGTH, ATTRIB, or ARRAY statement. However, a numeric variable always occupies 8 bytes in memory, regardless of its length attribute.

A character variable should be declared with a length equal to the longest value that the variable could hold. The length of a character variable can be declared in a LENGTH or ATTRIB statement or in various other statements.

Variable lengths are discussed in more detail in chapter 2, "The facts." The issue of the length of a character variable is discussed in chapter 14, "Data types."

Codes

If a variable has few enough possible values that they can all be listed, a code can be substituted for it. A code can sometimes be much more compact than the data it replaces. Up to 256 values can be represented by a 1-byte code.

For example, if a variable has the values 1 to 10, those values can be represented by the code '01'X = 1, '02'X = 2, etc. The use of codes is described in chapter 14, "Data types."

A value informat and value format can be used with a code variable of this sort. For example, the states of a traffic signal might be represented by this code:

State	Code
Red	'01'X
Green	'02'X
Yellow	'03'X
Flashing red	'04'X
Flashing yellow	'05'X
Dark	'00'X

You could read values into this code using this value informat

```
PROC FORMAT;
  INVALUE $SIGNAL (MIN=5)
      'Red'               = '01'X
      'Green'             = '02'X
      'Yellow'            = '03'X
      'Flashing red'      = '04'X
      'Flashing yellow'   = '05'X
```

```
        'Dark'              = '00'X
        ;
```

and write and display them using the corresponding value format

```
PROC FORMAT;
  VALUE $SIGNAL (MIN=5)
        '01'X = 'Red'
        '02'X = 'Green'
        '03'X = 'Yellow'
        '04'X = 'Flashing red'
        '05'X = 'Flashing yellow'
        '00'X = 'Dark'
        ;
```

Custom data types, such as integer variables and unions, can represent the most compact way to store certain variables. They are described in chapter 14.

Variables

Reducing the number of variables is one way to reduce the amount of data. If some variables in the input data are never used, you can simply not read them in. The KEEP= or DROP= dataset option can be used to select the variables from an input SAS dataset to be used, or to specify the variables to be written to an output SAS dataset.

If two variables are functionally related to each other, you might not need to have both of them. For example, in data about a circle, you probably do not need variables representing both the radius and the diameter, because the diameter is always 2 times the radius.

At the other extreme, if two variables are never used at the same time, you might be able to combine them. For example, a variable SSN might represent the Social Security number of a person or, in the case of a corporation, its employer identification number. This kind of combined variable is called a *union* and is described in chapter 14.

Special missing values allow a numeric variable also to contain "flags" that explain why a value is missing. Missing values are described in chapter 2, "The facts."

Observations

The number of observations affects the size of a file. It does not affect the use of memory.

As with variables, there is no need to hang onto observations just because they are there. If some of the input data is irrelevant to an analysis, you can use a subsetting IF statement to eliminate it.

If a file just has too many observations to work with comfortably, you might decide to discard most of them, just randomly. This suggestion might seem shocking, but it is often possible to get statistically valid results from an analysis of a random sample of observations. Random sampling is described in chapter 17, "Applications."

If a SAS dataset actually contains duplicate observations — the same data twice — they can be eliminated using the NODUPKEY option with the SORT proc. The NODUPKEY option eliminates observations for which (after sorting) the values of all the BY variables are the same as those in the previous observation. If you want to eliminate only observations in which the values of *all* the variables are the same, just list all the variables in the BY statement. Sorting is discussed in chapter 8.

Files

You can easily occupy any amount of storage space just by keeping duplicates or near-duplicates of data files. The "saving steps" philosophy described at the beginning of this chapter can help minimize this problem among temporary SAS datasets.

If one data file can easily be extracted from another, it might not be necessary to keep both files. It depends, in part, on how expensive storage is in comparison to run time. If storage space is at a premium, there is no need to keep a SAS dataset that is simply an "image" of an input file that is already being stored — or a SAS dataset that is just a subset of another SAS dataset. Just save the program step that creates each file, and create it again each time you need to work with it.

The compressed form of a SAS dataset might take less space than the standard form, and usually (because of being smaller) can be read and written faster than the standard form. SAS datasets with long character variables, small integer values, and repeated values tend to benefit from compression. However, you cannot use direct access techniques on a compressed file.

The right procs

This section lists some things to consider in making the most effective use of specific procs.

Many procs use formatted values of variables rather than their internal values, or optionally can do so. For those procs, it is often more effective to recode a variable using a format than by using a separate data step. On the other hand, using formatted values is slower than the internal values.

The FREQ and TABULATE procs produce tables with different general shapes, so for simple frequency tables, you should use the proc that is better suited for the tables you want to get. The FREQ proc is generally faster than the TABULATE proc, especially when few variables are used. The TABULATE proc has greater flexibility in the contents of the tables it produces.

In the SUMMARY proc and other procs that use the CLASS statement, the effect of the CLASS statement on the operation of the proc is very different from that of the BY statement. When a BY statement is used, only the classes belonging to one BY group are kept in memory at one time. This greatly reduces the memory use of the proc, and it results in slightly faster execution too. The use of the BY statement is thus more efficient than the CLASS statement. However, the BY statement requires that the input SAS dataset be grouped by the BY variables. It usually isn't efficient to sort a SAS dataset in order to do a proc step with BY variables instead of CLASS variables. However, that approach might be necessary if the proc runs out of memory using a CLASS statement.

For calculating descriptive statistics, the SUMMARY (or MEANS) proc is much faster than the UNIVARIATE proc. It is also more precise in its calculations of some statistics. The UNIVARIATE proc is really only appropriate when you are calculating quantiles.

The character-oriented PLOT and CHART procs are much simpler than the GPLOT and GCHART procs — but, of course, the latter procs produce graphically superior output.

Faster

You should not usually have to worry about the speed of a SAS program, beyond the principle of saving steps covered at the beginning of this chapter. However, there might be some programs whose speed becomes an issue, because they seem to take too long to run, or because they handle enormous amounts of data or are run frequently.

The program's log tells how much time each step takes. You should focus your efforts first on the longest running steps, because that is where the potential for saving time is. If one step takes 80 percent of the run time of a program, then speeding up all the other steps could not possibly decrease the program's run time by more than a fifth.

Saving steps provides the greatest potential for speeding up SAS programs. After that's done, you should focus on compressing the data and simplifying the program. If, after that, a step still isn't fast enough, the various techniques in this section might speed it up a bit more.

To make a program faster, you have to make things easier for the computer. What processes are faster for the computer may not be obvious, and vary from one computer to another, even within the same class of computers. The SAS log can help you determine experimentally what makes a step go faster. This section lists several general things to consider.

Informats and formats. Some informats, and the corresponding formats, are simpler than others. The $CHAR and RB informats and formats are the fastest of all, because they don't require any interpreting or formatting. The binary informats and formats and $, $HEX, and HEX are almost as fast. Informats and formats that use decimal digits are slower because of all the multiplication involved in converting between decimal forms and the floating point form. Other informats and formats require varying amounts of processing. Using a decimal specification with an informat or format slows it down a bit.

Character variables. Because of the advantages of the $CHAR informat and format, character variables can be more efficient than numeric variables. A number or digit string that is never (or rarely) used in arithmetic can be a character variable. This is especially useful with single-digit codes.

Unneeded variables. Omit variables if you don't need them. Read only the fields you will use from an input data file, skipping the others. Use the KEEP= dataset option to specify which variables to be saved in a SAS dataset and which variables to be used in an input SAS dataset. In a proc, use a VAR statement to specify which variables should be processed.

Temporary variables. Rather than doing exactly the same calculation several times, do it once and assign the result to a variable.

Reusing variables. If you can use the same variable for different things in different parts of a step, it could be faster than having two variables. DO loop index variables, especially, can be reused for several loops (though not, of course, for nested loops).

```
DO I = 1 TO 10; ...; END;
DO I = 1 TO N; ...; END;
```

Group processing. If a calculated variable is the same for every observation of a BY group, calculate it only once, at the beginning of the group.

```
RETAIN PERCENT;
SET INVEST;
BY RATE;
IF FIRST.RATE THEN PERCENT = RATE*.01;
```

Subset early. If you're going to discard an observation anyway, do so before you do any unnecessary work on it. This is especially important if you discard most observations in a step. You might even want to break up an INPUT statement so that you don't have to do all the interpreting for an input record you won't be using. For example, if you use only records in an input file that have a record ID of N, you could subset immediately after reading the record ID field:

```
INPUT @11 RECORDID $CHAR1. @;
IF RECORDID = 'N';
INPUT ...
```

(Remember that the single trailing @ does not hold an input record for the next observation. Only a trailing @@ does that. So this approach does not create an infinite loop.)

Sequential access. Sequential access is several times faster than direct access (the SET statement using the POINT= option). Thus, you should usually use sequential access when you want to access observations in the order in which they are stored, even if you don't want to use all the observations. The FIRSTOBS=, OBS=, and WHERE= dataset options can be helpful in selecting observations. For example, this

```
SET A (FIRSTOBS=1000 OBS=1099);
```

is much faster than this:

```
DO POINT=1000 TO 1099;
  SET A POINT=POINT;
  END;
```

Unroll loops. Going through a DO loop takes some work, to keep track of the index values and check the loop conditions for each repetition of the loop. Processes that repeat a fixed number of times run faster if coded as repeated statements rather than as a loop. However, you might have to sacrifice brevity.

```
* Using DO loop:;
DO I = 1 TO 5;
  A{I} = X**I;
  END;

* The same thing, but faster:;
A{1} = X;
A{2} = X**2;
A{3} = X**3;
A{4} = X**4;
A{5} = X**5;
```

Array references. Variable names execute faster than array references.

```
* Faster yet:;
A1 = X;
A2 = X**2;
A3 = X**3;
A4 = X**4;
A5 = X**5;
```

Arrays. Arrays require a certain amount of overhead, so if you can do without them, the program will run faster. Data arrays, defined using the _TEMPORARY_ keyword instead of variable names, are faster than the standard variable list arrays.

Array subscripts. Array subscripts conventionally start at 1, but they execute fastest if they start at 0.

Statistic functions. Statistic functions, such as the SUM function, calculate statistics faster than you can calculate them in a loop. Also, the possibility of using the OF keyword with an abbreviated variable list might eliminate the need for an array.

```
* The wrong way;
ARRAY A{14} A1-A14;
ATOTAL = 0;
DO I = 1 TO 14; ATOTAL + A{I}; END;
```

```
* Much better;
ATOTAL = SUM(OF A1-A14);
```

Initial value. The RETAIN statement is more efficient than an assignment statement for providing an initial value for a variable.

Renaming. Use the RENAME= dataset option to rename a variable, rather than creating a new variable and assigning it the value of the old variable.

```
* The wrong way;
DATA C (DROP=CC);
  SET A (KEEP=CC);
  C = CC;
  ...

* The right way;
DATA C;
  SET A (KEEP=CC RENAME=(CC=C));
  ...
```

Arithmetic. Most computers find dividing to be a slower process than multiplying, and exponentiating slower still. Addition, subtraction, and negation are much faster. You can sometimes use the faster operators in place of the slower ones. For example, you don't have to divide by a constant. Instead of

```
PERCENT = RATE/100;
```

you can code

```
PERCENT = RATE*.01;
```

Common control flow path. You should speed up processes that happen almost all the time, without much concern for things that hardly ever happen. If most observations follow the same control flow path in a step, you should see if you can simplify it for those cases.

SELECT block. In a SELECT block, the first WHEN statements are reached slightly faster than the later ones. The SELECT block will execute fastest if the WHEN statements appear in descending order of popularity.

Table lookup. Some table lookup methods are much faster than others. See chapter 15, and experiment if necessary.

System options. If you're not using macrolanguage, the NOMACRO system option eliminates the overhead of the macro processor. If you are using the MACRO option, the NOIMPLMAC option speeds up processing somewhat. All the system options that reduce the extent of the log, including NOMPRINT, NOSYMBOLGEN, NOSOURCE, NOSOURCE2 and NONOTES, speed things up by eliminating some of the processing and output associated with the log.

RETAIN. The SAS supervisor ordinarily sets some variables to missing at the top of the observation loop. Naming variables in a RETAIN statement prevents this from happening, speeding up the step the slightest bit. A global RETAIN statement provides the maximum advantage you can get from this, but be very sure that it's okay not to reset variables to missing before you put in a global RETAIN statement.

Bit testing. Bit testing is occasionally more efficient than other forms of comparison. You can use the comparison `X = '00'B` to find out if X is a multiple of 4, for example.

Sorting

Sorting a large file can take a long time. Many programs spend most of their run time sorting SAS datasets.

The first thing to consider to reduce the time spent sorting is the possibility of avoiding the sort steps. The SORT proc is not always necessary. Procs that use the CLASS statement, such as SUMMARY, can produce sorted output SAS datasets from unsorted input.

You might also be able to reduce the amount of data being sorted: discard unneeded variables and observations, and keep the data small, using the techniques described earlier in this chapter under "Compressing."

To add observations to a sorted SAS dataset, sort the observations to be added and then interleave. This is more efficient than concatenating the two SAS datasets and then sorting, because it requires sorting only the new observations.

Small files are easier to sort than large files, so if you need to combine the observations of several sizeable SAS datasets, you should sort them and then interleave, rather than concatenating and then sorting. (With small SAS datasets, concatenating and then sorting is faster because it involves fewer steps.)

```
* Faster for small SAS datasets:  fewer steps;
  DATA COMBINED;                                     * 1. Concatenate;
    SET A B C;
  PROC SORT DATA=COMBINED;                           * 2. Sort;
    BY ID;

* Faster for larger SAS datasets:  smaller sorts;
  PROC SORT DATA=A; BY ID;                           * 1. Sort;
  PROC SORT DATA=B; BY ID;
  PROC SORT DATA=C; BY ID;
  DATA COMBINED;                                     * 2. Interleave;
    SET A B C;
    BY ID;
```

Sorting can take longer (and might not work at all) if there is a shortage of either memory or storage space. If this might be a problem, you can allow for plenty of memory and storage for the sort step using the techniques described below. However, if there is already plenty of memory and storage, adding more will not make a sort go much faster.

The TAGSORT option usually speeds up sorting of large files. The TAGSORT option and some alternative ways of sorting, which work in certain specialized situations, are described in chapter 8.

Under the MVS operating system, there is a proc designed to speed up sort steps. The SYNCSORT proc, published by Syncsort Inc., is intended as a substitute for the SORT proc. According to Syncsort Inc., it is much faster than the SORT proc.

For tasks like match merging and printing a report in sorted order, indexing might be faster than sorting. Sorting is more efficient, though, if the key variables make up most of the width of an observation, or if the sorted SAS dataset will be read repeatedly. Also, indexes can only work with ascending order, but sorting can also be done in descending order. Indexing is described in chapter 8, "Groups And Sorting."

Memory

If a SAS program attempts to use more memory than is available, the SAS System will shut itself down, possibly in a very unfriendly way. Also, certain procs will not run or will not run as well if there is not enough memory.

There are also some fixed blocks of memory whose size limits the number of certain kinds of objects. In particular, the program data vector, or PDV, limits the combined length of variables that can be used in any step.

To conserve memory, avoid using objects that take up memory. Each step uses memory separately from other steps, so you should focus your efforts only on steps that seem problematic. In addition to the memory used by the steps, some memory is used by objects that survive from one step to the next.

The macro processor, macrovariables, macros being executed, display manager, and all current display manager windows take up considerable amounts of memory. If memory is tight, it is reasonable to run a program without the macro processor (with the NOMACRO configuration option) or display manager.

The use of %INCLUDE files takes up a certain amount of memory, for file pointers to all the program files. It might help to copy an entire program into a single file.

The amount of memory used by full-screen procs depends on the number of windows used and on the number of fields in each window. (A field is a specifically defined part of a line on the computer screen.) Thus, with the FSEDIT proc, for example, the amount of memory needed depends on the number of variables. With over a hundred variables, the normal amount of memory recommended for the SAS System might not be enough. The EDITOR proc is less friendly but uses much less memory.

In data steps, every token in the step requires some memory. This creates a theoretical limit to the length of a step, but the limit must be at least several thousand lines, because we've never found it. However, certain features of the data step can eat up memory much more quickly.

The values of variables are kept in the PDV, which is a fixed-size block. However, all the attributes of variables — name, type, position, length, label, informat, and format — also have to be kept in memory, and that can add up if there are hundreds of variables.

Arrays, for some reason, seem to take *lots* of memory! Eighty arrays doesn't seem like all that many, but it might be enough to make a data step crash even before it starts running. This is a peculiarity of the SAS language; ordinary SAS arrays are lists of variable names. Data arrays, defined using the _TEMPORARY_ keyword instead of variable names, use less memory.

Most character functions and operators take up a lot of memory, because they are designed to work with the maximum length of a SAS character string, which is 200 bytes. Using the SUBSTR pseudo-variable to do concatenation often uses less memory than the concatenation operator. Also, it is more efficient to use the PUT statement features to create output records in text files, rather than using assignment statements to assemble a character variable representing the records.

File pointers and I/O streams also take up a lot of memory. This is a good thing to keep in mind when you write a step that uses direct access SET statements to read from a SAS dataset. Each SET statement is a different input stream and has a different file pointer. There is no logical conflict in having more than one direct access SET statement referring to the same SAS dataset, but it can be less efficient. It is best if all the direct access references to the same SAS dataset can be done in a single SET statement.

If, even after simplifying, a data step still uses too much memory, you might have to break it up into two data steps, with a temporary SAS dataset conveying data from the first step to the second — the opposite of the "saving steps" process described at the beginning of this chapter.

Storage

Storage is mostly important because the use of storage affects run time. However, storage also costs money, and the amount of storage might be limited at the time a program is run.

Saving steps can reduce the use of temporary data storage considerably. Compressing the data can also be helpful. You might be able to use a random sample of a SAS dataset instead of keeping all the observations.

You can delete temporary SAS datasets that are no longer needed at critical points in a program — before sorting, for example, or before writing a large SAS dataset.

When a data step writes a very large SAS dataset, and you're concerned that the step might run out of storage space before it writes the entire SAS dataset, you can monitor the step's use of storage by writing notes in the log. For example, you could note each 10,000th observations with statements like these:

```
FILE LOG;
IF NOT MOD(_N_, 10000) THEN PUT _N_=;
```

Even if the SAS System crashes, the log will be mostly intact. So if the step crashes because it runs out of storage space, you can at least see how far it got.

Hardware

At some point, the desire to get the most efficient use out of a computer has to be weighed against the possibility of an additional investment in computer hardware. It might not be cost-effective, for example, to spend weeks making a program use a megabyte less memory if one megabyte of memory costs less than a day's pay. Similarly, buying more storage devices or using removable storage (such as tape and floppy disks) might be the best solution to a storage shortage.

Using a faster computer — or a fast microcomputer in place of a multiuser computer — might solve the problem of the program that runs too slow.

At the other extreme, if cost-cutting is your reason for seeking efficiency for a mainframe or minicomputer program, you might be able to move it to a less expensive microcomputer hardware platform. Microcomputers can be about as powerful as mainframes, but cost much less.

> Many organizations systematically underinvest in equipment and expect their employees to make the best of it — and you might have some sympathy for this approach, because an increased equipment budget might come out of a reduced payroll. So figure out what side you're on before you start this kind of financial analysis. If it's your money, though, by all means equip yourself as effectively as you can.

Some improvements in computer performance might be possible just by making the best use of the hardware that you already have. If you use several kinds of storage devices, for example, try to put the SAS System files and commonly used SAS data libraries (especially the WORK library) on the fastest device available. You might even be able to put some SAS datasets in a RAM disk.

On a microcomputer, certain kinds of utility programs, such as print spoolers, can use up memory. By removing those programs, you'll have a bit more memory to work with.

Going nowhere

Some programming is completely ineffective. Pointless SAS statements can result when a program is revised and formerly useful parts are not removed, because of confused macrolanguage programming, or just as the result of bad programming habits. Some surprisingly popular bad habits are noted here.

Disk exercise

The opposite extreme from saving steps is adding extra steps to a program that accomplish nothing at all. These steps go through the motions of an ordinary SAS step but produce nothing of interest as a result. It's the SAS equivalent of spinning your wheels.

The most ineffective SAS step we've ever seen goes something like this:

```
  DATA A;
    SET A;
RUN;
```

This step doesn't accomplish anything at all! And it takes a lot of work for the computer: reading the original SAS dataset, writing an exact copy, and then erasing the original. Yet there it is. In some cases it arises out the mistaken belief that the SET statement is necessary to "put" a SAS dataset into a proc step. (Usually, what you need is the DATA= option in the PROC statement.)

This step is only a slight improvement:

```
  DATA A;
    SET THERE.A;
RUN;
```

To the computer, this step is just like the previous one, except for the detail of erasing the original SAS dataset. SAS programmers explain this step as "bringing a SAS dataset into the WORK library." Actually, they are just making a copy of a SAS dataset. There is a mistaken belief that the WORK library is somehow "internal" or faster or virtuous in some way that other SAS data libraries do not share. In almost every case, though, the WORK library has the same physical characteristics as any other SAS data library in the program.

Usually the copying just isn't necessary. Because WORK.A is just an exact copy of THERE.A, using WORK.A is not an improvement over using THERE.A. If you wanted to say

```
    SET A;
```

you could just as well use

```
SET THERE.A;
```

And instead of

```
PROC SORT DATA=A;
```

you should use

```
PROC SORT DATA=THERE.A OUT=A;
```

In some cases copying is appropriate: if a SAS dataset is on a tape or floppy disk volume, or is a SAS data view, and will be used as input data for several steps, for direct access input, or for interactive editing. For copying SAS data files, the COPY or APPEND proc is more efficient.

Stating the obvious

The use of declaration statements — LENGTH, RETAIN, ARRAY, and so on — is a mark of a serious programmer. However, some programmers (trying to look serious, perhaps) use these statements in situations where they are not appropriate, making extra work for the SAS supervisor.

This LENGTH statement is superfluous:

```
DATA _NULL_;
  LENGTH A B C 5;          * Meaningless;
```

Declaring the length of a character variable is almost always appropriate. However, these are numeric variables, and the length attribute of a numeric variable only affects the amount of storage space it takes in an output SAS dataset. Numeric variables always take up the full 8 bytes in memory. Thus, declaring the length of a numeric variable is only appropriate in a step that creates a SAS dataset. It is a futile gesture in a `DATA _NULL_` step.

This step is not perfect:

```
 DATA _NULL_;
   ARRAY A{25} A1-A25;
   SET PART;
   TOTAL = SUM(OF A1-A25);
   PUT _N_= TOTAL=;
RUN;
```

The ARRAY statement should not be there. The array A is declared, but is never referenced in the step. Instead, the abbreviated variable list `A1-A25` is used to identify the variables directly.

This statement does not change the value of STRING:

```
STRING = TRIM(STRING);
```

It is true that the TRIM function removes trailing blanks from the STRING variable. However, because SAS character variables have fixed lengths, those blanks come right back when the value is blank padded to assign it to the variable. The result: no change at all.

Likewise, this assignment statement:

```
STRING = RIGHT(TRIM(STRING));
```

Some programmers think that the RIGHT function right-aligns a character variable. Actually, it works on an expression, not a variable. The length of the variable that the result is assigned to has no effect on the process. The RIGHT function works by moving blanks from the end of a string to the beginning. If there are no trailing blanks, it does nothing. And that's the case here, because the trailing blanks were removed by the TRIM function.

This statement is, at least, overkill:

```
STRING = REPEAT(' ', 131);
```

The programmer probably intends to create a variable of length 132, all blank. However, if the length of the variable has been declared (as in a LENGTH statement), you can simply assign it a single blank, and the rest of its length is filled in with blank padding:

```
STRING = ' ';
```

On the other hand, if the variable has not been declared already, the statement using the REPEAT function gives it a length of 200, because that is the memory length returned by that function.

PART FOUR: Working

What do people do with the SAS programming language?

17 Applications

SAS programmers address all kinds of problems in business and science. This chapter touches on a few of the subject areas of SAS programs.

Database programming

A database is an organized body of data. Although there are specialized software packages, called *database management systems* or *DBMSs*, that are designed to handle especially demanding database applications, a SAS programmer will often find it easier to handle ordinary database applications using the SAS System.

There are five essential parts of database programming, each of which can be done several ways in a SAS program:

Adding data: Data step with INPUT statement or WINDOW, FSEDIT proc, other editing proc

Changing data: Data step, FSEDIT proc, other editing proc, UPDATE statement

Deleting data: WHERE= dataset option, DROP= dataset option, subsetting IF and DELETE statements, FSEDIT proc

Changing the way data is organized: Merging, concatenating, interleaving, sorting, crossing, updating, reshaping, recoding, table lookup, etc.

Getting reports and summaries of data: FSEDIT proc, other editing procs, PRINT proc, other reporting procs, data steps

The SAS System's ability to produce reports from a database, in particular, distinguishes it from any DBMS package. Most DBMS software allows you only to create reports in formats foreseen by the software designers. SAS is a general programming language, so you can produce a report in any format *you* can imagine.

Tables

The primary form of data organization in database programming is a two-dimensional table, which in a SAS database would be a SAS dataset with variables and observations. The words *row* and *record* are often used instead of *observation* in database programming; variables are sometimes called *fields* or *columns*.

Typically, a table is kept in sorted order by one variable or a group of variables, to make it easy to find observations. In a SAS program, the SORT proc can be used to put a table in order when a table is created or modified.

> The database "table" is named after the report "table," but is not exactly the same thing.

Foreign tables

With the SAS interface engines, SAS steps can access tables created by other software, including the most popular DBMSs. SAS programs can even modify tables in some of these other formats. This allows the advantages of dedicated DBMS software to be combined with those of the SAS System. More importantly, it makes it easier for SAS programmers to analyze data kept in various database formats.

There are also SAS procs and other programs to translate tables between SAS dataset formats and other formats. The DBF proc is an example; it converts SAS datasets to dBASE files, and vice versa. Converting a SAS dataset to a dBASE III file is done by the single statement

```
PROC DBF DATA=SAS dataset DB3=fileref;
```

The reverse conversion is done with this statement:

```
PROC DBF DB3=fileref OUT=SAS dataset;
```

The DB2= or DB4= option can be used instead of the DB3= option to work with dBASE II and dBASE IV file formats.

Measurements

You can measure data either in SAS datasets or as it passes through a data step.

The CONTENTS proc provides the basic information about a SAS dataset: the number of observations, all the variable attributes, and so on. The descriptive statistics procs, such as FREQ and SUMMARY, can provide various pictures of the data values in a SAS dataset. The FREQ proc, for example, can provide a list of all the values of a variable (provided there aren't too many different values) and how many times each value appears. If the observations of the SAS dataset MEETINGS represent meetings, and the YEAR and MONTH variables identify the month in which the meeting occurs, then this step will tell you how many meetings there are in each month:

```
PROC FREQ DATA=MEETINGS;
  TABLES YEAR*MONTH / LIST;
```

Ideally, all the data you work with would be meaningful, accurate, and up-to-date. However, you might be supplied data by a process that does not assure this. You won't be able to detect everything that's wrong with the data, but you can identify and discard data that is obviously wrong.

A situation in which a program identifies input data as incorrect is called a *data error*. Data errors include situations when a code does not belong to set of codes, when a variable value does not belong to the meaningful range of values for the variable, when observations fail to match in a merging or lookup process, when there are duplicate observations, when a combination of variable values are not meaningful, and when a total does not match detail.

It is a good practice to put data errors in reports — either informally, in the log, or in a carefully designed report in its own print file. A report of a data error should include an error message and all the relevant data; in most cases, you can write the entire observation containing the error. An error message can be either a concise code or a short sentence, depending on what you find easier to work with.

These statements, for example, check for a data error in the PERCENT variable.

```
IF PERCENT < 0 OR PERCENT > 100 THEN DO;
  FILE LOG;
  PUT / 'Percent out of range.' / _ALL_;
  DELETE;
  END;
```

The exact process for handling errors in matching depends on what you expect. If three SAS datasets should each contain one observation for each of the same set of ID values, the error checking could look like this:

```
MERGE A (IN=IN1) B (IN=IN2) C (IN=IN3);
BY ID;
IF NOT (IN1 AND IN2 AND IN3) THEN DO;
  FILE LOG;
  PUT / 'Not found in all SAS datasets.' / _ALL_;
  DELETE;
  END;
IF NOT FIRST.ID THEN DO;
  FILE LOG;
  PUT / 'Duplicate found in at least one SAS dataset.' / _ALL_;
```

```
    DELETE;
    END;
```

The value of these error messages is twofold: First, you can see the number of data errors for each different reason, and perhaps investigate individual errors. Second, if the error rate is unexpectedly high or forms an unexpected pattern, that might indicate either a logical error in the program or a misunderstanding, an error in the documentation of the input data.

You can use a value informat to catch data errors at the input stage. You can just list all the valid input values in the informat definition, and the associate the OTHER range with a value (perhaps missing) that is distinct from any of the valid values.

For example, if the value of SWITCH can be only ON or OFF, you could use this value informat

```
PROC FORMAT;
  INVALUE $SWITCH (UPCASE JUST)
      'ON'  = 'ON'
      'OFF' = 'OFF'
      OTHER = ' ';
```

and then read the variable using this informat. Reading from a text file could be done using the $SWITCH informat:

```
  INPUT SWITCH $SWITCH3. ...;
  IF SWITCH = ' ' THEN DO;
    FILE LOG;
    PUT / 'SWITCH not set.' / _ALL_;
    DELETE;
    END;
```

If you associate this kind of value informat with a field on a defined screen used with the FSEDIT proc, the informat will turn the field blank after any OTHER value is entered, thus quietly but firmly hinting that the value was incorrect.

A value informat can be used together with a corresponding value format in order to compress a code variable. For example, if you used this value informat

```
PROC FORMAT;
  INVALUE $SWITCH
      'ON'  = '1'
      'OFF' = '0'
      OTHER = ' ';
```

you would have to write the value using this value format:

```
PROC FORMAT;
  VALUE $SWITCH
      '1' = 'ON'
      '0' = 'OFF'
      ;
```

In the process, you would shorten the variable to a length of 1 byte, with a resulting savings in storage use and run time.

If you give someone a database with code variables using value formats and value informats, you'll need to provide the informats and formats along with it. Conversely, if you receive a coded variable with a value format, you should check to make sure that the value format encompasses all the values of the variable. If you have the source code of the value format, you can make a list of the values of the variables using the FREQ proc (using a "neutral" format, such as `$CHAR.` or `BEST4.`) and compare the list of values against the ranges in the VALUE statement. Or you can use the FREQ proc with the value format associated with the variable, and see if any values have unexpected formatted values.

Comparing files

You might compare two files to verify that they are the same, to verify that they are different, or to find out how different they are. You might compare versions of a file from different times, or determine the effect of an update by comparing the "before" and "after" versions. Instead of comparing two files directly, you could compare summaries or statistics describing the files.

The most painstaking way to compare files is to print them both and compare the reports. This process can be simplified slightly by match merging the files in order to print them both on the same report. Taking this a step further, you can have the computer program do the comparison.

You could simply print all the observations that do not match, as in this step:

```
DATA _NULL_;
  MERGE NOW (RENAME=(AGE=AGENOW) IN=NOW)
       THEN (RENAME=(AGE=AGETHEN) IN=THEN);
  BY PERSON;
  IF NOW AND THEN THEN
  IF AGETHEN > AGENOW OR AGETHEN < AGENOW - 1 THEN DO;
    FILE LOG;
    PUT PERSON +2 'Age reported then: ' AGETHEN +3
        'Age reported now: ' AGENOW;
    END;
```

The COMPARE proc does a similar process, but works only for numeric variables.

Recordkeeping

A database is useless without an understanding of what the data in it represents. At the very least, someone must know what the variables are. Ideally, there are written descriptions of each variable, along with an explanation of the observations in each table.

After a conclusion has been reached from a data processing system, an *audit trail* is a set of information that shows how the conclusion was reached. It always includes the original input data, along with any documentation of it, and also includes programs or logs or intermediate data files, with enough detail that all the conclusions can be reconstructed by investigators. Maintaining audit trails is essential when working with accounting data and research data.

Statistics

The SAS System's first claim to fame is its collection of statistics procs. If you're a statistician, you'll find procs for curve fitting, time series, analysis of variance, nonparametrics, confidence intervals, hypothesis testing, and other statistics topics. If you're not a statistician, you'll probably be more interested in the descriptive statistics procs.

In addition to the use of procs, there can be some programming involved in statistics work. This section describes some of the specialized programming techniques that are used in statistics.

Samples

A random sample of a SAS dataset is another SAS dataset, containing the same variables and randomly selected observations. Random samples are often used for analysis when a SAS dataset is unnecessarily large. Random samples might also be generated as part of the design of an experiment.

If observations are already in random order, any chunk of them is a random sample. You can extract a random sample of any size using the FIRSTOBS= and OBS= dataset options.

```
PROC MEANS DATA=HEAVY (FIRSTOBS=45001 OBS=45200);
```

If the observations are not in random order, you can put them in random order. To do that, just use a randomly generated variable as the sort key.

```
DATA DISORDER;
  SET ORDER;
  RANDOM = RANUNI(8);
PROC SORT DATA=DISORDER OUT=CHAOS;
  BY RANDOM;
```

You can also select observations randomly. To select approximately one hundredth of the observations, you could use a subsetting IF statement comparing the RANUNI function to .01:

```
DATA SAMPLE;
  SET HEAVY;
  IF RANUNI(2) < .01 THEN OUTPUT SAMPLE;
```

Alternatively, you could select observations using a random POINT= value in a direct access SET statement. This allows the possibility that an observation might be selected more than once — *sampling with replacement,* in statistical terms. In assigning a value to the POINT= variable, be sure that the value is an observation number in the input SAS dataset. Also, as with any step with a direct access SET statement, make sure you arrange for the step to stop at some point.

This step selects 320 random observations from the SAS dataset HEAVY, to create the SAS dataset SAMPLEWR:

```
DATA SAMPLEWR;
  POINT = CEIL(NOBS*RANUNI(4));
  SET HEAVY POINT=POINT NOBS=NOBS;
  N + 1;
  IF N >= 320 THEN STOP;
```

To sample without replacement using a direct access SET statement, you can make sure you always increase the POINT= variable from one observation to the next. In essence, this is selecting at random intervals in the SAS dataset. This step, for each observation, randomly selects an observation from the next 240 observations after the previous selection:

```
POINT + CEIL(RANUNI(1)*240);
IF POINT > NOBS THEN STOP;
SET HEAVY POINT=POINT NOBS=NOBS;
```

Alternatively, you can divide the SAS dataset into intervals of a fixed size, selecting one observation from each interval. This process, selecting randomly from fixed intervals, does not produce a true random sample if the observations are not in random order to begin with, because consecutive observations are particularly unlikely to be selected.

```
POINT = CEIL((_N_ + RANUNI(8) - 1)*70);
IF POINT > NOBS THEN STOP;
SET HEAVY POINT=POINT NOBS=NOBS;
```

Another approach is periodic ("*n*thed") sampling. It is not a random process at all, but its simplicity is reassuring to some. It does produce a valid representative sample in some cases. For example, a periodic sample from a SAS dataset in ZIP code order would be representative of the geographic distribution of the SAS dataset.

Periodic sampling is done with a subsetting IF statement, using a modulus with the automatic variable _N_. The process depends on the variable N, which is the inverse of the proportion of observations to be selected. For example, to select one sixteenth of the observations, N would be 16. If N is a counting number, you can use this statement:

```
IF NOT MOD(_N_, N);  * integer N;
```

This slightly more complicated statement works for any number N greater than 1:

```
IF MOD(_N_, N) < 1;   * any N;
```

You can get another, different random sample of the same size by adding an offset value to this comparison. The sample will have no observations in common with the sample generated by the statement above if the offset value is between 1 and N.

```
* Variation, to get a completely different sample;
RETAIN OFFSET 1; * use a value between 1 and N;
IF (MOD(_N_, N) + OFFSET) < 1;
```

A more complicated approach programmers sometimes use is to select by proportion. The ratio of observations selected so far to the number of observations to be selected is compared to the ratio of the number of observations read so far to the total number of observations. This approach has the advantage of allowing the programmer to specify the exact number of observations to be selected.

The statements below select 390 observations periodically from the SAS dataset HEAVY. The variable SO_FAR keeps track of the number of observations that have been selected so far. NOBS is the total number of observations in HEAVY to select from.

```
RETAIN TARGET 390;
SET HEAVY NOBS=NOBS;
IF SO_FAR/TARGET < _N_/NOBS;
SO_FAR + 1;
```

A variation on this uses a forward-looking proportion. The ratio of the number of observations left to be selected to the number of observations to be selected is compared to the ratio of the number of observations left to be selected from to the total number of observations.

The variable TO_GO keeps track of the number of observations left to be selected.

```
RETAIN TARGET TO_GO 390;
SET HEAVY NOBS=NOBS;
IF TO_GO/TARGET > (NOBS - _N_)/NOBS;
TO_GO + -1;
```

Descriptive statistics

A *sample* is a set of values or measurements that is part of and is considered to represent in some way a larger set that is being studied. A *statistic* is a number that is mathematically derived from the values of a sample. A *descriptive statistic* is a statistic used to describe the characteristics of a sample.

The SAS statistic functions, SUM, N, STD, and so on, each calculate one descriptive statistic for a sample listed as the function's arguments. The statistic functions were described in chapter 3, "Programs on call."

Several procs, including SUMMARY and TABULATE, can calculate descriptive statistics, using all the values of a variable in a SAS dataset as a sample. It is also possible to program the calculations for those same descriptive statistics.

Calculating descriptive statistics in a data step has three important advantages: the input data does not have to be a numeric variable in a SAS dataset; the calculation can be added to any existing data step without much additional work for the program; and you can calculate other statistics that are not contained in the SAS System.

The step below calculates some descriptive statistics for one variable, A, in the SAS dataset A. These statistics match those calculated by descriptive statistics procs when the `VARDEF=DF` option is used.

```
DATA _NULL_;
  RETAIN;
  SET A (KEEP=A) END=LAST;
  * SET A  -  BY GROUP  -  for grouped statistics;
  IF MIN = . THEN MIN = A;
  IF A <= .Z THEN NMISS + 1;
  ELSE DO;
    N + 1;
    SUM + A;
    USS + A*A;
    SC + A*A*A;
    SF + A*A*A*A;
    MIN = MIN MIN A;
    MAX = MAX MAX A;
    END;
  IF LAST THEN DO;      * IF LAST.GROUP for grouped statistics;
    IF N >= 1 THEN DO;
      RANGE = MAX - MIN;
      MEAN = SUM/N;
      CSS = USS - MEAN*SUM;
      END;
    IF N >= 2 THEN DO;
      VAR = CSS/(N - 1);            * Sample variance;
      STD = SQRT(VAR);
      STDERR = SQRT(VAR/N);
      IF MEAN THEN CV = 100*STD/MEAN;     * % coeff. of variation;
      IF STD THEN DO;
        IF N >= 3 THEN SKEWNESS =
            (SC - 3*MEAN*USS + 2*MEAN*MEAN*SUM)
            / (VAR*STD) * N/((N - 1)*(N - 2));
        IF N >= 4 THEN KURTOSIS = (SF - 4*MEAN*SC
            + 6*MEAN*MEAN*USS - 3*MEAN*MEAN*MEAN*SUM)
            / (VAR*VAR) * N*(N + 1)/((N - 1)*(N - 2)*(N - 3))
            - 3*(N - 1)*(N - 1)/((N - 2)*(N - 3));
        T = MEAN/STDERR;
        PRT = 2*PROBT(-ABS(T), N - 1);
        END;
      END;
```

```
    PUT 'Descriptive Statistics Calculated In A Data Step' //
        N= / NMISS= / MIN= / MAX= / RANGE= /
        SUM= / MEAN= / USS= / CSS= / VAR= / STD= / STDERR= /
        CV= / SKEWNESS= / KURTOSIS= / T= / PRT= ;
    END;
```

```
Descriptive Statistics Calculated In A Data Step

N=44
NMISS=1
MIN=1
MAX=543
RANGE=542
SUM=1676
MEAN=38.090909091
USS=353216
CSS=289375.63636
VAR=6729.6659619
STD=82.034541273
STDERR=12.367172421
CV=215.36514415
SKEWNESS=5.6705758486
KURTOSIS=35.17943104
T=3.0800014583
PRT=0.003601016
```

Quantiles

Quantiles are statistics that divide a distribution into equal parts. The median, for example, divides a distribution into two equal parts; half the values are below it, and half are above it. Likewise, one fourth of the values are below the first quartile of a distribution, and three fourths are below the third quartile. Other commonly used quantiles are deciles, which divide a distribution into ten equal parts, and percentiles, which create 100 equal parts.

Quantiles cannot be calculated algebraically; the only way to determine a sample quantile is to put the values in the sample in order. If the sample is all the values of a variable in a SAS dataset, sort the SAS dataset by that variable, and then use a direct access SET statement to find a value at a particular location.

These steps find deciles of the SCORE variable:

```
PROC SORT DATA=MEASURE (KEEP=SCORE) OUT=ORDER;
  BY SCORE;
DATA _NULL_;
  DO DECILE = 1 TO 9;
    POINT = ROUND((NOBS + 1)*DECILE*.1);
    SET ORDER POINT=POINT NOBS=NOBS;
    PUT 'Decile ' DECILE 'is ' SCORE;
    END;
```

The UNIVARIATE proc reports a few select quantiles: the median, the 1st and 3rd quartiles, and the 1st, 5th, 10th, 90th, 95th, and 99th percentiles.

The range between two quantiles is a *quantile rank,* which is often just called a quantile. For example, a value below the 1st percentile may be considered to belong to the 1st percentile, just as a value below the median is described as belonging to the 1st half. The RANK proc assigns quantile ranks if the GROUPS= option is used; or you can do it using the SORT proc and a data step.

There are several differences in the details of the process, depending on which way you do it. The program below creates the variable DECILE which has values 1 to 10; it uses missing values, if there are any (assigning them to decile 1); it works for any variable, including character variables; and it can be used for a combination of variables (just by listing the variables in succession in the BY statement). It also results in sorted SAS dataset, which is sometimes useful for other reasons.

```
PROC SORT DATA=MEASURE;
  BY SCORE;
DATA QUANTILE;
  SET MEASURE NOBS=NOBS;
  DECILE = CEIL(_N_*10/NOBS); * For deciles 1 to 10;
```

The RANK proc with the `GROUPS=10` option, by contrast, creates a DECILE variable with values 0 through 9, instead of the more conventional 1 through 10. It ignores missing values. The RANK proc works only for numeric variables, but can calculate quantiles for several variables at the same time. It has a choice of ways to handle ties. It is usually faster because it does not require sorting a SAS dataset.

```
PROC RANK DATA=MEASURE OUT=QUANTILE GROUPS=10;
  VAR SCORE;
  RANKS DECILE;
```

Simulations

A computer simulation uses mathematically defined events to represent real-life events. The results of the mathematical events are used to predict the results of the real-life events.

There are two distinct kinds of simulations: a random, or stochastic, simulation, in which random numbers are used to generate the events, and an exhaustive simulation, in which every possible event is considered, according to the understanding of a real-life system. Random simulation is often called the *Monte Carlo method,* after a famous gambling resort.

The science of probability had its origins in games of chance, partly because some of them are very easy to describe probabilistically. Consider a coin toss, for example. It can be simulated using the SAS statements

```
IF RANUNI(5) < 0.5 THEN PUT 'Heads'; ELSE PUT 'Tails';
```

A series of coin tosses could be simulated using a DO loop:

```
HEADS = 0;
DO I = 1 TO 100; HEADS + (RANUNI(5) < 0.5); END;
TAILS = 100 - HEADS;
PUT HEADS= TAILS=;
```

There are six possible results of the roll of a die, each equally likely. Thus, the roll of a die can be simulated by this statement:

```
DIE = CEIL(RANUNI(5)*6);
```

Simulations of dice figure prominently in the more complex example that follows.

Risk

Risk is a global military strategy game marketed by Parker Brothers. The game is played on a stylized world map. The world is divided into 42 territories, each of which is occupied by the armies of one player. The game consists mainly of a series of battles between adjacent territories; the outcome of each battle is determined by the roll of several dice.

The attacking player can roll up to three dice, and the defending player, up to two. The number of dice is also limited by the number of armies on a territory.

The highest attacking die is compared to the highest defending die. If the attacking die is higher than the defending die, the attacker wins, and one defending army is removed. If the dice are equal or the defending die is higher, the defender wins, and one attacking army is removed. If each player rolled at least two dice, the second highest die is compared in the same way.

The objective of the following programs is to determine the probabilities of the different outcomes of a Risk battle, depending on the number of dice rolled by each player. The probabilities are first determined by an exhaustive simulation, in which every possible combination of dice is considered, and in the second program, by a stochastic simulation, in which rolls of the dice are randomly generated.

In the exhaustive simulation, an iterative DO loop is used to generate the six possible values of each die. The results are then determined inside the innermost loop. The two outermost loops represent the different numbers of dice the players can roll.

```
DATA _NULL_;
  FILE PRINT NOTITLES;
  RETAIN A 10 B 15 C 18 D 27 E 36 F 45 G 54;

  PUT / @C+4 'RISK BATTLE PROBABILITIES'
      // @A ' Dice ' @E '  Winner'
      / @A 'A' @B 'D'
      @C '    A' @D '    D' @E '    AA' @F '    AD' @G '    DD' /;
```

```
DO D_DICE = 1 TO 2; * Number of defending dice;
DO A_DICE = 1 TO 3; * Number of attacking dice;
  RES_A = 0; RES_AA = 0; RES_DD = 0;
  ARMIES = A_DICE MIN D_DICE; * Number of armies decided;
  N = 6**(A_DICE + D_DICE);   * Number of die combinations;
  *-----------------------------------------------------------*
  | All combinations of dice are generated using DO loops.    |
  | For dice being used, the loop bounds are 1 TO 6.          |
  | For dice not being used, the loop bounds are 0 TO 0.      |
  | After the dice rolls are generated, the top two dice on   |
  | side are identified.                                      |
  *-----------------------------------------------------------*;
  DO ROLL_D1 = 1 TO 6; * Defending dice roll;
  DO ROLL_D2 = (D_DICE = 2) TO 6*(D_DICE = 2); * 1-6 or 0-0;
    DEFEND1 = ROLL_D1 MAX ROLL_D2; *Defending dice, sorted;
    DEFEND2 = ROLL_D1 MIN ROLL_D2;
    DO ROLL_A1 = 1 TO 6; * Attacking dice;
    DO ROLL_A2 = (A_DICE >= 2) TO 6*(A_DICE >= 2);
    DO ROLL_A3 = (A_DICE >= 3) TO 6*(A_DICE >= 3);
      ATTACK1 = ROLL_A1 MAX ROLL_A2 MAX ROLL_A3;
      ATTACK2 = ROLL_A1 + ROLL_A2 + ROLL_A3 - ATTACK1
              - (ROLL_A1 MIN ROLL_A2 MIN ROLL_A3);
      * Count results;
      IF ARMIES = 1 THEN RES_A + (ATTACK1 > DEFEND1);
      ELSE DO; * 2 armies;
        RES_AA + ATTACK1 > DEFEND1 AND ATTACK2 > DEFEND2;
        RES_DD + ATTACK1 <= DEFEND1 AND ATTACK2 <= DEFEND2;
        END;
      END;
      END;
      END;
    END;
    END;
  IF ARMIES = 1 THEN DO;
    RES_D = N - RES_A;
    FREQ_A = RES_A/N;
    FREQ_D = RES_D/N;
    PUT / @A A_DICE 1. @B D_DICE 1.
          @C FREQ_A 8.7 @D FREQ_D 8.7
        / @A N COMMA6. @C RES_A COMMA6. @D RES_D COMMA6.;
    END;
  ELSE DO; * 2 armies;
    RES_AD = N - RES_AA - RES_DD;
    FREQ_AA = RES_AA/N;
    FREQ_AD = RES_AD/N;
    FREQ_DD = RES_DD/N;
    PUT / @A A_DICE 1. @B D_DICE 1.
          @E FREQ_AA 8.7 @F FREQ_AD 8.7 @G FREQ_DD 8.7
        / @A N COMMA6.
         @E RES_AA COMMA6. @F RES_AD COMMA6. @G RES_DD COMMA6.;
    END;
  END;
  END;

  PUT /// @C 'A, attacker' / @C 'D, defender';
  STOP;
RUN;
```

```
                    RISK BATTLE PROBABILITIES

 Dice                                    Winner
A     D         A          D          AA         AD         DD


1     1   .4166667  .5833333
     36         15        21

2     1   .5787037  .4212963
    216        125        91

3     1   .6597222  .3402778
  1,296        855       441

1     2   .2546296  .7453704
    216         55       161

2     2                        .2276235  .3240741  .4483025
  1,296                             295       420       581

3     2                        .3716564  .3357767  .2925669
  7,776                           2,890     2,611     2,275


              A, attacker
              D, defender
```

In the stochastic simulation below, expressions involving the RANUNI function replace the DO loops of the exhaustive simulation, and the structure of the program changes accordingly.

```
DATA _NULL_;
  FILE PRINT NOTITLES;
  RETAIN A 10 B 15 C 18 D 27 E 36 F 45 G 54;
  RETAIN N 160; * Number of battles simulated;
  PUT / @C+4 'RISK BATTLE PROBABILITIES'
      // @A ' Dice ' @E '  Winner'
      / @A 'A' @B 'D'
      @C '    A' @D '    D' @E '    AA' @F '    AD' @G '    DD' /;

  DO D_DICE = 1 TO 2; * Number of defending dice;
  DO A_DICE = 1 TO 3; * Number of attacking dice;
    RES_A = 0; RES_AA = 0; RES_DD = 0;
    ARMIES = A_DICE MIN D_DICE; * Number of armies decided;
    DO I = 1 TO N;
      ROLL_D1 = CEIL(6*RANUNI(7)); * Defending dice roll;
      IF D_DICE >= 2 THEN ROLL_D2 = CEIL(6*RANUNI(7));
      ELSE ROLL_D2 = 0;
      DEFEND1 = ROLL_D1 MAX ROLL_D2; *Defending dice, sorted;
      DEFEND2 = ROLL_D1 MIN ROLL_D2;
      ROLL_A1 = CEIL(6*RANUNI(7));    * Attacking dice;
      IF A_DICE >= 2 THEN ROLL_A2 = CEIL(6*RANUNI(7));
      ELSE ROLL_A2 = 0;
      IF A_DICE >= 3 THEN ROLL_A3 = CEIL(6*RANUNI(7));
      ELSE ROLL_A3 = 0;
      ATTACK1 = ROLL_A1 MAX ROLL_A2 MAX ROLL_A3;
```

```
        ATTACK2 = ROLL_A1 + ROLL_A2 + ROLL_A3 - ATTACK1
                  - (ROLL_A1 MIN ROLL_A2 MIN ROLL_A3);
        * Count results;
        IF ARMIES = 1 THEN RES_A + (ATTACK1 > DEFEND1);
        ELSE DO; * 2 armies;
          RES_AA + ATTACK1 > DEFEND1 AND ATTACK2 > DEFEND2;
          RES_DD + ATTACK1 <= DEFEND1 AND ATTACK2 <= DEFEND2;
          END;
        END;
      IF ARMIES = 1 THEN DO;
        RES_D = N - RES_A;
        FREQ_A = RES_A/N;
        FREQ_D = RES_D/N;
        PUT / @A A_DICE 1. @B D_DICE 1.
              @C FREQ_A 8.7 @D FREQ_D 8.7
            / @A N COMMA6. @C RES_A COMMA6. @D RES_D COMMA6.;
        END;
      ELSE DO; * 2 armies;
        RES_AD = N - RES_AA - RES_DD;
        FREQ_AA = RES_AA/N;
        FREQ_AD = RES_AD/N;
        FREQ_DD = RES_DD/N;
        PUT / @A A_DICE 1. @B D_DICE 1.
              @E FREQ_AA 8.7 @F FREQ_AD 8.7 @G FREQ_DD 8.7
            / @A N COMMA6.
             @E RES_AA COMMA6. @F RES_AD COMMA6. @G RES_DD COMMA6.;
        END;
      END;
      END;

    PUT /// @C 'A, attacker' / @C 'D, defender';
    STOP;
RUN;
```

```
                        RISK BATTLE PROBABILITIES

         Dice                           Winner
        A    D      A         D          AA        AD        DD


        1    1  .4375000 .5625000
           160        70        90

        2    1  .5562500 .4437500
           160        89        71

        3    1  .6812500 .3187500
           160       109        51

        1    2  .2875000 .7125000
           160        46       114

        2    2                      .2125000 .3187500 .4687500
           160                            34        51        75

        3    2                      .3312500 .3437500 .3250000
           160                            53        55        52
```

```
A, attacker
D, defender
```

In this case, the exhaustive simulation and the stochastic simulation produce similar results, but the exhaustive simulation takes slightly longer to run. However, for more complicated models, perhaps with ten dice instead of five, the exhaustive simulation might take much longer to run.

Input data

The Risk simulation above did not use any input data, but it is possible to do simulations with input data. You might do this, for example, in a marketing study that projects the results of a proposed marketing strategy by simulating the response of each customer, based on actual customer data.

Computer system management

It takes real work to manage multiuser computer systems. Management problems include accounting and billing, security, capacity planning, and performance measurements. SAS programs are widely used in all these aspects of computer system management.

The details vary considerably, depending on the operating system and hardware used. An organization's style and priorities also affect the way they manage their computer systems.

Under the MVS operating system, SMF is the most widely used utility program for monitoring the behavior of the computer. It keeps up a running commentary by writing records that describe system events such as jobs. SMF records are variable-length records with their own notoriously complex record formats. Because SMF records are so complicated, few people try to do anything with them with any software other than the SAS System.

MXG® is a book of SAS source code and advice that is very helpful in dealing with SMF records and other system monitoring data on IBM mainframes. Its proper name is *Merrill's Expanded Guide To Computer Performance Evaluation Using The SAS® System*; it is named after its author, Barry Merrill.

The SAS product SAS/CPE® can be used to do computer system management under the VMS operating system.

Word processing tools

Although you would probably not use the SAS System for word processing, SAS programs can be useful in analyzing the text of word processing documents. Each word processing program has its own file formats, but most of them allow you to save a a document in text form (sometimes called "text only" or "text with line breaks" or "ASCII" form), so that it can be used as input data for a SAS program.

Word count

Perhaps the most often calculated statistic in word processing is the number of words in a document. If a "word" is any sequence of characters separated by blanks or line breaks, they can be counted with this program:

```
  DATA _NULL_;
    LENGTH WORD $ 64;
    INFILE DOCUMENT EOF=EOF FLOWOVER;
    INPUT WORD $ @@;
    COUNT + 1;
    RETURN;
EOF: PUT 'Word count:   ' COUNT :COMMA14.;
    STOP;
```

```
Word count:  6,726
```

If a "word" has to contain at least one letter, the program is changed slightly:

```
  DATA _NULL_;
    LENGTH WORD $ 64;
    INFILE DOCUMENT EOF=EOF FLOWOVER;
    INPUT WORD $ @@;
    IF INDEXC(WORD,
            'ABCDEFGHIJKLMNOPQRSTUVWXYZabcdefghijklmnopqrstuvwxyz')
        THEN COUNT + 1;
    RETURN;
EOF: PUT 'Word count:   ' COUNT :COMMA14.;
    STOP;
```

```
Word count:  5,993
```

Word lengths

Often people are interested in how long the words in a document are. The mean word length is often taken as a measure of how difficult a document is to read.

This program counts the number of words of each length, and then describes the distribution of word lengths.

```
 DATA _NULL_;
   LENGTH WORD $ 64;
   RETAIN COUNT1-COUNT64 0  A 10  B 20  C 32;
   ARRAY COUNT{64};
   FILE PRINT;
   INFILE DOCUMENT EOF=EOF FLOWOVER;

   INPUT WORD $ @@;
   IF INDEXC(WORD,
           'ABCDEFGHIJKLMNOPQRSTUVWXYZabcdefghijklmnopqrstuvwxyz')
       THEN COUNT{LENGTH(WORD)} + 1;
   RETURN;
EOF:
   N = SUM(OF COUNT1-COUNT64);
   IF N < 1 THEN STOP;
   PUT @30 'Word Lengths' //
       @A 'Length' @B 'Frequency' @C 'Rel. Frequency' /;
   DO LENGTH = 1 TO 64;
     REL = COUNT{LENGTH}/N;
     IF COUNT{LENGTH} THEN PUT
         @A LENGTH 6. @B COUNT{LENGTH} COMMA9. @C REL 9.6;
     END;
   PUT / @A ' TOTAL' @B N COMMA9. /;

   SUM = 0; SS = 0; DIST = 0;
   DO LENGTH = 1 TO 64;
     SUM + COUNT{LENGTH}*LENGTH;
     SS + COUNT{LENGTH}*LENGTH*LENGTH;
     IF DIST < N*.5 THEN DO;    * Find median;
       DIST + COUNT{LENGTH};
       IF DIST >= N*.5 THEN MEDIAN = LENGTH;
       END;
     END;
   MEAN = SUM/N;
   STD = SQRT((SS - SUM*SUM/N)/N);
   PUT / @A 'Median word length:  ' MEDIAN
       / @A 'Mean word length:  ' MEAN :9.5
       / @A 'Standard deviation of word length:  ' STD :9.5;
   STOP;
```

We applied the program to an early draft of this chapter and got this output:

Word Lengths

Length	Frequency	Rel. Frequency
1	278	0.046387
2	1,020	0.170199
3	1,078	0.179877
4	840	0.140164
5	574	0.095778
6	531	0.088603
7	528	0.088103
8	363	0.060571
9	283	0.047222
10	198	0.033039
11	115	0.019189
12	86	0.014350
13	43	0.007175
14	16	0.002670
15	9	0.001502
16	2	0.000334
17	3	0.000501
18	8	0.001335
19	3	0.000501
20	4	0.000667
21	5	0.000834
22	1	0.000167
28	1	0.000167
55	2	0.000334
64	2	0.000334
TOTAL	5,993	

```
Median word length:  4
Mean word length:  5.01702
Standard deviation of word length:  3.29440
```

Word list

A similar objective would be to list all the words in a document, along with the number of times each one occurs. Leading and trailing punctuation marks are not considered part of words in the program below, and the list is presented in alphabetical order.

```
DATA WORD1;
  RETAIN ALFN
'ABCDEFGHIJKLMNOPQRSTUVWXYZabcdefghijklmnopqrstuvwxyz0123456789';
  LENGTH WORD $ 64 CAPITAL $ 24;
  INFILE DOCUMENT FLOWOVER;
  INPUT WORD $ @@;
  * Remove leading and trailing punctuation and blanks;
  WORD = SUBSTR(WORD, INDEXC(WORD, ALFN),
         66 - INDEXC(REVERSE(WORD), ALFN) - INDEXC(WORD, ALFN));
  CAPITAL = UPCASE(WORD); * Used for alphabetizing;
PROC SORT DATA=WORD1 OUT=WORD2;
  BY CAPITAL WORD;
```

```
TITLE1 'Word Frequencies';
  DATA _NULL_;
    FILE PRINT;
    SET WORD2 (KEEP=WORD);
    BY WORD NOTSORTED;
    IF FIRST.WORD THEN COUNT = 0;
    COUNT + 1;
    IF LAST.WORD THEN PUT COUNT 5. +2 WORD $CHAR64.;
```

```
   62  A
  199  a
    1  ability
    2  able
    2  about
...
```

Spelling

Another use of a word list is in spell checking. A spell checker compares the words in a document against a list of words, noting those that do not appear on the list.

The list of words in the program below is a SAS dataset that could be created by a step like this:

```
  DATA LEXICON;
    LENGTH CAPITAL $ 16;
    INPUT CAPITAL $;
CARDS;
A ABILITY ABLE ...
```

This program starts with the SAS dataset WORD2 created in the word list program above, matching it against a dictionary called LEXICON, and listing every word that does not match.

```
  DATA _NULL_;
    FILE PRINT;
    MERGE WORD2 (IN=USED) LEXICON (IN=OK);
    BY CAPITAL;
    IF USED AND NOT OK THEN PUT WORD $CHAR64.;
```

The SPELL proc, introduced with SAS release 6.06, does a similar process.

Of course, the dictionary probably would not contain every word used in a document, but it could contain almost all of them. This program would then produce a relatively short list of words, which a writer could scan carefully for misspellings.

Word frequencies

The spell checking program above uses a spelling dictionary, in the form of a SAS dataset called LEXICON. Such dictionaries are often created out of the most frequently used words in a set of documents supposed to be representative of documents in general.

Of course, there is no guarantee that all the words in a dictionary created this way would be spelled correctly, but in practice, it works reasonably well, provided that the documents that are analyzed to create the dictionary are chosen with care.

To make a spelling dictionary this way, you could modify the word list program above to create a list sorted by descending frequency, and then use only words with a frequency greater than 5 or so.

```
PROC FREQ DATA=WORD1 ORDER=INTERNAL;
  TABLES CAPITAL / NOPRINT OUT=WORDFREQ;
DATA LEXICON (KEEP=CAPITAL);
  SET WORDFREQ;
  IF COUNT > 5;
```

Form letters

Form letters can be created in a SAS program, and this might be the easiest approach when several variables in a SAS dataset affect the contents of the body of the letter. A form letter is a kind of prose report, as described in chapter 11.

18 User interface

The characteristics of an interactive program that are apparent when the program is running are called the program's *user interface.*

Users and programs

A user is a person who gets results from a computer without necessarily having any particular programming skill. The point of a user interface is to make a program easy to use. User interfaces for a SAS program can allow the user to control selected details of what the program does.

Many computer programs are user-directed: the program mainly responds to actions initiated by the user. User actions are at the center of the program. The Macintosh family of computers is known for having this kind of program almost exclusively. We emphasize the concept of a user-directed program because this is something a SAS program should not attempt to be. User-directed programs are written in structured programming languages using structured or object-oriented techniques. Even a simple user-directed program would tax the control flow of the SAS System. Instead, a SAS program should tell the user exactly what to decide and when to decide it.

Keeping the user interface separated from the rest of the program is a good practice. Have the user interface routines ask the user all the relevant questions up front, if possible. Then, the user won't have to sit there and wait for the next question while the program is processing data.

This approach has even more important advantages to the programmer. First, it lets you develop the functionality of a program separately from the user interface. It is the easiest way to add a user interface to an existing program. You can change the user interface without rewriting the program.

And you might be able to use the same or nearly the same user interface on different programs, saving work both for you and for any user who uses more than one of those programs.

> Keeping the user interface separate allows the possibility of using a SAS user interface with a non-SAS program or of using a non-SAS user interface with a SAS program.

Windows

In the 1980s, windows became the central feature of the user interfaces of most commercial computer programs. For our purposes, a *window* is a rectangular area displaying logically related data, part or all of which might be visible on the screen at one time.

A window usually contains one or more fields where the user can type. In a standard interaction with a window (on a keyboard-oriented computer) the user types something and presses the enter (or return) key, and the window goes away.

Usually a window is surrounded by a box, or frame, to show the user where the edges of the window are. This is especially helpful when more than one window might be visible at one time.

You should not use lots of different types of windows in a program. Use only as many as your program really needs, to keep things simple for the user. Usually a non-user-directed program can operate with just two types of windows: menus and dialog boxes.

A menu is a list of choices that the user can select from. The easiest way to implement a menu is to associate a code, usually one character, with each option. The user enters one of the codes in the selection field. The program then does whatever is the appropriate response to the user's selection.

```
Selection ===>

1  Print table
2  Print short report
3  Print long report
4  Redefine titles
E  Do something else
```

A menu

```
Selection ===> E

1  Print table
2  Print short report
3  Print long report
4  Redefine titles
E  Do something else
```

A menu selection

A dialog box can ask the user one or more questions, with fields for the user to fill in, or it might just inform the user of something.

```
Enter this month's interest
rate: [            ] percent

Press ENTER to continue.
```

A dialog box

A third type of window occasionally appears. Its main purpose is just to fill up the screen. This type of window is called a *splash* window.

Data step windows

The WINDOW and DISPLAY statements can be used to implement windows in a data step. The WINDOW statement defines a window; then the DISPLAY statement displays it. There are certain characteristics of data step windows that you should keep in mind when designing a program that will use them. A window can cover the whole screen or part of the screen. The first and last line and the first and last column are taken up by a border rectangle. The name of the window appears on the left side of the first line. The second line is taken up by a command line. The third line is reserved as a message area.

Once displayed, a window cannot be removed from the screen for the remainder of the data step. It is automatically removed at the end of the step. The window retains control until the user presses the enter (or return) key. If the window has data entry fields, the window does not return control to the program until the user has entered a value or pressed the enter key in *every* data entry field in the window. However, the user can make the window disappear and cancel the rest of the step at any point by entering the END command on the window's command line.

Because of the persistence of data step windows (and to conserve memory) a step should usually display only one window. The contents of the window can be varied to give the effect of different windows.

Optional fields in dialog boxes can be problematic, because a data step window does not treat any field as optional. To keep from confusing and alienating users, a dialog box with more than one field should not contain any optional fields. Put each optional field in a separate dialog box.

WINDOW

The form of the WINDOW statement is

```
WINDOW window name   COLOR=background color
  ROWS=n COLUMNS=n IROW=n ICOLUMN=n
  GROUP=group name   fields . . .
  ;
```

The window and group names are SAS names used to identify the window in the DISPLAY statement. The window name appears in the upper left corner of the window border, so choose a name that will mean something to the users.

The ROWS= and COLUMNS= options give the size of the window. The IROW= and ICOLUMN= options give the starting location of the window — the coordinates of the upper left corner. The border is not considered in defining the location and size of the window, so you should use at least `IROW=2` and `ICOLUMN=2` to allow one row and one column for the border. However, the command line and message line are included in determining the size of the window, so the number of rows should be at least 3 to allow one line for fields in the window. Also, the width of a window should be 18 or more, to allow the user to type at least 5 characters on the command line. If you omit all these options, reasonable default values are used.

A WINDOW statement typically contains several groups. Think of a group as a set of information that is displayed at one time, such as a menu or dialog box. A group consists of several fields. A field is a string of consecutive characters on one line of the window that are treated as a logical unit. There are three kinds of fields: constant fields, protected variable fields, and unprotected variable fields. The definition of a group also contains pointer controls that determine the location of fields.

The pointer controls used in the WINDOW statement are similar to those of the PUT statement. The # pointer control can be used with a numeric constant or numeric variable to move the line pointer to a particular line. The / pointer control moves the line pointer to the next line. The @ pointer control can be used with a numeric constant or numeric variable to move the column pointer to a particular column on the current line. The + pointer control can be used with a numeric constant or numeric variable to advance the column pointer a certain number of columns.

A constant field is specified as

character constant COLOR=*color*

A character constant is usually a character literal, enclosed in quotes. The COLOR= option specifies the color to be used for the characters in the field.

This group consists of a single constant field, displayed at row 5, column 21:

```
GROUP=HELLO #5 @21 'Greetings, human!'
```

A protected variable field displays the value of a variable. It is defined as

variable *format specification* COLOR=*color* PROTECT=YES

The variable and format specification follow the same rules as a PUT statement. The variable can be a variable name or an explicitly subscripted array reference. The format specification consists of a format name and period and perhaps a width or decimal specification. If the format specification is omitted, the format attribute of the variable is used. The format attribute of the variable could be specified in a FORMAT statement earlier in the step. The default format specifications are `BEST12.` for numeric variables and `$CHAR.` for character variables.

An unprotected variable field allows a value to be entered for a variable. It also displays the value of the variable. If you do not want to display the previous value of the variable, use an assignment statement to set the value to missing before the DISPLAY statement. An unprotected variable field is defined as

variable *format/informat specification* COLOR=*color*

The format and informat used must have the same name. To use an informat and a format that have different names, do not use a format/informat specification for the variable in the WINDOW statement. The variable's informat and format attributes will then be used. You can set those attributes by using an INFORMAT statement and a FORMAT statement earlier in the step.

The $CHAR format and informat are usually used for unprotected character variable fields. The $ format and informat can be used to left-align the field, preventing a user from entering leading blanks. For numeric variables, the BEST format and informat are usually used. (The BEST informat is equivalent to the standard numeric informat.)

A few options are sometimes useful with an unprotected variable field. The `DISPLAY=NO` option keeps the value entered by the user from being displayed, as might be done for a password. The `REQUIRED=YES` option prevents the user from leaving the field blank. The `AUTOSKIP=YES` option moves the cursor to the next unprotected field when the user types the last character in the field. Video features can be specified with the ATTR= option, including `ATTR=HIGHLIGHT` to make a field brighter, `ATTR=UNDERLINE` to underline a field, `ATTR=REV_VIDEO` to display a field in reverse video (with the character and background colors swapped), `ATTR=BLINK` to make the characters in a field blink, or `ATTR=(UNDERLINE, REV_VIDEO, HIGHLIGHT, BLINK)` to do all of these at once. These video features appear only if they are supported by the hardware and system software being used. Many video displays, in particular, do not do underlining.

The colors a window can use depend on the implementation and on the specific hardware you use. However, on color displays, the primary colors, RED, GREEN, and BLUE, the secondary colors, YELLOW, MAGENTA, and CYAN, and the gray scales WHITE, GRAY, and BLACK are usually supported. If you do not specify colors, the default background color is BLACK, and the default character color is WHITE.

DISPLAY

The DISPLAY statement displays a specified window and group, with the window name and group name separated by a period. The usual form of the statement is

```
DISPLAY window name.group name   BLANK;
```

The BLANK option erases the previous contents of the window; it is not necessary the first time a window is displayed or when you want to display the previous contents of the window along with the new fields. The NOINPUT option can be used to prevent the user from entering values into any of the fields in the window (even the command line). The BELL option can be used to make the computer beep when the window is displayed. The NOINPUT option is only really appropriate to display a status window while the user waits for the program to do some processing. The BELL option could be used, as on a toaster, to let the user know that a long process is completed.

In using a window with input fields, the tab key is useful for moving to the beginning of the next field. The user can enter display manager commands such as ZOOM on the command line. The user can enter END on the command line to stop the data step.

Two automatic character variables, _CMD_ and _MSG_, are associated with the first two lines of a window. If _MSG_ is given a value before a DISPLAY statement, that value is displayed on the second line of the window, the message line. If the user enters anything on the command line other than a recognized display manager command, that value is assigned to the _CMD_ variable, which can be used in program statements after the DISPLAY statement.

The first word of every display manager command is made up entirely of letters. Almost any single letter is recognized by display manager as a command, even if it is not valid as a display manager command. If you use the command line for the user to enter options in a window, as in the menus presented below, you must not use options that display manager will regard as its own commands. To be safe, you could avoid using single letters or alphabetic words as options. Numerals and punctuation marks are safe, although you should not try to use ";" or ":" in an option. A mixture of letters and digits in a word is also safe. If you want to use single-letter options, you can have the user precede them with a period or other punctuation mark, as in the example below.

Control flow for menus and dialog boxes

Menus and dialog boxes can be implemented directly using the features of the WINDOW and DISPLAY statement. Each different menu or dialog box is a different group in the window definition; the BLANK option on the DISPLAY statement is necessary when going from one menu or dialog box to another. A menu is followed by a SELECT block with a different WHEN statement for each option a user can choose from, and an OTHERWISE statement in case the user fails to enter an option or enters one incorrectly.

The program below does some simple arithmetic and demonstrates the control flow used with menus and dialog boxes. Because most users expect lowercase and uppercase letters to be equivalent in menus, we present the selection codes using uppercase letters, and then translate the user's response to uppercase using the UPCASE function. The quit option is presented as `.Q` instead of just `Q` because `Q` is recognized by display manager as a command.

The SCAN function is used to extract the first command from the command line. Thus, the option will still be recognized even if it is not entered at the left side of the command line or if another command follows it. The COMPRESS function is needed because the _CMD_ variable might include extra spaces under some SAS implementations.

The DISPLAY statement creates an observation loop just like that of the SET statement. Thus, the DISPLAY statement and the SELECT block that follow it are executed repeatedly, until either the user enters the END command, or the user enters the `.Q` option, which leads the program to the STOP statement.

It is sometimes necessary to set values to missing or zero before a DISPLAY statement for a dialog box, so that previously entered values will not be displayed again. In this case, it is done automatically by the observation loop.

```
OPTIONS MISSING=' ';
  DATA _NULL_;
    WINDOW MATH
        ROWS=6 COLUMNS=36 IROW=7 ICOLUMN=16
        GROUP=MENU
        #1 @2 '1   Add two numbers'
        #2 @2 '2   Multiply two numbers'
        #4 @2 '.Q  Quit'
        GROUP=ADD
        #1 @2 'Enter the two numbers to add.'
        #3 @2 TERM1 BEST15. ATTR=REV_VIDEO
        +1 '+'
        +1 TERM2 BEST15. ATTR=REV_VIDEO
        GROUP=SUM
        #1 @2 'The sum is ' SUM BEST16. PROTECT=YES
        #3 @2 'Press ENTER to continue.'
        GROUP=MULTIPLY
        #1 @2 'Enter the two numbers to multiply.'
        #3 @2 FACTOR1 BEST15. ATTR=REV_VIDEO
        +1 '+'
        +1 FACTOR2 BEST15. ATTR=REV_VIDEO
        GROUP=PRODUCT
        #1 @2 'The product is ' PRODUCT BEST18. PROTECT=YES
        #3 @2 'Press ENTER to continue.'
        ;
```

```
    DISPLAY MATH.MENU BLANK; * Menu;
    SELECT(SCAN(COMPRESS(UPCASE(_CMD_)), 1, ';'));
      WHEN('1') DO;
        DISPLAY MATH.ADD BLANK; * Addition dialog box;
        SUM = SUM(0, TERM1, TERM2);
        DISPLAY MATH.SUM BLANK; * Sum dialog box;
        END;
      WHEN('2') DO;
        DISPLAY MATH.MULTIPLY BLANK; * Multiply dialog box;
        IF FACTOR1 AND FACTOR2 THEN PRODUCT = FACTOR1*FACTOR2;
        ELSE PRODUCT = 0;
        DISPLAY MATH.PRODUCT BLANK; * Product dialog box;
        END;
      WHEN('.Q') STOP;
      OTHERWISE DO;
        IF _CMD_ = ' ' THEN _MSG_ = 'Enter option on line above.';
        ELSE _MSG_ = 'Option not recognized.';
        END;
      END;
RUN;
```

```
Command ===> 1

 1   Add two numbers
 2   Multiply two numbers

 .Q  Quit
```

```
Command ===>

 Enter the two numbers to add.

 [2               ]  +  [25              ]
```

```
Command ===>

 The sum is                 27

 Press ENTER to continue.
```

```
Command ===> 2

 1   Add two numbers
 2   Multiply two numbers

 .Q  Quit
```

```
Command ===>

Enter the two numbers to multiply.

 .125                  +  128
```

```
Command ===>

 The product is                       16

 Press ENTER to continue.
```

```
Command ===> .q

 1   Add two numbers
 2   Multiply two numbers

 .Q  Quit
```

Program parameters

A more typical use of a user interface for a SAS program involves one or more dialog boxes in which values are entered that become values for macrovariables that control the way the rest of the steps in the program operate.

The step below gets values for two macrovariables. It also provide an example of the use of a title in a dialog box. The title provides reassurance that the user is running the right program. The IF . . . THEN statement shows a simple form of validating the value of a variable entered on a screen; if the user did not enter a positive number, the program substitutes the value 1.

```
  DATA _NULL_;
    WINDOW REPORT
        ROWS=9 COLUMNS=52 IROW=2 ICOLUMN=17
        GROUP=PREL
        #1 @18 'Preliminary Report'
        #3 @2 'Name of input file: '
        FILE $31. ATTR=REV_VIDEO REQUIRED=YES
        #5 @2 'Number of copies of report: ' N 2. ATTR=REV_VIDEO
        #7 @2 'Press ENTER to continue.';
    DISPLAY REPORT.PREL;
    IF N <= 0 THEN N = 1;
    CALL SYMPUT('INFILE', FILE);
    CALL SYMPUT('NCOPIES', PUT(N, Z2.));
    STOP; * The STOP statement here is essential
            to keep the step from looping. ;
RUN;
```

```
Command ===>

                  Preliminary Report

 Name of input file: [                              ]

 Number of copies of report: [  ]

 Press ENTER to continue.
```

This use of macrovariables is discussed in chapter 12, "Flexcode." Any of the flexcode techniques can be given a friendlier appearance by combining them with the user interface techniques described in this chapter.

Program menu

You can use a menu together with an %INCLUDE statement to let a user execute several programs from the same initial menu. The user won't even have to think about the fact that they are separate programs.

```
DATA _NULL_;
  WINDOW BASEBALL COLOR=GREEN
      ROWS=13 COLUMNS=27 IROW=8 ICOLUMN=27
      GROUP=MENU
      #1 @2 '1   Batting'
      #2 @2 '2   Pitching'
      #3 @2 '3   Fielding'
      #4 @2 '4   Roster'
      #5 @2 '5   Coaches'
      #6 @2 '6   Office Staff'
      #7 @2 '7   Schedule'
      #8 @2 '8   Stadium'
      #9 @2 '9   Budget'
      #11 @2 '.Q  Quit'
      ;
  DISPLAY BASEBALL.MENU;
  SELECT(UPCASE(COMPRESS(_CMD_)));
    WHEN('1') CALL SYMPUT('PROGRAM', '%INCLUDE "BATTING.SAS" ');
    WHEN('2') CALL SYMPUT('PROGRAM', '%INCLUDE "PITCHING.SAS"');
    WHEN('3') CALL SYMPUT('PROGRAM', '%INCLUDE "FIELDING.SAS"');
    WHEN('4') CALL SYMPUT('PROGRAM', '%INCLUDE "ROSTER.SAS"  ');
    WHEN('5') CALL SYMPUT('PROGRAM', '%INCLUDE "COACH.SAS"   ');
    WHEN('6') CALL SYMPUT('PROGRAM', '%INCLUDE "STAFF.SAS"   ');
    WHEN('7') CALL SYMPUT('PROGRAM', '%INCLUDE "SCHEDULE.SAS"');
    WHEN('8') CALL SYMPUT('PROGRAM', '%INCLUDE "STADIUM.SAS" ');
    WHEN('9') CALL SYMPUT('PROGRAM', '%INCLUDE "BUDGET.SAS"  ');
    WHEN('.Q') CALL SYMPUT('PROGRAM', '');
    OTHERWISE DO;
      IF _CMD_ = ' ' THEN _MSG_ = 'Enter option on line above.';
      ELSE _MSG_ = 'Option not recognized.';
      DELETE;
      END;
    END;
```

```
    STOP;
RUN;
&PROGRAM;
```

```
Command ===> 5

 1   Batting
 2   Pitching
 3   Fielding
 4   Roster
 5   Coaches
 6   Office Staff
 7   Schedule
 8   Stadium
 9   Budget

 .Q  Quit
```

```
%INCLUDE "COACH.SAS";
```

Menu bars

Display manager windows can have menu bars instead of command lines. A menu bar gives the user a limited number of selections to choose from on a single line, with one option highlighted; the user can use the left and right cursor keys to move from one selection to the next, then press the enter key to make a selection.

The PMENU proc, introduced in SAS release 6.06, defines menu bars to be used with display manager windows. A menu bar can have vertically oriented "pull-down" menus and dialog boxes associated with it — a selection on a menu bar or pull-down menu can lead to a pull-down menu or dialog box. The new MENU= option in the WINDOW statement makes it possible to use a menu bar with a data step window.

The end result of a menu bar is the same as a command line: a string is returned to the program through the _CMD_ variable. However, the process looks different to the user.

A menu bar for the program above could be coded like this:

```
PROC PMENU CAT=WORK.BALL;
  MENU BASEBALL;
    ITEM 'Bat'      SELECTION=B1;
    ITEM 'Pitch'    SELECTION=B2;
    ITEM 'Field'    SELECTION=B3;
    ITEM 'Roster'   SELECTION=B4;
    ITEM 'Coach'    SELECTION=B5;
    ITEM 'Office'   SELECTION=B6;
    ITEM 'Schedule' SELECTION=B7;
    ITEM 'Stadium'  SELECTION=B8;
    ITEM 'Budget'   SELECTION=B9;
    ITEM 'Quit'     SELECTION=B10;
```

```
        SELECTION B1 '1';
        SELECTION B2 '2';
        SELECTION B3 '3';
        SELECTION B4 '4';
        SELECTION B5 '5';
        SELECTION B6 '6';
        SELECTION B7 '7';
        SELECTION B8 '8';
        SELECTION B9 '9';
        SELECTION B10 '.Q';
QUIT;
```

The CAT=WORK.BALL option identifies a catalog where the resulting menu definition will be stored. The MENU statement, because it is the first MENU statement in the run group, defines a menu bar. The ITEM statements identify the options to appear on the menu bar and associate a SELECTION statement with each one. The SELECTION statements identify the commands to be submitted — equivalent to the user typing that command on the command line.

The resulting menu would be associated with a window in a window definition like this one:

```
WINDOW BASEBALL COLOR=GREEN MENU=WORK.BALL.BASEBALL
    #1 'Baseball';
...
DISPLAY BASEBALL;
```

These statements could be substituted for the WINDOW and DISPLAY statements in the program above without making any other changes in the program. Notice that the complexity of the menu definition is made up for by a simplified window definition. (However, a window definition does have to have at least one field.)

Instead of being associated with a single selection, a menu item can be identified with a pull-down menu, using the MENU= option, or a dialog box, using the DIALOG= option. The pull-down menu would be defined using a MENU statement and ITEM statements later in the same run group. The dialog box would be defined by a combination of DIALOG, TEXT, CHECKBOX, RADIOBOX, and RBUTTON statements later in the same run group.

A PMENU dialog box can contain text fields, where a user can type information; *radio buttons,* to let the user pick one from a list; and *check boxes* for yes/no options. There are also two buttons in every PMENU dialog box: an OK button, to indicate that the user is done entering values, and a Cancel button, to return to the menu that brought up the dialog box.

In the PMENU proc, the first statements used in defining a dialog box are the DIALOG statement and a TEXT statement:

```
DIALOG name command;
  TEXT #line @column text;
```

The command is a quoted string that can contain references to the radio buttons, check boxes, and text fields in the dialog box. The TEXT statement contains a quoted string that appears in the dialog box to explain the purpose of the dialog box to the user. The # and @ controls have the same meaning as in the WINDOW statement. There can be several TEXT statements, if needed.

Additional TEXT statements can identify input fields. This form of the TEXT statement is:

```
TEXT #line @column LEN=length;
```

The # and @ terms identify the location of the field. The LEN= term specifies the length of the field.

The value entered in the text field is referred to in the command string by an at-sign followed by the number of the TEXT statement, counting only TEXT statements that contain input fields. For example, for the text field defined by the second input field TEXT statement in a dialog box, the characters `@2` would appear in the command string.

These statements define a dialog box that lets the user pick a number:

```
DIALOG PICK '.E=@1';
  TEXT #1 @1 'Pick a number from';
  TEXT #2 @1 '1 to 4:';
  TEXT #2 @9 LEN=1;
```

If the user types a 3, the command returned to the program, in the _CMD_ variable, is "`.E=3`". On the other hand, the user could just as easily type an M, and the dialog box would return the command "`.E=M`".

To let a user choose from among a short list of options, radio buttons can be used. A set of radio buttons is called a *radio box* and is defined by a RADIOBOX statement followed by several RBUTTON statements:

```
RADIOBOX DEFAULT=number;
  RBUTTON NONE #line @column string;
  RBUTTON #line @column string;
  RBUTTON #line @column string;
  ...
```

The DEFAULT= term identifies the radio button in the radio box that is selected when the dialog box is first displayed. Each RBUTTON statement identifies the location of the radio button and a text string. The string is displayed to the right of the radio button and is included in the command returned by the dialog box. In the command string, a number sign followed by the number of the RADIOBOX statement refers to the text values for that radio box. For example, the text from the first radio box would be referred to as `#1`. However, if the NONE option appears in the RBUTTON statement, the text from that radio button is not used in the command. By convention, the radio buttons in a radio box are usually oriented vertically — in the same column on subsequent lines.

The statements below define a dialog box in which a user can choose a number from 1 to 4 using radio buttons. The command returned is the same as with the text field.

```
DIALOG PICKRAD '.E=#1';
  TEXT #1 @1 'Pick a number:';
  RADIOBOX DEFAULT=1;
    RBUTTON #2 @2 '1';
    RBUTTON #3 @2 '2';
    RBUTTON #4 @2 '3';
    RBUTTON #5 @2 '4';
```

Finally, a check box is defined in a CHECKBOX statement, which is nearly identical to the RBUTTON statement. The statement is:

```
CHECKBOX #line @column string;
```

To have the check box on, or checked, when the dialog box is first displayed, use the ON option:

```
CHECKBOX ON #line @column string;
```

As with a radio button, the string is displayed next to the check box and is included in the command returned by the dialog box if the check box is selected. An ampersand followed by the number of the CHECKBOX statement refers to the check box string in the command string. For the first CHECKBOX statement in the dialog box, the characters `&1` would be used.

Putting this all together, these statements define a menu bar, pull-down menus, and dialog boxes that let the user pick a number from 1 to 4 in several different ways:

```
PROC PMENU CATALOG=WORK.DECISION;
  MENU NUMBER;
    ITEM 'Menu' MENU=M;
    ITEM 'Dialog' MENU=D;
    ITEM '1' SELECTION=PICK1;
    ITEM '2' SELECTION=PICK2;
    ITEM '3' SELECTION=PICK3;
    ITEM '4' SELECTION=PICK4;
    ITEM 'Quit' SELECTION=QUIT;
    SELECTION PICK1 '.E=1';
    SELECTION PICK2 '.E=2';
    SELECTION PICK3 '.E=3';
    SELECTION PICK4 '.E=4';
    SELECTION QUIT 'END';
  MENU M;
    ITEM '1' SELECTION=MPICK1;
    ITEM '2' SELECTION=MPICK2;
    ITEM '3' SELECTION=MPICK3;
    ITEM '4' SELECTION=MPICK4;
    SELECTION MPICK1 '.E=1';
    SELECTION MPICK2 '.E=2';
    SELECTION MPICK3 '.E=3';
    SELECTION MPICK4 '.E=4';
```

```
    MENU D;
      ITEM 'Text' DIALOG=TEXT;
      ITEM 'Boxes' DIALOG=BOXES;
    DIALOG TEXT '.E=@1';
      TEXT #1 @1 'Pick a number from';
      TEXT #2 @1 '1 to 4:';
      TEXT #2 @9 LEN=1;
    DIALOG BOXES '.-%1&1';
      TEXT #1 @1 'Describe number:';
      RADIOBOX DEFAULT=1;
        RBUTTON #2 @2 'Even';
        RBUTTON #3 @2 'Odd';
      CHECKBOX #5 @2 '>2';
QUIT;
```

The menu could be used with this data step:

```
DM 'PMENU ON';
  DATA _NULL_;
    WINDOW NUMBER MENU=WORK.DECISION.NUMBER #1 ' ';
    DISPLAY NUMBER;
    C = COMPRESS(_CMD_);
    SELECT;
      WHEN(C =: '.E=1') NUMBER = 1;
      WHEN(C =: '.E=2') NUMBER = 2;
      WHEN(C =: '.E=3') NUMBER = 3;
      WHEN(C =: '.E=4') NUMBER = 4;
      WHEN(C =: '.-') DO;
        NUMBER = 1;
        IF INDEX(C, 'Even') THEN NUMBER + 1;
        IF INDEX(C, '>2')   THEN NUMBER + 2;
        END;
      OTHERWISE NUMBER = 0;
      END;
    IF NUMBER THEN _MSG_ = 'Number ' || PUT(NUMBER, 1.);
RUN;
DM 'PMENU OFF';
```

The initial menu bar displayed in the window (in place of the command line) is:

```
Menu  Dialog  1  2  3  4  Quit
```

The exact appearance of PMENU menus varies by implementation.

If the user selects the `Menu` option (perhaps by using the arrow keys and enter key), this pull-down menu appears:

```
1
2
3
4
```

Selecting one of these items returns the command "`.E=1`", "`.E=2`", "`.E=3`", or "`.E=4`", respectively. The data step then checks for these values of _CMD_ in the SELECT block.

Selecting `Dialog` in the menu bar brings up this menu:

```
Text
Boxes
```

Selecting `Text` brings up the first dialog box, looking something like this:

```
Pick a number from
1 to 4: _

    OK     Cancel
```

If the user presses the `OK` button, the character entered in the text field, if any, is combined with the characters "`.E=`" to form the command that is returned. The user can also press the `Cancel` button to return to the menu.

Selecting `Boxes` brings up the second dialog box:

```
Describe number:
 * Even
 o Odd

 _ >2

   OK     Cancel
```

The other four options on the menu bar are associated with specific commands. The END command, associated with the `Quit` option, is actually a display manager command, so it is executed, rather than returning control to the data step. The END command ends the data step when it is entered in a display manager window.

After the user makes a selection, the corresponding command value is returned to the data step in the _CMD_ variable. The data step then has to make sense of it — not too difficult in this case, but potentially very complicated in a real application.

It is possible on some computers to associate a color with an item in a dialog box, using the COLOR= option on the TEXT, RBUTTON, or CHECKBOX statement.

Other windows

There are macro %WINDOW and %DISPLAY statements that correspond to the WINDOW and DISPLAY statements described above. They work in basically the same way and might be more convenient in programs where macrolanguage features are used for meta-control flow.

More intricate user interfaces can be defined using program screens created using the BUILD proc, which is part of the SAS/AF product. Program screens use a different language, Screen Control Language or SCL, which has many of the same characteristics as SAS data step syntax, but with completely different I/O syntax and several additional features. Each character position on a program screen can be assigned a color separately, and there is similarly detailed control of other features, including function keys. The BUILD proc creates a few other screen types, particularly menu screens.

However, SAS/AF windows have their drawbacks. They cannot be defined in a program file, so they tend to take longer to create, and integrating them into a SAS program is a relatively cumbersome process. They also use much more memory, take longer to run, have more bugs, and cannot be moved as easily from one operating system to another.

When they work, the simpler features of the data step windows are an advantage — and for most programs, they are all the user interface you will need.

Line mode

The SAS System can be run interactively with a line-mode or teletype-style user interface instead of the full-screen interface of display manager. The line-mode interface has the advantages of running faster and using less memory (and, in some SAS implementations, less temporary storage). However, line mode has none of the advantages that windows make possible. The configuration options necessary to run the SAS System in line mode vary by implementation.

In a data step, the INPUT and PUT statement can be used for line mode input from the user or output to the screen — which is called *console I/O*. The specific form of the FILENAME statements varies by operating system. Under MS-DOS, these statements can be used:

```
FILENAME STDIN TERMINAL;
FILENAME STDOUT TERMINAL;
```

Console I/O can be done even in a display manager session.

The mechanics of the line mode user interface are much like those of the data step windows. Compare this line mode version of the math program to the window version presented earlier:

```
DATA _NULL_;
  INFILE STDIN UNBUFFERED;
  FILE STDOUT;

  PUT 'MATH  Select option:'
      / @5 '1  Add two numbers'
      / @5 '2  Multiply two numbers'
      / @5 'Q  Quit';
  INPUT LINE $80.;
  SELECT(SCAN(UPCASE(LINE), 1, ' ;'));
    WHEN('1') DO;
      PUT 'Enter the two numbers to add.';
      INPUT LINE $80.;
      TERM1 = SCAN(LINE, 1, ' ,;+*&');
      TERM2 = SCAN(LINE, 2, ' ,;+*&');
      SUM = SUM(0, TERM1, TERM2);
      PUT 'The sum is ' SUM :BEST16.;
      END;
    WHEN('2') DO;
      PUT 'Enter the two numbers to multiply.';
      INPUT LINE $80.;
      FACTOR1 = SCAN(LINE, 1, ' ,;+*&');
      FACTOR2 = SCAN(LINE, 2, ' ,;+*&');
      IF FACTOR1 AND FACTOR2 THEN PRODUCT = FACTOR1*FACTOR2;
      ELSE PRODUCT = 0;
      PUT 'The product is ' PRODUCT :BEST18.;
      END;
    WHEN('Q') STOP;
    OTHERWISE ;
    END;
RUN;
```

```
MATH  Select option:
    1  Add two numbers
    2  Multiply two numbers
    Q  Quit
1
Enter the two numbers to add.
2, 25
The sum is 27
MATH  Select option:
    1  Add two numbers
    2  Multiply two numbers
    Q  Quit
2
Enter the two numbers to multiply.
  .125*128
The product is 16
MATH  Select option:
    1  Add two numbers
    2  Multiply two numbers
    Q  Quit
q
```

The baseball example is also readily translated to line mode:

```
  DATA _NULL_;
    INFILE STDIN UNBUFFERED;
    FILE STDOUT;

    PUT 'BASEBALL  Select option:'
        / '1  Batting'
        / '2  Pitching'
        / '3  Fielding'
        / '4  Roster'
        / '5  Coaches'
        / '6  Office Staff'
        / '7  Schedule'
        / '8  Stadium'
        / '9  Budget'
        / 'Q  Quit';
    INPUT ACTION $1.;
    SELECT(UPCASE(ACTION));
      WHEN('1') CALL SYMPUT('PROGRAM', '%INCLUDE "BATTING.SAS" ');
      WHEN('2') CALL SYMPUT('PROGRAM', '%INCLUDE "PITCHING.SAS"');
      WHEN('3') CALL SYMPUT('PROGRAM', '%INCLUDE "FIELDING.SAS"');
      WHEN('4') CALL SYMPUT('PROGRAM', '%INCLUDE "ROSTER.SAS"  ');
      WHEN('5') CALL SYMPUT('PROGRAM', '%INCLUDE "COACH.SAS"   ');
      WHEN('6') CALL SYMPUT('PROGRAM', '%INCLUDE "STAFF.SAS"   ');
      WHEN('7') CALL SYMPUT('PROGRAM', '%INCLUDE "SCHEDULE.SAS"');
      WHEN('8') CALL SYMPUT('PROGRAM', '%INCLUDE "STADIUM.SAS" ');
      WHEN('9') CALL SYMPUT('PROGRAM', '%INCLUDE "BUDGET.SAS"  ');
      WHEN('Q') CALL SYMPUT('PROGRAM', '');
      OTHERWISE DELETE;
      END;
    STOP;
RUN;
&PROGRAM;
```

```
BASEBALL  Select option:
1  Batting
2  Pitching
3  Fielding
4  Roster
5  Coaches
6  Office Staff
7  Schedule
8  Stadium
9  Budget
Q  Quit
8
```

```
%INCLUDE "STADIUM.SAS";
```

19 Power tools

This chapter is about the pragmatic details of a SAS programmer's work, other than programming. Having the right equipment and information and knowing the right people can make the job easier.

Hardware

To do ordinary computer programming, you need a computer, a screen, a keyboard, and so on — hardware.

Computers

Computers are, first of all, classified according to software compatibility. For example, a program compiled for MS-DOS computers will, if coded carefully, run on any MS-DOS computer, but not on other kinds of computers. Software compatibility depends on several factors in a computer's design, including the central processor, ROM, and numerous design details.

The central processor, or CPU, is the chip that actually runs programs, turning instructions into actions. Each processor model recognizes a certain set of instructions. Often the instruction set of a new processor includes all the instructions of another processor along with some new ones, a condition called *backward compatibility*. This is how a family of processors comes about.

The two most popular central processor families are the Intel 8086 family, including the 8088, 80286, 80386, and so on, used in almost all MS-DOS computers; and the Motorola 68000 family, including the 68020, 68030, and so on, used in most other microcomputers.

> Some people, including computer manufacturers, also use the term *CPU* to refer to the whole computer. They do this to emphasize the fact that the computer cannot be used without additional equipment, such as a screen and keyboard.

ROM is *read-only memory*. A computer's ROM usually contains the most important routines, especially those related to starting the computer and managing the most fundamental aspects of I/O. If programs use ROM routines directly, the programs will run correctly only on computers that have the specific ROM routines they use.

After computers are classified by software compatibility, they can be ranked according to power. Computers vary vastly in power, even within a software compatibility class. A simplified measure of the power of a computer is its mips rating, telling how many million instructions per second the computer could theoretically execute. Computers range in power from less than 1 mips to over 50 mips; the top end of the range goes up year by year.

The size of a computer used to be some indication of its power, but that is no longer reliable. Mainframes as a class were, not too long ago, a hundred times as powerful as microcomputers, but not any more; the power gap is now unremarkable, with some newer microcomputer models actually faster than some current mainframe models.

The model of central processor used is the main thing that determines the power of a computer. The clock speed, which determines how fast the central processor works, also makes a difference and is an often cited characteristic of a computer. Various details of the computer's design also affect its mips rating.

The mips rating of a computer is not a perfect indication of how it will perform on actual tasks. Other details, especially the amount of memory and the speed of storage devices, affect the speed of typical processing.

An especially important detail for programs that use floating-point numbers, including all SAS programs, is a math coprocessor, a second chip that works alongside the central processor. If a computer has a math coprocessor, that chip does floating point arithmetic and certain mathematical functions instead of the central processor. Each math coprocessor is designed to work with a specific central processor. Like central processors, math coprocessors have different models and clock speeds that determine how fast they work. The speed of a math coprocessor is rated in megaflops, millions of floating point operations per second.

The amount of RAM is an important consideration. RAM is random access memory, the ordinary memory used by programs. Running a typical SAS program, the SAS System might use 1 megabyte of RAM, but some programs require much more, and some procs run faster with more RAM available.

If you have to choose between computers on the basis of power, it's best if you can measure it yourself rather than relying on standardized ratings. First identify or construct a program that is typical of the kinds of things your programs, especially your more demanding programs, do. Run it on different computers, and then compare run times.

Screen

Computer screens differ mainly in their graphics capabilities.

Some screens can display only text, or characters, in fixed positions on the screen. Most screens, though, can display either text or graphics. Screens might have separate modes: a text mode, which is faster but can display only text, and a graphics mode. The text mode might allow the computer software to select between a few different character sets, or *fonts*, built into the display hardware.

Screens are also rated by the number of colors they can display. The simplest possibility, a monochrome screen, can display only two colors — which are usually described as black and white, regardless of what colors they actually are. Other screens can display 4, 16, 32, 256, or more colors simultaneously.

The resolution of a screen is important with graphics; it determines how precisely a graphic image can be shown. On the other hand, a higher resolution takes more processing for the computer and is correspondingly slower. The resolution of a screen is often expressed as the total number of dots or pixels across and down the screen. It can also be expressed in terms of the size of the pixels.

Sometimes screens have different modes, which work at different speeds and allow different numbers of colors or use different resolutions.

The SAS System is primarily text-oriented software, so it can be displayed acceptably on any ordinary computer screen. The SAS/GRAPH product, though, displays graphics only on specific kinds of screens.

Input devices

Computers are controlled through keyboards and other user input devices. If you are choosing a keyboard, you could look for the less common characters used in SAS programs, such as the braces, { and }, and the vertical bar. However, nearly all keyboards now have a more or less standard layout that includes these characters.

Several kinds of input devices can be used with some computers to identify positions on the screen. A mouse is a small device that is rolled around on any flat surface to move a pointer on the screen. A trackball is a ball that the user moves in any direction to move a pointer on the screen. A graphics tablet is a rectangle whose positions correspond to positions on the screen; the user identifies screen positions by pointing at the graphics tablet with a pen-like device.

Any one of these devices can be used to speed up processes like text editing, but the mouse is the simplest and most commonly used one. In the near future, the SAS Display Manager System will be supporting the use of a mouse for editing and menus.

Storage devices

Storage requires a medium and a device to access it. The most common storage mediums are disks, in various forms, and tape, either on reels or in cartridges.

Whatever their physical form, computer storage is measured by these characteristics:

- **fixed** or **removable**, whether the medium is a permanent part of the storage device or can be removed in order to use several volumes with the same device
- **read-only**, **write-once**, or **erasable**, whether a volume cannot be written to, can be written to only once, or can be erased and written to repeatedly
- **capacity**, the amount that can be stored on a volume
- **direct access** or **sequential only**, whether data on the volume can be accessed by address (usually true of disks), or only by reading through the volume in order (usually true of tapes)
- **access time**, the time it takes the storage device to find a location on the volume
- **transfer rate**, how fast data is transferred between the storage device and the computer, which might depend on whether you're reading or writing and on other things
- **sturdiness** of the device and the medium, the specific physical requirements they have about temperature, dust, humidity, handling, and so on, and how long they last

For heavily used files, such as the SAS System files, access time is the most critical characteristic. It can have as much impact on the speed of a program as the computer itself can. The transfer rate of the device a SAS dataset is on can also affect the speed of a program. The SAS System files and the WORK library should usually be installed on the fastest storage device connected to a computer.

No storage medium is completely safe. For this reason, it is standard practice to keep copies, called *backup copies* or *backups*, of all important data files. To protect important files from fire and other hazards, the backup copies can be kept at a separate location.

Backup copies do not necessarily have to be exact copies of files; you just have to be able to reconstruct a file from the backup data. For example, if the data in a SAS dataset is extracted from a text file, it might be adequate to keep the text file and the SAS program that creates the SAS dataset from it. Backup copies of files are often kept in compressed form.

Some computer systems have automatic backup systems that make copies of every file you create. If possible, you should have those systems skip over the files you use with the SAS System, especially the log and the WORK library. Normal-format SAS datasets contain header information that makes direct access of the SAS dataset possible. This header information becomes incorrect whenever the file is copied or moved, unless the copy is made by a SAS program. The COPY proc is the best way to make backup copies of SAS datasets.

As disk files are modified, they eventually get fragmented, with different parts of the file scattered around the disk. This uses up extra space on the disk and slows down file access, so many people periodically *defragment* their disks using a program usually described as a *disk optimizing program*. This program moves files around on the disk. However, moving a normal-format SAS dataset can invalidate any address information in its header. So you should not let the disk optimizing program work on some forms of SAS datasets. One approach you can take is to copy all the SAS datasets to another storage volume (using the COPY proc, of course) before optimizing, and then copy them back afterward.

Printers

Printers have the same characteristics of graphics, colors, fonts, and resolution that are described above for screens. Printers generally have fewer colors and higher resolution than screens. Many printers work only with a few specific paper sizes; others allow a range of paper sizes.

Printers also vary in the way they expect data to be sent to them. The special characteristics of a printer are usually handled by an operating system routine called a *printer driver*. Like computers, printers usually use either the ASCII or EBCDIC character sets or variations on them. Along with the text to be printed, printers also expect certain kinds of print control characters or else a set of commands in a particular page description language.

Some very old mainframe printers have a very limited character set, consisting of capital letters, digits, and a few punctuation marks. Other characters sent to those printers print either as blanks or not at all.

Multiuser computers and terminals

Multiuser computers tend to be mysterious. You don't ordinarily get to see the computer. It could be halfway around the world somewhere. You can't deal with it except through a terminal, which might be connected directly or indirectly to the computer. Unless you know the computer operators, it's hard to find out much about the computer. They could take away the computer and plug in a new one and not tell you, and you might never notice.

Nevertheless, it's a good idea to know the basic facts about the computer you work on, including its manufacturer and model name, the model names of the fixed storage devices you use, and the operating system(s), and the terminal type you use. This is the most important information in dealing with questions of efficiency and compatibility.

A terminal is usually just a screen, a keyboard, and a bit of communications hardware. However, it is also possible to use a computer as a terminal. This is called *terminal emulation*, and is usually done with a combination of hardware and software. If you're doing terminal emulation, you should know what kind of terminal you are emulating.

In sharing a computer with other users, the speed of the computer on your job depends on what else it's working on at the same time. Many systems slow down around 9 a.m., speed up a bit around lunchtime, slow down a lot by midafternoon, and then practically zip along by about suppertime. This pattern might be shifted some if most of the users are in a different time zone. It is helpful to know the performance patterns of the computer you work on.

Most multiuser computers have both a foreground and a background. Foreground programs let you interact with the screen while the program is running. Background jobs let you run a program completely independent of your terminal. At most computer systems, background jobs are encouraged, because they give the computer operators more flexibility in managing the system. If you really want to be nice, you can run all your large programs as background jobs overnight.

More than one computer system

If there are several computer systems around that you can use, you should try to learn their strengths and weaknesses. In particular, a mainframe might have more storage capacity, while a desktop computer is likely to have a faster response time for most work.

Software

The software you can use depends to a great extent on the computer you work on. On a single-user computer, you might be able to equip yourself with the specific software that will be most useful for you.

Software for multiuser computers tends to cost a small fortune, and the selection is pretty limited, but on the other hand, you can usually use all the software that anyone else has installed on the same system, at no extra charge. If you're interested in using a certain software package, you might ask about it rather than just assuming it isn't there. Sometimes the SAS System, for example, is installed on a mainframe by the system operators just for computer performance evaluation work, and they might not think to tell anyone else that it's there.

The SAS System

After you find the SAS System, your next question should be what SAS release you have and what SAS products are installed.

The SAS release number is announced at the beginning of the SAS log. The whole number part of the release number is the version number. Ideally, the SAS manuals you have should be for the same release, but they must at least be for the same version.

There is no simple way to find out what SAS products (other than base SAS) are installed on a computer. The best way is to try to run the procs in a product. Don't worry about syntax; just submit a step consisting of a PROC statement. If the SAS supervisor can't find the proc, it will say so. An error message saying that a statement or option is missing from the proc step is a likely sign that the product is installed.

Operating system

The operating system is the most fundamental software on a computer, after it's up and running. It intermediates between all other programs and the computer hardware. It also contains routines for handling files.

Almost every operating system has a command-line interface that lets you access operating system routines by entering commands. For example, there is usually a COPY command to copy files and other commands for that rename, list, and delete files.

In most environments, you can access the operating system in SAS programs using the X statement. Thus, operating system commands for file handling can be made part of a SAS program.

Text editor

Programming tends to involve a lot of text editing. As a programmer, you should use the best text editor you can find, and get to know all of its shortcuts that are useful to you. Being a power user of a text editor can make the editing process go twice as fast. (Typing skill helps too.)

Display manager's program editor window is significantly improved with release 6.06, and there's no reason not to use if it has the features that are important to you. Most full-page text editors, though, have friendlier file handling and more editing features and command-key shortcuts. On multiuser computers, there is probably a text editor on the system that almost everyone uses; you should see if you prefer it. For desktop computers, text editors are inexpensive programs. If you use a word processing program, you might like to use it for text editing. Also, most compilers come with text editors.

Sort package

Almost every computer system has sorting capabilities, either as an operating system command or as a separate program, or both. It's usually possible to do your sorting inside your SAS programs, using the SORT proc, but sometimes another sorting routine might do the job more easily or efficiently. You might, for example, sort a text file before reading it rather than sorting a SAS dataset.

Database management systems

In many organizations and projects, database management systems, or DBMSs, are where the interesting data is. Being conversant with the DBMSs around you can make it easier to get supplied with data. In some cases you might be able to access DBMS data directly in SAS programs using the appropriate interface engines.

Document processing

Word processing and page layout programs can be useful programs to use along with SAS programs in preparing reports. You can prepare a table in a SAS program, and then fine-tune its format in a word processing program, perhaps, or use a page layout program to combine it with other tables and text for printing.

RAM disk

A RAM disk is a block of memory set up to act like a storage device. The use of a RAM disk with a SAS program can speed it up considerably if you have RAM to spare.

Small, simple utility programs, usually distributed as part of a package of utility programs, set up RAM disks. Once set up, they can be used like a disk, but with two important differences: they are much faster, and they are erased when the computer is turned off or rebooted. Moderate-sized temporary data files are good candidates for being "stored" in a RAM disk; putting a frequently-used file in a RAM disk might speed up a program by a factor of 2 or more. But remember that RAM disks are volatile and might disappear in a system crash at any moment. Don't put anything in a RAM disk that you can't afford to lose.

Computer security

There are three main hazards in computer operations: data lost; secrets revealed; and unauthorized programs or uses that might do damage or use up computer resources. Backup copies are the main defense against loss of data. Computers can also have security systems that prevent certain people from erasing certain files. The same security systems can, to an extent, prevent unauthorized people from reading files. Files can also be protected by physically disconnecting them from the computer and locking them up. There are also encryption programs, which can actually make it impossible for a person who does not have the right password to read a file.

ID codes and secret passwords, if used correctly, keep unauthorized people from logging onto a multiuser computer. Computer system monitoring can look for patterns of unauthorized access. A single-user computer can be protected by various kinds of physical locks that prevent the computer from even being turned on. These devices can also guard against theft, which is a significant threat to computers in some places.

Viruses, self-replicating programs that can spread from one disk to another and often interfere with computer operations, are a threat to all classes of computers. For microcomputers, there are various antiviral programs that can be used to detect viruses, prevent them from spreading, and erase them. However, no antiviral program could protect against all unknown future strains of viruses. Viruses can only spread from one disk to another on a computer when the target disk is unlocked and mounted at the same time as the disk with the virus, so this is a situation you should avoid with suspicious programs and disks. This requires turning any fixed disks off, because they generally do not have any hardware-based write-protection.

If you like to start long programs and then walk away from the computer, other computer users in your office might be a threat to your programs. Desktop computers are associated in some people's minds with interaction, and if they watch the screen for a minute and nothing moves, they might conclude that no one is using the computer. If they try to type and still nothing happens, they might conclude that the computer has crashed. Yet this is exactly what they would find with an ordinary SAS program running. They might then restart the computer, forcing you to run your program all over again later. This is especially a threat if you dim the computer screen when you go away — a reasonable precaution to keep a CRT from burning out (or "burning in") sooner than it needs to.

So, if you work in an office where someone might come along and take your computer just because it doesn't look like anyone is using it, you should protect your program in your absence by putting up a warning sign in a prominent place — such as in front of the screen. We provide a professionally designed warning sign, suitable for reproducing on an office copier, at the end of this chapter.

Sources of information

You can learn about computers and programs by reading about them, talking to people about them, and trying them out.

Publications

Certain books are obligatory for a professional SAS programmer to have. There are others that might be useful.

The most important book (other than this one, of course) is *SAS Language: Reference*, in an edition corresponding to the SAS version you are using. This is the encyclopedia of SAS syntax and of all SAS routines other than procs. You also need at least one book on the procs of each SAS product you use, including base SAS.

SAS Institute publishes four main categories of SAS manuals. Reference guides are the most detailed and authoritative. Syntax guides cover syntax rules very concisely. Introductory guides and usage guides are oriented more toward beginners, although a usage guide can be useful when you want to write a very ordinary program using a specific proc that you are not familiar with, or as a way of learning the general features of a particular SAS product. There are also technical reports, which vary in length and cover various specialized and advanced topics not covered in the manuals.

You should have whatever manuals you need to get the best use of all the software you use, including operating systems, sort programs, text editors, word processors, page layout programs, and DBMSs. To use operating systems like Unix and MS-DOS, a reference book covering command syntax is essential.

SAS Institute publishes a slick quarterly called *SAS Communications®*, which is where they usually announce new products and enhancements. Articles also discuss future changes in the SAS System and other SAS Institute software. If you're waiting for a future software release from SAS Institute to solve your problems, you should write to SAS Institute to ask about getting *SAS Communications*.

SAS Institute's books and technical reports are all listed in the semiannual *Publications Catalog*. It's a good idea to refer to the catalog before buying books, to make sure that you're getting the most appropriate ones.

Help screens

Display manager's help screens, brought up by the HELP command, provide an extremely concise overview of some parts of the SAS System. They can help you remember the syntax of a statement if you've forgotten it and no manual is nearby.

People

If you want to write SAS programs, the most helpful people to know are SAS programmers. If they're doing work in the same industry or specialization as you, that's even better. Talking about programming can save you a lot of work and helps keep you on your toes. If you have a problem, another programmer might be able to tell you what you need to do differently.

SAS users who do work related in some way to yours can also be helpful when it comes to specific applications. There are numerous regional, local, and specialized SAS user groups that meet periodically; however, these groups tend not to have a programming emphasis.

Every SAS site is supposed to have a SAS Software Consultant, who is supposed to solve people's SAS problems. In practice, the system doesn't work very well. Even if you can identify your SAS Software Consultant, there's no guarantee that the SAS Software Consultant will be willing or able to help you.

If you are a SAS Software Consultant, you can talk to the technical support people at SAS Institute. Our experience is that they are pretty good at explaining what the SAS System does to people who are simply confused. The more confused you are, the more effective they will be. On the other hand, if you're not confused at all, which is usually the case with programmers by the time they get around to calling, there isn't much the technical support people can do. A typical programmer's problem is that a particular statement or option or proc is doing something peculiar some of the time for no reason at all. The programmer wants to know why. "Just because" is often the best answer there is.

Knowing a sales representative at SAS Institute can also be helpful. Sales representatives don't have the technical perspective that the technical support people have, but they might be the ones to talk to if you think getting another SAS product might solve your problem — especially if you're in a position to influence a decision to license SAS products for a multiuser computer.

If you have more money than time, you can consider trying to find an expert to solve a specific problem for you. Despite the old saying that no one wants to debug anyone else's programs, there are people who do things like that.

Experiment

The ultimate expert is reality itself. The SAS System does what it does even more reliably than it does what the books or experts say it does. Experimenting with any programming language will eventually establish what it does, but the SAS language is particularly well suited to this because of the log messages and the ease with which reports can be created.

Let's say you're wondering whether the FORMAT statement uses an equals sign between the variable name and the format specification. You can find out by reading the log of the program below. One of the two proc steps will generate a syntax error.

```
  DATA X;
    INPUT X @@;
CARDS;
1 2 3 4 5 6
  PROC PRINT DATA=X;
    FORMAT X=7.;
RUN;
  PROC PRINT DATA=X;
    FORMAT X 7.;
RUN;
```

There are many details of the SAS language that the manuals do not cover or are ambiguous about. For example, a LINESLEFT= variable tells the number of lines left on a page in a print file. Does that include the current line or not? Is the variable updated in the middle of a PUT statement, or only at the end of the PUT statement? Would assigning a value to the LINESLEFT= variable have any effect? Or would doing that be a syntax error or a runtime error? Don't go around asking people questions like these! Instead, develop a hypothesis or two, write the simplest possible program to test the hypothesis, and draw your own conclusions.

CAUTION

DO NOT DISTURB

Professional
SAS program
at work

20 Projects

There are different kinds of objectives a computer programming project can have. A simple project might answer a particular question or investigate a data file, and could be done by one person. A complicated project might create several related programs to be run routinely as part of the operation of a business (a *production system*) or a program to be used by an undetermined number of computer users (a *software package*), and might take the coordinated efforts of several people to do.

How carefully a project is managed depends on how important its objectives are and on how many different people are involved. It might also be affected by company policy. The formal approach involves distinct phases of design, coding and debugging, testing, and maintenance. In an informal project, the rule might be, "Code first, ask questions later." The different aspects of programming are still present, though, even though they might serve only as conceptual guides.

Design

After the objective of a project has been determined, the design fills in the realistic details. It describes standards for the input data and output data of a program and the processing it does. If there is a user interface, the design can include sketches and functional descriptions of each screen the users see. The design of reports produced by a program might be very general or very specific.

The number of different programs is usually specified as part of a design, but that characteristic is not as critical for a system of SAS programs. SAS programs can be combined and separated easily enough.

A program should be designed for the users. If a program will be used frequently or by many different people or by people with no particular training, making it easy to use is especially important. If it will be run frequently, making it run efficiently might be important. If it modifies an important database, making it reliable is important.

Coding

Coding is the most visible part of programming. It is what people picture when they think of programming. In coding, the programmer transforms the design of a program into a program.

A program is the link between people and computers. To be effective, it must communicate effectively in both directions, "making sense" both to the computer and to programmers. That is, it has to be *syntactically correct* — following the rules of syntax of an interpreter or compiler — and also *readable* — so that a programmer can determine easily enough what the program does.

Neatness alone goes a long way toward making a program readable. Habits of neatness, when used consistently, form a coding style. Our style in this book includes these standards:

Statements
Each statement usually starts on a separate line. In some cases,
a block or step or several closely related statements appear on the same line.
Statements are written in execution order when possible.
In a data step, statements are written in this order:

statements between steps
DATA statement
LENGTH statement
RETAIN statement
other nonexecutable statements
FILE statement (if one output text file is used throughout step)
other executable statements

Dataset options are used instead of the corresponding statements.

Indentation:

Statements that do not belong to a step (including CARDS and RUN)	0
DATA and PROC statements	2
Other statements in a step	4
Inside a block (including the END statement)	additional 2
Continuation of a statement	additional 4 (or aligned to show parallels)

Spacing:
around all operators except *, /, **, and unary + and –
around = when used in assignment, but not when used to associate
around + for sum statement
before semicolon in null statement
extra spacing used to show parallel constructions when appropriate

Equivalent symbols:
Braces are used for array subscripts.
Operators: AND, OR , NOT, MIN, MAX, <, <=, =, >=, >, NE

Names:
Words are written in uppercase letters.
When a variable or statement label is primarily associated with an option, it is usually given the same name as the option: `LL=LL`, `EOF=EOF`, etc. However, when the END= option is associated with the observation loop, the variable LAST is used.
The variables A, B, C, ... are used for column pointer locations.
The variables I, J, ... are used for nondescript indexes.

These standards, and the other ones we use, form a rather ordinary style that tends to be acceptable to professional SAS programmers. It is also designed for maximum portability. We use AND, OR, and NOT instead of &, |, and ^, for example, because many programmers recognize them more readily, because the misuse of & can cause macro processor problems, and because ^ is nonportable.

You might use a different style that you feel more comfortable with. What is important is that you have a consistent style. This makes your programs easier to read, for you and for anyone else reading your programs.

Some classic coding strategies are not as effective in SAS programming. Pseudocode, in which English-like statements represent processes to be coded, can cause trouble when done in SAS coding. Similarly, flow charts that show the order of execution of a program are not recommended. However, data flow charts can be helpful in breaking a program into steps. If each input and output file for each proc is identified by a symbol, you can see what other steps are needed in the program.

Debugging

The SAS log is the main tool to use in debugging a SAS program. It is a powerful debugging tool, especially if you don't use macros. It normally contains the source code of a program, messages that identify specific syntax errors and certain conditions that occur in processing, the run time of each step, the number of variables and observations in each SAS dataset created, the number and length of records in a text file, the names of files, and the amount of memory used by the program.

Removing syntax errors is the traditional first step in debugging SAS programs. Error messages usually identify the exact location of the syntax error. However, data errors can also produce syntax error messages. For example, if a BY variable is missing from an input SAS dataset, that is reported as a syntax error, even though it could be that the program is right and the input SAS dataset is wrong. Also, after one syntax error has been found, subsequent syntax checking might be biased.

After the syntax errors are gone, there are other things to check for in the log. These conditions that are reported in the log often indicate logical errors in a program:

- automatic conversion between data types
- missing values produced by operations on missing values
- incorrect arguments for a function or CALL routine
- INPUT or PUT statement flowing over the end of a line
- INPUT errors: incorrect data for informat
- division by 0
- exponentiation with negative base and non-whole number exponent
- exponentiation with zero base and nonpositive exponent
- apparent macrolanguage reference not resolved
- quoted string over 200 characters long
- END statement missing
- no observations in SAS dataset
- SAS dataset already sorted, on SORT proc step
- variable named in dataset option does not exist
- variable has not been initialized
- file not found

You can add whatever additional information you want to the log, without disrupting the functionality of the program. In a data step, you can write the values of variables in the log using these statements:

```
FILE LOG;
PUT ...;
```

Some terms you can use in the PUT statement for debugging are:

`_N_`	the automatic counter variable
`_ERROR_`	which indicates the presence of certain kinds of input errors
`_ALL_`	named output for all variables defined in the step
variable=	named output for a variable
`(_NUMERIC_) (=)`	named output for all numeric variables
`(_CHARACTER_) (=)`	named output for all character variables
`_INFILE_`	the most recently read record from the current INFILE

Between steps, you can use the %PUT statement to write in the log.

You can also add extra steps to report on the contents of a file. You can find out about a SAS dataset using the PRINT and CONTENTS procs. Or you can use this step:

```
DATA _NULL_; SET; PUT _ALL_;
```

Use the OBS= dataset options and other dataset options to have a step print only selected observations from a SAS dataset.

The system option OBS= can be useful for debugging. This option stops processing any step after that number of repetitions of the observation loop, which might make the program run faster. You can identify syntax errors in some programs using

```
OPTIONS OBS=0;
```

Further debugging and testing might be done with a moderate number of observations, such as `OBS=100`.

Documentation

Some documentation for programs might be necessary in addition to the descriptive names and comments used throughout your programs. You might put a general description of each program at the top of each program file. Many programmers like to add such information as their name and phone number, the name of the program, the date the program and any modifications were written, and descriptions of all input and output files. This seems an appropriate level of detail if you have no way of knowing who in a large organization might be maintaining the program next.

Documentation can also be separate from the program file. For a system that contains several programs, there should be system documentation that describes the actions of each program and all the input and output data.

If a program is designed to be used by people who are not programmers or computer system operators, it should have user documentation, which is usually in the form of a user manual. The purpose of user documentation is to make the program easy to use. A user manual often contains screen shots, printed representations of screen images, along with detailed instructions for using each screen.

Testing

Programs are tested in various different ways, but the most reputable form of testing involves two phases: *alpha* testing, which is done by people who are familiar with the technical details involved in designing and coding the program, followed by *beta* testing, which is done by people who have no particular knowledge of the program's internals but who represent typical users.

If you want to do a really thorough job of alpha testing, you can test all the components of the program separately. For example, you can test a single step by creating input data that covers all the important permutations of input data that the step should handle, and comparing that to the output data produced by the step to make sure that it's correct. You can do similar testing for informats and formats you create. You could even test SAS features to make sure they do what you think they do.

Beta testing tests the user documentation in addition to the program. Beta testers will tell you if something about the program or documentation confuses them; they also tend to use programs in ways that programmers did not anticipate, uncovering less obvious logical errors in the program.

Maintenance

After a program is finished and has been in use, it might be modified in some way — to add new capabilities, remove newly discovered bugs, adjust to changes in data formats, or take advantage of new SAS or operating system features. This kind of programming is called *maintenance programming.*

Maintenance programming involves the whole process of coding, debugging, documentation, and testing. You might be tempted to skip parts of the process, but doing so entails all the same risks that it entails in the original programming process.

Maintenance is made easier if the program and documentation are written well in the first place. Programs that are poorly documented can take longer to modify than they took to write.

The worst thing a maintenance programmer can do is to modify a program in such a way that it no longer works — and then be unable to restore it to working condition. To help keep this from happening, it is important to keep a copy of every working version of a program.

21 Languages

There are several reasons why a SAS programmer might work with other programming languages, including writing routines to be used in SAS programs, and translating programs between SAS and other languages. Some translating or rewriting might also be required in porting programs between different SAS implementations.

Porting SAS programs

Programmers frequently need to take an existing program and make it run in a different environment: on a different kind of computer, under a different operating system, or using a different compiler or interpreter. This process is called *porting*. A program that is easy to port or a programming language that makes porting easy is said to be *portable*.

The SAS language is relatively portable, as programming languages go, with syntax rules that are nearly the same on different computers. However, it does have nonportable features, and programs that use them might have to be partly rewritten to be ported.

Implementations

SAS Institute makes a distinction between SAS *versions*, which are identified by whole numbers, and SAS *releases*, which are identified by decimal fractions. The current SAS version is 6; it has had several releases, including 6.03, 6.04, and 6.06. Releases 6.04 and 6.06 are the latest SAS releases as we write this book; they are expected to be available for all of the SAS System's hardware platforms in 1990, except for Unix workstations, which are getting their own release (presumably release 6.07).

Each SAS release includes several implementations, for different types of computers and operating systems. The parts of the SAS Supervisor that deal with the hardware and operating system are different in each implementation, although most of those differences should not be apparent to the SAS programmer.

Each implementation also has features designed to take advantage of the distinctive characteristics of each operating system. Using these features might increase the efficiency or usefulness of a program, but they also make it nonportable.

X statement

The X statement is the most obviously nonportable SAS statement. *X* stands for *external*; the X statement passes commands to the operating system to be executed. For example, when SAS is running under MS-DOS, the statement

```
X 'DIR A:\7?C*.';
```

causes the MS-DOS command

```
DIR A:\7?C*.
```

to be executed. Under other operating systems, though, the result of that X statement would be various computerized versions of "Huh?"

Files

Every operating system has its own ways of defining and handling files. These differences can affect the statements in SAS programs that identify files — particularly the FILENAME, FILE, INFILE, LIBNAME, and PROC PRINTTO statements, and dataset options in other statements.

Some implementations support a sequential format for SAS datasets, for example, while others do not.

Graphics

Different operating systems and hardware have different graphics capabilities. Most of the SAS System makes relatively modest use of graphics, so it can operate pretty much the same in different implementations. However, the SAS/GRAPH procs use graphics intensively and, accordingly, vary between implementations.

Character set

A *character set* is a code for representing characters in digital form. Different computers use different character sets.

Computers for English-language users (and for most languages) use one byte for each character. That allows up to 256 characters, corresponding to the numbers 0 through 255.

The character set affects the way character values sort and compare. In that context, the term *collating sequence* is often used. (*Collating* is a rarely used euphemism for *sorting*.)

Most computers follow the ASCII standard for characters. However, the ASCII standard defines only half of the possible characters, from 0 through 127. Different computers have different uses for the other 128 characters.

The ASCII collating sequence is:

```
blank !"#%&'()*+,-./0123456789:;<=>?@
ABCDEFGHIJKLMNOPQRSTUVWXYZ[\]^_`
abcdefghijklmnopqrstuvwxyz{|}~
```

An older standard, EBCDIC, is still in use on IBM mainframes. It defines about 120 characters. The other characters are undefined, or "non-printing," characters.

```
blank ¢.<(+|&!$*);¬-/¦,%_>?`:#@'="
abcdefghijklmnopqr~stuvwxyz
{ABCDEFGHI}JKLMNOPQR\STUVWXYZ
0123456789
```

Both the ASCII and EBCDIC character sets include control characters, such as the tab character, that have particular meanings in files but are not intended to be visible.

Programs that rely on collating sequence characteristics may not be portable. For example, on an ASCII computer, the expression

```
'A' < 'a'
```

would be true, while on an EBCDIC computer, it would be false.

In the ASCII collating sequence, the expression

```
'A' <= CH <= 'Z'
```

can be used to test whether the one-character variable CH is a capital letter. In the EBCDIC collating sequence, though, that range also includes }, \, and several undefined characters.

The SAS System has the $ASCII and $EBCDIC informats and formats for converting between ASCII and EBCDIC characters.

The operations of SAS functions such as BYTE and SEQUENCE depend on the collating sequence, and programs that use them may not be portable.

> Some older mainframe hardware supports the brace characters { and } and lowercase letters poorly or not at all. Because of that, on some computers, it is conventional to use only uppercase letters and to use parentheses instead of braces.

Numeric Data

Different computers represent numeric data in slightly different ways. Normally, this should not concern a SAS programmer; however, it can be relevant whenever the informats and formats corresponding to those numeric forms, such as the PIB, IB, and RB informats and formats, are used.

The SAS System has a corresponding set of informats and formats that are designed to be portable. They do not necessarily correspond to a computer's internal numeric forms, but they operate in a standard way across different SAS implementations. The names of these informats and formats have the S370F prefix — for example, the S370FPIB informat, the portable informat that corresponds to the nonportable PIB informat. S370 stands for System/370, the IBM mainframe model whose numeric forms were taken as a standard. (F, perhaps, stands for family.)

Differing floating-point forms affect the precision of numeric variables, which is especially important in SAS datasets when short variable lengths are used. You might have to change LENGTH statements when porting a SAS program between computers — especially when porting programs from an IBM mainframe to another type of computer. A 7-digit integer, for example, can be stored precisely in a variable of length 4 on an IBM mainframe, but requires a length of 5 on most other computers.

The details of floating-point forms also determine the largest and smallest numbers a computer can represent and can affect the magnitude of rounding errors.

Compiled data steps

Compiled data steps cannot currently be moved between computers with different SAS implementations. To move compiled data steps to a different implementation, move the program that compiles the data steps to the appropriate SAS implementation and run it there to create compiled data steps for that implementation.

Moving data

Moving a system from one computer to another can involve moving both programs and data files. Different techniques are used for moving SAS datasets and text files.

SAS datasets

SAS datasets are stored in different formats for different SAS implementations, so they have to be translated when they are moved from one kind of computer to another or from one SAS version to another.

The SAS System handles the translation of SAS datasets using a transport engine. In SAS releases 6.03–6.04, the CPORT proc is used instead of an engine to write a SAS data library in transport format, and the CIMPORT proc to do the reverse. In SAS version 5, the TRANSPORT=YES dataset option and XCOPY proc (on EBCDIC machines) were used.

Text Files

File transfer and file exchange programs have a text mode that handles any translation needed between different computers' text file formats. For a text file transfer to work perfectly, all the characters in the file should be text characters that both computers' character sets share. (In addition, the EBCDIC ¬ character is sometimes equated with the ASCII ^ character. Some file transfer programs let you control the mapping of characters.) Usually there aren't any problems with program files and readable data files.

A different mode, often called binary mode, transfers files without translating. This sometimes works for moving files that contain binary data. However, binary fields can be troublesome (see "Numeric Data" above), so you might want to put data in a different format (perhaps hexadecimal) before moving it.

If you move a file containing text fields between ASCII and EBCDIC computers in binary form, you can use the $ASCII or $EBCDIC informat to translate the text between the different character sets.

Older SAS versions

Before SAS version 6, there were other SAS versions on mainframes and minicomputers. The earlier SAS language versions had most, but not all, of the features that SAS version 6 has. They also had some features that are not present in SAS version 6. These are the features that are most important to note if you are porting programs written in earlier SAS versions to version 6.

SAS version 5 for mainframes

The mainframe implementations of SAS version 5 were very different from the minicomputer implementations. The mainframe implementations had more features and were considered the standard SAS System at the time.

Macros

SAS version 5 for mainframes marked the first appearance of SAS macrolanguage, with features that were slightly different from the current macrolanguage.

SAS version 5 for mainframes also supported an older form of macro, which is called a *program macro* to distinguish it from a macrolanguage macro. The program macro was actually almost like a macrovariable, but unlike a macrovariable, it had to contain whole tokens. Program macros were defined with the MACRO statement, which had the form

```
MACRO name text %
```

> The MACRO statement ends in a percent sign instead of a semicolon to make it easy for program macros to contain semicolons. Two percent signs (%%) are used to represent a percent sign in a program macro definition.

This MACRO statement

```
MACRO RETUNE RETAIN A1-A100 0 B1-B100 100 %
```

creates the program macro RETUNE with the value

```
RETAIN A1-A100 0 B1-B100 100
```

Later, wherever the word RETUNE appears in the program, the value of the macro is substituted. For example, the line,

```
RETUNE THIS AND THAT;
```

would mean

```
RETAIN A1-A100 0 B1-B100 100 THIS AND THAT;
```

Obviously, after a program macro had been defined, its name could not be used as the name of a variable or anything else in the program. However, the recognition of a program macro name could be suspended temporarily with the %DEACTIVATE or %DEACT statement

```
%DEACT RETUNE;
```

or permanently with the %DELETE or %DEL statement. Temporarily suspended program macros could be restored with the %ACTIVATE or %ACT statement.

The %MLIST or %LISTM statement could be used to list a program macro or the directory of currently defined program macros in the log.

Arrays

SAS version 5 for mainframes did not support multidimensional arrays.

Windows

SAS version 5 had limited windowing capabilities. It did not have the WINDOW and DISPLAY statements, and its SAS/AF product had limited screen definition capabilities and did not include SCL.

BY statement

On mainframes, up to and including version 5, the BY statement in the data step had a different meaning than the BY statement in version 6 or on minicomputers. Each SAS dataset in the step had to have the BY variables, and a direct access SET statement could not appear in the same step as a BY statement.

I/O

Engines, views, SAS dataset indexes, and the SQL proc were all new with SAS release 6.06. The WHERE= dataset option was introduced with SAS release 6.03.

Functions

Two functions in SAS version 5 are not used in version 6. The SASVER function, which identified the SAS release number, is replaced by the SYSVER macrovariable. (Note the change in spelling.) The RESOLVE function in version 5 had the macro processor convert a macroexpression to constant text. Programming involving the RESOLVE function can usually be rewritten using the SYMGET function.

Add-on procs

Many mainframe installations had a group of SAS procs published by SUGI, called the SUGI Supplemental Library. It consists mainly of procs written by programmers for their own use. In addition, some installations had other procs that were written by programmers there or elsewhere. These version 5 procs cannot be used with SAS version 6.

The SUGI Supplemental Library is documented by a book called *SUGI Supplemental Library User's Guide, Version 5 Edition*. Some of the functionality of the SUGI Supplemental Library has been incorporated into SAS Institute procs.

SAS version 5 for minicomputers

Minicomputers got a minimal implementation of version 5. It did not have macrolanguage or program macros, but it did at least have the %INCLUDE statement. It had no implicitly subscripted arrays and no conditional SELECT block. There were other minor syntax differences between the minicomputer and mainframe implementations.

In some respects, the minicomputer implementations were more like the current SAS language than the mainframe implementations —

particularly the use of the multidimensional arrays and the meaning of the BY statement in the data step.

Updating from version 5 to version 6

On mainframes and minicomputers that supported SAS version 5, the V5TOV6 proc converts SAS data libraries from version 5 format to version 6 format. It also converts version 5 format libraries to version 6 catalogs.

SAS version 4

SAS version 4 preceded version 5 on minicomputers. Its syntax was nearly the same. Version 4 did not support multidimensional arrays.

SAS version 82

SAS version 82 preceded SAS version 5 on mainframes. It did not have macrolanguage; programmers used program macros and %INCLUDE statements instead. There were no explicitly subscripted arrays, ATTRIB statement, or SELECT block.

In version 82, character constants usually did not have to be quoted, except in expressions. The KEEP and DROP statements could be used in proc steps.

Other languages

Translating a program means making it work about the same way in a different programming language.

Programmers translate programs between languages for various reasons, which might include programmer or management preferences, habits, or conventions, the availability or price of a language on the hardware and operating system to be used, and the inherent, characteristic pluses and minuses of each language.

Advantages of other languages compared to SAS

The advantages of other languages compared to SAS may represent reasons to translate a SAS program to another language or, conversely, reasons not to translate a program to the SAS language.

Some languages have low-level control features allowing access to the computer screen, input devices, and operating system routines. These features allow a program to be user-directed and event-driven, to do sound and animation, and to use memory management techniques.

Most languages have more data types than the two SAS data types. The use of the integer data type, in particular, is essential for some applications. Some languages allow a user to define new data types. Also, most languages do not have the 200-character limit on the length of character variables or the 32,000-byte limit on the total size of all variables.

Most languages allow a program to be divided into routines, allowing structured programming techniques. This is very helpful in coding and debugging complicated programs. It also allows programs to be smaller.

For many applications, a stand-alone, compiled program is essential. SAS programs can only run where the SAS System in present, but a stand-alone program requires only the right hardware and operating system.

In applications where speed is critical, the runtime advantages of the integer data type, memory management, compiled programs, and structured programming techniques make it essential to use a language that has those features.

Advantages of SAS compared to other languages

The advantages of the SAS language represent reasons to translate a program to SAS or reasons not to translate a program from SAS to another language. The SAS procs are the most compelling reason. Using procs can save half of the coding in a program, or more. Conversely, coding the functional equivalent of a SAS proc in a particular language might be very difficult or impossible.

I/O flexibility is another outstanding feature of the SAS language. SAS is the language of choice for reading very complicated data files. Using SAS datasets can also simplify writing and reading temporary data files. Interface engines allow a SAS program to access the data in some databases directly, something that is impossible in most programming languages.

The control flow features within the data step are another advantage of the SAS language. The DO loop, in particular, has more flexibility than almost any loop structure in any language.

Translating from SAS to other languages

Translating a SAS program to another language requires a strong understanding of the SAS language, because all the automatic SAS features are no longer automatic in the translated program.

In the most direct way of translating, each SAS step becomes a routine. There is also the potential for combining steps that could not be combined in the SAS program.

The observation loop in each step can be coded as an ordinary loop, with the counter variable _N_ as the index variable. The close connection between control flow and input in the observation loop must be coded explicitly. Techniques for interleaving and match merging are shown in chapter 10, "File formats," and can be used as a guide in translating.

Most languages have floating point and character data types, so you can usually translate SAS numeric and character variables directly to those types. For variables used only as integers, it is usually better to translate them to an integer data type. You can consider the benefits of any other data types a language has.

Missing values are distinctively a SAS feature. For floating-point variables, if a language has direct support for nans, you can use nans to have any particular meaning corresponding to the meaning of a missing value. If there are values that are clearly out of the range of values of a variable, you could use them the same way. Otherwise, you might have to create a separate variable to indicate when a value is missing. Whatever code you use, you will need to check for it before a computation involving the variable, in order not to use the missing values in arithmetic.

Most languages have operators corresponding to most of the SAS operators. Some of the SAS operators might be implemented as functions.

Some rewriting will be necessary in translating control flow statements. In particular, the subsetting IF and DELETE statements will have to be written as another kind of branching, such as a GOTO statement. GOTO statements are also used to simulate blocks in languages that do not have anything that corresponds to the DO block. These SAS statements

```
IF condition THEN DO;
  block;
  END;
```

would have to be translated to something like

```
IF NOT condition THEN GOTO label
block
label:
```

Usually, a SELECT block is translated to an IF . . . THEN . . . ELSE kind of construction. However, a few languages, notably Pascal and C, have control flow statements that have some of the features of the SELECT block.

If you use LINK statements or the HEADER= option, those lines should be made into separate routines.

The effect of a BY statement takes some work to construct. The equivalents of FIRST. and LAST. variables can be created by comparing the values of BY variables to the preceding and following input observations. To compare a value to the value in the following observation, you'll have to be reading one observation ahead.

Input and output can be a real chore in other languages, compared to the use of the SAS I/O statements. Simple INPUT and PUT might be handled by the language's I/O statements. Most of the time, though, you will need to write a separate routine corresponding to each INPUT, SET, MERGE, UPDATE, PUT, and OUTPUT statement. Each informat and format can also be coded as a separate function. It's also up to you, usually, to open and close files, and to make sure that you don't read past the end of a file.

Using output and input to pass data between "steps" might not be necessary in another language, though, if you have enough memory to hold the data. Then you can use an array in memory instead of writing a file on a storage device.

Any SAS routine that is used in the SAS program has to be written in the translated program. Functions, informats, formats, and CALL routines are usually not too complicated and can be coded as functions. Some of them will already be present in the language's function library.

Procs are another matter. The complexity of the SAS procs might deter you from the whole idea of translating the program. However, you do not need to translate the whole SAS proc — just the specific features of it that you use.

Sorting is a particular problem. If the data is not too large, you should do sorting entirely in memory, using the techniques used for sorting arrays. If the sorting process seems too slow (as it probably will if you use the bubble sort described in chapter 8), you can read about the efficiency issues involved in sorting in any of the various books on sort algorithms. If you need to sort a data file, because it is too large to read into memory, you will probably prefer to use a packaged routine to do that.

You should not plan to translate an engine. Instead, take the form of the data file you use into account when you code specific I/O routines.

You can construct a rough equivalent of the SAS log if you need to. Just create a text output file, and write messages to it at appropriate places in the program. Your log will not contain program statements, but you can write notes indicating numbers of observations, data errors, and so on.

C

If you're looking for a language to translate a program to, the C programming language is a good all-around choice. It has all this to recommend it:

- efficient, compact, compiled, stand-alone programs
- structured programming, allowing separate compilations of routines
- low-level features and access to operating system routines
- elegant syntax
- a relatively standardized form for virtually all computers
- the language most widely used for serious software development

The discussion that follows is intended to help programmers with a working knowledge of C translate SAS programs to C. Some of the details are also applicable to translating to other languages.

The following table shows the most straightforward substitutions you can make for certain SAS features in translating a SAS program to C.

<table>
<tr><th>SAS feature</th><th>C feature</th></tr>
<tr><td>character variable</td><td>char variable, or array of char</td></tr>
<tr><td>numeric variable</td><td>integer or floating-point variable</td></tr>
<tr><td>hexadecimal constant '1201'X or 1201X</td><td>0x1201</td></tr>
<tr><td>arithmetic operators +, –, *, /</td><td>+, –, *, /</td></tr>
<tr><td>exponentiation X**Y</td><td>pow(X,Y)</td></tr>
<tr><td>comparison operators
<, <=, =, >=, >, NE</td><td>for numbers and characters:
<, <=, ==, >=, >, !=
for strings: strcmp function</td></tr>
<tr><td>logical operators AND, OR, NOT</td><td>&&, ||, !</td></tr>
<tr><td>assignment statement X = A;</td><td>X = A;</td></tr>
<tr><td>sum statement X + 1;</td><td>X++;</td></tr>
<tr><td>sum statement X + A;</td><td>X += A;</td></tr>
<tr><td>sum statement X + -A;</td><td>X -= A;</td></tr>
<tr><td>DO; ... END;</td><td>{ ... }</td></tr>
<tr><td>DO I = 1 TO 10; ... END;</td><td>for(i = 1; i <= 10; i++) { ... }</td></tr>
<tr><td>DO WHILE(...); ... END;</td><td>while(...) { ... }</td></tr>
<tr><td>DO UNTIL(...); ... END;</td><td>do { ... } while (! ...)</td></tr>
<tr><td>IF ... THEN ... ; ELSE ... ;</td><td>if(...) ... ; else ...</td></tr>
<tr><td>SELECT(integer);
WHEN(value) ... ;
OTHERWISE ... ;
END;</td><td>switch(integer)
{ case value: ... ; break;
default: ... ;
}</td></tr>
<tr><td>SELECT</td><td>if(...) { ... }
else if(...) { ... }
...</td></tr>
<tr><td>observation loop
DATA;
IF _N_ = 1 THEN initialize
... END=LAST;
...
IF LAST THEN final processing</td><td>initialize
for(n = 1; eof; N++)
{
...
}
final processing</td></tr>
<tr><td>step</td><td>function</td></tr>
<tr><td>proc</td><td>function</td></tr>
<tr><td>function</td><td>function</td></tr>
<tr><td>informat</td><td>function</td></tr>
<tr><td>format</td><td>function</td></tr>
<tr><td>CALL routine</td><td>function</td></tr>
<tr><td>LINK or HEADER=</td><td>function</td></tr>
<tr><td>SAS dataset</td><td>data file or array</td></tr>
<tr><td>observation</td><td>structure</td></tr>
</table>

C does not have any I/O statements, and its high-level input/output functions are not especially appropriate for use with fixed-field data files. A C translation of an INPUT statement tends to be rather detailed: first a record of a particular length is read, then each field is interpreted, one by one. A fixed-field record can be defined as a structure to make accessing the fields easier. The translation of a SET statement is done just like an INPUT statement, but with less interpreting to be done. A PUT or OUTPUT statement would be the reverse, putting fields into a record and then writing the record.

The example belows shows many of the techniques and problems of translating a SAS program to C. This SAS program reads data from a text file, summarizes it, and prints a report:

```
OPTIONS NOCENTER;
TITLE1 'The Number Of Fish In The Sea';
  DATA FISH;
    INFILE CENSUS MISSOVER;
    INPUT SEA $CHAR15.
        +8 HEMISPHR $CHAR1.
        VARIETY $CHAR16.
        COUNT 8.
        BOATS 4.
        DEPTH 5.;
  PROC SUMMARY DATA=FISH NWAY;
    CLASS HEMISPHR SEA;
    ID DEPTH;
    VAR COUNT BOATS;
    OUTPUT SUM= OUT=SEA;
  PROC PRINT DATA=SEA;
```

In the C translation below, the three steps of the SAS program become, roughly, the read_file, sum, and print functions.

```
/* structure definitions */
typedef struct
{     char sea[15];
      char region[8];
      char hemisphere;
      char variety[16];
      char fish_count[8];
      char boat_count[4];
      char depth[5];
} input_record;

typedef struct
{     char hemisphere;
      char sea[15];
      long fish_count;
      long boat_count;
      long depth;
} observation;

char *title = "The Number Of Fish In The Sea";

/* function declarations */
int read_file(observation *);
int getrecord(FILE *, char *, size_t);
long ctol(char *, size_t);
int seacompare(void *, void *);
int sum(observation *, int, observation *);
void print(observation *, FILE *);
void write_line(char *, observation *);
void ultoc(char *, long, long);
void error(int);
```

```
/* The main() function in a C program is the main program. */
main()
{
     observation table[1000], total[1];
     FILE *printfile;
     int n, end, nobs;

     nobs = read_file(table);
     if(nobs <= 0) error(-1);

     qsort((void *) table, nobs, sizeof(observation), seacompare);

     printfile = fopen("fish.prn", "w");
     if(printfile == NULL) error(10);

     do
     {    end = sum(table, nobs, total);
          print(total, printfile);
     } while(!end);
     fclose(printfile);
}

/* This function reads the input file and creates a table of data
   in memory. */
read_file(table)
     observation *table;
{
     input_record record;
     int n, eof;
     FILE *inputfile;

     inputfile = fopen("fish.census", "r");
     if(inputfile == NULL) error(4);

     for(n = 0; n < 1000; n++)
     {    eof = getrecord(inputfile,
               (char *) &record, sizeof(record));
          if(eof) break;
          memcpy((void *) table[n].sea, (void *) record.sea,
               sizeof(table->sea));
          table[n].hemisphere = toupper(record.hemisphere);
          table[n].fish_count = ctol(record.fish_count,
               sizeof(record.fish_count));
          table[n].boat_count = ctol(record.boat_count,
               sizeof(record.boat_count));
          table[n].depth = ctol(record.depth,
               sizeof(record.depth));
     }
     fclose(inputfile);
     return n;
}

/* This function simulates the effects of the MISSOVER and PAD
   options in reading a fixed-length record. */
getrecord(file, record, length)
     FILE *file;
```

```
     char *record;
     size_t length;
{
     int i, c;

     memset((void *) record, ' ', length);      /* blank fill */

     for(i = 0, c = 0; c !='\n' && c != EOF; i++)
     {    c = fgetc(file);
          if(c != EOF && c != '\n' && i < length)
               *(record++) = (char) c;
     }
     return  i <= 1 && c == EOF;       /* end of file, no data? */
}

/* This function converts a character array to a long integer. */
long ctol(c, length)
     char *c;
     size_t length;
{
     char string[33];
     if(length > 32) length = 32;
     memcpy(string, c, length);
     string[length] = '\0';
     return atol(string);
}

/* The compare function used by the qsort function. */
seacompare(x, y)
     void *x, *y;
{
     return memcmp(x, y, 16);
}

/* This function summarizes the sorted table by sea. */
sum(table, nobs, total)
     observation *table, *total;
     int nobs;
{
     static int n = 0;

     total->fish_count = 0;
     total->boat_count = 0;
     total->depth = 0;
     memcpy((void *) total, (void *) (table + n), 16);
     do
     {    total->fish_count += table[n].fish_count;
          total->boat_count += table[n].boat_count;
          if(total->depth < table[n].depth)
               total->depth = table[n].depth;
          n++;
     } while(!memcmp((void *) total, (void *) (table + n), 16)
          && n < nobs);
     return n >= nobs;
}
```

```
/* This function produces the print output. */
void print(sea, file)
     observation *sea;
     FILE *file;
{
     static int linesleft = 0;
     char record[53];

     if(!linesleft)
     {    fputs(title, file);
          fputc('\n', file); /* blank line */
          fputs(
           "Hemisphr Sea                    Depth      Count    Boats",
               file);
          fputc('\n', file);
          linesleft = 50;
     }
     write_line(record, sea);
     fputs(record, file);
     fputc('\n', file);
     linesleft--;
}

/* This function formats an ordinary table line. */
void write_line(record, sea)
     char *record;
     observation *sea;
{
     memset((void *) record, ' ', 52); /* blank fill */
     record[0] = sea->hemisphere;
     memcpy(record + 9, sea->sea, 15);
     ultoc(record + 25, (unsigned long) (sea->depth), 7);
     ultoc(record + 33, (unsigned long) (sea->fish_count), 10);
     ultoc(record + 44, (unsigned long) (sea->boat_count), 8);
     record[52] = '\0';
}

/* This function converts an integer to a numeral. */
void ultoc(c, n, length)
     char *c;
     long n, length;
{
     register int i;

     memset((void *) c, ' ', length);      /* blank fill */
     for(i = length - 1; i >= 0; i--)
     {    c[i] = '0' + (n % 10);           /* digits */
          n /= 10;
          if(!n) return;
     }
     memset((void *) c, '*', length);      /* overflow: star fill */
}
```

```
/* error messages */
void error(code)
     int code;
{
     switch(code)
     {    case -1: fputs("no input records", stderr); break;
          case 4: fputs("can't open input file", stderr); break;
          case 10: fputs("can't open output file", stderr); break;
     }
     exit();
}
```

You can see that the problem becomes much longer when coded in C. This is not because C is a wordy language; on the contrary, C is known for the conciseness of its syntax. It's just the effect of the automatic SAS features that have to be coded explicitly in C. The `main()` function of the C program is about the same length as the SAS program. Several of the other C functions are very general functions that could be used in almost any similar C program. The corresponding routines are invisible in the SAS program, because they are provided as part of the SAS System.

On the other hand, the lack of automatic features makes the C program much faster than the SAS program. The C program does not have the overhead of the SAS interpreter when it runs, and because its routines do not need to be very flexible, they do not need to include features not used by this particular program.

Translating from other languages to SAS

In rewriting existing programs as SAS programs, the program structure is usually the most significant challenge. Short, simple programs can usually be translated to a single SAS step. An example of this is shown in chapter 1, "Getting started." For more complicated programs, the program has to be broken up into steps in a sensible way, which often involves extensive changes in the program structure. This is especially true when the program being translated is a structured program; the difficulty of making it fit the step-structured SAS style might dissuade you from undertaking the translation.

However, with some ingenuity, it can often be done. You should look for loops that might work as observation loops, identifying the data that they work on as observations (or, in some cases, BY groups). Also look for segments of the program that correspond to SAS routines, especially functions and procs. Identify any table lookup activity in the program, and code it in the most appropriate way in the SAS program, regardless of how it is done in the original program. SAS table lookup techniques are discussed in chapter 15.

Assigning data types is usually not too difficult; you can usually treat all number-oriented, logical, and time variables as SAS numeric variables, and all other variables as SAS character variables. The alternatives discussed in chapter 14, "Data types," might be useful.

The SAS System does not allow large blocks of data in memory, so you might have to translate a large array into a SAS dataset. The program data vector can only hold a few thousand variables in any one step — and, of course, each element of a SAS array counts as a separate variable.

Translating a program to the SAS language essentially means rewriting the program, using the original program as a guide, so all the usual SAS programming techniques discussed throughout this book can be expected to apply.

SAS system programming

SAS routines — procs, engines, functions, CALL routines, formats, and informats — are just programs written by programmers. You can, if you want to, write your own routines and use them in your SAS programs. This section will not tell you exactly how to code and install SAS routines — that is a subject for another book — but will give you an idea of what is involved.

You should plan on coding the routines in the C programming language. It is possible to use other languages, especially PL/I, Fortran, and assembly language, for these routines, but they are usually easier to write and more portable as C programs.

Through SAS version 5, PL/I, Fortran, and assembly language were the languages used to code the SAS System, so you might find older routines that were coded in those languages. For SAS version 6, the entire SAS System was rewritten in C — an enormous undertaking that first required creating C compilers that were up to the task!

To run a C program, you need a C compiler, which converts the source code into a machine language file. Routines for the SAS System do not have a main function, which means that they cannot be run by themselves. However, the machine language files only need to be installed correctly, by moving them into the right library or directory, to be used in a SAS program.

Functions are the easiest routines to write. You can think of a function as a data step with a fixed number of input variables and only one output variable. The whole point of the function is to assign the right value to that output variable.

CALL routines are very much like functions, except that they do not return values. A CALL routine, might, however, change the value of one or more of its arguments.

Formats and informats are very much like functions. A format has one argument, which is a numeric or character value depending on whether the format is a numeric or character format, and it produces a character string. An informat has a character argument and produces a numeric or character result. In addition to the values they produce, informats and formats also have to be concerned with pointer movements. Certain kinds of informats and formats can be created using the FORMAT proc, as described in chapter 3, "Programs on call."

A proc can be just about any kind of program. However, a proc is more than just a program. It also has its own rules of syntax. The proc and the SAS supervisor collaborate on the complicated process of enforcing the proc's syntax rules, interpreting the proc step statements, and identifying the input data for the proc.

Engines are potentially the most complicated routines. Unlike the other routines, engines have to be able to do several different things: reading an observation, writing an observation, identifying variables, and so on. On the other hand, it should be possible to modify an already coded engine to read and write a similar kind of data file without doing any especially involved programming.

Many routines were written to be used with SAS version 5. After SAS Institute releases guidelines for programming portable add-on routines for version 6, which are expected in 1991, it is likely that even more routines will be written to be used with SAS version 6. SAS Institute's new SAS/TOOLKIT™ software product will include routines needed to create add-on procs.

22 Classic problems

This chapter consists of a set of programs that address problems that have been addressed often in the past, but rarely as SAS programs. These programs should give you an idea of the range and flexibility of the SAS programming language. At the same time, they serve as examples of ways to approach programming problems.

Prime number sieve

A prime number is a positive integer that cannot be obtained by multiplying any two other positive integers. By contrast, a composite number is an integer that is a product of two or more prime numbers. The number 1 is usually considered a special case, neither prime nor composite.

The purpose of a prime number sieve is to list the prime numbers. It is called a "sieve" because it finds prime numbers by identifying all the composite numbers. Numbers that "fall through" are primes. The process builds on itself, because the composite numbers are identified as multiples of the prime numbers.

This program's speed depends mainly on the processing speed of the computer. You can adjust it to generate a different number of prime numbers by assigning a different value to the macrovariable TOTAL.

The macrovariable DIM determines the size of the arrays P, the set of prime numbers, and M, the sieve, consisting of multiples of those same prime numbers. The value of DIM determines how far the program can go., The process eventually generates a composite number — the square of the 5,001st prime number, the next prime number beyond the last one in the array. The conditional STOP statement stops the program if that number is reached. In any case, the search for prime numbers stops at the highest double-precision odd number your computer can represent, which you can assign to the macrovariable MAXINT.

```
%LET TOTAL = 6000;
%LET DIM = 2000;
%LET MAXINT = 2E9;

  DATA _NULL_;
    ARRAY P{&DIM} _TEMPORARY_; * Prime numbers;
    ARRAY M{&DIM} _TEMPORARY_; * Multiples of prime numbers;
    FILE PRINT NOTITLES;
    SQUARE = 4;

    DO X = 2 TO &MAXINT; * Is X prime?;
      IF X = SQUARE THEN DO; * Extend sieve;
        IMAX + 1;
        IF IMAX >= &DIM THEN STOP; * Sieve limit reached;
        SQUARE = M{IMAX + 1};
        CONTINUE;
        END;
      IN_SIEVE = 0;
      * Find least prime factor;
      DO I = 1 TO IMAX UNTIL (IN_SIEVE);
        DO WHILE (M{I} < X); M{I} + P{I}; END;   * Update sieve;
        IF M{I} = X THEN IN_SIEVE = 1;
        END;
      IF IN_SIEVE THEN CONTINUE;
      * Add to list of prime numbers;
      PUT X @;
      N + 1;
      IF N >= &TOTAL THEN STOP;
      ELSE IF N <= &DIM THEN DO; P{N} = X; M{N} = X*X; END;
      END;
    STOP;
RUN;
```

```
2 3 5 7 11 13 17 19 23 29 31 37 41 43 47 53 59 61 67 71 73 79 83 89 97 101 103
107 109 113 127 131 137 139 149 151 157 163 167 173 179 181 191 193 197 199 211
223 227 229 233 239 241 251 257 263 269 271 277 281 283 293 307 311 313 317 331
337 347 349 353 359 367 373 379 383 389 397 401 409 419 421 431 433 439 443 449
457 461 463 467 479 487 491 499 503 509 521 523 541 547 557 563 569 571 577 587
593 599 601 607 613 617 619 631 641 643 647 653 659 661 673 677 683 691 701 709
719 727 733 739 743 751 757 761 769 773 787 797 809 811 821 823 827 829 839 853
857 859 863 877 881 883 887 907 911 919 929 937 941 947 953 967 971 977 983 991
997 1009 1013 1019 1021 1031 1033 1039 1049 1051 1061 1063 1069 1087 1091 1093
1097 1103 1109 1117 1123 1129 1151 1153 1163 1171 1181 1187 1193 1201 1213 1217
1223 1229 1231 1237 1249 1259 1277 1279 1283 1289 1291 1297 1301 1303 1307 1319
1321 1327 1361 1367 1373 1381 1399 1409 1423 1427 1429 1433 1439 1447 1451 1453
1459 1471 1481 1483 1487 1489 1493 1499 1511 1523 1531 1543 1549 1553 1559 1567
1571 1579 1583 1597 1601 1607 1609 1613 1619 1621 1627 1637 1657 1663 1667 1669
1693 1697 1699 1709 1721 1723 1733 1741 1747 1753 1759 1777 1783 1787 1789 1801
1811 1823 1831 1847 1861 1867 1871 1873 1877 1879 1889 1901 1907 1913 1931 1933
1949 1951 1973 1979 1987 1993 1997 1999 2003 2011 2017 2027 2029 2039 2053 2063
2069 2081 2083 2087 2089 2099 2111 2113 2129 2131 2137 2141 2143 2153 2161 2179
2203 2207 2213 2221 2237 2239 2243 2251 2267 2269 2273 2281 2287 2293 2297 2309
2311 2333 2339 2341 2347 2351 2357 2371 2377 2381 2383 2389 2393 2399 2411 2417
2423 2437 2441 2447 2459 2467 2473 2477 2503 2521 2531 2539 2543 2549 2551 2557
2579 2591 2593 2609 2617 2621 2633 2647 2657 2659 2663 2671 2677 2683 2687 2689
2693 2699 2707 2711 2713 2719 2729 2731 2741 2749 2753 2767 2777 2789 2791 2797
2801 2803 2819 2833 2837 2843 2851 2857 2861 2879 2887 2897 2903 2909 2917 2927
2939 2953 2957 2963 2969 2971 2999 3001 3011 3019 3023 3037 3041 3049 3061 3067
3079 3083 3089 3109 3119 3121 3137 3163 3167 3169 3181 3187 3191 3203 3209 3217
...
```

Life

There is a class of mathematical games called *cellular automatons*. A cellular automaton is "played" on a grid, with each square, or *cell*, in the grid having one of a set of allowed values, or *states*. On each move, each cell is given a new state that depends on its previous state and the previous states of the eight cells around it. This can be an arduous task to do manually, so the process is often computerized.

The most widely known cellular automaton is called Life. In Life, there are two states cells can have, usually identified as "live" and "dead." On each move, a dead cell becomes a live cell if exactly three of the eight cells it borders are alive. A live cell stays alive only if two or three of the bordering cells are alive.

The sequence of grids below demonstrate how this works, using one starting configuration on a 3 × 3 grid. The white squares are the live cells.

As usually happens, the grid is filled with dead squares after only a few moves. The challenge in Life is to choose starting configurations that yield interesting behavior — something that can be achieved easily by experimenting.

In a SAS program, the live and dead states can be represented by two characters. We'll use the at-sign (which does look slightly like an amoeba) for live cells, with dead cells left blank.

The program below uses a grid of 18 rows and 60 columns — a size chosen to fit on most computer screens. The grid is represented as an array of character strings of length 60 — a more practical approach than defining a two-dimensional array with a separate variable for each square. A window is used to set the initial value for the grid and to display the subsequent evolution of the grid.

The program centers around two infinite loops: the DO loop, which shows the subsequent states of the grid, and the observation loop, which allows the possibility of starting over with a fresh grid. The program depends on the DELETE statements (which could just as well be RETURN statements) and STOP statements to break out of these loops.

```
DATA _NULL_;
  LENGTH L1-L18 CURRENT ABOVE BELOW $ 60 NBRHOOD $ 9;
  ARRAY L{18} $ 60;

  WINDOW LIFE ROWS=20 COLUMNS=60 IROW=2 ICOLUMN=10
      GROUP=INIT
      #1  @1 L1  $CHAR60.
      #2  @1 L2  $CHAR60.
      #3  @1 L3  $CHAR60.
      #4  @1 L4  $CHAR60.
      #5  @1 L5  $CHAR60.
```

```
    #6  @1 L6  $CHAR60.
    #7  @1 L7  $CHAR60.
    #8  @1 L8  $CHAR60.
    #9  @1 L9  $CHAR60.
    #10 @1 L10 $CHAR60.
    #11 @1 L11 $CHAR60.
    #12 @1 L12 $CHAR60.
    #13 @1 L13 $CHAR60.
    #14 @1 L14 $CHAR60.
    #15 @1 L15 $CHAR60.
    #16 @1 L16 $CHAR60.
    #17 @1 L17 $CHAR60.
    #18 @1 L18 $CHAR60.
    GROUP=SHOW
    #1  @1 L1  $CHAR60. PROTECT=YES
    #2  @1 L2  $CHAR60. PROTECT=YES
    #3  @1 L3  $CHAR60. PROTECT=YES
    #4  @1 L4  $CHAR60. PROTECT=YES
    #5  @1 L5  $CHAR60. PROTECT=YES
    #6  @1 L6  $CHAR60. PROTECT=YES
    #7  @1 L7  $CHAR60. PROTECT=YES
    #8  @1 L8  $CHAR60. PROTECT=YES
    #9  @1 L9  $CHAR60. PROTECT=YES
    #10 @1 L10 $CHAR60. PROTECT=YES
    #11 @1 L11 $CHAR60. PROTECT=YES
    #12 @1 L12 $CHAR60. PROTECT=YES
    #13 @1 L13 $CHAR60. PROTECT=YES
    #14 @1 L14 $CHAR60. PROTECT=YES
    #15 @1 L15 $CHAR60. PROTECT=YES
    #16 @1 L16 $CHAR60. PROTECT=YES
    #17 @1 L17 $CHAR60. PROTECT=YES
    #18 @1 L18 $CHAR60. PROTECT=YES
    ;

* Set initial grid;
_MSG_ =  'Enter initial value for grid';
DISPLAY LIFE.INIT;
DO WHILE(1);
  CURRENT = ' ';
  DO ROW = 1 TO 18;
    ABOVE = CURRENT;
    CURRENT = L{ROW};
    IF ROW < 18 THEN BELOW = L{ROW + 1}; ELSE BELOW = ' ';
    IF NOT (ABOVE = ' ' AND CURRENT = ' ' AND BELOW = ' ') THEN
        DO COLUMN = 1 TO 60;
      * Count live cells in neighborhood;
      SELECT(COLUMN);
        WHEN(1)  DO; LEFT = 1;  WIDTH = 2; END;
        WHEN(60) DO; LEFT = 59; WIDTH = 2; END;
        OTHERWISE DO; LEFT = COLUMN - 1; WIDTH = 3; END;
        END;
      SUBSTR(NBRHOOD, 1, 3) = SUBSTR(ABOVE, LEFT, WIDTH);
      SUBSTR(NBRHOOD, 4, 3) = SUBSTR(CURRENT, LEFT, WIDTH);
      SUBSTR(NBRHOOD, 7, 3) = SUBSTR(BELOW, LEFT, WIDTH);
      COUNT = LENGTH(COMPRESS(NBRHOOD));
      * Assign live or dead state based on Life rules;
      SELECT(SUBSTR(CURRENT, COLUMN, 1));
        WHEN(' ') IF COUNT = 3 THEN
```

```
                SUBSTR(L{ROW}, COLUMN, 1) = '@'; * New live cell;
            OTHERWISE IF COUNT < 3 OR COUNT > 4 THEN
                SUBSTR(L{ROW}, COLUMN, 1) = ' '; * New dead cell;
            END;
          END;
          DISPLAY LIFE.SHOW NOINPUT;
        END;

      EXTINCT = 1;
      DO I = 1 TO 18; IF L{I} NE ' ' THEN EXTINCT = 0; END;

      * Display grid;
      IF EXTINCT THEN _MSG_ = 'END to quit.  Enter to start over.';
      ELSE _MSG_ =
        'END to quit.  RESTART to start over.  Enter to continue.';
      DISPLAY LIFE.SHOW;
      SELECT(SUBSTR(UPCASE(_CMD_), 1, 1));
        WHEN('Q') STOP;
        WHEN('E') STOP;
        WHEN('R') DELETE;
        OTHERWISE ;
        END;
      IF EXTINCT THEN DELETE;
      END;
RUN;
```

In using this program, it is important to enter a value or press the enter key at least once on every line on the screen to initialize the grid. This is because of the way the DISPLAY statement works. Avoid using up and down arrow keys when initializing the grid. Use the tab or return key to move from one row to the next. You can enter any nonblank characters in setting the initial live cells, but after that, any new live cells display as `@`.

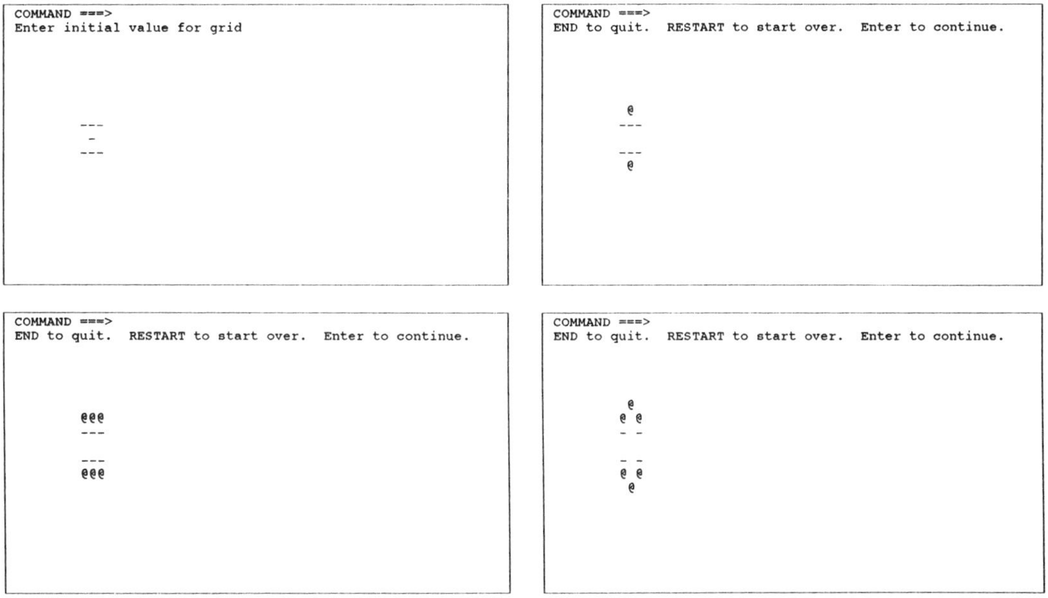

```
COMMAND ===>
END to quit.  RESTART to start over.  Enter to continue.



       @
      @ @



      @ @
       @
```

```
COMMAND ===>
END to quit.  RESTART to start over.  Enter to continue.



      @
      @



      @
      @
```

```
COMMAND ===> END
END to quit.  Enter to start over.
```

Only slight modifications would be needed to run another cellular automaton with this program.

Global distances

Calculating surface distances between places on Earth is a very practical problem, and one that can be addressed handily in a SAS program. This program starts with a list of major cities and their coordinates, and produces a report showing the distance between each pair of cities. Any locations of interest could be substituted in the input data.

This program makes the simplifying assumption that Earth is a perfect sphere. It isn't, of course; it is measurably flattened. However, the distances calculated by this program should be accurate enough for most purposes.

The first step creates the SAS dataset CITIES, which is a simple table containing observations with city name, longitude, and latitude. The second step crosses CITIES with itself to create the list of city pairs used in the report. The crossing technique is discussed in chapter 8, "Groups and sorting." The standard crossing technique is modified by the DO loop bounds so that each pair is only produced once, and a city is not paired with itself.

```
* Convert coordinates to degrees N and degrees E;
DATA CITIES (KEEP=CITY LATI LONG);
  INPUT CITY $CHAR20. LATI_D 2. +1 LATI_M 2. +1 LATI_NS $CHAR1.
                +1 LONG_D 3. +1 LONG_M 2. +1 LONG_EW $CHAR1.;
```

```
    LATI = LATI_D + LATI_M/60; IF LATI_NS = 'S' THEN LATI = -LATI;
    LONG = LONG_D + LONG_M/60; IF LONG_EW = 'W' THEN LONG = -LONG;
CARDS;---1----+----2----+----3----+-
Bombay              19°00'N  73°00'E
Cairo               30°00'N  31°15'E
Calcutta            22°30'N  88°15'E
Johannesburg        26°00'S  27°45'E
Lagos                6°15'N   3°30'E
London              51°30'N   0°00'W
Los Angeles         34°00'N 118°15'W
Mexico City         19°30'N  99°15'W
Moscow              55°45'N  37°30'E
New York            40°45'N  74°00'W
Sao Paulo           23°30'S  46°45'W
Shanghai            31°15'N 121°30'E
Sydney              34°00'S 151°15'E
Tokyo               35°45'N 139°45'E
;
OPTIONS NOCENTER NODATE NONUMBER;
TITLE 'Distances Between Cities';
  DATA _NULL_;
    RETAIN DIAMETER 12741; * Approximate Earth diameter (km);
    RETAIN R .017453292; * Factor to convert degrees to radians;
    FILE PRINT COLUMN=COLUMN;

    IF _N_ = NOBS THEN STOP;
    SET CITIES (RENAME=(CITY=CITY1 LATI=LATI1 LONG=LONG1));
    PUT / 'FROM ' CITY1 'TO:' +3 @;
    DO POINT = _N_ + 1 TO NOBS;
      SET CITIES (RENAME=(CITY=CITY2 LATI=LATI2 LONG=LONG2))
          POINT=POINT NOBS=NOBS;
      DISTANCE = DIAMETER*ARSIN(SQRT(
           (1 - COS(LATI1*R)*COS(LATI2*R)*COS((LONG1 - LONG2)*R)
              - SIN(LATI1*R)*SIN(LATI2*R))*.5));
      IF COLUMN > 60 - LENGTH(CITY2) THEN PUT / @2 @;
      PUT CITY2 DISTANCE :COMMA7. +2 @;
      END;
```

```
Distances Between Cities

FROM Bombay TO:   Cairo 4,371   Calcutta 1,632
 Johannesburg 6,993   Lagos 7,629   London 7,197
 Los Angeles 14,001   Mexico City 15,650   Moscow 5,046
 New York 12,547   Sao Paulo 13,794   Shanghai 5,027
 Sydney 10,150   Tokyo 6,722
FROM Cairo TO:   Calcutta 5,689   Johannesburg 6,238
 Lagos 3,923   London 3,508   Los Angeles 12,210
 Mexico City 12,375   Moscow 2,905   New York 9,023
 Sao Paulo 10,225   Shanghai 8,357   Sydney 14,419   Tokyo 9,566
FROM Calcutta TO:   Johannesburg 8,455   Lagos 9,204
 London 7,951   Los Angeles 13,134   Mexico City 15,273
 Moscow 5,538   New York 12,745   Sao Paulo 15,426
 Shanghai 3,423   Sydney 9,152   Tokyo 5,153
FROM Johannesburg TO:   Lagos 4,439   London 9,034
 Los Angeles 16,638   Mexico City 14,567   Moscow 9,136
 New York 12,802   Sao Paulo 7,419   Shanghai 11,799
 Sydney 11,070   Tokyo 13,561
```

```
FROM Lagos TO:   London 5,042   Los Angeles 12,440
 Mexico City 11,098   Moscow 6,268   New York 8,502
 Sao Paulo 6,377   Shanghai 12,234   Sydney 15,485   Tokyo 13,484
FROM London TO:   Los Angeles 8,767   Mexico City 8,938
 Moscow 2,485   New York 5,575   Sao Paulo 9,502   Shanghai 9,190
 Sydney 16,999   Tokyo 9,550
FROM Los Angeles TO:   Mexico City 2,473   Moscow 9,772
 New York 3,939   Sao Paulo 9,890   Shanghai 10,434
 Sydney 12,073   Tokyo 8,810
FROM Mexico City TO:   Moscow 10,712   New York 3,364
 Sao Paulo 7,433   Shanghai 12,890   Sydney 12,963   Tokyo 11,283
FROM Moscow TO:   New York 7,501   Sao Paulo 11,801
 Shanghai 6,824   Sydney 14,516   Tokyo 7,482
FROM New York TO:   Sao Paulo 7,679   Shanghai 11,851
 Sydney 15,991   Tokyo 10,836
FROM Sao Paulo TO:   Shanghai 18,570   Sydney 13,343
 Tokyo 18,515
FROM Shanghai TO:   Sydney 7,896   Tokyo 1,761
FROM Sydney TO:   Tokyo 7,847
```

This program could easily be modified to calculate distances on another planet by substituting a different value for DIAMETER in the RETAIN statement and a different set of locations in the input data.

BASIC interpreter

A programming language is executed either directly, by an interpreter, or indirectly, after being converted to machine language by a compiler. Interpreters and compilers are themselves computer programs, but they are often thought to belong in a class of their own, much too complicated for an ordinary programmer to attempt.

While it is true that writing a compiler requires a working knowledge of machine language and more of the details of computer science than most programmers need to know about, writing an interpreter does not. In fact, an interpreter is in some ways very much like an ordinary SAS program. The observation in the observation loop is just replaced by a program line.

In this section, a greatly simplified form of the BASIC programming language, which we call "B BASIC," is implemented by a SAS program. B BASIC recognizes the keywords

- IF, THEN, and ELSE, much the same as in SAS syntax
- PRINT
- LET, an optional verb used for assignment statements in BASIC
- REM, for a remark, which is what comments are called in BASIC
- FOR, TO, STEP, and NEXT, for loops, which can be nested, but have to be contained on a single line
- STOP and END to mark the end of a program

Parentheses are not recognized, and variable names can be only one letter, optionally followed by % for an integer variable or $ for a string variable. B BASIC has a large enough set of features for you to see how an interpreter works.

The interpreter works interactively, with a window in which a user can enter a program line. More than one statement can be included on a line if statements are separated by colons.

A complete explanation of the interpreter could fill up a book of its own. However, you might start by noting the four functional sections of the program. First, the user enters a BASIC program line; this is done in the DISPLAY statement at the beginning. Second, the program line is parsed, converting it into an array of tokens. Third, the line is executed. The fourth section, the expression evaluator, follows the EVALUATE statement label. It is used whenever it is needed in executing a program line.

```
* The B BASIC Interpreter
****************************************************************
The main variables used in this program:
LINE      BASIC line
UPLINE    BASIC line with letters converted to uppercase
C         index of characters in BASIC line
H         remaining part of BASIC line, uppercase
TOKEN{T}  token array
FLOAT{}   array of float variables
INT{}     array of integer variables
STRING{}  array of string variables
NUMERIC{}array of float and integer variables
T         index of token
LEN       length of string variable or constant, or other length
_MSG_     message to be displayed on screen at DISPLAY statement
IFS       count of the number of IF keywords in BASIC line
DO_ELSE   a Boolean variable indicating whether an ELSE action is executed,
          true only if the first IF condition in the preceding line was false
LEX       index of variable based on position of variable name in alphabet
VARTYPE   type of variable: blank for float, % for int, $ for string

Variables used with FOR/NEXT loops
FORLEVEL          level of nested FOR/NEXT loops: 0 outside loops
INDEXV{FORLEVEL}  index of index variable in FOR/NEXT loop
START{FORLEVEL}   beginning of loop
TO{FORLEVEL}, STEP{FORLEVEL} index values in loop

Additional variables are used with the expression evaluator.

A token is kept as a structure of length 3.  The first byte indicates the
type of token:
A  verb
K  other keyword
V  variable name
N  numeric constant
S  string constant
O  operator
E  END keyword
:  statement delimiter
blank  marks end of BASIC line

The meaning of the other two bytes depends on the type of token.
```

```
For keywords, they are the first one or two characters of the keyword.
For constants, byte 2 is the index of the beginning of the constant in the
BASIC line, in PIB1. format.  Byte 3 is the length of the constant.
For variables, byte 2 and 3 are the variable name.  Byte 2 is a capital
letter.  Byte 3 is the type:  blank, %, or $.
For operators, bytes 2 and 3 are the BASIC symbol for the operator.

String values are "C" strings.  The end of the string is marked by the
null character, '00'X.  See chapter 14, "Data Types."

When syntax errors are found in the BASIC line, an error message is assigned
to _MSG_ and the DELETE statement is executed so that the line is
redisplayed.  The line might already be partly executed.
B BASIC is forgiving in many matters of syntax.
The expression evaluator never finds an error in an expression, though it
returns 0 if it can't figure things out.
*****************************************************************;


DATA _NULL_;
  LENGTH LINE UPLINE H $ 100 STRING1-STRING26 $ 200
      SVALUE SOPERAND $ 200 XTYPE $ 1 XSTATE $ 2;
  RETAIN BNUMBER FLOAT1-FLOAT26 INT1-INT26 DO_ELSE 0
      STRING1-STRING26 '00'X ALFABET 'ABCDEFGHIJKLMNOPQRSTUVWXYZ'
      LINE;

  ARRAY STRING{26} $ STRING1-STRING26;
  ARRAY FLOAT{26} FLOAT1-FLOAT26;
  ARRAY INT{26} INT1-INT26;
  ARRAY NUMERIC{52} FLOAT1-FLOAT26 INT1-INT26;
  ARRAY TOKEN{84} $ 3 _TEMPORARY_;
  ARRAY INDEXV{8} _TEMPORARY_;
  ARRAY START{8} _TEMPORARY_;
  ARRAY TO{8} _TEMPORARY_;
  ARRAY STEP{8} _TEMPORARY_;
  WINDOW B_BASIC ROWS=3 COLUMNS=78 IROW=20 ICOLUMN=2
      GROUP=STATEMNT #1 @1 LINE $CHAR.;
  DISPLAY B_BASIC.STATEMNT;

  DO T = 1 TO 84; TOKEN{T} = '   '; END;
  * Parse;
  C = 1;
  UPLINE = UPCASE(LINE);
  DO T = 1 TO 84 WHILE(C <= 90 AND SUBSTR(UPLINE, C) NE '');
    * Find nonblank character;
    C + VERIFY(SUBSTR(LINE, C), ' ') - 1;
    H = SUBSTR(UPLINE, C);
    SELECT; * Identify tokens;
      WHEN(H =: ':')    DO; TOKEN{T} = ':  '; C + 1; END;
      * Comments;
      WHEN(H =: '!')    DO; TOKEN{T} = 'A! '; C = 99; END;
      WHEN(H =: 'REM')  DO; TOKEN{T} = 'A! '; C = 99; END;
      * Keywords;
      WHEN(H =: 'ELSE') DO; TOKEN{T} = 'AE '; C + 4; END;
      WHEN(H =: 'END')  DO; TOKEN{T} = 'END'; C = 99; END;
      WHEN(H =: 'FOR')  DO; TOKEN{T} = 'AF '; C + 3; END;
      WHEN(H =: 'IF')   DO; TOKEN{T} = 'AIF'; C + 2; END;
      WHEN(H =: 'LET')  DO; TOKEN{T} = 'AL '; C + 3; END;
```

```
    WHEN(H =: 'NEXT') DO; TOKEN{T} = 'AN '; C + 4; END;
    WHEN(H =: 'PRINT')DO; TOKEN{T} = 'AP '; C + 5; END;
    WHEN(H =: 'STOP') DO; TOKEN{T} = 'AS '; C + 4; END;
    WHEN(H =: 'STEP') DO; TOKEN{T} = 'KST'; C + 4; END;
    WHEN(H =: 'THEN') DO; TOKEN{T} = 'KTH'; C + 4; END;
    WHEN(H =: 'TO')   DO; TOKEN{T} = 'KTO'; C + 2; END;
    * Operators;
    WHEN(H =: '>=')   DO; TOKEN{T} = 'O>='; C + 2; END;
    WHEN(H =: '<=')   DO; TOKEN{T} = 'O<='; C + 2; END;
    WHEN(H =: '<>')   DO; TOKEN{T} = 'O<>'; C + 2; END;
    WHEN(INDEXC(SUBSTR(H, 1, 1), '=><+-*/^,;')) DO;
      TOKEN{T} = 'O' || SUBSTR(H, 1, 1) || ' ';
      C + 1;
      END;
    * Constants;
    WHEN(INDEXC(SUBSTR(H, 1, 1), '0123456789.')) DO;
      LEN = VERIFY(H, '0123456789.') - 1;
      IF NOT LEN THEN LEN = 81 - C;
      TOKEN{T} = 'N' || PUT(C, PIB1.) || PUT(LEN, PIB1.);
      C + LEN;
      END;
    WHEN(INDEXC(SUBSTR(H, 1, 1), '''"')) DO;
      IF C = 90 THEN LEN = 0;
      ELSE DO;  * find close quote;
        LEN = INDEXC(SUBSTR(H, 2), SUBSTR(H, 1, 1)) - 1;
        IF NOT LEN THEN LEN = 90 - C;
        END;
      TOKEN{T} = 'S' || PUT(C + 1, PIB1.) || PUT(LEN, PIB1.);
      C + LEN + 2;
      END;
    * Variable names;
    WHEN(INDEXC(SUBSTR(H, 1, 1), ALFABET)) SELECT;
      WHEN(C = 90) DO;
        TOKEN{T} = 'V' ||  SUBSTR(H, 1, 1) || ' ';
        C + 1;
        END;
      WHEN(INDEXC(SUBSTR(H, 2, 1), '$% ')) DO;
        TOKEN{T} = 'V' || UPCASE(SUBSTR(LINE, C, 2));
        C + 2;
        END;
      WHEN(INDEXC(SUBSTR(H, 2, 1),
          'ABCDEFGHIJKLMNOPQRSTUVWXYZ0123456789'))
          DO; _MSG_ = 'Unknown word'; DELETE; END;
      OTHERWISE DO;
        TOKEN{T} = 'V' || SUBSTR(H, 1, 1) || ' ';
        C + 1;
        END;
      END;
    OTHERWISE DO; _MSG_ = 'Unknown symbol'; DELETE; END;
    END;
  END;

* Check syntax and execute;
IF TOKEN{1} NE 'AE ' THEN DO_ELSE = 0;
IFS = 0; FORLEVEL = 0;
T = 1;
DO UNTIL(T > 84); * verb loop;
  SELECT(TOKEN{T});
```

```
WHEN('   ') T = 99; * End of line;
WHEN('A! ') T = 99; * Remark;
WHEN(':  ') T + 1; * End of statement;
WHEN('END') DO; * END statement;
  IF T = 1 THEN STOP;
  ELSE DO; _MSG_ = 'END ignored'; T = 99; END;
  END;
WHEN('AE ') DO; * ELSE statement;
  IF T = 1 AND DO_ELSE THEN DO; T + 1; DO_ELSE = 0; END;
  ELSE T = 99;
  END;
WHEN('AF ') DO; * FOR statement;
  FORLEVEL + 1;
  T + 1;
  IF TOKEN{T} NE: 'V' THEN
      DO; _MSG_ = 'Index variable expected'; DELETE; END;
  IF SUBSTR(TOKEN{T}, 3) = '$' THEN
      DO; _MSG_ = '$ index variable not allowed'; DELETE; END;
  INDEXV{FORLEVEL} = INDEXC(ALFABET, SUBSTR(TOKEN{T}, 2, 1))
      + 26*(SUBSTR(TOKEN{T}, 3, 1) = '%');
  T + 1;
  IF TOKEN{T} NE 'O= ' THEN DO; _MSG_ = '= expected'; DELETE; END;
  T + 1;
  LINK EVALUATE;
  NUMERIC{INDEXV{FORLEVEL}} = NVALUE;
  IF TOKEN{T} NE 'KTO' THEN DO; _MSG_ = 'TO expected'; DELETE; END;
  T + 1;
  LINK EVALUATE;
  TO{FORLEVEL} = NVALUE;
  IF TOKEN{T} = 'KST' THEN DO;
    T + 1;
    LINK EVALUATE;
    IF NOT NVALUE THEN
      DO; _MSG_ = 'Can''t STEP by 0'; DELETE; END;
    STEP{FORLEVEL} = NVALUE;
    END;
  ELSE STEP{FORLEVEL} = 1;
  IF SIGN(STEP{FORLEVEL}) =
      -SIGN(TO{FORLEVEL} - NUMERIC{INDEXV{FORLEVEL}}) THEN
      DO; _MSG_ = 'TO and STEP values inconsistent'; DELETE; END;
  IF TOKEN{T} NE ':' THEN
      DO; _MSG_ = ': expected after FOR statement'; DELETE; END;
  T + 1;
  START{FORLEVEL} = T;
  END;
WHEN('AIF') DO; * IF statement;
  IFS + 1;
  T + 1;
  LINK EVALUATE;
  IF TOKEN{T} NE 'KTH' THEN
      DO; _MSG_ = 'THEN expected'; DELETE; END;
  ELSE IF NVALUE THEN T + 1;
  ELSE DO; T = 99; IF IFS = 1 THEN DO_ELSE = 1; END;
  END;
WHEN('AL ') DO; * LET statement;
  T + 1;
  IF TOKEN{T} NE: 'V' THEN
      DO; _MSG_ = 'Variable name expected'; DELETE; END;
```

```
    LEX = INDEXC(ALFABET, SUBSTR(TOKEN{T}, 2, 1));
    VARTYPE = SUBSTR(TOKEN{T}, 3);
    T + 1;
    IF TOKEN{T} NE 'O= ' THEN DO; _MSG_ = '= expected'; DELETE; END;
    T + 1;
    LINK EVALUATE;
    SELECT(VARTYPE);
      WHEN('$') STRING{LEX} = SVALUE;
      WHEN('%') INT{LEX} = ROUND(NVALUE);
      OTHERWISE FLOAT{LEX} = NVALUE;
      END;
    END;
  WHEN('AN ') DO; * NEXT statement;
    IF FORLEVEL <= 0 THEN DO; _MSG_ =
        'FOR statement expected before NEXT statement'; DELETE; END;
    NUMERIC{INDEXV{FORLEVEL}} + STEP{FORLEVEL};
    IF (STEP{FORLEVEL} > 0 AND
        NUMERIC{INDEXV{FORLEVEL}} <= TO{FORLEVEL}) OR
       (STEP{FORLEVEL} < 0 AND
        NUMERIC{INDEXV{FORLEVEL}} >= TO{FORLEVEL}) THEN
        T = START{FORLEVEL};
    ELSE DO;
      FORLEVEL + -1;
      DO UNTIL(TOKEN{T} IN (' ', ':', 'A!') OR T >= 84); T + 1; END;
      END;
    END;
  WHEN('AP ') DO; * PRINT statement;
    T + 1;
    DO WHILE(TOKEN{T} NOTIN: (' ', ':', 'A!') AND T < 84);
      SELECT;
        WHEN(TOKEN{T} = 'O; ') DO; PUT ' ' @; T + 1; END;
        WHEN(TOKEN{T} = 'O, ') DO; PUT '     ' @; T + 1; END;
        WHEN(TOKEN{T} IN: ('S', 'N', 'O', 'V')) DO;
          LINK EVALUATE;
          SELECT(XTYPE);
            WHEN('S') DO;
              LENGTH = INDEXC(SVALUE, '00'X) - 1;
              IF LENGTH < 0 THEN LENGTH = 200;
              IF LENGTH > 0 THEN PUT SVALUE $VARYING200. LENGTH @;
              END;
            WHEN('N') PUT NVALUE :BEST16. @;
            OTHERWISE ;
            END;
          END;
        OTHERWISE ;
        END;
      END;
    PUT;
    END;
  WHEN('AS ') STOP; * STOP statement;
  OTHERWISE DO;
    IF TOKEN{T} =: 'V' THEN DO;  * implied LET statement;
      LEX = INDEXC(ALFABET, SUBSTR(TOKEN{T}, 2, 1));
      VARTYPE = SUBSTR(TOKEN{T}, 3);
      T + 1;
      IF TOKEN{T} NE 'O= ' THEN DO; _MSG_ = '= expected'; DELETE; END;
      T + 1;
      LINK EVALUATE;
```

```
          SELECT(VARTYPE);
            WHEN('$') STRING{LEX} = SVALUE;
            WHEN('%') INT{LEX} = ROUND(NVALUE);
            OTHERWISE FLOAT{LEX} = NVALUE;
            END;
          END;
        ELSE DO; _MSG_ = 'Verb expected'; DELETE; END;
        END;
      END;
    END;

  LINE = ''; DELETE; * Go on to next BASIC line;


*****************************************************************
Expression evaluator

This expression evaluator is used anywhere an expression should appear
in a BASIC statement.  It is state-oriented, with the top level of
branching done on XSTATE.
Ultimately, three values are returned:  XTYPE, NVALUE, and SVALUE.

These variables are used only with the expression evaluator:
NVALUE   the numeric value of the expression
SVALUE   the string value of the expression
XSTATE   a code containing the state of the evaluation:
          N if the expression so far produces a numeric value
          S if the expression so far produces a character value
          $+ if the last token was a concatenation operator
          an operator symbol if the last token was any other operator
          blank at the beginning of the expression
          X if an error has occurred in the expression
XTYPE    a code containing the type of the expression:  N, S, or blank
XSIGN    + or - if unary + or - operators are found
NOPERAND a numeric value used temporarily
SOPERAND a string value used temporarily

Release 6.06 and later: change all occurrences of COMMA32. to ?? COMMA32.
*****************************************************************;


EVALUATE:
    NVALUE = 0; SVALUE = '00'X;
    XSTATE = '  '; XTYPE = ' '; XSIGN = ' ';
    DO T = T TO 84 WHILE(TOKEN{T} IN: ('O', 'V', 'N', 'S')
                    AND TOKEN{T} NOTIN ('O, ', 'O; '));
      IF XSTATE IN ('N', 'S') THEN XSIGN = ' ';
      SELECT;
        WHEN(XSTATE = 'X ') ;
        WHEN(XSTATE NOTIN ('N', 'S') AND TOKEN{T} IN ('O+ ', 'O- ')) SELECT;
          WHEN(TOKEN{T} = 'O- ' AND XSIGN = '-') XSIGN = '+';
          WHEN(TOKEN{T} = 'O- ' OR XSIGN = '-') XSIGN = '-';
          OTHERWISE XSIGN = '+';
          END;
        WHEN(XSTATE = '  ') SELECT;
          WHEN(TOKEN{T} =: 'V' AND SUBSTR(TOKEN{T}, 3) = '$') DO;
            XTYPE = 'S'; XSTATE = 'S';
            SVALUE = STRING{INDEXC(ALFABET, SUBSTR(TOKEN{T}, 2, 1))};
            IF XSIGN NE ' ' THEN DO;
```

```
      XTYPE = 'N'; XSTATE = 'N';
      NVALUE = INPUT(LEFT(SVALUE), COMMA32.);
      IF NVALUE <= .Z THEN DO; NVALUE = 0; _ERROR_ = 0; END;
      IF XSIGN = '-' THEN NVALUE = -NVALUE;
      END;
    END;
  WHEN(TOKEN{T} =: 'V') DO;
    XTYPE = 'N'; XSTATE = 'N';
    IF SUBSTR(TOKEN{T}, 3) = '%' THEN
         NVALUE =   INT{INDEXC(ALFABET, SUBSTR(TOKEN{T}, 2, 1))};
    ELSE NVALUE = FLOAT{INDEXC(ALFABET, SUBSTR(TOKEN{T}, 2, 1))};
    IF XSIGN = '-' THEN NVALUE = -NVALUE;
    END;
  WHEN(TOKEN{T} =: 'S' AND XSIGN = ' ') DO;
    XTYPE = 'S'; XSTATE = 'S';
    SVALUE = SUBSTR(LINE, INPUT(SUBSTR(TOKEN{T}, 2, 1), PIB1.),
        INPUT(SUBSTR(TOKEN{T}, 3), PIB1.)) || '00'X;
    END;
  WHEN(TOKEN{T} IN: ('N', 'S')) DO;
    XTYPE = 'N'; XSTATE = 'N';
    SOPERAND = SUBSTR(LINE, INPUT(SUBSTR(TOKEN{T}, 2, 1), PIB1.),
                        INPUT(SUBSTR(TOKEN{T}, 3), PIB1.));
    NVALUE = INPUT(LEFT(SOPERAND), COMMA32.);
    IF NVALUE <= .Z THEN DO; NVALUE = 0; _ERROR_ = 0; END;
    IF XSIGN = '-' THEN NVALUE = -NVALUE;
    END;
  OTHERWISE XSTATE = 'X';
  END;
WHEN(XSTATE = 'N ') SELECT;
  WHEN(TOKEN{T} =: 'O') XSTATE = SUBSTR(TOKEN{T}, 2);
  OTHERWISE XSTATE = 'X';
  END;
WHEN(XSTATE = 'S ') SELECT;
  WHEN(TOKEN{T} = 'O+ ') XSTATE = '$+'; * Concatenation;
  WHEN(TOKEN{T} IN ('O<', 'O<=', 'O=', 'O>=', 'O>', 'O<>'))
      XSTATE = SUBSTR(TOKEN{T}, 2);  * Character comparison;
  WHEN(TOKEN{T} =: 'O') DO; * Numeric operator;
    XTYPE = 'N';
    NVALUE = INPUT(LEFT(SVALUE), COMMA32.);
    IF NVALUE <= .Z THEN DO; NVALUE = 0; _ERROR_ = 0; END;
    XSTATE = SUBSTR(TOKEN{T}, 2);
    END;
  OTHERWISE XSTATE = 'X';
  END;
WHEN(XSTATE = '$+') SELECT; * Concatenation;
  WHEN(TOKEN{T} =: 'V' AND SUBSTR(TOKEN{T}, 3) = '$') DO;
    LEN = INDEXC(SVALUE, '00'X);
    IF LEN THEN SUBSTR(SVALUE, LEN) =
        STRING{INDEXC(ALFABET, SUBSTR(TOKEN{T}, 2, 1))};
    END;
  WHEN(TOKEN{T} =: 'V') DO;
    LEN = INDEXC(SVALUE, '00'X);
    IF LEN THEN SUBSTR(SVALUE, LEN) = SCAN(PUT(
        NUMERIC{INDEXC(ALFABET, SUBSTR(TOKEN{T}, 2, 1))
                + 26*(SUBSTR(TOKEN{T}, 3) = '%')},
        BEST16.), 1, ' ') || '00'X;
    END;
  WHEN(TOKEN{T} =: 'S' AND XSIGN = ' ') DO;
```

```
      LEN = INDEXC(SVALUE, '00'X);
      IF LEN THEN SUBSTR(SVALUE, LEN) =
          SUBSTR(LINE, INPUT(SUBSTR(TOKEN{T}, 2, 1), PIB1.),
                       INPUT(SUBSTR(TOKEN{T}, 3), PIB1.)) || '00'X;
      END;
    WHEN(TOKEN{T} IN: ('N', 'S')) DO; * Concatenate numeral;
      LEN = INDEXC(SVALUE, '00'X);
      IF LEN THEN DO;
        SOPERAND = SUBSTR(LINE, INPUT(SUBSTR(TOKEN{T}, 2, 1), PIB1.),
                                INPUT(SUBSTR(TOKEN{T}, 3), PIB1.));
        NOPERAND = INPUT(LEFT(SOPERAND), COMMA32.);
        IF NOPERAND <= .Z THEN DO; NOPERAND = 0; _ERROR_ = 0; END;
        IF XSIGN = '-' THEN NOPERAND = -NOPERAND;
        SUBSTR(SVALUE, LEN) =
            SCAN(PUT(NOPERAND, BEST16.), 1, ' ') || '00'X;
        END;
      END;
    OTHERWISE XSTATE = 'X';
    END;
  WHEN(XSTATE IN ('< ', '<=', '= ', '>=', '> ', '<>') AND XTYPE = 'S')
      DO;
    SELECT;
      WHEN(TOKEN{T} IN: ('S', 'N')) DO;
        IF TOKEN{T} =: 'S' AND XSIGN = ' ' THEN SOPERAND =
            SUBSTR(LINE, INPUT(SUBSTR(TOKEN{T}, 2, 1), PIB1.),
                         INPUT(SUBSTR(TOKEN{T}, 3), PIB1.)) || '00'X;
        ELSE DO;
          SOPERAND = SUBSTR(LINE,
                         INPUT(SUBSTR(TOKEN{T}, 2, 1), PIB1.),
                         INPUT(SUBSTR(TOKEN{T}, 3), PIB1.));
          NOPERAND = INPUT(LEFT(SOPERAND), COMMA32.);
          IF NOPERAND <= .Z THEN DO; NOPERAND = 0; _ERROR_ = 0; END;
          IF XSIGN = '-' THEN NOPERAND = -NOPERAND;
          SOPERAND = SCAN(PUT(NOPERAND, BEST16.), 1, ' ') || '00'X;
          END;
        END;
      WHEN(TOKEN{T} =: 'V' AND SUBSTR(TOKEN{T}, 3) = '$') DO;
        SOPERAND = STRING{INDEXC(ALFABET, SUBSTR(TOKEN{T}, 2, 1))};
        IF XSIGN NE ' ' THEN DO;
          NOPERAND = INPUT(LEFT(SOPERAND), COMMA32.);
          IF NOPERAND <= .Z THEN DO; NOPERAND = 0; _ERROR_ = 0; END;
          IF XSIGN = '-' THEN NOPERAND = -NOPERAND;
          SOPERAND = SCAN(PUT(NOPERAND, BEST16.), 1, ' ') || '00'X;
          END;
        END;
      WHEN(TOKEN{T} =: 'V') DO;
        NOPERAND = NUMERIC{INDEXC(ALFABET, SUBSTR(TOKEN{T}, 2, 1))
                     + 26*(SUBSTR(TOKEN{T}, 3) = '%')};
        IF XSIGN = '-' THEN NOPERAND = -NOPERAND;
        SOPERAND = SCAN(PUT(NOPERAND, BEST16.), 1, ' ') || '00'X;
        END;
      OTHERWISE XSTATE = 'X';
      END;
    SELECT(XSTATE);
      WHEN('< ') NVALUE = SVALUE <  SOPERAND;
      WHEN('<=') NVALUE = SVALUE <= SOPERAND;
      WHEN('= ') NVALUE = SVALUE =  SOPERAND;
      WHEN('>=') NVALUE = SVALUE >= SOPERAND;
```

```
      WHEN('> ') NVALUE = SVALUE >  SOPERAND;
      WHEN('<>') NVALUE = SVALUE NE SOPERAND;
      OTHERWISE XSTATE = 'X';
      END;
    IF XSTATE NE 'X' THEN DO; XTYPE = 'N'; XSTATE = 'N'; END;
    END;
  WHEN(XSTATE IN ('< ', '<=', '= ', '>=', '> ', '<>', '+ ', '- ',
                  '* ', '/ ', '^ ')) DO; * Numeric operation;
    IF XTYPE = 'S' THEN DO; * Convert string value to number;
      LEN = INDEXC(SVALUE, '00'X);
      IF LEN THEN SUBSTR(SVALUE, LEN) = ' ';
      NVALUE = INPUT(LEFT(SVALUE), COMMA32.);
      IF NVALUE <= .Z THEN DO; NVALUE = 0; _ERROR_ = 0; END;
      END;
    SELECT;
      WHEN(TOKEN{T} IN: ('S', 'N')) DO;
        SOPERAND = SUBSTR(LINE,
                     INPUT(SUBSTR(TOKEN{T}, 2, 1), PIB1.),
                     INPUT(SUBSTR(TOKEN{T}, 3), PIB1.));
        NOPERAND = INPUT(LEFT(SOPERAND), COMMA32.);
        IF NOPERAND <= .Z THEN DO; NOPERAND = 0; _ERROR_ = 0; END;
        IF XSIGN = '-' THEN NOPERAND = -NOPERAND;
        END;
      WHEN(TOKEN{T} =: 'V' AND SUBSTR(TOKEN{T}, 3) = '$') DO;
        SOPERAND = STRING{INDEXC(ALFABET, SUBSTR(TOKEN{T}, 2, 1))};
        LEN = INDEXC(SOPERAND, '00'X);
        IF LEN THEN SUBSTR(SOPERAND, LEN) = ' ';
        NOPERAND = INPUT(LEFT(SOPERAND), COMMA32.);
        IF NOPERAND <= .Z THEN DO; NOPERAND = 0; _ERROR_ = 0; END;
        IF XSIGN = '-' THEN NOPERAND = -NOPERAND;
        END;
      WHEN(TOKEN{T} =: 'V') DO;
        NOPERAND = NUMERIC{INDEXC(ALFABET, SUBSTR(TOKEN{T}, 2, 1))
                       + 26*(SUBSTR(TOKEN{T}, 3) = '%')};
        IF XSIGN = '-' THEN NOPERAND = -NOPERAND;
        END;
      OTHERWISE XSTATE = 'X';
      END;
    SELECT(XSTATE);
      WHEN('< ') NVALUE = NVALUE <  NOPERAND;
      WHEN('<=') NVALUE = NVALUE <= NOPERAND;
      WHEN('= ') NVALUE = NVALUE =  NOPERAND;
      WHEN('>=') NVALUE = NVALUE >= NOPERAND;
      WHEN('> ') NVALUE = NVALUE >  NOPERAND;
      WHEN('<>') NVALUE = NVALUE NE NOPERAND;
      WHEN('+ ') NVALUE = NVALUE +  NOPERAND;
      WHEN('- ') NVALUE = NVALUE -  NOPERAND;
      WHEN('* ') NVALUE = NVALUE *  NOPERAND;
      WHEN('/ ') NVALUE = NVALUE /  NOPERAND;
      WHEN('^ ') NVALUE = NVALUE ** NOPERAND;
      OTHERWISE XSTATE = 'X';
      END;
    IF XSTATE NE 'X' THEN DO; XTYPE = 'N'; XSTATE = 'N'; END;
    IF NVALUE <= .Z THEN DO; NVALUE = 0; _ERROR_ = 0; END;
    END;
  OTHERWISE XSTATE = 'X';
  END;
END;
```

```
    * Expression evaluator returns both numeric and string values;
    SELECT(XTYPE);
      WHEN('N') SVALUE = SCAN(PUT(NVALUE, BEST16.), 1, ' ');
      WHEN('S') DO;
        SOPERAND = SVALUE;
        LEN = INDEXC(SOPERAND, '00'X);
        IF LEN THEN SUBSTR(SOPERAND, LEN) = ' ';
        NOPERAND = INPUT(LEFT(SOPERAND), COMMA32.);
        IF NOPERAND <= .Z THEN DO; NOPERAND = 0; _ERROR_ = 0; END;
        END;
      OTHERWISE DO; SVALUE = '00'X; NVALUE = 0; END;
      END;
    RETURN;
RUN;
```

The B BASIC interpreter demonstrates the complexity of control flow that a data step can have. Each of the three large parts of the step is implemented as a SELECT block within a DO loop. Within the SELECT blocks, some of the WHEN actions include other SELECT blocks. The LINK statement is used to access the expression evaluator, keeping it separate from the rest of the step.

The implementation of FOR/NEXT loops demonstrates one way a complicated feature can be simple to program. The use of the arrays with the index values FORLEVEL makes nested FOR/NEXT loops almost as easy as a single FOR/NEXT loop would be. Conversely, the expression evaluator shows how complicated a simple feature can prove to be. The expression evaluator is over 200 lines but still does not implement all the features usually allowed in BASIC expressions. A more structured approach would have to be taken to code a comprehensive expression evaluator.

As written, the interpreter uses a very simple application of a data step window. The window consists of only one field, in addition to the command line and message line.

The B BASIC interpreter can be used to run BASIC statements like the ones below, entering one line at a time in the B_BASIC window:

```
LET A% = 1
LET B% = 3
LET P = 3.14159265358979  ! pi
FOR R = A% TO B%:PRINT R;P/4*R*R;R*R:NEXT:!print r,circle,square
```

```
1  0.78539816339745  1
2  3.14159265358979  4
3  7.06858347057703  9
```

```
FOR I = 2 TO 10:S = 0:FOR X = 1 TO I:S = S + X:NEXT:PRINT I;S:NEXT
```

```
2  3
3  6
4  10
5  15
```

```
6  21
7  28
8  36
9  45
10  55
```

```
LET Q = 15      ! quantity
IF Q >= 12 THEN D% = Q/12:D = D%*3.39:I=-D%*12+Q*.30:PRINT Q;D+I
ELSE PRINT Q;Q*.30
```

```
15  4.29
```

You can also enter lines containing B BASIC syntax errors in order to see how the error handling logic works. In reading the syntax/execution part of the interpreter, you can note that there is no fundamental difference between executing a syntactically correct statement and issuing an error message for a line that contains an error.

```
Command ===>

IF Q >= 12
```

```
Command ===>
THEN expected
IF Q >= 12
```

There are many ways in which the B BASIC interpreter could be modified. To add statements, you would just need to add the keywords to the SELECT block that does parsing and then add the execution of the statement to the syntax/execution part of the program. The interpreter could be revised to run with a line mode interface instead of using display manager windows, following the example of the revised math program in chapter 18, "User interface."

Program file features could be added. You could have the program copy the BASIC lines that are entered to the log or to another file by using a PUT statement with the LINE variable right after the DISPLAY statement. To have the interpreter execute a program from a file, you could replace the DISPLAY statement with an INPUT statement. You could also add support for the BASIC INPUT statement to allow a BASIC program to read data from an input file.

There is no reason why the parsing and interpreting logic in the interpreter has to be used to run BASIC programs. You could modify it to run a programming language of your own design. More practically, you could use the same general approach to implement a simpler command syntax to be used in a user interface for a SAS program, allowing users to issue commands to the program.

Update

Many new features were added in releases 6.08–6.10, some of them quite useful to SAS programmers. The biggest new feature is the REPORT proc.

The REPORT proc

Designed as an interactive way to generate reports, the REPORT proc is perhaps even more valuable to programmers. Use the NOWD option to bypass the proc windows and send output directly to the standard print file.

By default, the proc produces the same kind of listing as the _ALL_ keyword of the PUT statement. With additional statements, however, it produces tables and gives you much more control over their appearance than the PRINT proc allows.

Tables

Unlike most procs that produce tables, the REPORT proc is designed around columns rather than variables. Instead of a VAR statement, you list variables in the COLUMN statement and define them further in DEFINE statements.

The COLUMN statement lists the columns of the report and determines the order in which they appear. In simple cases, the columns are simply variables from the SAS dataset named in the PROC statement. The COLUMN statement also includes any header that spans columns. In parentheses, list the header and columns it covers. For a header of more than one line, simply use more than one character constant.

Each variable is listed again in its own DEFINE statement. The DEFINE statement is the word DEFINE, the variable name from the COLUMN statement, a slash, and any options that apply to the variable. The possible options include one or more character constants as a column header, the

FORMAT= or F= option with a format specification or the WIDTH= option to set the column width, the SPACING= option to set the number of spaces to the left of the column, the FLOW option for word wrap when the value is wider than the column, LEFT, CENTER, or RIGHT for alignment, and PAGE to begin the column on a new page. The DEFINE statement may be omitted if there are no options to declare for a variable.

Even in this simple example, the REPORT proc goes beyond what the PRINT proc can do:

```
TITLE1 'Your Elected Officials';
  PROC REPORT DATA=POLS NOWD;
    COLUMN NAME OFFICE DISTRICT ('Elections' ELECTED NEXT);
    DEFINE NAME / 'Name' WIDTH=23;
    DEFINE OFFICE / 'Office' WIDTH=15 SPACING=1;
    DEFINE DISTRICT / 'District' WIDTH=11 SPACING=1;
    DEFINE ELECTED / 'Last' FORMAT=YEAR4.;
    DEFINE NEXT / 'Next' FORMAT=YEAR4.;
RUN;
```

```
                        Your Elected Officials

                                                         Elections
    Name                   Office          District      Last  Next
    Public, Joe            Mayor           Anytown       1993  1998
    Sharp, Guy             Sen.            FL            1990  1996
    Badley, Sue            Sen.            NY            1992     .
    Doppler, Elizabeth     Rep.            MD 37         1994  1996
    North, Jerome          Pres.           USA              .  1996
    LaFemme, Churchill     V.P.            USA              .  1996
```

Several PROC statement options affect the appearance of the table. To set off the column headers, use the HEADLINE option for a line and the HEADSKIP option for a blank line. To produce a table with no headers, use the NOHEADER option. You can change the default column width and spacing with the COLWIDTH= and SPACING= options. The CENTER, LS=, PS=, WRAP, PANELS=, and PSPACE= options affect the layout of the page.

Aliases

Because each column has its own DEFINE statement, the REPORT proc can print the same variable twice with two different formats. But if the same variable appears twice, how do you know which DEFINE statement belongs to which column? That's what aliases are for. An equals sign and an alias follow the variable name in the COLUMN statement, and you use the alias in the DEFINE statement.

```
TITLE1 'Your Elected Officials';
  PROC REPORT DATA=POLS NOWD HEADLINE;
    COLUMN NAME OFFICE ('Last Elected' ELECTED=MONTH ELECTED=YEAR);
    DEFINE NAME / 'Name' WIDTH=23;
    DEFINE OFFICE / 'Office' Width=17 SPACING=1;
    DEFINE MONTH / 'Month' FORMAT=MONNAME9.;
    DEFINE YEAR / 'Year' FORMAT=YEAR4.;
```

```
RUN;
```

```
                    Your Elected Officials

                                                Last Elected
Name                     Office                 Month  Year
------------------------------------------------------------
Public, Joe              Mayor               November  1993
Sharp, Guy               Sen.                November  1990
Badley, Sue              Sen.                November  1992
Doppler, Elizabeth       Rep.                November  1994
North, Jerome            Pres.                      .     .
LaFemme, Churchill       V.P.                       .     .
```

Usage

One of the options that can appear in a DEFINE statement is the *usage* of a variable, a code that determines what part of the report the column is. In a regular table report, the usage of every variable is DISPLAY, and you don't have to specify it. Other usages that can appear in a regular table report are ORDER and COMPUTED.

Order variables

An order variable differs from a display variable in two ways. First, it changes the order of rows in the table. That is, the table is sorted according to the order variable. If there are several order variables, they take precedence in sorting according to their order of appearance in the COLUMN statement.

Second, each value of an order variable appears only once, on the first row with that value. The column is blank in subsequent rows that have the same value. (However, when an order variable is displayed in a row, all order variables to its right are also displayed.) Even if the SAS dataset is already sorted, you can define a variable as an order variable in order to have each value of the variable appear only once, not repeated on every line.

Computed variables

You can display variables that are based on other variables in the report or in the SAS dataset. A computed variable has the usage COMPUTED in its DEFINE statement and gets its value in a code segment.

A code segment is a group of general programming statements, much the same as in the data step. It can include the data step assignment, sum, LENGTH, and CALL statements, along with control flow statements other than those that refer to the observation loop of the data step.

A code segment is preceded by a COMPUTE statement and followed by an ENDCOMP statement to form a COMPUTE block. The COMPUTE statement names the variable being computed and, for a character variable, sets the length of the variable in the /LENGTH= option. This is an example of a DEFINE statement and COMPUTE block to compute a numeric variable:

```
DEFINE T_KELVIN / COMPUTED WIDTH=8;
COMPUTE T_KELVIN;
  T_KELVIN = (T_FAHREN + 459.67)*5/9;
  IF .Z < T_KELVIN < 0 THEN T_KELVIN = 0;
  ENDCOMP;
```

A COMPUTE block can create and use variables other than ones that appear in the report. Those variables survive from one code segment to the next, so variables created in one code segment can be used in a subsequent code segment. The REPORT proc computes columns from left to right in each row, so a COMPUTE block can only rely on values to its left — variables listed in the COLUMN statement to the left of the variable being computed, and variables computed in those columns' COMPUTE blocks. If you need to base a computation on a variable in the SAS dataset that does not appear in the report, list the variable in the COLUMN statement and define it with the appropriate usage and the NOPRINT option.

Conditional formatting

Among several ways you can format a variable differently in different rows of a report, the most direct is with the DEFINE routine. This CALL routine can only be used in the code segments of the REPORT proc. Its first argument is the number or name of a column. The second argument, when setting a format, is the code string `'FORMAT'`. The third argument is a format specification. The routine changes the format of the column for one row only. To be effective, the routine must execute to the left of the column.

The following example simply blanks out a column, using the $BLANK format, based on a condition of a variable in the SAS dataset. Two columns with the NOPRINT option make the computation possible: CONFIRM, a variable from the SAS dataset used in the computation, and BLANK, which provides an anchor for the execution of COMPUTE block.

```
  PROC FORMAT;
    VALUE $BLANK OTHER=' ';
RUN;
TITLE 'Scheduled Events';
  PROC REPORT DATA=FUTURE NOWD NOHEADER;
    COLUMN DATE CONFIRM BLANK CITY SPONSOR;
    DEFINE DATE / ORDER FORMAT=DATE9. ORDER=INTERNAL;
    DEFINE CONFIRM / DISPLAY NOPRINT;
    DEFINE BLANK / COMPUTED NOPRINT;
    DEFINE CITY / WIDTH=15;
    DEFINE SPONSOR / WIDTH=15;
    COMPUTE BLANK;
      IF NOT CONFIRM THEN
          CALL DEFINE('SPONSOR', 'FORMAT', '$BLANK.');
      ENDCOMP;
RUN;
```

```
                         Scheduled Events

          21JAN1997  NEW YORK          Bjorn's Pizza
          28JAN1997  DAYTONA BEACH
          06JUL1997  HALIFAX           Devon Island Fr
          08JUL1997  HAGERSTOWN, MD    Parker & Locker
```

The LINE statement

COMPUTE blocks can also execute at the beginning or end of the report or at the beginning or end of each value of an ORDER variable. There, COMPUTE blocks are not necessarily used to compute new variables. More often, they put additional lines, called *break lines*, in the report. They do that with the LINE statement.

The LINE statement implements a subset of the features of the PUT statement. The LINE statement can include character constants, repeated character constants, the @ and + pointer controls, and variables with formats. Unlike the PUT statement, the LINE statement is not an executable statement. It cannot be made conditional, because it is not affected by control flow statements. The following example produces a line of periods between values of the ORDER variable DATE:

```
COMPUTE AFTER DATE;
  LINE @11 60*'.';
  ENDCOMP;
```

Use multiple LINE statements to print multiple lines.

Blank lines

If you just want a blank line between groups, you can do that with a BREAK statement. Its options determine actions that happen between groups. Use the SKIP option for a blank line:

```
BREAK AFTER DATE / SKIP
```

Other break options are PAGE, for a page break, SUMMARIZE to print a summary line, OL, UL, DOL, and DUL for lines over or under the break lines or summary line, and SUPPRESS to keep the break variable from being printed on the summary line.

A break can also happen at the beginning or end of the report. Use the RBREAK BEFORE or RBREAK AFTER statement with break options and COMPUTE blocks with the keyword BEFORE or AFTER, but without a variable name.

Summary lines

When you use the SUMMARIZE option on the RBREAK statement, the report includes a summary line. The traditional use of the summary line is for a line of totals at the end of the report, as in the example below. This example also demonstrates the use of the PANELS= option to divide the page into columns.

```
TITLE1 'State Names';
  PROC REPORT DATA=STATES NOWD
      LS=80 PS=30 PANELS=2 PSPACE=12 HEADSKIP;
    COLUMN NAME LETTERS;
    DEFINE NAME / WIDTH=18;
    DEFINE LETTERS / WIDTH=7;
    RBREAK AFTER / OL SUMMARIZE;
RUN;
```

```
                              State Names

  NAME                LETTERS            NAME                LETTERS

  Alabama                   7            Nebraska                  8
  Alaska                    6            Nevada                    6
  Arizona                   7            New Hampshire            12
  Arkansas                  8            New Jersey                9
  California               10            New Mexico                9
  Colorado                  8            New York                  7
  Connecticut              11            North Carolina           13
  Delaware                  8            North Dakota             11
  Florida                   7            Ohio                      4
  Georgia                   7            Oklahoma                  8
  Hawaii                    6            Oregon                    6
  Idaho                     5            Pennsylvania             12
  Illinois                  8            Rhode Island             11
  Indiana                   7            South Carolina           13
  Iowa                      4            South Dakota             11
  Kansas                    6            Tennessee                 9
  Kentucky                  8            Texas                     5
  Louisiana                 9            Utah                      4
  Maine                     5            Vermont                   7
  Maryland                  8            Virginia                  8
  Massachusetts            13            Washington               10
  Michigan                  8            West Virginia            12
  Minnesota                 9            Wisconsin                 9
  Mississippi              11            Wyoming                   7
  Missouri                  8                                -------
  Montana                   7                                    412
```

Summary lines can also appear at the end of a group if you use the SUMMARIZE option in the BREAK statement, or at the beginning of the report or a group if you specify BEFORE instead of AFTER in the RBREAK or BREAK statement.

Analysis variables

In the previous example, because of the SUMMARIZE option, the variable LETTERS is an analysis variable instead of a display variable. An analysis variable has a statistic applied to it before it is printed — in this case, the default statistic, SUM. A more complete DEFINE statement would read:

```
DEFINE LETTERS / WIDTH=7 ANALYSIS SUM;
```

The detail rows in the report actually calculate the statistic on the single value of the observation shown in the row. Because the SUM statistic of a single value is the value itself, the detail rows look the same as if the variable were a simple display variable. Other statistics that may make sense to use in a regular table report are MIN, MAX, and MEAN. You can select the statistic in the DEFINE statement or in the COLUMN statement, putting a comma between the variable and the statistic.

Summary reports

If you eliminate the detail lines from a report, keeping only the summary lines, you have a summary report. In a summary report, group and analysis variables take the place of order and display variables. The report displays one row of summary statistics per group instead of one row per observation. If there is only one observation per group, the summary report may be the same as a detail report of the same SAS dataset.

You can't tell by looking at the following report that it is a summary report. The group and analysis variables are presented just the same as order and display variables.

```
  PROC REPORT DATA=ION NOWD;
    COLUMN SCHEME ELEMENT COUNT;
    DEFINE SCHEME / 'Scheme' GROUP WIDTH=6;
    DEFINE ELEMENT / 'Element' GROUP WIDTH=7;
    DEFINE COUNT / 'Count' ANALYSIS SUM FORMAT=COMMA9.;
    BREAK AFTER SCHEME / SKIP;
RUN;
```

```
                  Ion Counts

         Scheme  Element      Count
         A       H           18,294
                 He           3,181
                 Li           1,928
                 Other        2,437

         B       H            9,647
                 He           3,534
                 Li           1,929
                 Other        2,006
```

In a summary report, you might want to display several columns with different statistics for the same variable. You can use parentheses in the COLUMN statement to associate a list of variables with a list of statistics, as:

```
COLUMN GROUP (LENGTH WIDTH),(MIN MEAN MAX);
```

A comma between two items in the COLUMN statement means that the items share the same column. With parentheses for grouping, all combinations of the two groups are formed.

An across variable is just a group variable displayed horizontally rather than vertically. It is associated with an analysis variable to make a two-dimensional table of statistics, similar to the TABULATE proc. For that kind of report, list the across variable after the group variables, because the across variable appears to the right of the group variables in the report. In the following example, SCHEME is the across variable, and it is grouped with the analysis variable COUNT and the statistic N. When not associated with an analysis variable, N produces a frequency count.

There are several other things to notice in the following example. Aliases are used for the statistic N, which appears twice in the COLUMN statement. The header defined for SCHEME begins and ends with a hyphen, which is repeated in the report to fill the width of its header space; this helps the reader identify which columns SCHEME covers. The COMPUTE block uses the DEFINE routine with the BLANK format to blank out the N columns in the summary rows, where they aren't meaningful. A summary row is identified when the value of the last group variable is missing. Column numbers, rather than names, are used to identify the columns because, with the across variable, more than one column has the same name. When counting columns to determine the column arguments for the DEFINE routine, you have to count the BLANK column, even though it is not displayed in the report.

```
  PROC FORMAT;
    VALUE BLANK OTHER=' ';
RUN;
TITLE 'Ion Counts';
  PROC REPORT DATA=ION NOWD;
    COLUMN ELEMENT SITE BLANK SCHEME,(COUNT N=N1) N=N2;
    DEFINE SCHEME / '- Scheme -' ACROSS WIDTH=6;
    DEFINE ELEMENT / 'Element' GROUP WIDTH=7;
    DEFINE SITE / 'Site' GROUP WIDTH=4;
    DEFINE BLANK / COMPUTED NOPRINT;
    DEFINE COUNT / 'Count' ANALYSIS SUM FORMAT=COMMA9.;
    DEFINE N1 / 'Trials' FORMAT=COMMA6.;
    DEFINE N2 / 'Total' 'Trials' FORMAT=COMMA7.;
    BREAK AFTER ELEMENT / SUMMARIZE SUPPRESS SKIP;
    RBREAK AFTER / SUMMARIZE PAGE;
    COMPUTE BLANK;
      IF SITE = '' THEN DO I = 5, 7, 8;
        CALL DEFINE(I, 'FORMAT', 'BLANK.');
        END;
      ENDCOMP;
RUN;
```

```
                               Ion Counts

                   -------------- Scheme --------------
                              A                       B              Total
 Element  Site          Count  Trials          Count  Trials        Trials
 H           1         17,770       3          9,268       3             6
             2            310       3            209       3             6
             3            214       3            170       3             6
```

		18,294		9,647		
He	1	2,981	3	3,336	3	6
	2	105	3	104	3	6
	3	95	3	94	3	6
		3,181		3,534		
Li	1	1,876	3	1,848	3	6
	2	33	3	45	3	6
	3	19	2	36	3	5
		1,928		1,929		
Other	1	1,749	3	1,367	3	6
	2	287	3	281	3	6
	3	401	3	358	3	6
		2,437		2,006		
		25,840		17,116		

If you define a table with only group variables, the table is a list of the values of the group variables. You can make it a frequency table by adding the column N or by using an across variable. If you define a table with only analysis variables, the table shows one row of statistics calculated over the entire SAS dataset. Computed variables and break lines can also appear in a summary report and work the same way as in a listing report.

Data step features

The new features of data step syntax shouldn't fundamentally change your approach to SAS programming, but they present major improvements in a few specialized areas.

Indexed table lookup

The KEY= option of the SET statement makes it possible to do an indexed table lookup from a SAS data file. This is easier to code and usually runs faster than the other storage table lookup techniques described in chapter 15.

The KEY= option names an index of the SAS dataset. The SET statement then looks for an observation whose key values match the value of the same variables in the data step. Use the /UNIQUE option after the KEY= option to indicate that you are looking for just one observation. The automatic variable _IORC_ is 0 if the observation is found, a nonzero return code if it is not found.

The following example puts all this together. Suppose you want to summarize account data by customer, looking up the customer ID and name in an account table. The account data is the SAS dataset CURRENT, the account table is ACCT, and it has a simple index on ACCOUNT.

```
DATA CUSTCUR;
  SET CURRENT;
  * Add customer ID and name from account table;
  SET ACCT (KEEP=ACCOUNT CUSTID CUSTNAME) KEY=ACCOUNT/UNIQUE;
```

```
    IF _IORC_ THEN DO; * Account not found in account table;
      CUSTID = '';
      CUSTNAME = '';
      END;
RUN;
  PROC SUMMARY DATA=CUSTCUR PRINT SUM N;
    CLASS CUSTID;
    ID CUSTNAME;
RUN;
```

If you want to look up more than one observation with the same key value, omit the /UNIQUE option and put the SET statement in a DO loop that repeats until _IORC_ is a nonzero return code.

MODIFY statement

The introduction of the MODIFY statement makes it possible to use the same physical SAS dataset for input and output in a data step. Effectively, you can use a data step to edit a SAS dataset. Name the SAS dataset in the DATA statement and again in the MODIFY statement, which acts basically like the SET statement. Then, based on data step logic, you can write out modified observations with the REPLACE statement, remove observations with the REMOVE statement, and add new observations with the OUTPUT statement.

Suppose, for example, you want to delete from the SAS dataset XFER.RECENT all observations that are more than a year old, based on the value of the variable INITDATE. You could do that with this step:

```
  DATA XFER.RECENT;
    MODIFY XFER.RECENT;
    IF INITDATE < "&SYSDATE"D - 365 THEN REMOVE;
RUN;
```

The REPLACE statement would be useful, for example, if you want to correct missing and negative values of the variable COUNT, setting them to 0. After the DATA and MODIFY statements, the statements would be:

```
IF COUNT < 0 THEN DO;
  COUNT = 0;
  REPLACE;
  END;
```

The MODIFY statement is usually faster than the SET statement for this kind of task. With the SET statement, the data step write the entire SAS dataset; with the MODIFY statement, it writes only the parts that are changed.

The MODIFY statement can also be used with the WHERE= option or the KEY= option (described above for the SET statement) to edit only selected observations of a SAS dataset. Other observations in the SAS dataset are not affected by the data step. For example, the INITDATE example above could have been written:

```
  DATA XFER.RECENT;
    MODIFY XFER.RECENT (WHERE=(INITDATE < "&SYSDATE"D - 365));
    REMOVE;
RUN;
```

The MODIFY statement can also be used with two SAS datasets and a BY statement. In this form, it resembles the behavior of the UPDATE statement, using nonmissing values in the second SAS dataset to update values from the first SAS dataset. However, although you can change the values of existing variables by using the REPLACE statement, you cannot add new variables to the SAS dataset named in the MODIFY statement, and you can add new observations only at the end of the SAS dataset.

Routines

The number of routines in the SAS System continues to increase. These are some of the most useful new routines.

EXECUTE

The EXECUTE routine is another useful tool for flexcode and macro programming. Used in the CALL routine in a data step, it takes one argument, a character value. It resolves any macrolanguage references in the value. The resulting SAS statements, if any, are executed after the data step executes. The resulting statements must be complete statements. The EXECUTE routine is the only way to access the macro processor during the execution of a data step. Be sure to use a RUN statement at the end of a data step that uses the EXECUTE routine.

The EXECUTE routine offers a better way to stop a program based on a data step condition. The statement is:

```
IF condition THEN CALL EXECUTE('ENDSAS;');
```

The program then stops at the conclusion of the data step.

Bitwise functions

A new set of functions does bitwise operations on the set of integers from 0 to $2^{32} - 1$, treating a number as a string of 32 bits. Bitwise logical operations apply logical operators independently to each of the 32 bits in the integer. Bit shifting removes some of the bits at the left or the right and moves the rest of them over in that direction. These are the bitwise functions:

Function call	Description
BAND(*n*, *n*)	bitwise logical AND
BOR(*n*, *n*)	bitwise logical OR
BXOR(*n*, *n*)	bitwise logical exclusive OR (bitwise ≠)
BNOT(*n*)	bitwise NOT
BLSHIFT(*n*, *d*)	shift left *d* bits
BRSHIFT(*n*, *d*)	shift right *d* bits

String functions

New functions fill in some of the gaps in the SAS System's string processing. The LOWCASE function is the lowercase counterpart to the UPCASE function. The TRIMN function goes beyond the TRIM function to convert a blank value to a null string. The TRANWRD function is similar to the TRANSLATE function, but replaces substrings rather than individual characters. The INDEXW function is like the INDEX function, but looks for the substring as an entire word in the string.

The QUOTE and DEQUOTE functions turn a character value into a SAS character constant and vice versa. These functions are useful when exchanging data with other programs in comma-delimited files.

Finally, the SOUNDEX function encodes a word with a modified Soundex encoding, which is traditionally used to find out whether two words are likely to sound similar.

International dates

Release 6.10 introduced international informats and formats. Primarily, they read and write dates in various languages. The routine names have the form *lan*`DF`*ir*, where *lan* is one of the language codes listed below and *ir* is a code identifying the international informat or format. The codes are:

Code	Language
DAN	Danish
DES	Swiss_German
DEU	German
ENG	English
ESP	Spanish
FIN	Finnish
FRA	French
FRS	Swiss_French
ITA	Italian
NLD	Dutch
NOR	Norwegian
PTG	Portuguese
SVE	Swedish

Code	International Informat
DE	DATE
DT	DATETIME
MY	MONYY

Code	International Format
DD	DDMMYY
DE	DATE
DN	WEEKDAY
DT	DATETIME
DWN	DOWNAME
MN	MONNAME
MY	MONYY
WKX	WEEKDATX
WDX	WORDDATX

For example, use the format DEUDFMN to write the German name of the month of a SAS date value.

The language that the international informats and formats use is determined by the system option DFLANG=, which selects one of the languages listed above. The default in English-speaking countries is `DFLANG=English`.

Glossary

across variable, *n.* in the REPORT proc, a variable that forms groups of observations for analysis whose values form columns rather than rows.

action, *n.* a statement or block used as the part of a control flow statement that is executed conditionally.

address, *n.* an index indicating the location of an object, especially in memory or on a storage volume.

algorithm, *n.* a sequence of instructions for completing a task.

analysis variable, *n.* a variable used to calculate statistics or for other computations.

application, *n.* 1. a more or less specific use of a computer. 2. a computer program with a more or less specific purpose.

argument, *n.* a value provided to a function or other routine by the program calling it

array, *n.* 1. in the SAS programming language, a list of variables that can be identified under a common name (the **array name**), as defined in an ARRAY statement, with the specific variable being referred to identified by one or more subscripts. 2. in other programming languages, a variable that has several values, which are distinguished from each other by the use of one or more subscripts.

ASCII, *adj.* having to do with a standard character set, used on most computers, that associates specific characters with the numbers 0–127.

assembler, *n.* 1. a program for converting assembly language to machine language. 2. assembly language.

assembly language, *n.* any low-level language in which program lines correspond directly to machine language instructions.

assignment statement, *n.* a statement whose second term is an equals sign, that assigns the value of the expression on the right side to the variable, array reference, or pseudo-variable on the left side.

at-sign, *n.* the character "@".

attribute, *n.* a fixed characteristic of a SAS variable, as its name, type, length, informat, format, or label.

automated, *adj.* not requiring the attention or effort of a person while a process takes place. Cf. **manual**, **computerized**.

automatic, *adj.* happening by default; happening without the intervention of a person.

automatic variable, *n.* a variable that a process creates without mentioning the variable by name.

background, *adj.* of a program, executing without any direct association with a screen display. Cf. **foreground**.

backslash, *n.* the character "\".

base SAS, see **SAS product**.

base, *n.* 1. a number to which an exponent is applied; the number to the left of the exponentiation operator. 2. the number used in defining a system of numerals, as the number 10 in decimal numerals. 3. a SAS dataset to which the observations of another SAS dataset are appended.

BASIC, *n.* a programming language, usually implemented as an interpreter, often used to teach beginning programmers about computers and programming.

batch, *adj.* 1. run without user interaction. 2. grouped to be processed together.

binary, *adj.* 1. having to do with the quantity two. 2. using a set of two digits, 0 and 1, to represent numbers or other information. 3. (of an operator) having two operands. 4. (of a file) considered as a sequence of bytes.

binary search, *n.* a search of a sorted file or array that progressively reduces the range of elements under consideration by determining which half of the remaining range the element being sought is in.

bit, *n.* a binary digit; the smallest possible unit of information, having only two possible values.

bitwise, *adj.* operating on the individual bits of a value.

blank, *n.* the character used to indicate an empty position on a page or screen.

block, *n.* several statements that are treated as one statement for control flow purposes. See **DO block**.

Boolean, *adj.* having to do with the use of 1 to represent true and 0 to represent false, and the mathematical treatment of logical problems.

brace, *n.* either of the characters "{" (**left brace**) and "}" (**right brace**); used to enclose array subscripts

bracket, *n.* either of the characters "[" (**left bracket**) and "]" (**right bracket**); may be used to enclose array subscripts in some SAS implementations.

branch, *v.* 1. to cause execution to continue at another place, or conditionally at one of several places. *n.* 2. an instance of branching.

bubble sort, *n.* a simple sort algorithm, which repeatedly compares each consecutive pair of objects, exchanging them when indicated

bug, *n.* unintended or undocumented behavior of a computer program. **buggy**, *adj.*

bullet, *n.* the character "•", often used to indicate the beginning of an item in a list (a **bulleted list**)

BY group, *n.* a group of consecutive observations in a SAS dataset with the same values of one or more variables, when so identified by a BY statement.

byte, *n.* an amount of information equal to 8 bits.

byte variable, *n.* a one-byte variable considered as an integer, either unsigned or signed.

C, *n.* a programming language, used for most software development and popular on microcomputers and under the Unix operating system, known for its simplicity, portability, and low-level access to data; the language in which the SAS System, beginning with version 6, is written.

CALL routine, *n.* a routine used in a CALL statement, which usually has arguments and might modify one or more of its arguments.

call, *v.* 1. to cause (a program, function, or routine) to be executed. *n.* 2. an instance of calling.

card, *n.* a record, especially in a text file.

catalog, *n.* 1. a list of files. 2. a SAS file that can contain screens and other data objects.

cell, *n.* the intersection of a row and a column in a table or grid.

character set, *n.* the set of characters used by a computer, printer, terminal, screen, etc., often including the numbers used to represent each of the characters.

character, *n.* 1. a symbol intended to be printed or displayed or having some special meaning in a file, usually represented as one byte. 2. a byte considered as a character. *adj.* 3. having to do with the SAS data type used to hold characters and other data

Cobol, *n.* a compiled programming language, usually nonstructured, known for its wordy, sentence-like syntax, widely used on mainframes and for financial programming.

code, *n.* 1. a particular standard for representing information in symbols. 2. a set of symbols representing information in a particular code. 3. source code. *v.* 4. to write code. 5. to represent using a code; encode.

collating sequence, *n.* 1. a character set, considered in terms of its effect on character comparisons. 2. a rule used to resolve character comparisons, overriding the values used to represent the characters.

colon, *n.* the character ":", used to separate a statement from a statement label

command, *n.* a sequence of characters telling a computer program to take a particular immediate action.

comment, *n.* a string of characters, usually descriptive, that appear in a program file but are marked as not belonging to the program, as a **delimited comment**, between the symbols "/*" and "*/", or a **comment statement**, beginning with "*" and ending with ";".

compiler, *n.* a program or routine that translates a high-level language to machine language.

computed variable, *n.* a variable whose values are assigned based on programming statements.

computerized, *adj.* requiring the use of a computer. Cf. **automated**.

concatenate, *v.* to combine two or more objects of the same type, end to end to form a single object of the same type. **concatenation**, *n.*

condition, *n.* an expression representing a logical true or false value, especially when used in a control flow statement, such as an IF … THEN statement.

conditional, *adj.* depending on a condition.

constant, *n.* a value that does not change in the course of running a program.

control flow, *n.* the order of execution of instructions in a program.

control report, *n.* a report that contains general information on the actions of a computer program or other process.

counter, *n.* a variable that counts the number of occurrences of something.

counting number, *n.* a number used in counting; positive integer.

cross, *v.* to combine two objects in a way that pairs each element of one object with each object of the other.

crosstabulate, *v.* to create a table showing the results of crossing. **crosstabulation**, *n.*

data step, *n.* a SAS step, identified by a DATA statement, in which programming can be done. Cf. **proc step**.

data type, *n.* See **type**.

database, *n.* a quantity of organized data, considered as a unit.

dataset option, *n.* an option that affects the input or output of a SAS dataset, used by listing it in parentheses following the SAS dataset name in a DATA, SET, MERGE, PROC, or other statement.

database management system, *n.* A program designed to manage and operate databases. Also, **DBMS**.

DDname, *n.* under the MVS operating system, a name temporarily associated with a file, corresponding to a fileref, libref, etc.

debug, *v.* to remove bugs.

decimal, *adj.* using a set of 10 digits (0–9) in numerals to represent numbers

decimal point, *n.* 1. the position in a numeral between the digits that represent the integer part (on the left) and the digits that represent a fractional part (on the right). 2. a period used to indicate this position. Also, *informal*, **point**.

default, *n.* 1. an action or condition that holds in the absence of an explicit decision. 2. an instance of using a default. *v.* 3. to use a default.

delimiter, *n.* 1. a character, such as a blank or comma, that indicates the end of a token or term. 2. a symbol, usually a blank, used to indicate the division between values in input data. **delimit**, *v.*

dialog, *n.* a user interface with a dynamic resembling a conversation between the user and the program.

digit, *n.* a character or symbol used in representing magnitude in a numeral, especially the 10 digits (0–9) used in decimal numerals. Cf. **decimal**, **bit**.

digit string, *n.* a character string consisting of digits, used as a code.

direct access, *n.* 1. access of an object by the object's address. *adj.* 2. able to be accessed by address. 3. allowing access by address.

directory, *n.* a list of files including information about the files, such as their size and location.

display manager, *n.* the part of the supervisor that provides the main full-screen interface for running SAS programs, including the program editor, log, output, help, keys, and other related windows. Also, **SAS Display Manager System**.

display variable, *n.* in the REPORT proc, a variable from the input SAS dataset whose values are directly displayed in the report for each observation.

DO block, *n.* a block consisting of the DO and END statements and any statements in between; treated as a single statement for control flow purposes.

DO loop, *n.* a DO block modified by an index variable or WHILE or UNTIL condition to execute repeatedly.

document, *v.* to write a description of; especially, to write a description of (a program) so that a programmer can understand it or so that a user can use it. **documentation**, *n.*

domain, *adj.* the range of values that can be used as an argument to a particular function.

dot, *n. informal.* a period used as a separator, especially in a name.

double precision, *adj.* having to do with the use of 8 bytes to represent numbers in floating point form; the way the SAS System represents numeric values in memory.

EBCDIC, *adj.* having to do with a character set used mainly on IBM mainframes.

element, *n.* 1. in the SAS programming language, one of the variable in an array. 2. one of the values in an array or structure.

end, *v.* (of a program) to stop executing, returning control to the calling program; something almost all programs, other than operating systems, are expected to do. Also, **stop**.

engine, *n.* a routine that controls access to SAS datasets.

engineering notation, *n.* a form of scientific notation using exponents that are multiples of 3.

error, *n.* 1. also, **syntax error**. an instance of a program failing to follow the syntax rules of a programming language. 2. also, **error condition**, **data error**. an unexpected program state resulting from invalid input data. 3. also, **logical error**. an instance of a program behaving in an unexpected way because it is coded incorrectly.

error code, *n.* a return code in which a nonzero value represents an error condition.

exclamation point, *n.* the character "!". Also, **exclamation mark**.

exhaustive, *adj.* considering or encompassing all possibilities.

explicitly subscripted array, *n.* an array whose subscript is the value of an expression that is part of the array reference. Cf. **implicitly subscripted array**.

exponent, *n.* 1. in exponentiation, the number indicating the number of times the base is multiplied; the number to the right of the exponentiation operator. 2. in scientific notation, the number indicating the power of 10 to be used. 3. in the floating point form, the number indicating the power of 2 to be used.

exponentiation, *n.* the process of multiplying a number together a specified number of times; raising a number to a power; indicated by the operator "**".

extension, *n.* the second part of an MS-DOS file name, having up to three characters.

field, *n.* a set of consecutive character positions that form a logical unit, especially in a record or screen.

file, *n.* a group of logically related stored data, treated as a unit by I/O routines, usually having a name.

fileref, *n.* a name temporarily associated with an input or output text file by a FILENAME statement or by similar means.

flexcode, *n.* a program that modifies itself as it runs.

floating point, *adj.* having to do with a method for representing numbers in binary form having a mantissa, an exponent representing the power of 2 to be multiplied by the mantissa to yield the number being represented, and a sign bit.

footnote, *n.* a note at the bottom of a page or table.

footnote lines, *n.* lines printed at the bottom of a page in a print file, defined by FOOTNOTE statements.

foreground, *adj.* of a program, having or being associated with a simultaneous screen display. Cf. **background**.

format, *n.* 1. also, **form**. a particular way of organizing data as a sequence of character or bytes, as in a file, record, or field. 2. a routine for converting a data value into characters. *v.* 4. to convert data into a particular format.

format option, *n.* an option associated with the definition of a format in a VALUE or PICTURE statement.

format specification, *n.* a specification for formatting, including a format name, an optional width specification, and sometimes an optional decimal specification; used in the PUT statement and the PUT function and as the format attribute of a variable.

formatted cell dataset, *n.* a SAS dataset containing formatted values for cells to be printed in a table report and indexes indicating where the cells appear.

Fortran, *n.* a programming language, usually structured, widely used on all kinds of computers for scientific and mathematical programming; used for writing SAS functions through SAS version 5.

function, *n.* 1. a routine, especially one that has arguments and returns a value based on the value of the arguments. 2. in mathematics, a mapping from one set to another, or a rule or formula for mapping.

gigabyte, *n.* an amount of information equal to 1,000 or 1,024 megabytes.

group variable, *n.* in the REPORT proc, a variable that forms groups of observations for analysis and also determines the order of rows.

hard-code, *v.* to include data values in a program's source code.

hardware, *n.* computers and the machines, connectors, etc., used with them.

heading, *n.* text at the top of a table or page. Also, **header**.

hexadecimal, *adj.* using a set of 16 digits (0–9, A–F) to represent numbers. Also, informally, **hex**.

hierarchical, *adj.* consisting of consecutive levels, with each object in a level associated with a specific object in the next higher level. **hierarchy**, *n.*

high-level, *adj.* of a computer language, designed to be comprehensible to programmers.

I/O, *n.* input and output, considered together.

implementation, *n.* 1. a particular SAS release in the form used for a particular computer class and operating system. 2. a compiler or interpreter for a particular programming language, as distinguished from different compilers and interpreters for that language.

implicitly subscripted array, *n.* an array whose subscript is the value of a specified variable. Cf. **explicitly subscripted array**.

implied decimal point, *n.* a decimal point not indicated by a period or other symbol.

index, *n.* 1. a number assigned sequentially to one of a set of objects, processes, etc. 2. a structure of a SAS dataset that lists the locations of observations having each different value of one or more key variables. *v.* 3. to create an index.

index variable, *n.* 1. a variable that takes on different values for repeated executions of a loop. 2. a variable used as the index of an array.

infinite loop, *n.* a loop whose structure does not include a provision for stopping.

informat option, *n.* an option associated with the definition of an informat in an INVALUE statement.

informat specification, *n.* a specification for interpreting, including an informat name, an optional width specification, and sometimes an optional decimal specification; used in the INPUT statement and the INPUT function and as the informat attribute of a variable.

informat, *n.* a routine used to convert data in a particular format to a SAS character or numeric value.

input, *n.* the process of moving data into a computer's memory from storage or other external devices.

install, *v.* to prepare for operation at a particular place or for use with specific equipment.

installation, *n.* 1. the process of or an instance of installing. 2. a place where or computer on which something is installed.

instruction, *n.* 1. a unit of machine language, usually one or more bytes, executed as a single process by a processor. 2. an assembly language code representing a machine language instruction.

integer, *n.* 1. a whole number or the negative of a whole number; a number with no fractional part. *adj.* 2. having to do with a method for representing numbers in binary form, using each bit as a binary digit, except for one bit sometimes used as a sign bit.

interactive, *adj.* of a program, using or expecting input from a user in the course of executing.

interleave, *v.* to combine sorted SAS datasets to create a single SAS dataset that contains all the observations of each of the SAS datasets and has the same sorted order, or a similar process with similar objects.

interpret, *v.* to determine the meaning of; to convert data into a more usable form.

interpreter, *n.* a program for executing programs in a particular programming language.

invoke, *v.* to make something, such as a macro, active by using its name. **invocation**, *n.*

job, *n.* a logically separate unit of processing; especially one treated as a separate process by the operating system of a multiuser computer.

keyword, *n.* a word with a specific syntactic meaning.

key, *n.* a variable, variables, field, etc., whose value is considered in matching and sorting.

kilobyte, *n.* an amount of information equal to 1,000 or 1,024 bytes.

label, *n.* 1. a character string, usually descriptive, associated with an object such as a variable or SAS dataset. 2. also, **statement label**. a word associated with a statement, preceding it and followed by a colon, used to identify the statement in GOTO statements and other branching.

leading blank, *n.* a blank or one of several blanks at the beginning of a character string.

leading zero, *n.* a zero digit at the beginning of a numeral.

length, *n.* 1. the length of a character value, as **visual length**, the index of the last nonblank character in a character string; **memory length**, the number of bytes of memory assigned to hold a value; **expression length**, the total number of characters in a character value. 2. an attribute of a SAS variable indicating the number of bytes used to store the variable in a SAS dataset, and for a character variable also determining the memory length and expression length of the variable.

library, *n.* a group of related files.

libref, *n.* a name temporarily associated with a SAS data library by a LIBREF statement or other method, and used as the first level of multi-level SAS file names.

line, *n.* 1. a sequence of characters aligned horizontally on a page or screen. 2. a record in a text file, considered as corresponding to a line on a printed page.

linear search, *n.* the process of finding an object in an array or file by checking each object in turn until the correct object is found.

list input, *n.* input of a variable from an input text file by the use of a variable name in an INPUT statement with no associated informat specification or columns given for the variable.

list output, *n.* output of a variable to an output text file by the use of a variable name in an PUT statement with no associated format specification or columns given for the variable.

log, *n.* a file created by the SAS supervisor that contains SAS program lines and messages about the execution of the program.

logical, *adj.* having or having to do with true and false values.

logically, *adv.* having to do with the purpose or meaning of something.

lookup, *n.* table lookup.

loop, *n.* 1. a control structure that makes a sequence of actions in a program execute repeatedly. 2. the sequence of actions that is executed repeatedly in a loop. *v.* 3. to execute a sequence of actions repeatedly.

low-level, *adj.* of a computer language, designed around the instruction set of a microprocessor.

machine language, *n.* a language consisting of the instructions that can be executed by a particular computer; executable code. Also, **machine code**.

macro compilation, *n.* the process of parsing and storing a macro.

macro execution, *n.* the process of converting a stored macro to SAS source code.

macro processor, *n.* the part of the SAS supervisor that handles macrolanguage objects.

macro, *n.* 1. a stored macrolanguage object defined by the %MACRO and %MEND statements. 2. program macro.

macrolanguage, *n.* a language consisting of statements and objects that create SAS source code.

macrovariable, *n.* a macrolanguage object associating a string of characters with a name, kept in memory.

mainframe, *n.* one of a class of usually multiuser computers characterized by complex architecture, fast processor and I/O speeds, and extremely high prices.

maintenance programming, *n.* revisions of a program and modifications done after the program is already in operation.

mantissa, *n.* 1. in floating-point form, a factor to be multiplied by a power of 2 to yield the magnitude of the number being represented. 2. a number having a similar function in notational forms similar to floating-point.

manual, *adj.* 1. requiring the attention or effort of a person while a process takes place. Cf. **automated**. *n.* 2. a book describing the use of a product, supplied by the people who supply the product.

match, *v.* 1. to have the same key value. 2. to associate two or more matching objects. *n.* 3. an instance of matching.

match cross, *v.* 1. to cross the BY groups of two or more SAS datasets. *n.* 2. an instance of match crossing.

match merge, *v.* 1. to merge in a way that matches objects according to their key values. *n.* 2. an instance of match merging.

megabyte, *n.* an amount of information equal to 1,000 or 1,024 kilobytes.

member, *n.* a SAS file belonging to a SAS data library.

memory, *n.* space for information in electrical devices, especially silicon chips. Cf. **storage**.

merge, *v.* 1. to combine SAS datasets or similar objects by combining the observations or other elements of the objects. *n.* 2. an instance of merging.

microcomputer, *n.* an ordinary computer; generally smaller and simpler in architecture than a minicomputer or mainframe, and designed to be used by one person at a time

minicomputer, *n.* a small or medium-sized multiuser computer, or a computer with an architecture more complicated than that of a microcomputer but less complicated than that of a mainframe.

missing value, *n.* 1. a nan used to represent the absence of a value in a SAS numeric value. 2. a blank character value, or a character value of length 0.

modular, *adj.* divided into physically and operationally separate parts.

module, *n.* one of the parts in a modular object, especially a routine in a structured programming language.

MS-DOS, *n.* a Microsoft operating system, the most widely used operating system to date.

multiuser, *adj.* designed for use by several users at the same time.

MVS, *n.* an IBM mainframe operating system, including the variants MVS/XA and MVS/ESA.

name, *n.* a word associated with an object, used to identify it.

nan, *n.* a floating point value associated with an error condition or used as a missing value rather than representing a number.

named input, *n.* in earlier SAS versions and some Fortran implementations, the ability to assign values to variables by reading input lines in which a variable name is followed by an equals sign and a value to be assigned to the variable.

named output, *n.* output to a text file in which a variable name is followed by an equals sign and the value of the variable.

native, *adj.* (of a SAS dataset) in a form specified by the SAS System.

non-print file, *n.* a text file not containing print control characters.

null, *n.* 1. a zero byte, considered as a character. 2. a missing value in SQL. 3. a macroexpression of length 0. *adj.* 4. having to do with a null.

numeral, *n.* a representation of a number using characters or symbols.

numeric, *adj.* having to do with the SAS data type used to represent numbers.

object, *n.* something that occupies or is associated with space in memory, as a variable, file, statement, file, constant, function, etc.

observation, *n.* 1. an instance of values of the variables in a SAS dataset. 2. the input data of one execution of an observation loop. 3. one item in a sample.

observation loop, *n.* 1. a loop that processes one observation in each repetition. 2. the automatic input-driven loop of most SAS steps.

one-to-one merge, *n.* a merge in which elements are combined sequentially, beginning with the first ones.

operand, *n.* a value used with an operator.

operating system, *n.* a program that controls the hardware of a computer and allows other programs to execute.

operator, *n.* 1. a token representing a mathematical or other process to be done on one or two operands. 2. a person who operates a computer or other equipment; user.

option, *n.* a value, usually set in a statement or command, that controls the way a program or process executes.

order variable, *n.* in the REPORT proc, a variable used to determine the order of rows

OS, *n.* 1. operating system. 2. An IBM mainframe operating system, the precursor of MVS.

OS/2, *n.* a microcomputer operating system, intended as a successor to MS-DOS.

output manager, *n.* a part of display manager that can be used to display, copy, and delete parts of the standard print file.

output, *n.* the process of moving data from a computer's memory to storage or other external devices.

pad, *v.* to extend to a certain length by adding blanks, zeros, etc., to the beginning or end of a value.

page, *n.* 1. one side of a sheet of paper, for the purposes of writing or printing. 2. a part of a print file between two consecutive new page characters.

panel, *n.* in the REPORT proc, a horizontal division of a page.

parameter, *n.* 1. a value that controls the actions of a program. 2. a value that varies the form of a probability distribution. 3. an argument of a SAS macro. Also, informally, **parm**.

parenthesis, *n.*, *pl.* **parentheses**. either of the characters "(" (**left parenthesis**) and ")" (**right parenthesis**), used for grouping and to enclose arguments.

parse, *v.* to divide a computer program, statement, or other character string into its meaningful components according to a set of rules. **parser**, *n.*

Pascal, *n.* a structured programming language, often used to teach structured programming techniques to students, and on microcomputers.

PDV, *n.* program data vector.

percent sign, *n.* the character "%".

picture, *n.* a character string containing formatting instructions for the picture processor, used in a picture format.

picture format, *n.* a numeric format defined by the PICTURE statement in the FORMAT proc, which associates ranges of values to be formatted with pictures.

picture option, *n.* an option associated with a picture in a picture format.

picture processor, *n.* the routine that uses a picture in a picture format to format a numeric value.

PL/1, *n.* a structured programming language, known for the diversity of its syntax features, formerly popular on mainframes; the language in which most of the SAS System, through version 5, was written. Also, **PL/I**.

pointer control, *n.* a term in an INPUT or PUT statement used to change the position of the column pointer or the line pointer.

population, *n.* a set to be studied statistically; especially a set from which a sample is drawn.

port, *v.* to move (source code) from one computer to another or from one compiler or interpreter to another.

portable, *adj.* able to be ported easily.

print file, *n.* a file containing special characters (**print control characters**) that communicate formatting information such as page breaks to a printer.

print output, *n.* text output from a program, suitable for printing

priority, *n.* 1. the state or condition of happening first. 2. a characteristic of an operator that determines whether it is executed before or after other operators in the same expression.

proc step, *n.* a step, identified by a PROC statement, that executes a proc.

proc, *n.* a routine used in a proc step. Also, formally, **procedure**.

program data vector, *n.* the block of memory that holds the values of all variables in a SAS step.

program macro, *n.* in SAS version 5 and earlier on mainframes, a form of macro consisting of part of a program, defined using the MACRO statement; after it is defined in a program, it can be invoked by using its name.

program, *n.* 1. a sequence of actions by a computer to achieve a particular result; routine. 2. a symbolic representation of this, as in a programming language. *v.* 3. to write or otherwise create a program.

pseudo-array, *n.* a structure used in a way that resembles the use of an array.

pseudo-variable, *n.* a part of a character variable to which a value is assigned when the SUBSTR function is used on the left side of an assignment statement.

quantile, *n.* 1. one of a set of values marking the division of a distribution into equal parts, as a **median**, which divides a distribution into two equal parts; **quartiles**, which divide a distribution into four equal parts; **percentiles**, which divide a distribution into 100 equal parts; etc. 2. also, **quantile rank**. one of the equal parts of a distribution between successive quantiles.

quote, *n.* 1. also, **quote mark**, **quotation mark**. either of the characters " ' " (**single quote**) and " " " (**double quote**), either of which may be used in a matched pair to enclose a character constant or any of certain other types of constants. *v.* 2. to enclose in quotes. 3. to cause to be treated as a constant in a manner similar to enclosing in quotes.

random number, *n.* a number selected randomly.

random sample, *n.* a sample selected randomly from a population, and therefore expected to be representative of the population in certain ways.

range, *n.* 1. a set of values treated together, as in a format definition. 2. the set of values that an array subscript may correctly take on.

recode, *n.* to replace one code with another.

record layout, *n.* a table defining the location and contents of the fields in a record. Also, **record format**.

record, *n.* a sequence of characters in a file treated as a unit by I/O routines; often, a sequence of characters between control characters used to mark record boundaries.

remark, *n.* a comment in a BASIC program.

release, *n.* a minor change in the SAS System, identified by a fractional number, such as 6.06, usually encompassing several implementations for different computers and operating systems.

report, *n.* output from a computer program intended to be read by a person.

return, *n.* 1. to resume execution or cause execution to be resumed at the place of an earlier branch, as with a LINK statement, or at the place a routine was called after the routine ends. 2. (of a function) to provide (a value) to the calling routine or program when returning. *n.* 3. an instance of returning. Cf. **call**.

return code, *n.* a value returned by a routine that indicates the success or failure of the process carried out by the routine.

round, *v.* to change a numeric value to a nearby value that belongs to a specified set of numbers, such as integers or double precision numbers.

rounding error, *n.* the difference between a number and the number used in a computer to represent that number.

routine, *n.* a sequence of actions taken by a computer to achieve a particular result, especially when used as part of a larger program.

run time, *n.* 1. the period of time when a program runs. 2. the length of time it takes a program to run. *adj.* 3. having to do with or occurring in run time. Also, **runtime**.

sample, *n.* a subset of a population.

SAS data library, *n.* a group of related SAS files.

SAS dataset, *n.* a data file organized in a way that can be used by the specialized I/O syntax of the SAS system, as the DATA and SET statements, and as input to SAS procs.

SAS date, *n.* a date or point in time expressed as the number of days since January 1, 1960.

SAS datetime, *n.* a measurement of a point in time expressed as the number of seconds since the beginning of January 1, 1960.

SAS file, *n.* a native SAS dataset, SAS catalog, or other file that can be a member of a SAS data library.

SAS product, *n.* one of a group of separately licensed and documented products that make up the SAS System, as **base SAS**, which includes the SAS supervisor, functions, CALL routines, informats, formats, engines, and the most generally useful procs; and **SAS/STAT®**, **SAS/AF®**, **SAS/OR®**, **SAS/ETS®**, **SAS/GRAPH®**, **SAS/QC®**, **SAS/FSP®**, etc., which are each a collection of specialized SAS procs.

SAS programmer, *n.* a person who writes SAS programs.

SAS site, *n.* a place or company where the SAS System is installed.

SAS Software Consultant, *n.* a person designated at a SAS site to provide technical support for SAS users at that site.

SAS System, *n.* a software system published by SAS Institute, Inc., implementing the SAS programming language, consisting of the SAS supervisor and programs to be used with it; comprising all the SAS products.

SAS time, *n.* a time of day represented as a duration of time in seconds since midnight.

SAS user, *n.* a person who uses the SAS System to solve problems primarily by means other than programming.

SAS version 5, *n.* a SAS version used on mainframes and minicomputers before the release of version 6 for those computers.

SAS version 6, *n.* a SAS version used on microcomputers beginning in 1985, and on other computers by 1990.

SAS weekday, *n.* one of the integers 1–7 used to represent the days of the week, from Sunday to Saturday.

scanning control, *n.* either of the symbols "&" and ":" used with a variable in an INPUT statement to indicate that the input value representing the variable's value in the input record is terminated by one delimiter (with ":") or two consecutive delimiters (with "&").

scientific notation, *n.* a way of writing numbers in which a number is represented as a number times a stated power of 10; notated in various ways.

screen catalog, *n.* a SAS catalog used to hold screens.

screen, *n.* 1. a device used to display information on a computer. 2. an organized display of information on a screen; a window that fills the entire screen. 3. an object defining a way of arranging information on a screen.

search method, *n.* an algorithm for finding a particular element of an array or object in a set of objects.

semicolon, *n.* the character ";", used to mark the end of statements.

sign, *n.* 1. a symbol. 2. either of the characters "+" and "–", used to indicate whether a number is positive or negative. 3. also, **sign bit**. a bit in a binary representation of a number used to indicate whether the number is negative. 4. (of a number) the condition of being positive or negative.

signed, *adj.* having a sign bit.

session, *n.* the period of time or sequence of events between starting the SAS System and ending it, between logging on and logging off, etc.; a continuous period of use of an interactive program.

simulation, *n.* a mathematical representation of a real-world, hypothesized, or imaginary phenomenon.

single-user, *adj.* designed for use by one user at a time.

slash, *n.* the character "/".

software, *n.* computer programs and data; information used with hardware.

sort, *v.* 1. to put the objects in an array, file, etc., in a particular order. *n.* 2. an instance of or the process of sorting. 3. an algorithm for sorting.

source code, *n.* symbols that represent a computer program in a programming language.

space, *n.* the blank character, considered as representing a horizontal displacement between characters, especially in proportional fonts.

special missing value, *n.* any of the missing values represented in a SAS program by a period followed by a letter or underscore.

SQL, *n.* a special-purpose high-level language that acts on tables. Also, **Structured Query Language**.

standard missing value, *n.* the missing value represented in SAS programs by a period, often generated automatically in a SAS program.

standard print file, *n.* the print file normally used to hold the results of SAS procs, addressed as file PRINT in data steps.

statement option, *n.* an option that is part of the syntax of a SAS statement, affecting the way the statement executes.

statement, *n.* a meaningful unit of a high-level language, usually representing one action to be carried out.

statistic, *n.* a value derived from the values of a sample.

step boundary, *n.* a point in a SAS program corresponding to the beginning or end of a step.

step, *n.* a separately executed part of a SAS program, consisting of a DATA or PROC statement and usually several other statements.

stochastic, *adj.* random.

storage, *n.* space for information on electromechanical devices, especially disks and tape. Cf. **memory**.

stratify, *v.* to divide into layers; to classify into ranges according to magnitude.

string, *n.* one or several consecutive characters or other objects, considered as a unit.

structure, *n.* a composite data type, consisting of several elements that might be of various types.

structured, *adj.* having separate processes in a program carried out in separate program units.

subscript, *n.* a number, or one of a group of numbers, indicating which element of an array is to be used.

SUGI, *n.* the largest SAS user group, which holds large annual conferences in the United States.

sum statement, *n.* a statement whose second term is a plus sign, that adds the value of the expression on the right side to the numeric variable or array reference on the left side.

supervisor, *n.* the central program of the SAS System, including the interpreter, display manager, macro processor, picture processor, linker, etc., and routines used to interface with the operating system and hardware.

syntax, *n.* the rules for the formation of statements and programs in a programming language.

syntax error, *n.* an instance of failing to follow a rule of syntax.

system, *n.* a group of interrelated objects.

system option, *n.* an option affecting the way the SAS System operates, that can be changed in the course of a SAS program using the OPTIONS statement or in similar ways.

tab, *n.* a character used to indicate various amounts of horizontal displacement, depending on the context; often used to separate fields in data files (**tab-delimited** files).

table, *n.* 1. a two-dimensional array of text, with rows and columns, used to report data. 2. a data file or structure with a similar two-dimensional organization.

table lookup, *n.* determining a value based on a key value by finding the key value in a list.

tabulate, *v.* to create a table; to put (data) into a table. **tabulation**, *n.*

term, *n.* a meaningful part of a statement, consisting of one or more tokens.

terminal, *n.* 1. a device at the end of a communications link, especially one used by a person to communicate with a computer. 2. also, **console**. the screen and keyboard of a computer, considered as resembling a terminal.

test, *v.* 1. to determine a particular quality of something. *n.* 2. an instance of testing.

text editor, *n.* a program that allows a person to edit text files.

text file, *n.* a file containing readable characters and often control characters used in displaying or printing.

text wrap, *n.* word wrap.

title lines, *n.* lines printed at the top of a page in a print file, defined by TITLE statements.

token, *n.* the smallest meaningful division of a program, consisting of one or more characters that form a word, operator, constant, etc.

trailing blank, *n.* a blank or one of several blanks at the end of a character string.

truncate, *v.* 1. to shorten an object by omitting part of it. 2. to convert a real number to an integer by rounding toward 0. 3. to erase one or more of the least significant bytes of a floating-point number. 4. to omit characters from the end of a character string. **truncation**, *n.*

type, *n.* a particular standard for representing data in binary form. Also, **data type**, **memory type**, **storage type**.

unary, *adj.* (of an operator) having one operand.

Unix, *n.* an operating system published by AT&T, and variants of it, used especially on minicomputers and workstations.

unsigned, *adj.* not having a sign bit; assumed to be nonnegative.

user, *n.* a person who gets results from a computer, other than by programming.

user interface, *n.* the aspects of a program that are apparent to a user.

value format, *n.* a format defined in a VALUE statement in the FORMAT proc, which associates ranges of values to be formatted with formatted values.

value informat, *n.* an informat defined in an INVALUE statement in the FORMAT proc, which associates input strings to be interpreted with specific values.

value, *n.* any of the various states that a particular data type can have.

variable, *n.* 1. a name in a computer program associated with a block of memory used as a particular data type, that can take on different values in the course of running the program. 2. a field in each observation of a SAS dataset, associated with a name and other attributes.

verb, *n.* a keyword identifying a BASIC statement.

version, *n.* a major change in the SAS System, identified by a whole number, usually encompassing several releases.

vertical bar, *n.* the character "|", two of which form the concatenation operator.

whole number, *n.* a number that can represent the result of counting, as 0, 1, 2, 3, etc.

window, *n.* a part of a computer screen, usually rectangular, in which a program displays logically related data.

word, *n.* 1. in a SAS program, a token beginning with an alphabetic character, as a name or keyword. 2. a sequence of characters identified by a parser as a unit.

word processor, *n.* a text editor that recognizes and acts on words, or a more powerful program that may also allow editing of formatting information, footnotes, graphics, etc.

word wrap, *n.* the process of dividing a character string into lines of approximately a certain length by putting line breaks at the beginnings of selected words.

workstation, *n.* 1. an assembly of furniture and equipment at which a person works, especially in an office. 2. a powerful computer used by one user at a time for a specialized application such as engineering, graphics, or word processing, formerly considered a separate class of computers, but now usually considered as specialized uses of microcomputers.

wrap, *v.* to do word wrap to.

Index

About the authors

Programmers, developers, and consultants, Rick Aster and Rhena Seidman have long advocated the use of the SAS language in serious software development. They have been writing SAS programs since version 82, working on a wide range of computer hardware.

Rhena Seidman has worked on many of the most popular applications of SAS programming, including direct marketing, clinical research, computer performance evaluation, project management, accounting, inventory control, databases, and statistical analysis. A physicist by training, she has written programs for Fermilab and NASA. She is a resident of New York City.

Rick Aster attributes his success in programming to his ability to think like a computer. His programs are used in the banking and insurance industries; in government; and in marketing, music, graphics, and nuclear waste applications. He has been involved in writing documentation for and translating and porting software systems. He lives in a forest in Chester County, Pennsylvania.

Either author can be contacted at Breakfast Communications Corporation, P.O. Box 176, Paoli, Pennsylvania 19301.

DISK WARRANTY

This software is protected by both United States copyright law and international copyright treaty provision. You must treat this software just like a book, except that you may copy it into a computer in order to be used and you may make archival copies of the software for the sole purpose of backing up our software and protecting your investment from loss.

By saying "just like a book," McGraw-Hill means, for example, that this software may be used by any number of people and may be freely moved from one computer location to another, so long as there is no possibility of its being used at one location or on one computer while it also is being used at another. Just as a book cannot be read by two different people in two different places at the same time, neither can the software be used by two different people in two different places at the same time (unless, of course, McGraw-Hill's copyright is being violated).

LIMITED WARRANTY

McGraw-Hill takes great care to provide you with top-quality software, thoroughly checked to prevent virus infections. McGraw-Hill warrants the physical diskette(s) contained herein to be free of defects in materials and workmanship for a period of sixty days from the purchase date. If McGraw-Hill receives written notification within the warranty period of defects in materials or workmanship, and such notification is determined by McGraw-Hill to be correct, McGraw-Hill will replace the defective diskette(s). Send requests to:

McGraw-Hill
Customer Services
P.O. Box 545
Blacklick, OH 43004-0545

The entire and exclusive liability and remedy for breach of this Limited Warranty shall be limited to replacement of defective diskette(s) and shall not include or extend to any claim for or right to cover any other damages, including but not limited to, loss of profit, data, or use of the software, or special, incidental, or consequential damages or other similar claims, even if McGraw-Hill has been specifically advised of the possibility of such damages. In no event will McGraw-Hill's liability for any damages to you or any other person ever exceed the lower of suggested list price or actual price paid for the license to use the software, regardless of any form of the claim.

MCGRAW-HILL SPECIFICALLY DISCLAIMS ALL OTHER WARRANTIES, EXPRESS OR IMPLIED, INCLUDING, BUT NOT LIMITED TO, ANY IMPLIED WARRANTY OF MERCHANTABILITY OR FITNESS FOR A PARTICULAR PURPOSE.

Specifically, McGraw-Hill makes no representation or warranty that the software is fit for any particular purpose and any implied warranty of merchantability is limited to the sixty-day duration of the Limited Warranty covering the physical diskette(s) only (and not the software) and is otherwise expressly and specifically disclaimed.

This limited warranty gives you specific legal rights; you may have others which may vary from state to state. Some states do not allow the exclusion of incidental or consequential damages, or the limitation on how long an implied warranty lasts, so some of the above may not apply to you.